FUNDAMENTALS OF MACHINE LEARNING FOR PREDICTIVE DATA ANALYTICS

FUNDAMENTALS OF MACHINE LEARNING FOR PREDICTIVE DATA ANALYTICS
Algorithms, Worked Examples, and Case Studies

John D. Kelleher
Brian Mac Namee
Aoife D'Arcy

The MIT Press
Cambridge, Massachusetts
London, England

MIT Press books may be purchased at special quantity discounts for business or sales promotional use. For information, please email special_sales@mitpress.mit.edu

This book was set in the LATEX programming language by the author. Printed and bound in the United States of America.

Library of Congress Cataloging-in-Publication Data

Kelleher, John D., 1974
Fundamentals of machine learning for predictive data analytics : algorithms, worked examples, and case studies / John D. Kelleher, Brian Mac Namee, and Aoife DArcy.
  pages cm
Includes bibliographical references and index.
ISBN 978-0-262-02944-5 (hardcover : alk. paper) 1. Machine learning. 2. Data mining. 3. Prediction theory. I. Mac Namee, Brian, 1978 II. DArcy, Aoife, 1978 III. Title.
Q325.5.K455 2015
006.3'1—dc23

                                        2014046123

10 9 8 7 6 5

To my wife and family,
thank you for your love, support, and patience.
John

To my family.
Brian

To Grandad D'Arcy, for the inspiration.
Aoife

Contents

Preface

In writing this book our target was to deliver an accessible, introductory text on the fundamentals of machine learning, and the ways that machine learning is used in practice to solve predictive data analytics problems in business, science, and other organizational contexts. As such, the book goes beyond the standard topics covered in machine learning books and also covers the lifecycle of a predictive analytics project, data preparation, feature design, and model deployment.

The book is intended for use on machine learning, data mining, data analytics, or artificial intelligence modules on undergraduate and post-graduate computer science, natural and social science, engineering, and business courses. The fact that the book provides case studies illustrating the application of machine learning within the industry context of data analytics also makes it a suitable text for practitioners looking for an introduction to the field and as a text book for industry training courses in these areas.

The design of the book is informed by our many years of experience in teaching machine learning, and the approach and material in the book has been developed and road-tested in the classroom. In writing this book we have adopted the following guiding principles to make the material accessible:

1. Explain the most important and popular algorithms clearly, rather than overview the full breadth of machine learning. As teachers we believe that giving a student deep knowledge of the core concepts underpinning a field provides them with a solid basis from which they can explore the field themselves. This sharper focus allows us to spend more time introducing, explaining, illustrating and contextualizing the algorithms that are fundamental to the field, and their uses.

2. Informally explain what an algorithm is trying to do before presenting the technical formal description of how it does it. Providing this informal introduction to each topic gives students a solid basis from which to attack the more technical material. Our experience with teaching this material to mixed audiences of undergraduates, post-graduates and professionals has shown that these informal introductions enable students to easily access the topic.

3. Provide *complete* worked examples. In this book we have presented complete workings for all examples, because this enables the reader to check their understanding in detail.

Structure of the Book

When teaching a technical topic, it is important to show the application of the concepts discussed to real-life problems. For this reason, we present machine learning within the context of predictive data analytics, an important and growing industry application of machine learning. The link between machine learning and data analytics runs through every chapter in the book. In Chapter 1 we introduce machine learning and explain the role it has within a standard data analytics project lifecycle. In Chapter 2 we provide a framework for designing and constructing a predictive analytics solution, based on machine learning, that meets a business need. All machine-learning algorithms assume a dataset is available for training, and in Chapter 3 we explain how to design, construct, and quality check a dataset before using it to a build prediction model.

Chapters 4, 5, 6, and 7 are the main machine learning chapters in the book. Each of these chapters presents a different approach to machine learning: Chapter 4, learning through information gathering; Chapter 5, learning through analogy; Chapter 6, learning by predicting probable outcomes; and Chapter 7, learning by searching for solutions that minimize error. All of these chapters follow the same two part structure

- Part 1 presents an informal introduction to the material presented in the chapter, followed by a detailed explanation of the fundamental technical concepts required to understand the material, and then a standard machine learning algorithm used in that learning approach is presented, along with a detailed worked example.

- Part 2 of each chapter explains different ways that the standard algorithm can be extended and well-known variations on the algorithm.

The motivation for structuring these technical chapters in two parts is that it provides a natural break in the chapter material. As a result, a topic can be included in a course by just covering Part 1 of a chapter ('Big Idea', fundamentals, standard algorithm and worked example); and then—time permitting—the coverage of the topic can be extended to some or all of the material in Part 2. Chapter 8 explains how to evaluate the performance of prediction models, and presents a range of different evaluation metrics. This chapter also adopts the two part structure of standard approach followed by extensions and variations. Throughout these technical chapters the link to the broader predictive analytics context is maintained through detailed and complete real-world examples, along with references to the datasets and/or papers that the examples are based on.

The link between the broader business context and machine learning is most clearly seen in the case studies presented in Chapters 9 (predicting customer churn) and 10 (galaxy classification). In particular, these case studies highlight how a range of issues and tasks beyond model building—such as business understanding, problem definition, data gathering and preparation, and communication of insight—are crucial to the success of a predictive analytics project. Finally, Chapter 11 discusses a range of fundamental topics in machine learning and also highlights that the selection of an appropriate machine learning approach for a given task involves factors beyond model accuracy—we must also match the characteristics of the model to the needs of the business.

How to Use this Book

Through our years of teaching this material we have developed an understanding of what is a reasonable amount of material to cover in a one-semester introductory module and on two-semester more advanced modules. To facilitate the use of the book in these different contexts, the book has been designed to be modular—with very few dependencies between chapters. As a result, a lecturer using this book can plan their course by simply selecting the sections of the book they wish to cover and not worry about the dependencies between the sections. When presented in class, the material in Chapters 1, 2, 9, 10 and 11 typically take two to three lecture hours to cover; and the material in Chapters 3, 4, 5, 6, 7, 8 normally take four to six lecture hours to cover.

In Table 1 we have listed a number of suggested course plans targeting different contexts. All of these courses include Chapter 1 (Machine Learning for Predictive Data Analytics) and Chapter 11 (The Art of Machine Learning for Predictive Data Analytics). The first course listed (*M.L. short deep*) is designed to be a one-semester machine learning course with a focus on giving the students a deep understanding of two approaches to machine learning, along with an understanding of the correct methodology to use when evaluating a machine learning model. In our suggested course we have chosen to cover all of Chapters 4 (Information-based Learning) and 7 (Error-based Learning). However, Chapter 5 (Similarity-based Learning) and/or 6 (Probability-based Learning) could be used instead. The *M.L. short deep* is also an ideal course plan for a short (1 week) professional training course. The second course (*M.L. short broad*) is another one-semester machine learning course. Here, however, the focus is on covering a range of machine learning approaches and, again, evaluation is covered in detail. For a longer two-semester machine learning course (*M.L. long*) we suggest covering data preparation (Section 3.6), all the machine learning chapters, and the evaluation chapter.

There are contexts, however, where the focus of a course is not primarily on machine learning. We also present to course paths that focus on the context of predictive data analytics. The course *P.D.A short* defines a one-semester course. This course gives students an introduction to predictive data analytics, a solid understanding of how machine learning solutions should be designed to meet a business need, insight into how prediction models work and should be evaluated, and includes one of the case studies. The *P.D.A short* is also an ideal course plan for a short (1 week) professional training course. If there is more time available then *P.D.A long* expands on the *P.D.A. short* course so that students gain a deeper and broader understanding of machine learning, and also includes the second case study.

Online Resources

The website:

www.machinelearningbook.com

provides access to a wide range of material that supports the book. This material includes: lecture slides, the complete set of images used in the book, video lectures based on the book, code samples, and an errata list (hopefully short). Worked solutions for all end of chapter exercises are available. For questions that are not marked with an ✳ a solutions manual is available from the book website. Solutions for those questions that are marked with an ✳ are contained in an instructors manual available from MIT Press on request.

Acknowledgements

We knew when we began writing this book that it would take a huge amount of work to complete. We underestimated, however, the amount of support we would need and receive from other people. We are delighted to take this opportunity to acknowledge these contributions to the book. We would like to thank our colleagues and students for the help and patience they extended to us over the last few years. We would also like to thank the staff at MIT Press, particularly Marie Lufkin Lee, and our copy editor Melanie Mallon. We are also very grateful to the two anonymous reviewers who provided insightful and helpful comments on an early draft of the manuscript. Each of us has also been fortunate to have the support of close friends and family which was invaluable in completing the book.

John would like to thank Robert Ross, Simon Dobnik, Josef van Genabith, Alan Mc Donnell, Lorraine Byrne, and all his friends from basketball. He would also like to thank his parents (John and Betty) and his sisters, without their support he would not have gotten past long-division and basic spelling. Finally, he would like to acknowledge and thank Aphra, this book would not have been started without her inspiration and would not have been completed without her patience.

Brian would like to thank his parents (Liam and Roisín) and family for all of their support, and acknowledge Pádraig Cunningham and Sarah Jane Delany who opened his eyes to machine learning.

Aoife would like to thank her parents (Michael and Mairead) and family, and all of the people who have supported her through her career—especially the much valued customers of The Analytics Store who give her data to play with!

Table 1

Suggested course syllabi.

Chapter	Section	M.L. (short) (deep)	M.L. (short) (broad)	M.L. (long)	P.D.A. (short)	P.D.A (long)
1		●	●	●	●	●
2					●	●
3	3.1, 3.2				●	●
	3.3, 3.4				●	●
	3.5				●	●
	3.6	●	●	●		●
4	4.1, 4.2, 4.3	●	●	●	●	●
	4.4.1	●		●		
	4.4.2	●		●		
	4.4.3	●		●		
	4.4.4	●	●	●		
	4.4.5	●	●	●		●
5	5.1, 5.2, 5.3		●	●		●
	5.4.1		●	●		●
	5.4.2			●		
	5.4.3		●	●		●
	5.4.4			●		
	5.4.5			●		
	5.4.6		●	●		●
6	6.1, 6.2, 6.3		●	●		●
	6.4.1		●	●		●
	6.4.2			●		
	6.4.3			●		
	6.4.4			●		
7	7.1, 7.2, 7.3	●	●	●	●	●
	7.4.1	●		●		●
	7.4.2	●		●		●
	7.4.3	●		●		●
	7.4.4	●	●	●		●
	7.4.5	●	●	●		
	7.4.6	●	●	●		
	7.4.7	●	●	●		
8	8.1, 8.2, 8.3	●	●	●	●	●
	8.4.1	●	●	●		●
	8.4.2	●	●	●		●
	8.4.3	●	●	●		●
	8.4.4	●	●	●		●
	8.4.5	●	●	●		●
	8.4.6					●
9					●	●
10						●
11		●	●	●	●	●

Notation

In this section we provide a short overview of the technical notation used throughout this book.

Notational Conventions

Throughout this book we discuss the use of machine learning algorithms to train prediction models based on datasets. The following list explains the notation used to refer to different elements in a dataset. Figure 1[xix] illustrates the key notation using a simple sample dataset.

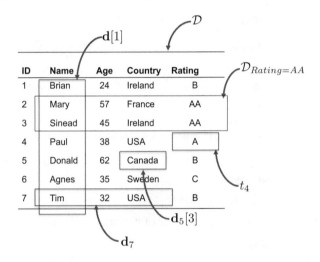

Figure 1

How the notation used in the book relates to the elements of a dataset.

Datasets

- The symbol $\mathcal{D}$ denotes a dataset.
- A dataset is composed of n instances, $(\mathbf{d}_1, t_1)$ to $(\mathbf{d}_n, t_n)$, where $\mathbf{d}$ is a set of m descriptive features and t is a target feature.
- A subset of a dataset is denoted using the symbol $\mathcal{D}$ with a subscript to indicate the definition of the subset. For example, $\mathcal{D}_{f=l}$ represents the subset of instances from the dataset $\mathcal{D}$ where the feature f has the value l.

Vectors of Features

- Lowercase boldface letters refer to a vector of features. For example, $\mathbf{d}$ denotes a vector of descriptive features for an instance in a dataset, and $\mathbf{q}$ denotes a vector of descriptive features in a query.

Instances

- Subscripts are used to index into a list of instances.
- $\mathbf{x}_i$ refers to the ith instance in a dataset.
- $\mathbf{d}_i$ refers to the descriptive features of the ith instance in a dataset.

Individual Features

- Lowercase letters represent a single feature (e.g., $f, a, b, c \ldots$).
- Square brackets [] are used to index into a vector of features (e.g., $\mathbf{d}[j]$ denotes the value of the jth feature in the vector $\mathbf{d}$).
- t represents the target feature.

Individual Features in a Particular Instance

- $\mathbf{d}_i[j]$ denotes the value of the jth descriptive feature of the ith instance in a dataset.
- a_i refers to the value for feature a of the ith instance in a dataset.
- t_i refers to the value of the target feature of the ith instance in a dataset

Indexes

- Typically i is used to index instances in a dataset, and j is used to index features in a vector.

Models

- We use $\mathbb{M}$ to refer to a model.
- $\mathbb{M}_\mathbf{w}$ refers to a model $\mathbb{M}$ parameterized by a parameter vector $\mathbf{w}$.
- $\mathbb{M}_\mathbf{w}(\mathbf{d})$ refers to the output of a model $\mathbb{M}$ parameterized by parameters $\mathbf{w}$ for descriptive features $\mathbf{d}$.

Set Size

- Vertical bars $|\ \ |$ refer to counts of occurrences (e.g., $|a = l|$ represents the number of times that $a = l$ occurs in a dataset).

Feature Names and Feature Values

- We use a specific typography when referring to a feature by name in the text (e.g., POSITION, CREDITRATING, and CLAIM AMOUNT).

- For categorical features, we use a specific typography to indicate the levels in the domain of the feature when referring to a feature by name in the text (e.g., *center*, *aa*, and *soft tissue*).

Notational Conventions for Probabilities

For clarity there are some extra notational conventions used in Chapter 6[247] on probability.

Generic Events

- Uppercase letters denote generic events where an unspecified feature (or set of features) is assigned a value (or set of values). Typically we use letters from the end of the alphabet—e.g., X, Y, Z—for this purpose.

- We use subscripts on uppercase letters to iterate over events. So, $\sum_i P(X_i)$ should be interpreted as summing over the set of events that are a complete assignment to the features in X (i.e., all the possible combinations of value assignments to the features in X).

Named Features

- Features explicitly named in the text are denoted by the uppercase initial letters of their names. For example, a feature named MENINGITIS is denoted by M.

Events Involving Binary Features

- Where a named feature is binary, we use the lowercase initial letter of the name of the feature to denote the event where the feature is true and the lowercase initial letter preceded by the $\neg$ symbol to denote the event where it is false. So, m will represent the event MENINGITIS $= true$, and $\neg m$ will denote MENINGITIS $= false$.

Events Involving Non-Binary Features

- We use lowercase letters with subscripts to iterate across values in the domain of a feature.

- So $\sum_i P(m_i) = P(m) + P(\neg m)$.
- In situations where a letter, for example X, denotes a joint event, then $\sum_i P(X_i)$ should be interpreted as summing over all the possible combinations of value assignments to the features in X.

Probability of an Event

- The probability that the feature f is equal to the value v is written $P(f = v)$.

Probability Distributions

- We use bold notation $\mathbf{P}()$ to distinguish a probability distribution from a probability mass function $P()$.
- We use the convention that the first element in a probability distribution vector is the probability for a true value. For example, the probability distribution for a binary feature, A, with a probability of 0.4 of being true would be written as $\mathbf{P}(A) = <0.4, 0.6>$.

1 Machine Learning for Predictive Data Analytics

Study the past if you would define the future.
—Confucius

Modern organizations collect massive amounts of data. For data to be of value to an organization, they must be analyzed to extract **insights** that can be used to make better decisions. The progression from **data** to **insights** to **decisions** is illustrated in Figure 1.1[1]. Extracting insights from data is the job of **data analytics**. This book focuses on **predictive data analytics**, which is an important subfield of data analytics.

Figure 1.1
Predictive data analytics moving from **data** to **insight** to **decision**.

1.1 What Is Predictive Data Analytics?

Predictive data analytics is the art of building and using **models** that make predictions based on patterns extracted from historical data. Applications of predictive data analytics include

- **Price Prediction:** Businesses such as hotel chains, airlines, and online retailers need to constantly adjust their prices in order to maximize returns based on factors such as seasonal changes, shifting customer demand, and the occurrence of special events. Predictive analytics models can be trained to predict optimal prices based on historical sales records. Businesses can then use these predictions as an input into their pricing strategy decisions.

- **Dosage Prediction:** Doctors and scientists frequently decide how much of a medicine or other chemical to include in a treatment. Predictive analytics models can be used to assist this decision making by predicting optimal dosages based on data about past dosages and associated outcomes.

- **Risk Assessment:** Risk is one of the key influencers in almost every decision an organization makes. Predictive analytics models can be used to predict the risk associated with decisions such as issuing a loan or underwriting an insurance policy. These models are trained using historical data from which they extract the key indicators of risk. The output from risk prediction models can be used by organizations to make better risk judgements.

- **Propensity Modeling:** Most business decision making would be made much easier if we could predict the likelihood, or **propensity**, of individual customers to take different actions. Predictive data analytics can be used to build models that predict future customer actions based on historical behavior. Successful applications of **propensity modeling** include predicting the likelihood of customers to leave one mobile phone operator for another, to respond to particular marketing efforts, or to buy different products.

- **Diagnosis:** Doctors, engineers, and scientists regularly make diagnoses as part of their work. Typically, these diagnoses are based on their extensive training, expertise, and experience. Predictive analytics models can help professionals make better diagnoses by leveraging large collections of historical examples at a scale beyond anything one individual would see over his or her career. The diagnoses made by predictive analytics models usually become an input into the professional's existing diagnosis process.

- **Document Classification:** Predictive data analytics can be used to automatically classify documents into different categories. Examples include email spam filtering, news sentiment analysis, customer complaint redirection, and medical decision making. In fact, the definition of a document can be expanded to include images, sounds, and videos, all of which can be classified using predictive data analytics models.

All these examples have two things in common. First, in each case a model is used to make a prediction to help a person or organization make a decision. In predictive data analytics we use a broad definition of the word **prediction**. In everyday usage, the word prediction has a temporal aspect—we predict what will happen in the future. However, in data analytics a prediction is the assignment of a value to any unknown variable. This could be predicting the price that something will be sold for in the future or, alternatively, it could mean predicting the type of document. So, in some cases prediction has a temporal aspect but not in all. The second thing that the examples listed above have in common is that a model is trained to make predictions based on a set of historical examples. We use **machine learning** to train these models.

1.2   What Is Machine Learning?

Machine learning is defined as an automated process that extracts patterns from data. To build the models used in predictive data analytics applications, we use **supervised machine learning**. Supervised machine learning[1] techniques automatically learn a model of the relationship between a set of **descriptive features** and a **target feature** based on a set of historical examples, or **instances**. We can then use this model to make predictions for new instances. These two separate steps are shown in Figure 1.2[3].

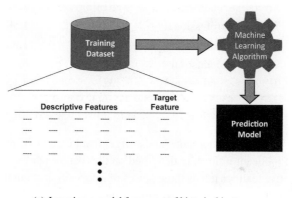

(a) Learning a model from a set of historical instances

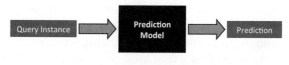

(b) Using a model to make predictions

Figure 1.2
The two steps in supervised machine learning.

   Table 1.1[4] lists a set of historical instances, or **dataset**, of mortgages that a bank has granted in the past.[2] This dataset includes descriptive features that

1 Other types of machine learning include **unsupervised learning**, **semi-supervised learning**, and **reinforcement learning**. In this book, however, we focus exclusively on supervised machine learning and use the terms supervised machine learning and machine learning interchangeably.

2 This dataset has been artificially generated for this example. Siddiqi (2005) gives an excellent overview of building predictive data analytics models for financial credit scoring.

Table 1.1

A credit scoring dataset.

ID	OCCUPATION	AGE	LOAN-SALARY RATIO	OUTCOME
1	industrial	34	2.96	repay
2	professional	41	4.64	default
3	professional	36	3.22	default
4	professional	41	3.11	default
5	industrial	48	3.80	default
6	industrial	61	2.52	repay
7	professional	37	1.50	repay
8	professional	40	1.93	repay
9	industrial	33	5.25	default
10	industrial	32	4.15	default

describe the mortgage, and a target feature that indicates whether the mortgage applicant ultimately defaulted on the loan or paid it back in full. The descriptive features tell us three pieces of information about the mortgage: the OCCUPATION (which can be *professional* or *industrial*) and AGE of the applicant and the ratio between the applicant's salary and the amount borrowed (LOAN-SALARY RATIO). The target feature, OUTCOME, is set to either *default* or *repay*. In machine learning terms, each row in the dataset is referred to as a **training instance**, and the overall dataset is referred to as a **training dataset**.

An example of a very simple prediction model for this domain would be

if LOAN-SALARY RATIO > 3 **then**
    OUTCOME = *default*
else
    OUTCOME = *repay*

We can say that this model is **consistent** with the dataset as there are no instances in the dataset for which the model does not make a correct prediction. When new mortgage applications are made, we can use this model to predict whether the applicant will repay the mortgage or default on it and make lending decisions based on this prediction.

Machine learning algorithms automate the process of learning a model that captures the relationship between the descriptive features and the target feature in a dataset. For simple datasets like the one in Table 1.1[4], we may be able to manually create a prediction model, and in an example of this scale, machine learning has little to offer us.

Consider, however, the dataset in Table 1.2[6], which shows a more complete representation of the same problem. This dataset lists more instances, and there are extra descriptive features describing the AMOUNT that a mortgage holder borrows, the mortgage holder's SALARY, the type of PROPERTY that the mortgage relates to (which can be *farm*, *house*, or *apartment*) and the TYPE of mortgage (which can be *ftp* for first-time buyers or *stb* for second-time buyers).

The simple prediction model using only the loan-salary ratio feature is no longer consistent with the dataset. It turns out, however, that there is at least one prediction model that is consistent with the dataset; it is just a little harder to find than the previous one:

> **if** LOAN-SALARY RATIO < 1.5 **then**
>   OUTCOME = *repay*
> **else if** LOAN-SALARY RATIO > 4 **then**
>   OUTCOME = *default*
> **else if** AGE < 40 **and** OCCUPATION $=$*industrial* **then**
>   OUTCOME = *default*
> **else**
>   OUTCOME = *repay*

To manually learn this model by examining the data is almost impossible. For a machine learning algorithm, however, this is simple. When we want to build prediction models from large datasets with multiple features, machine learning is the solution.

1.3   How Does Machine Learning Work?

Machine learning algorithms work by searching through a set of possible prediction models for the model that best captures the relationship between the descriptive features and target feature in a dataset. An obvious criteria for driving this search is to look for models that are consistent with the data. There are,

Table 1.2
A more complex credit scoring dataset.

ID	AMOUNT	SALARY	LOAN-SALARY RATIO	AGE	OCCUPATION	PROPERTY	TYPE	OUTCOME
1	245,100	66,400	3.69	44	industrial	farm	stb	repay
2	90,600	75,300	1.20	41	industrial	farm	stb	repay
3	195,600	52,100	3.75	37	industrial	farm	ftb	default
4	157,800	67,600	2.33	44	industrial	apartment	ftb	repay
5	150,800	35,800	4.21	39	professional	apartment	stb	default
6	133,000	45,300	2.94	29	industrial	farm	ftb	default
7	193,100	73,200	2.64	38	professional	house	ftb	repay
8	215,000	77,600	2.77	17	professional	farm	ftb	repay
9	83,000	62,500	1.33	30	professional	house	ftb	repay
10	186,100	49,200	3.78	30	industrial	house	ftb	default
11	161,500	53,300	3.03	28	professional	apartment	stb	repay
12	157,400	63,900	2.46	30	professional	farm	stb	repay
13	210,000	54,200	3.87	43	professional	apartment	ftb	repay
14	209,700	53,000	3.96	39	industrial	farm	ftb	default
15	143,200	65,300	2.19	32	industrial	apartment	ftb	default
16	203,000	64,400	3.15	44	industrial	farm	ftb	repay
17	247,800	63,800	3.88	46	industrial	house	stb	repay
18	162,700	77,400	2.10	37	professional	house	ftb	repay
19	213,300	61,100	3.49	21	industrial	apartment	ftb	default
20	284,100	32,300	8.80	51	industrial	farm	ftb	default
21	154,000	48,900	3.15	49	professional	house	stb	repay
22	112,800	79,700	1.42	41	professional	house	ftb	repay
23	252,000	59,700	4.22	27	professional	house	stb	default
24	175,200	39,900	4.39	37	professional	apartment	stb	default
25	149,700	58,600	2.55	35	industrial	farm	stb	default

however, at least two reasons why just searching for consistent models is not sufficient in order to learn useful prediction models. First, when we are dealing with large datasets, it is likely that there will be **noise**[3] in the data, and prediction models that are consistent with noisy data will make incorrect predictions. Second, in the vast majority of machine learning projects, the training set represents only a small sample of the possible set of instances in the domain. As a result, machine learning is an **ill-posed problem**. An ill-posed problem is

---

3 For example, some of the feature values will be mislabeled.

Table 1.3

A simple retail dataset

ID	BBY	ALC	ORG	GRP
1	no	no	no	couple
2	yes	no	yes	family
3	yes	yes	no	family
4	no	no	yes	couple
5	no	yes	yes	single

a problem for which a unique solution cannot be determined using only the information that is available.

We can illustrate how machine learning is an ill-posed problem using an example in which the analytics team at a supermarket chain wants to be able to classify customer households into the demographic groups *single*, *couple*, or *family*, based solely on their shopping habits.[4] The dataset in Table 1.3[7] contains descriptive features describing the shopping habits of 5 customers. The descriptive features measure whether a customer buys baby food, BBY, alcohol, ALC, or organic vegetable products, ORG. Each feature can take one of the two values: *yes* or *no*. Alongside these descriptive features is a target feature, GRP, that describes the demographic group for each customer (*single*, *couple*, or *family*). The dataset in Table 1.3[7] is referred to as a **labeled dataset** because it includes values for the target feature.

Imagine we attempt to learn a prediction model for this retail scenario by searching for a model that is consistent with the dataset. The first thing we need to do is figure out many different possible models actually exist for the scenario. This defines the set of prediction models the machine learning algorithm will search. From the perspective of searching for a consistent model, the most important property of a prediction model is that it defines a mapping from every possible combination of descriptive feature values to a prediction for the target feature. For the retail scenario, there are only three binary descriptive features, so there are $2^3 = 8$ possible combinations of descriptive feature

4 This kind of classification is not unusual given that supermarket chains can collect huge amounts of data about customers' shopping habits through a loyalty card scheme but find it expensive and time consuming to collect more personal data, such as demographic classifications. Demographic classifications, however, are extremely useful to marketing departments when designing special offers and other customer incentives.

Table 1.4

Potential prediction models (a) before and (b) after training data becomes available.

(a)

BBY	ALC	ORG	GRP	$\mathbb{M}_1$	$\mathbb{M}_2$	$\mathbb{M}_3$	$\mathbb{M}_4$	$\mathbb{M}_5$	...	$\mathbb{M}_{6\,561}$
no	no	no	?	couple	couple	single	couple	couple	...	couple
no	no	yes	?	single	couple	single	couple	couple	...	single
no	yes	no	?	family	family	single	single	single	...	family
no	yes	yes	?	single	single	single	single	single	...	couple
yes	no	no	?	couple	couple	family	family	family	...	family
yes	no	yes	?	couple	family	family	family	family	...	couple
yes	yes	no	?	single	family	family	family	family	...	single
yes	yes	yes	?	single	single	family	family	couple	...	family

(b)

BBY	ALC	ORG	GRP	$\mathbb{M}_2$	$\mathbb{M}_4$	$\mathbb{M}_5$	...
no	no	no	couple	couple	couple	couple	...
no	no	yes	couple	couple	couple	couple	...
no	yes	no	?	family	single	single	...
no	yes	yes	single	single	single	single	...
yes	no	no	?	couple	family	family	...
yes	no	yes	family	family	family	family	...
yes	yes	no	family	family	family	family	...
yes	yes	yes	?	single	family	couple	...

values. However, for each of these 8 possible descriptive feature value combinations, there are 3 possible target feature values, so this means that there are $3^8 = 6,561$ possible prediction models that could be used. Table 1.4(a)[8] illustrates the relationship between descriptive feature value combinations and prediction models for the retail scenario. The descriptive feature combinations are listed on the left hand side of the table and the set of potential models for this domain are shown as $\mathbb{M}_1$ to $\mathbb{M}_{6,561}$ on the right hand side of the table. Using the training dataset from Table 1.3[7] a machine learning algorithm will reduce the full set of 6,561 possible prediction models for this scenario down to just those that are consistent with the training instances. Table 1.4(b)[8], illustrates this; the blanked out columns in the table indicate the models that are not consistent with the training data.

Table 1.4(b)[8] also illustrates the fact that the training dataset does not contain an instance for every possible descriptive feature value combination and that there are still a large number of potential prediction models that remain consistent with the training dataset after the inconsistent models have been excluded.[5] Specifically, there are three remaining descriptive feature value combinations for which the correct target feature value is not known, and therefore there are $3^3 = 27$ potential models that remain consistent with the training data. Three of these—$\mathbb{M}_2$, $\mathbb{M}_4$, and $\mathbb{M}_5$—are shown in Table 1.4(b)[8]. Because a single consistent model cannot be found based on the sample training dataset alone, we say that machine learning is fundamentally an **ill-posed problem**.

We might be tempted to think that having multiple models that are consistent with the data is a good thing. The problem is, however, that although these models agree on what predictions should be made for the instances in the training dataset, they disagree with regard to what predictions should be returned for instances that are not in the training dataset. For example, if a new customer starts shopping at the supermarket and buys baby food, alcohol, and organic vegetables, our set of consistent models will contradict each other with respect to what prediction should be returned for this customer, for example, $\mathbb{M}_2$ will return GRP = *single*, $\mathbb{M}_4$ will return GRP = *family*, and $\mathbb{M}_5$ will return GRP = *couple*.

The criterion of consistency with the training data doesn't provide any guidance with regard to which of the consistent models to prefer when dealing with queries that are outside the training dataset. As a result, we cannot use the set of consistent models to make predictions for these queries. In fact, searching for predictive models that are consistent with the dataset is equivalent to just memorizing the dataset. As a result, no learning is taking place because the set of consistent models tells us nothing about the underlying relationship between the descriptive and target features beyond what a simple look-up of the training dataset would provide.

If a predictive model is to be useful, it must be able to make predictions for queries that are not present in the data. A prediction model that makes the correct predictions for these queries captures the underlying relationship between the descriptive and target features and is said to **generalize** well. Indeed, the goal of machine learning is to find the predictive model that generalizes best.

---

5   In this simple example it is easy to imagine collecting a training instance to match every possible combination of descriptive features; because there are only 3 binary descriptive features, there are only $2^3 = 8$ combinations. In more realistic scenarios, however, there are usually many more descriptive features, which means many more possible combinations. In the credit scoring dataset in Table 1.2[6], for example, a conservative estimate of the number of possible combinations of descriptive features is over 3.6 billion!

In order to find this single best model, a machine learning algorithm must use some criteria for choosing among the candidate models it considers during its search.

Given that consistency with the dataset is not an adequate criterion to select the best prediction model, what criteria should we use? There are a lot of potential answers to this question, and that is why there are a lot of different machine learning algorithms. Each machine learning algorithm uses different model selection criteria to drive its search for the best predictive model. So, when we choose to use one machine learning algorithm instead of another, we are, in effect, choosing to use one model selection criterion instead of another.

All the different model selection criteria consist of a set of assumptions about the characteristics of the model that we would like the algorithm to induce. The set of assumptions that defines the model selection criteria of a machine learning algorithm is known as the **inductive bias**[6] of the machine learning algorithm. There are two types of inductive bias that a machine learning algorithm can use, a restriction bias and a preference bias. A **restriction bias** constrains the set of models that the algorithm will consider during the learning process. A **preference bias** guides the learning algorithm to prefer certain models over others. For example, in Chapter 7[323] we introduce a machine learning algorithm called **multivariable linear regression with gradient descent**, which implements the restriction bias of only considering prediction models that produce predictions based on a linear combination of the descriptive feature values and applies a preference bias over the order of the linear models it considers in terms of a gradient descent approach through a weight space. As a second example, in Chapter 4[117] we introduce the **Iterative Dichotomizer 3** (**ID3**) machine learning algorithm, which uses a restriction bias of only considering tree prediction models where each branch encodes a sequence of checks on individual descriptive features but also utilizes a preference bias by considering shallower (less complex) trees over larger trees. It is important to recognize that using an inductive bias is a necessary prerequisite for learning to occur; without inductive bias, a machine learning algorithm cannot learn anything beyond what is in the data.

In summary, machine learning works by searching through a set of potential models to find the prediction model that best generalizes beyond the dataset.

6 Learning a general rule from a finite set of examples is called **inductive learning**. This is why machine learning is sometimes described as inductive learning, and the set of assumptions used by the machine algorithm that biases it towards selecting a single model is called the **inductive bias** of the algorithm.

Machine learning algorithms use two sources of information to guide this search, the training dataset and the inductive bias assumed by the algorithm.

1.4   What Can Go Wrong with Machine Learning?

Different machine learning algorithms encode different inductive biases. Because a machine learning algorithm encodes an inductive bias, it can induce models that generalize beyond the instances in a training dataset. An inappropriate inductive bias, however, can lead to mistakes. It has been shown that there is no particular inductive bias that on average is the best one to use.[7] Also, in general, there is no way of knowing for a given predictive task which inductive bias will work best. Indeed, the ability to select the appropriate machine learning algorithm (and hence inductive bias) to use for a given predictive task is one of the core skills that a data analyst must develop.

There are two kinds of mistakes that an inappropriate inductive bias can lead to: **underfitting** and **overfitting**. Underfitting occurs when the prediction model selected by the algorithm is too simplistic to represent the underlying relationship in the dataset between the descriptive features and the target feature. Overfitting, by contrast, occurs when the prediction model selected by the algorithm is so complex that the model fits to the dataset too closely and becomes sensitive to noise in the data.

To understand underfitting and overfitting, consider the task of inducing a model to predict a person's INCOME (the target feature) based on AGE (a single descriptive feature). Table 1.5[12] lists a simple dataset that gives ages and salaries for five people. A visualization[8] of this dataset is shown in Figure 1.3(a)[13].

The line in Figure 1.3(b)[13] represents one model of the relationship between the AGE and INCOME features. This line illustrates a very simple linear function that maps AGE to INCOME. Although this simple model goes some way toward capturing the general trend of the relationship between AGE and INCOME, it does not manage to capture any of the subtlety of the relationship. This model is said to underfit the data as it is not complex enough to fully capture the relationship between the descriptive feature and the target feature. By

7 This is known as the **No Free Lunch Theorem** (Wolpert, 1996).

8 We discuss this exact type of visualization, a scatter plot, in detail in Chapter 3[55]. For this example it is sufficient to say that a point is shown for each person in the dataset placed to represent their age (horizontally) and their salary (vertically).

Table 1.5

The age-income dataset.

ID	AGE	INCOME
1	21	24,000
2	32	48,000
3	62	83,000
4	72	61,000
5	84	52,000

contrast, the model shown in Figure 1.3(c)[13], while consistent with the training instances, seems much more complicated than necessary. This model is said to overfit the training data.

Models that either underfit or overfit do not **generalize** well and so will not be able to make good predictions for query instances beyond what was in the training dataset. The prediction model shown in Figure 1.3(d)[13], however, is a **Goldilocks model**: it is *just right*, striking a good balance between underfitting and overfitting. We find these Goldilocks models by using machine learning algorithms with appropriate inductive biases. This is one of the great arts of machine learning and something that we return to throughout this book.

1.5   The Predictive Data Analytics Project Lifecycle: CRISP-DM

Building predictive data analytics solutions for the kinds of applications described in Section 1.1[1] involves a lot more than just choosing the right machine learning algorithm. Like any other significant project, the chances of a predictive data analytics project being successful are greatly increased if a standard process is used to manage the project through the project lifecycle. One of the most commonly used processes for predictive data analytics projects is the **Cross Industry Standard Process for Data Mining (CRISP-DM)**.[9] Key features of the CRISP-DM process that make it attractive to data analytics practitioners are that it is non-proprietary; it is application, industry, and tool neutral; and it explicitly views the data analytics process from both an application-focused and a technical perspective.

---

9 While the name CRISP-DM refers to **data mining** (a field that overlaps significantly with predictive data analytics), it is equally applicable to predictive analytics projects.

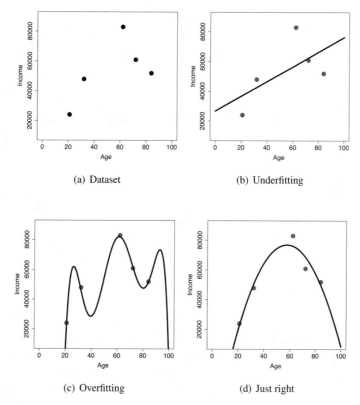

(a) Dataset   (b) Underfitting

(c) Overfitting   (d) Just right

Figure 1.3

Striking a balance between overfitting and underfitting when trying to predict income from age.

Figure 1.4[14] shows six key phases of the predictive data analytics project lifecycle that are defined by the CRISP-DM:

- **Business Understanding:** Predictive data analytics projects never start out with the goal of building a prediction model. Instead, they are focused on things like gaining new customers, selling more products, or adding efficiencies to a process. So, during the first phase in any analytics project, the primary goal of the data analyst is to fully understand the business (or organizational) problem that is being addressed, and then to design a data analytics solution for it.

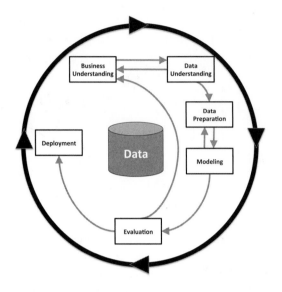

Figure 1.4

A diagram of the CRISP-DM process that shows the six key phases and indicates the important relationships between them. This figure is based on Figure 2 of Wirth and Hipp (2000).

- **Data Understanding:** Once the manner in which predictive data analytics will be used to address a business problem has been decided, it is important that the data analyst fully understand the different data sources available within an organization and the different kinds of data that are contained in these sources.

- **Data Preparation:** Building predictive data analytics models requires specific kinds of data, organized in a specific kind of structure known as an **analytics base table (ABT)**.[10] This phase of CRISP-DM includes all the activities required to convert the disparate data sources that are available in an organization into a well-formed ABT from which machine learning models can be induced.

- **Modeling:** The modeling phase of the CRISP-DM process is when the machine learning work occurs. Different machine learning algorithms are used to build a range of prediction models from which the best model will be selected for deployment.

---

10 All datasets presented in this chapter have been structured as ABTs.

- **Evaluation:** Before models can be deployed for use within an organization, it is important that they are fully evaluated and proved to be fit for the purpose. This phase of CRISP-DM covers all the evaluation tasks required to show that a prediction model will be able to make accurate predictions after being deployed and that it does not suffer from overfitting or underfitting.

- **Deployment:** Machine learning models are built to serve a purpose within an organization, and the last phase of CRISP-DM covers all the work that must be done to successfully integrate a machine learning model into the processes within an organization.

Figure 1.4[14] also illustrates the flow between each of these phases and emphasizes that data is at the heart of the process. Certain phases in CRISP-DM are more closely linked together than others. For example, Business Understanding and Data Understanding are tightly coupled, and projects typically spend some time moving back and forth between these phases. Similarly, the Data Preparation and Modeling phases are closely linked, and analytics projects often spend some time iterating between these two phases. Using the CRISP-DM process improves the likelihood that predictive data analytics projects will be successful, and we recommend its use.

1.6 Predictive Data Analytics Tools

Throughout this book we discuss the many different ways we can use machine learning techniques to build predictive data analytics models. In these discussions we do not refer to specific tools or implementations of these techniques. There are, however, many different, easy-to-use options for implementing machine learning models that interested readers can use to follow along with the examples in this book.

The first decision that must be made in choosing a machine learning platform is whether to use an application-based solution or to use a programming language. We will look at application-based solutions first. Well-designed application-based, or *point-and-click*, tools make it very quick and easy to develop and evaluate models, and to perform associated data manipulation tasks. Using one of these tools, it is possible to train, evaluate, and deploy a predictive data analytics model in less than an hour! Important application-based solutions for building predictive data analytics models include IBM SPSS, Knime Analytics Platform, RapidMiner Studio, SAS Enterprise Miner, and

Weka.[11] The tools by IBM and SAS are enterprise-wide solutions that integrate with the other offerings by these companies. Knime, RapidMiner, and Weka are interesting as they are all open-source, freely available solutions that readers can begin to use without any financial investment.

An interesting alternative to using an application-based solution for building predictive data analytics models is to use a programming language. Two of the most commonly used programming languages for predictive data analytics are R and Python.[12] Building predictive data analytics models using a language like R or Python is not especially difficult. For example, the following simple lines of code use the R language to build a predictive model for a simple task:

```
creditscoring.train <- read.csv("creditScoringTrain.csv")
glm.mod <- glm(Outcome~Amount+Salary+Age+LoanSalaryRatio,
    family=binomial(link="logit"), data=creditscoring.train)
creditscoring.test <- read.csv("creditScoringTest.csv")
predicted.values <- predict(glm.mod, creditscoring.test)
```

The advantage of using a programming language for predictive data analytics projects is that it gives the data analyst huge flexibility. Anything that the analyst can imagine can be implemented. This is in contrast to application-based solutions, in which the analyst can only really achieve what the tool developers had in mind when they designed the tool. The other main advantage of using a programming language is that, in most cases, the newest advanced analytics techniques will become available in programming languages long before they will be implemented in application-based solutions.

Obviously, though, using programming languages also has disadvantages associated with it. The main disadvantage is that programming is a skill that takes time and effort to learn. Using a programming language for advanced analytics has a significantly steeper learning curve than using an application-based solution. The second disadvantage is that using a programming language means we have very little of the infrastructural support, such as data management, that is present in application-based solutions available to us. This puts an extra burden on developers to implement these supports themselves.

11 For further details, see www.ibm.com/software/ie/analytics/spss, www.knime.org, www.rapidminer.com, www.sas.com, and www.cs.waikato.ac.nz/ml/weka.

12 The website kdnuggets.com runs a regular poll on the most popular programming languages for predictive data analytics, which R and Python regularly top www.kdnuggets.com/polls/2013/languages-analytics-data-mining-data-science.html. For further details about R and Python, see www.r-project.org and www.python.org.

1.7   The Road Ahead

Predictive data analytics projects use machine learning algorithms to induce prediction models from historical data. The insights that these prediction models produce are used to help organizations make data-driven decisions. Machine learning algorithms learn prediction models by inducing a generalized model of the relationship between a set of descriptive features and a target feature from a set of specific training instances. Machine learning, however, is made difficult because there is usually more than one model that is consistent with the training dataset—because of this, machine learning is often described as an ill-posed problem. Machine learning algorithms address this issue by encoding an inductive bias—or set of assumptions—that guide the algorithm to prefer certain models over others. We will see as we proceed through this book that the selection of a machine learning algorithm is not the only way that we can bias the predictive data analytics process. All the other choices that we make, such as the data to use, the descriptive features to use, and the way in which we deploy a model bias the outcome of the overall process, and this is something we need to be keenly aware of.

The purpose of this book is to give readers a solid grounding in the theoretical underpinnings of the most commonly used machine learning techniques and a clear view of how machine learning techniques are used in practice in predictive data analytics projects. With this in mind, readers can view the book as three parts that are mapped to the phases of the CRISP-DM process.

The first part—Chapters 2[21] and 3[55]—covers the Business Understanding, Data Understanding, and Data Preparation phases of the process. In this part we discuss how a business problem is converted into a data analytics solution, how data can be prepared for this task, and the data exploration tasks that should be performed during these phases.

The second part of the book covers the Modeling phase of CRISP-DM. We consider four main families of machine learning algorithm:

- Information-based learning (Chapter 4[117])
- Similarity-based learning (Chapter 5[179])
- Probability-based learning (Chapter 6[247])
- Error-based learning (Chapter 7[323])

By looking at these four key families, we cover the most commonly used approaches to inductive machine learning that can be used to build most predictive data analytics solutions.

The third part of the book covers the Evaluation and Deployment phases of CRISP-DM. Chapter 8[397] describes a range of different approaches to evaluating prediction models. Chapters 9[463] and 10[483] present case studies describing specific predictive analytics projects from Business Understanding right up to Deployment. These case studies will demonstrate how everything described in the preceding chapters comes together in a successful predictive data analytics project.

Finally, Chapter 11[511] provides some overarching perspectives on machine learning for predictive data analytics and summarizes some of the key differences between the different approaches covered in this book.

1.8   Exercises

1. What is **predictive data analytics**?

2. What is **supervised machine learning**?

3. Machine learning is often referred to as an **ill-posed problem**. What does this mean?

4. The following table lists a dataset from the credit scoring domain we discussed in the chapter. Underneath the table we list two prediction models that are consistent with this dataset, **Model 1** and **Model 2**.

ID	OCCUPATION	AGE	LOAN-SALARY RATIO	OUTCOME
1	industrial	39	3.40	default
2	industrial	22	4.02	default
3	professional	30	2.70	repay
4	professional	27	3.32	default
5	professional	40	2.04	repay
6	professional	50	6.95	default
7	industrial	27	3.00	repay
8	industrial	33	2.60	repay
9	industrial	30	4.50	default
10	professional	45	2.78	repay

Model 1
if LOAN-SALARY RATIO > 3.00 **then**
    OUTCOME = *default*
else
    OUTCOME = *repay*

Model 2
if AGE$= 50$ **then**
    OUTCOME = *default*
else if AGE$= 39$ **then**
    OUTCOME = *default*
else if AGE$= 30$ **and** OCCUPATION = *industrial* **then**
    OUTCOME = *default*
else if AGE$= 27$ **and** OCCUPATION = *professional* **then**
    OUTCOME = *default*
else
    OUTCOME = *repay*

a. Which of these two models do you think will generalise better to instances not contained in the dataset?

b. Propose an inductive bias that would enable a machine learning algorithm to make the same preference choice as you did in part (a).

c. Do you think that the model that you rejected in part (a) of this question is overfitting or underfitting the data?

∗ 5. What is meant by the term **inductive bias**?

∗ 6. How do machine learning algorithms deal with the fact that machine learning is an **ill-posed problem**?

∗ 7. What can go wrong when an inappropriate **inductive bias** is used?

∗ 8. It is often said that 80% of the work done on predictive data analytics projects is done in the Business Understanding, Data Understanding, and Data Preparation phases of **CRISP-DM**, and just 20% is spent on the Modeling, Evaluation, and Deployment phases. Why do you think this would be the case?

2 Data to Insights to Decisions

We cannot solve our problems with the same thinking we used when we created them.
—Albert Einstein

Predictive data analytics projects are not handed to data analytics practitioners fully formed. Rather, analytics projects are initiated in response to a business problem, and it is our job—as analytics practitioners—to decide how to address this business problem using analytics techniques. In the first part of this chapter we present an approach to developing **analytics solutions** that address specific **business problems**. This involves an analysis of the needs of the business, the data we have available for use, and the capacity of the business to use analytics. Taking these factors into account helps to ensure that we develop analytics solutions that are effective and fit for purpose. In the second part of this chapter we move our attention to the data structures that are required to build predictive analytics models, and in particular the **analytics base table** (**ABT**). Designing ABTs that properly represent the characteristics of a **prediction subject** is a key skill for analytics practitioners. We present an approach in which we first develop a set of **domain concepts** that describe the prediction subject, and then expand these into concrete **descriptive features**. Throughout the chapter we return to a case study that demonstrates how these approaches are used in practice.

2.1 Converting Business Problems into Analytics Solutions

Organizations don't exist to do predictive data analytics. Organizations exist to do things like make more money, gain new customers, sell more products, or reduce losses from fraud. Unfortunately, the predictive analytics models that we can build do not do any of these things. The models that analytics practitioners build simply make predictions based on patterns extracted from historical datasets. These predictions do not solve business problems; rather, they provide insights that help the organization make better decisions to solve their business problems.

A key step, then, in any data analytics project is to understand the **business problem** that the organization wants to solve and, based on this, to determine the kind of insight that a predictive analytics model can provide to help the organization address this problem. This defines the **analytics solution** that the analytics practitioner will set out to build using machine learning. Defining the analytics solution is the most important task in the **Business Understanding** phase of the CRISP-DM process.

In general, converting a business problem into an analytics solution involves answering the following key questions:

1. **What is the business problem? What are the goals that the business wants to achieve?** These first two questions are not always easy to answer. In many cases organizations begin analytics projects because they have a clear issue that they want to address. Sometimes, however, organizations begin analytics projects simply because somebody in the organization feels that this is an important new technique that they should be using. Unless a project is focused on clearly stated goals, it is unlikely to be successful. The business problem and goals should always be expressed in business terms and not yet be concerned with the actual analytics work at this stage.

2. **How does the business currently work?** It is not feasible for an analytics practitioner to learn everything about the businesses with which they work as they will probably move quickly between different areas of an organization, or even different industries. Analytics practitioners must, however, possess what is referred to as **situational fluency**. This means that they understand enough about a business so that they can converse with partners in the business in a way that these business partners understand. For example, in the insurance industry, insurance policy holders are usually referred to as *members* rather than *customers*. Although from an analytics perspective, there is really little difference, using the correct terminology makes it much easier for business partners to engage with the analytics project. Beyond knowing the correct terminology to use, an analytics practitioner who is situationally fluent will have sufficient knowledge of the quirks of a particular domain to be able to competently build analytics solutions for that domain.

3. **In what ways could a predictive analytics model help to address the business problem?** For any business problem, there are a number of different analytics solutions that we could build to address it. It is important to explore these possibilities and, in conjunction with the business, to agree on the most suitable solution for the business. For each proposed solution, the following points should be described: (1) the predictive model that will be built; (2) how the predictive model will be used by the business; and (3) how using the predictive model will help address the original business

problem. The next section provides a case study of the process for converting a business problem into a set of candidate analytics solutions.

2.1.1   Case Study: Motor Insurance Fraud

Consider the following business problem: in spite of having a fraud investigation team that investigates up to 30% of all claims made, a motor insurance company is still losing too much money due to fraudulent claims. The following predictive analytics solutions could be proposed to help address this business problem:

- **[Claim prediction]** A model could be built to predict the likelihood that an insurance claim is fraudulent. This model could be used to assign every newly arising claim a fraud likelihood, and those that are most likely to be fraudulent could be flagged for investigation by the insurance company's claims investigators. In this way the limited claims investigation time could be targeted at the claims that are most likely to be fraudulent, thereby increasing the number of fraudulent claims detected and reducing the amount of money lost to fraud.

- **[Member prediction]** A model could be built to predict the propensity of a member[1] to commit fraud in the near future. This model could be run every quarter to identify those members most likely to commit fraud, and the insurance company could take a risk mitigation action ranging from contacting the member with some kind of warning to canceling the member's policies. By identifying members likely to make fraudulent claims before they make them, the company could save significant amounts of money.

- **[Application prediction]** A model could be built to predict, at the point of application, the likelihood that a policy someone has applied for will ultimately result in a fraudulent claim. The company could run this model every time a new application is made and reject those applications that are predicted likely to result in a fraudulent claim. The company would therefore reduce the number of fraudulent claims and reduce the amount of money they would lose to these claims.

- **[Payment prediction]** Many fraudulent insurance claims simply over-exaggerate the amount that should actually be paid out. In these cases the insurance company goes through an expensive investigation process but still

---

1 Remember that in insurance we don't refer to customers!

must make a reduced payment in relation to a claim. A model could be built to predict the amount most likely to be paid out by an insurance company after having investigated a claim. This model could be run whenever new claims arise, and the policy holder could be offered the amount predicted by the model as settlement as an alternative to going through a claims investigation process. Using this model, the company could save on claims investigations and reduce the amount of money paid out on fraudulent claims.

2.2   Assessing Feasibility

Once a set of candidate analytics solutions that address a business problem have been defined, the next task is to evaluate the feasibility of each solution. This involves considering the following questions:

- Is the data required by the solution available, or could it be made available?
- What is the capacity of the business to utilize the insights that the analytics solution will provide?

The first question addresses data availability. Every analytics solution will have its own set of data requirements, and it is useful, as early as possible, to determine if the business has sufficient data available to meet these requirements. In some cases a lack of appropriate data will simply rule out proposed analytics solutions to a business problem. More likely, the easy availability of data for some solutions might favor them over others. In general, evaluating the feasibility of an analytics solution in terms of it data requirements involves aligning the following issues with the requirements of the analytics solution:

- **The key objects in the company's data model and the data available regarding them.** For example, in a bricks-and-mortar retail scenario, the key objects are likely to be customers, products, sales, suppliers, stores, and staff. In an insurance scenario, the key objects are likely to be policy holders, policies, claims, policy applications, investigations, brokers, members, investigators, and payments.
- **The connections that exist between key objects in the data model.** For example, in a banking scenario is it possible to connect the multiple accounts that a single customer might own? Similarly, in an insurance scenario is it possible to connect the information from a policy application with the details (e.g., claims, payments, etc) of the resulting policy itself?

- **The granularity of the data that the business has available.** In a bricks-and-mortar retail scenario, data on sales might only be stored as a total number of sales per product type per day, rather than as individual items sold to individual customers.

- **The volume of data involved.** The amount of data that is available to an analytics project is important because (a) some modern datasets are so large that they can stretch even state of the art machine learning tools; and (b) conversely, very small datasets can limit our ability to evaluate the expected performance of a model after deployment.

- **The time horizon for which data is available.** It is important that the data available covers the period required for the analytics solution. For example, in an online gaming scenario, it might be possible to find out every customer's account balance today but utterly impossible to find out what their balance was last month, or even yesterday.

The second issue affecting the feasibility of an analytics solution is the ability of the business to utilize the insight that the solution provides. If a business is required to drastically revise all their processes to take advantage of the insights that can be garnered from a predictive model, the business may not be ready to do this no matter how good the model is. In many cases the best predictive analytics solutions are those that fit easily into an existing business process.

Based on analysis of the associated data and capacity requirements, the analytics practitioner can assess the feasibility of each predictive analytics solution proposed to address a business problem. This analysis will eliminate some solutions altogether and for those solutions that appear feasible will generate a list of the data and capacity required for successful implementation. Those solutions that are deemed feasible should then be presented to the business, and one or more should be selected for implementation.

As part of the process of agreeing on the solution to pursue, the analytics practitioner must agree with the business, as far as possible, the goals that will define a successful model implementation. These goals could be specified in terms of the required accuracy of the model and/or the impact of the model on the business.

2.2.1   Case Study: Motor Insurance Fraud

Returning to the motor insurance fraud detection case study, below we evaluate
the feasibility of each proposed analytics solution in terms of data and business
capacity requirements.

- **[Claim prediction]** *Data Requirements:* This solution would require that
  a large collection of historical claims marked as *fraudulent* and *non-
  fraudulent* exist. Similarly, the details of each claim, the related policy, and
  the related claimant would need to be available. *Capacity Requirements:*
  Given that the insurance company already has a claims investigation team,
  the main requirements would be that a mechanism could be put in place to
  inform claims investigators that some claims were prioritized above others.
  This would also require that information about claims become available in
  a suitably timely manner so that the claims investigation process would not
  be delayed by the model.

- **[Member prediction]** *Data Requirements*: This solution would not only
  require that a large collection of claims labeled as either *fraudulent* or *non-
  fraudulent* exist with all relevant details, but also that all claims and policies can be connected to an identifiable member. It would also require that
  any changes to a policy are recorded and available historically. *Capacity
  Requirements:* This solution first assumes that it is possible to run a process
  every quarter that performs an analysis of the behavior of each customer.
  More challenging, there is the assumption that the company has the capacity
  to contact members based on this analysis and can design a way to discuss this issue with customers highlighted as likely to commit fraud without
  damaging the customer relationship so badly as to lose the customer. Finally,
  there are possibly legal restrictions associated with making this kind of contact.

- **[Application prediction]** *Data Requirements:* Again, a historical collection
  of claims marked as *fraudulent* or *non-fraudulent* along with all relevant
  details would be required. It would also be necessary to be able to connect
  these claims back to the policies to which they belong and to the application details provided when the member first applied. It is likely that the
  data required for this solution would stretch back over many years as the
  time between making a policy application and making a claim could cover
  decades. *Capacity Requirements:* The challenge in this case would be to

integrate the automated application assessment process into whatever application approval process currently exists within the company.

- **[Payment prediction]** *Data Requirements:* This solution would require the full details of policies and claims as well as data on the original amount specified in a claim and the amount ultimately paid out. *Capacity Requirements:* Again, this solution assumes that the company has the potential to run this model in a timely fashion whenever new claims rise and also has the capacity to make offers to claimants. This assumes the existence of a customer contact center or something similar.

For the purposes of the case study, we assume that after the feasibility review, it was decided to proceed with the **claim prediction** solution, in which a model will be built that can predict the likelihood that an insurance claim is fraudulent.

2.3   Designing the Analytics Base Table

Once we have decided which analytics solution we are going to develop in response to a business problem, we need to begin to design the data structures that will be used to build, evaluate, and ultimately deploy the model. This work sits primarily in the **Data Understanding** phase of the **CRISP-DM** process (see Figure 1.4[14]) but also overlaps with the **Business Understanding** and **Data Preparation** phases (remember that the CRISP-DM process is not strictly linear).

The basic data requirements for predictive models are surprisingly simple. To build a predictive model, we need a large dataset of historical examples of the scenario for which we will make predictions. Each of these historical examples must contain sufficient data to describe the scenario and the outcome that we are interested in predicting. So, for example, if we are trying to predict whether or not insurance claims are fraudulent, we require a large dataset of historical insurance claims, and for each one we must know whether or not that claim was found to be fraudulent.

The basic structure in which we capture these historical datasets is the **analytics base table** (**ABT**), a schematic of which is shown in Table 2.1[28]. An analytics base table is a simple, flat, tabular data structure made up of rows and columns. The columns are divided into a set of **descriptive features** and a single **target feature**. Each row contains a value for each descriptive feature

Table 2.1
The basic structure of an analytics base table—descriptive features and a target feature.

			Descriptive Features				Target Feature
───	───	───	───	───	───	───	───
───	───	───	───	───	───	───	───
───	───	───	───	───	───	───	───
───	───	───	───	───	───	───	───

and the target feature and represents an **instance** about which a prediction can be made.

Although the ABT is the key structure that we use in developing machine learning models, data in organizations is rarely kept in neat tables ready to be used to build predictive models. Instead, we need to construct the ABT from the raw data sources that are available in an organization. These may be very diverse in nature. Figure 2.1[28] illustrates some of the different data sources that are typically combined to create an ABT.

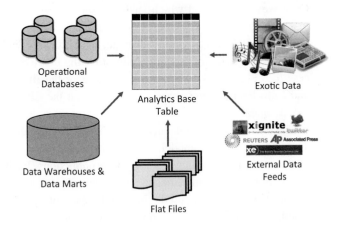

Figure 2.1
The different data sources typically combined to create an analytics base table.

Before we can start to aggregate the data from these different sources, how-ever, a significant amount of work is required to determine the appropriate design for the ABT. In designing an ABT, the first decision an analytics practi-tioner needs to make is on the **prediction subject** for the model they are trying to build. The prediction subject defines the basic level at which predictions are made, and each row in the ABT will represent one instance of the prediction subject—the phrase **one-row-per-subject** is often used to describe this structure. For example, for the analytics solutions proposed for the motor insurance fraud scenario, the prediction subject of the claim prediction and payment prediction models would be an insurance claim; for the member prediction model, the prediction subject would be a member; and for the application prediction model, it would be an application.

Each row in an ABT is composed of a set of descriptive features and a target feature. The actual features themselves can be based on any of the data sources within an organization, and defining them can appear a mammoth task at first. This task can be made easier by making a hierarchical distinction between the actual features contained in an ABT and a set of **domain concepts** upon which features are based—see Figure 2.2[29].

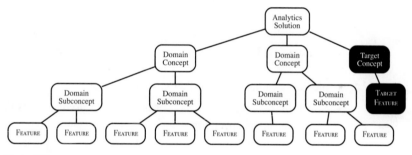

Figure 2.2

The hierarchical relationship between an analytics solution, domain concepts, and descriptive features.

A domain concept is a high-level abstraction that describes some characteristic of the prediction subject from which we derive a set of concrete features that will be included in an ABT. If we keep in mind that the ultimate goal of an analytics solution is to build a predictive model that predicts a target feature from a set of descriptive features, domain concepts are the characteristics of the prediction subject that domain experts and analytics experts believe are likely to be useful in making this prediction. Often, in a collaboration between analytics experts and domain experts, we develop a hierarchy of domain concepts that starts from the analytics solution, proceeds through a small number of levels of abstraction to result in concrete descriptive features. Examples of domain concepts include *customer value*, *behavioral change*, *product usage mix*, and *customer lifecycle stage*. These are abstract concepts that are understood to be likely important factors in making predictions. At this stage we do not worry too much about exactly how a domain concept will be converted into a concrete feature, but rather try to enumerate the different areas from which features will arise.

Obviously, the set of domain concepts that are important change from one analytics solution to another. However, there are a number of general domain concepts that are often useful:

- **Prediction Subject Details:** Descriptive details of any aspect of the prediction subject.

- **Demographics:** Demographic features of users or customers such as age, gender, occupation, and address.

- **Usage:** The *frequency* and *recency* with which customers or users have interacted with an organization. The *monetary value* of a customer's interactions with a service. The *mix* of products or services offered by the organization that a customer or user has used.

- **Changes in Usage:** Any changes in the frequency, recency, or monetary value of a customer's or user's interactions with an organization (for example, has a cable TV subscriber changed packages in recent months?).

- **Special Usage:** How often a user or customer used services that an organization considers special in some way in the recent past (for example, has a customer called a customer complaints department in the last month?).

- **Lifecycle Phase:** The position of a customer or user in their lifecycle (for example, is a customer a new customer, a loyal customer or a lapsing customer?).

- **Network Links:** Links between an item and other related items (for example, links between different customers or different products, or social network links between customers).

The actual process for determining domain concepts is essentially one of **knowledge elicitation**—attempting to extract from domain experts the knowledge about the scenario we are trying to model. Often, this process will take place across multiple meetings, involving the analytics and domain experts, where the set of relevant domain concepts for the analytics solution are developed and refined.

2.3.1 Case Study: Motor Insurance Fraud

At this point in the motor insurance fraud detection project, we have decided to proceed with the proposed **claim prediction** solution, in which a model will be built that can predict the likelihood that an insurance claim is fraudulent. This system will examine new claims as they arise and flag for further investigation those that look like they might be fraud risks. In this instance the prediction subject is an insurance claim, and so the ABT for this problem will contain details of historical claims described by a set of descriptive features that capture likely indicators of fraud, and a target feature indicating whether a claim was ultimately considered fraudulent. The domain concepts in this instance will be concepts from within the insurance domain that are likely to be important in determining whether a claim is fraudulent. Figure 2.3[31] shows some domain concepts that are likely to be useful in this case. This set of domain concepts would have been determined through consultations between the analytics practitioner and domain experts within the business.

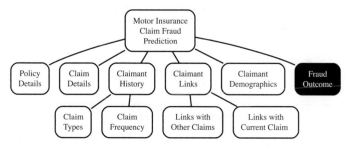

Figure 2.3
Example domain concepts for a motor insurance fraud prediction analytics solution.

The domain concepts shown here are *Policy Details*, which covers information relating to the policy held by the claimant (such as the age of the policy and the type of the policy); *Claim Details*, which covers the details of the claim itself (such as the incident type and claim amount); *Claimant History*, which includes information on previous claims made by the claimant (such as the different types of claims they have made in the past and the frequency of past claims); *Claimant Links*, which captures links between the claimant and any other people involved in the claim (for example, the same people being involved in multiple insurance claims together is often an indicator of fraud); and *Claimant Demographics*, which covers the demographic details of the claimant (such as age, gender, and occupation). Finally, a domain concept,

Fraud Outcome, is included to cover the target feature. It is important that this is included at this stage because target features often need to be derived from multiple raw data sources, and the effort that will be involved in this should not be forgotten.

In Figure 2.3[31] the domain concepts *Claimant History* and *Claimant Links* have both been broken down into a number of **domain subconcepts**. In the case of *Claimant History*, the domain subconcept of *Claim Types* explicitly recognizes the importance of designing descriptive features to capture the different types of claims the claimant has been involved in in the past, and the *Claim Frequency* domain subconcept identifies the need to have descriptive features relating to the frequency with which the claimant has been involved in claims. Similarly, under *Claimant Links* the *Links with Other Claims* and *Links with Current Claim* domain subconcepts highlight the fact that the links to or from this claimant can be broken down into links related to the current claim and links relating to other claims. The expectation is that each domain concept, or domain subconcept, will lead to one or more actual descriptive features derived directly from organizational data sources. Together these descriptive features will make up the ABT.

2.4   Designing and Implementing Features

Once domain concepts have been agreed on, the next task is to design and implement concrete features based on these concepts. A feature is any measure derived from a domain concept that can be directly included in an ABT for use by a machine learning algorithm. Implementing features is often a process of approximation through which we attempt to express as much of each domain concept as possible from the data sources that are available to us. Often it will take multiple features to express a domain concept. Also, we may have to use some **proxy features** to capture something that is closely related to a domain concept when direct measurement is not possible. In some extreme cases we may have to abandon a domain concept completely if the data required to express it isn't available. Consequently, understanding and exploring the data sources related to each domain concept that are available within an organization is a fundamental component of feature design. Although all the factors relating to data that were considered during the feasibility assessment of the analytics solution[2] are still relevant, three key data considerations are particularly important when we are designing features.

The first consideration is **data availability**, because we must have data available to implement any feature we would like to use. For example, in an online payments service scenario, we might define a feature that calculates the average of a customer's account balance over the past six months. Unless the company maintains a historical record of account balances covering the full six-month period, however, it will not be possible to implement this feature.

The second consideration is the **timing** with which data becomes available for inclusion in a feature. With the exception of the definition of the target feature, data that will be used to define a feature must be available before the event around which we are trying to make predictions occurs. For example, if we were building a model to predict the outcomes of soccer matches, we might consider including the attendance at the match as a descriptive feature. The final attendance at a match is not available until midway through the game, so if we were trying to make predictions before kick-off, this feature would not be feasible.

The third consideration is the **longevity** of any feature we design. There is potential for features to go stale if something about the environment from which they are generated changes. For example, to make predictions of the outcome of loans granted by a bank, we might use the borrower's salary as a descriptive feature. Salaries, however, change all the time based on inflation and other socio-economic factors. If we were to use a model that includes salary values over an extended period (for example, 10 years) the salary values used to initially train the model may have no relationship to the values that would be presented to the model later on. One way to extend the longevity of a feature is to use a derived ratio instead of a raw feature. For example, in the loan scenario a ratio between salary and requested loan amount might have a much longer useful life span than the salary and loan amount values alone.

As a result of these considerations, feature design and implementation is an iterative process in which data exploration informs the design and implementation of features, which in turn inform further data exploration, and so on.

---

2 See the discussion in Section 2.1[21] relating to data availability, data connections, data granularity, data volume, and data time horizons.

2.4.1   Different Types of Data

The data that the features in an ABT contain can be of a number of different types:

- **Numeric:** True numeric values that allow arithmetic operations (e.g., price, age)
- **Interval:** Values that allow ordering and subtraction, but do not allow other arithmetic operations (e.g., date, time)
- **Ordinal:** Values that allow ordering but do not permit arithmetic (e.g., size measured as small, medium, or large)
- **Categorical:** A finite set of values that cannot be ordered and allow no arithmetic (e.g., country, product type)
- **Binary:** A set of just two values (e.g., gender)
- **Textual:** Free-form, usually short, text data (e.g., name, address)

Figure 2.4[35] shows examples of these different data types. We often reduce this categorization to just two data types: **continuous** (encompassing the numeric and interval types), and **categorical** (encompassing the categorical, ordinal, binary, and textual types). When we talk about categorical features, we refer to the set of possible values that a categorical feature can take as the **levels** of the feature or the **domain** of the feature. For example, in Figure 2.4[35] the levels of the CREDIT RATING feature are {*aa*, *a*, *b*, *c*} and the levels of the GENDER feature are {*male, female*}. As we will see when we look at the machine learning algorithms covered in Chapters 4[117] to 7[323], the presence of different types of descriptive and target features can have a big impact on how an algorithm works.

2.4.2   Different Types of Features

The features in an ABT can be of two types: **raw features** or **derived features**. Raw features are features that come directly from raw data sources. For example, customer age, customer gender, loan amount, or insurance claim type are all descriptive features that we would most likely be able to transfer directly from a raw data source to an ABT.

Derived descriptive features do not exist in any raw data source, so they must be constructed from data in one or more raw data sources. For example, average customer purchases per month, loan-to-value ratios, or changes in

Ordinal Ordinal Categorical

ID	NAME	DATE OF BIRTH	GENDER	CREDIT RATING	COUNTRY	SALARY
0034	Brian	22/05/78	male	aa	ireland	67,000
0175	Mary	04/06/45	female	c	france	65,000
0456	Sinead	29/02/82	female	b	ireland	112,000
0687	Paul	11/11/67	male	a	usa	34,000
0982	Donald	01/12/75	male	b	australia	88,000
1103	Agnes	17/09/76	female	aa	sweden	154,000

Textual Interval Binary Numeric

Figure 2.4
Sample descriptive feature data illustrating numeric, binary, ordinal, interval, categorical, and textual types.

usage frequencies for different periods are all descriptive features that could be useful in an ABT but that most likely need to be be derived from multiple raw data sources. The variety of derived features that we might wish to use is limitless. For example, consider the number of features we can derive from the monthly payment a customer makes on an electricity bill. From this single raw data point, we can easily derive features that store the average payment over six months; the maximum payment over six months; the minimum payment over six months; the average payment over three months; the maximum payment over three months; the minimum payment over three months; a flag to indicate that a missed payment has occurred over the last six months; a mapping of the last payment made to a *low*, *medium*, or *high* level; the ratio between the current and previous bill payments, and many more.

Despite this limitless variety, however, there are a number of common derived feature types:

- **Aggregates:** These are aggregate measures defined over a group or period and are usually defined as the count, sum, average, minimum, or maximum of the values within a group. For example, the total number of insurance claims that a member of an insurance company has made over his or her lifetime might be a useful derived feature. Similarly, the average amount of money spent by a customer at an online retailer over periods of one, three, and six months might make an interesting set of derived features.

- **Flags:** Flags are binary features that indicate presence or absence of some characteristic within a dataset. For example, a flag indicating whether or not a bank account has ever been overdrawn might be a useful descriptive feature.

- **Ratios:** Ratios are continuous features that capture the relationship between two or more raw data values. Including a ratio between two values can often be much more powerful in a predictive model than including the two values themselves. For example, in a banking scenario, we might include a ratio between a loan applicant's salary and the amount for which they are requesting a loan rather than including these two values themselves. In a mobile phone scenario, we might include three ratio features to indicate the mix between voice, data, and SMS services that a customer uses.

- **Mappings:** Mappings are used to convert continuous features into categorical features and are often used to reduce the number of unique values that a model will have to deal with. For example, rather than using a continuous feature measuring salary, we might instead map the salary values to *low*, *medium*, and *high* levels to create a categorical feature.

- **Other:** There are no restrictions to the ways in which we can combine data to make derived features. One especially creative example of feature design was when a large retailer wanted to use the level of activity at a competitor's stores as a descriptive feature in one of their analytics solutions. Obviously, the competitor would not give them this information, and so the analytics team at the retailer sought to find some proxy feature that would give them much the same information. Being a large retailer, they had considerable resources at their disposable, one of which was the ability to regularly take high-resolution satellite photos. Using satellite photos of their competitor's premises, they were able to count the number of cars in their competitor's parking lots and use this as a proxy measure of activity within their competitor's stores!

Although in some applications the target feature is a raw value copied directly from an existing data source, in many others it must be derived. Implementing the target feature for an ABT can demand significant effort. For example, consider a problem in which we are trying to predict whether a customer will default on a loan obligation. Should we count one missed payment as a default or, to avoid predicting that good customers will default, should we consider a customer to have defaulted only after they miss three consecutive payments? Or three payments in a six-month period? Or two payments in a five-month period? Just like descriptive features, target features are based on a domain concept, and we must determine what actual implementation is useful, feasible, and correct according to the specifics of the domain in question. In defining target features, it is especially important to seek input from domain experts.

2.4.3   Handling Time

Many of the predictive models that we build are **propensity models**, which predict the likelihood (or propensity) of a future outcome based on a set of descriptive features describing the past. For example, the goal in the insurance claim fraud scenario we have been considering is to make predictions about whether an insurance claim will turn out to be fraudulent after investigation based on the details of the claim itself and the details of the claimant's behavior in *the time preceding the claim*. Propensity models inherently have a temporal element, and when this is the case, we must take time into account when designing the ABT. For **propensity modeling**, there are two key periods: the **observation period**, over which descriptive features are calculated, and the **outcome period**, over which the target feature is calculated.[3]

In some cases the observation period and outcome period are measured over the same time for all prediction subjects. Consider the task of predicting the likelihood that a customer will buy a new product based on past shopping behavior: features describing the *past shopping behavior* are calculated over the observation period, while the outcome period is the time during which we observe whether the customer bought the product. In this situation, the observation period for all the prediction subjects, in this case customers, might be defined as the six months prior to the launch of the new product, and the outcome period might cover the three months after the launch. Figure 2.5(a)[38] shows these two different periods, assuming that the customer's shopping behavior was measured from August 2012 through January 2013, and whether they bought the product of interest was observed from February 2013 through

---

3 It is important to remember for this discussion that all the data from which we construct an ABT for training and evaluating a model will be historical data.

April 2013; and Figure 2.5(b)[38] illustrates how the observation and outcome period for multiple customers are measured over the same period.

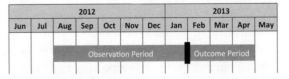

(a) Observation period and outcome period

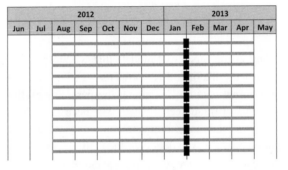

(b) Observation and outcome periods for multiple customers (each line represents a customer)

Figure 2.5
Modeling points in time using an observation period and an outcome period.

Often, however, the observation period and outcome period will be measured over different dates for each prediction subject. Figure 2.6(a)[39] shows an example in which, rather than being defined by a fixed date, the observation period and outcome period are defined relative to an event that occurs at different dates for each prediction subject. The insurance claims fraud scenario we have been discussing throughout this section is a good example of this. In this example the observation period and outcome period are both defined relative to the date of the claim event, which will happen on different dates for different claims. The observation period is the time before the claim event, across which the descriptive features capturing the claimant's behavior are calculated, while the outcome period is the time immediately after the claim event, during which it will emerge whether the claim is fraudulent or genuine. Figure 2.6(a)[39] shows an illustration of this kind of data, while Figure 2.6(b)[39] shows how this is aligned so that descriptive and target features can be extracted to build an ABT. Note that in Figure 2.6(b)[39] the month names have been abstracted and are now defined relative to the transition between the observation and outcome periods.

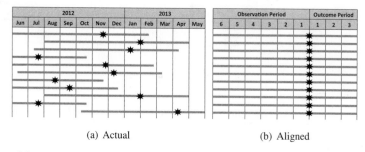

(a) Actual   (b) Aligned

Figure 2.6

Observation and outcome periods defined by an event rather than by a fixed point in time (each line represents a prediction subject and stars signify events).

When time is a factor in a scenario, the descriptive features and the target feature will not necessarily both be time dependent. In some cases only the descriptive features have a time component to them, and the target feature is time independent. Conversely, the target feature may have a time component and the descriptive features may not.

Next-best-offer models provide an example scenario where the descriptive features are time dependent but the target feature is not. A next-best-offer model is used to determine the least expensive incentive that needs to be offered to a customer who is considering canceling a service, for example, a mobile phone contract, in order to make them reconsider and stay. In this case the customer contacting the company to cancel their service is the key event in time. The observation period that the descriptive features will be based on is the customer's entire behavior up to the point at which they make this contact. There is no outcome period as the target feature is determined by whether the company is able to entice the customer to reconsider and, if so, the incentive that was required to do this. Figure 2.7[40] illustrates this scenario.

Loan default prediction is an example where the definition of the target feature has a time element but the descriptive features are time independent. In loan default prediction, the likelihood that an applicant will default on a loan is predicted based on the information the applicant provides on the application form. There really isn't an observation period in this case as all descriptive features will be based on information provided by the applicant on the

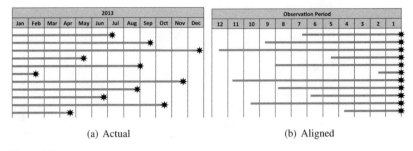

(a) Actual   (b) Aligned

Figure 2.7

Modeling points in time for a scenario with no real outcome period (each line represents a customer, and stars signify events).

application form, rather than on observing the applicant's behavior over time.[4] The outcome period in this case is considered the period of the lifetime of the loan during which the applicant will have either fully repaid or defaulted on the loan. In order to build an ABT for such a problem, a historical dataset of application details and subsequent repayment behavior is required (this might stretch back over multiple years depending on the terms of the loans in question). This scenario is illustrated in Figure 2.8[40].

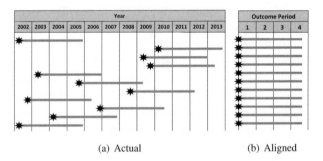

(a) Actual   (b) Aligned

Figure 2.8

Modeling points in time for a scenario with no real observation period (each line represents a customer, and stars signify events).

4 Some might argue that the information on the application form summarizes an applicant's entire life, so this constitutes the observation period in this case!

2.4.4 Legal Issues

Data analytics practitioners can often be frustrated by legislation that stops them from including features that appear to be particularly well suited to an analytics solution in an ABT. Organizations must operate within the relevant legislation that is in place in the jurisdictions in which they operate, and it is important that models are not in breach of this. There are significant differences in legislation in different jurisdictions, but a couple of key relevant principles almost always apply.

The first is related to **anti-discrimination legislation**. Anti-discrimination legislation in most jurisdictions prohibits discrimination on the basis of some set of the following grounds: sex, age, race, ethnicity, nationality, sexual orientation, religion, disability, and political opinions. For example, the United States Civil Rights Act of 1964[5] made it illegal to discriminate against a person on the basis of race, color, religion, national origin, or sex. Subsequent legislation has added to this list (for example, disability was later added as a further basis for non-discrimination). In the European Union the 1999 Treaty of Amsterdam[6] prohibits discrimination on the basis of sex, racial or ethnic origin, religion or belief, disability, age, or sexual orientation. The exact implementation details of anti-discrimination law change, however, across the countries in the European Union.

The impact this has on designing features for inclusion in an ABT is that the use of some features in analytics solutions that leads to some people being given preferential treatment is in breach of anti-discrimination law. For example, credit scoring models such as the one discussed in Section 1.2[3] cannot use race as a descriptive feature because this would discriminate against people on this basis.

The second important principle relates to **data protection legislation**, and in particular the rules surrounding the use of **personal data**. Personal data is defined as data that relates to an identified or identifiable individual, who is known as a **data subject**. Although, data protection legislation changes significantly across different jurisdictions, there are some common tenets on which there is broad agreement. The Organisation for Economic Co-operation and

---

5 The full text of the Civil Rights Act of 1964 is available at www.gpo.gov/fdsys/granule/STATUTE-78/STATUTE-78-Pg241/content-detail.html.

6 The full text of the EU Treaty of Amsterdam is available at www.europa.eu/eu-law/decision-making/treaties/pdf/treaty_of_amsterdam/treaty_of_amsterdam_en.pdf.

Development (OECD, 2013) defines a set of eight general principles of data protection legislation.[7] For the design of analytics base tables, three are especially relevant: the **collection limitation principle**, the **purpose specification principle**, and the **use limitation principle**.

The collection limitation principle states that personal data should only be obtained by lawful means with the knowledge and consent of a data subject. This can limit the amount of data that an organization collects and, sometimes, restricts implementing features to capture certain domain concepts because consent has not been granted to collect the required data. For example, the developers of a smartphone app might decide that by turning on location tracking, they could gather data that would be extremely useful in predicting future usage of the app. Doing this without the permission of the users of the app, however, would be in breach of this principle.

The purpose specification principle states that data subjects should be informed of the purpose for which data will be used at the time of its collection. The use limitation principle adds that collected data should not subsequently be used for purposes other than those stated at the time of collection. Sometimes this means that data collected by an organization cannot be included in an ABT because this would be incompatible with the original use for which the data was collected. For example, an insurance company might collect data on customers' travel behaviors through their travel insurance policy and then use this data in a model that predicts personalized prices for life insurance. Unless, however, this second use was stated at the time of collection, this use would be in breach of this principle.

The legal considerations surrounding predictive analytics are of growing importance and need to be seriously considered during the design of any analytics project. Although larger organizations have legal departments to whom proposed features can be handed over for assessment, in smaller organizations analysts are often required to make these assessments themselves, and consequently they need to be aware of the legal implications relating to their decisions.

---

7 The full discussion of these principles is available at www.oecd.org/sti/ieconomy/privacy.htm.

2.4.5   Implementing Features

Once the initial design for the features in an ABT has been completed, we can begin to implement the technical processes that are needed to extract, create, and aggregate the features into an ABT. It is at this point that the distinction between raw and derived features becomes apparent. Implementing a raw feature is simply a matter of copying the relevant raw value into the ABT. Implementing a derived feature, however, requires data from multiple sources to be combined into a set of single feature values.

A few key **data manipulation** operations are frequently used to calculate derived feature values: joining data sources, filtering rows in a data source, filtering fields in a data source, deriving new features by combining or transforming existing features, and aggregating data sources. Data manipulation operations are implemented in and performed by **database management systems**, **data management tools**, or **data manipulation tools**, and are often referred to as an **extract-transform-load** (**ETL**) process.

2.4.6   Case Study: Motor Insurance Fraud

Let's return to the motor insurance fraud detection solution to consider the design and implementation of the features that will populate the ABT. As we noted in our discussion regarding handling time, the motor insurance claim prediction scenario is a good example of a situation in which the observation period and outcome period are measured over different dates for each insurance claim (the prediction subject for this case study). For each claim the observation and output periods are defined relative to the specific date of that claim. The observation period is the time prior to the claim event, over which the descriptive features capturing the claimant's behavior are calculated, and the outcome period is the time immediately after the claim event, during which it will emerge whether the claim is fraudulent or genuine.

The *Claimant History* domain concept that we developed for this scenario indicates the importance of information regarding the previous claims made by the claimant to the task of identifying fraudulent claims. This domain concept is inherently related to the notion of an observation period, and as we will see, the descriptive features derived from the domain subconcepts under *Claimant History* are time dependent. For example, the *Claim Frequency* domain subconcept under the *Claimant History* concept should capture the fact that the number of claims a claimant has made in the past has an impact on the likelihood of a new claim being fraudulent. This could be expressed in a single descriptive feature counting the number of claims that the claimant has made in the past. This single value, however, may not capture all the relevant information. Adding extra descriptive features that give a more complete picture of a domain concept can lead to better predictive models. In this example we might also include the number of claims made by the claimant in the last three months, the average number of claims made by the claimant per year, and the ratio of the average number of claims made by the claimant per year to the claims made by the claimant in the last twelve months. Figure 2.9[44] shows these descriptive features in a portion of the domain concept diagram.

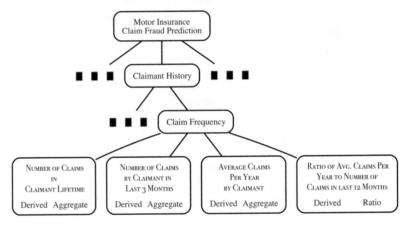

Figure 2.9

A subset of the domain concepts and related features for a motor insurance fraud prediction analytics solution.

The *Claim Types* subconcept of the *Claim History* is also time dependent. This domain subconcept captures the variety of claim types made by the claimant in the past, as these might provide evidence toward possible fraud. The features included under this subconcept, all of which are derived features, are shown in Figure 2.10[45]. The features place a particular emphasis on claims relating to soft tissue injuries (for example, whiplash) because it is understood within the insurance industry that these are frequently associated with fraudulent claims. The number of soft tissue injury claims the claimant has made in the past and the ratio between the number of soft tissue injury claims and other claims made by the claimant are both included as descriptive features in the ABT. A flag is also included to indicate that the claimant has had at least one claim refused in the past, because this might be indicative of a pattern of making speculative claims. Finally, a feature is included that expresses the variety of different claim types made by the claimant in the past. This uses the **entropy** measure that is discussed in Section 4.2[120] as it does a good job of capturing in a single number the variety in a set of objects.

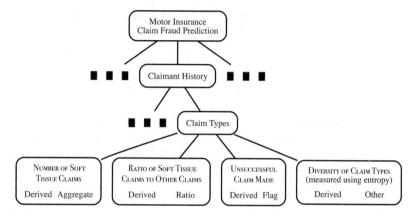

Figure 2.10

A subset of the domain concepts and related features for a motor insurance fraud prediction analytics solution.

However, not all the domain concepts in this scenario are time dependent. The *Claim Details* domain concept, for example, highlights the importance of the details of the claim itself in distinguishing between fraudulent and genuine claims. The type of the claim and amount of the claim are raw features calculated directly from a claims table contained in one of the insurance company's operational databases. A derived feature containing the ratio between the claim amount and the total value of the premiums paid to date on the policy is included. This is based on an expectation that fraudulent claims may be made early in the lifetime of a policy before too much has been spent on premiums. Finally, the insurance company divides their operations into a number of geographic areas defined internally based on the location of their branches, and a feature is included that maps raw address data to these regions.

Table 2.2[47] illustrates the structure of the final ABT that was designed for the motor insurance claims fraud detection solution.[8] The table contains more descriptive features than the ones we have discussed in this section.[9] The table

8 The table is too wide to fit on a page, so it has been split into three sections.

9 The mapping between the features we have discussed here and the column names in Table 2.2[47] is as follows: Number of Claimants: Num. Clmnts.; Number of Claims in Claimant

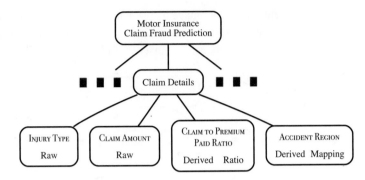

Figure 2.11

A subset of the domain concepts and related features for a motor insurance fraud prediction analytics solution.

also shows the first four instances. If we examine the table closely, we see a number of strange values (for example, $-99,999$) and a number of missing values. In the next chapter, we describe the process we should follow to evaluate the quality of the data in the ABT and the actions we can take if the quality isn't good enough.

2.5 Summary

It is important to remember that predictive data analytics models built using machine learning techniques are tools that we can use to help make better decisions within an organization and are not an end in themselves. It is paramount that, when tasked with creating a predictive model, we fully understand the business problem that this model is being constructed to address and ensure that it does address it. This is the goal behind the process of *converting business problems into analytics solutions* as part of the Business Understanding phase of the CRISP-DM process. When undertaking this process, it is important to take into account the availability of data and the capacity of a business

---

LIFETIME: NUM. CLAIMS; NUMBER OF CLAIMS BY CLAIMANT IN LAST 3 MONTHS: NUM. CLAIMS 3 MONTHS; AVERAGE CLAIMS PER YEAR BY CLAIMANT: AVG. CLAIMS PER YEAR; RATIO OF AVERAGE CLAIMS PER YEAR TO NUMBER OF CLAIMS IN LAST 12 MONTHS: AVG. CLAIMS RATIO; NUMBER OF SOFT TISSUE CLAIMS: NUM. SOFT TISSUE; RATIO OF SOFT TISSUE CLAIMS TO OTHER CLAIMS: % SOFT TISSUE; UNSUCCESSFUL CLAIM MADE: UNSUCC. CLAIMS; DIVERSITY OF CLAIM TYPES: CLAIM DIV.; CLAIM AMOUNT: CLAIM AMT.; CLAIM TO PREMIUM PAID RATIO: CLAIM TO PREM.; ACCIDENT REGION: REGION.

Table 2.2

The ABT for the motor insurance claims fraud detection solution.

ID	TYPE	INC.	MARITAL STATUS	NUM. CLMNTS.	INJURY TYPE	HOSPITAL STAY	CLAIM AMT.
1	ci	0		2	soft tissue	no	1,625
2	ci	0		2	back	yes	15,028
3	ci	54,613	married	1	broken limb	no	-99,999
4	ci	0		3	serious	yes	270,200
⋮					⋮		

ID	TOTAL CLAIMED	NUM. CLAIMS	NUM. CLAIMS 3 MONTHS	AVG. CLAIMS PER YEAR	AVG. CLAIMS RATIO	NUM. SOFT TISSUE	% SOFT TISSUE
1	3,250	2	0	1	1	2	1
2	60,112	1	0	1	1	0	0
3	0	0	0	0	0	0	0
4	0	0	0	0	0	0	0
⋮				⋮			

ID	UNSUCC. CLAIMS	CLAIM AMT. REC.	CLAIM DIV.	CLAIM TO PREM.	REGION	FRAUD FLAG
1	2	0	0	32.500	mn	1
2	0	15,028	0	57.140	dl	0
3	0	572	0	-89.270	wat	0
4	0	270,200	0	30.186	dl	0
⋮				⋮		

to take advantage of insights arising from analytics models as otherwise it is possible to construct an apparently accurate prediction model that is in fact useless.

Predictive data analytics models are reliant on the data that is used to build them—the **analytics base table** (**ABT**) is the key data resource in this regard. An ABT, however, rarely comes directly from a single source already existing within an organization. Instead, the ABT has to be created by combining a range of operational data sources together. The manner in which these data

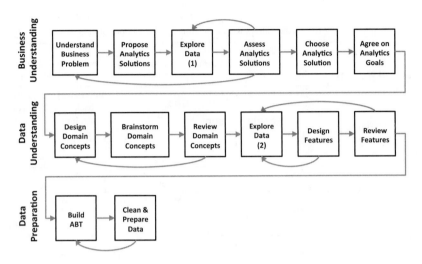

Figure 2.12
A summary of the tasks in the Business Understanding, Data Understanding, and Data Preparation phases of the CRISP-DM process.

resources should be combined must be designed and implemented by the analytics practitioner in collaboration with domain experts. An effective way in which to do this is to start by defining a set of **domain concepts** in collaboration with the business, and then designing **features** that express these concepts in order to form the actual ABT. Domain concepts cover the different aspects of a scenario that are likely to be important in the modeling task at hand.

Features (both descriptive and target) are concrete numeric or symbolic representations of domain concepts. Features can be of many different types, but it is useful to think of a distinction between **raw features** that come directly from existing data sources and **derived features** that are constructed by manipulating values from existing data sources. Common manipulations used in this process include aggregates, flags, ratios, and mappings, although any manipulation is valid. Often multiple features are required to fully express a single domain concept.

The techniques described in this chapter cover the **Business Understanding**, **Data Understanding**, and (partially) **Data Preparation** phases of the **CRISP-DM** process. Figure 2.12[48] shows how the major tasks described in this chapter align with these phases. The next chapter will describe the data understanding and data preparation techniques mentioned briefly in this chapter in much more detail. It is important to remember that in reality, the **Business Understanding**, **Data Understanding**, and **Data Preparation** phases of the CRISP-DM process are performed iteratively rather than linearly. The curved arrows in Figure 2.12[48] show the most common iterations in the process.

2.6 Further Reading

On the topic of converting business problems into analytics solutions, Davenport (2006) and Davenport and Kim (2013) are good business-focused sources. Levitt and Dubner (2005), Ayres (2008), Silver (2012), and Siegel (2013) all provide nice dicusssions of different applications of predictive data analytics.

The CRISP-DM process documentation (Chapman et al., 2000) is surprisingly readable, and adds a lot of extra detail to the tasks described in this chapter. For details on developing business concepts and designing features, Svolba (2007) is excellent (the approaches described can be applied to any tool, not just SAS, which is the focus of Svolba's book).

For further discussion of the legal issues surrounding data analytics, Tene and Polonetsky (2013) and Schwartz (2010) are useful. Chapter 2 of Siegel (2013) discusses the ethical issues surrounding predictive analytics.

2.7   Exercises

1. An online movie streaming company has a business problem of growing **customer churn**—subscription customers canceling their subscriptions to join a competitor. Create a list of ways in which predictive data analytics could be used to help address this business problem. For each proposed approach, describe the predictive model that will be built, how the model will be used by the business, and how using the model will help address the original business problem.

2. A national revenue commission performs audits on public companies to find and fine tax defaulters. To perform an audit, a tax inspector visits a company and spends a number of days scrutinizing the company's accounts. Because it takes so long and relies on experienced, expert tax inspectors, performing an audit is an expensive exercise. The revenue commission currently selects companies for audit at random. When an audit reveals that a company is complying with all tax requirements, there is a sense that the time spent performing the audit was wasted, and more important, that another business who is not tax compliant has been spared an investigation. The revenue commissioner would like to solve this problem by targeting audits at companies who are likely to be in breach of tax regulations, rather than selecting companies for audit at random. In this way the revenue commission hopes to maximize the yield from the audits that it performs.

   To help with **situational fluency** for this scenario here is a brief outline of how companies interact with the revenue commission. When a company is formed, it registers with the company registrations office. Information provided at registration includes the type of industry the company is involved in, details of the directors of the company, and where the company is located. Once a company has been registered, it must provide a tax return at the end of every financial year. This includes all financial details of the company's operations during the year and is the basis of calculating the tax liability of a company. Public companies also must file public documents every year that outline how they have been performing, details of any changes in directorship, and so on.

a. Propose two ways in which predictive data analytics could be used to help address this business problem.[10] For each proposed approach, describe the predictive model that will be built, how the model will be used by the business, and how using the model will help address the original business problem.

b. For each analytics solution you have proposed for the revenue commission, outline the type of data that would be required.

c. For each analytics solution you have proposed, outline the capacity that the revenue commission would need in order to utilize the analytics-based insight that your solution would provide.

3. The table below shows a sample of a larger dataset containing details of policy holders at an insurance company. The descriptive features included in the table describe each policy holders' ID, occupation, gender, age, the value of their car, the type of insurance policy they hold, and their preferred contact channel.

ID	OCCUPATION	GENDER	AGE	MOTOR VALUE	POLICY TYPE	PREF CHANNEL
1	lab tech	female	43	42,632	planC	sms
2	farmhand	female	57	22,096	planA	phone
3	biophysicist	male	21	27,221	planA	phone
4	sheriff	female	47	21,460	planB	phone
5	painter	male	55	13,976	planC	phone
6	manager	male	19	4,866	planA	email
7	geologist	male	51	12,759	planC	phone
8	messenger	male	49	15,672	planB	phone
9	nurse	female	18	16,399	planC	sms
10	fire inspector	male	47	14,767	planC	email

a. State whether each descriptive feature contains numeric, interval, ordinal, categorical, binary, or textual data.

b. How many levels does each categorical and ordinal feature have?

---

10 Revenue commissioners around the world use predictive data analytics techniques to keep their processes as efficient as possible. Cleary and Tax (2011) is a good example.

4. Select one of the predictive analytics models that you proposed in your answer to Question 2 about the revenue commission for exploration of the design of its **analytics base table** (**ABT**).

   a. What is the prediction subject for the model that will be trained using this ABT?

   b. Describe the domain concepts for this ABT.

   c. Draw a domain concept diagram for the ABT.

   d. Are there likely to be any legal issues associated with the domain concepts you have included?

* 5. Although their sales are reasonable, an online fashion retailer is struggling to generate the volume of sales that they had originally hoped for when launching their site. List a number of ways in which predictive data analytics could be used to help address this business problem. For each proposed approach, describe the predictive model that will be built, how the model will be used by the business, and how using the model will help address the original business problem.

* 6. An oil exploration company is struggling to cope with the number of exploratory sites that they need to drill in order to find locations for viable oil wells. There are many potential sites that geologists at the company have identified, but undertaking exploratory drilling at these sites is very expensive. If the company could increase the percentage of sites at which they perform exploratory drilling that actually lead to finding locations for viable wells, they could save a huge amount of money.

   Currently geologists at the company identify potential drilling sites by manually examining information from a variety of different sources. These include ordinance survey maps, aerial photographs, characteristics of rock and soil samples taken from potential sites, and measurements from sensitive gravitational and seismic instruments.

   a. Propose two ways in which predictive data analytics could be used to help address the problem that the oil exploration company is facing. For each proposed approach, describe the predictive model that will be built, how the model will be used by the company, and how using the model will help address the original problem.

   b. For each analytics solution you have proposed, outline the type of data that would be required.

    c. For each analytics solution you have proposed, outline the capacity that would be needed in order to utilize the analytics-based insight that your solution would provide.

∗ 7. Select one of the predictive analytics models that you proposed in your answer to the previous question about the oil exploration company for exploration of the design of its **analytics base table**.

    a. What is the prediction subject for the model that will be trained using this ABT?

    b. Describe the domain concepts for this ABT.

    c. Draw a domain concept diagram for the ABT.

    d. Are there likely to be any legal issues associated with the domain concepts you have included?

3 Data Exploration

Fail to prepare, prepare to fail.
—Roy Keane

In Chapter 2[21] we described the process of moving from a business problem to an analytics solution and, from there, to the design and construction of an **analytics base table** (**ABT**). An ABT for a predictive analytics solution contains a set of instances that are represented by a set of descriptive features and a target feature. Before attempting to build predictive models based on an ABT it is important that we undertake some exploratory analysis, or **data exploration**, of the data contained in the ABT. **Data exploration** is a key part of both the **Data Understanding** and, **Data Preparation** phases of CRISP-DM.

There are two goals in data exploration. The first goal is to fully understand the characteristics of the data in the ABT. It is important that for each feature in the ABT, we understand characteristics such as the types of values a feature can take, the ranges into which the values in a feature fall, and how the values in a dataset for a feature are distributed across the range that they can take. We refer to this as *getting to know* the data. The second goal of data exploration is to determine whether or not the data in an ABT suffer from any **data quality issues** that could adversely affect the models that we build. Examples of typical data quality issues include an instance that is missing values for one or more descriptive features, an instance that has an extremely high value for a feature, or an instance that has an inappropriate level for a feature. Some data quality issues arise due to invalid data and will be corrected as soon as we discover them. Others, however, arise because of perfectly valid data that may cause difficulty to some machine learning techniques. We note these types of data quality issues during exploration for potential handling when we reach the modeling phase of a project.

The most important tool used during data exploration is the **data quality report**. This chapter begins by describing the structure of a data quality report and explaining how it is used to *get to know* the data in an ABT and to identify data quality issues. We then describe a number of strategies for handling data quality issues and when it is appropriate to use them. Throughout the discussion of the data quality report and how we use it, we return to the motor insurance fraud case study from Chapter 2[21]. Toward the end of the chapter, we introduce some more advanced data exploration techniques that, although not part of the standard data quality report, can be useful at this stage of an analytics project and present some data preparation techniques that can be applied to the data in an ABT prior to modeling.

3.1   The Data Quality Report

The **data quality report** is the most important tool of the data exploration process. A data quality report includes tabular reports (one for continuous features and one for categorical features) that describe the characteristics of each feature in an ABT using standard statistical measures of **central tendency** and **variation**. The tabular reports are accompanied by data visualizations that illustrate the distribution of the values in each feature in an ABT. Readers who are not already familiar with standard measures of central tendency (**mean**, **mode**, and **median**), standard measures of variation (**standard deviation** and **percentiles**), and standard data visualization plots (**bar plots**, **histograms**, and **box plots**) should read Appendix A[525] for the necessary introduction.

The table in a data quality report that describes continuous features should include a row containing the minimum, 1st quartile, mean, median, 3rd quartile, maximum, and standard deviation statistics for that feature as well as the total number of instances in the ABT, the percentage of instances in the ABT that are missing a value for each feature and the **cardinality** of each feature, (cardinality measures the number of distinct values present in the ABT for a feature). Table 3.1(a)[57] shows the structure of the table in a data quality report that describes continuous features.

The table in the data quality report that describes categorical features should include a row for each feature in the ABT that contains the two most frequent levels for the feature (the mode and 2nd mode) and the frequency with which these appear (both as raw frequencies and as a proportion of the total number of instances in the dataset). Each row should also include the percentage of instances in the ABT that are missing a value for the feature and the cardinality of the feature. Table 3.1(b)[57] shows the structure of the table in a data quality report that describes categorical features.

The data quality report should also include a histogram for each continuous feature in an ABT. For continuous features with cardinality less than 10, we use bar plots instead of histograms as this usually produces more informative data visualization. For each categorical feature in an ABT, a bar plot should be included in the data quality report.

Table 3.1

The structures of the tables included in a data quality report to describe (a) continuous features and (b) categorical features.

(a) Continuous Features

Feature	Count	% Miss.	Card.	Min.	1st Qrt.	Mean	Median	3rd Qrt.	Max.	Std. Dev.
——	——	——	——	——	——	——	——	——	——	——
——	——	——	——	——	——	——	——	——	——	——
——	——	——	——	——	——	——	——	——	——	——

(b) Categorical Features

Feature	Count	% Miss.	Card.	Mode	Mode Freq.	Mode %	2nd Mode	2nd Mode Freq.	2nd Mode %
——	——	——	——	——	——	——	——	——	——
——	——	——	——	——	——	——	——	——	——
——	——	——	——	——	——	——	——	——	——

3.1.1 Case Study: Motor Insurance Fraud

Table 3.2[58] shows a portion of the ABT that has been developed for the motor insurance claims fraud detection solution based on the design described in Section 2.4.6[43].[1] The data quality report for this ABT is shown across Table 3.3[59] (tabular reports for continuous and categorical features) and Figure 3.1[60] (data visualizations for each feature in the dataset).

---

1 In order to allow this dataset fit on one page, only a subset of the features described in the domain concept diagrams in Figures 2.9[44], 2.10[45], and 2.11[46] are included.

Table 3.2
Portions of the ABT for the motor insurance claims fraud detection problem discussed in Section 2.4.6[43].

ID	TYPE	INC.	MARITAL STATUS	NUM. CLMNTS.	INJURY TYPE	HOSPITAL STAY	CLAIM AMT.	TOTAL CLAIMED	NUM CLAIMS	NUM. SOFT TISS.	% SOFT TISS.	CLAIM AMT. RCVD.	FRAUD FLAG
1	ci	0		2	soft tissue	no	1,625	3,250	2	2	1.0	0	1
2	ci	0		2	back	yes	15,028	60,112	1	0	0	15,028	0
3	ci	54,613	married	1	broken limb	no	-99,999	0	0	0	0	572	0
4	ci	0		4	broken limb	yes	5,097	11,661	1	1	1.0	7,864	0
5	ci	0		4	soft tissue	no	8,869	0	0	0	0	0	1
					...	...					...		
300	ci	0		2	broken limb	no	2,244	0	0	0	0	2,244	0
301	ci	0		1	broken limb	no	1,627	92,283	3	0	0	1,627	0
302	ci	0		3	serious	yes	270,200	0	0	0	0	270,200	0
303	ci	0		1	soft tissue	no	7,668	92,806	3	0	0	7,668	0
304	ci	46,365	married	1	back	no	3,217	0	0	0	0	1,653	0
			...			...					...		
458	ci	48,176	married	3	soft tissue	yes	4,653	8,203	1	0	0	4,653	0
459	ci	0		1	soft tissue	yes	881	51,245	3	0	0	0	1
460	ci	0		3	back	no	8,688	729,792	56	5	0.08	8,688	0
461	ci	47,371	divorced	1	broken limb	yes	3,194	11,668	1	0	0	3,194	0
462	ci	0		1	soft tissue	no	6,821	0	0	0	0	0	1
			...			...					...		
496	ci	0		1	soft tissue	no	2,118	0	0	0	0	0	1
497	ci	29,280	married	4	broken limb	yes	3,199	0	0	0	0	0	1
498	ci	0		1	broken limb	yes	32,469	0	0	0	0	16,763	0
499	ci	46,683	married	1	broken limb	no	179,448	0	0	0	0	179,448	0
500	ci	0		1	broken limb	no	8,259	0	0	0	0	0	1

Table 3.3

A data quality report for the motor insurance claims fraud detection ABT displayed in Table 3.2[58].

(a) Continuous Features

Feature	Count	% Miss.	Card.	Min	1st Qrt.	Mean	Median	3rd Qrt.	Max	Std. Dev.
INCOME	500	0.0	171	0.0	0.0	13,740.0	0.0	33,918.5	71,284.0	20,081.5
NUM. CLAIMANTS	500	0.0	4	1.0	1.0	1.9	2	3.0	4.0	1.0
CLAIM AMOUNT	500	0.0	493	-99,999	3,322.3	16,373.2	5,663.0	12,245.5	270,200.0	29,426.3
TOTAL CLAIMED	500	0.0	235	0.0	0.0	9,597.2	0.0	11,282.8	729,792.0	35,655.7
NUM. CLAIMS	500	0.0	7	0.0	0.0	0.8	0.0	1.0	56.0	2.7
NUM. SOFT TISSUE	500	2.0	6	0.0	0.0	0.2	0.0	0.0	5.0	0.6
% SOFT TISSUE	500	0.0	9	0.0	0.0	0.2	0.0	0.0	2.0	0.4
AMOUNT RECEIVED	500	0.0	329	0.0	0.0	13,051.9	3,253.5	8,191.8	295,303.0	30,547.2
FRAUD FLAG	500	0.0	2	0.0	0.0	0.3	0.0	1.0	1.0	0.5

(b) Categorical Features

Feature	Count	% Miss.	Card.	Mode	Mode Freq.	Mode %	2nd Mode	2nd Mode Freq.	2nd Mode %
INSURANCE TYPE	500	0.0	1	ci	500	100.0	–	–	–
MARITAL STATUS	500	61.2	4	married	99	51.0	single	48	24.7
INJURY TYPE	500	0.0	4	broken limb	177	35.4	soft tissue	172	34.4
HOSPITAL STAY	500	0.0	2	no	354	70.8	yes	146	29.2

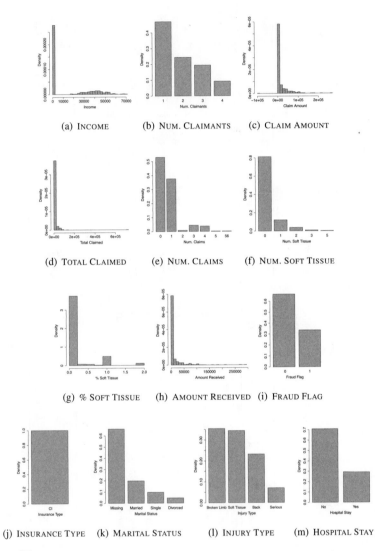

Figure 3.1

Visualizations of the continuous and categorical features in the motor insurance claims fraud detection ABT in Table 3.2[58].

3.2 Getting to Know the Data

The data quality report gives an in-depth picture of the data in an ABT, and we should study it in detail in order to *get to know* the data that we will work with. For each feature, we should examine the central tendency and variation to understand the types of values that each feature can take. For categorical features, we should first examine the mode, 2nd mode, mode %, and 2nd mode % in the categorical features table in the data quality report. These tell us the most common levels within these features and will identify if any levels dominate the dataset (these levels will have a very high mode %). The bar plots shown in the data quality report are also very useful here. They give us a quick overview of all the levels in the domain of each categorical feature and the frequencies of these levels.

For continuous features we should first examine the mean and standard deviation of each feature to get a sense of the central tendency and variation of the values within the dataset for the feature. We should also examine the minimum and maximum values to understand the range that is possible for each feature. The histograms for each continuous feature included in a data quality report are a very easy way for us to understand how the values for a feature are distributed across the range they can take.[2] When we generate histograms of features, there are a number of common, well-understood shapes that we should look out for. These shapes relate to well-known standard **probability distributions**,[3] and recognizing that the distribution of the values in an ABT for a feature closely matches one of these standard distributions can help us when building machine learning models. During data exploration we don't need to go any further than simply recognizing that features seem to follow particular distributions, and this can be done from examining the histogram for each feature. Figure 3.2[62] shows a selection of histogram shapes that exhibit characteristics commonly seen when analyzing features and that are indicative of standard, well-known probability distributions.

Figure 3.2(a)[62] shows a histogram exhibiting a **uniform distribution**. A uniform distribution indicates that a feature is equally likely to take a value in any of the ranges present. Sometimes a uniform distribution is indicative of

---

2 Note that in a density histogram, the height of each bar represents the likelihood that a value in the range defining that bar will occur in a data sample, see Section A.4.2[535].

3 We discuss probability distributions in more depth in Chapter 6[247].

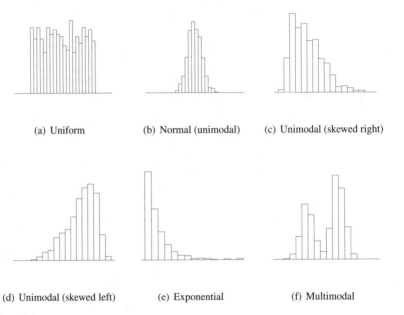

(a) Uniform   (b) Normal (unimodal)   (c) Unimodal (skewed right)

(d) Unimodal (skewed left)   (e) Exponential   (f) Multimodal

Figure 3.2

Histograms for six different sets of data, each of which exhibit well-known, common characteristics.

a descriptive feature that contains an ID rather than a measure of something more interesting.

Figure 3.2(b)[62] shows a shape indicative of a **normal distribution**. Features following a normal distribution are characterized by a strong tendency toward a central value and symmetrical variation to either side of this central tendency. Naturally occurring phenomena—for example, the heights or weights of a randomly selected group of men or women—tend to follow a normal distribution. Histograms that follow a normal distribution can also be described as **unimodal** because they have a single peak around the central tendency. Finding features that exhibit a normal distribution is a good thing, as many of the modeling techniques we discuss in later chapters work particularly well with normally distributed data.

Figures 3.2(c)[62] and 3.2(d)[62] show unimodal histograms that exhibit **skew**. Skew is simply a tendency toward very high (**right skew** as seen in Figure

3.2(c)[62]) or very low (**left skew** as seen in Figure 3.2(d)[62]) values. Features recording salaries often follow a right skewed, distribution as most people are paid salaries near a well-defined central tendency, but there are usually a small number of people who are paid very large salaries. Skewed distributions are often said to have **long tails** toward these very high or very low values.

In a feature following an **exponential distribution**, as shown in Figure 3.2(e)[62], the likelihood of low values occurring is very high but diminishes rapidly for higher values. Features such as the number of times a person has made an insurance claim or the number of times a person has been married tend to follow an exponential distribution. Recognizing that a feature follows an exponential distribution is another clear warning sign that outliers are likely. As shown in Figure 3.2(e)[62], exponential distributions have a long tail, and so very high values are not uncommon.

Finally, a feature characterized by a **multimodal distribution** has two or more very commonly occurring ranges of values that are clearly separated. Figure 3.2(f)[62] shows a **bi-modal distribution** with two clear peaks—we can think of this as two normal distributions pushed together. Multimodal distributions tend to occur when a feature contains a measurement made across a number of distinct groups. For example, if we were to measure the heights of a randomly selected group of Irish men and women, we would expect a bi-modal distribution with a peak at around 1.635m for women and 1.775m for men.

Observing a multimodal distribution is cause for both caution and optimism. The caution comes from the fact that measures of central tendency and variation tend to break down for multimodal data. For example, consider that the mean value of the distribution shown in Figure 3.2(f)[62] is likely to sit right in the valley between the two peaks, even though very few instances actually have this value. The optimism associated with finding multimodally distributed data stems from the fact that, if we are lucky, the separate peaks in the distribution will be associated with the different target levels we are trying to predict. For example, if we were trying to predict gender from a set of physiological measurements, height would most likely be a very predictive value, as it would separate people into male and female groups.

This stage of data exploration is mostly an information-gathering exercise, the output of which is just a better understanding of the contents of an ABT. It does, however, also present a good opportunity to discuss anything unusual that we notice about the central tendency and variation of features within the ABT. For example, a salary feature with a mean of 40 would seem unlikely (40,000 would seem more reasonable) and should be investigated.

3.2.1   The Normal Distribution

The **normal distribution** (also known as a **Gaussian distribution**) is so important that it is worth spending a little extra time discussing its characteristics. Standard probability distributions have associated **probability density functions**, which define the characteristics of the distribution. The probability density function for the normal distribution is

$$N(x, \mu, \sigma) = \frac{1}{\sigma \sqrt{2\pi}} e^{-\frac{(x-\mu)^2}{2\sigma^2}} \tag{3.1}$$

where x is any value, and μ and σ are parameters that define the shape of the distribution. Given a probability density function, we can plot the **density curve** associated with a distribution, which gives us a different way to visualize standard distributions like the normal. Figure 3.3[65] shows the density curves for a number of different normal distributions. The higher the curve for a particular value on the horizontal axis, the more likely that value is.

The curve defined by a normal probability distribution is symmetric around a single peak value. The location of the peak value is defined by the parameter μ (pronounced *mu*), which denotes the **population mean** (in other words, the mean value of the feature if we had access to every value that could possibly occur). The height and slope of the curve is dependent on the parameter σ (pronounced *sigma*), which denotes the **population standard deviation**. The larger the value of σ, the lower the maximum height of the curve and the shallower the slope. Figure 3.3(a)[65] illustrates how the location of the peak moves as the value for μ changes, and Figure 3.3(b)[65] illustrates how the shape of the curve changes as we vary the value for σ. Notice that in both figures, the normal distribution plotted with the continuous black line has mean $\mu = 0$ and standard deviation $\sigma = 1$. This normal distribution is known as the **standard normal distribution**. The notation X is $N(\mu, \sigma)$ is often used as a shorthand for X is a *normally distributed feature with mean μ and standard deviation σ.*[4] One important characteristic of the normal distribution is often described as the 68−95−99.7 **rule**. The rule states that approximately 68% of the values in a sample that follows a normal distribution will be within one σ of μ, 95% of the values will be within two σ of μ, and 99.7% of values will be within three σ of μ. Figure 3.4[65] illustrates this rule. This rule highlights that in data that

---

4 Sometimes, the variance of a feature, σ^2, rather than its standard deviation, σ, is listed as the parameter for the normal distribution. In this text we always use the standard deviation σ.

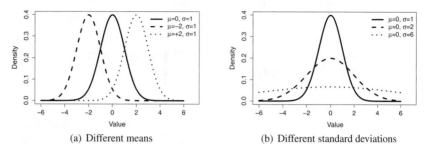

(a) Different means   (b) Different standard deviations

Figure 3.3

(a) Three normal distributions with different means but identical standard deviations; (b) three normal distributions with identical means but different standard deviations.

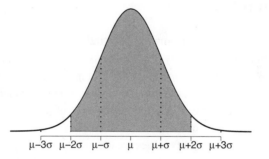

Figure 3.4

An illustration of the 68−95−99.7 rule. The gray region defines the area where 95% of values in a sample are expected.

follows a normal distribution, there is a very low probability of observations occurring that differ from the mean by more than two standard deviations.

3.2.2   Case Study: Motor Insurance Fraud

The data quality report in Table 3.3[59] and in Figure 3.1[60] and allows us to very quickly become familiar with the central tendency and variation of each feature in the ABT. These were all broadly as the business expected. In the bar plots in Figure 3.1[60], the different levels in the domain of each categorical feature, and how these levels are distributed, are obvious. For example, INJURY TYPE has four levels. Three of these, *broken limb*, *soft tissue*, and *back*, are quite frequent in the ABT, while *serious* is quite rare. The distribution of INSURANCE TYPE is a little strange, as it displays only one level.

From the histograms in Figure 3.1[60], we see that all the continuous features except for INCOME and FRAUD FLAG seem to follow an exponential distribution pretty closely. INCOME is interesting as it seems to follow what looks like a normal distribution except that there is one large bar at about 0. The distribution of the FRAUD FLAG feature that can be seen in its histogram is not typical of a continuous feature.

By analyzing the data quality report, we are able to understand the characteristics of the data in the ABT. We will return to the features that seemed to have slightly peculiar distributions.

3.3   Identifying Data Quality Issues

After getting to know the data, the second goal of data exploration is to identify any data quality issues in an ABT. A **data quality issue** is loosely defined as anything *unusual* about the data in an ABT. The most common data quality issues, however, are **missing values**, **irregular cardinality** problems, and **outliers**. In this section we describe each of these data quality issues and outline how the data quality report can be used to identify them.

The data quality issues we identify from a data quality report will be of two types: data quality issues due to **invalid data** and data quality issues due to **valid data**. Data quality issues due to invalid data typically arise because of errors in the process used to generate an ABT, usually in relation to calculating derived features. When we identify data quality issues due to invalid data, we should take immediate action to correct them, regenerate the ABT, and re-create the data quality report. Data quality issues due to valid data can arise for a range of domain-specific reasons (we discuss some of these later in this section), and we do not necessarily need to take any corrective action to address these issues. We do not correct data quality issues due to valid data unless the predictive models we will use the data in the ABT to train require that particular data quality issues be corrected. For example, we cannot train error-based models with data that contains missing values, and data that contains outliers significantly damages the performance of similarity-based models. At this stage we simply record any data quality issues due to valid data in a **data quality plan** so that we remain aware of them and can handle them later if required. Table 3.4[67] shows the structure of a data quality plan. For each of

Table 3.4
The structure of a data quality plan.

Feature	Data Quality Issue	Potential Handling Strategies
——	———	—————
——	———	—————
——	———	—————
——	———	—————

the data quality issues found, we include the feature it was found in and the details of the data quality issue. Later we add information on potential handling strategies for each data quality issue.

3.3.1 Missing Values

Often when an ABT is generated, some instances will be missing values for one or more features. The **% Miss.** columns in the data quality report highlight the percentage of missing values for each feature (both continuous and categorical) in an ABT, and so it is very easy to identify which features suffer from this issue. If features have missing values, we must first determine why the values are missing. Often missing values arise from errors in data integration or in the process of generating values for derived fields. If this is the case, these missing values are due to invalid data, so the data integration errors can be corrected, and the ABT can be regenerated to populate the missing values. Missing values can also arise for legitimate reasons, however. Sometimes in an organization, certain values will only have been collected after a certain date, and the data used to generate an ABT might cover time both before and after this date. In other cases, particularly where data arises from manual entry, certain personally sensitive values (for example, salary, age, or weight) may be entered only for a small number of instances. These missing values are due to valid data, so they do not need to be handled but should instead be recorded in the data quality plan.

There is one case in which we might deal directly with missing values that arise from valid data during data exploration. If the proportion of missing values for a feature is very high, a good rule of thumb is anything in excess of 60%, then the amount of information stored in the feature is so low that it is probably a good idea to simply remove that feature from the ABT.

3.3.2   Irregular Cardinality

The **Card.** column in the data quality report shows the number of distinct values present for a feature within an ABT. A data quality issue arises when the cardinality for a feature does not match what we expect, a mismatch called an **irregular cardinality**. The first things to check the cardinality column for are features with a cardinality of 1. This indicates a feature that has the same value for every instance and contains no information useful for building predictive models. Features with a cardinality of 1 should first be investigated to ensure that the issue is not due to an ABT generation error. If this is the case, then the error should be corrected, and the ABT should be regenerated. If the generation process proves to be error-free, then features with a cardinality of 1, although valid, should be removed from an ABT because they will not be of any value in building predictive models.

The second things to check for in the cardinality column are categorical features incorrectly labeled as continuous. Continuous features will usually have a cardinality value close to the number of instances in the dataset. If the cardinality of a continuous feature is significantly less than the number of instances in the dataset, then it should be investigated. Sometimes a feature is actually continuous but in practice can assume only a small range of values—for example, the number of children a person has. In this case there is nothing wrong, and the feature should be left alone. In other cases, however, a categorical feature will have been developed to use numbers to indicate categories and might be mistakenly identified as a continuous feature in a data quality report. Checking for features with a low cardinality will highlight these features. For example, a feature might record gender using 1 for female and 0 for male. If treated as a continuous feature in a data quality report, this would have a cardinality of 2. Once identified, these features should be recoded as categorical features.

The third way in which a data quality issue can arise due to an irregular cardinality is if a categorical feature has a much higher cardinality than we would expect given the definition of the feature. For example, a categorical feature storing gender with a cardinality of 6 is worthy of further investigation. This issue often arises because multiple levels are used to represent the same thing—for example, in a feature storing gender, we might find levels of *male*, *female, m, f, M*, and *F*, which all represent male and female in slightly different ways. This is another example of a data quality issue due to invalid data. It should be corrected through a mapping to a standard set of levels, and the ABT should be regenerated.

The final example of a data quality issue due to an irregular cardinality is when a categorical feature simply has a very high number of levels—anything over 50 is worth investigation. There are many genuine examples of features that will have such high cardinality, but some of the machine learning algorithms that we will look at will struggle to effectively use features with such high cardinality. This is an example of a data issue due to valid data, so if this occurs for features in an ABT, it should be noted in the data quality plan.

3.3.3 Outliers

Outliers are values that lie far away from the central tendency of a feature. There are two kinds of outliers that might occur in an ABT: **invalid outliers** and **valid outliers**. Invalid outliers are values that have been included in a sample through error and are often referred to as noise in the data. Invalid outliers can arise for all sorts of different reasons. For example, during a manual data entry process, a *fat fingered*[5] analyst may have entered 100,000 instead of 1,000. Valid outliers are correct values that are simply very different from the rest of the values for a feature, for example, a billionaire who has a massive salary compared to everyone else in a sample.

There are two main ways that the data quality report can be used to identify outliers within a dataset. The first is to examine the minimum and maximum values for each feature and use domain knowledge to determine whether these are plausible values. For example, a minimum age value of -12 would jump out as an error. Outliers identified in this way are likely to be invalid outliers and should immediately be either corrected, if data sources allow this, or removed and marked as missing values if correction is not possible. In some cases we might even remove a complete instance from a dataset based on the presence of an outlier.

The second approach to identifying outliers is to compare the gaps between the median, minimum, maximum, 1st quartile, and 3rd quartile values. If the gap between the 3rd quartile and the maximum value is noticeably larger than the gap between the median and the 3rd quartile, this suggests that the maximum value is unusual and is likely to be an outlier. Similarly, if the gap between the 1st quartile and the minimum value is noticeably larger than the gap between the median and the 1st quartile, this suggests that the minimum

5 *Fat finger* is a phrase often used in financial trading to refer to mistakes that arise when a trader enters extra zeros by mistake and buys or sells much more of a stock than intended.

value is unusual and is likely to be an outlier. The outliers shown in box plots also help to make this comparison. Exponential or skewed distributions in histograms are also good indicators of the presence of outliers.

It is likely that outliers found using the second approach are valid outliers, so they are a data quality issue due to valid data. Some machine learning techniques do not perform well in the presence of outliers, so we should note these in the data quality plan for possible handling later in the project.

3.3.4   Case Study: Motor Insurance Fraud

Using the data quality report in Table 3.3[59] and Figure 3.1[60] together with the ABT extract in Table 3.2[58], we can perform an analysis of this ABT for data quality issues. We do this by describing separately missing values, irregular cardinality, and outliers.

3.3.4.1   Missing Values

The **% Miss.** column of the data quality report in Table 3.3[59] shows that MARITAL STATUS and NUM. SOFT TISSUE are the only features with an obvious problem with missing values. Indeed, over 60% of the values for MARITAL STATUS are missing, so this feature should almost certainly be removed from the ABT (we return to this feature shortly). Only 2% of the values for the NUM. SOFT TISSUE feature are missing, so removal would be extreme in this case. This issue should be noted in the data quality plan.

An examination of the histogram for the INCOME feature (shown in Figure 3.1(a)[60]) and the actual data for this feature in Table 3.2[58] reveals an interesting pattern. In the histogram we can see an unusual number of zero values for INCOME that seems set apart from the central tendency of the data, which appears to be at about 40,000. Examining the INCOME row in the data quality report also shows a large difference between the mean and median values, which is unusual. Examining the actual raw data in Table 3.2[58] shows that these zeros always co-occur with missing values in the MARITAL STATUS feature. This pattern was investigated with the business to understand whether this was an issue due to valid or invalid data. It was confirmed by the business that the zeros in the INCOME feature actually represent missing values and that MARITAL STATUS and INCOME were collected together, leading to their both being missing for the same instances in the ABT. No other data source existed from which these features could be populated, so it was decided to remove both of them from the ABT.

3.3.4.2 Irregular Cardinality

Reading down the **Card.** column of the data quality report, we can see that the cardinality of the INSURANCE TYPE feature is 1, aa obvious data problem that needs investigation. The cardinality value indicates that every instance has the same value for this feature, *ci*. Investigation of this issue with the business revealed that nothing had gone wrong during the ABT generation process, and that *ci* refers to *car insurance*. Every instance in this ABT should have that value, and this feature was removed from the ABT.

Many of the continuous features in the dataset also have very low cardinality values. NUM. CLAIMANTS, NUM. CLAIMS, NUM. SOFT TISSUE, % SOFT TISSUE, and FRAUD FLAG all have cardinality less than 10, which is unusual in a dataset of 500 instances. These low cardinalities were investigated with the business. The low cardinality for the NUM. CLAIMANTS, NUM. CLAIMS, and NUM. SOFT TISSUE features was found to be valid, because these are categorical features and can only take values in a small range as people tend not to make very many claims. The % SOFT TISSUE feature is a ratio of the NUM. CLAIMS and NUM. SOFT TISSUE features, and its low cardinality arises from their low cardinality.

The cardinality of 2 for the FRAUD FLAG feature highlights the fact that this is not really a continuous feature. Rather, FRAUD FLAG is a categorical feature that just happens to use *0* and *1* as its category labels which has led to its being treated as continuous in the ABT. FRAUD FLAG was changed to be a categorical feature. This is particularly important in this case because FRAUD FLAG is the target feature, and as we will see in upcoming chapters, the type of the target feature has a big impact on how we apply machine learning techniques.

3.3.4.3 Outliers

From an examination of the minimum and maximum values for each continuous feature in Table 3.3(a)[59], CLAIM AMOUNT jumps out as having an unusual minimum value of −99,999. A little investigation revealed that this minimum value arises from $\mathbf{d}_3$ in Table 3.2[58]. The absence of a large bar at −99,999 in Figure 3.1(c)[60] confirms that there are not multiple occurrences of this value. The pattern 99,999 also suggests that this is most likely a data entry error or a system default remaining in the ABT. This was confirmed with the business in this case, and this value was treated as a invalid outlier and replaced with a missing value.

Table 3.5

The data quality plan for the motor insurance fraud prediction ABT.

Feature	Data Quality Issue	Potential Handling Strategies
NUM. SOFT TISSUE	Missing values (2%)	
CLAIM AMOUNT	Outliers (high)	
AMOUNT RECEIVED	Outliers (high)	

CLAIM AMOUNT, TOTAL CLAIMED, NUM. CLAIMS and AMOUNT RECEIVED all seem to have unusually high maximum values, especially when compared to their median and 3rd quartile values. To investigate outliers, we should always start by locating the instance in the dataset that contains the strange maximum or minimum values. In this case the maximum values for TOTAL CLAIMED and NUM. CLAIMS both come from $\mathbf{d}_{460}$ in Table 3.2[58]. This policy holder seems to have made many more claims than anyone else, and the total amount claimed reflects this. This deviation from the norm was investigated with the business, and it turned out that although these figures were correct, this policy was actually a company policy rather than an individual policy, which was included in the ABT by mistake. For this reason, instance $\mathbf{d}_{460}$ was removed from the ABT.

The offending large maximums for CLAIM AMOUNT and AMOUNT RECEIVED both come from $\mathbf{d}_{302}$ in Table 3.2[58]. Investigation of this claim with the business revealed that this is in fact a valid outlier and represents an unusually large claim for a very serious injury. Examination of the histograms in Figures 3.1(c)[60] and 3.1(h)[60] show that the CLAIM AMOUNT and AMOUNT RECEIVED features have a number of large values (evidenced by the small bars to the right hand side of these histograms) and that $\mathbf{d}_{302}$ is not unique. These outliers should be noted in the data quality plan for possible handling later in the project.

3.3.4.4   The Data Quality Plan

Based on the analysis described in the preceding sections, the data quality plan shown in Table 3.5[72] was created. This records each of the data quality issues due to valid data that have been identified in the motor insurance fraud ABT. During the Modeling phase of the project, we will use this table as a reminder of data quality issues that could affect model training. At the end of the next section we complete this table by adding potential handling strategies.

3.4   Handling Data Quality Issues

When we find data quality issues due to valid data during data exploration, we should note these issues in a data quality plan for potential handling later in the project. The most common issues in this regard are missing values and outliers, which are both examples of **noise** in the data. Although we usually delay handling noise issues until the modeling phase of a project (different predictive model types require different levels of noise handling, and we should in general do as little noise handling as we can), in this section we describe the most common techniques used to handle missing values and outliers. It is a good idea to add suggestions for the best technique to handle each data quality issue in the data quality plan during data exploration as it will save time during modeling.

3.4.1   Handling Missing Values

The simplest approach to handling missing values is to simply drop from an ABT any features that have them. This, however, can result in massive, and frequently needless, loss of data. For example, if in an ABT containing 1,000 instances, one value is missing for a particular feature, it would be pretty extreme to remove that whole feature. As a general rule of thumb, only features that are missing in excess of 60% of their values should be considered for complete removal, and more subtle handling techniques should be used for features missing less data.

An alternative to entirely deleting features that suffer from large numbers of missing values is to a derive a missing indicator feature from them. This is a binary feature that flags whether the value was present or missing in the original feature. This can be useful if the reason that specific values for a feature are missing might have some relationship to the target feature—for example, if a feature that has missing values represented sensitive personal data, people's readiness to provide this data (or not) might tell us something about them. When missing indicator features are used, the original feature is usually discarded.

Another simple approach to handling missing values is **complete case analysis**, which deletes from an ABT any instances that are missing one or more feature values. This approach, however, can result in significant amounts of data loss and can introduce a bias into the dataset if the distribution of missing values in the dataset is not completely random. In general, we recommend the use of complete case analysis only to remove instances that are missing the value of the target feature. Indeed, any instances with a missing value for the target feature should always be removed from an ABT.

Imputation replaces missing feature values with a plausible estimated value based on the feature values that are present. The most common approach to imputation is to replace missing values for a feature with a measure of the central tendency of that feature. For continuous features, the mean or median are most commonly used, and for categorical features, the mode is most commonly used.

Imputation, however, should not be used for features that have very large numbers of missing values because imputing a very large number of missing values will change the central tendency of a feature too much. We would be reluctant to use imputation on features missing in excess of 30% of their values and would strongly recommend against the use of imputation on features missing in excess of 50% of their values.

There are other, more complex approaches to imputation. For example, we can actually build a predictive model that estimates a replacement for a missing value based on the feature values that are present in a dataset for a given instance. We recommend, however, using simple approaches first and turning to more complex ones only if required.

Imputation techniques tend to give good results and avoid the data loss associated with deleting features or complete case analysis. It is important to note, however, that all imputation techniques suffer from the fact that they change the underlying data in an ABT and can cause the variation within a feature to be underestimated, which can negatively bias the relationships between a descriptive feature and a target feature.

3.4.2   Handling Outliers

The easiest way to handle outliers is to use a **clamp transformation**. This clamps all values above an upper threshold and below a lower threshold to these threshold values, thus removing the offending outliers:

$$a_i = \begin{cases} lower & \text{if } a_i < lower \\ upper & \text{if } a_i > upper \\ a_i & otherwise \end{cases} \quad (3.2)$$

where a_i is a specific value of feature a, and *lower* and *upper* are the lower and upper thresholds.

The upper and lower thresholds can be set manually based on domain knowledge or can be calculated from data. One common way to calculate clamp thresholds is to set the lower threshold to the 1st quartile value minus 1.5 times the **inter-quartile range** and the upper threshold to the 3rd quartile plus 1.5 times the inter-quartile range . This works effectively and takes into account the fact that the variation in a dataset can be different to either side of a central tendency.

If this approach were to be used for the CLAIM AMOUNT feature from the motor claims insurance fraud detection scenario, then the upper and lower thresholds would be defined as follows:

$$lower = \quad 3{,}322.3 - 1.5 \times 8{,}923.2 = -10{,}062.5$$
$$upper = 12{,}245.5 + 1.5 \times 8{,}923.2 = \quad 25{,}630.3$$

where the values used are extracted from Table 3.3[59]. Any values outside these thresholds would be converted to the threshold values. Examining the histogram in Figure 3.1(c)[60] is useful in considering the impact of applying the clamp transformation using these thresholds. Locating 25,630.3 on the horizontal axis shows that this upper threshold would cause a relatively large number of values to be changed. The impact of the clamp transformation can be reduced by changing the multiplier used to calculate the thresholds from 1.5 to a larger value.

Another commonly used approach to setting the upper and lower thresholds is to use the mean value of a feature plus or minus 2 times the standard deviation.[6] Again this works well, but it does assume that the underlying data follows a normal distribution.

If this approach were to be used for the AMOUNT RECEIVED feature from the motor claims insurance fraud detection scenario, then the upper and lower thresholds would be defined as follows:

$$lower = 13{,}051.9 - 2 \times 30{,}547.2 = -48{,}042.5$$
$$upper = 13{,}051.9 + 2 \times 30{,}547.2 = \quad 74{,}146.3$$

where the values used are again extracted from Table 3.3[59]. Examining the histogram in Figure 3.1(h)[60] is again a good indication of the impact of using

---

6 Recall that in Section 3.2[61] we discussed the 68−95−99.7 rule associated with the normal distribution. This approach to handling outliers is based directly on this rule.

this transformation. This impact can be reduced by changing the multiplier used to calculate the thresholds from 2 to a larger value.

Opinions vary widely on when transformations like the clamp transformation should be used to handle outliers in data. Many argue that performing this type of transformation may remove the most interesting and, from a predictive modeling point of view, informative instances from a dataset. On the other hand, some of the machine learning techniques that we discuss in upcoming chapters perform poorly in the presence of outliers. We recommend only applying the clamp transformation in cases where it is suspected that a model is performing poorly due to the presence of outliers. The impact of the clamp transformation should then be evaluated by comparing the performance of different models trained on datasets where the transformation has been applied and where it has not.

3.4.3   Case Study: Motor Insurance Fraud

If we needed to do it, the most sensible approach to handling the missing values in the NUM. SOFT TISSUE feature would be to use imputation. There are very few missing values for this feature (2%), so replacing them with an imputed value should not excessively affect the variance of the feature. In this case the median value of 0.0 (shown in Table 3.3(a)[59]) is the most appropriate value to use to replace the missing values; because this feature only actually takes discrete values, the mean value of 0.2 never naturally occurs in the dataset.

The outliers present in the CLAIM AMOUNT and AMOUNT RECEIVED features could be easily handled using a clamp transformation. Both features follow a broadly exponential distribution, however, which means that the methods described for setting the thresholds of the clamp will not work especially well (both methods work best for normally distributed data). Therefore, manually setting upper and lower thresholds based on domain knowledge is most appropriate in this case. The business advised that for both features, a lower threshold of 0 and an upper threshold of 80,000 would make sense.

We completed the data quality plan by including these potential handling strategies. The final data quality plan is shown in Table 3.6[77]. Together with the data quality report, these are the outputs of the data exploration work for the motor insurance fraud detection project.

Table 3.6

The data quality plan with potential handling strategies for the motor insurance fraud prediction ABT.

Feature	Data Quality Issue	Potential Handling Strategies
NUM. SOFT TISSUE	Missing values (2%)	Imputation (median: 0.0)
CLAIM AMOUNT	Outliers (high)	Clamp transformation (manual: 0, 80,000)
AMOUNT RECEIVED	Outliers (high)	Clamp transformation (manual: 0, 80,000)

3.5   Advanced Data Exploration

All the descriptive statistics and data visualization techniques that we have used in the previous sections of this chapter have focused on the characteristics of individual features. This section will introduce techniques that enable us to examine relationships between pairs of features.

3.5.1   Visualizing Relationships Between Features

In preparing to create predictive models, it is always a good idea to investigate the relationships between pairs of features. This can help indicate which descriptive features might be useful for predicting a target feature and help find pairs of descriptive features that are closely related. Identifying pairs of closely related descriptive features is one way to reduce the size of an ABT because if the relationship between two descriptive features is strong enough, we may not need to include both. In this section we describe approaches to visualizing the relationships between pairs of continuous features, pairs of categorical features, and pairs including one categorical and one continuous feature.

For the examples in this section, we introduce a new dataset. Table 3.7[78] shows the details of thirty players in a professional basketball team. The dataset includes the HEIGHT, WEIGHT, and AGE of each player; the POSITION that the player normally plays (*guard*, *center*, or *forward*); the CAREER STAGE of the player (*rookie*, *mid-career*, or *veteran*); the average weekly SPONSORSHIP EARNINGS of each player; and whether the player has a SHOE SPONSOR (*yes* or *no*).

Table 3.7
The details of a professional basketball team.

ID	POSITION	HEIGHT	WEIGHT	CAREER STAGE	AGE	SPONSORSHIP EARNINGS	SHOE SPONSOR
1	forward	192	218	veteran	29	561	yes
2	center	218	251	mid-career	35	60	no
3	forward	197	221	rookie	22	1,312	no
4	forward	192	219	rookie	22	1,359	no
5	forward	198	223	veteran	29	362	yes
6	guard	166	188	rookie	21	1,536	yes
7	forward	195	221	veteran	25	694	no
8	guard	182	199	rookie	21	1,678	yes
9	guard	189	199	mid-career	27	385	yes
10	forward	205	232	rookie	24	1,416	no
11	center	206	246	mid-career	29	314	no
12	guard	185	207	rookie	23	1,497	yes
13	guard	172	183	rookie	24	1,383	yes
14	guard	169	183	rookie	24	1,034	yes
15	guard	185	197	mid-career	29	178	yes
16	forward	215	232	mid-career	30	434	no
17	guard	158	184	veteran	29	162	yes
18	guard	190	207	mid-career	27	648	yes
19	center	195	235	mid-career	28	481	no
20	guard	192	200	mid-career	32	427	yes
21	forward	202	220	mid-career	31	542	no
22	forward	184	213	mid-career	32	12	no
23	forward	190	215	rookie	22	1,179	no
24	guard	178	193	rookie	21	1,078	no
25	guard	185	200	mid-career	31	213	yes
26	forward	191	218	rookie	19	1,855	no
27	center	196	235	veteran	32	47	no
28	forward	198	221	rookie	22	1,409	no
29	center	207	247	veteran	27	1,065	no
30	center	201	244	mid-career	25	1,111	yes

3.5.1.1   Visualizing Pairs of Continuous Features

The scatter plot is one of the most important tools in data visualization. A scatter plot is based on two axes: the horizontal axis represents one feature, and the vertical axis represents a second. Each instance in a dataset is represented by a point on the plot determined by the values for that instance of the two features being plotted. Figure 3.5(a)[79] shows an example scatter plot for the HEIGHT and WEIGHT features from the dataset in Table 3.7[78]. The points in this scatter plot are arranged in a broadly linear pattern diagonally across the scatter plot. This suggests that there is a strong, positive, linear relationship between the HEIGHT and WEIGHT features—as height increases, so does weight. We say that features with this kind of relationship are positively covariant. Figure 3.5(b)[79] shows a scatter plot for the SPONSORSHIP EARNINGS and AGE features from Table 3.7[78]. These features are strongly negatively covariant. Figure 3.5(c)[79] shows a scatter plot of the HEIGHT and AGE features. These features are not strongly covariant either positively or negatively.

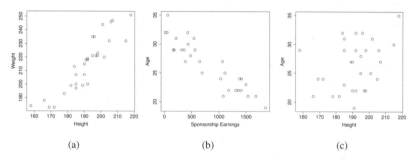

(a)   (b)   (c)

Figure 3.5

Example scatter plots for pairs of features from the dataset in Table 3.7[78], showing (a) the strong positive covariance between HEIGHT and WEIGHT; (b) the strong negative covariance between SPONSORSHIP EARNINGS and AGE; and (c) the lack of strong covariance between HEIGHT and AGE.

A **scatter plot matrix (SPLOM)** shows scatter plots for a whole collection of features arranged into a matrix. This is useful for exploring the relationships between groups of features—for example, all the continuous features in an ABT. Figure 3.6[80] shows an example scatter plot matrix for the continuous features from the professional basketball team dataset in Table 3.7[78]: HEIGHT, WEIGHT, AGE, and SPONSORSHIP EARNINGS. Each row and column represent the feature named in the cells along the diagonal. The cells above and below the diagonal show scatter plots of the features in the row and column that meet at that cell.

A scatter plot matrix is a very quick way to explore the relationships within a whole set of continuous features. The effectiveness of scatter plot matrices, however, diminishes once the number of features in the set goes beyond 8 because the graphs become too small. Using interactive tools that aid data exploration can help overcome this limitation.

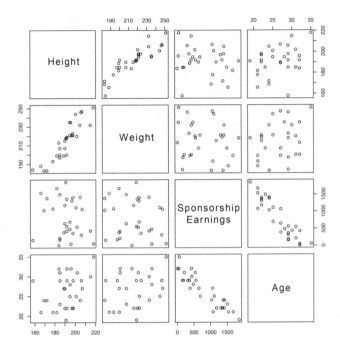

Figure 3.6

A scatter plot matrix showing scatter plots of the continuous features from the professional basketball team dataset in Table 3.7[78].

3.5.1.2   Visualizing Pairs of Categorical Features

The simplest way to visualize the relationship between two categorical features is to use a collection of bar plots. This is often referred to as a **small multiples** visualization. First, we draw a simple bar plot showing the densities of the different levels of the first feature. Then, for each level of the second feature, we draw a bar plot of the first feature using only the instances in the dataset for which the second feature has that level. If the two features being visualized have a strong relationship, then the bar plots for each level of the second feature will look noticeably different to one another and to the overall bar plot for the first feature. If there is no relationship, then we should expect that the levels of the first feature will be evenly distributed amongst the instances having the different levels of the second feature, so all bar plots will look much the same.

Figure 3.7(a)[81] shows an example for the CAREER STAGE and SHOE SPONSOR features from the professional basketball team dataset in Table 3.7[78]. The bar plot on the left shows the distribution of the different levels of the CAREER STAGE feature across the entire dataset. The two plots on the right show the distributions for those players with and without a shoe sponsor. Since all three plots show very similar distributions, we can conclude that no real relationship exists between these two features and that players of any career stage are equally likely to have a shoe sponsor or not.

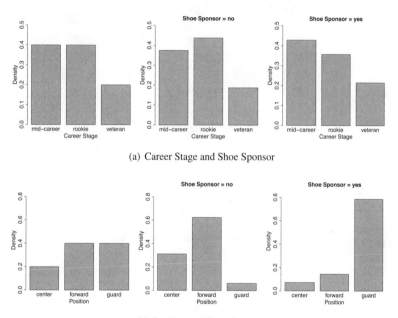

(a) Career Stage and Shoe Sponsor

(b) Position and Shoe Sponsor

Figure 3.7

Examples of using small multiple bar plot visualizations to illustrate the relationship between two categorical features: (a) the CAREER STAGE and SHOE SPONSOR features; and (b) the POSITION and SHOE SPONSOR features. All data comes from Table 3.7[78].

Figure 3.7(b)[81] shows another example, for the POSITION and SHOE SPONSOR features from the same dataset. In this case, the three plots are very different, so we can conclude that there is a relationship between these two features. It seems that players who play in the guard position are much more likely to have a shoe sponsor than forwards or centers.

When using small multiples, it is important that all the small charts are kept consistent because this ensures that only genuine differences within the data are highlighted, rather than differences that arise from formatting. For example,

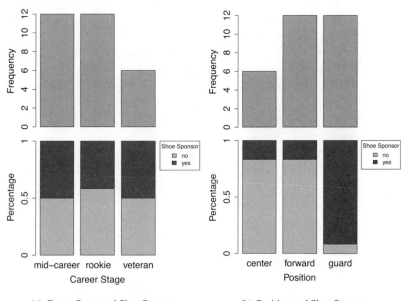

(a) Career Stage and Shoe Sponsor   (b) Position and Shoe Sponsor

Figure 3.8

Examples of using stacked bar plot visualizations to illustrate the relationship between two categorical features: (a) CAREER STAGE and SHOE SPONSOR features; and (b) POSITION and SHOE SPONSOR features, all from Table 3.7[78].

the scales of the axes must always be kept consistent, as should the order of the bars in the individual bar plots. It is also important that densities are shown rather than frequencies as the overall bar plots on the left of each visualization cover much more of the dataset than the other two plots, so frequency-based plots would look very uneven.

If the number of levels of one of the features being compared is small (we recommend no more than three), we can use **stacked bar plots** as an alternative to the small multiples bar plots approach. When this approach is used, we show a bar plot of the first feature above a bar plot that shows the relative distribution of the levels of the second feature within each level of the first. Because relative distributions are used, the bars in the second bar plot cover the full range of the space available—these are often referred to as 100% stacked bar plots. If two features are unrelated, then we would expect to see the same proportion of each level of the second feature within the bars for each level of the first.

Figure 3.8[82] shows two examples of using stacked bar plots. In the first example, Figure 3.8(a)[82], a bar plot of the CAREER STAGE feature is shown above a 100% stacked bar plot showing how the levels of the SHOE SPONSOR feature are distributed in instances having each level of CAREER STAGE. The distributions of the levels of SHOE SPONSOR are almost the same for each level of CAREER STAGE, and therefore we can conclude that there is no relationship between these two features. The second example, Figure 3.8(b)[82], shows the POSITION and SHOE SPONSOR features. In this case we can see that distributions of the levels of the SHOE SPONSOR feature are not the same for each position. From this we can again conclude that guards are more likely to have a shoe sponsor than players in the other positions.

3.5.1.3 Visualizing a Categorical Feature and a Continuous Feature

The best way to visualize the relationship between a continuous feature and a categorical feature is to use a small multiples approach, drawing a density histogram of the values of the continuous feature for each level of the categorical feature. Each histogram includes only those instances in the dataset that have the associated level of the categorical feature. Similar to using small multiples for categorical features, if the features are unrelated (or independent) then the histograms for each level should be very similar. If the features are related, however, then the shapes and/or the central tendencies of the histograms will be different.

Figure 3.9(a)[84] shows a histogram of the AGE feature from the dataset in Table 3.7[78]. We can see from this histogram that AGE follows a uniform distribution across a range from about 19 to about 35. Figure 3.9(c)[84] shows small multiple histograms for values of AGE broken down by the different levels of the POSITION feature. These histograms show a slight tendency for centers to be a little older than guards and forwards, but the relationship does not appear very strong as each of the smaller histograms are similar to the overall uniform distribution of the AGE feature. Figures 3.9(b)[84] and 3.9(d)[84] show a second example, this time for the HEIGHT and POSITION features. From Figure 3.9(b)[84] we can see that HEIGHT follows a normal distribution centered around a mean of approximately 194. The three smaller histograms depart from this distribution and suggest that centers tend to be taller than forwards, who in turn tend to be taller than guards.

An alternative approach to using small multiples to visualize the relationship between a categorical feature and a continuous feature is to use a collection of

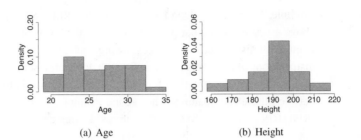

(a) Age   (b) Height

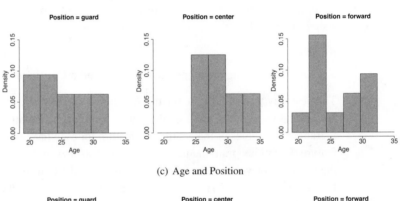

(c) Age and Position

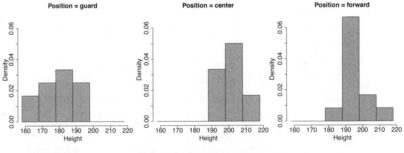

(d) Height and Position

Figure 3.9

Example of using small multiple histograms to visualize the relationship between a categorical feature and a continuous feature. All examples use data from the professional basketball team dataset in Table 3.7[78]: (a) a histogram of the AGE feature; (b) a histogram of the HEIGHT feature; (c) histograms of the AGE feature for instances displaying each level of the POSITION feature; and (d) histograms of the HEIGHT feature for instances displaying each level of the POSITION feature.

box plots. For each level of the categorical feature, a box plot of the corresponding values of the continuous feature is drawn. This gives multiple box plots that offer an easy comparison of how the central tendency and variation of the continuous feature change for the different levels of the categorical feature. When a relationship exists between the two features, the box plots should show differing central tendencies and variations. When no relationship exists, the box plots should all appear similar.

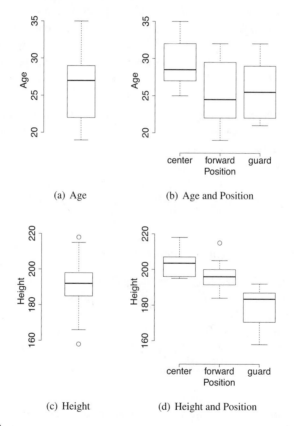

(a) Age   (b) Age and Position

(c) Height   (d) Height and Position

Figure 3.10

Using box plots to visualize the relationships between categorical and continuous features from Table 3.7[78]: (a) the relationship between the POSITION feature and the AGE feature; and (b) the relationship between the POSITION feature and the HEIGHT feature.

In Figures 3.10(a)[85] and 3.10(b)[85] we illustrate the multiple box plot approach using the AGE and POSITION features from the dataset in Table

$3.7^{[78]}$. Figure $3.10(a)^{[85]}$ shows a box plot for AGE across the full dataset, while Figure $3.10(b)^{[85]}$ shows individual box plots for AGE for each level of the POSITION feature. Similar to the histograms in Figure $3.9^{[84]}$, this visualization shows a slight indication that centers tend to be older than forwards and guards, but the three box plots overlap significantly, suggesting that this relationship is not very strong.

Figures $3.10(c)^{[85]}$ and $3.10(d)^{[85]}$ show a similar pair of visualizations for the HEIGHT and POSITION features. Figure $3.10(d)^{[85]}$ is typical of a series of box plots showing a strong relationship between a continuous and a categorical feature. We can see that the average height of centers is above that of forwards, which in turn is above that of guards. Although the whiskers show that there is some overlap between the three groups, they do appear to be well separated.

Histograms show more detail than box plots, so small multiple histograms offer a more detailed view of the relationship between two features. The differences in central tendency and variation between levels can, however, be easier to see in box plots. Box plots are also better suited when the categorical feature has many levels—beyond four levels, small multiple histograms tend to be difficult to interpret. A good approach is to use box plots to initially determine which pairs of features might have a strong relationship and then further investigate these pairs using small multiple histograms.

3.5.2   Measuring Covariance and Correlation

As well as visually inspecting scatter plots, we can calculate formal measures of the relationship between two continuous features using **covariance** and **correlation**. For two features, a and b, in a dataset of n instances, the **sample covariance** between a and b is

$$cov(a,b) = \frac{1}{n-1} \sum_{i=1}^{n} \left((a_i - \overline{a}) \times \left(b_i - \overline{b} \right) \right) \tag{3.3}$$

where a_i and b_i are values of features a and b for the ith instance in a dataset, and $\overline{a}$ and $\overline{b}$ are the sample means of features a and b. Covariance values fall into the range $[-\infty, \infty]$ where negative values indicate a negative relationship, positive values indicate a positive relationship, and values near zero indicate that there is little or no relationship between the features.

Table $3.8^{[87]}$ shows the workings for the calculation of the covariance between the HEIGHT feature and the WEIGHT and AGE features from the

Table 3.8

Calculating covariance.

ID	HEIGHT (h)	$h - \bar{h}$	WEIGHT (w)	$w - \bar{w}$	$(h - \bar{h}) \times (w - \bar{w})$	AGE (a)	$a - \bar{a}$	$(h - \bar{h}) \times (a - \bar{a})$
1	192	0.9	218	3.0	2.7	29	2.6	2.3
2	218	26.9	251	36.0	967.5	35	8.6	231.3
3	197	5.9	221	6.0	35.2	22	-4.4	-26.0
4	192	0.9	219	4.0	3.6	22	-4.4	-4.0
5	198	6.9	223	8.0	55.0	29	2.6	17.9
				...				
26	191	-0.1	218	3.0	-0.3	19	-7.4	0.7
27	196	4.9	235	20.0	97.8	32	5.6	27.4
28	198	6.9	221	6.0	41.2	22	-4.4	-30.4
29	207	15.9	247	32.0	508.3	27	0.6	9.5
30	201	9.9	244	29.0	286.8	25	-1.4	-13.9
Mean	191.1		215.0			26.4		
Std. Dev.	13.6		19.8			4.2		
Sum					7,009.9			570.8

The table shows how the $\left((a_i - \bar{a}) \times (b_i - \bar{b})\right)$ portion of Equation (3.3)[86] is calculated for each instance in a dataset to arrive at the sum required in the calculation. The relevant means and standard deviations are also shown (standard deviation is not required to calculate covariance but is included as it will be useful later for calculating correlation).

dataset in Table 3.7[78]. The table shows how the $\left((a_i - \bar{a}) \times (b_i - \bar{b})\right)$ portion of Equation (3.3)[86] is calculated for each instance in the dataset for the two covariance calculations. Given this table we can calculate the covariances as follows:

$$cov(\text{HEIGHT}, \text{WEIGHT}) = \frac{7,009.9}{29} = 241.72$$

$$cov(\text{HEIGHT}, \text{AGE}) = \frac{570.8}{29} = 19.7$$

These figures indicate that there is a strong positive relationship between the height and weight of a player, and a much smaller positive relationship between height and age. This supports the relationships suggested by the scatter plots of these pairs of features shown in Figures 3.5(a)[79] and 3.5(c)[79].

This example also illustrates a problem with using covariance. Covariance is measured in the same units as the features that it measures. As a result, comparing the covariance between pairs of features only makes sense if each pair of features is composed of the same mixture of units. Correlation[7] is a normalized form of covariance that ranges between -1 and $+1$. We calculate the correlation between two features by dividing the covariance between the two features by the product of their standard deviations. The correlation between two features, a and b, can be calculated as

$$corr(a,b) = \frac{cov(a,b)}{sd(a) \times sd(b)} \tag{3.4}$$

where $cov(a,b)$ is the covariance between features a and b and $sd(a)$ and $sd(b)$ are the standard deviations of a and b respectively. Because correlation is normalized, it is dimensionless and, consequently, does not suffer from the interpretability difficulties associated with covariance. Correlation values fall into the range $[-1, 1]$, where values close to -1 indicate a very strong negative correlation (or covariance), values close to 1 indicate a very strong positive correlation, and values around 0 indicate no correlation. Features that have no correlation are said to be **independent.**

The correlations between the HEIGHT and WEIGHT and AGE features can be calculated, using the covariances and standard deviations from Table 3.8[87], as follows:

$$corr(Height, Weight) = \frac{241.72}{13.6 \times 19.8} = 0.898$$
$$corr(Height, Age) = \frac{19.7}{13.6 \times 4.2} = 0.345$$

These correlation values are much more useful than the covariances calculated previously because they are on a normalized scale, which allows us compare the strength of the relationships to each other. There is a strong positive correlation between HEIGHT and WEIGHT features, but very little correlation between HEIGHT and AGE.

In the majority of ABTs there are multiple continuous features between which we would like to explore relationships. Two tools that can be useful for this are the covariance matrix and the correlation matrix. A covariance matrix contains a row and column for each feature, and each element of the matrix lists the covariance between the corresponding pairs of features. As a result, the elements along the main diagonal list the covariance between a feature and

---

7 The correlation coefficient presented here is more fully known as the Pearson product-moment correlation coefficient or Pearson's r and is named after Karl Pearson, one of the giants of statistics.

itself, in other words, the variance of the feature. The covariance matrix, usually denoted as $\sum$, between a set of continuous features, $\{a, b, \ldots, z\}$, is given as

$$\sum_{\{a,b,\ldots,z\}} = \begin{bmatrix} var(a) & cov(a,b) & \cdots & cov(a,z) \\ cov(b,a) & var(b) & \cdots & cov(b,z) \\ \vdots & \vdots & \ddots & \vdots \\ cov(z,a) & cov(z,b) & \cdots & var(z) \end{bmatrix} \qquad (3.5)$$

Similarly, the correlation matrix is just a normalized version of the covariance matrix and shows the correlation between each pair of features:

$$correlation\ matrix_{\{a,b,\ldots,z\}} = \begin{bmatrix} corr(a,a) & corr(a,b) & \cdots & corr(a,z) \\ corr(b,a) & corr(b,b) & \cdots & corr(b,z) \\ \vdots & \vdots & \ddots & \vdots \\ corr(z,a) & corr(z,b) & \cdots & corr(z,z) \end{bmatrix} \qquad (3.6)$$

The covariance and correlation matrices for the HEIGHT, WEIGHT and AGE features are

$$\sum_{\{Height,Weight,Age\}} = \begin{bmatrix} 185.128 & 241.72 & 19.7 \\ 241.72 & 392.102 & 24.469 \\ 19.7 & 24.469 & 17.697 \end{bmatrix}$$

and

$$correlation\ matrix_{\{Height,Weight,Age\}} = \begin{bmatrix} 1.0 & 0.898 & 0.345 \\ 0.898 & 1.0 & 0.294 \\ 0.345 & 0.294 & 1.0 \end{bmatrix}$$

The scatter plot matrices (SPLOMs) described in Section 3.5.1[77] are really a visualization of the correlation matrix. This can be made more obvious by including the correlation coefficients in SPLOMs in the cells above the diagonal. In Figure 3.11[90] the cells above the diagonal show the correlation coefficients for each pair of features. The font sizes of the correlation coefficients are scaled according to the absolute value of the strength of the correlation to draw attention to those pairs of features with the strongest relationships.

Correlation is a good measure of the relationship between two continuous features, but it is not by any means perfect. First, the correlation measure given in Equation (3.4)[88] responds only to linear relationships between features. In a linear relationship between two features, as one feature increases or decreases, the other feature increases or decreases by a corresponding amount.

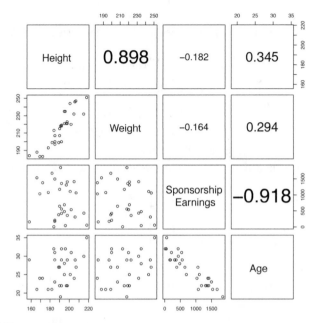

Figure 3.11
A scatter plot matrix showing scatter plots of the continuous features from the professional basketball team dataset in Table 3.7[78] with correlation coefficients included.

Frequently, features will have very strong non-linear relationships that correlation does not respond to. Also, peculiarities in a dataset can affect the calculation of the correlation between two features. This problem is illustrated
very clearly in the famous example of Anscombe's quartet,[8] shown in Figure
3.12[91]. This is a series of four pairs of features that all have the same correlation value of 0.816, even though they exhibit very different relationships.

    Perhaps the most important thing to remember in relation to correlation is
that *correlation does not necessarily imply causation*. Just because the values
of two features are correlated does not mean that an actual causal relationship
exists between the two. There are two main ways in which causation can be
mistakenly assumed. The first is by mistaking the order of a causal relationship.
For example, based on correlations tests alone, we might conclude that the
presence of swallows cause hot weather, that spinning windmills cause wind,

8 Francis Anscombe was a famous statistician who published his quartet in 1973 (Anscombe,
1973).

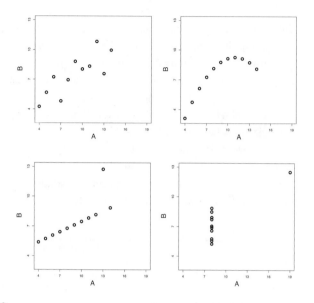

Figure 3.12

Anscombe's quartet. For all four samples, the correlation measure returns the same value (0.816) even though the relationship between the features is very different in each case.

and that playing basketball causes people to be tall. In fact, swallows migrate to warmer countries, windmills are made to spin by wind, and tall people often choose to play basketball because of the advantage their height gives them in that game.

The second kind of mistake that makes people incorrectly infer causation between two features is ignoring a third important, but hidden, feature. In a famous example of this, an article was published in the prestigious journal *Nature* outlining a causal relationship between young children sleeping with a night-light turned on and these children developing short-sightedness in later life (Quinn et al., 1999). Later studies (Gwiazda et al., 2000; Zadnik et al., 2000), however, could not replicate this link, and eventually a more plausible explanation for the correlation between night-light use and short-sightedness was uncovered. Short-sighted parents, because of their poor night vision, tend to favor the use of night-lights to help them find their way around their children's bedrooms at night. Short-sighted parents are more likely to have short-sighted children, and it is this that accounts for the correlation between night-light use and short-sightedness in children, rather than any causal link. This is an example of a confounding feature, a feature that influences two others and so leads to the appearance of a causal relationship. Confounding features are a common explanation of mistaken conclusions about causal relationships. The lesson to be learned here is that before causation is concluded based on a strong correlation between two features, in-depth studies involving domain experts are required—correlation alone is just not enough. In spite of these difficulties, for machine learning purposes, correlation is a very good measure of the relationship between two continuous features.[9]

3.6   Data Preparation

Instead of explicitly handling problems like noise within the data in an ABT, some data preparation techniques change the way data is represented just to make it more compatible with certain machine learning algorithms. This section describes two of the most common such techniques: binning and normalization. Both techniques focus on transforming an individual feature in some way. There are also situations, however, where we wish to change the size and/or the distributions of target values within the ABT. We describe a range of different **sampling** techniques that can be used to do this. As with the techniques described in the previous section, sometimes these techniques are performed as part of the Data Preparation phase of CRISP-DM, but sometimes they are performed as part of the Modeling phase.

3.6.1   Normalization

Having continuous features in an ABT that cover very different ranges can cause difficulty for some machine learning algorithms. For example, a feature representing customer ages might cover the range $[16, 96]$, whereas a feature

---

9 There are approaches to formally measuring the relationship between a pair of categorical features (for example, the χ^2 test) and for measuring the relationship between a categorical feature and a continuous feature (for example, the **ANOVA test**). We do not cover these in this book, however, and readers are directed to the further reading section at the end of this chapter for information on these approaches.

Table 3.9

A small sample of the HEIGHT and SPONSORSHIP EARNINGS features from the professional basketball team dataset in Table 3.7[78], showing the result of range normalization and standardization.

	HEIGHT			SPONSORSHIP EARNINGS		
	Values	Range	Standard	Values	Range	Standard
	192	0.500	-0.073	561	0.315	-0.649
	197	0.679	0.533	1,312	0.776	0.762
	192	0.500	-0.073	1,359	0.804	0.850
	182	0.143	-1.283	1,678	1.000	1.449
	206	1.000	1.622	314	0.164	-1.114
	192	0.500	-0.073	427	0.233	-0.901
	190	0.429	-0.315	1,179	0.694	0.512
	178	0.000	-1.767	1,078	0.632	0.322
	196	0.643	0.412	47	0.000	-1.615
	201	0.821	1.017	1,111	0.652	0.384
Max	206			1,678		
Min	178			47		
Mean	193			907		
Std. Dev.	8.26			532.18		

representing customer salaries might cover the range $[10{,}000, 100{,}000]$. **Normalization** techniques can be used to change a continuous feature to fall within a specified range while maintaining the relative differences between the values for the feature. The simplest approach to normalization is **range normalization**, which performs a linear scaling of the original values of the continuous feature into a given range. We use range normalization to convert a feature value into the range $[low, high]$ as follows:

$$a_i' = \frac{a_i - min(a)}{max(a) - min(a)} \times (high - low) + low \qquad (3.7)$$

where a_i' is the normalized feature value, a_i is the original value, $min(a)$ is the minimum value of feature a, $max(a)$ is the maximum value of feature a, and *low* and *high* are the minimum and maximum values of the desired range. Typical ranges used for normalizing feature values are $[0,1]$ and $[-1,1]$. Table 3.9[93] shows the effect of applying range normalization to a small sample of the HEIGHT and SPONSORSHIP EARNINGS features from the dataset in Table 3.7[78].

Range normalization has the drawback that it is quite sensitive to the presence of outliers in a dataset. Another way to normalize data is to **standardize** it into **standard scores**.[10] A standard score measures how many standard deviations a feature value is from the mean for that feature. To calculate a standard score, we compute the mean and standard deviation for the feature and normalize the feature values using the following equation:

$$a_i' = \frac{a_i - \bar{a}}{sd(a)} \tag{3.8}$$

where a_i' is the normalized feature value, a_i is the original value, $\bar{a}$ is the mean for feature a, and $sd(a)$ is the standard deviation for a. Standardizing feature values in this ways squashes the values of the feature so that the feature values have a mean of 0 and a standard deviation of 1. This results in the majority of feature values being in a range of $[-1,1]$. We should take care when using standardization as it assumes that data is normally distributed. If this assumption does not hold, then standardization may introduce some distortions. Table 3.9[93] also shows the effect of applying standardization to the HEIGHT and SPONSORSHIP EARNINGS features.

In upcoming chapters we use normalization to prepare data for use with machine learning algorithms that require descriptive features to be in particular ranges. As is so often the case in data analytics, there is no hard and fast rule that says which is the best normalization technique, and this decision is generally made based on experimentation.

3.6.2   Binning

Binning involves converting a continuous feature into a categorical feature. To perform binning, we define a series of ranges (called **bins**) for the continuous feature that correspond to the levels of the new categorical feature we are creating. The values for the new categorical feature are then created by assigning to instances in the dataset the level of the new feature that corresponds to the range that their value of the continuous feature falls into. There are many different approaches to binning. We will introduce two of the more popular: **equal-width binning** and **equal-frequency binning**.

Both equal-width and equal-frequency binning require that we manually specify how many bins we would like to use. Deciding on the number of bins can be difficult. The general trade-off is this:

---

10 A standard score is equivalent to a **z-score**, and standardizing in the way described here is also known as applying a **z-transform** to the data.

- If we set the number of bins to a very low number—for example 2 or 3 bins—(in other words, we abstract to a very low level of resolution), we may lose a lot of information with respect to the distribution of values in the original continuous feature. Using a small number of bins, however, has the advantage of having a large number of instances in each bin.

- If we set the number of bins to a high number—for example 10 or more— then, just because there are more bin boundaries, it is more likely that at least some of our bins will align with interesting features of the distribution of the original continuous feature. This means that our binning categories will provide a better representation of this distribution. However, the more bins we have, the fewer instances we will have in each bin. Indeed, as the number of bins grows, we can end up with empty bins.

Figure 3.13[96] illustrates the effect of using different numbers of bins.[11] In this example, the dashed line represents a multimodal distribution from which a set of continuous feature values has been generated. The histogram represents the bins. Ideally the histogram heights should follow the dashed line. In Figure 3.13(a)[96] there are three bins that are each quite wide, and the histogram heights don't really follow the dashed line. This indicates that this binning does not accurately represent the real distribution of values in the underlying continuous feature. In Figure 3.13(b)[96] there are 14 bins. In general, the histogram heights follow the dashed line, so the resulting bins can be considered a reasonable representation of the continuous feature. Also, there are no gaps between the histogram bars, which indicates that there are no empty bins. Finally, Figure 3.13(c)[96] illustrates what happens when we used 60 bins. The histogram heights fit the contour line to an extent, but there is a greater variance in the heights across the bins in this image. Some of the bins are very tall and other bins are empty, as indicated by the gaps between the bars. When we compare, the three images, 14 bins seems to best model the data. Unfortunately, there is no guaranteed way of finding the optimal number of bins for a set of values for a continuous feature. Often, choosing the number of bins comes down to intuition and a process of trial and error experimentation.

Once the number of bins, b, has been chosen, the equal-width binning algorithm splits the range of the feature values into b bins each of size $\frac{range}{b}$. For example, if the values for a feature fell between zero and 100 and we wished to

---

11 These images were generated using equal-width binning. However, the points discussed in the text are also relevant to equal-frequency binning.

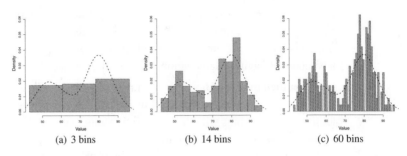

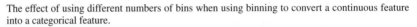

(a) 3 bins   (b) 14 bins   (c) 60 bins

Figure 3.13

The effect of using different numbers of bins when using binning to convert a continuous feature into a categorical feature.

have 10 bins, then bin 1 would cover the interval[12] $[0,10)$, bin 2 would cover the interval $[10,20)$, and so on, up to bin 10, which would cover the interval $[90,100]$. Consequently, an instance with a feature value of 18 would be placed into bin 2.

Equal-width binning is simple and intuitive, and can work well in practice. However, as the distribution of values in the continuous feature moves away from a uniform distribution, then some bins will end up with very few instances in them, and other bins will have a lot of instances in them. For example, imagine our data followed a normal distribution: then the bins covering the intervals of the feature range at the tails of the normal distribution will have very few instances, and the bins covering the intervals of the feature range near the mean will contain a lot of instances. This scenario is illustrated in Figures 3.14(a)[97] to 3.14(c)[97], which shows a continuous feature following a normal distribution converted into different numbers of bins using equal-width binning. The problem with this is that we are essentially wasting bins because some of the bins end up representing a very small number of instances (the height of the bars in the diagram shows the number of instances in each bin). If we were able to merge the bins in the regions where there are very few instances, then the resulting spare bins could be used to represent the differences between instances in the regions where lots of instances are clustered together. Equal-frequency binning does this.

12 In interval notation, a square bracket, [or], indicates that the boundary value is included in the interval, and a curved bracket, (or), indicates that it is excluded from the interval.

Equal-frequency binning first sorts the continuous feature values into ascending order and then places an equal number of instances into each bin, starting with bin 1. The number of instances placed in each bin is simply the total number of instances divided by the number of bins, b. For example, if we had 10,000 instances in our dataset and we wish to have 10 bins, then bin 1 would contain the 1,000 instances with the lowest values for the feature, and so on, up to bin 10, which would contain the 1,000 instances with the highest feature values. Figures 3.14(d)[97] to 3.14(f)[97] show the same normally distributed continuous feature mentioned previously binned into different numbers of bins using equal-frequency binning.[13]

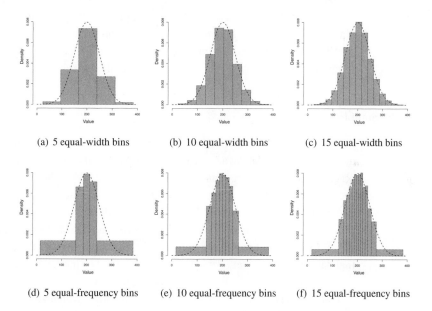

(a) 5 equal-width bins   (b) 10 equal-width bins   (c) 15 equal-width bins

(d) 5 equal-frequency bins   (e) 10 equal-frequency bins   (f) 15 equal-frequency bins

Figure 3.14

(a)–(c) Equal-frequency binning of normally distributed data with different numbers of bins; (d)–(f) the same data binned into the same number of bins using equal-width binning. The dashed lines illustrate the distribution of the original continuous feature values, and the gray boxes represent the bins.

Using Figure 3.14[97] to compare these two approaches to binning, we can see that by varying the width of the bins, equal-frequency binning uses bins to

---

13 The bins created when equal frequency binning is used are equivalent to percentiles (discussed in Section A.1[525]).

more accurately model the heavily populated areas of the range of values the continuous feature can take. The downside to this is that the resulting bins can appear slightly less intuitive because they are of varying sizes.

Regardless of the binning approach used, once the values for a continuous feature have been binned, the continuous feature is discarded and replaced by a categorical feature, which has a level for each bin—the bin numbers can be used or a more meaningful label can be manually generated. We will see in forthcoming chapters that using binning to transform a continuous feature into a categorical feature is often the easiest way for some of the machine learning approaches to handle a continuous feature. Another advantage of binning, especially equal-frequency binning, is that it goes some way toward handling outliers. Very large or very small values simply end up in the highest or lowest bin. It is important to remember though that no matter how well it is done, binning always discards information from the dataset because it abstracts from a continuous representation to a coarser categorical resolution.

3.6.3   Sampling

In some predictive analytics scenarios, the dataset we have is so large that we do not use all the data available to us in an ABT and instead **sample** a smaller percentage from the larger dataset. We need to be careful when sampling, however, to ensure that the resulting datasets are still representative of the original data and that no unintended bias is introduced during this process. Biases are introduced when, due to the sampling process, the distributions of features in the sampled dataset are very different to the distributions of features in the original dataset. The danger of this is that any analysis or modeling we perform on this sample will not be relevant to the overall dataset.

The simplest form of sampling is **top sampling**, which simply selects the top $s\%$ of instances from a dataset to create a sample. Top sampling runs a serious risk of introducing bias, however, as the sample will be affected by any ordering of the original dataset. For this reason, we recommend that top sampling be avoided.

A better choice, and our recommended default, is **random sampling**, which randomly selects a proportion of $s\%$ of the instances from a large dataset to create a smaller set. Random sampling is a good choice in most cases as the random nature of the selection of instances should avoid introducing bias.

Sometimes there are very specific relationships in a dataset that we want to maintain in a sample. For example, if we have a categorical target feature, we may want to ensure that the sample has exactly the same distribution of the different levels of the target feature as the original dataset. In most cases random sampling will maintain distributions; however, if there are one or more levels of a categorical feature that only a very small proportion of instances in a dataset have, there is a chance that these will be omitted or underrepresented by random sampling. **Stratified sampling** is a sampling method that ensures that the relative frequencies of the levels of a specific stratification feature are maintained in the sampled dataset.

To perform stratified sampling, the instances in a dataset are first divided into groups (or strata), where each group contains only instances that have a particular level for the stratification feature. The $s\%$ of the instances in each stratum are then randomly selected, and these selections are combined to give an overall sample of $s\%$ of the original dataset. Remember that each stratum will contain a different number of instances, so by sampling on a percentage basis from each stratum, the number of instances taken each from stratum will be proportional to the number of instances in each stratum. As a result, this sampling strategy is guaranteed to maintain the relative frequencies of the different levels of the stratification feature.

In contrast to stratified sampling, sometimes we would like a sample to contain different relative frequencies of the levels of a particular feature to the distribution in the original dataset. For example, we may wish to create a sample in which the levels of a particular categorical feature are represented equally, rather than with whatever distribution they had in the original dataset. To do this, we can use **under-sampling** or **over-sampling**.

Like stratified sampling, under-sampling begins by dividing a dataset into groups, where each group contains only instances that have a particular level for the feature to be under-sampled. The number of instances in the *smallest* group is the under-sampling target size. Each group containing more instances than the smallest one is then randomly sampled by the appropriate percentage to create a subset that is the under-sampling target size. These under-sampled groups are then combined to create the overall under-sampled dataset.

Over-sampling addresses the same issue as under-sampling but in the opposite way around. After dividing the dataset into groups, the number of instances in the *largest* group becomes the over-sampling target size. From each smaller group, we then create a sample containing that number of instances. To create a sample that is larger than the size of the group that we are sampling from, we use random sampling with replacement. This means that when an instance is randomly selected from the original dataset, it is replaced into the dataset so that it might be selected again. The consequence of this is that each instance from the original dataset can appear more than once in the sampled dataset.[14] After having created the larger samples from each group, we combine these to form the overall over-sampled dataset.

Sampling techniques can be used to reduce the size of a large ABT to make exploratory analysis easier, to change the distributions of target features in an ABT, and to generate different portions of an ABT to use for training and evaluating a model.

3.7   Summary

For a data analytics practitioner, the key outcomes of the **data exploration** process (which straddles the **Data Understanding** and **Data Preparation** phases of **CRISP-DM**) are that the practitioner should

1. Have *gotten to know* the features within the ABT, especially their central tendencies, variations, and **distributions**.
2. Have identified any **data quality issues** within the ABT, in particular **missing values**, **irregular cardinality**, and **outliers**.
3. Have corrected any data quality issues due to **invalid data**.
4. Have recorded any data quality issues due to **valid data** in a **data quality plan** along with potential handling strategies.
5. Be confident that enough good quality data exists to continue with a project.

Although the **data quality report** is just a collection of simple descriptive statistics and visualizations of the features in an **analytics base table**, it is a very powerful tool and the key to achieving the outcomes listed above. By examining the data quality report, analytics practitioners can get a complete picture of the data that they will work with for the rest of an analytics project. In this chapter we have focused on using the data quality report to explore the data in an ABT. A data quality report, however, can also be used to explore any dataset and is commonly used to understand the data in the raw data sources that are used to populate an ABT.

We also took our first steps toward building predictive models in this chapter when we looked at **correlation**. A descriptive feature that correlates strongly

---

14 Although we didn't mention it explicitly in other cases where we mentioned random sampling, we meant random sampling without replacement.

with a target feature would be a good place to start building a predictive model, and we return to correlations in later chapters. Examining correlation between features as part of data exploration allows us to add extra outcomes to the list at the beginning of this section:

1. Be aware of the relationships between features in an ABT.
2. Have begun the **feature selection** exercise by removing some features from the ABT.

The previous section of the chapter (Section 3.6[92]) focused on **data preparation** techniques that we can use on the data in an ABT. It is important to remember that when we perform data preparations (such as those in Section 3.6[92] or those described in Section 3.4[73]), we are changing the data that we will use to subsequently train predictive models. If we change the data too much, then the models that we build will not relate well to the original data sources when we deploy them. There is, therefore, a delicate balance that we need to strike between preparing the data so that it is appropriate for use with machine learning algorithms and keeping the data true to the underlying processes that generate it. Well designed evaluation experiments are the best way to find this balance (we discuss evaluation in detail in Chapter 8[397]).

The last point worth mentioning is that this chapter relates to deployment. The data in an ABT is historical data from the disparate data sources within an organization. We use this data to train and evaluate a machine learning model that will then be deployed for use on newly arising data. For example, in the motor insurance fraud detection example that we used in this chapter, the claims in the ABT were all historical. The prediction model that we would build using this data would be deployed to predict whether newly arising claims are likely to be fraudulent. It is important that the details of any data preparation techniques we perform on the data in the ABT be saved (usually in the data quality plan) so that we can also apply the same techniques to newly arising data. This is an important detail of model deployment that is sometimes overlooked, which can lead to strange model performance.

3.8   Further Reading

The basis of data exploration is statistics. Montgomery and Runger (2010) is an excellent applied introductory text in statistics and covers, in more detail, all the basic measures used in this chapter. It also covers advanced topics, such

as the χ^2 test and **ANOVA test** mentioned in the notes for Section 3.5.2[86].
Rice (2006) provides a good—if more theoretical—treatment of statistics.

For the practical details of building a data quality report, Svolba (2007, 2012) are very good, even if the SAS language is not being used. Similarly, Dalgaard (2008) is very good even if the R language is not being used. As an example of a detailed investigation into the impact of applying data preparation techniques, Batista and Monard (2003) is interesting.

Data visualization is a mix of statistics, graphic design, art, and psychology. Chang (2012) and Fry (2007) both provide great detail on visualization in general and the R language in particular (the visualizations in this book are almost all generated in R). For more conceptual discussions of data visualization, Tufte (2001) and Bertin (2010) are important works in the field.

3.9   Exercises

1. The table below shows the age of each employee at a cardboard box factory.

ID	1	2	3	4	5	6	7	8	9	10
AGE	51	39	34	27	23	43	41	55	24	25

ID	11	12	13	14	15	16	17	18	19	20
AGE	38	17	21	37	35	38	31	24	35	33

Based on this data calculate the following **summary statistics** for the AGE feature:

   a. Minimum, maximum and range

   b. Mean and median

   c. Variance and standard deviation

   d. 1st quartile (25th percentile) and 3rd quartile (75th percentile)

   e. Inter-quartile range

   f. 12th percentile

2. The table below shows the policy type held by customers at a life assurance company.

ID	POLICY	ID	POLICY	ID	POLICY
1	Silver	8	Silver	15	Platinum
2	Platinum	9	Platinum	16	Silver
3	Gold	10	Platinum	17	Platinum
4	Gold	11	Silver	18	Platinum
5	Silver	12	Gold	19	Gold
6	Silver	13	Platinum	20	Silver
7	Bronze	14	Silver		

   a. Based on this data calculate the following **summary statistics** for the POLICY feature:

      i. Mode and 2nd mode

      ii. Mode % and 2nd mode %

   b. Draw a **bar plot** for the POLICY feature.

3. An analytics consultant at an insurance company has built an **ABT** that will be used to train a model to predict the best communications channel to use to contact a potential customer with an offer of a new insurance product.[15] The following table contains an extract from this ABT—the full ABT contains 5,200 instances.

ID	OCC	GENDER	AGE	LOC	MOTOR INS	MOTOR VALUE	HEALTH INS	HEALTH TYPE	HEALTH DEPS ADULTS	HEALTH DEPS KIDS	PREF CHANNEL
1	Student	female	43	urban	yes	42,632	yes	PlanC	1	2	sms
2		female	57	rural	yes	22,096	yes	PlanA	1	2	phone
3	Doctor	male	21	rural	yes	27,221	no				phone
4	Sheriff	female	47	rural	yes	21,460	yes	PlanB	1	3	phone
5	Painter	male	55	rural	yes	13,976	no				phone
			⋮			⋮			⋮		
14		male	19	rural	yes	48,66	no				email
15	Manager	male	51	rural	yes	12,759	no				phone
16	Farmer	male	49	rural	no		no				phone
17		female	18	urban	yes	16,399	no				sms
18	Analyst	male	47	rural	yes	14,767	no				email
			⋮			⋮			⋮		
2747		female	48	rural	yes	35,974	yes	PlanB	1	2	phone
2748	Editor	male	50	urban	yes	40,087	no				phone
2749		female	64	rural	yes	156,126	yes	PlanC	0	0	phone
2750	Reporter	female	48	urban	yes	27,912	yes	PlanB	1	2	email
			⋮			⋮			⋮		
4780	Nurse	male	49	rural	no		yes	PlanB	2	2	email
4781		female	46	rural	yes	18,562	no				phone
4782	Courier	male	63	urban	no		yes	PlanA	2	0	email
4783	Sales	male	21	urban	no		no				sms
4784	Surveyor	female	45	rural	yes	17,840	no				sms
			⋮			⋮			⋮		
5199	Clerk	male	48	rural	yes	19,448	yes	PlanB	1	3	email
5200	Cook	47	female	rural	yes	16,393	yes	PlanB	1	2	sms

The descriptive features in this dataset are defined as follows:

- AGE: The customer's age

---

15 The data used in this question has been artificially generated for this book. Channel propensity modeling is used widely in industry; for example, see Hirschowitz (2001).

- GENDER: The customer's gender (*male* or *female*)
- LOC: The customer's location (*rural* or *urban*)
- OCC: The customer's occupation
- MOTORINS: Whether the customer holds a motor insurance policy with the company (*yes* or *no*)
- MOTORVALUE: The value of the car on the motor policy
- HEALTHINS: Whether the customer holds a health insurance policy with the company (*yes* or *no*)
- HEALTHTYPE: The type of the health insurance policy (*PlanA*, *PlanB*, or *PlanC*)
- HEALTHDEPSADULTS: How many dependent adults are included on the health insurance policy
- HEALTHDEPSKIDS: How many dependent children are included on the health insurance policy
- PREFCHANNEL: The customer's preferred contact channel (*email*, *phone*, or *sms*)

The consultant generated the following **data quality report** from the ABT (visualizations of binary features have been omitted for space saving).

Feature	Count	% Miss.	Card.	Min.	1st Qrt.	Mean	Median	3rd Qrt.	Max.	Std. Dev.
AGE	5,200	0	51	18	22	41.59	47	50	80	15.66
MOTORVALUE	5,200	17.25	3,934	4,352	15,089.5	23,479	24,853	32,078	166,993	11,121
HEALTHDEPSADULTS	5,200	39.25	4	0	0	0.84	1	1	2	0.65
HEALTHDEPSKIDS	5,200	39.25	5	0	0	1.77	2	3	3	1.11

Feature	Count	% Miss.	Card.	Mode	Mode Freq.	Mode %	2nd Mode	2nd Mode Freq.	2nd Mode %
GENDER	5,200	0	2	female	2,626	50.5	male	2,574	49.5
LOC	5,200	0	2	urban	2,948	56.69	rural	2,252	43.30
OCC	5,200	37.71	1,828	Nurse	11	0.34	Sales	9	0.28
MOTORINS	5,200	0	2	yes	4,303	82.75	no	897	17.25
HEALTHINS	5,200	0	2	yes	3,159	60.75	no	2,041	39.25
HEALTHTYPE	5,200	39.25	4	PlanB	1,596	50.52	PlanA	796	25.20
PREFCHANNEL	5,200	0	3	email	2,296	44.15	phone	1,975	37.98

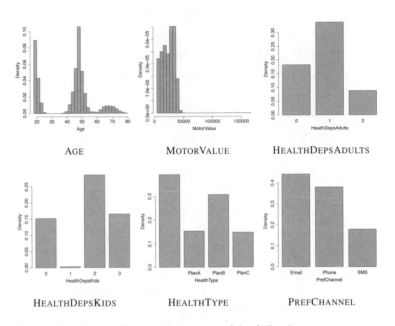

AGE   MOTORVALUE   HEALTHDEPSADULTS

HEALTHDEPSKIDS   HEALTHTYPE   PREFCHANNEL

Discuss this data quality report in terms of the following:

a. Missing values

b. Irregular cardinality

c. Outliers

d. Feature distributions

4. The following **data visualizations** are based on the channel prediction dataset given in Question 3. Each visualization illustrates the relationship between a descriptive feature and the target feature, PREFCHANNEL. Each visualization is composed of four plots: one plot of the distribution of the descriptive feature values in the entire dataset, and three plots illustrating the distribution of the descriptive feature values for each level of the target. Discuss the strength of the relationships shown in each visualizations.

a. The visualization below illustrates the relationship between the continuous feature AGE and the target feature, PREFCHANNEL.

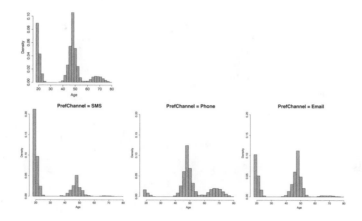

b. The visualization below illustrates the relationship between the categorical feature GENDER and the target feature PREFCHANNEL.

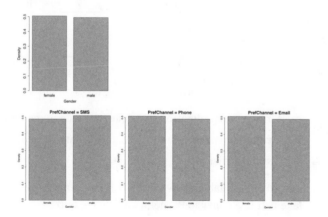

c. The visualization below illustrates the relationship between the categorical feature LOC and the target feature, PREFCHANNEL.

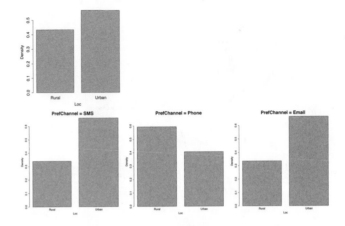

5. The table below shows the scores achieved by a group of students on an exam.

ID	1	2	3	4	5	6	7	8	9	10
SCORE	42	47	59	27	84	49	72	43	73	59

ID	11	12	13	14	15	16	17	18	19	20
SCORE	58	82	50	79	89	75	70	59	67	35

Using this data, perform the following tasks on the SCORE feature:

a. A **range normalization** that generates data in the range $(0, 1)$

b. A **range normalization** that generates data in the range $(-1, 1)$

c. A **standardization** of the data

6. The following table shows the IQs for a group of people who applied to take part in a television general knowledge quiz.

ID	1	2	3	4	5	6	7	8	9	10
IQ	92	107	83	101	107	92	99	119	93	106

ID	11	12	13	14	15	16	17	18	19	20
IQ	105	88	106	90	97	118	120	72	100	104

Using this dataset, generate the following **binned** versions of the IQ feature:

a. An **equal-width binning** using 5 bins.

b. An **equal-frequency binning** using 5 bins

* 7. Comment on the **distributions** of the features shown in each of the following histograms.

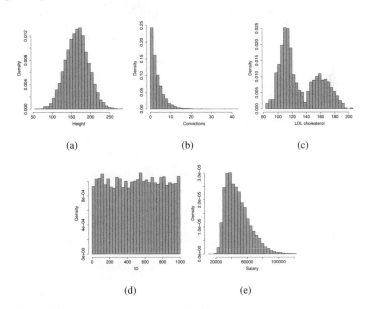

a. The height of employees in a truck driving company.

b. The number of prior criminal convictions held by people given prison sentences in a city district over the course of a full year.

c. The LDL cholesterol values for a large group of patients, including smokers and non-smokers.

d. The employee ID numbers of the academic staff at a university.

e. The salaries of motor insurance policy holders.

✳ 8. The table below shows socio-economic data for a selection of countries for
      the year 2009,[16] using the following features:

      - COUNTRY: The name of the country

      - LIFEEXPECTANCY: The average life expectancy (in years)

      - INFANTMORTALITY: The infant mortality rate (per 1,000 live births)

      - EDUCATION: Spending per primary student as a percentage of GDP

      - HEALTH: Health spending as a percentage of GDP

      - HEALTHUSD: Health spending per person converted into US dollars

COUNTRY	LIFE EXPECTANCY	INFANT MORTALITY	EDUCATION	HEALTH	HEALTH USD
Argentina	75.592	13.500	16.841	9.525	734.093
Cameroon	53.288	67.700	7.137	4.915	60.412
Chile	78.936	7.800	17.356	8.400	801.915
Colombia	73.213	16.500	15.589	7.600	391.859
Cuba	78.552	4.800	44.173	12.100	672.204
Ghana	60.375	52.500	11.365	5.000	54.471
Guyana	65.560	31.200	8.220	6.200	166.718
Latvia	71.736	8.500	31.364	6.600	756.401
Malaysia	74.306	7.100	14.621	4.600	316.478
Mali	53.358	85.500	14.979	5.500	33.089
Mongolia	66.564	26.400	15.121	5.700	96.537
Morocco	70.012	29.900	16.930	5.200	151.513
Senegal	62.653	48.700	17.703	5.700	59.658
Serbia	73.532	6.900	61.638	10.500	576.494
Thailand	73.627	12.700	24.351	4.200	160.136

   a. Calculate the **correlation** between the LIFEEXPECTANCY and INFANT-
       MORTALITY features.

   b. The image below shows a **scatter plot matrix** of the continuous fea-
       tures from this dataset (the correlation between LIFEEXPECTANCY
       and INFANTMORTALITY has been omitted). Discuss the relationships
       between the features in the dataset that this scatter plot highlights.

16 The data listed in this table is real and was amalgamated from a number of reports that were
retrieved from Gapminder (www.gapminder.org). The EDUCATION data is based on a report
from the World Bank (data.worldbank.org/indicator/SE.XPD.PRIM.PC.ZS); the
HEALTH and HEALTHUSD data are based on reports from the World Health Organization (www.
who.int); all the other features are based on reports created by Gapminder.

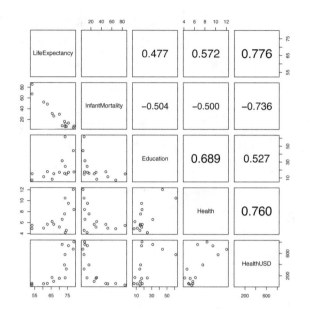

* 9. Tachycardia is a condition that causes the heart to beat faster than normal at rest. The occurrence of tachycardia can have serious implications including increased risk of stroke or sudden cardiac arrest. An analytics consultant has been hired by a major hospital to build a predictive model that predicts the likelihood that a patient at a heart disease clinic will suffer from tachycardia in the month following a visit to the clinic. The hospital will use this model to make predictions for each patient when they visit the clinic and offer increased monitoring for those deemed to be at risk. The analytics consultant has generated an ABT to be used to train this model.[17] The descriptive features in this dataset are defined as follows:

- AGE: The patient's age
- GENDER: The patient's gender (*male* or *female*)
- WEIGHT: The patient's weight
- HEIGHT: The patient's height
- BMI: The patient's body mass index (BMI) which is calculated as $\frac{weight}{height^2}$ where weight is measured in kilograms and height in meters.

---

17 The data used in this question has been artificially generated for this book. This type of application of machine learning techniques, however, is common; for example see Osowski et al. (2004).

- SYS. B.P.: The patient's systolic blood pressure
- DIA. B.P.: The patient's diastolic blood pressure
- HEART RATE: The patient's heart rate
- H.R. DIFF.: The difference between the patient's heart rate at this visit and at their last visit to the clinic
- PREV. TACHY.: Has the patient suffered from tachycardia before?
- TACHYCARDIA: Is the patient at high risk of suffering from tachycardia in the next month?

The following table contains an extract from this ABT—the full ABT contains 2,440 instances.

ID	AGE	GENDER	WEIGHT	HEIGHT	BMI	SYS. B.P.	DIA. B.P.	HEART RATE	H.R. DIFF.	PREV. TACHY.	TACHYCARDI
1	6	male	78	165	28.65	161	97	143			true
2	5	m	117	171	40.01	216	143	162	17	true	true
⋮					⋮			⋮			
143	5	male	108	1.88	305,568.13	139	99	84	21	false	true
144	4	male	107	183	31.95	1,144	90	94	-8	false	true
⋮					⋮			⋮			
1,158	6	female	92	1.71	314,626.72	111	75	75	-5		false
1,159	3	female	151	1.59	596,495.39	124	91	115	23	true	true
⋮					⋮			⋮			
1,702	3	male	86	193	23.09	138	81	83		false	false
1,703	6	f	73	166	26.49	134	86	84	-4		false
⋮					⋮			⋮			

The consultant generated the following **data quality report** from the ABT.

Feature	Count	% Miss.	Card.	Mode	Mode Freq.	Mode %	2nd Mode	2nd Mode Freq.	2n Moc
GENDER	2,440	0.00	4	male	1,591.00	65.20	female	647.00	26.5
PREV. TACHY.	2,440	44.02	3	false	714.00	52.27	true	652.00	47.7
TACHYCARDIA	2,440	2.01	3	false	1,205.00	50.40	true	1,186.00	49.6

Feature	Count	% Miss.	Card.	Min.	1st Qrt.	Mean	Median	3rd Qrt.	Max.	Std. Dev.
AGE	2,440	0.00	7	1.00	3.00	3.88	4.00	5.00	7.00	1.22
WEIGHT	2,440	0.00	174	0.00	81.00	95.70	95.00	107.00	187.20	20.89
HEIGHT	2,440	0.00	109	1.47	162.00	162.21	171.50	179.00	204.00	41.06
BMI	2,440	0.00	1,385	0.00	27.64	18,523.40	32.02	38.57	596,495.39	77,068.75
SYS .B.P.	2,440	0.00	149	62.00	115.00	127.84	124.00	135.00	1,144.00	29.11
DIA. B.P.	2,440	0.00	109	46.00	77.00	86.34	84.00	92.00	173.60	14.25
HEART RATE	2,440	0.00	119	57.00	91.75	103.28	100.00	110.00	190.40	18.21
H.R. DIFF.	2,440	13.03	78	-50.00	-4.00	3.00	1.00	8.00	47.00	12.38

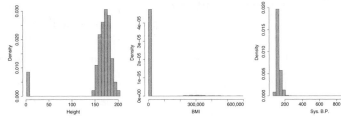

AGE   GENDER   WEIGHT

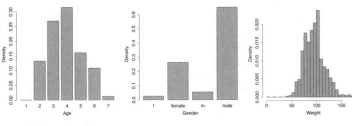

HEIGHT   BMI   SYS. B.P.

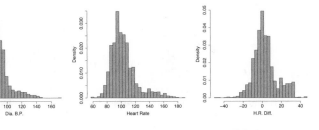

DIA. B.P.   HEART RATE   H.R DIFF.

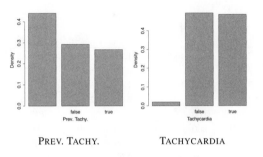

PREV. TACHY.   TACHYCARDIA

Discuss this data quality report in terms of the following:

a. Missing values

b. Irregular cardinality

c. Outliers

d. Feature distributions

* 10. The following data visualizations are based on the tachycardia prediction dataset from Question 9 (after the instances with missing TACHYCARDIA values have been removed and all outliers have been handled). Each visualization illustrates the relationship between a descriptive feature and the target feature, TACHYCARDIA and is composed of three plots: a plot of the distribution of the descriptive feature values in the full dataset, and plots showing the distribution of the descriptive feature values for each level of the target. Discuss the relationships shown in each visualizations.

a. The visualization below illustrates the relationship between the continuous feature DIA. B.P. and the target feature, TACHYCARDIA.

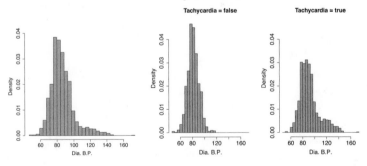

b. The visualization below illustrates the relationship between the continuous HEIGHT feature and the target feature TACHYCARDIA.

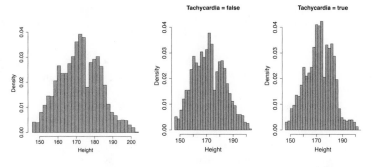

c. The visualization below illustrates the relationship between the categorical feature PREV. TACHY. and the target feature, TACHYCARDIA.

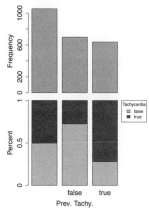

4   Information-based Learning

Information is the resolution of uncertainty.
—Claude Elwood Shannon

In this chapter we discuss the ways in which concepts from **information the-ory** can be used to build prediction models. We start by discussing **decision trees**, the fundamental structure used in information-based machine learning, before presenting the fundamental measures of information content that are used: **entropy** and **information gain**. We then present the **ID3** algorithm, the standard algorithm used to induce a decision tree from a dataset. The exten-sions and variations to this standard approach that we present describe how different data types can be handled, how overfitting can be avoided using deci-sion tree **pruning**, and how multiple prediction models can be combined in **ensembles** to improve prediction accuracy.

4.1   Big Idea

We'll start off by playing a game. *Guess Who* is a two-player game in which one player chooses a card with a picture of a character on it from a deck and the other player tries to guess which character is on the card by asking a series of questions to which the answer can only be yes or no. The player asking the questions wins by guessing who is on the card within a small number of questions and loses otherwise. Figure 4.1[118] shows the set of cards that we will use for our game. We can represent these cards using the dataset given in Table 4.1[118].

Now, imagine that we have picked one of these cards and you have to guess which one by asking questions. Which of the following questions would you ask first?

1. Is it a man?

2. Does the person wear glasses?

Most people would ask Question 1 first. Why is this? At first, this choice of question might seem ineffective. For example, if you ask Question 2, and we answer *yes*, you can be sure that we have picked *Brian* without asking any more questions. The problem with this reasoning, however, is that, on average, the answer to Question 2 will be *yes* only one out of every four times you play. That means that three out of every four times you ask Question 2, the answer

Figure 4.1

Cards showing character faces and names for the *Guess Who* game.

Table 4.1

A dataset that represents the characters in the *Guess Who* game.

Man	Long Hair	Glasses	Name
Yes	No	Yes	Brian
Yes	No	No	John
No	Yes	No	Aphra
No	No	No	Aoife

will be *no*, and you will still have to distinguish between the three remaining characters.

Figure 4.2[119] illustrates the possible question sequences that can follow in a game beginning with Question 2. In Figure 4.2(a)[119] we next ask, *Is it a man?* and then, if required, *Do they have long hair?* In Figure 4.2(b)[119] we reverse this order. In both of these diagrams, one path to an answer about the character on a card is 1 question long, one path is 2 questions long, and two paths are 3 questions long. Consequently, if you ask Question 2 first, the average number of questions you have to ask per game is

$$\frac{1+2+3+3}{4} = 2.25$$

On the other hand, if you ask Question 1 first, there is only one sequence of questions with which to follow it. This sequence is shown in Figure 4.3[120]. Irrespective of the answers to the questions, you always have to follow a path through this sequence that is 2 questions long to reach an answer about the character on a card. This means that if you always ask Question 1 first, the average number of questions you have to ask per game is

$$\frac{2+2+2+2}{4} = 2$$

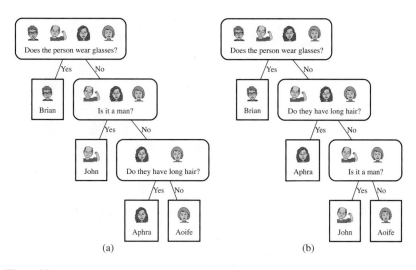

Figure 4.2
The different question sequences that can follow in a game of *Guess Who* beginning with the question *Does the person wear glasses?*

What is interesting here is that no matter what question you ask, the answer is always either *yes* or *no*, but, on average, an answer to Question 1 seems to carry more information than an answer to Question 2. This is not because of the literal message in the answer (either *yes* or *no*). Rather, it is because of the way that the answer to each question splits the character cards into different sets based on the value of the descriptive feature the question is asked about (MAN, LONG HAIR or GLASSES) and the likelihood of each possible answer to the question.

An answer to Question 1, *Is it a man?*, splits the game domain into two sets of equal size: one containing *Brian* and *John* and one containing *Aphra* and *Aoife*. One of these sets contains the solution, which leaves you with just one more question to ask to finish the game. By contrast, an answer to Question 2 splits the game domain into one set containing one element, *Brian*, and another set containing three elements: *John*, *Aphra*, and *Aoife*. This works out really well when the set containing the single element contains the solution. In the more likely case that the set containing three elements contains the solution, however, you may have to ask two more questions to uniquely identify the answer. So, when you consider both the likelihood of an answer and how an answer splits up the domain of solutions, it becomes clear that an answer to

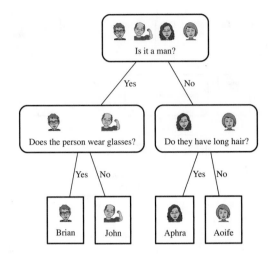

Figure 4.3

The different question sequences that can follow in a game of *Guess Who* beginning with the question *Is it a man?*

Question 2 leaves you with more work to do to solve the game than an answer to Question 1.

So, the big idea here is to figure out which features are the most informative ones to ask questions about by considering the effects of the different answers to the questions, in terms of how the domain is split up after the answer is received and the likelihood of each of the answers. Somewhat surprisingly, people seem to be able to easily do this based on intuition. Information-based machine learning algorithms use the same idea. These algorithms determine which descriptive features provide the most information about a target feature and make predictions by sequentially testing the features in order of their informativeness.

4.2   Fundamentals

In this section we introduce Claude Shannon's approach to measuring information,[1] in particular his model of **entropy** and how it is used in the **information**

1 Claude Shannon is considered to be the father of information theory. Shannon worked for AT&T Bell Labs, where he worked on the efficient encoding of messages for telephone communication. It

Table 4.2

An email spam prediction dataset.

ID	SUSPICIOUS WORDS	UNKNOWN SENDER	CONTAINS IMAGES	CLASS
376	true	false	true	spam
489	true	true	false	spam
541	true	true	false	spam
693	false	true	true	ham
782	false	false	false	ham
976	false	false	false	ham

gain measure to capture the informativeness of a descriptive feature. Before this we introduce **decision trees**, the actual prediction models that we are trying to build.

4.2.1   Decision Trees

Just as we did when we played *Guess Who*, an effective way to generate a prediction is to carry out a series of tests on the values of the descriptive features describing a query instance, and use the answers to these tests to determine the prediction. **Decision trees** take this approach. To illustrate how a decision tree works, we will use the dataset listed in Table 4.2[121]. This dataset contains a set of training instances that can be used to build a model to predict whether emails are *spam* or *ham* (genuine). The dataset has three binary descriptive features: SUSPICIOUS WORDS is *true* if an email contains one or more words that are typically found in spam email (e.g., *casino, viagra, bank*, or *account*); UNKNOWN SENDER is *true* if the email is from an address that is not listed in the contacts of the person who received the email; and CONTAINS IMAGES is *true* if the email contains one or more images.

Figure 4.4[122] shows two decision trees that are **consistent** with the spam dataset. Decision trees look very like the game trees that we developed for the *Guess Who* game. As with all tree representations, a decision tree consists of a **root node** (or starting node), **interior nodes**, and **leaf nodes** (or terminating nodes) that are connected by **branches**. Each non-leaf node (root and interior)

---

was this focus on encoding that motivated his approach to measuring information. In information theory, the meaning of the word **information** deliberately excludes the psychological aspects of the communication and should be understood as measuring the optimal encoding length of a message given the set of possible messages that could be sent within the communication.

in the tree specifies a test to be carried out on a descriptive feature. The number of possible levels that a descriptive feature can take determines the number of downward branches from a non-leaf node. Each of the leaf nodes specifies a predicted level of the target feature.

In the diagrams in Figure 4.4[122], ellipses represent root or interior nodes, and rectangles represent leaf nodes. The labels of the ellipses indicate which descriptive feature is tested at that node. The labels on the each branch indicate one of the possible feature levels that the descriptive feature at the node above can take. The labels on the rectangular leaf nodes indicate the target level that should be predicted when the tests on the interior nodes create a path that terminates at that leaf node.

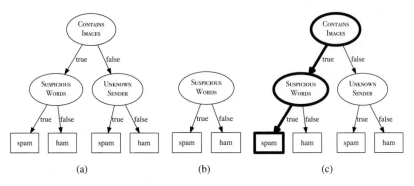

Figure 4.4

Two decision trees (a) and (b) that are consistent with the instances in the spam dataset; (c) the path taken through the tree shown in (a) to make a prediction for the query instance SUSPICIOUS WORDS = *true*, UNKNOWN SENDER = *true*, CONTAINS IMAGES = *true*.

The process of using a decision tree to make a prediction for a query instance starts by testing the value of the descriptive feature at the root node of the tree. The result of this test determines which of the root node's children the process should then descend to. These two steps of testing the value of a descriptive feature and descending a level in the tree are then repeated until the process comes to a leaf node at which a prediction can be made.

To demonstrate how this process works, imagine we were given the query email SUSPICIOUS WORDS = *true*, UNKNOWN SENDER = *true*, CONTAINS IMAGES = *true*, and asked to predict whether it is *spam* or *ham*. Applying the decision tree from Figure 4.4(a)[122] to this query, we see that the root node of this tree tests the CONTAINS IMAGES feature. The query instance value for CONTAINS IMAGES is *true* so the process descends the left branch from the root node, labeled *true*, to an interior node that tests the SUSPICIOUS WORDS feature. The query instance value for this feature is *true*, so based on the result of the test at this node, the process descends the left branch, labeled *true*, to a leaf node labeled *spam*. As the process has arrived at a leaf node, it terminates, and the target level indicated by the leaf node, *spam*, is predicted for the query instance. The path through the decision tree for this query instance is shown in figure 4.4(c)[122].

The decision tree in Figure 4.4(b)[122] would have returned the same prediction for the query instance. Indeed, both of the decision trees in Figures 4.4(a)[122] and 4.4(b)[122] are consistent with the dataset in Table 4.2[121] and can generalize sufficiently to make predictions for query instances like the one considered in our example. The fact that there are, at least, two decision trees that can do this raises the question: How do we decide which is the best decision tree to use?

We can apply almost the same approach that we used in the *Guess Who* game to make this decision. Looking at the decision trees in Figures 4.4(a)[122] and 4.4(b)[122], we notice that the tree in Figure 4.4(a)[122] performs tests on two features in order to make a prediction, while the decision tree in Figure 4.4(b)[122] only ever needs to test the value of one feature. The reason for this is that SUSPICIOUS WORDS, the descriptive feature tested at the root node of the tree in Figure 4.4(b)[122], perfectly splits the data into a pure group of *spam* emails and a pure group of *ham* emails. We can say that because of the purity of the splits that it makes, the SUSPICIOUS WORDS feature provides more information about the value of the target feature for an instance than the CONTAINS IMAGES feature, so a tree that tests this descriptive feature at the root node is preferable.

This gives us a way to choose between a set of different decision trees that are all consistent with a set of training instances. We can introduce a preference for decision trees that use fewer tests, in other words, trees that are on average shallower.[2] This is the primary inductive bias that a machine learning algorithm taking an information-based approach encodes. To build shallow trees, we need to put the descriptive features that best discriminate between instances that have different target feature values toward the top of the tree. To do this we

---

2 In fact, it can be argued that a preference toward shallower decision trees is a good idea in general and can be viewed as following **Occam's razor**. Occam's razor is the principle of keeping theories as simple as possible. It is named after a fourteenth century Franciscan monk, William of Occam (sometimes spelled Ockham), who was one of the first to formulate this principle. The *razor* in the title comes from the idea of shaving off any unnecessary assumptions from a theory.

need a formal measure of how well a descriptive feature discriminates between the levels of the target feature. Similar to the way we analyzed the questions in the *Guess Who* game, we will measure the discriminatory power of a descriptive feature by analyzing the size and probability of each set of instances created when we test the value of the feature and how pure each set of instances is with respect to the target feature values of the instances it contains. The formal measure we will use to do this is Shannon's entropy model.

4.2.2   Shannon's Entropy Model

Claude Shannon's entropy model defines a computational measure of the impurity of the elements in a set. Before we examine the mathematical definition of entropy, we will first provide an intuitive explanation of what it means. Figure 4.5[125] illustrates a collection of sets of playing cards of contrasting entropy. An easy way to understand the entropy of a set is to think in terms of the uncertainty associated with guessing the result if you were to make a random selection from the set. For example, if you were to randomly select a card from the set in Figure 4.5(a)[125], you would have zero uncertainty, as you would know for sure that you would select an ace of spades. So, this set has zero entropy. If, however, you were to randomly select an element from the set in Figure 4.5(f)[125], you would be very uncertain about any prediction as there are twelve possible outcomes, each of which is equally likely. This is why this set has very high entropy. The other sets in Figure 4.5[125] have entropy values between these two extremes.

This gives us a clue as to how we should define a computational model of entropy. We can transform the probabilities[3] of the different possible outcomes when we randomly select an element from a set to entropy values. An outcome with a large probability should map to a low entropy value, while an outcome with a small probability should map to a large entropy value. The mathematical **logarithm**, or **log**, function[4] does almost exactly the transformation that we need.

---

3 We use some simple elements of probability theory in this chapter. Readers unfamiliar with the way probabilities are calculated based on the relative frequencies of events should read the first section of Appendix B[541] before continuing with this chapter.

4 The *log* of a to the base b, written as $log_b(a)$, is the number to which we must raise b to get a. For example, $log_2(8) = 3$ because $2^3 = 8$ and $log_5(625) = 4$ because $5^4 = 625$.

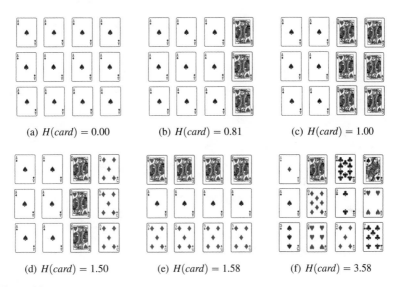

(a) $H(card) = 0.00$ (b) $H(card) = 0.81$ (c) $H(card) = 1.00$

(d) $H(card) = 1.50$ (e) $H(card) = 1.58$ (f) $H(card) = 3.58$

Figure 4.5

The entropy of different sets of playing cards measured in bits.

If we examine the graph of the **binary logarithm** (a logarithm to the base 2) of probabilities ranging from 0 to 1 in Figure 4.6(a)[126], we see that the logarithm function returns large negative numbers for low probabilities, and small negative numbers for high probabilities. Ignoring the fact that the logarithm function returns negative numbers, the magnitude of the numbers it returns is ideal as a measure of entropy: large numbers for low probabilities and small numbers (near zero) for high probabilities. It should also be noted that the range of values for the binary logarithm of a probability, $[-\infty, 0]$, is much larger than those taken by the probability itself $[0, 1]$. This is also an attractive characteristic of this function. It will be more convenient for us to convert the output of the log function to positive numbers by multiplying them by -1. Figure 4.6(b)[126] shows the impact of this.

Shannon's model of entropy is a weighted sum of the logs of the probabilities of each possible outcome when we make a random selection from a set. The weights used in the sum are the probabilities of the outcomes themselves so that outcomes with high probabilities contribute more to the overall entropy of a set than outcomes with low probabilities. Shannon's model of entropy is

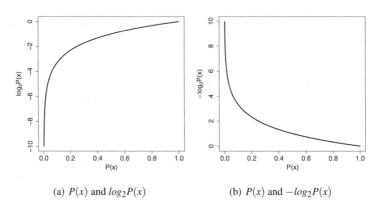

(a) $P(x)$ and $log_2 P(x)$ (b) $P(x)$ and $-log_2 P(x)$

Figure 4.6

(a) A graph illustrating how the value of a binary log (the log to the base 2) of a probability changes across the range of probability values; (b) the impact of multiplying these values by -1.

defined as

$$H(t) = -\sum_{i=1}^{l} (P(t=i) \times log_s(P(t=i))) \qquad (4.1)$$

where $P(t=i)$ is the probability that the outcome of randomly selecting an element t is the type i, l is the number of different types of things in the set, and s is an arbitrary logarithmic base. The minus sign at the beginning of the equation is simply added to convert the negative numbers returned by the log function to positive ones (as described above). We will always use 2 as the base, s, when we calculate entropy, which means that we measure entropy in **bits**.[5] Equation (4.1)[126] is the cornerstone of modern **information theory** and is an excellent measure of the impurity, **heterogeneity**, of a set.

To understand how Shannon's entropy model works, consider the example of a set of 52 different playing cards. The probability of randomly selecting any specific card i from this set, $P(card = i)$, is quite low, just $\frac{1}{52}$. The entropy

---

5 Using binary logs, the maximum entropy for a set with two types of elements is 1.00 bit, but the entropy for a set with more than two types of elements may be greater than 1.00 bit. The choice of base when using Shannon's model in the context that it will be used later in this chapter is arbitrary. The choice of base 2 is partly due to a conventional computer science background and partly because it allows us to use the *bits* unit of information.

of the set of 52 playing cards is calculated as

$$H(card) = -\sum_{i=1}^{52} P(card = i) \times log_2(P(card = i))$$

$$= -\sum_{i=1}^{52} 0.019 \times log_2(0.019)$$

$$= -\sum_{i=1}^{52} -0.1096$$

$$= 5.700 \; bits$$

In this calculation, for each possible card Shannon's model multiplies a small probability, $P(card) = i$, by a large negative number, $log_2(P(card) = i)$, resulting in a relatively large negative number. The individual relatively large negative numbers calculated for each card are then summed to return one large negative number. The sign of this is inverted to give a large positive value for the entropy of this very impure set.

By contrast, consider the example of calculating the entropy of a set of 52 playing cards if we only distinguish between cards based on their suit (hearts ♥, clubs ♣, diamonds ♦ or, spades ♠). This time there are only 4 possible outcomes when a random card is selected from this set, each with a reasonably large probability of $\frac{13}{52}$. The entropy associated with this set can be calculated as

$$H(suit) = -\sum_{l \in \{♥,♣,♦,♠\}} P(suit = l) \times log_2(P(suit = l))$$

$$= -\left((P(♥) \times log_2(P(♥))) + (P(♣) \times log_2(P(♣))) \right.$$
$$\left. + (P(♦) \times log_2(P(♦))) + (P(♠) \times log_2(P(♠))) \right)$$

$$= -\left(\left({}^{13}/_{52} \times log_2({}^{13}/_{52}) \right) + \left({}^{13}/_{52} \times log_2({}^{13}/_{52}) \right) \right.$$
$$\left. + \left({}^{13}/_{52} \times log_2({}^{13}/_{52}) \right) + \left({}^{13}/_{52} \times log_2({}^{13}/_{52}) \right) \right)$$

$$= -((0.25 \times -2) + (0.25 \times -2) + (0.25 \times -2) + (0.25 \times -2))$$

$$= 2 \; bits$$

In this calculation Shannon's model multiples the large probability of selecting a specific suit, $P(suit = l)$, by a small negative number, $log_2(P(suit = l))$, to return a relatively small negative number. The relatively small negative numbers associated with each suit are summed to result in a small negative number overall. Again, the sign of this number is inverted to result in a small positive value for the entropy of this much purer set.

To further explore the entropy, we can return to look at the entropy values of each set of cards shown in Figure 4.5[125]. In the set in Figure 4.5(a)[125], all the cards are identical. This means that there is no uncertainty as to the result when a selection is made from this set. Shannon's model of information is designed to reflect this intuition, and the entropy value for this set is 0.00 bits. In the sets in Figures 4.5(b)[125] and 4.5(c)[125], there is a mixture of two different types of cards, so these have higher entropy values, in these instances, 0.81 bits and 1.00 bit. The maximum entropy for a set with two types of elements is 1.00 bit, which occurs when there are equal numbers of each type in the set.

The sets in Figures 4.5(d)[125] and 4.5(e)[125] both have three types of cards. The maximum entropy for sets with three elements is 1.58 and occurs when there are equal numbers of each type in the set, as is the case in Figure 4.5(e)[125]. In Figure 4.5(d)[125] one card type is more present than the others, so the overall entropy is slightly lower, 1.50 bits. Finally, the set in Figure 4.5(f)[125] has a large number of card types, each represented only once, which leads to the high entropy value of 3.58 bits.

This discussion highlights the fact that entropy is essentially a measure of the heterogeneity of a set. As the composition of the sets changed from the set with only one type of element (Figure 4.5(a)[125]) to a set with many different types of elements each with an equal likelihood of being selected (Figure 4.5(f)[125]), the entropy score for the sets increased.

4.2.3   Information Gain

What is the relationship between a measure of heterogeneity of a set and predictive analytics? If we can construct a sequence of tests that splits the training data into pure sets with respect to the target feature values, then we can label queries by applying the same sequence of tests to a query and labeling it with the target feature value of instances in the set it ends up in.

To illustrate this we'll return to the spam dataset from Table 4.2[121]. Figure 4.7[129] shows how the instances in the spam dataset are split when we partition it using each of the three descriptive features. Looking at 4.7(a)[129], we can see that splitting the dataset based on the SUSPICIOUS WORDS feature provides a lot of information about whether an email is spam or ham. In fact, partitioning the data by this feature creates two pure sets: one containing only instances with the target level *spam* and the other set containing only instances with the

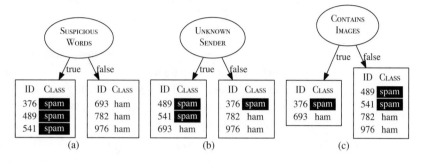

Figure 4.7

How the instances in the spam dataset split when we partition using each of the different descriptive features from the spam dataset in Table 4.2[121].

target level *ham*. This indicates that the SUSPICIOUS WORDS feature is a good feature to test if we are trying to decide whether a new email—not listed in the training dataset—is spam or not.

What about the other features? Figure 4.7(b)[129] shows how the UNKNOWN SENDER feature partitions the dataset. The resulting sets both contain a mixture of *spam* and *ham* instances. This indicates that the UNKNOWN SENDER feature is not as good at discriminating between spam and ham emails as the SUSPICIOUS WORDS feature. Although there is a mixture in each of these sets, however, it seems to be the case that when UNKNOWN SENDER = *true*, the majority of emails are *spam*, and when UNKNOWN SENDER = *false*, the majority of emails are *ham*. So although this feature doesn't perfectly discriminate between spam and ham it does give us some information that we might be able to use in conjunction with other features to help decide whether a new email is spam or ham. Finally, if we examine the partitioning of the dataset based on the CONTAINS IMAGES feature, Figure 4.7(c)[129], it looks like this feature is not very discriminatory for *spam* and *ham* at all. Both of the resulting sets contain a balanced mixture of spam and ham instances.

What we need to do now is to develop a formal model that captures the intuitions about the informativeness of these features described above. Unsurprisingly, we do this using Shannon's entropy model. The measure of informativeness that we will use is known as **information gain** and is a measure of the reduction in the overall entropy of a set of instances that is achieved by testing on a descriptive feature. Computing information gain is a three-step process:

1. Compute the entropy of the original dataset with respect to the target feature. This gives us an measure of how much information is required in order to organize the dataset into pure sets.

2. For each descriptive feature, create the sets that result by partitioning the instances in the dataset using their feature values, and then sum the entropy scores of each of these sets. This gives a measure of the information that remains required to organize the instances into pure sets after we have split them using the descriptive feature.

3. Subtract the remaining entropy value (computed in step 2) from the original entropy value (computed in step 1) to give the information gain.

We need to define three equations to formally specify information gain (one for each step). The first equation calculates the entropy for a dataset with respect to a target feature[6]

$$H(t, \mathcal{D}) = - \sum_{l \in levels(t)} (P(t = l) \times log_2(P(t = l))) \qquad (4.2)$$

where $levels(t)$ is the set of levels in the domain of the target feature t, and $P(t = l)$ is the probability of a randomly selected instance having the target feature level l.

The second equation defines how we compute the entropy remaining after we partition the dataset using a particular descriptive feature d. When we partition the dataset $\mathcal{D}$ using the descriptive feature d we create a number of partitions (or sets) $\mathcal{D}_{d=l_1} \ldots \mathcal{D}_{d=l_k}$, where $l_1 \ldots l_k$ are the k levels that feature d can take. Each partition, $\mathcal{D}_{d=l_i}$, contains the instances in $\mathcal{D}$ that have a value of level l_i for the d feature. The entropy remaining after we have tested d is a weighted sum of the entropy, still with respect to the target feature, of each partition. The weighting is determined by the size of each partition—so a large partition should contribute more to the overall remaining entropy than a smaller partition. We use the term $rem(d, \mathcal{D})$ to denote this quantity and define it formally as

$$rem(d, \mathcal{D}) = \sum_{l \in levels(d)} \underbrace{\frac{|\mathcal{D}_{d=l}|}{|\mathcal{D}|}}_{\text{weighting}} \times \underbrace{H(t, \mathcal{D}_{d=l})}_{\substack{\text{entropy of} \\ \text{partition } \mathcal{D}_{d=l}}} \qquad (4.3)$$

---

6 This is almost identical to the definition of Shannon's entropy model given in Equation (4.1)[126]. We have extended the definition to include an explicit parameter for the dataset $\mathcal{D}$ for which we are computing the entropy, and we have specified the base as 2.

Using Equation $(4.2)^{[130]}$ and Equation $(4.3)^{[130]}$, we can now formally define information gain made from splitting the dataset $\mathcal{D}$ using the feature d as

$$IG(d, \mathcal{D}) = H(t, \mathcal{D}) - rem(d, \mathcal{D}) \qquad (4.4)$$

To illustrate how information gain is calculated, and to check how well it models our intuitions described at the beginning of this section, we will compute the information gain for each descriptive feature in the spam dataset. The first step is to compute the entropy for the whole dataset using Equation $(4.2)^{[130]}$:

$$
\begin{aligned}
H(t, \mathcal{D}) &= -\sum_{l \in \{spam, ham\}} \left(P(t = l) \times log_2(P(t = l)) \right) \\
&= -\left(\left(P(t = spam) \times log_2(P(t = spam)) \right. \right. \\
&\qquad \left. \left. + \left(P(t = ham) \times log_2(P(t = ham)) \right) \right) \right) \\
&= -\left(\left({}^3/_6 \times log_2({}^3/_6) \right) + \left({}^3/_6 \times log_2({}^3/_6) \right) \right) \\
&= 1 \ bit
\end{aligned}
$$

The next step is to compute the entropy remaining after we split the dataset using each of the descriptive features. The computation for the SUSPICIOUS WORDS feature is[7]

$$
\begin{aligned}
&rem(\text{WORDS}, \mathcal{D}) \\
&= \left(\frac{|\mathcal{D}_{\text{WORDS}=true}|}{|\mathcal{D}|} \times H(t, \mathcal{D}_{\text{WORDS}=true}) \right) \\
&\quad + \left(\frac{|\mathcal{D}_{\text{WORDS}=false}|}{|\mathcal{D}|} \times H(t, \mathcal{D}_{\text{WORDS}=false}) \right) \\
&= \left({}^3/_6 \times \left(-\sum_{l \in \{spam, ham\}} P(t = l) \times log_2(P(t = l)) \right) \right) \\
&\quad + \left({}^3/_6 \times \left(-\sum_{l \in \{spam, ham\}} P(t = l) \times log_2(P(t = l)) \right) \right) \\
&= \left({}^3/_6 \times \left(-\left(\left({}^3/_3 \times log_2({}^3/_3) \right) + \left({}^0/_3 \times log_2({}^0/_3) \right) \right) \right) \right) \\
&\quad + \left({}^3/_6 \times \left(-\left(\left({}^0/_3 \times log_2({}^0/_3) \right) + \left({}^3/_3 \times log_2({}^3/_3) \right) \right) \right) \right) \\
&= 0 \ bits
\end{aligned}
$$

---

7 Note that we have shortened feature names in these calculations to save space.

The remaining entropy for the UNKNOWN SENDER feature is

$$
\begin{aligned}
rem\,(\text{SENDER}, \mathcal{D}) \\
&= \left(\frac{|\mathcal{D}_{\text{SENDER}=true}|}{|\mathcal{D}|} \times H\left(t, \mathcal{D}_{\text{SENDER}=true}\right) \right) \\
&\quad + \left(\frac{|\mathcal{D}_{\text{SENDER}=false}|}{|\mathcal{D}|} \times H\left(t, \mathcal{D}_{\text{SENDER}=false}\right) \right) \\
&= \left({}^{3}/_{6} \times \left(- \sum_{l \in \{spam,ham\}} P(t=l) \times log_2(P(t=l)) \right) \right) \\
&\quad + \left({}^{3}/_{6} \times \left(- \sum_{l \in \{spam,ham\}} P(t=l) \times log_2(P(t=l)) \right) \right) \\
&= \left({}^{3}/_{6} \times \left(- \left(\left({}^{2}/_{3} \times log_2({}^{2}/_{3}) \right) + \left({}^{1}/_{3} \times log_2({}^{1}/_{3}) \right) \right) \right) \right) \\
&\quad + \left({}^{3}/_{6} \times \left(- \left(\left({}^{1}/_{3} \times log_2({}^{1}/_{3}) \right) + \left({}^{2}/_{3} \times log_2({}^{2}/_{3}) \right) \right) \right) \right) \\
&= 0.9183 \; bits
\end{aligned}
$$

The remaining entropy for the CONTAINS IMAGES feature is

$$
\begin{aligned}
rem\,(\text{IMAGES}, \mathcal{D}) \\
&= \left(\frac{|\mathcal{D}_{\text{IMAGES}=true}|}{|\mathcal{D}|} \times H\left(t, \mathcal{D}_{\text{IMAGES}=true}\right) \right) \\
&\quad + \left(\frac{|\mathcal{D}_{\text{IMAGES}=false}|}{|\mathcal{D}|} \times H\left(t, \mathcal{D}_{\text{IMAGES}=false}\right) \right) \\
&= \left({}^{2}/_{6} \times \left(- \sum_{l \in \{spam,ham\}} P(t=l) \times log_2(P(t=l)) \right) \right) \\
&\quad + \left({}^{4}/_{6} \times \left(- \sum_{l \in \{spam,ham\}} P(t=l) \times log_2(P(t=l)) \right) \right) \\
&= \left({}^{2}/_{6} \times \left(- \left(\left({}^{1}/_{2} \times log_2({}^{1}/_{2}) \right) + \left({}^{1}/_{2} \times log_2({}^{1}/_{2}) \right) \right) \right) \right) \\
&\quad + \left({}^{4}/_{6} \times \left(- \left(\left({}^{2}/_{4} \times log_2({}^{2}/_{4}) \right) + \left({}^{2}/_{4} \times log_2({}^{2}/_{4}) \right) \right) \right) \right) \\
&= 1 \; bit
\end{aligned}
$$

We can now complete the information gain calculation for each descriptive feature as

$$IG(\text{WORDS}, \mathcal{D}) = H(\text{CLASS}, \mathcal{D}) - rem(\text{WORDS}, \mathcal{D})$$
$$= 1 - 0$$
$$= 1 \; bit$$
$$IG(\text{SENDER}, \mathcal{D}) = H(\text{CLASS}, \mathcal{D}) - rem(\text{SENDER}, \mathcal{D})$$
$$= 1 - 0.9183$$
$$= 0.0817 \; bits$$
$$IG(\text{IMAGES}, \mathcal{D}) = H(\text{CLASS}, \mathcal{D}) - rem(\text{IMAGES}, \mathcal{D})$$
$$= 1 - 1$$
$$= 0 \; bits$$

The information gain of the SUSPICIOUS WORDS feature is 1 bit. This is equivalent to the total entropy for the entire dataset. An information gain score for a feature that matches the entropy for the entire dataset indicates that the feature is perfectly discriminatory with respect to the target feature values. Unfortunately, in more realistic datasets, finding a feature as powerful as the SUSPICIOUS WORDS feature is very rare. The feature UNKNOWN SENDER has an information gain of 0.0817 bits. An information gain score this low suggests that although splitting on this feature provides some information, it is not particularly useful. Finally, the CONTAINS IMAGES feature has an information gain score of 0 bits. This ranking of the features by information gain mirrors the intuitions we developed about the usefulness of these features during our earlier discussion.

We started this section with the idea that if we could construct a sequence of tests that splits the training data into pure sets with respect to the target feature values, then we can do prediction by applying the same sequence of tests to the prediction queries and labeling them with the target feature of the set they end up in. A key part of doing this is being able to decide which tests should be included in the sequence and in what order. The information gain model we have developed allows us to decide which test we should add to the sequence next because it enables us to select the best feature to use on a given dataset. In the next section, we introduce the standard algorithm for growing decision trees in this way.

4.3   Standard Approach: The ID3 Algorithm

Assuming that we want to use shallow decision trees, is there a way in which we can automatically create them from data? One of the best known decision tree induction algorithms is the **Iterative Dichotomizer 3** (**ID3**) algorithm.[8] This algorithm attempts to create the shallowest decision tree that is consistent with the data given.

The ID3 algorithm builds the tree in a recursive, depth-first manner, beginning at the root node and working down to the leaf nodes. The algorithm begins by choosing the best descriptive feature to test (i.e., the best question to ask first). This choice is made by computing the **information gain** of the descriptive features in the training dataset. A root node is then added to the tree and labeled with the selected test feature. The training dataset is then partitioned using the test. There is one partition created for each possible test result, which contains the training instances that returned that result. For each partition a branch is grown from the node. The process is then repeated for each branch using the relevant partition of the training set in place of the full training set and with the selected test feature excluded from further testing. This process is repeated until all the instances in a partition have the same target level, at which point a leaf node is created and labeled with that level.

The design of the ID3 algorithm is based on the assumption that a correct decision tree for a domain will classify instances from that domain in the same proportion as the target level occurs in the domain. So, given a dataset $\mathcal{D}$ representing a domain with two target levels C_1 and C_2, an arbitrary instance from the domain should be classified as being associated with target level C_1 with the probability $\frac{|C_1|}{|C_1|+|C_2|}$ and to target level C_2 with the probability $\frac{|C_2|}{|C_1|+|C_2|}$, where $|C_1|$ and $|C_2|$ refer to the number of instances in $\mathcal{D}$ associated with C_1 and C_2 respectively. To ensure that the resulting decision tree classifies in the correct proportions, the decision tree is constructed by repeatedly partitioning[9] the training dataset, until every instance in a partition maps to the same target level.

Algorithm 4.1[135] lists a pseudocode description of the ID3 algorithm. Although the algorithm looks quite complex, it essentially does one of two things each time it is invoked: it either stops growing the current path in the

---

8 This algorithm was first published in Quinlan (1986).

9 Hence the name **Iterative Dichotomizer**.

tree by adding a leaf node to the tree, Lines 1–6, or it extends the current path by adding an interior node to the tree and growing the branches of this node by repeatedly rerunning the algorithm, Lines 7–13.

Algorithm 4.1 Pseudocode description of the ID3 algorithm.

Require: set of descriptive features $\mathbf{d}$
Require: set of training instances $\mathcal{D}$

  1: **if** all the instances in $\mathcal{D}$ have the same target level C **then**
  2:     **return** a decision tree consisting of a leaf node with label C
  3: **else if $\mathbf{d}$ is empty then**
  4:     **return** a decision tree consisting of a leaf node with the label of the majority target level in $\mathcal{D}$
  5: **else if $\mathcal{D}$ is empty then**
  6:     **return** a decision tree consisting of a leaf node with the label of the majority target level of the dataset of the immediate parent node
  7: **else**
  8:     $\mathbf{d}\,[best] \;\leftarrow\; \underset{d \in \mathbf{d}}{\arg\max}\, IG\,(d, \mathcal{D})$
  9:     make a new node, $Node_{\mathbf{d}[best]}$, and label it with $\mathbf{d}\,[best]$
10:     partition $\mathcal{D}$ using $\mathbf{d}\,[best]$
11:     remove $\mathbf{d}\,[best]$ from $\mathbf{d}$
12:     **for** each partition $\mathcal{D}_i$ of $\mathcal{D}$ **do**
13:         grow a branch from $Node_{\mathbf{d}[best]}$ to the decision tree created by rerunning *ID3* with $\mathcal{D} = \mathcal{D}_i$

Lines 1–6 of Algorithm 4.1[135] control when a new leaf node is created in the tree. We have already mentioned that the ID3 algorithm constructs the decision tree by recursively partitioning the dataset. An important decision to be made when designing any recursive process is what the base cases that stop the recursion will be. In the ID3 algorithm the base cases are the situations where we stop splitting the dataset and construct a leaf node with an associated target level. There are two important things to remember when designing these base cases. First, the dataset of training instances considered at each of the interior nodes in the tree is not the complete dataset; rather, it is the subset of instances considered at its parent node that had the relevant feature value for the branch from the parent to the current node. Second, once a feature has been tested, it is not considered for selection again along that path in the tree. A feature will only be tested once on any path in the tree, but it may occur several times in the tree on different paths. Based on these constraints, the algorithm defines three situations where the recursion stops and a leaf node is constructed:

1. All the instances in the dataset have the same target feature level. In this situation, the algorithm returns a single leaf node tree with that target level as its label (Algorithm 4.1[135] Lines 1–2).

2. The set of features left to test is empty. This means that we have already tested every feature on the path between the root node and the current node. We have no more features we can use to distinguish between the instances, so we return a single leaf node tree with the majority target level of the dataset as its target level (Algorithm 4.1[135] Lines 3–4).

3. The dataset is empty. This can occur when, for a particular partition of the dataset, there are no instances that have a particular feature value. In this case we return a single leaf node tree with the majority target level of the dataset at the parent node that made the recursive call (Algorithm 4.1[135] Lines 5–6).

If none of these cases hold, the algorithm continues to recursively create interior nodes, Lines 7–13 of Algorithm 4.1[135]. The first step in creating an interior node is to decide which descriptive feature should be tested at this node (Line 8 of Algorithm 4.1[135]). When we first mentioned the ID3 algorithm, we stated that it tries to create the shallowest decision tree that is consistent with the data given. The feature of the ID3 algorithm that biases it toward shallow trees is the mechanism that it uses to determine which descriptive feature is the *most informative* one to test at a new node. The ID3 algorithm uses the **information gain** metric to choose the best feature to test at each node in the tree. Consequently, the selection of the best feature to split a dataset on is based on the purity, or homogeneity, of the resulting partitions in the datasets. Again, remember that each node is constructed in a context consisting of a dataset of instances containing a subset of the instances used to construct its parent node and the set of descriptive features that have not been tested on the path between the root node and parent node. As a result, the information gain for a particular descriptive feature may be different at different nodes in the tree because it will be computed on different subsets of the full training dataset. One consequence of this is that a feature with a low information gain at the root node (when the full dataset is considered) may have a high information gain score at one of the interior nodes because it is predictive on the subset of instances that are considered at that interior node.

Once the most informative feature, **d** [*best*], has been chosen, the algorithm adds a new node, labeled with the feature **d** [*best*], to the tree (Line 9). It then splits the dataset that was considered at this node, $\mathcal{D}$, into partitions, $\mathcal{D}_1, \ldots, \mathcal{D}_k$, according to the levels that **d** [*best*] can take, $\{l_1, \ldots, l_k\}$ (Line 10). Next, it removes the feature **d** [*best*] from the set of features considered for testing later on this path in the tree; this enforces the constraint that a feature can be tested only once on any particular path in the tree (Line 11). Finally, in Lines 12 and 13, the algorithm grows a branch in the tree for each of the values in the domain of **d** [*best*] by recursively calling itself for each of the partitions created at Line 10. Each of these recursive calls uses the partition it is called on as the dataset it considers and is restricted to selecting from the set of features that have not been tested so far on the path from the root node. The node returned by the recursive call to the algorithm may be the root of a subtree or a leaf node. Either way, it is joined to the current node with a branch labeled with the appropriate level of the selected feature.

4.3.1   A Worked Example: Predicting Vegetation Distributions

In this section we will work through an example to illustrate how the ID3 is used to induce a decision tree. This example is based on **ecological modeling**, an area of scientific research that applies statistical and analytical techniques to model ecological processes. One of the problems faced by ecological management practitioners is that it is often too expensive to do large-scale, high-resolution land surveys. Using predictive analytics, however, the results of small-scale surveys can be used to create predictive models that can be applied across large regions. These models are used to inform resource management and conservation activities[10], such as managing the distribution of animal species and vegetation across geographic regions. The descriptive features used by these models are often features that can be automatically extracted from digitized maps, aerial photographs, or satellite imagery—for example, the elevation, steepness, color, and spectral reflection of the terrain, and the presence or absence of features such as rivers, roads, or lakes.

Table 4.3 lists an example dataset from the ecological modeling domain.[11] In this example, the prediction task is to classify the type of vegetation that

---

10 See Guisan and Zimmermann (2000) and Franklin (2009) for an introduction to uses of predictive analytics in ecological modeling.

11 This artificially generated example dataset is inspired by the research reported in Franklin et al. (2000).

Table 4.3

The vegetation classification dataset.

ID	STREAM	SLOPE	ELEVATION	VEGETATION
1	false	steep	high	chapparal
2	true	moderate	low	riparian
3	true	steep	medium	riparian
4	false	steep	medium	chapparal
5	false	flat	high	conifer
6	true	steep	highest	conifer
7	true	steep	high	chapparal

is likely to be growing in areas of land based only on descriptive features extracted from maps of the areas. Ecological modelers can use information about the type of vegetation that grows in a region as a direct input into their animal species management and conservation programs because areas covered in different types of vegetation support different animal species. By using a predictive model that only requires features from maps, the ecological modelers can avoid expensive ground-based or aerial surveys. There are three types of vegetation that should be recognized by this model. First, *chapparal* is a type of evergreen shrubland that can be fire-prone. The animal species typically found in this vegetation include gray foxes, bobcats, skunks, and rabbits. Second, *riparian* vegetation occurs near streams and is characterized by trees and shrubs. It is usually home to small animals, including raccoons, frogs, and toads. Finally, *conifer* refers to forested areas that contain a variety of tree species (including pine, cedar, and fir trees), with a mixture of shrubs on the forest floor. The animals that may be found in these forests include bears, deer, and cougars. The type of vegetation in an area is stored in the target feature, VEGETATION.

There are three descriptive features in the dataset. STREAM is a binary feature that describes whether or not there is a stream in the area. SLOPE describes the steepness of the terrain in an area and has the levels *flat*, *moderate*, and *steep*. ELEVATION describes the elevation of an area and has the levels *low*, *medium*, *high*, and *highest*.

The first step in building the decision tree is to determine which of the three descriptive features is the best one to split the dataset on at the root node. The algorithm does this by computing the information gain for each feature. The total entropy for this dataset, which is required to calculate information gain,

Table 4.4

Partition sets (Part.), entropy, remainder (Rem.), and information gain (Info. Gain) by feature for the dataset in Table 4.3[138].

Split by Feature	Level	Part.	Instances	Partition Entropy	Rem.	Info. Gain
STREAM	*true*	$\mathcal{D}_1$	$\mathbf{d}_2, \mathbf{d}_3, \mathbf{d}_6, \mathbf{d}_7$	1.5000	1.2507	0.3060
	false	$\mathcal{D}_2$	$\mathbf{d}_1, \mathbf{d}_4, \mathbf{d}_5$	0.9183		
SLOPE	*flat*	$\mathcal{D}_3$	$\mathbf{d}_5$	0.0	0.9793	0.5774
	moderate	$\mathcal{D}_4$	$\mathbf{d}_2$	0.0		
	steep	$\mathcal{D}_5$	$\mathbf{d}_1, \mathbf{d}_3, \mathbf{d}_4, \mathbf{d}_6, \mathbf{d}_7$	1.3710		
ELEVATION	*low*	$\mathcal{D}_6$	$\mathbf{d}_2$	0.0	0.6793	0.8774
	medium	$\mathcal{D}_7$	$\mathbf{d}_3, \mathbf{d}_4$	1.0		
	high	$\mathcal{D}_8$	$\mathbf{d}_1, \mathbf{d}_5, \mathbf{d}_7$	0.9183		
	highest	$\mathcal{D}_9$	$\mathbf{d}_6$	0.0		

is computed as

$$
H(\text{VEGETATION}, \mathcal{D})
$$

$$
= - \sum_{l \in \left\{ \begin{array}{l} chapparal, \\ riparian, \\ conifer \end{array} \right\}} P(\text{VEGETATION} = l) \times log_2 \left(P(\text{VEGETATION} = l) \right)
$$

$$
= - \left(\left(\frac{3}{7} \times log_2 \left(\frac{3}{7} \right) \right) + \left(\frac{2}{7} \times log_2 \left(\frac{2}{7} \right) \right) + \left(\frac{2}{7} \times log_2 \left(\frac{2}{7} \right) \right) \right)
$$

$$
= 1.5567 \ bits
$$

(4.5)

Table 4.4[139] shows the calculation of the information gain for each feature using this result.

We can see from Table 4.4[139] that ELEVATION has the largest information gain of the three features and so is selected by the algorithm at the root node of the tree. Figure 4.8[140] illustrates the state of the tree after the dataset is split using ELEVATION. Notice that the full dataset has been split into four partitions (labeled $\mathcal{D}_6$, $\mathcal{D}_7$, $\mathcal{D}_8$, and $\mathcal{D}_9$ in Table 4.4[139]) and that the feature ELEVATION is no longer listed in these partitions as it has already been used to split the data. The $\mathcal{D}_6$ and $\mathcal{D}_9$ partitions each contain just one instance. Consequently, they are pure sets, and these partitions can be converted into leaf nodes. The $\mathcal{D}_7$ and $\mathcal{D}_8$ partitions, however, contain instances with a mixture of target feature levels, so the algorithm needs to continue splitting these partitions. To do this,

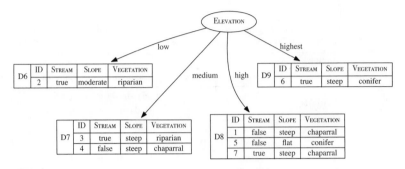

Figure 4.8

The decision tree after the data has been split using ELEVATION.

Table 4.5

Partition sets (Part.), entropy, remainder (Rem.), and information gain (Info. Gain) by feature for the dataset $\mathcal{D}_7$ in Figure 4.8[140].

Split by Feature	Level	Part.	Instances	Partition Entropy	Rem.	Info. Gain
STREAM	*true*	$\mathcal{D}_{10}$	$\mathbf{d}_3$	0.0	0.0	1.0
	false	$\mathcal{D}_{11}$	$\mathbf{d}_4$	0.0		
SLOPE	*flat*	$\mathcal{D}_{12}$		0.0	1.0	0.0
	moderate	$\mathcal{D}_{13}$		0.0		
	steep	$\mathcal{D}_{14}$	$\mathbf{d}_3, \mathbf{d}_4$	1.0		

the algorithm needs to decide which of the remaining descriptive features has the highest information gain for each partition.

To address partition $\mathcal{D}_7$, first the algorithm computes the entropy of $\mathcal{D}_7$ as

$$H\left(\text{VEGETATION}, \mathcal{D}_7\right)$$

$$= -\sum_{l \in \left\{\begin{array}{l} \textit{chapparal,} \\ \textit{riparian,} \\ \textit{conifer} \end{array}\right\}} P(\text{VEGETATION} = l) \times log_2\left(P(\text{VEGETATION} = l)\right)$$

$$= -\left(\left(^1/_2 \times log_2(^1/_2)\right) + \left(^1/_2 \times log_2(^1/_2)\right) + \left(^0/_2 \times log_2(^0/_2)\right)\right)$$

$$= 1.0 \ bits$$

(4.6)

The information gained by splitting $\mathcal{D}_7$ for using STREAM and SLOPE is then computed as detailed in Table 4.5[140].

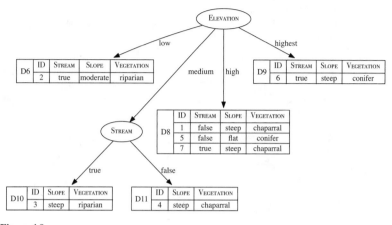

Figure 4.9

The state of the decision tree after the $\mathcal{D}_7$ partition has been split using STREAM.

The calculations in Table 4.5[140] show that STREAM has a higher information gain than SLOPE and so is the best feature with which to split $\mathcal{D}_7$. Figure 4.9[141] depicts the state of the decision tree after the $\mathcal{D}_7$ partition has been split. Splitting $\mathcal{D}_7$ creates two new partitions ($\mathcal{D}_{10}$ and $\mathcal{D}_{11}$). Notice that SLOPE is the only descriptive feature that is listed in $\mathcal{D}_{10}$ and $\mathcal{D}_{11}$. This reflects the fact that ELEVATION and STREAM have already been used on the path from the root node to each of these partitions and so cannot be used again. Both of these new partitions are pure sets with respect to the target feature (indeed, they only contain one instance each), and consequently, these sets do not need to be split any further and can be converted into leaf nodes.

At this point $\mathcal{D}_8$ is the only partition that is not a pure set. There are two descriptive features that can be used to split $\mathcal{D}_8$: STREAM and SLOPE. The decision regarding which of these features to split on is made by calculating which feature has the highest information gain for $\mathcal{D}_8$. The overall entropy for

Table 4.6

Partition sets (Part.), entropy, remainder (Rem.), and information gain (Info. Gain) by feature for the dataset $\mathcal{D}_8$ in Figure 4.9[141].

Split by Feature	Level	Part.	Instances	Partition Entropy	Rem.	Info. Gain
STREAM	*true*	$\mathcal{D}_{15}$	$\mathbf{d}_7$	0.0	0.6666	0.2517
	false	$\mathcal{D}_{16}$	$\mathbf{d}_1, \mathbf{d}_5$	1.0		
SLOPE	*flat*	$\mathcal{D}_{17}$	$\mathbf{d}_5$	0.0	0.0	0.9183
	moderate	$\mathcal{D}_{18}$		0.0		
	steep	$\mathcal{D}_{19}$	$\mathbf{d}_1, \mathbf{d}_7$	0.0		

$\mathcal{D}_8$ is calculated as

$$
H(\text{VEGETATION}, \mathcal{D}_8)
$$
$$
= - \sum_{l \in \left\{ \begin{matrix} chapparal, \\ riparian, \\ conifer \end{matrix} \right\}} P(\text{VEGETATION} = l) \times log_2\left(P(\text{VEGETATION} = l)\right)
$$
$$
= - \left(\left({}^2/_3 \times log_2({}^2/_3) \right) + \left({}^0/_3 \times log_2({}^0/_3) \right) + \left({}^1/_3 \times log_2({}^1/_3) \right) \right)
$$
$$
= 0.9183 \; bits
$$

$$(4.7)$$

Table 4.6[142] details the calculation of the information gain for each descriptive feature in $\mathcal{D}_8$ using this result. It is clear from Table 4.6[142] that in the context of $\mathcal{D}_8$, SLOPE has a higher information gain than STREAM.

Figure 4.10[143] illustrates the state of the decision tree after $\mathcal{D}_8$ has been split. Notice that one of the partitions created by splitting $\mathcal{D}_8$ based on SLOPE is empty: $\mathcal{D}_{18}$. This is because there were no instances in $\mathcal{D}_8$ that had a value of *moderate* for the SLOPE feature. This empty partition will result in a leaf node that returns a prediction of the majority target level in $\mathcal{D}_8$, *chapparal*. The other two partitions created by splitting $\mathcal{D}_8$ are pure with respect to the target feature: $\mathcal{D}_{17}$ contains one instance with a *conifer* target level, and $\mathcal{D}_{19}$ contains two instances, both of which have a *chapparal* target level.

At this point all the remaining partitions are pure with respect to the target feature. Consequently, the algorithm now converts each partition into a leaf node and returns the final decision tree. Figure 4.11[143] shows this decision tree. If the prediction strategy encoded in this tree is applied to the original dataset in Table 4.3[138], it will correctly classify all the instances in the dataset.

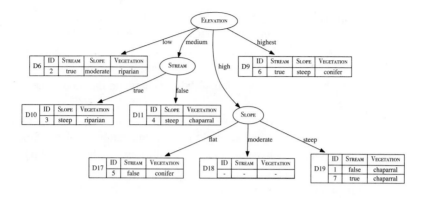

Figure 4.10

The state of the decision tree after the $\mathcal{D}_8$ partition has been split using SLOPE.

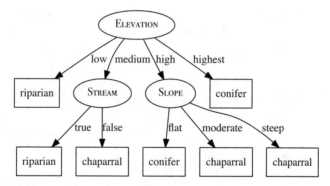

Figure 4.11

The final vegetation classification decision tree.

In machine learning terms, the induced model is **consistent** with the training data.

One final point: remember that the empty partition in Figure 4.10[143] ($\mathcal{D}_{18}$) has been converted into a leaf node that returns the *chapparal* target level. This is because *chapparal* is the majority target level in the partition at the parent node ($\mathcal{D}_8$) of this leaf node. Consequently, this tree will return a prediction of VEGETATION = *chapparal* for the following query:

$$\text{STREAM} = \textit{true}, \text{SLOPE} = \textit{moderate}, \text{ELEVATION} = \textit{high}$$

This is interesting because there are no instances listed in Table 4.3[138] where SLOPE = *moderate* and VEGETATION = *chapparal*. This example illustrates one way in which the predictions made by the model generalize beyond the dataset. Whether the generalizations made by the model are correct will depend on whether the assumptions used in generating the model (i.e., the **inductive bias**) are appropriate.

The ID3 algorithm works in exactly the same way for larger, more complicated datasets; there is simply more computation involved. Since it was first proposed, there have been many modifications to the original ID3 algorithm to handle variations that are common in real-world datasets. We explore the most important of these modifications in the following sections.

4.4   Extensions and Variations

The ID3 decision tree induction algorithm described in the previous section provides the basic approach to decision tree induction: a top-down, recursive, depth-first partitioning of the dataset beginning at the root node and finishing at the leaf nodes. Although this algorithm works quite well as presented, it assumes categorical features and clean data. It is relatively easy, however, to extend the ID3 algorithm to handle continuous descriptive features and continuous target features. A range of techniques can also be used to make a decision tree more robust to noise in the data. In this section we describe the techniques used to address these issues as well as the use of ensemble methods that allow us to combine the predictions made by multiple models. We begin, however, by introducing some of the metrics, other than entropy-based information gain, that can be used to select which feature to split on next as we build the tree.

4.4.1   Alternative Feature Selection and Impurity Metrics

The information gain measure described in Section 4.2.3[128] uses entropy to judge the impurity of the partitions that result from splitting a dataset using a particular feature. Entropy-based information gain, however, does have some drawbacks. In particular, it preferences features with many levels because these features will split the data into many small subsets, which will tend to be pure, irrespective of any correlation between the descriptive feature and the target feature. One way of addressing this issue is to use **information gain ratio** instead of entropy. The information gain ratio is computed by dividing the

information gain of a feature by the amount of information used to determine
the value of the feature

$$GR\,(d,\mathcal{D}) = \frac{IG\,(d,\mathcal{D})}{-\sum\limits_{l \in levels(d)} (P(d = l) \times log_2(P(d = l)))} \qquad (4.8)$$

where $IG\,(d,\mathcal{D})$ is the information gain of the feature d for the dataset $\mathcal{D}$ (computed using Equation (4.4)[131] from Section 4.2.3[128]), and the divisor is the
entropy of the dataset $\mathcal{D}$ with respect to the feature d (note that *levels*(d) is
the set of levels that the feature d can take). This divisor biases information
gain ratio away from features that take on a large number of values and as such
counteracts the bias in information gain toward these features.

To illustrate how information gain ratio is computed, we will compute the
information gain ratio for the descriptive features STREAM, SLOPE, and ELE-
VATION in the vegetation classification dataset in Table 4.3[138]. We already
know the information gain for these features (see Table 4.4[139]):

$$IG\,(\text{STREAM}, \mathcal{D}) = 0.3060$$
$$IG\,(\text{SLOPE}, \mathcal{D}) = 0.5774$$
$$IG\,(\text{ELEVATION}, \mathcal{D}) = 0.8774$$

To convert these information gain scores into information gain ratios, we need
to compute the entropy of each feature and then divide the information gain
scores by the respective entropy values. The entropy calculations for these
descriptive features are

$$H\,(\text{STREAM}, \mathcal{D})$$
$$= - \sum_{l \in \{ \substack{true, \\ false} \}} P(\text{STREAM} = l) \times log_2\,(P(\text{STREAM} = l))$$
$$= - \left(\left({}^4/_7 \times log_2\left({}^4/_7 \right) \right) + \left({}^3/_7 \times log_2\left({}^3/_7 \right) \right) \right)$$
$$= 0.9852 \; bits$$

$$H\,(\text{SLOPE}, \mathcal{D})$$

$$= - \sum_{l \in \left\{ \substack{\textit{flat,} \\ \textit{moderate,} \\ \textit{steep}} \right\}} P(\text{SLOPE} = l) \times log_2\left(P(\text{SLOPE} = l)\right)$$

$$= - \left(\left({}^1\!/_7 \times log_2\left({}^1\!/_7 \right) \right) + \left({}^1\!/_7 \times log_2\left({}^1\!/_7 \right) \right) \right.$$
$$\left. + \left({}^5\!/_7 \times log_2\left({}^5\!/_7 \right) \right) \right)$$

$$= 1.1488 \textit{ bits}$$

$$H\,(\text{ELEVATION}, \mathcal{D})$$

$$= - \sum_{l \in \left\{ \substack{\textit{low,} \\ \textit{medium,} \\ \textit{high,} \\ \textit{highest}} \right\}} P(\text{ELEVATION} = l) \times log_2\left(P(\text{ELEVATION} = l)\right)$$

$$= - \left(\left({}^1\!/_7 \times log_2\left({}^1\!/_7 \right) \right) + \left({}^2\!/_7 \times log_2\left({}^2\!/_7 \right) \right) \right.$$
$$\left. + \left({}^3\!/_7 \times log_2\left({}^3\!/_7 \right) \right) + \left({}^1\!/_7 \times log_2\left({}^1\!/_7 \right) \right) \right)$$

$$= 1.8424 \textit{ bits}$$

Using these results, we can now compute the information gain ratio for each descriptive feature by dividing the feature's information gain by the entropy for that feature:

$$GR\,(\text{STREAM}, \mathcal{D}) = \frac{0.3060}{0.9852} = 0.3106$$

$$GR\,(\text{SLOPE}, \mathcal{D}) = \frac{0.5774}{1.1488} = 0.5026$$

$$GR\,(\text{ELEVATION}, \mathcal{D}) = \frac{0.8774}{1.8424} = 0.4762$$

From these calculations we can see that SLOPE has the highest information gain ratio score, even though ELEVATION has the highest information gain. The implication of this is that if we build a decision tree for the dataset in Table 4.3[138] using information gain ratio, then SLOPE (rather than ELEVATION) would be the feature chosen for the root of the tree. Figure 4.12[147] illustrates the tree that would be generated for this dataset using information gain ratio.

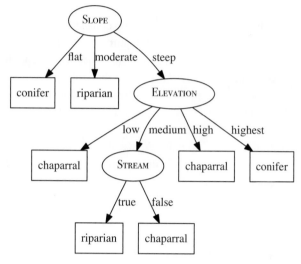

Figure 4.12

The vegetation classification decision tree generated using information gain ratio.

Notice that there is a *chapparal* leaf node at the end of the branch ELEVA-TION = *low* even though there are no instances in the dataset where ELEVA-TION = *low* and VEGETATION = *chapparal*. This leaf node is the result of an empty partition being generated when the partition at the ELEVATION node was split. This leaf node was assigned the target level *chapparal* because this was the majority target level in the partition at the ELEVATION node.

If we compare this decision tree to the decision tree generated using infor-mation gain (see Figure 4.11[143]), it is obvious that the structure of the two trees is very different. This difference illustrates the effect of the metric used to select which feature to split on during tree construction. Another interesting point of comparison between these two trees is that even though they are both consistent with the dataset in Table 4.3[138], they do not always return the same prediction. For example, given the following query:

STREAM = *false*, SLOPE = *moderate*, ELEVATION = *highest*

the tree generated using information gain ratio (Figure 4.12[147]) will return VEGETATION = *riparian*, whereas the tree generated using information gain (Figure 4.11[143]) will return VEGETATION = *conifer*. The combination of fea-tures listed in this query does not occur in the dataset. Consequently, both of the trees are attempting to generalize beyond the dataset. This illustrates how two different models that are both consistent with a dataset can make different generalizations.[12] So, which feature selection metric should be used, information gain or information gain ratio? Information gain has the advantage that it is computationally less expensive than information gain ratio. If there is variation across the number of values in the domain of the descriptive features in a dataset, however, information gain ratio may be a better option. These factors aside, the effectiveness of descriptive feature selection metrics can vary from domain to domain. So we should experiment with different metrics to find which one results in the best models for each dataset.

Another commonly used measure of impurity is the **Gini index**:

$$Gini\,(t, \mathcal{D}) = 1 - \sum_{l \in levels(t)} P(t = l)^2 \qquad (4.9)$$

where $\mathcal{D}$ is a dataset with a target feature t; $levels(t)$ is the set of levels in the domain of the target feature; and $P(t = l)$ is the probability of an instance of $\mathcal{D}$ having the target level l. The Gini index can be understood as calculating how often the target levels of instances in a dataset would be misclassified if predictions were made based only on the distribution of the target levels in the dataset. For example, if there were two target levels with equal likelihood in a dataset, then the expected rate of misclassification would be 0.5, and if there were four target levels with equal likelihood, then the expected rate of misclassification would be 0.75. The Gini index is 0 when all the instances in the dataset have the same target level and $1 - \frac{1}{k}$ when there are k possible target levels with equal likelihood. Indeed, a nice feature of the Gini index is that Gini index scores are always between 0 and 1, and in some contexts this may make it easier to compare Gini indexes across features. We can calculate

---

12 This is an example of how machine learning is an **ill-posed problem**, as discussed in Section 1.3[5].

Table 4.7

Partition sets (Part.), entropy, Gini index, remainder (Rem.), and information gain (Info. Gain) by feature for the dataset in Table 4.3[138].

Split by Feature	Level	Part.	Instances	Partition Gini Index	Rem.	Info. Gain
STREAM	*true*	$\mathcal{D}_1$	d_2, d_3, d_6, d_7	0.6250	0.5476	0.1054
	false	$\mathcal{D}_2$	d_1, d_4, d_5	0.4444		
SLOPE	*flat*	$\mathcal{D}_3$	d_5	0.0	0.4000	0.2531
	moderate	$\mathcal{D}_4$	d_2	0.0		
	steep	$\mathcal{D}_5$	d_1, d_3, d_4, d_6, d_7	0.5600		
ELEVATION	*low*	$\mathcal{D}_6$	d_2	0.0	0.3333	0.3198
	medium	$\mathcal{D}_7$	d_3, d_4	0.5000		
	high	$\mathcal{D}_8$	d_1, d_5, d_7	0.4444		
	highest	$\mathcal{D}_9$	d_6	0.0		

the Gini index for the dataset in Table 4.3[138] as

$$Gini\left(\text{VEGETATION}, \mathcal{D}\right)$$

$$= 1 - \sum_{l \in \left\{\begin{array}{l} chapparal, \\ riparian, \\ conifer \end{array}\right\}} P(\text{VEGETATION} = l)^2$$

$$= 1 - \left(\left(^3/_7\right)^2 + \left(^2/_7\right)^2 + \left(^2/_7\right)^2\right)$$

$$= 0.6531$$

The information gain for a feature based on the Gini index can be calculated in the same way as it is using entropy: calculate the Gini index for the full dataset and then subtract the sum of the weighted Gini index scores for the partitions created by splitting with the feature. Table 4.7[149] shows the calculation of the information gain using the Gini index for the descriptive features in the vegetation classification dataset. Comparing these results to the information gain calculated using entropy (see Table 4.4[139]), we can see that although the resulting numbers are different, the relative ranking of the features is the same—in both cases ELEVATION has the highest information gain. Indeed, for the vegetation dataset, the decision tree that will be generated using information gain based on the Gini index will be identical to the one generated using information gain based on entropy (see Figure 4.11[143]).

So, which impurity measure should be used, Gini or entropy? The best advice that we can give is that it is good practice when building decision tree models to try out different impurity metrics and compare the results to see which suits a dataset best.

4.4.2 Handling Continuous Descriptive Features

The easiest way to handle a continuous descriptive feature in a decision tree is to define a threshold within the range of values that the continuous feature can take and use this threshold to partition the instances based on whether their values for the feature are above or below the threshold.[13] The only challenge is to determine the best threshold to use. Ideally, we should use the threshold that results in the highest information gain when the feature is used to split the dataset. The problem, however, is that with a continuous feature, there is an infinite number of thresholds to choose from.

There is, though, a simple way to find the optimal threshold, which avoids testing an infinite number of possible thresholds. First, the instances in the dataset are sorted according to the values of the continuous feature. The adjacent instances in the ordering that have different target feature levels are then selected as possible threshold points. It can be shown that the optimal threshold value must lie at one of the boundaries between adjacent instances with different target levels. The optimal threshold is found by computing the information gain for each of the target level transition boundaries and selecting the boundary with the highest information gain as the threshold. Once a threshold has been set, the continuous feature can compete with the other categorical features for selection as the splitting feature at any node. To illustrate how this is done, we will use a modified version of the vegetation classification dataset from Table 4.3[138] in which the ELEVATION feature now contains actual elevations in feet. This dataset is listed in Table 4.8[151].

To select the best feature to use at the root of the tree, we need to calculate the information gain for each feature. We know from our earlier calculations that the entropy for this dataset is 1.5567 bits (see Equation (4.5)[139]) and that the information gain for the categorical features are $IG\,(\text{STREAM}, \mathcal{D}) = 0.3060$ and $IG\,(\text{SLOPE}, \mathcal{D}) = 0.5774$ (see Table 4.4[139]). This leaves us with the tasks of calculating the best threshold on which to split the ELEVATION feature, and

---

13 This approach is related to **binning** as described in Section 3.6.2[94]. Simply binning continuous features to convert them into categorical features is another valid approach to handling continuous features in decision trees.

Table 4.8

Dataset for predicting the vegetation in an area with a continuous ELEVATION feature (measured in feet).

ID	STREAM	SLOPE	ELEVATION	VEGETATION
1	false	steep	3,900	chapparal
2	true	moderate	300	riparian
3	true	steep	1,500	riparian
4	false	steep	1,200	chapparal
5	false	flat	4,450	conifer
6	true	steep	5,000	conifer
7	true	steep	3,000	chapparal

Table 4.9

Dataset for predicting the vegetation in an area sorted by the continuous ELEVATION feature.

ID	STREAM	SLOPE	ELEVATION	VEGETATION
2	true	moderate	300	riparian
4	false	steep	1,200	chapparal
3	true	steep	1,500	riparian
7	true	steep	3,000	chapparal
1	false	steep	3,900	chapparal
5	false	flat	4,450	conifer
6	true	steep	5,000	conifer

calculating the information gain when we partition the dataset with ELEVA-TION using this optimal threshold. Our first task, is to sort the dataset based on the ELEVATION feature. This is shown in Table 4.9[151].

Once the instances have been sorted, we look for adjacent pairs that have different target levels. In Table 4.9[151] we can see that four pairs of adjacent instances have a transition between the target levels, instances d_2 and d_4, d_4 and d_3, d_3 and d_7, and d_1 and d_5. The boundary value between each of these pairs is simply the average of their ELEVATION values:

- the boundary between d_2 and d_4 is $\frac{300 + 1,200}{2} = 750$

- the boundary between d_4 and d_3 is $\frac{1,200 + 1,500}{2} = 1,350$

- the boundary between d_3 and d_7 is $\frac{1,500 + 3,000}{2} = 2,250$

- the boundary between d_1 and d_5 is $\frac{3,900 + 4,450}{2} = 4,175$

Table 4.10

Partition sets (Part.), entropy, remainder (Rem.), and information gain (Info. Gain) for the candidate ELEVATION thresholds: $\geqslant 750$, $\geqslant 1{,}350$, $\geqslant 2{,}250$ and $\geqslant 4{,}175$.

Split by Threshold	Part.	Instances	Partition Entropy	Rem.	Info. Gain
$\geqslant 750$	$\mathcal{D}_1$	$\mathbf{d}_2$	0.0	1.2507	0.3060
	$\mathcal{D}_2$	$\mathbf{d}_4, \mathbf{d}_3, \mathbf{d}_7, \mathbf{d}_1, \mathbf{d}_5, \mathbf{d}_6$	1.4591		
$\geqslant 1{,}350$	$\mathcal{D}_3$	$\mathbf{d}_2, \mathbf{d}_4$	1.0	1.3728	0.1839
	$\mathcal{D}_4$	$\mathbf{d}_3, \mathbf{d}_7, \mathbf{d}_1, \mathbf{d}_5, \mathbf{d}_6$	1.5219		
$\geqslant 2{,}250$	$\mathcal{D}_5$	$\mathbf{d}_2, \mathbf{d}_4, \mathbf{d}_3$	0.9183	0.9650	0.5917
	$\mathcal{D}_6$	$\mathbf{d}_7, \mathbf{d}_1, \mathbf{d}_5, \mathbf{d}_6$	1.0		
$\geqslant 4{,}175$	$\mathcal{D}_7$	$\mathbf{d}_2, \mathbf{d}_4, \mathbf{d}_3, \mathbf{d}_7, \mathbf{d}_1$	0.9710	0.6935	0.8631
	$\mathcal{D}_8$	$\mathbf{d}_5, \mathbf{d}_6$	0.0		

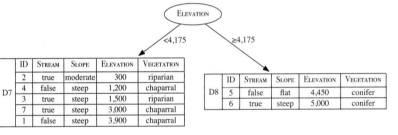

Figure 4.13

The vegetation classification decision tree after the dataset has been split using ELEVATION $\geqslant$ 4,175.

This results in four candidate thresholds: $\geqslant 750$, $\geqslant 1{,}350$, $\geqslant 2{,}250$, and $\geqslant 4{,}175$. Table 4.10[152] shows the computation of information gain for a split using each of these thresholds. The threshold $\geqslant 4{,}175$ has the highest information gain of any of the candidate thresholds (0.8631 bits), and this information gain is also higher than the information gain for either of the other two descriptive features. So, we should use ELEVATION $\geqslant 4{,}175$ as the test at the root node of the tree, as shown in Figure 4.13[152].

Unlike categorical features, continuous features can be used at multiple points along a path in a decision tree, although the threshold applied to the feature at each of these tests will be different. This is important as it allows multiple splits within a range of a continuous feature to be considered on a path. Consequently, as we build the rest of the tree, we may reuse the ELEVATION

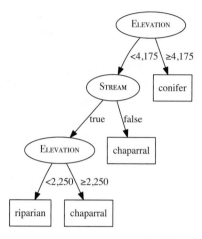

Figure 4.14

The decision tree that would be generated for the vegetation classification dataset listed in Table 4.9[151] using information gain.

feature. This is why that ELEVATION feature is listed in both the partitions ($\mathcal{D}_7$ and $\mathcal{D}_8$) in Figure 4.13[152]. We can continue to build the tree by recursively extending each branch as we did in the previous decision tree examples. Figure 4.14[153] shows the decision tree that is ultimately generated from this process. Notice that the tree uses a mixture of continuous and categorical features and that the ELEVATION feature is used twice with different thresholds in each case.

4.4.3 Predicting Continuous Targets

When we use a decision tree to make predictions for a continuous target, we refer to the tree as a **regression tree**.[14] Typically the value output by the leaf node of a regression tree is the mean of the target feature values of the instances from the training set that reached that node. This means that the error of a regression tree when making a prediction for a query instance is the difference between the mean of the training instances that reached the leaf node that returns the prediction and the correct value that should have been returned for that query. Assuming that the set of training instances reaching a leaf node are

---

14 Sometimes the task of predicting a continuous target is referred to as a **regression task**.

indicative of the queries that will be labeled by the node, it makes sense to construct regression trees in a manner that reduces the **variance** in the target feature values of the set of training instances at each leaf node in the tree. We can do this by adapting the ID3 algorithm to use a measure of variance[15] rather than a measure of entropy when selecting the best feature. Using variance as our measure of impurity, the impurity at a node can be calculated as

$$var\,(t,\mathcal{D}) = \frac{\sum_{i=1}^{n}(t_i - \bar{t})^2}{n-1} \tag{4.10}$$

where $\mathcal{D}$ is the dataset that has reached the node, n is the number of instances in $\mathcal{D}$, $\bar{t}$ is the mean of the target feature for the dataset $\mathcal{D}$, and t_i iterates across the target value of each instance in $\mathcal{D}$. Using variance as our measure of impurity, we can select which feature to split on at a node by selecting the feature that minimizes the weighted variance across the resulting partitions. The **weighted variance** is computed by summing the variance of the target feature within each partition created by splitting a dataset on a descriptive feature multiplied by the fraction of the dataset in each partition. So, at each node the algorithm will choose the feature to split on by selecting the feature with the lowest weighted variance for the target feature:

$$\mathbf{d}\,[best] = \underset{d\in\mathbf{d}}{\arg\min} \sum_{l\in levels(d)} \frac{|\mathcal{D}_{d=l}|}{|\mathcal{D}|} \times var(t, \mathcal{D}_{d=l}) \tag{4.11}$$

where $var\,(t, \mathcal{D}_{d=l})$ is the variance of the target feature in the partition of the dataset $\mathcal{D}$ containing the instances where $d = l$, $|\mathcal{D}_{d=l}|$ is the size of this partition and $|\mathcal{D}|$ is the size of the dataset. This means that at each decision node, the algorithm will select the feature that partitions the dataset to most reduce the weighted variance of the partitions. This causes the algorithm to cluster instances with similar target feature values. As a result, leaf nodes with small variance in the target feature values across the set of instances at the node are preferred over leaf nodes where the variance in the target feature values across the set of instances at the node is large. To change the ID3 algorithm in Algorithm 4.1[135] to select features to split on based on variance, we replace Line 8 with Equation 4.11[154].

---

15 We introduce **variance** in Section A.1.2[527], and although we extend the formal definition of variance here to include a dataset parameter $\mathcal{D}$—we do this to explicitly highlight the fact that we are calculating the variance of a feature within a particular dataset, usually the dataset at a node in the tree—the measure of variance we are using is identical to the variance defined in Equation (3)[528].

The other change we need to make to Algorithm 4.1[135] to handle continuous targets relates to the base cases that cause the algorithm to stop processing data partitions and to create a leaf node. In the ID3 algorithm we created a leaf node when there were no instances left in the partition being processed (Line 5), when there were no features left on which to split the data (Line 3), or when we had created a pure partition of the dataset with respect to the target feature levels (Line 1). An algorithm to learn decision trees for a continuous target can use the first two base cases. When these cases occur, the algorithm will create a leaf node that returns the mean value of the target feature in a data partition, rather than the majority level. For continuous targets there is no such thing as a pure split, so we will need to change the final base case.

Figure 4.15[156] illustrates the type of partitioning we are trying to achieve when we use a variance measure to select the features to split on in a decision tree. Figure 4.15(a)[156] depicts a set of instances on the continuous number line. Figure 4.15(b)[156] depicts one of the extremes for grouping these instances, where we treat them all as belonging to one partition. The large gap between the two apparent clusters in this dataset results in a large variance, which indicates that we are probably underfitting with this grouping. In Figure 4.15(c)[156] the instances have been gathered into two groups that have a relatively low variance compared to the single group in Figure 4.15(b)[156]. Intuitively we can see that this grouping is, as Goldilocks put it, *just right* and is the type of grouping we are trying to generate when we use a variance measure to select the splitting point.

Figure 4.15(d)[156] depicts one of the problems that can arise when a variance measure is used to split a continuous target feature. In this example each instance has been put into an individual partition, and although these partitions each have a variance of zero, this is indicative of overfitting the data. This extreme partitioning of the dataset into sets of single instances can happen if there are a lot of descriptive features in the dataset, or if there are one or more continuous descriptive features that the algorithm is allowed to split on repeatedly. The reason that partitioning the dataset into single instances is indicative of overfitting is that if there is any noise in the training data (something that is likely in real applications), then the leaf nodes generated due to noisy instances will result in unreliable predictions for queries. To avoid this kind of extreme partitioning, we introduce an **early stopping criterion** into the algorithm for building regression trees. The simplest early stopping criterion is to stop partitioning the dataset if the number of training instances in the partition at the node we are processing is less than some threshold, usually around 5% of the

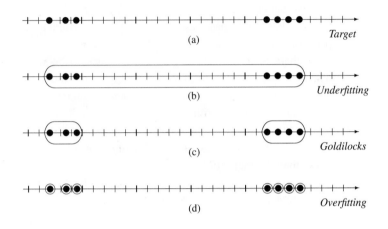

Figure 4.15

(a) A set of instances on a continuous number line; (b), (c), and (d) depict some of the potential groupings that could be applied to these instances.

Table 4.11

A dataset listing the number of bike rentals per day.

ID	SEASON	WORK DAY	RENTALS	ID	SEASON	WORK DAY	RENTALS
1	winter	false	800	7	summer	false	3,000
2	winter	false	826	8	summer	true	5,800
3	winter	true	900	9	summer	true	6,200
4	spring	false	2,100	10	autumn	false	2,910
5	spring	true	4,740	11	autumn	false	2,880
6	spring	true	4,900	12	autumn	true	2,820

overall dataset size.[16] This early stopping criterion replaces the base case on Line 1 of the ID3 algorithm.

The change to the mechanism for selecting the best feature to split on (made on Line 8) and the introduction of an early stopping criterion (which replaces Line 1) are the only modifications we need to make to the ID3 algorithm (Algorithm 4.1[135]) to allow it to handle continuous target features. To see how this

---

16 It is also common to use a minimum partition variance as an early stopping criterion. If the variance in the partition being processed is below a set threshold, then the algorithm will not partition the data and will instead create a leaf node.

Table 4.12

The partitioning of the dataset in Table 4.11[156] based on SEASON and WORK DAY features and the computation of the weighted variance for each partitioning.

Split by Feature	Level	Part.	Instances	$\dfrac{|\mathcal{D}_{d=l}|}{|\mathcal{D}|}$	$var\,(t, \mathcal{D})$	Weighted Variance
SEASON	winter	$\mathcal{D}_1$	d_1, d_2, d_3	0.25	2,692	
	spring	$\mathcal{D}_2$	d_4, d_5, d_6	0.25	2,472,533	1,379,331
	summer	$\mathcal{D}_3$	d_7, d_8, d_9	0.25	3,040,000	
	autumn	$\mathcal{D}_4$	d_{10}, d_{11}, d_{12}	0.25	2,100	
WORK DAY	true	$\mathcal{D}_5$	$d_3, d_5, d_6, d_8, d_9, d_{12}$	0.50	4,026,346	2,551,813
	false	$\mathcal{D}_6$	$d_1, d_2, d_4, d_7, d_{10}, d_{11}$	0.50	1,077,280	

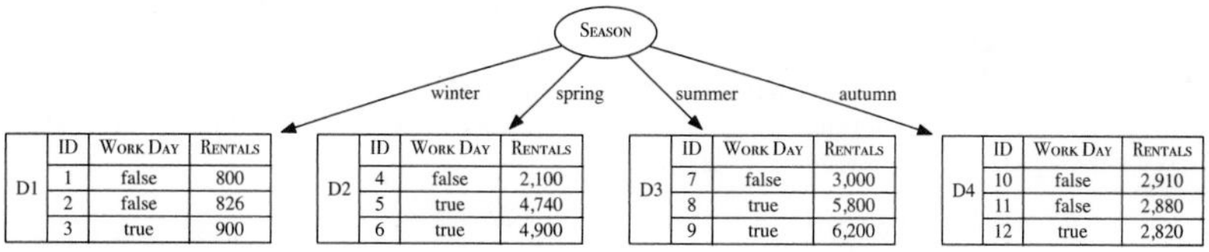

Figure 4.16

The decision tree resulting from splitting the data in Table 4.11[156] using the feature SEASON.

revised algorithm can induce a decision tree, we will use the example of predicting the number of bike rentals per day for a city bike sharing program based on the SEASON and whether it is a WORK DAY. Predicting the number of bike rentals on a given day is useful because it can give the administrators of the bike sharing program an insight into the number of resources they need to have ready each day. Table 4.11[156] lists a small dataset from this domain.[17]

Table 4.12[157] illustrates the computation of the weighted variance that results from partitioning the data by SEASON and WORK DAY. It is evident from Table 4.12[157] that partitioning the data using SEASON results in a lower weighted variance than partitioning by WORK DAY. This tells us that splitting by SEASON results in a better clustering of the target data than splitting by WORK DAY. Figure 4.16[157] illustrates the state of the decision tree after the root node has been created using SEASON.

---

17 This example is inspired by the research reported in Fanaee-T and Gama (2014). The dataset presented here is synthesized for this example; however, a real bike sharing dataset for this task is available through the UCI Machine Learning Repository (Bache and Lichman, 2013) at `archive.ics.uci.edu/ml/datasets/Bike+Sharing+Dataset`.

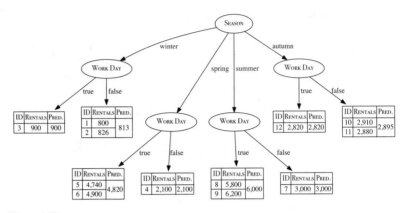

Figure 4.17
The final decision tree induced from the dataset in Table 4.11[156]. To illustrate how the tree generates predictions, this tree lists the instances that ended up at each leaf node and the prediction (PRED.) made by each leaf node.

Figure 4.17[158] illustrates the final decision tree that will be generated for this dataset. This tree will predict the mean target feature value of the leaf node indicated by the descriptive features of a query instance. For example, given a query instance with SEASON = *summer* and WORK DAY = *true*, this decision tree will predict that there will be 6,000 bike rentals on that day.

4.4.4   Tree Pruning

A predictive model **overfits** the training set when at least some of the predictions it returns are based on spurious patterns present in the training data used to induce the model. Overfitting happens for a number of reasons, including **sampling variance**[18] and noise in the training set.[19] The problem of overfitting can affect any machine learning algorithm; however, the fact that decision tree induction algorithms work by recursively splitting the training data means that they have a natural tendency to segregate noisy instances and to create leaf nodes around these instances. Consequently, decision trees overfit by splitting the data on irrelevant features that only appear relevant due to noise or

---

18 This means that the distribution over the target feature will be different between a training set sample and the full population.

19 For example, there might be errors in the target feature or descriptive feature values of one or more of the training instances.

sampling variance in the training data. The likelihood of overfitting occurring increases as a tree gets deeper because the resulting predictions are based on smaller and smaller subsets as the dataset is partitioned after each feature test in the path.

Tree pruning identifies and removes subtrees within a decision tree that are likely to be due to noise and sample variance in the training set used to induce it. In cases where a subtree is deemed to be overfitting, pruning the subtree means replacing the subtree with a leaf node that makes a prediction based on the majority target feature level (or average target feature value) of the dataset created by merging the instances from all the leaf nodes in the subtree. Obviously, pruning will result in decision trees being created that are not consistent with the training set used to build them. In general, however, we are more interested in creating prediction models that generalize well to new data rather than that are strictly consistent with training data, so it is common to sacrifice consistency for generalization capacity.

The simplest way to prune a decision tree is to introduce **early stopping criteria** (similar to the one discussed in the previous section) into the tree induction algorithm. This is often known as **pre-pruning**. There are a range of simple pre-pruning strategies. For example, we can stop creating subtrees when the number of instances in a partition falls below a threshold, when the information gain (or whatever other feature selection metric is being used) measured at a node is not deemed to be sufficient to make partitioning the data worthwhile,[20] or when the depth of the tree goes beyond a predefined limit. More advanced approaches to pre-pruning use statistical significance tests to determine the importance of subtrees, for example, χ^2 **pruning** (pronounced *chi-squared*).[21]

Pre-pruning approaches are computationally efficient and can work well for small datasets. By stopping the partitioning of the data early, however, induction algorithms that use pre-pruning can fail to create the most effective trees because they miss interactions between features that emerge within subtrees that are not obvious when the parent nodes are being considered. Pre-pruning can mean that these useful subtrees are never created.

Post-pruning is an alternative approach to tree pruning in which the tree induction algorithm is allowed to grow a tree to completion, and then each

---

20 **Critical value pruning** (Mingers, 1987) is a well known version of this pruning technique.

21 See Frank (2000) for a detailed discussion and analysis on the use of statistical tests in decision tree pruning.

branch on the tree is examined in turn. Branches that are deemed likely to be due to overfitting are pruned. Post-pruning relies on a criteria that can distinguish between subtrees that model relevant aspects of the data and subtrees that model irrelevant random patterns in the data. There are a range of different criterion that can be used from a very simple threshold on the number of instances at a node in the tree, to statistical significance texts like χ^2. We recommend the use of criteria that compare the **error rate** in the predictions made by a decision tree when a given subtree is included and when it is pruned. To measure error rate, we set aside some of the training data as a **validation dataset**[22] that is not used during tree induction. We can measure the performance of a decision tree by presenting the instances in the validation to the decision tree and comparing the predictions made for these instances with the actual target feature values in the dataset. The error rate measures the number of predictions made by the tree that are incorrect. A subtree is pruned if the error rate on the validation set of the decision tree with the subtree removed is no greater than the error rate of the decision tree when the subtree is included. Because the instances in the validation set are not used during training, the error rate on the validation set provides a good estimate of the generalization capability of a decision tree.

Reduced error pruning (Quinlan, 1987) is a popular version of post-pruning based on error rates. In reduced error pruning, a decision tree is built to completion and then the tree is searched in an iterative, bottom-up, left-to-right manner for subtrees that can be pruned. The error rate resulting from predictions for the instances in the validation dataset made at the root node of each subtree is compared to the error rate resulting from predictions made at the leaves of the subtree. If the error rate at the subtree root node is less than or equal to the combined error rate at the leaves, the subtree is pruned.

To show how reduced error pruning works, we will consider the task of predicting whether a post-operative patient should be sent to an intensive care unit (ICU) or to a general ward for recovery.[23] Hypothermia is a major concern for post-operative patients, so many of the descriptive features relevant to this domain relate to a patient's body temperature. In our example CORE-TEMP

---

22 In the context of decision tree pruning, the validation set is often referred to as the **pruning dataset**.

23 The example of predicting where post-operative patients should be sent is inspired by the research reported in Woolery et al. (1991). A real dataset related to this research is available through the UCI Machine Learning Repository (Bache and Lichman, 2013) at `archive.ics.uci.edu/ml/datasets/Post-Operative+Patient/`.

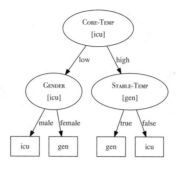

Figure 4.18

The decision tree for the post-operative patient routing task.

Table 4.13

An example validation set for the post-operative patient routing task.

ID	CORE-TEMP	STABLE-TEMP	GENDER	DECISION
1	high	true	male	gen
2	low	true	female	icu
3	high	false	female	icu
4	high	false	male	icu
5	low	false	female	icu
6	low	true	male	icu

describes the core temperature of the patient (which can be *low* or *high*) and
STABLE-TEMP describes whether the patient's current temperature is stable
(*true* or *false*). We also include the GENDER of the patient (*male* or *female*).
The target feature in this domain, DECISION, records the decision of whether
the patient is sent to the *icu* or to a general ward (*gen*) for recovery. Figure
4.18[161] illustrates a decision tree that has been trained for this post-operative
patient routing task. The target level in square brackets at each interior node in
the tree shows the majority target level for the data partition at that node.

Table 4.13[161] lists a validation dataset for this domain, and Figure 4.19[162]
illustrates how this validation dataset is used to perform reduced error pruning. In Figure 4.19(a)[162] the pruning algorithm considers the subtree under the
GENDER node for pruning. The path through the tree to make predictions for
instances d_2, d_5, and d_6 from the validation dataset leads to this subtree. The
majority target level predicted at the root node of this subtree (the GENDER
node) gives a correct prediction of *icu* for each of the three instances, so the
error rate on the validation set for the root node of the subtree is 0. In contrast,

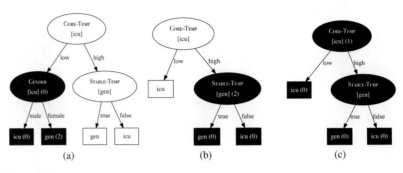

Figure 4.19
The iterations of reduced error pruning for the decision tree in Figure 4.18[161] using the validation set in Table 4.13[161]. The subtree that is being considered for pruning in each iteration is highlighted in black. The prediction returned by each non-leaf node is listed in square brackets. The error rate for each node is given in round brackets.

the predictions made at the leaf nodes of this subtree are incorrect for d_2 and d_5 (because these patients are *female*, the prediction made is *gen* which does not match the validation dataset), so the error rate for the leaf nodes of this subtree is $0 + 2 = 2$. Because the error rate for the leaf nodes is higher than the error rate for the root node of the subtree, this subtree is pruned and replaced by a leaf node. The result of this pruning is visible on the left branch of the tree in Figure 4.19(b)[162].

In the second iteration of the algorithm, the subtree under the STABLE-TEMP node is considered for pruning (highlighted in Figure 4.19(b)[162]). In this instance, the error rate for the root node of this subtree (the STABLE-TEMP node) is 2, whereas the error rate of the leaf nodes of the tree is $0 + 0 = 0$. As the error rate of the root node of the subtree is higher than the error rate of the leaf nodes, the tree is not pruned. Figure 4.19(c)[162] illustrates the final iteration of the algorithm. In this iteration the subtree underneath the root node of the decision tree (the CORE-TEMP node) is considered for pruning (i.e., the full decision tree). In this iteration, the error rate of the root node (1) is greater than the error rate of the three leaf nodes, $(0 + 0 + 0 = 0)$, so the tree is left unchanged.

Post-pruning using an error rate criteria is probably the most popular way to prune decision trees.[24] One of the advantages of pruning decision trees is that

---

24 See Esposito et al. (1997) and Mingers (1989) for overviews and empirical comparisons of a range of decision tree pruning methods based on error rate.

it keeps trees smaller, which in turn makes them easier to interpret. Another advantage is that pruning often increases the accuracy of the trees when there is noise in the training dataset. This is because pruning typically affects the lower parts of the decision tree, where noisy training data is most likely to cause overfitting. As such, pruning can be viewed as a **noise dampening mechanism** that removes nodes that have been created because of a small set of noisy instances.

4.4.5   Model Ensembles

Much of the focus of machine learning is on developing the single most accurate prediction model possible for a given task. The techniques we introduce in this section take a slightly different approach. Rather than creating a single model, they generate a set of models and then make predictions by aggregating the outputs of these models. A prediction model that is composed of a set of models is called a **model ensemble**.

The motivation behind using ensemble methods is the idea that a committee of experts working together on a problem are more likely to solve it successfully than a single expert working alone. As is always the case when a committee is working together, however, steps should be taken to guard against **group think**. In the context of ensemble models, this means that each model should make predictions independently of the other models in the ensemble. Given a large population of independent models, an ensemble can be very accurate even if the individual models in the ensemble perform only marginally better than random guessing.

There are two defining characteristics of ensemble models:

1. They build multiple different models from the same dataset by inducing each model using a modified version of the dataset.

2. They make a prediction by aggregating the predictions of the different models in the ensemble. For categorical target features, this can be done using different types of voting mechanisms, and for continuous target features, this can be done using a measure of the central tendency of the different model predictions, such as the mean or the median.

There are two standard approaches to creating ensembles: **boosting** and **bagging**. The remainder of this section explains each of these.

4.4.5.1   Boosting

When we use **boosting**,[25] each new model added to an ensemble is biased to pay more attention to instances that previous models misclassified. This is done by incrementally adapting the dataset used to train the models. To do this we use a **weighted dataset** where each instance has an associated weight $\mathbf{w}_i \geq 0$, initially set to $\frac{1}{n}$ where n is the number of instances in the dataset. These weights are used as a distribution over which the dataset is sampled to create a **replicated training set**, in which the number of times an instance is replicated is proportional to its weight.

Boosting works by iteratively creating models and adding them to the ensemble. The iteration stops when a predefined number of models have been added. During each iteration the algorithm does the following:

1. Induces a model using the weighted dataset and calculates the total error, ϵ, in the set of predictions made by the model for the instances in the training dataset.[26] The ϵ value is calculated by summing the weights of the training instances for which the predictions made by the model are incorrect.

2. Increases the weights for the instances misclassified by the model using

$$\mathbf{w}[i] \leftarrow \mathbf{w}[i] \times \left(\frac{1}{2 \times \epsilon} \right) \tag{4.12}$$

and decreases the weights for the instances correctly classified by the model using[27]

$$\mathbf{w}[i] \leftarrow \mathbf{w}[i] \times \left(\frac{1}{2 \times (1 - \epsilon)} \right) \tag{4.13}$$

3. Calculates a **confidence factor**, α, for the model such that α increases as ϵ decreases. A common way to calculate the confidence factor is

$$\alpha = \frac{1}{2} \times log_e \left(\frac{1 - \epsilon}{\epsilon} \right) \tag{4.14}$$

Once the set of models has been created, the ensemble makes predictions using a weighted aggregate of the predictions made by the individual models.

25 Schapire (1999) gives a readable introduction to boosting by one of the originators of the technique.

26 Normally in machine learning, we do not test a model using the same dataset that we use to train it. Boosting, however, is an exception to this rule.

27 Updating the weights using Equations (4.12)[164] and (4.13)[164] ensures that the weights always sum to 1.

The weights used in this aggregation are the confidence factors associated with each model. For categorical target features, the ensemble returns the majority target level using a weighted vote, and for continuous target features, the ensemble returns the weighted mean.

4.4.5.2 Bagging

When we use **bagging** (or **bootstrap aggregating**), each model in the ensemble is trained on a random sample[28] of the dataset where, importantly, each random sample is the same size as the dataset and **sampling with replacement** is used. These random samples are known as **bootstrap samples**, and one model is induced from each bootstrap sample. The reason that we sample with replacement is that this will result in duplicates within each of the bootstrap samples, and consequently, every bootstrap sample will be missing some of the instances from the dataset. As a result, each bootstrap sample will be different, and this means that models trained on different bootstrap samples will also be different.[29]

Decision tree induction algorithms are particularly well suited to use with bagging. This is because decision trees are very sensitive to changes in the dataset: a small change in the dataset can result in a different feature being selected to split the dataset at the root, or high up in the tree, and this can have a ripple effect throughout the subtrees under this node. Frequently, when bagging is used with decision trees, the sampling process is extended so that each bootstrap sample only uses a randomly selected subset of the descriptive features in the dataset. This sampling of the feature set is known as **subspace sampling**. Subspace sampling further encourages the diversity of the trees within the ensemble and has the advantage of reducing the training time for each tree.

Figure 4.20[166] illustrates the process of creating a model ensemble using bagging and subspace sampling. The combination of bagging, subspace sampling, and decision trees is known as a **random forest** model. Once the individual models have been induced, the ensemble makes predictions by returning the majority vote or the median depending on the type of prediction required. For continuous target features, the median is preferred to the mean because the mean is more heavily affected by outliers.

---

28 See Section 3.6.3[98].

29 If we have a very large dataset we may—for computational reasons—want to create bootstrap samples that are smaller than the original dataset. If this is the case, then **sampling without replacement** is preferred. This is called **subbagging**.

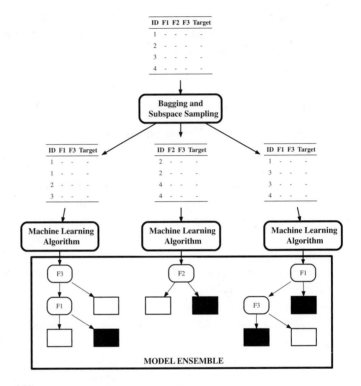

Figure 4.20
The process of creating a model ensemble using bagging and subspace sampling.

4.4.5.3   Summary

Which approach should we use? Bagging is simpler to implement and paral-
lelize than boosting, so it may be better with respect to ease of use and training
time. With respect to the general ability of bagging and boosting ensembles to
make accurate predictions, the results reported in Caruana et al. (2008) indicate
that boosted decision tree ensembles were the best performing model of those
tested for datasets containing up to 4,000 descriptive features. For datasets containing more that 4,000 features, random forest ensembles (based on bagging)
performed better. Caruana et al. (2008) suggest that a potential explanation
for this pattern of results is that boosted ensembles are prone to overfitting,

and in domains with large numbers of features, overfitting becomes a serious problem.[30]

4.5 Summary

We have introduced information theory as a method of determining the shortest sequence of descriptive feature tests required to make a prediction. We have also introduced **decision tree** models, which make predictions based on sequences of tests on the descriptive feature values of a query. Consequently, decision trees naturally lend themselves to being trained using information-based metrics. We also introduced the **ID3** algorithm as a standard algorithm for inducing decision trees from a dataset. The ID3 algorithm uses a top-down, recursive, depth-first partitioning of the dataset to build a tree model beginning at the root node and finishing at the leaf nodes. Although this algorithm works quite well as presented, it assumes categorical features with no missing values and clean data. The algorithm can, however, be extended to handle continuous descriptive features and continuous target features. We also discussed how **tree pruning** can be used to help with the problem of overfitting.

The **C4.5** algorithm is a well-known variant of the ID3 algorithm that uses these extensions to handle continuous and categorical descriptive features and missing features. It also uses post-pruning to help with overfitting. **J48** is an open source implementation of the C4.5 algorithm that is used in many data analytics toolkits. Another well-known variant of the ID3 algorithm is the **CART** algorithm. The CART algorithm uses the **Gini index** (introduced in Section 4.4.1[144]) instead of information gain to select features to add to the tree. This algorithm can also handle continuous target features. The variant of the decision tree algorithm that should be used for a particular problem depends on the nature of the problem and the dataset being used. Performing evaluation experiments using different model types is really the only way to determine which variant will work best for a specific problem.

The main advantage of decision tree models is that they are interpretable. It is relatively easy to understand the sequences of tests a decision tree carried out in order to make a prediction. This interpretability is very important in some domains. For example, if a prediction model is being used as a diagnostic tool in a medical scenario, it is not sufficient for the system to simply

---

30 Question 5, at the end of this chapter, explores model ensembles in more detail, and worked examples are provided in the solution.

return a diagnosis. In these contexts both the doctor and the patient would want the system to provide some explanation of how it arrives at the predictions it makes. Decision tree models are ideal for these scenarios.

Decision tree models can be used for datasets that contain both categorical and continuous descriptive features. A real advantage of the decision tree approach is that it has the ability to model the interactions between descriptive features. This arises from the fact that the tests carried out at each node in the tree are performed in the context of the results of the tests on the other descriptive features that were tested at the preceding nodes on the path from the root. Consequently, if there is an **interaction effect** between two or more descriptive features, a decision tree can model this. It is worth noting that this ability is diminished if **pre-pruning** is employed, as pre-pruning may stop subtrees that capture descriptive feature interactions from forming. Finally, as noted earlier, decision tree induction is, relatively, robust to noise in the dataset if **pruning** is used.

There are, however, some situations where decision tree models are not the best option. Although decision trees can handle both categorical and continuous features, they tend to become quite large when dealing with continuous descriptive features. This can result in trees becoming difficult to interpret. Consequently, if dealing with purely continuous data, other prediction models may be more appropriate, for example, the error-based models we will see in Chapter 7[323].

Decision trees also have difficulty with domains that have a large number of descriptive features, particularly if the number of instances in the training dataset is small. In these situations overfitting becomes very likely. The probability-based models we will see in Chapter 6[247] do a better job of handling high-dimensional data.

Another potential issue with decision trees is that they are eager learners. As such, they are not suitable for modeling concepts that change over time, because they will need to be retrained. In these scenarios, the similarity-based prediction models that are the topic of the next chapter, Chapter 5[179], perform better, as these models can be incrementally retrained.

We concluded this chapter by explaining **model ensembles**. We can build a model ensemble using any type of prediction model—or, indeed, a mixture of model types. We don't have to use decision trees. However, decision trees are often used in model ensembles, due to the sensitivity of tree induction to changes in the dataset, and this is why we have introduced model ensembles in this chapter. Model ensembles are amongst the most powerful machine learning algorithms: Caruana and Niculescu-Mizil (2006) report a large-scale comparison between seven different types of prediction model in which bagged and boosted tree ensembles are reported as among the best performing. The cost of this high performance, however, is increased learning and model complexity.

4.6   Further Reading

Gleick (2011) provides an excellent and accessible introduction to information theory and its history. Shannon and Weaver (1949) is taken as the foundational book in information theory, and Cover and Thomas (1991) is a well-regarded textbook on the topic. MacKay (2003) is an excellent textbook on information theory and machine learning.

Quinlan (1986) originally described the ID3 algorithm, and Quinlan (1993) and Breiman (1993) are two of the best-known books on decision trees. Loh (2011) provides a good overview of more recent developments in tree induction algorithms.

Schapire (1990) is an example of some of the early work on weak learners and computational learning theory. Freund and Schapire (1995) introduced the **AdaBoost** algorithm, which is one of the seminal boosting algorithms. Friedman et al. (2000) generalized the AdaBoost algorithm and developed another popular boosting algorithm, the **LogitBoost** algorithm. Breiman (1996) developed the use of bagging for prediction, and Breiman (2001) introduced **random forests**. Kuncheva (2004) and Zhou (2012) both provide good overviews of ensemble learning.

4.7   Exercises

1. The image below shows a set of eight Scrabble pieces.

a. What is the **entropy** in bits of the letters in this set?

b. What would be the reduction in entropy (i.e., the **information gain**) in bits if we split these letters into two sets, one containing the vowels and the other containing the consonants?

c. What is the maximum possible entropy in bits for a set of eight Scrabble pieces?

d. In general, which is preferable when you are playing Scrabble: a set of letters with high entropy or a set of letters with low entropy?

2. A convicted criminal who reoffends after release is known as a *recidivist*. The table below lists a dataset that describes prisoners released on parole, and whether they reoffended within two years of release.[31]

ID	GOOD BEHAVIOR	AGE < 30	DRUG DEPENDENT	RECIDIVIST
1	false	true	false	true
2	false	false	false	false
3	false	true	false	true
4	true	false	false	false
5	true	false	true	true
6	true	false	false	false

This dataset lists six instances where prisoners were granted parole. Each of these instances are described in terms of three binary descriptive features

31 This example of predicting recidivism is based on a real application of machine learning: parole boards do rely on machine learning prediction models to help them when they are making their decisions. See Berk and Bleich (2013) for a recent comparison of different machine learning models used for this task. Datasets dealing with prisoner recidivism are available online, for example: catalog.data.gov/dataset/prisoner-recidivism/. The dataset presented here is not based on real data.

(GOOD BEHAVIOR, AGE < 30, DRUG DEPENDENT) and a binary target feature, RECIDIVIST. The GOOD BEHAVIOR feature has a value of *true* if the prisoner had not committed any infringements during incarceration, the AGE < 30 has a value of *true* if the prisoner was under 30 years of age when granted parole, and the DRUG DEPENDENT feature is *true* if the prisoner had a drug addiction at the time of parole. The target feature, RECIDIVIST, has a *true* value if the prisoner was arrested within two years of being released; otherwise it has a value of *false*.

a. Using this dataset, construct the decision tree that would be generated by the **ID3** algorithm, using entropy-based information gain.

b. What prediction will the decision tree generated in part (a) of this question return for the following query?

$$\text{GOOD BEHAVIOR} = \textit{false}, \text{AGE} < 30 = \textit{false},$$
$$\text{DRUG DEPENDENT} = \textit{true}$$

c. What prediction will the decision tree generated in part (a) of this question return for the following query?

$$\text{GOOD BEHAVIOR} = \textit{true}, \text{AGE} < 30 = \textit{true},$$
$$\text{DRUG DEPENDENT} = \textit{false}$$

3. The table below lists a sample of data from a census.[32]

ID	AGE	EDUCATION	MARITAL STATUS	OCCUPATION	ANNUAL INCOME
1	39	bachelors	never married	transport	25K–50K
2	50	bachelors	married	professional	25K–50K
3	18	high school	never married	agriculture	<25K
4	28	bachelors	married	professional	25K–50K
5	37	high school	married	agriculture	25K–50K
6	24	high school	never married	armed forces	<25K
7	52	high school	divorced	transport	25K–50K
8	40	doctorate	married	professional	>50K

There are four descriptive features and one target feature in this dataset:

- AGE, a continuous feature listing the age of the individual

---

[32] This census dataset is based on the Census Income Dataset (Kohavi, 1996), which is available from the UCI Machine Learning Repository (Bache and Lichman, 2013) at `archive.ics.uci.edu/ml/datasets/Census+Income/`.

- EDUCATION, a categorical feature listing the highest education award achieved by the individual (*high school*, *bachelors*, *doctorate*)
- MARITAL STATUS (*never married*, *married*, *divorced*)
- OCCUPATION (*transport* = works in the transportation industry; *professional* = doctors, lawyers, etc.; *agriculture* = works in the agricultural industry; *armed forces* = is a member of the armed forces)
- ANNUAL INCOME, the target feature with 3 levels (*<25K*, *25K–50K*, *>50K*)

a. Calculate the **entropy** for this dataset.

b. Calculate the **Gini index** for this dataset.

c. When building a decision tree, the easiest way to handle a continuous feature is to define a threshold around which splits will be made. What would be the optimal threshold to split the continuous AGE feature (use information gain based on entropy as the feature selection measure)?

d. Calculate **information gain** (based on entropy) for the EDUCATION, MARITAL STATUS, and OCCUPATION features.

e. Calculate the **information gain ratio** (based on entropy) for EDUCATION, MARITAL STATUS, and OCCUPATION features.

f. Calculate **information gain** using the **Gini index** for the EDUCATION, MARITAL STATUS, and OCCUPATION features.

4. The diagram below shows a decision tree for the task of predicting heart disease.[33] The descriptive features in this domain describe whether the patient suffers from chest pain (CHEST PAIN) as well as the blood pressure of the patient (BLOOD PRESSURE). The binary target feature is HEART DISEASE. The table beside the diagram lists a pruning set from this domain.

---

33 This example is inspired by the research reported in Palaniappan and Awang (2008).

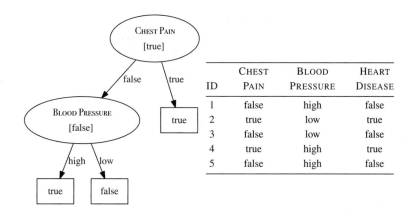

ID	CHEST PAIN	BLOOD PRESSURE	HEART DISEASE
1	false	high	false
2	true	low	true
3	false	low	false
4	true	high	true
5	false	high	false

Using the pruning set, apply **reduced error pruning** to the decision tree. Assume that the algorithm is applied in a bottom-up, left-to-right fashion. For each iteration of the algorithm, indicate the subtrees considered as pruning candidates, explain why the algorithm chooses to prune or leave these subtrees in the tree, and illustrate the tree that results from each iteration.

5. The following table[34] lists a dataset containing the details of five participants in a heart disease study, and a target feature RISK which describes their risk of heart disease. Each patient is described in terms of four binary descriptive features

- EXERCISE, how regularly do they exercise
- SMOKER, do they smoke
- OBESE, are they overweight
- FAMILY, did any of their parents or siblings suffer from heart disease

ID	EXERCISE	SMOKER	OBESE	FAMILY	RISK
1	daily	false	false	yes	low
2	weekly	true	false	yes	high
3	daily	false	false	no	low
4	rarely	true	true	yes	high
5	rarely	true	true	no	high

34 The data in this table has been artificially generated for this question, but is inspired by the results from the Framingham Heart Study: www.framinghamheartstudy.org.

a. As part of the study researchers have decided to create a predictive model to screen participants based on their risk of heart disease. You have been asked to implement this screening model using a **random forest**. The three tables below list three bootstrap samples that have been generated from the above dataset. Using these bootstrap samples create the decision trees that will be in the random forest model (use entropy based information gain as the feature selection criterion).

ID	EXERCISE	FAMILY	RISK
1	daily	yes	low
2	weekly	yes	high
2	weekly	yes	high
5	rarely	no	high
5	rarely	no	high

Bootstrap Sample A

ID	SMOKER	OBESE	RISK
1	false	false	low
2	true	false	high
2	true	false	high
4	true	true	high
5	true	true	high

Bootstrap Sample B

ID	OBESE	FAMILY	RISK
1	false	yes	low
1	false	yes	low
2	false	yes	high
4	true	yes	high
5	true	no	high

Bootstrap Sample C

b. Assuming the random forest model you have created uses majority voting, what prediction will it return for the following query:

EXERCISE=*rarely*, SMOKER=*false*, OBESE=*true*, FAMILY=*yes*

* 6. The following table lists a dataset containing the details of six patients. Each patient is described in terms of three binary descriptive features (OBESE, SMOKER, and DRINKS ALCOHOL) and a target feature (CANCER RISK).[35]

ID	OBESE	SMOKER	DRINKS ALCOHOL	CANCER RISK
1	true	false	true	low
2	true	true	true	high
3	true	false	true	low
4	false	true	true	high
5	false	true	false	low
6	false	true	true	high

35 The data in this table has been artificially generated for this question. The American Cancer Society does, however, provide information on the causes of cancer: www.cancer.org/cancer/cancercauses/.

a. Which of the descriptive features will the **ID3** decision tree induction algorithm choose as the feature for the root node of the decision tree?

b. When designing a dataset, it is generally a bad idea if all the descriptive features are indicators of the target feature taking a particular value. For example, a potential criticism of the design of the dataset in this question is that all the descriptive features are indicators of the CANCER RISK target feature taking the same level, *high*. Can you think of any descriptive features that could be added to this dataset that are indicators of the *low* target level?

* 7. The following table lists a dataset collected in an electronics shop showing details of customers and whether they responded to a special offer to buy a new laptop.

ID	AGE	INCOME	STUDENT	CREDIT	BUYS
1	< 31	high	no	bad	no
2	< 31	high	no	good	no
3	31 – 40	high	no	bad	yes
4	> 40	med	no	bad	yes
5	> 40	low	yes	bad	yes
6	> 40	low	yes	good	no
7	31 – 40	low	yes	good	yes
8	< 31	med	no	bad	no
9	< 31	low	yes	good	yes
10	> 40	med	yes	bad	yes
11	< 31	med	yes	good	yes
12	31 – 40	med	no	good	yes
13	31 – 40	high	yes	bad	yes
14	> 40	med	no	good	no

This dataset has been used to build a decision tree to predict which customers will respond to future special offers. The decision tree, created using the **ID3** algorithm, is shown below.

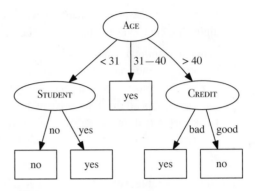

a. The **information gain** (calculated using entropy) of the feature AGE at the root node of the tree is 0.247. A colleague has suggested that the STUDENT feature would be better at the root node of the tree. Show that this is not the case.

b. Yet another colleague has suggested that the ID feature would be a very effective at the root node of the tree. Would you agree with this suggestion?

∗ 8. This table lists a dataset of the scores students achieved on an exam described in terms of whether the student studied for the exam (STUDIED) and the energy level of the lecturer when grading the student's exam (ENERGY).

ID	STUDIED	ENERGY	SCORE
1	yes	tired	65
2	no	alert	20
3	yes	alert	90
4	yes	tired	70
5	no	tired	40
6	yes	alert	85
7	no	tired	35

Which of the two descriptive features should we use as the testing criterion at the root node of a decision tree to predict students' scores?

＊ 9. Calculate the probability of a **model ensemble** that uses simple majority voting making an incorrect prediction in the following scenarios. (Hint: Understanding how to use the **binomial distribution** will be useful in answering this question.)

  a. The ensemble contains 11 independent models, all of which have an error rate of 0.2.

  b. The ensemble contains 11 independent models, all of which have an error rate of 0.49.

  c. The ensemble contains 21 independent models, all of which have an error rate of 0.49.

5 Similarity-based Learning

When I see a bird that walks like a duck and swims like a duck and quacks like a duck, I call that bird a duck.
—James Whitcomb Riley

Similarity-based approaches to machine learning come from the idea that the best way to make a predictions is to simply look at what has worked well in the past and predict the same thing again. The fundamental concepts required to build a system based on this idea are **feature spaces** and **measures of similarity**, and these are covered in the fundamentals section of this chapter. These concepts allow us to understand the standard approach to building similarity-based models: the **nearest neighbor algorithm**. After covering the standard algorithm, we then look at extensions and variations that allow us to handle noisy data (the *k* **nearest neighbor**, or *k*-**NN**, algorithm), to make predictions more efficiently (*k-d* **trees**), to predict continuous targets, and to handle different kinds of descriptive features with varying **measures of similarity**. We also take the opportunity to introduce the use of **data normalization** and **feature selection** in the context of similarity-based learning. These techniques are generally applicable to all machine learning algorithms but are especially important when similarity-based approaches are used.

5.1 Big Idea

The year is 1798, and you are Lieutenant-Colonel David Collins of HMS *Calcutta* exploring the region around Hawkesbury River, in New South Wales. One day, after an expedition up the river has returned to the ship, one of the men from the expedition tells you that he saw a strange animal near the river. You ask him to describe the animal to you, and he explains that he didn't see it very well because, as he approached it, the animal growled at him, so he didn't approach too closely. However, he did notice that the animal had webbed feet and a duck-billed snout.

In order to plan the expedition for the next day, you decide that you need to classify the animal so that you can determine whether it is dangerous to approach it or not. You decide to do this by thinking about the animals you can remember coming across before and comparing the features of these animals with the features the sailor described to you. Table 5.1[180] illustrates this process by listing some of the animals you have encountered before and how they compare with the growling, web-footed, duck-billed animal that the sailor

Table 5.1
Matching animals you remember to the features of the unknown animal described by the sailor.

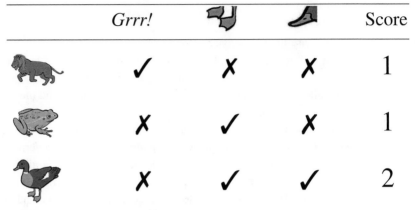

	Grrr!			Score
	✓	✗	✗	1
	✗	✓	✗	1
	✗	✓	✓	2

Images created by Jan Gillbank, English for the Australian Curriculum website (www.e4ac. edu.au). Used under Creative Commons Attribution 3.0 license.

described. For each known animal, you count how many features it has in common with the unknown animal. At the end of this process, you decide that the unknown animal is most similar to a duck, so that is what it must be. A duck, no matter how strange, is not a dangerous animal, so you tell the men to get ready for another expedition up the river the next day.

The process of classifying an unknown animal by matching the features of the animal against the features of animals you have encountered before neatly encapsulates the big idea underpinning similarity-based learning: if you are trying to make a prediction for a current situation then you should search your memory to find situations that are similar to the current one and make a prediction based on what was true for the most similar situation in your memory. In this chapter we are going to see how this type of reasoning can be implemented as a machine learning algorithm.

5.2   Fundamentals

As the name similarity-based learning suggests, a key component of this approach to prediction is defining a computational measure of similarity between instances. Often this measure of similarity is actually some form of

distance measure. A consequence of this, and a somewhat less obvious requirement of similarity-based learning, is that if we are going to compute distances
between instances, we need to have a concept of space in the representation of
the domain used by our model. In this section we introduce the concept of a
feature space as a representation for a training dataset and then illustrate how
we can compute measures of similarity between instances in a feature space.

5.2.1 Feature Space

Table 5.2[182] lists an example dataset containing two descriptive features, the
SPEED and AGILITY ratings for college athletes (both measures out of 10), and
one target feature that lists whether the athletes were drafted to a professional
team.[1] We can represent this dataset in a **feature space** by taking each of the
descriptive features to be the axes of a **coordinate system**. We can then place
each instance within the feature space based on the values of its descriptive
features. Figure 5.1[182] is a scatter plot to illustrate the resulting feature space
when we do this using the data in Table 5.2[182]. In this figure SPEED has been
plotted on the horizontal axis, and AGILITY has been plotted on the vertical
axis. The value of the DRAFT feature is indicated by the shape representing
each instance as a point in the feature space: triangles for *no* and crosses for
yes.

There is always one dimension for every descriptive feature in a dataset.
In this example, there are only two descriptive features, so the feature space is
two-dimensional. Feature spaces can, however, have many more dimensions—
in document classification tasks, for example, it is not uncommon to have
thousands of descriptive features and therefore thousands of dimensions in the
associated feature space. Although we can't easily draw feature spaces beyond
three dimensions, the ideas underpinning them remain the same.

We can formally define a feature space as an abstract *m*-dimensional space
that is created by making each descriptive feature in a dataset an axis of an
m-dimensional coordinate system and mapping each instance in the dataset to
a point in this coordinate system based on the values of its descriptive features.

For similarity-based learning, the nice thing about the way feature spaces
work is that if the values of the descriptive features of two or more instances in
the dataset are the same, then these instances will be mapped to same point in

---

1 This example dataset is inspired by the use of analytics in professional and college sports, often
referred to as **sabremetrics**. Two accessible introductions to this field are Lewis (2004) and Keri
(2007).

Table 5.2
The SPEED and AGILITY ratings for 20 college athletes and whether they were drafted by a professional team.

ID	SPEED	AGILITY	DRAFT	ID	SPEED	AGILITY	DRAFT
1	2.50	6.00	no	11	2.00	2.00	no
2	3.75	8.00	no	12	5.00	2.50	no
3	2.25	5.50	no	13	8.25	8.50	no
4	3.25	8.25	no	14	5.75	8.75	yes
5	2.75	7.50	no	15	4.75	6.25	yes
6	4.50	5.00	no	16	5.50	6.75	yes
7	3.50	5.25	no	17	5.25	9.50	yes
8	3.00	3.25	no	18	7.00	4.25	yes
9	4.00	4.00	no	19	7.50	8.00	yes
10	4.25	3.75	no	20	7.25	5.75	yes

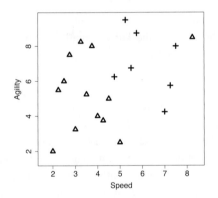

Figure 5.1
A feature space plot of the college athlete data in Table 5.2[182].

the feature space. Also, as the differences between the values of the descriptive features of two instances grows, so too does the distance between the points in the feature space that represent these instances. So the distance between two points in the feature space is a useful measure of the similarity of the descriptive features of the two instances.

5.2.2 Measuring Similarity Using Distance Metrics

The simplest way to measure the similarity between two instances, **a** and **b**, in a dataset is to measure the distance between the instances in a feature space. We can use a **distance metric** to do this: $metric(\mathbf{a}, \mathbf{b})$ is a function that returns the distance between two instances **a** and **b**. Mathematically, a **metric** must conform to the following four criteria:

1. **Non-negativity**: $metric(\mathbf{a}, \mathbf{b}) \geqslant 0$
2. **Identity**: $metric(\mathbf{a}, \mathbf{b}) = 0 \Longleftrightarrow \mathbf{a} = \mathbf{b}$
3. **Symmetry**: $metric(\mathbf{a}, \mathbf{b}) = metric(\mathbf{b}, \mathbf{a})$
4. **Triangular Inequality**: $metric(\mathbf{a}, \mathbf{b}) \leqslant metric(\mathbf{a}, \mathbf{c}) + metric(\mathbf{b}, \mathbf{c})$

One of the best known distance metrics is **Euclidean distance**, which computes the length of the straight line between two points. Euclidean distance between two instances **a** and **b** in an m-dimensional feature space is defined as

$$Euclidean(\mathbf{a}, \mathbf{b}) = \sqrt{\sum_{i=1}^{m} (\mathbf{a}\,[i] - \mathbf{b}\,[i])^2} \qquad (5.1)$$

The descriptive features in the college athlete dataset are both continuous, which means that the feature space representing this data is technically known as a **Euclidean coordinate space**, and we can compute the distance between instances in it using Euclidean distance. For example, the Euclidean distance between instances $\mathbf{d}_{12}$ (SPEED = 5.00, AGILITY = 2.50) and $\mathbf{d}_5$ (SPEED = 2.75, AGILITY = 7.50) from Table 5.2[182] is

$$Euclidean(\mathbf{d}_{12}, \mathbf{d}_5) = \sqrt{(5.00 - 2.75)^2 + (2.50 - 7.50)^2}$$
$$= \sqrt{30.0625} = 5.4829$$

Another, less well-known, distance metric is the **Manhattan distance**.[2] The Manhattan distance between two instances **a** and **b** in a feature space with m dimensions is defined as

$$Manhattan(\mathbf{a}, \mathbf{b}) = \sum_{i=1}^{m} abs(\mathbf{a}\,[i] - \mathbf{b}\,[i]) \qquad (5.2)$$

---

2 The Manhattan distance, or **taxi-cab distance**, is so called because it is the distance that a taxi driver would have to cover if going from one point to another on a road system that is laid out in blocks, like the Manhattan road system.

where the *abs*() function returns the absolute value. For example, the Manhattan distance between instances $\mathbf{d}_{12}$ (SPEED = 5.00, AGILITY = 2.50) and $\mathbf{d}_5$ (SPEED = 2.75, AGILITY = 7.50) in Table 5.2[182] is

$$Manhattan(\mathbf{d}_{12}, \mathbf{d}_5) = abs(5.00 - 2.75) + abs(2.5 - 7.5)$$
$$= 2.25 + 5 = 7.25$$

Figure 5.2(a)[184] illustrates the difference between the Manhattan and Euclidean distances between two points in a two-dimensional feature space. If we compare Equation (5.1)[183] and Equation (5.2)[183], we can see that both distance metrics are essentially functions of the differences between the values of the features. Indeed, the Euclidean and Manhattan distances are special cases of the **Minkowski distance**, which defines a family of distance metrics based on differences between features.

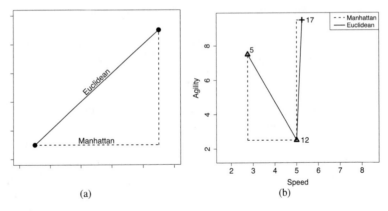

(a)   (b)

Figure 5.2

(a) A generalized illustration of the Manhattan and Euclidean distances between two points; (b) a plot of the Manhattan and Euclidean distances between instances $\mathbf{d}_{12}$ and $\mathbf{d}_5$ and between $\mathbf{d}_{12}$ and $\mathbf{d}_{17}$ from Table 5.2[182].

The **Minkowski distance** between two instances **a** and **b** in a feature space with m descriptive features is defined as

$$Minkowski(\mathbf{a}, \mathbf{b}) = \left(\sum_{i=1}^{m} abs(\mathbf{a}[i] - \mathbf{b}[i])^p \right)^{\frac{1}{p}} \qquad (5.3)$$

where the parameter p is typically set to a positive value and defines the behavior of the distance metric. Different distance metrics result from adjusting the value of p. For example, the Minkowski distance with $p = 1$ is the Manhattan distance, and with $p = 2$ is the Euclidean distance. Continuing in this manner, we can define an infinite number of distance metrics.

The fact that we can define an infinite number of distance metrics is not merely an academic curiosity. In fact, the predictions produced by a similarity-based model will change depending on the exact Minkowski distance used (i.e., $p = 1, 2, \ldots, \infty$). Larger values of p place more emphasis on large differences between feature values than smaller values of p because all differences are raised to the power of p. Consequently, the Euclidean distance (with $p = 2$) is more strongly influenced by a single large difference in one feature than the Manhattan distance (with $p = 1$).[3]

We can see this if we compare the Euclidean and Manhattan distances between instances $\mathbf{d}_{12}$ and $\mathbf{d}_5$ with the Euclidean and Manhattan distances between instances $\mathbf{d}_{12}$ and $\mathbf{d}_{17}$ (SPEED = 5.25, AGILITY = 9.50). Figure 5.2(b)[184] plots the Manhattan and Euclidean distances between these pairs of instances.

The Manhattan distances between both pairs of instances are the same: 7.25. It is striking, however, that the Euclidean distance between $\mathbf{d}_{12}$ and $\mathbf{d}_{17}$ is 8.25, which is greater than the Euclidean distance between $\mathbf{d}_{12}$ and $\mathbf{d}_5$, which is just 5.48. This is because the maximum difference between $\mathbf{d}_{12}$ and $\mathbf{d}_{17}$ for any single feature is 7 units (for AGILITY), whereas the maximum difference between $\mathbf{d}_{12}$ and $\mathbf{d}_5$ on any single feature is just 5 units (for AGILITY). Because these differences are squared in the Euclidean distance calculation, the larger maximum single difference between $\mathbf{d}_{12}$ and $\mathbf{d}_{17}$ results in a larger overall distance being calculated for this pair of instances. Overall the Euclidean distance weights features with larger differences in values more than features with smaller differences in values. This means that the Euclidean difference is more influenced by a single large difference in one feature rather than a lot of small differences across a set of features, whereas the opposite is true of Manhattan distance.

Although we have an infinite number of Minkowski-based distance metrics to choose from, Euclidean distance and Manhattan distance are the most commonly used of these. The question of which is the best one to use, however, still remains. From a computational perspective, the Manhattan distance has a

3 In the extreme case with $p = \infty$ the Minkowski metric simple returns the maximum difference between any of the features. This is known as the **Chebyshev distance** but is also sometimes called the **chessboard distance** because it is the number of moves a king must make in chess to go from one square on the board to any other square.

slight advantage over the Euclidean distance—the computation of the squaring and the square root is saved—and computational considerations can become important when dealing with very large datasets. Computational considerations aside, Euclidean distance is often used as the default.

5.3   Standard Approach: The Nearest Neighbor Algorithm

We now understand the two fundamental components of similarity-based learning: a feature space representation of the instances in a dataset and a measure of similarity between instances. We can put these components together to define the standard approach to similarity-based learning: the **nearest neighbor algorithm**. The training phase needed to build a nearest neighbor model is very simple and just involves storing all the training instances in memory. In the standard version of the algorithm, the data structure used to store training data is a simple list. In the prediction stage, when the model is used to make predictions for new query instances, the distance in the feature space between the query instance and each instance in memory is computed, and the prediction returned by the model is the target feature level of the instance that is nearest to the query in the feature space. The default distance metric used in nearest neighbor models is Euclidean distance. Algorithm 5.1[186] provides a pseudocode definition of the algorithm for the prediction stage. The algorithm really is very simple, so we can move straight to looking at a worked example of it in action.

Algorithm 5.1 Pseudocode description of the nearest neighbor algorithm.

Require: a set of training instances
Require: a query instance
  1: Iterate across the instances in memory to find the nearest neighbor—this is the instance with the shortest distance across the feature space to the query instance.
  2: Make a prediction for the query instance that is equal to the value of the target feature of the nearest neighbor.

5.3.1   A Worked Example

Assume that we are using the dataset in Table 5.2[182] as our labeled training dataset, and we want to make a prediction to tell us whether a query instance with SPEED $= 6.75$ and AGILITY $= 3.00$ is likely to be drafted or not. Figure 5.3[187] illustrates the feature space of the training dataset with the query, represented by the **?** marker.

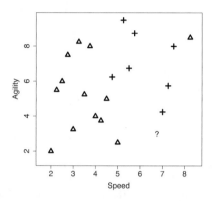

Figure 5.3
A feature space plot of the data in Table 5.2[182], with the position in the feature space of the query represented by the ? marker.

Just by visually inspecting Figure 5.3[187], we can see that the nearest neighbor to the query instance has a target level of *yes*, so this is the prediction that the model should return. However, let's step through how the algorithm makes this prediction. Remember that during the prediction stage, the nearest neighbor algorithm iterates across all the instances in the training dataset and computes the distance between each instance and the query. These distances are then ranked from lowest to highest to find the nearest neighbor. Table 5.3[188] shows the distances between our query instance and each instance from Table 5.2[182] ranked from lowest to highest. Just as we saw in Figure 5.3[187], this shows that the nearest neighbor to the query is instance $\mathbf{d}_{18}$, with a distance of 1.2749 and a target level of *yes*.

When the algorithm is searching for the nearest neighbor using Euclidean distance, it is partitioning the feature space into what is known as a **Voronoi tessellation**[4], and it is trying to decide which **Voronoi region** the query belongs to. From a prediction perspective, the Voronoi region belonging to

---

4 A Voronoi tessellation is a way of decomposing a space into regions where each region belongs to an instance and contains all the points in the space whose distance to that instance is less than the distance to any other instance.

Table 5.3

The distances (Dist.) between the query instance with SPEED = 6.75 and AGILITY = 3.00 and each instance in Table 5.2[182].

ID	SPEED	AGILITY	DRAFT	Dist.	ID	SPEED	AGILITY	DRAFT	Dist.
18	7.00	4.25	yes	1.27	11	2.00	2.00	no	4.85
12	5.00	2.50	no	1.82	19	7.50	8.00	yes	5.06
10	4.25	3.75	no	2.61	3	2.25	5.50	no	5.15
20	7.25	5.75	yes	2.80	1	2.50	6.00	no	5.20
9	4.00	4.00	no	2.93	13	8.25	8.50	no	5.70
6	4.50	5.00	no	3.01	2	3.75	8.00	no	5.83
8	3.00	3.25	no	3.76	14	5.75	8.75	yes	5.84
15	4.75	6.25	yes	3.82	5	2.75	7.50	no	6.02
7	3.50	5.25	no	3.95	4	3.25	8.25	no	6.31
16	5.50	6.75	yes	3.95	17	5.25	9.50	yes	6.67

a training instance defines the set of queries for which the prediction will be determined by that training instance. Figure 5.4(a)[189] illustrates the Voronoi tessellation of the feature space using the training instances from Table 5.2[182] and shows the position of our sample query instance within this decomposition. We can see in this figure that the query is inside a Voronoi region defined by an instance with a target level of *yes*. As such, the prediction for the query instance should be *yes*.

The nearest neighbor prediction algorithm creates a set of **local models**, or neighborhoods, across the feature space where each model is defined by a subset of the training dataset (in this case, one instance). Implicitly, however, the algorithm is also creating a global prediction model based on the full dataset. We can see this if we highlight the decision boundary within the feature space. The **decision boundary** is the boundary between regions of the feature space in which different target levels will be predicted. We can generate the decision boundary by aggregating the neighboring local models (in this case Voronoi regions) that make the same prediction. Figure 5.4(b)[189] illustrates the decision boundary within the feature space for the two target levels in the college athlete dataset. Given that the decision boundary is generated by aggregating the Voronoi regions, it is not surprising that the query is on the side of the decision boundary representing the *yes* target level. This illustrates that a decision boundary is a global representation of the predictions made by the local models associated with each instance in the training set. It also highlights the fact that the nearest neighbor algorithm uses multiple local models to create an implicit global model to map from the descriptive feature values to the target feature.

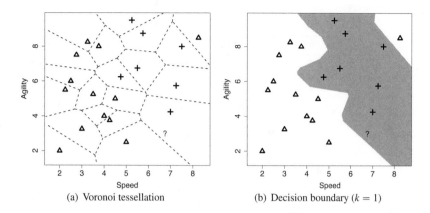

(a) Voronoi tessellation   (b) Decision boundary ($k = 1$)

Figure 5.4

(a) The Voronoi tessellation of the feature space for the dataset in Table 5.2[182] with the position of the query represented by the ? marker; (b) the decision boundary created by aggregating the neighboring Voronoi regions that belong to the same target level.

One of the advantages of the nearest neighbor approach to prediction is that it is relatively straightforward to update the model when new labeled instances become available—we simply add them to the training dataset. Table 5.4[190] lists the updated dataset when the example query instance with its prediction of *yes* is included.[5] Figure 5.5(a)[191] illustrates the Voronoi tessellation of the feature space that results from this update, and Figure 5.5(b)[191] presents the updated decision boundary. Comparing Figure 5.5(b)[191] with Figure 5.4(b)[189], we can see that the main difference is that the decision boundary in the bottom right region of the feature space has moved to the left. This reflects the extension of the *yes* region due to the inclusion of the new instance.

In summary, the inductive bias underpinning similarity-based machine learning algorithms is that things that are similar (i.e., instances that have similar descriptive features) also have the same target feature values. The nearest neighbor algorithm creates an implicit global predictive model by aggregating local models, or neighborhoods. The definition of these neighborhoods is based on similarity within the feature space to the labeled training instances.

---

5 Instances should only be added to the training dataset if we have determined after making the prediction that the prediction was, in fact, correct. In this example, we assume that at the draft, the query player was drafted.

Table 5.4

The extended version of the college athletes dataset.

ID	SPEED	AGILITY	DRAFT	ID	SPEED	AGILITY	DRAFT
1	2.50	6.00	no	12	5.00	2.50	no
2	3.75	8.00	no	13	8.25	8.50	no
3	2.25	5.50	no	14	5.75	8.75	yes
4	3.25	8.25	no	15	4.75	6.25	yes
5	2.75	7.50	no	16	5.50	6.75	yes
6	4.50	5.00	no	17	5.25	9.50	yes
7	3.50	5.25	no	18	7.00	4.25	yes
8	3.00	3.25	no	19	7.50	8.00	yes
9	4.00	4.00	no	20	7.25	5.75	yes
10	4.25	3.75	no	21	6.75	3.00	yes
11	2.00	2.00	no				

Predictions are made for a query instance using the target level of the training instance defining the neighborhood in the feature space that contains the query.

5.4   Extensions and Variations

We now understand the standard nearest neighbor algorithm. The algorithm, as presented, can work well with clean, reasonably sized datasets containing continuous descriptive features. Often, however, datasets are noisy, very large, and may contain a mixture of different data types. As a result, a lot of extensions and variations of the algorithm have been developed to address these issues. In this section we describe the most important of these.

5.4.1   Handling Noisy Data

Throughout our worked example using the college athlete dataset, the top right corner of the feature space contained a *no* region (see Figure 5.4[189]). This region exists because one of the *no* instances occurs far away from the rest of the instances with this target level. Considering that all the immediate neighbors of this instance are associated with the *yes* target level, it is likely that either this instance has been incorrectly labeled and should have a target feature value of *yes*, or one of the descriptive features for this instance has an incorrect value and hence it is in the wrong location in the feature space. Either way, this instance is likely to be an example of **noise** in the dataset.

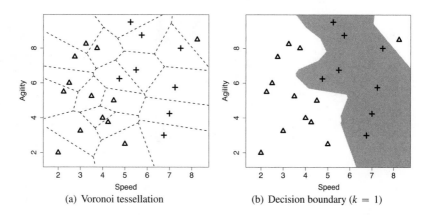

Figure 5.5

(a) The Voronoi tessellation of the feature space when the dataset has been updated to include the query instance; (b) the updated decision boundary reflecting the addition of the query instance in the training set.

Fundamentally, the nearest neighbor algorithm is a set of local models, each defined using a single instance. Consequently, the algorithm is sensitive to noise because any errors in the description or labeling of training data results in erroneous local models and hence incorrect predictions. The most direct way of mitigating against the impact of noise in the dataset on a nearest neighbor algorithm is to dilute the dependency of the algorithm on individual (possibly noisy) instances. To do this we simply modify the algorithm to return the majority target level within the set of **k nearest neighbors** to the query **q**:

$$\mathbb{M}_k(\mathbf{q}) = \underset{l \in levels(t)}{\arg \max} \sum_{i=1}^{k} \delta(t_i, l) \tag{5.4}$$

where $\mathbb{M}_k(\mathbf{q})$ is the prediction of the model $\mathbb{M}$ for the query **q** given the parameter of the model k; $levels(t)$ is the set of levels in the domain of the target feature, and l is an element of this set; i iterates over the instances $\mathbf{d}_i$ in increasing distance from the query **q**; t_i is the value of the target feature for instance $\mathbf{d}_i$; and $\delta(t_i, l)$ is the **Kronecker delta** function, which takes two parameters and returns 1 if they are equal and 0 otherwise. Figure 5.6(a)[192] demonstrates how this approach can regularize the decision boundary for the dataset in Table 5.4[190]. In this figure we have set $k = 3$, and this modification has resulted in the *no* region in the top right corner of the feature space disappearing.

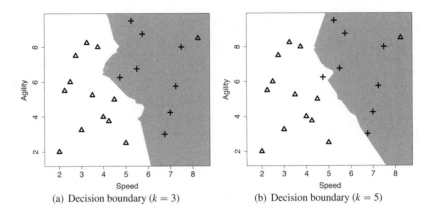

(a) Decision boundary ($k = 3$)   (b) Decision boundary ($k = 5$)

Figure 5.6
The decision boundary using majority vote of the nearest 3 and 5 instances.

Although, in our example, increasing the set of neighbors from 1 to 3 removed the noise issue, $k = 3$ does not work for every dataset. There is always a trade-off in setting the value of k. If we set k too, low we run the risk of the algorithm being sensitive to noise in the data and overfitting. Conversely, if we set k too high, we run the risk of losing the true pattern of the data and under-fitting. For example, Figure 5.6(b)[192] illustrates what happens to the decision boundary in our example feature space when $k = 5$. Here we can see that the decision boundary may have been pushed too far back into the *yes* region (one of the crosses is now on the wrong side of the decision boundary). So, even a small increase in k can have a significant impact on the decision boundary.

The risks associated with setting k to a high value are particularly acute when we are dealing with an **imbalanced dataset**. An imbalanced dataset is a dataset that contains significantly more instances of one target level than another. In these situations, as k increases, the majority target level begins to dominate the feature space. The dataset in the college athlete example is imbalanced—there are 13 *no* instances and only 7 *yes* instances. Although this differential between the target levels in the dataset may not seem substantial, it does have an impact as k increases. Figure 5.7(a)[193] illustrates the decision boundary when $k = 15$. Clearly, large portions of the *yes* region are now on the wrong side of the decision boundary. Moreover, if k is set to a value larger than 15, the majority target level dominates the entire feature space. Given the sensitivity of the algorithm to the value of k, how should we set this parameter? The

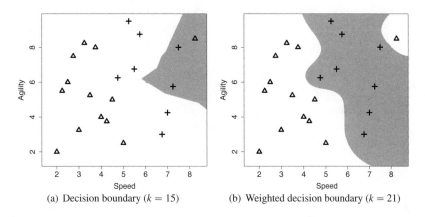

(a) Decision boundary ($k = 15$) (b) Weighted decision boundary ($k = 21$)

Figure 5.7

(a) The decision boundary using majority vote of the nearest 15 neighbors; (b) the weighted k nearest neighbor model decision boundary (with $k = 21$).

most common way to tackle this issue is to perform evaluation experiments to investigate the performance of models with different values for k and to select the one that performs best. We return to these kinds of evaluation experiments in Chapter 8[397].

Another way to address the problem of how to set k is to use a **weighted k nearest neighbor** approach. The problem with setting k to a high value arises because the algorithm starts taking into account neighbors that are far away from the query instance in the feature space. As a result, the algorithm tends toward the majority target level in the dataset. One way of counterbalancing this tendency is to use a **distance weighted k nearest neighbor** approach. When a distance weighted k nearest neighbor approach is used, the contribution of each neighbor to the prediction is a function of the inverse distance between the neighbor and the query. So when calculating the overall majority vote across the k nearest neighbors, the votes of the neighbors that are close to the query get a lot of weight, and the votes of the neighbors that are further away from the query get less weight. The easiest way to implement this weighting scheme is to weight each neighbor by the reciprocal[6] of the squared

6 When using the reciprocal of the squared distance as a weighting function, we need to be careful to avoid division by zero in the case where the query is exactly the same as its nearest neighbor. Typically this problem case is handled by assigning the query the target level of the training instance **d** that it exactly matches.

distance between the neighbor **d** and the query **q**:

$$\frac{1}{dist(\mathbf{q},\mathbf{d})^2} \tag{5.5}$$

Using the distance weighted k nearest neighbor approach, the prediction returned for a given query is the target level with the highest score when we sum the weights of the votes of the instances in the neighborhood of k nearest neighbors for each target level. The weighted k nearest neighbor model is defined as

$$\mathbb{M}_k(\mathbf{q}) = \underset{l\in levels(t)}{\arg\max} \sum_{i=1}^{k} \frac{1}{dist(\mathbf{q},\mathbf{d_i})^2} \times \delta(t_i,l) \tag{5.6}$$

where $\mathbb{M}_k(\mathbf{q})$ is the prediction of the model $\mathbb{M}$ for the query $\mathbf{q}$ given the parameter of the model k; $levels(t)$ is the set of levels in the domain of the target feature, and l is an element of this set; i iterates over the instances $\mathbf{d}_i$ in increasing distance from the query $\mathbf{q}$; t_i is the value of the target feature for instance $\mathbf{d}_i$; and $\delta(t_i,l)$ is the **Kronecker delta** function, which takes two parameters and returns 1 if they are equal and 0 otherwise. The reason we multiply by the Kronecker delta function is to ensure that in calculating the score for each of the candidate target levels, we include only the weights for the instances whose target feature value matches that level.

When we weight the contribution to a prediction of each of the neighbors by the reciprocal of the distance to the query, we can actually set k to be equal to the size of the training set and therefore include all the training instances in the prediction process. The issue of losing the true pattern of the data is less acute now because the training instances that are very far away from the query naturally won't have much of an effect on the prediction.

Figure 5.7(b)[193] shows the decision boundary for a weighted k nearest neighbor model for the dataset in Table 5.4[190] with $k = 21$ (the size of the dataset) and weights computed using the reciprocal of the squared distance. One of the most striking things about this plot is that the top-right region of the feature space again belongs to the *no* region. This may not be a good thing if this instance is due to noise in the data, and this demonstrates that there is no *silver bullet* solution to handling noise in datasets. This is one of the reasons that creating a data quality report[7] and spending time on cleaning the dataset is such an important part of any machine learning project. That said, there are some other features of this plot that are encouraging. For example, the size of a *no* region

7 See Section 3.1[56].

in the top right of the feature space is smaller than the corresponding region for the nearest neighbor model with $k = 1$ (see Figure 5.4(b)[189]). So by giving all the instances in the dataset a weighted vote, we have a least reduced the impact of the noisy instance. Also, the decision boundary is much smoother than the decision boundaries of the other models we have looked at in this section. This may indicate that the model is doing a better job of modeling the transition between the different target levels.

Using a weighted k nearest neighbor model does not require that we set k equal to the size of the dataset, as we did in this example. It may be possible to find a value for k—using evaluation experiments—that eliminates, or further reduces, the effect of the noise on the model. As is so often the case in machine learning, fitting the parameters of a model is as important as selecting which model to use.

Finally, it is worth mentioning two situations where this weighted k nearest neighbor approach can be problematic. The first is if the dataset is very imbalanced, then even with a weighting applied to the contribution of the training instances, the majority target level may dominate. The second is when the dataset is very large, which means that computing the reciprocal of squared distance between the query and all the training instances can become too computationally expensive to be feasible.

5.4.2 Efficient Memory Search

The fact that the nearest neighbor algorithm stores the entire training dataset in memory has a negative effect on the time complexity of the algorithm. In particular, if we are working with a large dataset, the time cost in computing the distances between a query and all the training instances and retrieving the k nearest neighbors may be prohibitive. Assuming that the training set will remain relatively stable, this time issue can be offset by investing in some one-off computation to create an index of the instances that enables efficient retrieval of the nearest neighbors without doing an exhaustive search of the entire dataset.

The ***k-d* tree**,[8] which is short for *k-dimensional* tree, is one of the best known of these indices. A *k-d* tree is a balanced **binary tree**[9] in which each of the nodes in the tree (both interior and leaf nodes) index one of the instances in a training dataset. The tree is constructed so that nodes that are nearby in the tree index training instances that are nearby in the feature space.

To construct a *k-d* tree, we first pick a feature and split the data into two partitions using the median value of this feature.[10] We then recursively split each of the two new partitions, stopping the recursion when there are fewer than two instances in a partition. The main decision to be made in this process is how to select the feature to split on. The most common way to do this is to define an arbitrary order over the descriptive features before we begin building the tree. Then, using the feature at the start of the list for the first split, we select the next feature in the list for each subsequent split. If we get to a point where we have already split on all the features, we go back to the start of the feature list.

Every time we partition the data, we add a node with two branches to the *k-d* tree. The node indexes the instance that had the median value of the feature, the left branch holds all the instances that had values less than the median, and the right branch holds all the instances that had values greater than the median. The recursive partitioning then grows each of these branches in a depth-first manner.

Each node in a *k-d* tree defines a boundary that partitions the feature space along the median value of the feature the data was split on at that node. Technically these boundaries are **hyperplanes**[11] and, as we shall see, play an important role when we are using the *k-d* tree to find the nearest neighbor for a query. In particular, the hyperplane at a node defines the boundary between the instances stored on each of the subtrees below the node. We will find this

8 The primary papers introducing *k-d* trees are Bentley (1975) and Friedman et al. (1977). Also, note that the *k* here has no relationship with the *k* used in *k* nearest neighbor. It simply specifies the number of levels in the depth of the tree, which is arbitrary and typically determined by the algorithm that constructs the tree.

9 A binary tree is simply a tree where every node in the tree has at most two branches.

10 We use the median value as the splitting threshold because it is less susceptible to the influence of outliers than the mean, and this helps keep the tree as balanced as possible—having a balanced tree helps with the efficiency in retrieval. If more than one instance in a dataset has the median value for a feature we are splitting on, then we select one of these instances to represent the median and place the other instances with the median value in the set containing the instances whose values are greater than the median.

11 A **hyperplane** is a geometric concept that generalizes the idea of a plane into different dimensions. For example, a hyperplane in 2D space is a line and in a 3D space is a plane.

useful when we are trying to decide whether to search both branches of a node when we are looking for the nearest neighbor or whether we can prune one of them.

Figure 5.8[198] illustrates the creation of the first two nodes of a *k-d* tree for the college athlete dataset in Table 5.4[190]. In generating this figure we have assumed that the algorithm selected the features to split on using the following ordering over the features: SPEED, AGILITY. The non-leaf nodes in the trees list the ID of the instance the node indexes and the feature and value pair that define the hyperplane partition on the feature space defined by the node. Figure 5.9(a)[199] shows the complete *k-d* tree generated for the dataset, and Figure 5.9(b)[199] shows the partitioning of the feature space as defined by the *k-d* tree. The lines in this figure indicate the hyperplanes partitioning the feature space that were created by the splits encoded in the non-leaf nodes in the tree. The heavier the weight of the line used to plot the hyperplane, the earlier in the tree the split occurred.

Once we have stored the instances in a dataset in a *k-d* tree, we can use the tree to quickly retrieve the nearest neighbor for a query instance. Algorithm 5.2[200] lists the algorithm we use to retrieve the nearest neighbor for a query. The algorithm starts by descending through the tree from the root node, taking the branch at each interior node that matches the value of the query for the feature tested at that node, until it comes to a leaf node (Line 3 of the algorithm). The algorithm stores the instance indexed by the leaf node in the *best* variable and sets the *best-distance* variable to the distance between the instance indexed by the leaf node and the query instance (Lines 5, 6, and 7). Unfortunately, there is no guarantee that this instance will be the nearest neighbor, although it should be a good approximate neighbor for the query. So the algorithm then searches the tree looking for instances that are closer to the query than the instance stored in *best* (Lines 4-11 of the algorithm control this search).

At each node encountered in the search, the algorithm does three things. First, it checks that the node is not NULL. If this is the case, then the algorithm has reached the parent node of the root of the tree and should terminate (Line 4) by returning the instance stored in *best* (Line 12). Second, the algorithm checks if the instance indexed by the node is closer to the query than the instance at the current best node. If it is, *best* and *best-distance* are updated to reflect this (Lines 5, 6, and 7). Third, the algorithm chooses which node it should move to next: the parent of the node or a node in the subtree under the other branch of the node (Lines 8, 9, 10, 11).

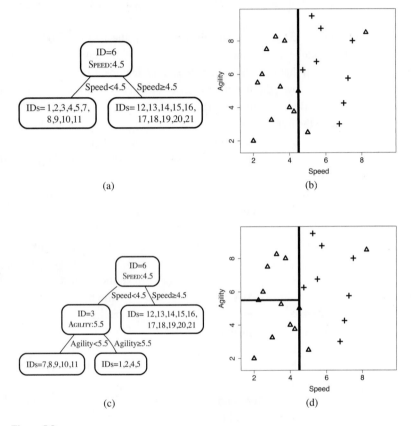

Figure 5.8

(a) The *k-d* tree generated for the dataset in Table 5.4[190] after the initial split using the SPEED feature with a threshold of 4.5; (b) the partitioning of the feature space by the *k-d* tree in (a); (c) the *k-d* tree after the dataset at the left child of the root has been split using the AGILITY feature with a threshold of 5.5; and (d) the partitioning of the feature space by the *k-d* tree in (c).

The decision of which node to move to next is made by checking if any instances indexed by nodes in the subtree on the other branch of the current node could be the nearest neighbor. The only way that this can happen is if there is at least one instance on the other side of the hyperplane boundary that bisects the node that is closer to the query than the current *best-distance*. Fortunately, because the hyperplanes created by the *k-d* tree are all axis-aligned,

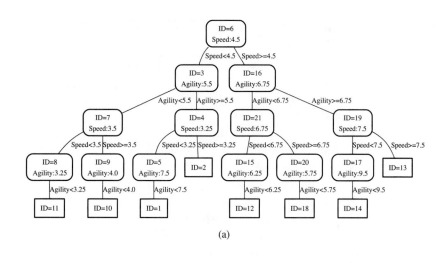

(a)

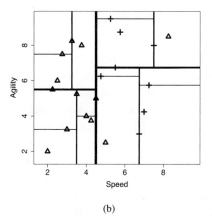

(b)

Figure 5.9

(a) The final *k-d* tree generated for the dataset in Table 5.4[190]; (b) the partitioning of the feature space defined by this *k-d* tree.

the algorithm can test for this condition quite easily. The hyperplane boundary bisecting a node is defined by the value used to split the descriptive feature at the node. This means that we only need to test whether the difference between the value for this feature for the query instance and the value for this feature that defines the hyperplane is less than the *best-distance* (Line 8). If this test succeeds, the algorithm descends to a leaf node of this subtree, using the same

---

Algorithm 5.2 Pseudocode description of the *k-d* tree nearest neighbor retrieval algorithm.

Require: query instance **q** and a *k-d* tree **kdtree**

  1: best = null

  2: best-distance = ∞

  3: node = descendTree(kdtree,q)

  4: **while** node! = NULL **do**

  5:    **if** distance(q,node) < best-distance **then**

  6:       best = node

  7:       best-distance = distance(q,node)

  8:    **if** boundaryDist(q, node) < best-distance **then**

  9:       node = descendtree(node,q)

10:    **else**

11:       node = parent(node)

12: **return** best

---

process it used to find the original leaf node (Line 9). If this test fails, the algorithm ascends the tree to the parent of the current node and prunes the subtree containing the region on the other side of the hyperplane without testing the instances in that region (Line 11). In either case, the search continues from the new node as before. The search finishes when it reaches the root node and both its branches have been either searched or pruned. The algorithm returns the instance stored in the *best* variable as the nearest neighbor.

We can demonstrate how this retrieval algorithm works by showing how the algorithm finds the nearest neighbor for a query instance with SPEED = 6.00 and AGILITY = 3.50. Figure 5.10(a)[201] illustrates the first stage of the retrieval of the nearest neighbor. The bold lines show the path taken to descend the tree from the root to a leaf node based on the values of the query instance (use Figure 5.9(a)[199] to trace this path in detail). This leaf node indexes instance d_{12} (SPEED = 5.00, AGILITY = 2.50). Because this is the initial descent down the tree, *best* is automatically set to d_{12}, and *best-distance* is set to the distance between instance d_{12} and the query, which is 1.4142 (we use Euclidean distance throughout this example). At this point the retrieval process will have executed Lines 1–7 of the algorithm.

Figure 5.10(b)[201] illustrates the location of the query in the feature space (the ?). The dashed circle centered on the query location has a radius equal to the *best-distance*. We can see in Figure 5.10(b)[201] that this circle intersects

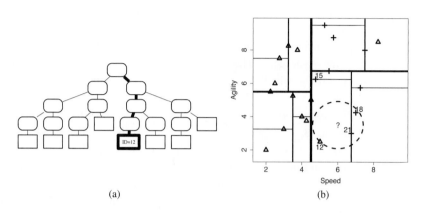

(a)   (b)

Figure 5.10

(a) The path taken from the root node to a leaf node when we search the tree with a query SPEED = 6.00, AGILITY = 3.50; (b) the ? marks the location of the query, the dashed circle plots the extent of the target, and for convenience in the discussion, we have labeled some of the nodes with the IDs of the instances they index (12, 15, 18, and 21).

with the triangle marking the location of $\mathbf{d}_{12}$, which is currently stored in *best* (i.e., it is our current best guess for the nearest neighbor). This circle covers the area in the feature space that we know must contain all the instances that are closer to the query than *best*. Although this example is just two dimensional, the *k-d* tree algorithm can work in a many dimensional feature space, so we will use the term **target hypersphere**[12] to denote the region around the query that is inside the *best-distance*. We can see in Figure 5.10(b)[201] that instance $\mathbf{d}_{12}$ is not the true nearest neighbor to the query—several other instances are inside the target hypersphere.

The search process must now move to a new node (Lines 8, 9, 10, and 11). This move is determined by Line 8, which checks if the distance between the query and the hyperplane[13] defined by the current node is less than the value of *best-distance*. In this case, however, the current node is a leaf node, so it

12 Similar to a hyperplane, a hypersphere is a generalization of the geometric concept of a sphere across multiple dimensions. So, in a 2D space the term hypersphere denotes a circle, in 3D it denotes a sphere, and so on.

13 Recall that each non-leaf node in the tree indexes an instance in the dataset and also defines a hyperplane that partitions the feature space. For example, the horizontal and vertical lines in Figure 5.9(b)[199] plot the hyperplanes defined by the non-leaf nodes of the *k-d* tree in Figure 5.9(a)[199].

does not define a hyperplane on the feature space. As a result, the condition checked in Line 8, fails and the search moves to the parent node of the current node (Line 11).

This new node indexes $\mathbf{d}_{15}$. The node is not NULL, so the **while** loop on Line 4 succeeds. The distance between instance $\mathbf{d}_{15}$ and the query instance is 3.0208, which is not less than the current value of *best-distance*, so the **if** statement on Line 5 will fail. We can see this easily in Figure 5.10(b)[201], as $\mathbf{d}_{15}$ is well outside the target hypersphere. The search will then move to a new node (Lines 8, 9, 10, and 11). To calculate the distance between the query instance and the hyperplane defined by the node indexing $\mathbf{d}_{15}$ (the boundaryDist function on Line 8), we use only the AGILITY feature as it is the splitting feature at this node. This distance is 2.75, which is greater than *best-distance* (we can see this in Figure 5.10(b)[201], as the hyperplane defined at the node indexing $\mathbf{d}_{15}$ does not intersect with the target hypersphere). This means that the **if** statement on Line 8 fails, and the search moves to the parent of the current node (Line 11).

This new node indexes $\mathbf{d}_{21}$, which is not NULL, so the **while** loop on Line 4 succeeds. The distance between the query instance and $\mathbf{d}_{21}$ is 0.9014, which is less than the value stored in *best-distance* (we can see this in Figure 5.10(b)[201], as $\mathbf{d}_{21}$ is inside the target hypersphere). Consequently, the **if** statement on Line 5 succeeds, and *best* is set to $\mathbf{d}_{21}$, and *best-distance* is set to 0.9014 (Lines 6 and 7). Figure 5.11(a)[203] illustrates the extent of the revised target hypersphere once these updates have been made.

The **if** statement on Line 8, which tests the distance between the query and the hyperplane defined by the current *best* node, is executed next. The distance between the query instance and the hyperplane defined by the node that indexes instance $\mathbf{d}_{21}$ is 0.75 (recall that because the hyperplane at this node is defined by the SPEED value of 6.75, we only compare this to the SPEED value of the query instance, 6.00). This distance is less than the current *best-distance* (in Figure 5.11(a)[203], the hyperplane defined by the node that indexes instance $\mathbf{d}_{21}$ intersects with the target hypersphere). The **if** statement on line 8 will succeed, and the search process will descend down the other branch of the current node (line 9), because there is possibly an instance closer than the current best instance stored down this branch.

It is obvious from Figure 5.11(a)[203] that the search process will not find any instances closer to the query than $\mathbf{d}_{21}$ nor are there any other hyperplanes that intersect with the target hypersphere. So the rest of the search process will involve a descent down to the node, indexing $\mathbf{d}_{18}$ and a direct ascent to the root node where the search process will then terminate and return $\mathbf{d}_{21}$ as the nearest neighbor (we will skip the details of these steps). Figure 5.11(b)[203] illustrates the parts of the *k-d* tree that were checked or pruned during the search process.

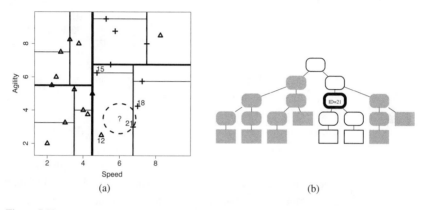

(a)   (b)

Figure 5.11

(a) The target hypersphere after instance $\mathbf{d}_{21}$ has been stored as *best*, and *best-distance* has been updated; (b) the extent of the search process: white nodes were checked by the search process, and the node with the bold outline indexed instance $\mathbf{d}_{21}$, which was returned as the nearest neighbor to the query. Grayed-out branches indicate the portions of the *k-d* tree pruned from the search.

In this example, using a *k-d* tree saved us calculating the distance between the query node and fourteen of the instances in the dataset. This is the benefit of using a *k-d* tree and becomes especially apparent when datasets are very large. However, using a *k-d* tree is not always appropriate; *k-d* trees are reasonably efficient when there are a lot more instances than there are features. As a rough rule of thumb, we should have around 2^m instances for *m* descriptive features. Once this ratio drops, the efficiency of the *k-d* tree diminishes. Other approaches to efficient memory access have been developed, for example, locality sensitive hashing, R-Trees, B-Trees, M-Trees, and VoRTrees among others. All these approaches are similar to *k-d* trees in that they are trying to set up indexes that enable efficient retrieval from a dataset. Obviously, the differences between them make them more or less appropriate for a given dataset, and it often requires some experiments to figure out which is the best one for a given problem.

We can extend this algorithm to retrieve the *k* nearest neighbors by modifying the search to use distance of the kth closest instance found as *best-distance*.

Table 5.5

A dataset listing salary and age information for customers and whether they purchased a product.

ID	SALARY	AGE	PURCH	ID	SALARY	AGE	PURCH
1	53,700	41	no	6	55,900	57	yes
2	65,300	37	no	7	48,600	26	no
3	48,900	45	yes	8	72,800	60	yes
4	64,800	49	yes	9	45,300	34	no
5	44,200	30	no	10	73,200	52	yes

We can also add instances to the tree after if has been created. This is important because one of the key advantages of a nearest neighbor approach is that
it can be updated with new instances as more labeled data arrive. To add a new
instance to the tree, we start at the root node and descend to a leaf node, taking the left or right branch of each node depending on whether the value of
the instance's feature is less than or greater than the splitting value used at the
node. Once we get to a leaf node, we simply add the new instance as either the
left or the right child of the leaf node. Unfortunately, adding nodes in this way
results in the tree becoming unbalanced, which can have a detrimental effect
on the efficiency of the tree. So if we add a lot of new instances, we may find
that the tree has become too unbalanced and that we will need to construct a
new tree from scratch using the extended dataset to restore the efficiency of the
retrieval process.

5.4.3   Data Normalization

A financial institution is planning a direct marketing campaign to sell a pension
product to its customer base. In preparation for this campaign, the financial
institution has decided to create a nearest neighbor model using a Euclidean
distance metric to predict which customers are most likely to respond to direct
marketing. This model will be used to target the marketing campaign only at
those customers that are most likely to purchase the pension product. To train
the model, the institution has created a dataset from the results of previous
marketing campaigns that list customer information—specifically the annual
salary (SALARY) and age (AGE) of the customer—and whether the customer
bought a product after they had been contacted via a direct marketing message
(PURCH). Table 5.5[204] lists a sample from this dataset.

Using this nearest neighbor model, the marketing department wants to
decide whether they should contact a customer with the following profile:

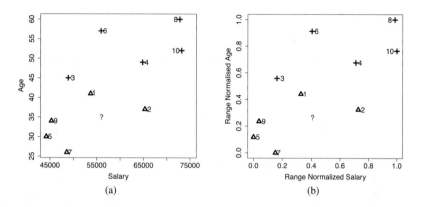

Figure 5.12

(a) The feature space defined by the SALARY and AGE features in Table 5.5[204]; (b) the normalized SALARY and AGE feature space based on the normalized data in Table 5.7[208]. The instances are labeled with their IDs; triangles represent instances with the *no* target level; and crosses represent instances with the *yes* target level. The location of the query SALARY = 56,000, AGE = 35 is indicated by the ?.

SALARY = 56,000 and AGE = 35. Figure 5.12(a)[205] presents a plot of the feature space defined by the SALARY and AGE features, containing the dataset in Table 5.5[204]. The location of the query customer in the feature space is indicated by the ?. From inspecting Figure 5.12(a)[205], it would appear as if instance d_1—which has a target level *no*—is the closest neighbor to the query. So we would expect that the model would predict *no* and that the customer would not be contacted.

The model, however, will actually return a prediction of *yes*, indicating that the customer should be contacted. We can analyze why this happens if we examine the Euclidean distance computations between the query and the instances in the dataset. Table 5.6[207] lists these distances when we include both the SALARY and AGE features, only the SALARY features, and only the AGE feature in the distance calculation. The nearest neighbor model uses both the SALARY and AGE features when it calculates distances to find the nearest neighbor to the query. The SALARY and AGE section of Table 5.6[207] lists these distances and the ranking that the model applies to the instances in the dataset using them. From the rankings we can see that the nearest neighbor to the query is instance d_6 (indicated by its rank of 1). Instance d_6 has a target value of *yes*, and this is why the model will return a positive prediction for the query.

Considering the distribution of the instances in the feature space as depicted in Figure 5.12(a)[205], the result that instance $\mathbf{d}_6$ is the nearest neighbor to the query is surprising. Several other instances appear to be much closer to the query, and importantly, several of these instances have a target level of *no*, for example, instance $\mathbf{d}_1$. Why do we get this strange result?

We can get a hint about what is happening by comparing the distances computed using both the SALARY and AGE features with the distances computed using the SALARY feature only, that listed in the SALARY Only section of Table 5.6[207]. The distances calculated using only the SALARY feature are almost exactly the same as the distances calculated using both the SALARY and AGE features. This is happening because the salary values are much larger than the age values. Consequently, the SALARY feature dominates the computation of the Euclidean distance whether we include the AGE feature or not. As a result, AGE is being virtually ignored by the metric. This dominance is reflected in the ranking of the instances as neighbors. In Table 5.6[207], if we compare the rankings based on SALARY and AGE with the rankings based solely on SALARY, we see that the values in these two columns are identical. The model is using only the SALARY feature and is ignoring the AGE feature when it makes predictions.

This dominance of the distance computation by a feature based solely on the fact that it has a larger range of values than other features is not a good thing. We do not want our model to bias toward a particular feature simply because the values of that feature happen to be large relative to the other features in the dataset. If we allowed this to happen, then our model will be affected by accidental data collection factors, such as the units used to measure something. For example, in a model that is sensitive to the relative size of the feature values, a feature that was measured in millimeters would have a larger effect on the resulting model predictions than a feature that was measured in meters.[14] Clearly we need to address this issue.

Fortunately, we have already discussed the solution to this problem. The problem is caused by features having different **variance**. In Section 3.6.1[92] we discussed variance and introduced a number of **normalization** techniques that

---

14 Figure 5.12(a)[205] further misleads us because when we draw scatter plots, we scale the values to make the plot fit in a square-shaped image. If we were to plot the axis for the SALARY feature to the same scale as the AGE feature in Figure 5.12(a)[205], it would stretch over almost 400 pages.

Table 5.6

The dataset from Table 5.5[204] with the Euclidean distance between each instance and the query SALARY = 56,000, AGE = 35 when we use both the SALARY and AGE features, just the SALARY feature, and just the AGE feature.

	Dataset			SALARY and AGE		SALARY Only		AGE Only	
ID	SALARY	AGE	PURCH	Dist.	Rank	Dist.	Rank	Dist.	Rank
1	53,700	41	no	2,300.0078	2	2,300	2	6	4
2	65,300	37	no	9,300.0002	6	9,300	6	2	2
3	48,900	45	yes	7,100.0070	3	7,100	3	10	6
4	64,800	49	yes	8,800.0111	5	8,800	5	14	7
5	44,200	30	no	11,800.0011	8	11,800	8	5	5
6	55,900	57	yes	102.3914	1	100	1	22	9
7	48,600	26	no	7,400.0055	4	7,400	4	9	3
8	72,800	60	yes	16,800.0186	9	16v800	9	25	10
9	45,300	34	no	10,700.0000	7	10,700	7	1	1
10	73,200	52	yes	17,200.0084	10	17,200	10	17	8

The Rank columns rank the distances of each instance to the query (1 is closest, 10 is furthest away).

normalize the variances in a set of features. The basic normalization technique we introduced was **range normalization**,[15] and we can apply it to the pension plan prediction dataset to normalize the variance in the SALARY and AGE features. For example, range normalization using the range $[0, 1]$ is applied to instance $\mathbf{d}_1$ from Table 5.5[204] as follows:

$$\text{SALARY:} \left(\frac{53,700 - 44,200}{73,200 - 44,200} \right) \times (1.0 - 0.0) + 0 = 0.3276$$

$$\text{AGE:} \quad \left(\frac{41 - 26}{60 - 26} \right) \times (1.0 - 0.0) + 0 \quad = 0.4412$$

Table 5.7[208] lists the dataset from Table 5.5[204] after we have applied range normalization using a range of $[0, 1]$ to the SALARY and AGE features. When we normalize the features in a dataset, we also need to normalize the features in any query instances using the same normalization process and parameters. We

15 For convenience we repeat Equation (3.7)[93] for range normalization here:
$$a'_i = \frac{a_i - min(a)}{max(a) - min(a)} \times (high - low) + low$$

Table 5.7

The updated version of Table 5.6[207] once we have applied range normalization to the SALARY and AGE features in the dataset and to the query instance.

	Normalized Dataset			SALARY and AGE		SALARY Only		AGE Only	
ID	SALARY	AGE	PURCH	Dist.	Rank	Dist.	Rank	Dist.	Rank
1	0.3276	0.4412	no	0.1935	1	0.0793	2	0.17647	4
2	0.7276	0.3235	no	0.3260	2	0.3207	6	0.05882	2
3	0.1621	0.5588	yes	0.3827	5	0.2448	3	0.29412	6
4	0.7103	0.6765	yes	0.5115	7	0.3034	5	0.41176	7
5	0.0000	0.1176	no	0.4327	6	0.4069	8	0.14706	3
6	0.4034	0.9118	yes	0.6471	8	0.0034	1	0.64706	9
7	0.1517	0.0000	no	0.3677	3	0.2552	4	0.26471	5
8	0.9862	1.0000	yes	0.9361	10	0.5793	9	0.73529	10
9	0.0379	0.2353	no	0.3701	4	0.3690	7	0.02941	1
10	1.0000	0.7647	yes	0.7757	9	0.5931	10	0.50000	8

The Rank columns rank the distances of each instance to the query (1 is closest, 10 is furthest away).

normalize the query instance with SALARY =56,000 and AGE = 35 as follows:

$$\text{SALARY:} \left(\frac{56{,}000 - 44{,}200}{73{,}200 - 44{,}200} \right) \times (1.0 - 0.0) + 0 = 0.4069$$

$$\text{AGE:} \quad \left(\frac{35 - 26}{60 - 26} \right) \times (1.0 - 0.0) + 0 \quad = 0.2647$$

Figure 5.12(b)[205] shows a plot of the feature space after the features have been normalized. The major difference between Figure 5.12(a)[205] and Figure 5.12(b)[205] is that the axes are scaled differently. In Figure 5.12(a)[205] the SALARY axis ranged from 45,000 to 75,000, and the AGE axis ranged from 25 to 60. In Figure 5.12(b)[205], however, both axes range from 0 to 1. Although this may seem like an insignificant difference, the fact that both features now cover the same range has a huge impact on the performance of a similarity-based prediction model that uses this data.

Table 5.7[208] also repeats the calculations from Table 5.6[207] using the normalized dataset and the normalized query instance. In contrast with Table 5.6[207], where there was a close match between the SALARY and AGE distances and the SALARY only distances and related rankings, in Table 5.7[208] there is much more variation between the SALARY and AGE distances and the SALARY only distances. This increased variation is mirrored in the fact that the rankings based on the distances calculated using the SALARY and AGE features are quite different from the rankings based on the distances calculated using SALARY only. These changes in the rankings of the instances is a direct result of normalizing the features and reflects the fact that the distance calculations are no longer dominated by the SALARY feature. The nearest neighbor model is now factoring both SALARY and AGE into the ranking of the instances. The net effect of this is that instance $\mathbf{d}_1$ is now ranked as the nearest neighbor to the query—this is in line with the feature space representation in Figure 5.12(b)[205]. Instance $\mathbf{d}_1$ has a target level of *no*, so the nearest neighbor model now predicts a target level of *no* for the query, meaning that the marketing department won't include the customer in their list of direct marketing prospects. This is the opposite of the prediction made using the original dataset.

In summary, distance computations are sensitive to the value ranges of the features in the dataset. This is something we need to control for when we are creating a model, as otherwise we are allowing an unwanted bias to affect the learning process. When we normalize the features in a dataset, we control for the variation across the variances of features and ensure that each feature can contribute equally to the distance metric. Normalizing the data is an important thing to do for almost all machine learning algorithms, not just nearest neighbor.

5.4.4   Predicting Continuous Targets

It is relatively easy to adapt the k nearest neighbor approach to handle continuous target features. To do this we simply change the approach to return a prediction of the average target value of the nearest neighbors, rather than the majority target level. The prediction for a continuous target feature by a k nearest neighbor model is therefore

$$\mathbb{M}_k(\mathbf{q}) = \frac{1}{k} \sum_{i=1}^{k} t_i \tag{5.7}$$

where $\mathbb{M}_k(\mathbf{q})$ is the prediction returned by the model using parameter value k for the query $\mathbf{q}$, i iterates over the k nearest neighbors to $\mathbf{q}$ in the dataset, and t_i is the value of the target feature for instance i.

Let's look at an example. Imagine that we are dealers in rare whiskey, and we would like some assistance in setting the reserve price for bottles of whiskey that we are selling at auction. We can use a k nearest neighbor model to predict the likely sale price of a bottle of whiskey based on the prices achieved by

Table 5.8

A dataset of whiskeys listing the age (in years), the rating (between 1 and 5, with 5 being the best), and the bottle price of each whiskey.

ID	AGE	RATING	PRICE	ID	AGE	RATING	PRICE
1	0	2	30.00	11	19	5	500.00
2	12	3.5	40.00	12	6	4.5	200.00
3	10	4	55.00	13	8	3.5	65.00
4	21	4.5	550.00	14	22	4	120.00
5	12	3	35.00	15	6	2	12.00
6	15	3.5	45.00	16	8	4.5	250.00
7	16	4	70.00	17	10	2	18.00
8	18	3	85.00	18	30	4.5	450.00
9	18	3.5	78.00	19	1	1	10.00
10	16	3	75.00	20	4	3	30.00

similar bottles at previous auctions.[16] Table 5.8[210] lists a dataset of whiskeys described by the RATING they were given in popular whiskey enthusiasts magazine and their AGE (in years). The PRICE achieved at auction by the each bottle is also included.

One thing that is immediately apparent in Table 5.8[210] is that the AGE and RATING features have different ranges. We should normalize these features before we build a model. Table 5.9[211] lists the whiskey dataset after the descriptive features have been normalized, using range normalization to the range $[0, 1]$.

Let's now make a prediction using this model for a 2-year-old bottle of whiskey that received a magazine rating of 5. Having normalized the dataset, we first need to normalize the descriptive feature values of this query instance using the same normalization process. This results in a query with AGE = 0.0667 and RATING = 1.00. For this example we set $k = 3$. Figure 5.13[212] shows the neighborhood that this defines around the query instance. The three closest neighbors to the query are instances $\mathbf{d}_{12}$, $\mathbf{d}_{16}$ and $\mathbf{d}_3$. Consequently, the model will return a price prediction that is the average price of these three

---

16 The example given here is based on artificial data generated for the purposes of this book. Predicting the prices of assets such as whiskey or wine using machine learning is, however, done in reality. For example, Ashenfelter (2008) deals with predicting wine prices and was covered in Ayres (2008).

Table 5.9
The whiskey dataset after the descriptive features have been normalized.

ID	AGE	RATING	PRICE	ID	AGE	RATING	PRICE
1	0.0000	0.25	30.00	11	0.6333	1.00	500.00
2	0.4000	0.63	40.00	12	0.2000	0.88	200.00
3	0.3333	0.75	55.00	13	0.2667	0.63	65.00
4	0.7000	0.88	550.00	14	0.7333	0.75	120.00
5	0.4000	0.50	35.00	15	0.2000	0.25	12.00
6	0.5000	0.63	45.00	16	0.2667	0.88	250.00
7	0.5333	0.75	70.00	17	0.3333	0.25	18.00
8	0.6000	0.50	85.00	18	1.0000	0.88	450.00
9	0.6000	0.63	78.00	19	0.0333	0.00	10.00
10	0.5333	0.50	75.00	20	0.1333	0.50	30.00

neighbors:

$$\mathbb{M}_3(\langle 0.0667, 1.00 \rangle) = \frac{200.00 + 250.00 + 55.00}{3} = 168.33$$

We can also use a **weighted k nearest neighbor** model to make predictions for continuous targets that take into account the distance from the query instance to the neighbors (just like we did for categorical target features in Section 5.4.1[190]). To do this, the model prediction equation in Equation (5.7)[209] is changed to

$$\mathbb{M}_k(\mathbf{q}) = \frac{\sum_{i=1}^{k} \frac{1}{dist(\mathbf{q}, \mathbf{d}_i)^2} \times t_i}{\sum_{i=1}^{k} \frac{1}{dist(\mathbf{q}, \mathbf{d}_i)^2}} \tag{5.8}$$

where $dist(\mathbf{q}, \mathbf{d}_i)$ is the distance between the query instance and its ith nearest neighbor. This is a weighted average of the target values of the k nearest neighbors, as opposed to the simple average in Equation (5.7)[209].

Table 5.10[213] shows the calculation of the numerator and denominator of Equation (5.8)[211] for our whiskey bottle example, using the normalized dataset with k set to 20 (the full size of the dataset). The final prediction for the price of the bottle of whiskey we plan to sell is

$$\frac{16{,}249.85}{99.2604} = 163.71$$

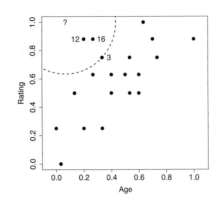

Figure 5.13

The AGE and RATING feature space for the whiskey dataset. The location of the query instance is indicated by the ? symbol. The circle plotted with a dashed line demarcates the border of the neighborhood around the query when $k = 3$. The three nearest neighbors to the query are labeled with their ID values.

The predictions using the $k = 3$ nearest neighbor model and the weighted k nearest neighbor model with k set to the size of the dataset are quite similar: 168.33 and 163.71. So, which model is making the better prediction? In this instance, to find out which model is best, we would really need to put the bottle of whiskey up for auction and see which model predicted the closest price. In situations where we have a larger dataset, however, we could perform evaluation experiments[17] to see which value of k leads to the best performing model. In general, standard k nearest neighbor models and weighted k nearest neighbor models will produce very similar results when a feature space is well populated. For datasets that only sparsely populate the feature space, however, weighted k nearest neighbor models usually make more accurate predictions as they take into account the fact that some of the *nearest* neighbors can actually be quite far away.

5.4.5   Other Measures of Similarity

So far we have discussed and used the Minkowski-based Euclidean and Manhattan distance metrics to compute the similarity between instances in a

---

17 These will be covered in Section 8.4.1[405].

Table 5.10

The calculations for the weighted k nearest neighbor prediction.

ID	PRICE	Distance	Weight	PRICE × Weight
1	30.00	0.7530	1.7638	52.92
2	40.00	0.5017	3.9724	158.90
3	55.00	0.3655	7.4844	411.64
4	550.00	0.6456	2.3996	1319.78
5	35.00	0.6009	2.7692	96.92
6	45.00	0.5731	3.0450	137.03
7	70.00	0.5294	3.5679	249.75
8	85.00	0.7311	1.8711	159.04
9	78.00	0.6520	2.3526	183.50
10	75.00	0.6839	2.1378	160.33
11	500.00	0.5667	3.1142	1557.09
12	200.00	0.1828	29.9376	5987.53
13	65.00	0.4250	5.5363	359.86
14	120.00	0.7120	1.9726	236.71
15	12.00	0.7618	1.7233	20.68
16	250.00	0.2358	17.9775	4494.38
17	18.00	0.7960	1.5783	28.41
18	450.00	0.9417	1.1277	507.48
19	10.00	1.0006	0.9989	9.99
20	30.00	0.5044	3.9301	117.90
		Totals:	99.2604	16,249.85

dataset. There are, however, many other ways in which the similarity between instances can be measured. In this section we introduce some alternative measures of similarity and discuss when it is appropriate to use them. Any of these measures of similarity can simply replace the Euclidean measure we used in our demonstrations of the nearest neighbor algorithm.

Throughout this section we use the terms similarity and distance almost interchangeably, because we often judge the similarity between two instances in terms of the distance between them in a feature space. The only difference to keep in mind is that when we use distances, smaller values mean that instances are closer together in a feature space, whereas when we use similarities, larger values indicate this. We will, however, be specific in distinguishing between **metrics** and **indexes**. Recall that in Section 5.2.2[183] we defined four criteria that a metric must satisfy: **non-negativity**, **identity**, **symmetry**, and **triangular inequality**. It is possible, however, to successfully use measures of similarity in similarity-based models that do not satisfy all four of these criteria. We refer to measures of similarity of this type as **indexes**. Most of the time the technical distinction between a metric and an index is not that important; we simply focus on choosing the right measure of similarity for the type of instances we are comparing. It is important, however, to know if a measure is a metric or an index as there are some similarity-based techniques that strictly require measures of similarity to be metrics. For example, the *k-d* **trees** described in Section 5.4.2[195] require that the measure of similarity used be a metric (in particular that the measure conform to the triangular inequality constraint).

5.4.5.1   Similarity Indexes for Binary Descriptive Features

There are lots of datasets that contain binary descriptive features—categorical features that have only two levels. For example, a dataset may record whether or not someone liked a movie, a customer bought a product, or someone visited a particular webpage. If the descriptive features in a dataset are binary, it is often a good idea to use a **similarity index** that defines similarity between instances specifically in terms of **co-presence** or **co-absence** of features, rather than an index based on distance.

To illustrate a series of similarity indexes for binary descriptive features, we will use an example of predicting **upsell** in an online service. A common business model for online services is to allow users a free trial period after which time they have to *sign up* to a paid account to continue using the service. These businesses often try to predict the likelihood that users coming to the end of the trial period will accept the upsell offer to move to the paid service. This insight into the likely future behavior of a customer can help a marketing department decide which customers coming close to the end of their trial period the department should contact to promote the benefits of signup to the paid service.

Table 5.11[215] lists a small binary dataset that a nearest neighbor model could use to make predictions for this scenario. The descriptive features in this dataset are all binary and record the following information about the behavior of past customers:

- PROFILE: Did the user complete the profile form when registering for the free trial?
- FAQ: Did the user read the frequently asked questions page?
- HELPFORUM: Did the user post a question on the help forum?

Table 5.11

A binary dataset listing the behavior of two individuals on a website during a trial period and whether they subsequently signed up for the website.

ID	PROFILE	FAQ	HELPFORUM	NEWSLETTER	LIKED	SIGNUP
1	true	true	true	false	true	yes
2	true	false	false	false	false	no

- NEWSLETTER: Did the user sign up for the weekly newsletter?
- LIKED: Did the user *Like* the website on Facebook?

The target feature, SIGNUP, indicates whether the customers ultimately signed up to the paid service or not (*yes* or *no*).

The business has decided to use a nearest neighbor model to predict whether a current trial user whose free trial period is about the end is likely to sign up for the paid service. The query instance, q, describing this user is:

$$\text{PROFILE} = true, \text{FAQ} = false, \text{HELPFORUM} = true,$$
$$\text{NEWSLETTER} = false, \text{LIKED} = false$$

Table 5.12[216] presents a pairwise analysis of similarity between the current trial user, q, and the two customers in the dataset in Table 5.11[215] in terms of

- **co-presence** (CP), how often a true value occurred for the same feature in both the query data q and the data for the comparison user (d_1 or d_2)
- **co-absence** (CA), how often a false value occurred for the same feature in both the query data q and the data for the comparison user (d_1 or d_2)
- **presence-absence** (PA), how often a true value occurred in the query data q when a false value occurred in the data for the comparison user (d_1 or d_2) for the same feature
- **absence-presence** (AP), how often a false value occurred in the query data q when a true value occurred in the data for the comparison user (d_1 or d_2) for the same feature

One way of judging similarity is to focus solely on co-presence. For example, in an online retail setting, co-presence could capture what two users jointly viewed, liked, or bought. The **Russel-Rao** similarity index focuses on this and is measured in terms of the ratio between the number of co-presences and the

Table 5.12

The similarity between the current trial user, **q**, and the two users in the dataset, d_1 and d_2, in terms of co-presence (CP), co-absence (CA), presence-absence (PA), and absence-presence (AP).

		q					**q**	
		Pres.	Abs.				Pres.	Abs.
d_1	Pres.	CP = 2	PA = 0		d_2	Pres.	CP = 1	PA = 1
	Abs.	AP = 2	CA = 1			Abs.	AP = 0	CA = 3

total number of binary features considered:

$$sim_{RR}(\mathbf{q}, \mathbf{d}) = \frac{CP(\mathbf{q}, \mathbf{d})}{|\mathbf{q}|} \tag{5.9}$$

where **q** and **d** are two instances, $|\mathbf{q}|$ is the total number of features in the dataset, and $CP(\mathbf{q}, \mathbf{d})$ measures the total number of co-presences between **q** and **d**. Using Russel-Rao, **q** has a higher similarity to d_1 than to d_2:

$$sim_{RR}(\mathbf{q}, \mathbf{d_1}) = \frac{2}{5} = 0.4$$

$$sim_{RR}(\mathbf{q}, \mathbf{d_2}) = \frac{1}{5} = 0.2$$

This means that the current trial user is judged to be more similar to the customer represented by instance d_1 than the customer represented by instance d_2.

In some domains co-absence is important. For example, in a medical domain when judging the similarity between two patients, it may be as important to capture the fact that neither patient had a particular symptom as it is to capture the symptoms that the patients have in common. The **Sokal-Michener** similarity index takes this into account and is defined as the ratio between the total number of co-presences and co-absences and the total number of binary features considered:

$$sim_{SM}(\mathbf{q}, \mathbf{d}) = \frac{CP(\mathbf{q}, \mathbf{d}) + CA(\mathbf{q}, \mathbf{d})}{|\mathbf{q}|} \tag{5.10}$$

Using Sokal-Michener for our online services example $\mathbf{q}$, is judged to be more similar to instance $\mathbf{d}_2$ than instance $\mathbf{d}_1$:

$$sim_{SM}(\mathbf{q}, \mathbf{d}_1) = \frac{3}{5} = 0.6$$

$$sim_{SM}(\mathbf{q}, \mathbf{d}_2) = \frac{4}{5} = 0.8$$

Sometimes, however, co-absences aren't that meaningful. For example, we may be in a retail domain in which there are so many items that most people haven't seen, listened to, bought, or visited the vast majority of them, and as a result, the majority of features will be co-absences. The technical term to describe a dataset in which most of the features have zero values is **sparse data**. In these situations we should use a metric that ignores co-absences. The **Jaccard** similarity index is often used in these contexts. This index ignores co-absences and is defined as the ratio between the number of co-presences and the total number of features, excluding those that record a co-absence between a pair of instances:[18]

$$sim_J(\mathbf{q}, \mathbf{d}) = \frac{CP(\mathbf{q}, \mathbf{d})}{CP(\mathbf{q}, \mathbf{d}) + PA(\mathbf{q}, \mathbf{d}) + AP(\mathbf{q}, \mathbf{d})} \tag{5.11}$$

Using Jaccard similarity, the current trial user in the online retail example is judged to be equally similar to instance $\mathbf{d}_1$ and $\mathbf{d}_2$:

$$sim_J(\mathbf{q}, \mathbf{d}_1) = \frac{2}{4} = 0.5$$

$$sim_J(\mathbf{q}, \mathbf{d}_2) = \frac{1}{2} = 0.5$$

The fact that the judgment of similarity between current trial user and the other users in the dataset changed dramatically depending on which similarity index was employed illustrates the importance of choosing the correct index for the task. Unfortunately, beyond highlighting that the Jaccard index is useful for sparse binary data, we cannot give a hard and fast rule for how to choose between these indexes. As is so often the case in predictive analytics, making the right choice requires an understanding of the requirements of the task that

---

18 One note of caution. The Jaccard similarity index is undefined for pairs of instances where all the features manifest co-absence as this leads to a division by zero.

we are trying to accomplish and matching these requirements with the features
we want to emphasize in our model.

5.4.5.2   Cosine Similarity

Cosine similarity is an index that can be used as a measure of the similarity
between instances with continuous descriptive features. The cosine similarity
between two instances is the **cosine** of the inner angle between the two **vectors** that extend from the origin of a feature space to each instance. Figure
5.14(a)[220] illustrates the inner angle, θ, between the vector from the origin to
two instances in a feature space defined by two descriptive features, SMS and
VOICE.

Cosine similarity is an especially useful measure of similarity when the
descriptive features describing instances in a dataset are related to each other.
For example, in a mobile telecoms scenario, we could represent customers with
just two descriptive features: the average number of SMS messages a customer
sends per month, and the average number of VOICE calls a customer makes
per month. In this scenario it is interesting to take a perspective on the similarity between customers that focuses on the mix of these two types of services
they use, rather than the volumes of the services they use. Cosine similarity
allows us to do this. The instances shown in Figure 5.14(a)[220] are based on this
mobile telecoms scenario. The descriptive feature values for $\mathbf{d}_1$ are SMS = 97
and VOICE = 21, and for $\mathbf{d}_2$ are SMS = 181 and VOICE = 184.

We compute the cosine similarity between two instances as the normalized
dot product of the descriptive feature values of the instances. The dot product
is normalized by the product of the lengths of the descriptive feature value
vectors.[19] The dot product of two instances, $\mathbf{a}$ and $\mathbf{b}$, defined by m descriptive
features is

$$\mathbf{a} \cdot \mathbf{b} = \sum_{i=1}^{m} (\mathbf{a}[i] \times \mathbf{b}[i]) = (\mathbf{a}[1] \times \mathbf{b}[1]) + \cdots + (\mathbf{a}[m] \times \mathbf{b}[m]) \qquad (5.12)$$

---

19 The length of a vector, $|\mathbf{a}|$, is computed as the square root of the sum of the elements of the
vector squared: $|\mathbf{a}| = \sum_{i=1}^{m} \mathbf{a}[i]^2$.

Geometrically, the dot product can be interpreted as equivalent to the cosine of the angle between the two vectors multiplied by the length of the two vectors:

$$\mathbf{a} \cdot \mathbf{b} = \sqrt{\sum_{i=1}^{m} \mathbf{a}[i]^2} \times \sqrt{\sum_{i=1}^{m} \mathbf{b}[i]^2} \times cos(\theta) \qquad (5.13)$$

We can rearrange Equation (5.13)[219] to calculate the cosine of the inner angle between two vectors as the normalized dot product:

$$\frac{\mathbf{a} \cdot \mathbf{b}}{\sqrt{\sum_{i=1}^{m} \mathbf{a}[i]^2} \times \sqrt{\sum_{i=1}^{m} \mathbf{b}[i]^2}} = cos(\theta) \qquad (5.14)$$

So, in an m-dimensional feature space, the cosine similarity between two instances $\mathbf{a}$ and $\mathbf{b}$ is defined as

$$
\begin{aligned}
sim_{COSINE}(\mathbf{a}, \mathbf{b}) &= \frac{\mathbf{a} \cdot \mathbf{b}}{\sqrt{\sum_{i=1}^{m} \mathbf{a}[i]^2} \times \sqrt{\sum_{i=1}^{m} \mathbf{b}[i]^2}} \\
&= \frac{\sum_{i=1}^{m} (\mathbf{a}[i] \times \mathbf{b}[i])}{\sqrt{\sum_{i=1}^{m} \mathbf{a}[i]^2} \times \sqrt{\sum_{i=1}^{m} \mathbf{b}[i]^2}}
\end{aligned}
\qquad (5.15)
$$

The cosine similarity between instances will be in the range $[0, 1]$, where 1 indicates maximum similarity and 0 indicates maximum dissimilarity.[20] We can calculate the cosine similarity between $\mathbf{d}_1$ and $\mathbf{d}_2$ from Figure 5.14(a)[220] as

$$
\begin{aligned}
sim_{COSINE}(\mathbf{d}_1, \mathbf{d}_1) &= \frac{(97 \times 181) + (21 \times 184)}{\sqrt{97^2 + 21^2} \times \sqrt{181^2 + 184^2}} \\
&= 0.8362
\end{aligned}
$$

20 If either vector used to calculate a cosine similarity contains negative feature values, then the cosine similarity will actually be in the range $[-1, 1]$. As before, 1 indicates high similarity, and 0 indicates dissimilarity, but it can be difficult to interpret negative similarity scores. Negative similarity values can be avoided, however, if we use range normalization (see Section 3.6.1[92]) to ensure that descriptive feature values always remain positive.

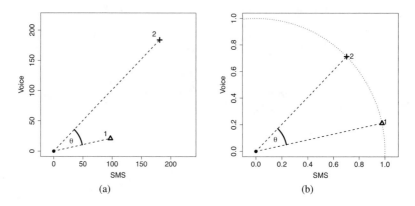

Figure 5.14

(a) The θ represents the inner angle between the vector emanating from the origin to instance $\mathbf{d}_1$ and the vector emanating from the origin to instance $\mathbf{d}_2$; (b) shows $\mathbf{d}_1$ and $\mathbf{d}_2$ normalized to the unit circle.

Figure 5.14(b)[220] highlights the normalization of descriptive feature values that takes place as part of calculating cosine similarity. This is different from the normalization we have looked at elsewhere in this chapter as it takes place within an instance rather than across all the values of a feature. All instances are normalized so as to lie on a **hypersphere** of radius 1.0 with its center at the origin of the feature space. This normalization is what makes cosine similarity so useful in scenarios in which we are interested in the relative spread of values across a set of descriptive features rather than the magnitudes of the values themselves. For example, if we have a third instance with SMS = 194 and VOICE = 42, the cosine similarity between this instance and $\mathbf{d}_1$ will be 1.0, because even though the magnitudes of their feature values are different, the relationship between the feature values for both instances is the same: both customers use about four times as many SMS messages as VOICE calls. Cosine similarity is also an appropriate similarity index for sparse data with non-binary features (i.e., datasets with lots of zero values) because the dot product will essentially ignore co-absences in its computation ($0 \times 0 = 0$).

5.4.5.3 Mahalanobis Distance

The final measure of similarity that we will introduce is the **Mahalanobis distance**, which is a metric that can be used to measure the similarity between instances with continuous descriptive features. The Mahalanobis distance is different from the other distance metrics we have looked at because it allows us to take into account how spread out the instances in a dataset are when judging similarities. Figure 5.15[221] illustrates why this is important. This figure shows scatter plots for three bivariate datasets that have the same central tendency, marked A and located in the feature space at $(50, 50)$, but whose instances are spread out differently across the feature space. In all three cases the question we would like to answer is, are instance B, located at at $(30, 70)$, and instance C, located at $(70, 70)$, likely to be from the same population from which the dataset has been sampled? In all three figures, B and C are equidistant from A based on Euclidean distance.

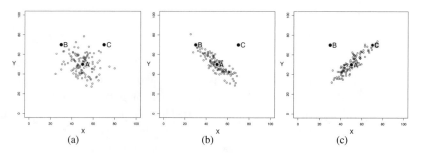

Figure 5.15

Scatter plots of three bivariate datasets with the same center point A and two queries B and C both equidistant from A; (a) a dataset uniformly spread around the center point; (b) a dataset with negative covariance; and (c) a dataset with positive covariance.

The dataset in Figure 5.15(a)[221] is equally distributed in all directions around A, and as a result, we can say that B and C are equally likely to be from the same population as the dataset. The dataset in Figure 5.15(b)[221], however, demonstrates a strong negative **covariance**[21] between the features. In this context, instance B is much more likely to be a member of the dataset than instance C. Figure 5.15(c)[221] shows a dataset with a strong positive covariance, and for this dataset, instance C is much more likely to be a member than instance B.

---

21 Covariance between features means that knowing the value of one feature tells us something about the value of the other feature. See Section 3.5.2[86] for more information.

What these examples demonstrate is that when we are trying to decide whether a query belongs to a group, we need to consider not only the central tendency of the group, but also how spread out the members in a group are. These examples also highlight that covariance is one way of measuring the spread of a dataset.

The Mahalanobis distance uses covariance to scale distances so that distances along a direction where the dataset is very spread out are scaled down, and distances along directions where the dataset is tightly packed are scaled up. For example, in Figure 5.15(b)[221] the Mahalanobis distance between B and A will be less than the Mahalanobis distance between C and A, whereas in Figure 5.15(c)[221] the opposite will be true. The Mahalanobis distance is defined as

$$Mahalanobis(\mathbf{a}, \mathbf{b}) =$$

$$\sqrt{\left[\mathbf{a}\,[1] - \mathbf{b}\,[1]\,, \ldots, \mathbf{a}\,[m] - \mathbf{b}\,[m]\right] \times \sum\nolimits^{-1} \times \begin{bmatrix} \mathbf{a}\,[1] - \mathbf{b}\,[1] \\ \vdots \\ \mathbf{a}\,[m] - \mathbf{b}\,[m] \end{bmatrix}} \qquad (5.16)$$

Let's step through Equation (5.16)[222] bit by bit. First, this equation computes a distance between two instances $\mathbf{a}$ and $\mathbf{b}$, each with m descriptive features. The first big term we come to in the equation is $\left[\mathbf{a}\,[1] - \mathbf{b}\,[1]\,, \ldots, \mathbf{a}\,[m] - \mathbf{b}\,[m]\right]$. This is a row vector that is created by subtracting each descriptive feature value of instance $\mathbf{b}$ from the corresponding feature values of $\mathbf{a}$. The next term in the equation, $\sum^{-1}$, represents the **inverse covariance matrix**[22] computed across all instances in the dataset. Multiplying the difference in feature values by the inverse covariance matrix has two effects. First, the larger the **variance** of a feature, the less weight the difference between the values for that feature will contribute to the distance calculation. Second, the larger the correlation between two features, the less weight they contribute to the distance. The final

---

22 We explain **covariance matrices** in Section 3.5.2[86]. The **inverse covariance matrix** is the matrix such that when the covariance matrix is multiplied by its inverse, the result is the **identity matrix**: $\sum \times \sum^{-1} = \mathbb{I}$. The identity matrix is a square matrix in which all the elements of the main diagonal are 1, and all other elements are 0. Multiplying any matrix by the identity matrix leaves the original matrix unchanged—this is the equivalent of multiplying by 1 for real numbers. So the effect of multiplying feature values be an inverse covariance matrix is to rescale the variances of all features to 1 and to set the covariance between all feature pairs to 0. Calculating the inverse of a matrix involves solving systems of linear equations and requires the use of techniques from linear algebra such as **Gauss-Jordan elimination** or **LU decomposition**. We do not cover these techniques here, but they are covered in most standard linear algebra textbooks such as Anton and Rorres (2010).

element of the equation is a column vector that is created in the same way as the row vector at the beginning of the equation—by subtracting each feature value from **b** from the corresponding feature value from **a**. The motivation for using a row vector to hold one copy of the feature differences and a column vector to hold the second copy of the features differences is to facilitate matrix multiplication. Now that we know that the row and column vector both contain the difference between the feature values of the two instances, it should be clear that, similar to Euclidean distance, the Mahalanobis distance squares the differences of the features. The Mahalanobis distance, however, also rescales the differences between feature values (using the inverse covariance matrix) so that all the features have unit variance, and the effects of covariance are removed.

The Mahalanobis distance can be understood as defining an orthonormal coordinate system with (1) an origin at the instance we are calculating the distance from (**a** in Equation (5.16)[222]); (2) a primary axis aligned with the direction of the greatest spread in the dataset; and (3) the units of all the axes scaled so that the dataset has unit variance along each axis. The rotation and scaling of the axes are the result of the multiplication by the inverse covariance matrix of the dataset ($\sum^{-1}$). So, if the inverse covariance matrix is the identity matrix $\mathbb{I}$, then no scaling or rotation occurs. This is why for datasets such as the one depicted in Figure 5.15(a)[221], where there is no covariance between the features, the Mahalanobis distance is simply the Euclidean distance.[23]

Figure 5.16[224] illustrates how the Mahalanobis distance defines this coordinate system, which is translated, rotated, and scaled with respect to the standard coordinates of a feature space. The three scatter plots in this image are of the dataset in Figure 5.15(c)[221]. In each case we have overlaid the coordinate system defined by the Mahalanobis distance from a different origin. The origins used for the figures were (a) $(50, 50)$, (b) $(63, 71)$, and (c) $(42, 35)$. The dashed lines plot the axes of the coordinate system, and the ellipses plot the 1, 3, and 5 unit distance contours. Notice how the orientation of the axes and the scaling of the distance contours are consistent across the figures. This is because the same inverse covariance matrix based on the entire dataset was used in each case.

---

23 The inverse of the identity matrix $\mathbb{I}$ is $\mathbb{I}$. So, if there is no covariance between the features, both the covariance and the inverse covariance matrix will be equal to $\mathbb{I}$.

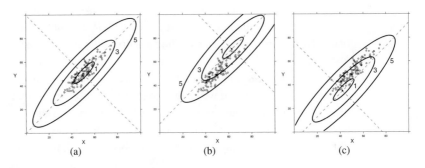

Figure 5.16
The coordinate systems defined by the Mahalanobis distance using the co-variance matrix for the dataset in Figure 5.15(c)[221] using three different origins: (a) $(50, 50)$, (b) $(63, 71)$, (c) $(42, 35)$. The ellipses in each figure plot the 1, 3, and 5 unit distance contours.

Let's return to the original question depicted in Figure 5.15[221]: Are B and C likely to be from the same population from which the dataset has been sampled? Focusing on Figure 5.15(c)[221], for this dataset it appears reasonable to conclude that instance C is a member of the dataset but that B is probably not. To confirm this intuition we can calculate the Mahalanobis distance between A and B and A and C using Equation (5.16)[222] as

$$Mahalanobis(A, B)$$

$$= \sqrt{[50 - 30, 50 - 70] \times \begin{bmatrix} 0.059 & -0.521 \\ -0.521 & 0.0578 \end{bmatrix} \times \begin{bmatrix} 50 - 30 \\ 50 - 70 \end{bmatrix}}$$

$$= 9.4049$$

$$Mahalanobis(A, C)$$

$$= \sqrt{[50 - 70, 50 - 70] \times \begin{bmatrix} 0.059 & -0.521 \\ -0.521 & 0.0578 \end{bmatrix} \times \begin{bmatrix} 50 - 70 \\ 50 - 70 \end{bmatrix}}$$

$$= 2.2540$$

where the inverse covariance matrix used in the calculations is based on the covariance matrix[24] calculated directly from the dataset: $\begin{bmatrix} 82.39 & 74.26 \\ 74.26 & 84.22 \end{bmatrix}$

Figure 5.17[225] shows a contour plot of these Mahalanobis distances. In this figure, A indicates the central tendency of the dataset in Figure 5.15(c)[221], and the ellipses plot the Mahalanobis distance contours that the distances from A to the instances B and C lie on. These distance contours were calculated using the inverse covariance matrix for the dataset and point A as the origin. The result is that instance C is much closer to A than B and so should be considered a member of the same population as this dataset.

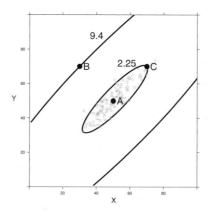

Figure 5.17

The effect of using a Mahalanobis versus Euclidean distance. A marks the central tendency of the dataset in Figure 5.15(c)[221]. The ellipses plot the Mahalanobis distance contours from A that B and C lie on. In Euclidean terms, B and C are equidistant from A; however, using the Mahalanobis distance, C is much closer to A than B.

To use Mahalanobis distance in a nearest neighbor model, we simply use the model in exactly the same way as described previously but substitute Mahalanobis distance for Euclidean distance.

5.4.5.4   Summary

In this section we have introduced a number of commonly used metrics and indexes for judging similarity between instances in a feature space. These are

---

24 Section 3.5.2[86] describes the calculation of covariance matrices. The inverse covariance matrix was calculated using the *solve* function from the **R** programming language.

typically used in situations where a Minkowski distance is not appropriate. For example, if we are dealing with binary features, it may be more appropriate to use the Russel-Rao, Sokal-Michener or Jaccard similarity metric. Or it may be that the features in the dataset are continuous—typically indicating that a Minkowski distance metric is appropriate—but that the majority of the descriptive features for each instance have zero values,[25] in which case we may want to use a similarity index that ignores descriptive features with zero values in both features, for example, **cosine similarity**. Alternatively, we may be dealing with a dataset where there is covariance between the descriptive features, in which case we should consider using the **Mahalanobis distance** as our measure of similarity. There are many other indexes and metrics we could have presented, for example, **Tanimoto similarity** (which is a generalization of the Jaccard similarity to non-binary data), and **correlation**-based approaches such as the **Pearson correlation**. The key things to remember, however, are that it is important to choose a similarity metric or index that is appropriate for the properties of the dataset we are using (be it binary, non-binary, sparse, covariant, etc.) and second, experimentation is always required to determine which measure of similarity will be most effective for a specific prediction model.

5.4.6   Feature Selection

Intuitively, adding more descriptive features to a dataset provides more information about each instance and should result in more accurate predictive models. Surprisingly, however, the number of descriptive features in a dataset increases, there often comes a point at which continuing to add new features to the dataset results in a decrease in the predictive power of the induced models. The reason for this phenomenon is that, fundamentally, the predictive power of an induced model is based on one of the following:

1. Partitioning the feature space into regions based on clusters of training instances with the same target value, and assigning a query located in a region the target value of the cluster that defines that region.

---

25 Recall that a dataset where the majority of descriptive features have zero as the value is known as **sparse data**. This often occurs in **document classification** problems, when a **bag-of-words** representation is used to represent documents as the frequency of occurrence of each word in a dictionary (the eponymous bag-of-words). The bag-of-words representation is covered more in Question 2[240] at the end of this chapter. One problem with sparse data is that with so few non-zero values, the variation between two instances may be dominated by noise.

2. Assigning a query a target value interpolated (for instance, by majority vote or average) from the target values of individual training instances that are near the query in the feature space.

Both of these strategies depend on a reasonable **sampling density** of the training instances across the feature space. The sampling density is the average density of training instances across the feature space. If the sampling density is too low, then large regions of the feature space do not contain any training instances, and it doesn't make sense to associate such a region with any cluster of training instances nor to look for training instances that are nearby. In such instances a model is essentially reduced to guessing predictions. We can measure the **sampling density** across a feature space in terms of the average density of a **unit hypercube**[26] in the feature space. The density of a unit hypercube is equal to

$$density = k^{\left(\frac{1}{m}\right)} \qquad (5.17)$$

where k is the number of instances inside the hypercube, and m is the number of dimensions of the feature space.

Figure 5.18[229] provides a graphical insight into the relationship between the number of descriptive features in a dataset and the sampling density of the feature space. Figure 5.18(a)[229] plots a one-dimensional dataset consisting of 29 instances spread evenly between 0.0 and 3.0. We have marked the unit hypercube covering the interval 0 to 1 in this figure. The density of this unit hypercube is $10^{\frac{1}{1}} = 10$ (there are 10 instances inside the hypercube). If we increase the number of descriptive features, the dimensionality of the feature space increases. Figures 5.18(b)[229] and 5.18(c)[229] illustrate what happens if we increase the number of descriptive features in a dataset but do not increase the number of instances. In Figure 5.18(b)[229] we have added a second descriptive feature, Y, and assigned each of the instances in the dataset a random Y value in the range $[0.0, 3.0]$. The instances have moved away from each other, and the sampling density has decreased. The density of the marked unit hypercube is now $4^{\frac{1}{2}} = 2$ (there are only 4 instances inside the hypercube). Figure 5.18(c)[229] illustrates the distribution of the original 29 instances when we move to a three-dimensional feature space (each instance has been given a random value in the range $[0.0, 3.0]$ for the Z feature). It is evident that the instances are getting

---

26 A hypercube is a generalization of the geometric concept of a cube across multiple dimensions. So in a two-dimensional space, the term hypercube denotes a square, in three-dimensional space, it denotes a cube, and so on. A unit hypercube is a hypercube in which the length of every side is 1 unit.

farther and farther away from each other, and the feature space is becoming very sparsely populated, with relatively large areas where there are no or very few instances. This is reflected in a further decrease in the sampling density. The density of the marked hypercube is $2^{\frac{1}{3}} = 1.2599$.

Figures 5.18(d)[229] and 5.18(e)[229] illustrate the cost we would have to incur in extra instances if we wished to maintain the sampling density in the dataset in line with each increase in the dimensionality of the feature space. In the two-dimensional feature space in Figure 5.18(d)[229], we have maintained the sampling density (the density of the marked unit hypercube is $100^{\frac{1}{2}} = 10$) at the expense of a very large increase in the number of instances—there are $29 \times 29 = 841$ instances plotted in this figure. This is quite a dramatic increase; however, it gets even more dramatic when we increase from two to three descriptive features. In Figure 5.18(e)[229] we have, again, maintained the sampling density (the density of the marked unit hypercube is $1000^{\frac{1}{3}} = 10$) at the expense of a very large increase in the number of instances—there are $29 \times 29 \times 29 = 24{,}389$ instances in this figure!

So, in order to maintain the sampling density of the feature space as the number of descriptive features increases, we need to dramatically, indeed exponentially, increase the number of instances. If we do not do this, then as we continue to increase the dimensionality of the feature space, the instances will continue to spread out until we reach a point in a high-dimensional feature space where most of the feature space is empty. When this happens, most of the queries will be in locations where none of the training instances are nearby, and as a result, the predictive power of the models based on these training instances will begin to decrease. This trade-off between the number of descriptive features and the density of the instances in the feature space is known as the **curse of dimensionality**.

Typically, we are not able to increase the number of instances in our dataset, and we face the scenario of a sparsely populated feature space,[27] as illustrated in Figures 5.18(b)[229] and 5.18(c)[229]. Fortunately, several features of real data can help us to induce reasonable models in high-dimensional feature spaces.[28] First, although real data does spread out, it doesn't spread out quite as randomly and quickly as we have illustrated here. Real instances tend to cluster. The net effect of this is that the distribution of real data tends to have a lower

---

27 This should not be confused with the concept of **sparse data** that was introduced earlier.

28 The discussion relating to the features of real data that help with the induction of models in high-dimensional spaces is based on Bishop (2006), pages 33–38.

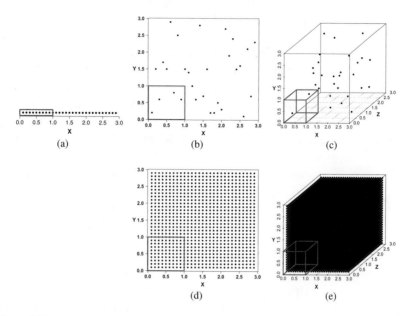

Figure 5.18
A set of scatter plots illustrating the curse of dimensionality. Across (a), (b), and (c), the number of instances remains the same, so the density of the marked unit hypercubes decreases as the number of dimensions increases; (d) and (e) illustrate the cost we must incur, in terms of the number of extra instances required, if we wish to maintain the density of the instances in the feature space as its dimensionality increases.

effective dimensionality than the dimensionality of the feature space. Second, within any small region or neighborhood of the feature space, real data tends to manifest a smooth correlation between changes in descriptive feature values and the values of the target feature. In other words, small changes in descriptive features result in small changes in the target feature. This means that we can generate good predictions for queries by interpolating from nearby instances with known target values.

Another factor that can help us deal with the curse of dimensionality is that some learning algorithms have a natural resistance to the problem. For example, the decision tree learning algorithms we looked at in the last chapter worked by selecting subsets of features from which to build predictive trees and so naturally reduce dimensionality. Even these algorithms, however, do eventually succumb to the curse as the dimensionality grows. Other algorithms, such as the nearest neighbor algorithm, that use all the descriptive features when making a prediction are particularly sensitive to the curse. The moral here is that the curse of dimensionality is a problem for all inductive learning approaches, and given that acquiring new labeled instances is typically not an option, the best way to avoid it is to restrict the number of descriptive features in a dataset to the smallest set possible, while still providing the learning algorithm with enough information about the instances to be able to build a useful model. This is difficult, however, because when we design descriptive features, we tend not to know exactly which ones will be predictive and which ones will not.

Fortunately, we can use **feature selection**[29] to help reduce the number of descriptive features in a dataset to just the subset that is most useful. Before we begin our discussion of approaches to feature selection, it is useful to distinguish between different types of descriptive features.

- **Predictive**: a predictive descriptive feature provides information that is useful in estimating the correct value of a target feature.

- **Interacting**: by itself, an interacting descriptive feature is not informative about the value of the target feature. In conjunction with one or more other features, however, it becomes informative.

- **Redundant**: a descriptive feature is redundant if it has a strong correlation with another descriptive feature.

- **Irrelevant**: an irrelevant descriptive feature does not provide information that is useful in estimating the value of the target feature.

The goal of any feature selection approach is to identify the smallest subset of descriptive features that maintains overall model performance. Ideally, a feature selection approach will return the subset of features that includes the predictive and interacting features while excluding the irrelevant and redundant features.

The most popular and straight forward approach to feature selection is to **rank and prune**. In this approach the features are ranked using a measure of their predictiveness, and any feature outside the top $X\%$ of the features in the list is pruned. The measures of predictiveness are called **filters** because they are used to filter apparently irrelevant features before learning occurs. Technically, a filter can be defined as a heuristic rule that assesses the predictiveness of

---

29 Feature selection is sometimes also known as **variable selection**.

a feature using only the intrinsic properties of the data, independently of the learning algorithm that will use the features to induce the model. For example, we can use **information gain**[30] as a filter in a rank and prune approach.

Although rank and prune approaches using filters are computationally efficient, they suffer from the fact that the predictiveness of each feature is evaluated in isolation from the other features in the dataset. This leads to the undesirable result that ranking and pruning can exclude interacting features and include redundant features.

To find the ideal subset of descriptive features to use to train a model, we could attempt to build a model using every possible subset, evaluate the performance of all these models, and select the feature subset that leads to the best model. This is unfeasible, however, as for d features, there are 2^d different possible feature subsets, which is far too many to evaluate unless d is very small. For example, with just 20 descriptive features, there are $2^{20} = 1,048,576$ possible feature subsets. Instead, feature selection algorithms often frame feature selection as a **greedy local search problem**, where each state in the search space specifies a subset of possible features. For example, Figure 5.19[232] illustrates a **feature subset space** for a dataset with three descriptive features: X, Y, and Z. In this figure each rectangle represents a state in the search space that is a particular feature subset. For instance, the rectangle on the very left represents the feature subset that includes no features at all, and the rectangle at the top of the second column from the left represents the feature subset including just the feature X. Each state is connected to all the other states that can be generated by adding or removing a single feature from that state. A greedy local search process moves across a feature subset space like this search in order to find the best feature subset.

When framed as a greedy local search problem, feature selection is defined in terms of an iterative process consisting of the following components:

1. **Subset Generation**: This component generates a set of candidate feature subsets that are successors of the current best feature subset.

2. **Subset Selection**: This component selects the feature subset from the set of candidate feature subsets generated by the subset generation component that is the most desirable for the search process to move to. One way to do this (similar to the ranking and pruning approach described previously) is to use a filter to evaluate the predictiveness of each candidate set of features

---

30 See Section 4.2.3[128].

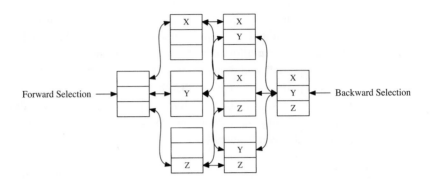

Figure 5.19
Feature subset space for a dataset with three features X, Y, and Z.

and select the most predictive one. A more common approach is to use a **wrapper**. A wrapper evaluates a feature subset in terms of the potential performance of the models that can be induced using that subset. This involves performing an evaluation experiment[31] for each candidate feature subset, in which a model is induced using only the features in the subset, and its performance is evaluated. The candidate feature subset that leads to the best performing model is then selected. Wrapper approaches are more computationally expensive than filters, as they involve training multiple models during each iteration. The argument for using a wrapper approach is that to get the best predictive accuracy, the inductive bias of the particular machine learning algorithm that will be used should be taken into consideration during feature selection. That said, filter approaches are faster and often result in models with good accuracy.

3. **Termination Condition**: This component determines when the search process should stop. Typically we stop when the subset selection component indicates that none of the feature subsets (search states) that can be generated from the current feature subset is more desirable than the current subset. Once the search process is terminated, the features in the dataset that are not members of the selected feature subset are pruned from the dataset before the prediction model is induced.

---

31 We discuss the design of evaluation experiments in details in Chapter 8[397].

Forward sequential selection is a commonly used implementation of the greedy local search approach to feature selection. In forward sequential selection, the search starts in a state with no features (shown on the left of Figure 5.19[232]). In the subset generation component of forward sequential selection, the successors of the current best feature subset are the set of feature subsets that can be generated from the current best subset by adding just a single extra feature. For example, after beginning with the feature subset including no features, the forward sequential search process generates three feature subsets, each containing just one of X, Y, or Z (shown in the second column of Figure 5.19[232]). The subset selection component in forward sequential selection can use any of the approaches described above and moves the search process to a new feature subset. For example, after starting with the feature subset including no features, the process will move to the most desirable of the feature subsets containing just one feature. Forward sequential selection terminates when no accessible feature subset is better than the current subset.

Backward sequential selection is a popular alternative to forward sequential selection. In backward sequential selection, we start with a feature subset including all the possible features in a dataset (shown on the right of Figure 5.19[232]). The successors of the current best feature subset generated in backward sequential selection are the set of feature subsets that can be generated from the current best subset by removing just a single extra feature. Backward sequential selection terminates when no accessible feature subset is better than or as good as the current subset.

Neither forward nor backward sequential selection consider the effect of adding or removing combinations of features, and as a result, they aren't guaranteed to find the absolute optimal subset of features. So which approach should we use? Forward sequential selection is a good approach if we expect lots of irrelevant features in the dataset, because typically it results in a lower overall computational cost for feature selection due to the fact that on average it generates smaller feature subsets. This efficiency gain, however, is at the cost of the likely exclusion of interacting features. Backward sequential selection has the advantage that it allows for the inclusion of sets of interacting features that individually may not be predictive (because all features are included at the beginning), with the extra computational cost of evaluating larger feature subsets. So if model performance is more important than computational considerations, backward sequential selection may be the better option; otherwise use forward sequential selection.

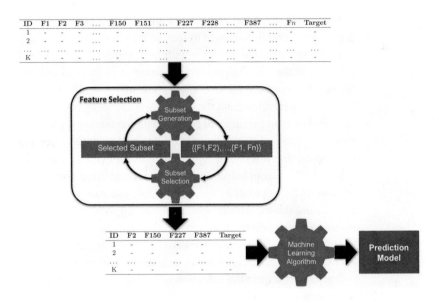

Figure 5.20
The process of model induction with feature selection.

Figure 5.20[234] illustrates how filter selection fits into the model induction process. It is important to remember that feature selection can be used in conjunction with almost any machine learning algorithm, not just similarity-based approaches. Feature selection is appropriate when there are large numbers of features, so we do not present a worked example here. We do, however, discuss the application of feature selection in the case study in Chapter 10[483].

5.5   Summary

Similarity-based prediction models attempt to mimic a very human way of reasoning by basing predictions for a target feature value on the most similar instances in memory. The fact that similarity-based models attempt to mimic a way of reasoning that is natural to humans makes them easy to interpret and understand. This advantage should not be underestimated. In a business context where people are using models to inform decision making, being able to understand how the model works gives people more confidence in the model and, hence, in the insight that it provides.

The standard approach to implementing a similarity-based prediction model is the **nearest neighbor algorithm**. This algorithm is built on two fundamental concepts: (1) a **feature space**, and (2) measures of similarity between instances within the feature space. In this chapter we presented a range of measures of similarity, including **distance metrics** (such as the **Euclidean**, **Manhattan**, and **Mahalanobis**) and **similarity indexes** (such as the **Russel-Rao**, **Sokal-Michener**, **Jaccard**, and **Cosine**). Each of these measures is suitable for different types of data, and matching the appropriate measure to the data is an important step in inducing an accurate similarity-based prediction model.

A point that we didn't discuss in this chapter is that it is possible to create custom measures for datasets with both continuous and categorical descriptive features by combining measures. For example, we might use a Euclidean distance metric to handle the continuous features in a dataset and the Jaccard similarity index to handle the categorical features. The overall measure of similarity could then be based on a weighted combination of the two. By combining measures in this way, we can apply nearest neighbor models to any dataset.

Custom metrics aside, the standard distance metrics and similarity indexes weight all features equally. Consequently, the predictions made by a nearest neighbor model are based on the full set of descriptive features in a dataset. This is not true of all prediction models. For example, the predictions made by decision tree models are based on the subset of descriptive features tested on the path from the root of the tree to the leaf node that specifies the prediction. The fact that nearest neighbor models use the full set of descriptive features when making a prediction makes them particularly sensitive to the occurrence of missing descriptive feature values. In Section 3.4[73] we introduced a number of techniques for handling **missing values**, and particular care should be taken to handle missing values if a nearest neighbor model is being used. The same is true for large range variations across the descriptive features in a dataset and **normalization** techniques (like those described in Section 3.6.1[92]) should almost always be applied when nearest neighbor models are used.

Nearest neighbor models are essentially a composition of a set of local models (recall our discussion on **Voronoi tessellation**) with the predictions made being a function of the target feature value of the instance in the dataset closest to the query. As a result, these models are very sensitive to noise in the target feature. The easiest way to solve this problem is to employ a k **nearest neighbor** model, which uses a function of the target feature values of the k closest instances to a query. Care must be taken, however, when selecting the parameter k, particularly when working with imbalanced datasets.

Nearest neighbor models are also sensitive to the presence of redundant and irrelevant descriptive features in training data. Consequently, **feature selection** is a particularly important process for nearest neighbor algorithms. Feature selection excludes redundant and irrelevant features from the induction process and by doing so alleviates the **curse of dimensionality**. The fact that we have emphasized feature selection in this chapter does not mean that it is not important to predictive analytics in general. The issue with redundant and irrelevant features is inherent in any large dataset, and the feature selection techniques described in this chapter are generally applicable when any type of machine learning algorithm is being used.

Finally, the nearest neighbor algorithm is what is known as a **lazy learner**. This contrasts with **eager learners**, such as the information-based (Chapter 4[117]), probability-based (Chapter 6[247]), and error-based (Chapter 7[323]) approaches to machine learning described in other chapters in this book. The distinction between easy learners and lazy learners is based on when the algorithm abstracts from the data. The nearest neighbor algorithm delays abstracting from the data until it is asked to make a prediction. At this point the information in the query is used to define a neighborhood in the feature space, and a prediction is made based on the instances in this neighborhood. Eager learners abstract away from the data during training and use this abstraction to make predictions, rather than directly comparing queries with instances in the dataset. The decision trees described in Chapter 4[117] are an example of this type of abstraction. One consequence of abstracting away from the training data is that models induced using an eager learning algorithm are typically faster at making predictions than models based on a lazy learner. In the case of a nearest neighbor algorithm, as the number of instances becomes large, the model will become slower because it has more instances to check when defining the neighborhood. Techniques such as the *k-d* **tree** can help with this issue by creating a fast index at the cost of some preprocessing. This means that a nearest neighbor model may not be appropriate in domains where speed of prediction is of the essence.

An advantage of the lazy learning strategy, however, is that similarity-based machine learning approaches are robust to concept drift. **Concept drift** is a phenomenon that occurs when the relationship between the target feature and the descriptive features changes over time. For example, the characteristics of spam emails change both cyclically through the year (typical spam emails at Christmas time are different to typical spam at other times of the year) and also longitudinally (spam in 2014 is very different from spam in 1994). If a prediction task is affected by concept drift, an eager learner may not be appropriate because the abstraction induced during training will go out of date, and the model will need to be retrained at regular intervals, a costly exercise. A nearest neighbor algorithm can be updated without retraining. Each time a prediction is made, the query instance can be added into the dataset and used in subsequent predictions.[32] In this way, a nearest neighbor model can be easily updated, which makes it relatively robust to concept drift (we will return to concept drift in Section 8.4.6[447]).

To conclude, the weaknesses of similarity-based learning approaches are that they are sensitive to the curse of dimensionality, they are slower than other models at making predictions (particularly with very large datasets), and they may not be able to achieve the same levels of accuracy as other learning approaches. The strengths of these models, however, are that they are easy to interpret, they can handle different types of descriptive features, they are relatively robust to noise (when k is set appropriately), and they may be more robust to concept drift than models induced by eager learning algorithms.

5.6 Further Reading

Nearest neighbor models are based on the concepts of a feature space and measures of similarity within this feature space. We have claimed that this is a very natural way for humans to think, and indeed, there is evidence from cognitive science to support a geometric basis to human thought (Gädenfors, 2004). Gädenfors (2004) also provides an excellent introduction and overview of distance metrics.

Chapter 13 of Hastie et al. (2009) gives an introduction to the statistical theory underpinning nearest neighbor models. The measure used to judge similarity is a key element in a nearest neighbor model. In this chapter, we have described a number of different distance metrics and similarity indexes. Cunningham (2009) provides, a broader introduction to the range of metrics and indexes that are available.

Efficiently indexing and accessing memory is an important consideration in scaling nearest neighbor models to large datasets. In this chapter we have shown how k-d trees (Bentley, 1975; Friedman et al., 1977) can be used to

---

32 Obviously we must verify that the prediction made was correct before adding a new instance to the dataset.

speed up the retrieval of nearest neighbors. There are, however, alternatives to *k-d* trees. Samet (1990) gives an introduction to **r-trees** and other related approaches. More recently, hash- based indexes, such as **locality sensitive hashing**, have been developed. Andoni and Indyk (2006) provides a survey of these hash based approaches. Another approach to scaling nearest neighbor models is to remove redundant or noisy instances from the dataset in which we search for neighbors. For example, the **condensed nearest neighbor** approach (Hart, 1968) was one of the earliest attempts at this and removes the that instances not near target level boundaries in a feature space as they are not required to make predictions. More recent attempts to do this include Segata et al. (2009) and Smyth and Keane (1995).

Nearest neighbor models are often used in text analytics applications. Daelemans and van den Bosch (2005) discuss why nearest neighbor models are so suitable for text analytics. Widdows (2004) provides a very readable and interesting introduction to geometry and linguistic meaning; see, in particular, Chapter 4 for an excellent introduction to similarity and distance. For a more general textbook on **natural language processing**, we recommend Jurafsky and Martin (2008). Finally, nearest neighbor models are the basis of **case-based reasoning** (**CBR**), which is an umbrella term for applications based on similarity-based machine learning. Richter and Weber (2013) is a good introduction, and overview, to CBR.

5.7   Epilogue

Returning to 1798 and HMS *Calcutta*, the next day you accompany your men on the expedition up the river, and you encounter the strange animal the sailor had described to you. This time when you see the animal yourself, you realize that it definitely isn't a duck! It turns out that you and your men are the first Europeans to encounter a platypus.[33]

This epilogue illustrates two important, and related, aspects of supervised machine learning. First, supervised machine learning is based on the **stationarity assumption** which states that the data doesn't change—it remains

---

33 The story recounted here of the discovery of the platypus is loosely based on real events. See Eco (1999) for a more faithful account of what happened and for a discussion of the implications of this discovery for classification systems in general. The platypus is not the only animal from Australia whose discovery by Europeans has relevance to predictive machine learning. See Taleb (2008) regarding the discovery of black swans and its relevance to predictive models.

Figure 5.21
A duck-billed platypus. This platypus image was created by Jan Gillbank, English for the Australian Curriculum website (`www.e4ac.edu.au`). Used under Creative Commons Attribution 3.0 license.

stationary—over time. One implication of this assumption is that supervised machine learning assumes that new target levels—such as previously unknown animals—don't suddenly appear in the data from which queries that are input to the model are sampled. Second, in the context of predicting categorical targets, supervised machine learning creates models that distinguish between the target levels that are present in the dataset from which they are induced. So if a prediction model is trained to distinguish between lions, frogs and ducks, the model will classify every query instance as being either a lion, a frog, or a duck—even if the query is actually a platypus.

Creating models that can identify queries as being sufficiently different from what was in a training dataset so as to be considered a new type of entity is a difficult research problem. Some of the areas of research relevant to this problem include **outlier detection** and **one-class classification**.

5.8   Exercises

1. The table below lists a dataset that was used to create a nearest neigh-
bour model that predicts whether it will be a good day to go surfing.

ID	WAVE SIZE (FT)	WAVE PERIOD (SECS)	WIND SPEED (MPH)	GOOD SURF
1	6	15	5	yes
2	1	6	9	no
3	7	10	4	yes
4	7	12	3	yes
5	2	2	10	no
6	10	2	20	no

Assuming that the model uses Euclidean distance to find the nearest neigh-
bour, what prediction will the model return for each of the following query
instances.

ID	WAVE SIZE (FT)	WAVE PERIOD (SECS)	WIND SPEED (MPH)	GOOD SURF
Q1	8	15	2	?
Q2	8	2	18	?
Q3	6	11	4	?

2. Email spam filtering models often use a **bag-of-words** representation
for emails. In a bag-of-words representation, the descriptive features that
describe a document (in our case, an email) each represent how many
times a particular word occurs in the document. One descriptive feature
is included for each word in a predefined dictionary. The dictionary is typically defined as the complete set of words that occur in the training dataset.
The table below lists the bag-of-words representation for the following five
emails and a target feature, SPAM, whether they are spam emails or genuine
emails:

- *"money, money, money"*
- *"free money for free gambling fun"*
- *"gambling for fun"*
- *"machine learning for fun, fun, fun"*
- *"free machine learning"*

ID	MONEY	FREE	FOR	Bag-of-Words GAMBLING	FUN	MACHINE	LEARNING	SPAM
1	3	0	0	0	0	0	0	true
2	1	2	1	1	1	0	0	true
3	0	0	1	1	1	0	0	true
4	0	0	1	0	3	1	1	false
5	0	1	0	0	0	1	1	false

a. What target level would a nearest neighbor model using **Euclidean distance** return for the following email: "*machine learning for free*"?

b. What target level would a k-NN model with $k = 3$ and using **Euclidean distance** return for the same query?

c. What target level would a **weighted k-NN** model with $k = 5$ and using a weighting scheme of the reciprocal of the squared Euclidean distance between the neighbor and the query, return for the query?

d. What target level would a k-NN model with $k = 3$ and using **Manhattan distance** return for the same query?

e. There are a lot of zero entries in the spam bag-of-words dataset. This is indicative of **sparse data** and is typical for text analytics. **Cosine similarity** is often a good choice when dealing with sparse non-binary data. What target level would a 3-NN model using cosine similarity return for the query?

3. The predictive task in this question is to predict the level of corruption in a country based on a range of macro-economic and social features. The table below lists some countries described by the following descriptive features:

- LIFE EXP., the mean life expectancy at birth
- TOP-10 INCOME, the percentage of the annual income of the country that goes to the top 10% of earners
- INFANT MORT., the number of infant deaths per 1,000 births
- MIL. SPEND, the percentage of GDP spent on the military
- SCHOOL YEARS, the mean number years spent in school by adult females

The target feature is the **Corruption Perception Index** (CPI). The CPI measures the perceived levels of corruption in the public sector of countries and ranges from 0 (highly corrupt) to 100 (very clean).[34]

COUNTRY ID	LIFE EXP.	TOP-10 INCOME	INFANT MORT.	MIL. SPEND	SCHOOL YEARS	CPI
Afghanistan	59.61	23.21	74.30	4.44	0.40	1.5171
Haiti	45.00	47.67	73.10	0.09	3.40	1.7999
Nigeria	51.30	38.23	82.60	1.07	4.10	2.4493
Egypt	70.48	26.58	19.60	1.86	5.30	2.8622
Argentina	75.77	32.30	13.30	0.76	10.10	2.9961
China	74.87	29.98	13.70	1.95	6.40	3.6356
Brazil	73.12	42.93	14.50	1.43	7.20	3.7741
Israel	81.30	28.80	3.60	6.77	12.50	5.8069
U.S.A	78.51	29.85	6.30	4.72	13.70	7.1357
Ireland	80.15	27.23	3.50	0.60	11.50	7.5360
U.K.	80.09	28.49	4.40	2.59	13.00	7.7751
Germany	80.24	22.07	3.50	1.31	12.00	8.0461
Canada	80.99	24.79	4.90	1.42	14.20	8.6725
Australia	82.09	25.40	4.20	1.86	11.50	8.8442
Sweden	81.43	22.18	2.40	1.27	12.80	9.2985
New Zealand	80.67	27.81	4.90	1.13	12.30	9.4627

We will use Russia as our query country for this question. The table below lists the descriptive features for Russia.

COUNTRY ID	LIFE EXP.	TOP-10 INCOME	INFANT MORT.	MIL. SPEND	SCHOOL YEARS	CPI
Russia	67.62	31.68	10.00	3.87	12.90	?

a. What value would a 3-nearest neighbor prediction model using Euclidean distance return for the CPI of Russia?

b. What value would a **weighted k-NN** prediction model return for the CPI of Russia? Use $k = 16$ (i.e., the full dataset) and a weighting scheme of

34 The data listed in this table is real and is for 2010/11 (or the most recent year prior to 2010/11 when the data was available). The data for the descriptive features in this table was amalgamated from a number of surveys retrieved from **Gapminder** (www.gapminder.org). The Corruption Perception Index is generated annually by **Transparency International** (www.transparency.org).

the reciprocal of the squared Euclidean distance between the neighbor and the query.

c. The descriptive features in this dataset are of different types. For example, some are percentages, others are measured in years, and others are measured in counts per 1,000. We should always consider normalizing our data, but it is particularly important to do this when the descriptive features are measured in different units. What value would a 3-nearest neighbor prediction model using Euclidean distance return for the CPI of Russia when the descriptive features have been normalized using range normalization?

d. What value would a **weighted k-NN** prediction model—with $k = 16$ (i.e., the full dataset) and using a weighting scheme of the reciprocal of the squared Euclidean distance between the neighbor and the query—return for the CPI of Russia when it is applied to the range-normalized data?

e. The actual 2011 CPI for Russia was 2.4488. Which of the predictions made was the most accurate? Why do you think this was?

* 4. You have been given the job of building a recommender system for a large online shop that has a stock of over 100,000 items. In this domain the behavior of customers is captured in terms of what items they have bought or not bought. For example, the following table lists the behavior of two customers in this domain for a subset of the items that at least one of the customers has bought.

ID	ITEM 107	ITEM 498	ITEM 7256	ITEM 28063	ITEM 75328
1	true	true	true	false	false
2	true	false	false	true	true

a. The company has decided to use a similarity-based model to implement the recommender system. Which of the following three similarity indexes do you think the system should be based on?

$$\text{Russell-Rao}(X,Y) = \frac{CP(X,Y)}{P}$$

$$\text{Sokal-Michener}(X,Y) = \frac{CP(X,Y) + CA(X,Y)}{P}$$

$$\text{Jaccard}(X,Y) = \frac{CP(X,Y)}{CP(X,Y) + PA(X,Y) + AP(X,Y)}$$

b. What items will the system recommend to the following customer? Assume that the recommender system uses the similarity index you chose in the first part of this question and is trained on the sample dataset listed above. Also assume that the system generates recommendations for query customers by finding the customer most similar to them in the dataset and then recommending the items that this similar customer has bought but that the query customer has not bought.

ID	ITEM 107	ITEM 498	ITEM 7256	ITEM 28063	ITEM 75328
Query	true	false	true	false	false

∗ 5. You are working as an assistant biologist to Charles Darwin on the *Beagle* voyage. You are at the Galápagos Islands, and you have just discovered a new animal that has not yet been classified. Mr. Darwin has asked you to classify the animal using a nearest neighbor approach, and he has supplied you the following dataset of already classified animals.

ID	BIRTHS LIVE YOUNG	LAYS EGGS	FEEDS OFFSPRING OWN MILK	WARM-BLOODED	COLD-BLOODED	LAND AND WATER BASED	HAS HAIR	HAS FEATHERS	CLASS
1	true	false	true	true	false	false	true	false	mammal
2	false	true	false	false	true	true	false	false	amphibian
3	true	false	true	true	false	false	true	false	mammal
4	false	true	false	true	false	true	false	true	bird

The descriptive features of the mysterious newly discovered animal are as follows:

ID	BIRTHS LIVE YOUNG	LAYS EGGS	FEEDS OFFSPRING OWN MILK	WARM-BLOODED	COLD-BLOODED	LAND AND WATER BASED	HAS HAIR	HAS FEATHERS	CLASS
Query	false	true	false	false	false	true	false	false	?

a. A good measure of distance between two instances with categorical features is the **overlap metric** (also known as the **hamming distance**), which simply counts the number of descriptive features that have *different* values. Using this measure of distance, compute the distances between the mystery animal and each of the animals in the animal dataset.

b. If you used a 1-NN model, what class would be assigned to the mystery animal?

c. If you used a 4-NN model, what class would be assigned to the mystery animal? Would this be a good value for k for this dataset?

∗ 6. You have been asked by a San Francisco property investment company to create a predictive model that will generate house price estimates for properties they are considering purchasing as rental properties. The table below lists a sample of properties that have recently been sold for rental in the city. The descriptive features in this dataset are SIZE (the property size in square feet) and RENT (the estimated monthly rental value of the property in dollars). The target feature, PRICE, lists the prices that these properties were sold for in dollars.

ID	SIZE	RENT	PRICE
1	2,700	9,235	2,000,000
2	1,315	1,800	820,000
3	1,050	1,250	800,000
4	2,200	7,000	1,750,000
5	1,800	3,800	1,450,500
6	1,900	4,000	1,500,500
7	960	800	720,000

a. Create a *k-d* **tree** for this dataset. Assume the following order over the features: RENT then SIZE.

b. Using the *k-d* tree that you created in the first part of this question, find the nearest neighbor to the following query: SIZE = 1,000, RENT = 2,200.

6   Probability-based Learning

When my information changes, I alter my conclusions. What do you do, sir?
—John Maynard Keynes

In this chapter we introduce probability-based approaches to machine learning. Probability-based prediction approaches are heavily based on **Bayes' Theorem**, and the fundamentals section of this chapter introduces this important cornerstone of computer science after covering some other fundamentals of **probability theory**. We then present the **naive Bayes model**, the standard approach to using probability-based approaches to machine learning. The extensions and variations to this standard approach that we describe are the use of **smoothing** to combat overfitting, the modifications required to the standard naive Bayes model to allow it to handle continuous features, and **Bayesian network** models that give us more control than a naive Bayes model over the assumptions that are encoded in a model.

6.1   Big Idea

Imagine that you are at a county fair and a stall owner is offering all comers a game of *find the lady*. *Find the lady* is a card game that hucksters have been using to earn money from unsuspecting marks for centuries.[1] In a game, the dealer holds three cards—one queen and two aces (as shown in Figure 6.1(a)[248])—and, typically with a little bit of flair, quickly drops these cards face down onto a table. Faced with the backs of three cards (as shown in Figure 6.1(b)[248]), the player then has to guess where the queen has landed. Usually the player bets money on their ability to do this, and the dealer uses a little manual trickery to misdirect the player toward the wrong card.

When you first see the game played, because the dealer lays out the three cards so quickly, you think that there is no way to tell where the queen lands. In this case you can only assume that the queen is equally likely to be in any of the three possible positions: *left*, *center*, or *right*. This is shown in the bar plot in Figure 6.1(c)[248], which shows an equal likelihood for each position. Not feeling quite brave enough to play a game, you decide to instead study the dealer playing games with other people.

---

1 It is appropriate to use a game involving gambling to introduce probability-based machine learning. The origins of probability theory come from attempts to understand gambling and games of chance, in particular, the work of Gerolamo Cardano and the later work of Pierre de Fermat and Blaise Pascal.

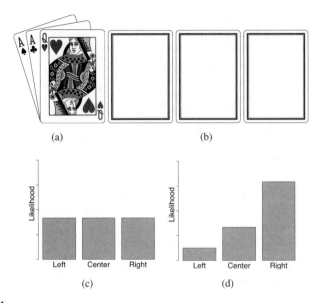

Figure 6.1

A game of *find the lady*: (a) the cards used; (b) the cards dealt face down on a table; (c) the initial likelihoods of the queen ending up in each position; (d) a revised set of likelihoods for the position of the queen based on evidence collected.

After watching the dealer play 30 games with other players, you notice that he has a tendency to drop the queen in the position on the right (19 times) more than the left (3 times) or center (8 times). Based on this, you update you beliefs about where the queen is likely to land based on the evidence that you have collected. This is shown in Figure 6.1(d)[248], where the bars have been redistributed to illustrate the revised likelihoods.

Confident that your study will help you, you lay a dollar down to play a game, ready to guess that the queen is in the position on the right. This time, however, as the dealer drops the cards onto the table, a sudden gust of wind turns over the card on the right to reveal that it is the ace of spades (shown in Figure 6.2(a)[249]). The extra piece of evidence means that you need to revise your belief about the likelihoods of where the queen will be once again. These revised likelihoods are shown in Figure 6.2(b)[249]. As you know that the card is not in the position on the right the likelihood of that you had associated with this position is redistributed amongst the other two possibilities. Based on the new likelihoods, you guess that the queen is in the center position, and happily,

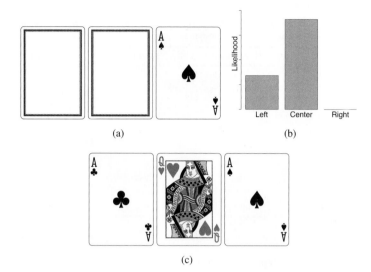

Figure 6.2

(a) The set of cards after the wind blows over the one on the right; (b) the revised likelihoods for the position of the queen based on this new evidence; (c) the final positions of the cards in the game.

this turns out to be correct (see Figure 6.2(c)[249]). The dealer encourages you to play again, but you know that you've got to know when to walk away, so you head on with an extra dollar in your pocket.

This illustrates the big idea underlying probability-based machine learning. We can use estimates of likelihoods to determine the most likely predictions that should be made. Most importantly, though, we revise these predictions based on data we collect and whenever extra evidence becomes available.

6.2 Fundamentals

In this section we describe **Bayes' Theorem** and the important fundamentals of probability theory that are required to use it. This section assumes a basic understanding of probability theory, including the basics of calculating probabilities based on **relative frequencies**, calculating **conditional probabilities**, the probability **product rule**, the probability **chain rule**, and the **Theorem of Total Probability**. Appendix B[541] provides a comprehensive introduction to

Table 6.1

A simple dataset for MENINGITIS diagnosis with descriptive features that describe the presence or absence of three common symptoms of the disease: HEADACHE, FEVER, and VOMITING.

ID	HEADACHE	FEVER	VOMITING	MENINGITIS
1	true	true	false	false
2	false	true	false	false
3	true	false	true	false
4	true	false	true	false
5	false	true	false	true
6	true	false	true	false
7	true	false	true	false
8	true	false	true	true
9	false	true	false	false
10	true	false	true	true

these aspects of probability theory, so we recommend that readers unfamiliar with them review this appendix before continuing with this chapter.

We will use the dataset[2] in Table 6.1[250] to illustrate how the terminology of probability is mapped into the language of machine learning for predictive data analytics. The target being predicted in this dataset is whether a patient is suffering from MENINGITIS, and the descriptive features are common symptoms associated with this disease (HEADACHE, FEVER, and VOMITING).

From a probability point of view, each feature in a dataset is a **random variable**, and the **sample space** for the domain associated with a prediction problem is the set of all possible combinations of assignments of values to features. Each row in a dataset represents an **experiment**, which associates a target feature value with a set of descriptive feature values, and the assignment of a set of descriptive features with values is an **event**. So, for example, each row in Table 6.1[250] represents an experiment and the assignment of the descriptive features to the values shown in each row can be referred to as a distinct event.

A **probability function**, $P()$, returns the probability of an event. For example, $P(\text{FEVER} = true)$ returns the probability of the FEVER feature taking the value *true*. This probability, which is 0.4, can be counted directly from the dataset. Probability functions for categorical features are referred to as **probability mass functions**, while probability functions for continuous features are known as **probability density functions**. In the early part

---

2 This data has been artificially generated for this example.

of this chapter, we focus on categorical features, but we return to continuous features in Section 6.4[272]. A **joint probability** refers to the probability of an assignment of specific values to multiple different features, for example, $P(\text{MENINGITIS} = true, \text{HEADACHE} = true) = 0.2$. Last, a **conditional probability** refers to the probability of one feature taking a specific value given that we already know the value of a different feature, for example, $P(\text{MENINGITIS} = true \mid \text{HEADACHE} = true) = 0.2857$.

It is often useful to talk about the probabilities for all the possible assignments to a feature. To do this we use the concept of a **probability distribution**. A probability distribution is a data structure that describes the probability of each possible value a feature can take. For example, the probability distribution for the binary feature MENINGITIS from Table 6.1[250] is $\mathbf{P}(\text{MENINGITIS}) = \langle 0.3, 0.7 \rangle$ (by convention we give the *true* probability first). We use bold notation to distinguish between a probability distribution, $\mathbf{P}()$, and a probability function, $P()$. The sum of a probability distribution must equal 1.0.

A **joint probability distribution** is a probability distribution over more than one feature assignment and is written as a multi-dimensional matrix in which each cell lists the probability of a particular combination of feature values being assigned. The dimensions of the matrix are dependent on the number of features and the number of values in the domains of the features. The sum of all the cells in a joint probability distribution must be 1.0. For example, the joint probability distribution for the four binary features from Table 6.1[250] (HEADACHE, FEVER, VOMITING, and MENINGITIS) is written as[3]

$$\mathbf{P}(H, F, V, M) = \begin{bmatrix} P(h,f,v,m), & P(\neg h,f,v,m) \\ P(h,f,v,\neg m), & P(\neg h,f,v,\neg m) \\ P(h,f,\neg v,m), & P(\neg h,f,\neg v,m) \\ P(h,f,\neg v,\neg m), & P(\neg h,f,\neg v,\neg m) \\ P(h,\neg f,v,m), & P(\neg h,\neg f,v,m) \\ P(h,\neg f,v,\neg m), & P(\neg h,\neg f,v,\neg m) \\ P(h,\neg f,\neg v,m), & P(\neg h,\neg f,\neg v,m) \\ P(h,\neg f,\neg v,\neg m), & P(\neg h,\neg f,\neg v,\neg m) \end{bmatrix} \qquad (6.1)$$

[3] To save space, throughout this chapter, named features are denoted by the uppercase initial letters of their names (e.g., the MENINGITIS feature is denoted M). Where a named feature is binary, we use the lowercase initial letter of the feature name to denote the feature being *true* and the lowercase initial letter preceded by the $\neg$ symbol to denote it being *false* (e.g., m denotes MENINGITIS $= true$, and $\neg m$ denotes MENINGITIS $= false$).

Given a joint probability distribution, we can compute the probability of any event in the domain that it covers by summing over the cells in the distribution where that event is true. For example, to compute the probability of $P(h)$ in the domain specified by the joint probability distribution $\mathbf{P}(H, F, V, M)$, we simply sum the values in the cells containing h (the cells in the first column). Calculating probabilities in this way is known as **summing out**. We can also use summing out to compute conditional probabilities from a joint probability distribution. To calculate the probability $P(h \mid f)$ from $\mathbf{P}(H, F, V, M)$, we sum the values in all the cells where h and f are the case (the top four cells in the first column).

We are now ready to take on Bayes' Theorem!

6.2.1   Bayes' Theorem

Bayes' Theorem[4] is so elegant and intuitive that it can be stated in one sentence of plain English:

the probability that an event has happened given a set of evidence for it is equal to the probability of the evidence being caused by the event multiplied by the probability of the event itself

or slightly more succinctly:

$$P(\text{an event given evidence}) = P(\text{the evidence given the event})$$
$$\times\ P(\text{the event})$$

Reading from left to right, the theorem shows us how to calculate the probability of an event given the evidence we have of that event in terms of the likelihood of the event causing this evidence. This is useful because reasoning from the evidence to events (**inverse reasoning**) is often much more difficult than reasoning from an event to the evidence it causes (**forward reasoning**). Bayes' Theorem allows us to easily swap back and forth between these two types of reasoning.

The formal definition of **Bayes' Theorem** is

$$P(X \mid Y) = \frac{P(Y \mid X)P(X)}{P(Y)} \tag{6.2}$$

4 Bayes' Theorem is named after the Reverend Thomas Bayes, who wrote an essay that described how to update beliefs as new information arises. After Thomas Bayes died, this essay was edited and published by the Reverend Richard Price (Bayes and Price, 1763). The modern mathematical form of Bayes' Theorem, however, was developed by Simon Pierre Laplace.

Bayes' Theorem defines the conditional probability of an event, X, given some evidence, Y, in terms of the product of the inverse conditional probability, $P(Y \mid X)$, and the prior probability of the event $P(X)$.

For an illustrative example of Bayes' Theorem in action, imagine that after a yearly checkup, a doctor informs a patient that there is both bad news and good news. The bad news is that the patient has tested positive for a serious disease and that the test the doctor used is 99% accurate (i.e., the probability of testing positive when a patient has the disease is 0.99, as is the probability of testing negative when a patient does not have the disease). The good news, however, is that the disease is extremely rare, striking only 1 in 10,000 people. So what is the actual probability that the patient has the disease? And why is the rarity of the disease good news given that the patient has tested positive for it?

We can use Bayes' Theorem to answer both of these questions. To calculate the probability that the patient actually has the disease based on the evidence of the test result, $P(d \mid t)$, we apply Bayes' Theorem:

$$P(d \mid t) = \frac{P(t \mid d)P(d)}{P(t)}$$

The information about the scenario gives us the probability of having the disease as $P(d) = 0.0001$ and the probability of not having the disease as $P(\neg d) = 0.9999$. The accuracy of the test is captured as $P(t \mid d) = 0.99$ and $P(t \mid \neg d) = 0.01$. The overall probability of the test returning a positive value, $P(t)$, is not given in the description above, but it can be easily calculated using the **Theorem of Total Probability**[5] as

$$\begin{aligned}
P(t) &= P(t \mid d)P(d) + P(t \mid \neg d)P(\neg d) \\
&= (0.99 \times 0.0001) + (0.01 \times 0.9999) \\
&= 0.0101
\end{aligned}$$

We can insert these probabilities into the application of Bayes' Theorem to give

$$\begin{aligned}
P(d \mid t) &= \frac{0.99 \times 0.0001}{0.0101} \\
&= 0.0098
\end{aligned}$$

5 The **Theorem of Total Probability** is explained in detail in Section B.3[548] of Appendix B[541].

So, the probability of actually having the disease, in spite of the positive test result, is less than 1%. This is why the doctor said the rarity of the disease was such good news. One of the important characteristics of Bayes' Theorem is its explicit inclusion of the prior probability of an event when calculating the likelihood of that event based on evidence.[6]

Let's look at Bayes' Theorem in a little more detail. Bayes' Theorem is easily derived from the **product rule**.[7] We know from the product rule and the logical symmetry of the *and* operation[8] that

$$P(Y \mid X)P(X) = P(X \mid Y)P(Y)$$

If we divide both sides of this equation by the prior probability on the left hand side, $P(Y)$, we get

$$\frac{P(X \mid Y)P(Y)}{P(Y)} = \frac{P(Y \mid X)P(X)}{P(Y)}$$

The $P(Y)$ terms on the left hand side of this equation, however, cancel each other out to give us Bayes' Theorem

$$\frac{P(X \mid Y)\cancel{P(Y)}}{\cancel{P(Y)}} = \frac{P(Y \mid X)P(X)}{P(Y)}$$

$$\Rightarrow P(X \mid Y) = \frac{P(Y \mid X)P(X)}{P(Y)}$$

There are two important observations regarding the division in Bayes' Theorem by the denominator $P(Y)$. The first is that this division functions as a normalization mechanism ensuring that

$$0 \leqslant P(X \mid Y) \leqslant 1$$

and

$$\sum_i P(X_i \mid Y) = 1.0$$

where $\sum_i P(X_i)$ should be interpreted as summing over the set of events that are a complete assignment to the features in X. The reason that the division functions as a normalization mechanism is that the prior probability of the

---

6 Famously, an experiment in which doctors were asked this question about the probability of the patient having the disease showed that most of them got this question wrong (Casscells et al., 1978).

7 The **product rule** is explained in detail in Section B.3[548] of Appendix B[541].

8 That is, a and $b = b$ and a.

evidence, $P(Y)$, is not conditional on X_i, and as a result, it is constant for all X_i.

The second interesting observation about the division of the right hand side of Bayes' Theorem by $P(Y)$ is that we can calculate $P(Y)$ in two different ways. First, we can calculate $P(Y)$ directly from a dataset as

$$P(Y) = \frac{|\{\text{rows where Y is the case}\}|}{|\{\text{rows in the dataset}\}|} \qquad (6.3)$$

Alternatively, we can use the **Theorem of Total Probability** to calculate $P(Y)$:

$$P(Y) = \sum_i P(Y \mid X_i)P(X_i) \qquad (6.4)$$

Notice that ignoring the subscripts, the expression we are summing in Equation (6.4)[255] is identical to the numerator in Bayes' Theorem. This gives us a way to calculate the **posterior probability distribution** over the possible assignment of values to the features in event X conditioned on the event Y, that is, $\mathbf{P}(X \mid Y)$, that avoids explicitly calculating $P(Y)$. If we let

$$\eta = \frac{1}{\sum_i P(Y \mid X_i)P(X_i)} \qquad (6.5)$$

then

$$P(X_i \mid Y) = \eta \times P(Y \mid X_i)P(X_i) \qquad (6.6)$$

where the term η explicitly represents a normalization constant. Because Bayes' Theorem can be calculated in this way, it is sometimes written as

$$P(X \mid Y) = \eta \times P(Y \mid X)P(X) \qquad (6.7)$$

where η is as defined in Equation (6.5)[255].

So we have two different definitions of Bayes' Theorem (Equation (6.2)[252] and Equation (6.7)[255]), but which one should we use? The choice is really a matter of convenience. If we are calculating the probability of a single event given some evidence, then calculating $P(Y)$ directly from the data using Equation (6.2)[252] is the easier option. If, however, we need to calculate the posterior probability distribution over X given Y, that is $\mathbf{P}(X \mid Y)$, then we will be actually calculating each of the $P(Y \mid X_i)P(X_i)$ values in Equation (6.5)[255] as part of this calculation, and it is more efficient to use Equation (6.7)[255].

We are now ready to use Bayes' Theorem to generate predictions based on a dataset. The next section will examine how this is done.

6.2.2   Bayesian Prediction

To make Bayesian predictions, we generate the probability of the event that a target feature, t, takes a specific level, l, given the assignment of values to a set of descriptive features, $\mathbf{q}$, from a query instance. We can restate Bayes' Theorem using this terminology and generalize the definition of Bayes' Theorem so that it can take into account more than one piece of evidence (each descriptive feature value is a separate piece of evidence). The **Generalized Bayes' Theorem** is defined as

$$P(t = l \mid \mathbf{q}[1], \ldots, \mathbf{q}[m]) = \frac{P(\mathbf{q}[1], \ldots, \mathbf{q}[m] \mid t = l)P(t = l)}{P(\mathbf{q}[1], \ldots, \mathbf{q}[m])} \tag{6.8}$$

To calculate a probability using the **Generalized Bayes' Theorem**, we need to calculate three probabilities:

1. $P(t = l)$, the **prior probability** of the target feature t taking the level l

2. $P(\mathbf{q}[1], \ldots, \mathbf{q}[m])$, the **joint probability** of the descriptive features of a query instance taking a specific set of values

3. $P(\mathbf{q}[1], \ldots, \mathbf{q}[m] \mid t = l)$, the **conditional probability** of the descriptive features of a query instance taking a specific set of values given that the target feature takes the level l

The first two of these probabilities are easy to calculate. $P(t = l)$ is simply the relative frequency with which the target feature takes the level l in a dataset. $P(\mathbf{q}[1], \ldots, \mathbf{q}[m])$ can be calculated as the relative frequency in a dataset of the joint event that the descriptive features of an instance take on the values $\mathbf{q}[1], \ldots, \mathbf{q}[m]$. As discussed in the previous section, it can also be calculated using the **Theorem of Total Probability** (in this instance, summing over all the target levels $\sum_{k \in levels(t)} P(\mathbf{q}[1], \ldots, \mathbf{q}[m] \mid t = k)P(t = k)$), or replaced entirely with a **normalization constant**, η.

The final probability that we need to calculate, $P(\mathbf{q}[1], \ldots, \mathbf{q}[m] \mid t = l)$, can be calculated either directly from a dataset (by calculating the relative frequency of the joint event $\mathbf{q}[1], \ldots, \mathbf{q}[m]$ within the set of instances where $t = l$), or alternatively, it can be calculated using the probability **chain rule**.[9] The chain rule states that the probability of a joint event can be rewritten as a

---

9 The probability **chain rule** is explained in detail in Section B.3[548] of Appendix B[541].

product of conditional probabilities. So, we can rewrite $P(\mathbf{q}[1],\ldots,\mathbf{q}[m])$ as

$$P(\mathbf{q}[1],\ldots,\mathbf{q}[m]) =$$
$$P(\mathbf{q}[1]) \times P(\mathbf{q}[2] \mid \mathbf{q}[1]) \times \cdots \times P(\mathbf{q}[m] \mid \mathbf{q}[m-1],\ldots,\mathbf{q}[2],\mathbf{q}[1])$$

We can use the chain rule for conditional probabilities by just adding the conditioning term to each term in the expression, so

$$P(\mathbf{q}[1],\ldots,\mathbf{q}[m] \mid t = l) =$$
$$P(\mathbf{q}[1] \mid t = l) \times P(\mathbf{q}[2] \mid \mathbf{q}[1], t = l) \times \ldots \qquad (6.9)$$
$$\cdots \times P(\mathbf{q}[m] \mid \mathbf{q}[m-1],\ldots,\mathbf{q}[3],\mathbf{q}[2],\mathbf{q}[1], t = l)$$

This transformation from a joint probability conditioned on a single event into a product of conditional probabilities with just one event being conditioned in each term may not appear to achieve much. We will see shortly, however, that this transformation is incredibly useful.

Let's look at an example of how we can now use Bayes' Theorem to make predictions based on the meningitis diagnosis dataset in Table 6.1[250] for a query instance with HEADACHE $= true$, FEVER $= false$, and VOMITING $= true$. Returning to the shortened notation that we used previously, a predicted diagnosis for this query instance can be given using Bayes' Theorem as

$$P(M \mid h, \neg f, v) = \frac{P(h, \neg f, v \mid M) \times P(M)}{P(h, \neg f, v)}$$

There are two values in the domain of the MENINGITIS feature, $true$ and $false$, so we have to do this calculation once for each. Considering first the calculation for m, we need the following probabilities, which can be computed directly from Table 6.1[250]

$$P(m) = \frac{|\{\mathbf{d}_5, \mathbf{d}_8, \mathbf{d}_{10}\}|}{|\{\mathbf{d}_1, \mathbf{d}_2, \mathbf{d}_3, \mathbf{d}_4, \mathbf{d}_5, \mathbf{d}_6, \mathbf{d}_7, \mathbf{d}_8, \mathbf{d}_9, \mathbf{d}_{10}\}|} = \frac{3}{10} = 0.3$$

$$P(h, \neg f, v) = \frac{|\{\mathbf{d}_3, \mathbf{d}_4, \mathbf{d}_6, \mathbf{d}_7, \mathbf{d}_8, \mathbf{d}_{10}\}|}{|\{\mathbf{d}_1, \mathbf{d}_2, \mathbf{d}_3, \mathbf{d}_4, \mathbf{d}_5, \mathbf{d}_6, \mathbf{d}_7, \mathbf{d}_8, \mathbf{d}_9, \mathbf{d}_{10}\}|} = \frac{6}{10} = 0.6$$

We also need to calculate the likelihood of the descriptive feature values of the query given that the target is $true$. We could calculate this directly from the dataset, but in this example, we will illustrate the chain rule approach just described. Using the chain rule approach, we compute the overall likelihood of the descriptive feature values given a target value of *true* as the product of a set of conditional probabilities that are themselves calculated from the dataset

$$P(h, \neg f, v \mid m) = P(h \mid m) \times P(\neg f \mid h, m) \times P(v \mid \neg f, h, m)$$
$$= \frac{|\{\mathbf{d_8}, \mathbf{d_{10}}\}|}{|\{\mathbf{d_5}, \mathbf{d_8}, \mathbf{d_{10}}\}|} \times \frac{|\{\mathbf{d_8}, \mathbf{d_{10}}\}|}{|\{\mathbf{d_8}, \mathbf{d_{10}}\}|} \times \frac{|\{\mathbf{d_8}, \mathbf{d_{10}}\}|}{|\{\mathbf{d_8}, \mathbf{d_{10}}\}|}$$
$$= \frac{2}{3} \times \frac{2}{2} \times \frac{2}{2} = 0.6666$$

We can now combine the three probabilities just calculated to calculate the overall probability of the target feature taking the level *true* given the query instance

$$P(m \mid h, \neg f, v) = \frac{P(h, \neg f, v \mid m) \times P(m)}{P(h, \neg f, v)}$$
$$= \frac{0.6666 \times 0.3}{0.6} = 0.3333$$

The corresponding calculation for $P(\neg m \mid h, \neg f, v)$ is:

$$P(\neg m \mid h, \neg f, v) = \frac{P(h, \neg f, v \mid \neg m) \times P(\neg m)}{P(h, \neg f, v)}$$
$$= \frac{\left(\begin{array}{c} P(h \mid \neg m) \times P(\neg f \mid h, \neg m) \\ \times P(v \mid \neg f, h, \neg m) \times P(\neg m) \end{array} \right)}{P(h, \neg f, v)}$$
$$= \frac{0.7143 \times 0.8 \times 1.0 \times 0.7}{0.6} = 0.6667$$

These calculations tell us that it is twice as probable that the patient does not have meningitis as it is that the patient does. This might seem a little surprising given that the patient is suffering from a headache and is vomiting, two key symptoms of meningitis. Indeed, we have a situation where the posterior for a given prediction given the evidence is quite low (here $P(m \mid h, \neg f, v) = 0.3333$), even though the likelihood of the evidence if we assume the prediction to be correct is quite high, $P(h, \neg f, v \mid m) = 0.6666$.

What is happening here is that, as Bayes' Theorem states, when calculating a posterior prediction, we weight the likelihood of the evidence given the prediction by the prior of the prediction. In this case, although the likelihood of suffering from a headache and vomiting is quite high when someone has meningitis, the prior probability of having meningitis is quite low. So, even when we take the evidence into account, the posterior probability of having meningitis remains low. This can seem counter-intuitive at first. The mistake is to confuse the probability of a prediction given the evidence with the probability of the evidence given the prediction and is another example of the **paradox of the false positive**.[10]

Calculating exact probabilities for each of the possible target levels is often very useful to a human decision maker, for example, a doctor. However, if we are trying to build a predictive model that automatically assigns a target level to a query instance, then we need to decide how the model will make a prediction based on the computed probabilities. The obvious way to do this is to have the model return the target level that has the highest posterior probability given the state of the descriptive features in the query. A prediction model that works in this way is making a **maximum a posteriori** (**MAP**) prediction.[11] We can formally define a Bayesian MAP prediction model as

$$\mathbb{M}(\mathbf{q}) = \underset{l \in levels(t)}{\arg\max} \, P(t = l \mid \mathbf{q}[1], \ldots, \mathbf{q}[m])$$
$$= \underset{l \in levels(t)}{\arg\max} \, \frac{P(\mathbf{q}[1], \ldots, \mathbf{q}[m] \mid t = l) \times P(t = l)}{P(\mathbf{q}[1], \ldots, \mathbf{q}[m])} \tag{6.10}$$

where $\mathbb{M}(\mathbf{q})$ is the prediction returned by the model $\mathbb{M}$ using a MAP prediction mechanism for a query, $\mathbf{q}$, composed of $\mathbf{q}[1], \ldots, \mathbf{q}[m]$ descriptive features; $levels(t)$ is the set of levels the target feature can take; and $\arg\max_{l \in levels(t)}$ specifies that we return the level, l, that has the maximum value computed using the function on the right of the arg max term.

Notice that the denominator in Equation (6.10)[259] is not dependent on the target feature, so it is functioning as a normalization constant. Furthermore, if we want to make a MAP prediction, we don't necessarily have to calculate the actual probabilities for each level in the target domain; we simply need to know which of the levels in the target domain has the largest probability. Consequently, we don't necessarily have to normalize the scores for each target level—something we would have to do if we wanted the actual probabilities.

---

10 The **paradox of the false positive** states that in order to make predictions about a rare event, the model has to be as accurate as the prior of the event is rare or there is a significant chance of **false positive** predictions (i.e., predicting the event when it is not the case). Doctorow (2010) provides an interesting discussion of this phenomenon.

11 The MAP prediction is the prediction mechanism that we assume throughout this book. An alternative mechanism is the **Bayesian optimal classifier**, but we won't discuss it in this text. See Mitchell (1997) for more details.

Instead we can simply return the target level that has the highest score from the numerator term. Using this simplification, the **Bayesian MAP prediction model** can be restated as

$$\mathbb{M}(\mathbf{q}) = \underset{l \in levels(t)}{\arg \max} \, P(\mathbf{q}[1], \dots, \mathbf{q}[m] \mid t = l) \times P(t = l) \quad (6.11)$$

Although it might seem that we now have a good solution for building probability-based prediction models, we are not quite done yet. There is one fundamental flaw with the approach that we have developed. To illustrate this, we will consider a second query instance for the meningitis diagnosis problem, this time with descriptive feature values HEADACHE = *true*, FEVER = *true*, and VOMITING = *false*. The probability of MENINGITIS = *true* given this query is

$$P(m \mid h, f, \neg v) = \frac{\left(\begin{array}{c} P(h \mid m) \times P(f \mid h, m) \\ \times P(\neg v \mid f, h, m) \times P(m) \end{array} \right)}{P(h, f, \neg v)}$$

$$= \frac{0.6666 \times 0 \times 0 \times 0.3}{0.1} = 0$$

and for MENINGITIS = *false*

$$P(\neg m \mid h, f, \neg v) = \frac{\left(\begin{array}{c} P(h \mid \neg m) \times P(f \mid h, \neg m) \\ \times P(\neg v \mid f, h, \neg m) \times P(\neg m) \end{array} \right)}{P(h, f, \neg v)}$$

$$= \frac{0.7143 \times 0.2 \times 1.0 \times 0.7}{0.1} = 1.0$$

The calculated posterior probabilities indicate that it is a certainty that the patient does not have meningitis! This is because as we progress along the sequence of conditional probabilities specified by the chain rule, the size of the set of conditioning events for each term increases. As a result, the set of events that fulfill the conditions for each conditional probability in the sequence, and hence that are considered when we compute the probability, get smaller and smaller as more and more conditions are added. The technical term for this splitting of the data into smaller and smaller sets based on larger and larger sets of conditions is **data fragmentation**. Data fragmentation is essentially an instance of the **curse of dimensionality**. As the number of descriptive features grows, the number of potential conditioning events grows. Consequently, an exponential increase is required in the size of the dataset as each new descriptive feature is added to ensure that for any conditional probability, there are enough instances in the training dataset matching the conditions so that the resulting probability is reasonable.

Returning to our example query, in order to calculate $P(h, f, \neg v \mid m)$, the chain rule requires us to define three conditional probabilities, $P(h \mid m)$, $P(f \mid h, m)$, and $P(\neg v \mid f, h, m)$. For the first of these terms, $P(h \mid m)$, only three instances in the dataset fulfill the condition of m ($\mathbf{d}_5$, $\mathbf{d}_8$ and $\mathbf{d}_{10}$). In two out of these three rows ($\mathbf{d}_8$ and $\mathbf{d}_{10}$), h is the case, so the conditional probability $P(h \mid m) = 0.6666$. These are also the only two rows that fulfill the conditions of the second term in the chain sequence, $P(f \mid h, m)$. In neither of these rows is f the case, so the conditional probability for $P(f \mid h, m)$ is 0. Because the chain rule specifies the product of a sequence of probabilities, if any of the probabilities in the sequence is zero, then the overall probability will be zero. Even worse, because there are no rows in the dataset where f, h, and m are true, there are no rows in the dataset where the conditions for the third term $P(\neg v \mid f, h, m)$ hold, so this probability is actually undefined as calculating it involves a division by zero. Trying to compute the probability of $P(h, f, \neg v \mid m)$ directly from the data rather than using the chain rule also suffers from the same problem.

In summary, whether we compute the likelihood term for this example using the chain rule or directly from the dataset, we will end up with a probability of zero, or worse, an undefined probability. This is because there are no instances in the dataset where a patient that had meningitis was suffering from a headache and had a fever but wasn't vomiting. Consequently, the probability for the MENINGITIS feature being *true* given the evidence in the query using this dataset was zero.

Clearly, the probability of a patient who has a headache and a fever having meningitis should be greater than zero. The problem here is that our dataset is not large enough to be truly representative of the meningitis diagnosis scenario, and our model is **overfitting** to the training data. The problem is even more serious than this, however, as in practice, it is almost never possible to collect a dataset that is big enough to sufficiently cover all the possible combinations of descriptive feature values that can occur in a dataset so as to avoid this. All is not lost, however, as the concepts of **conditional independence** and **factorization** can help us overcome this flaw of our current approach.

6.2.3   Conditional Independence and Factorization

So far our treatment of probability has assumed that the evidence we have collected affects the probability of the event we are trying to predict. This is not always the case. For example, it would seem reasonable to argue that the behavior of an octopus in a swimming tank should not affect the outcome of a soccer match.[12] If knowledge of one event has no effect on the probability of another event, and vice versa, then the two events are said to be **independent** of each other. If two events X and Y are independent, then

$$P(X \mid Y) = P(X)$$
$$P(X, Y) = P(X) \times P(Y)$$

Full independence between events is quite rare. A more common phenomenon is that two, or more, events may be independent if we know that a third event has happened. This is known as **conditional independence**. The typical situation where conditional independence holds between events is when the events share the same cause. For example, consider the symptoms of meningitis. If we don't know whether the patient has meningitis, then knowing that the patient has a headache may increase the probability we assign to the patient of suffering from a fever. This is because having a headache increases the probability of the patient having meningitis, which in turn increases the probability of the patient having a fever. However, if we already know that the patient has meningitis, then also knowing that the patient has a headache will not affect the probability of the patient having a fever. This is because the information we get from knowing that the patient has a headache is already contained within the information that the patient has meningitis. In this situation, knowing that someone has meningitis makes the events of them having a headache and having a fever independent of each other. For two events, X and Y, that are conditionally independent given knowledge of a third event, here Z,

---

12 During the European Soccer Championships in 2008 and the 2010 Soccer World Cup, an octopus in Germany, called Paul, was attributed with achieving an 85% success rate at predicting the results of the matches involving Germany. Paul's impressive accuracy should not be taken to suggest that octopus behavior affects soccer matches but rather that independent events may be correlated, at least for an interval of time, without the events actually being dependent. As the oft quoted maxim states: correlation does not imply causation! (See Section 3.5.2[86] for further discussion.)

we can say that

$$P(X \mid Y, Z) = P(X \mid Z)$$
$$P(X, Y \mid Z) = P(X \mid Z) \times P(Y \mid Z)$$

This allows us an important reformulation of the **chain rule** for situations in which conditional independence applies. Recall that the chain rule for calculating the probability that a set of descriptive features, $\mathbf{q}[1], \ldots, \mathbf{q}[m]$, takes a specific set of values when a target feature, t, takes a specific level, l, is

$$
\begin{aligned}
P(\mathbf{q}[1], \ldots, \mathbf{q}[m] \mid t = l) = & \\
P(\mathbf{q}[1] \mid t = l) \times P(\mathbf{q}[2] \mid \mathbf{q}[1], t = l) \times \ldots & \\
\cdots \times P(\mathbf{q}[m] \mid \mathbf{q}[m-1], \ldots, \mathbf{q}[3], \mathbf{q}[2], \mathbf{q}[1], t = l) &
\end{aligned} \tag{6.12}
$$

If the event of the target feature t taking the level l causes the assignment of values to the descriptive features, $\mathbf{q}[1], \ldots, \mathbf{q}[m]$, then the events of each descriptive feature taking a value are conditionally independent of each other given the value of the target feature. This means that the chain rule definition can be simplified as follows:

$$
\begin{aligned}
P(\mathbf{q}[1], \ldots, \mathbf{q}[m] \mid t = l) & \\
= P(\mathbf{q}[1] \mid t = l) \times P(\mathbf{q}[2] \mid t = l) \times \cdots \times P(\mathbf{q}[m] \mid t = l) & \\
= \prod_{i=1}^{m} P(\mathbf{q}[i] \mid t = l) &
\end{aligned} \tag{6.13}
$$

The reason that this simplification is so important is that it allows us to simplify the calculations in Bayes' Theorem, under the assumption of conditional independence between the descriptive features, given the level l of the target feature, from

$$
P(t = l \mid \mathbf{q}[1], \ldots, \mathbf{q}[m]) = \frac{\left(\begin{array}{l} P(\mathbf{q}[1] \mid t = l) \times P(\mathbf{q}[2] \mid \mathbf{q}[1], t = l) \times \\ \cdots \times P(\mathbf{q}[m] \mid \mathbf{q}[m-1], \ldots, \mathbf{q}[1], t = l) \\ \times P(t = l) \end{array} \right)}{P(\mathbf{q}[1], \ldots, \mathbf{q}[m])}
$$

to

$$
P(t = l \mid \mathbf{q}[1], \ldots, \mathbf{q}[m]) = \frac{\left(\prod_{i=1}^{m} P(\mathbf{q}[i] \mid t = l) \right) \times P(t = l)}{P(\mathbf{q}[1], \ldots, \mathbf{q}[m])} \tag{6.14}
$$

Where appropriate, conditional independence not only simplifies the calculations but also enables us to compactly represent the full joint probability distribution for a domain. Rather than calculating and storing the probabilities of all the joint events in a domain, we can break up the distribution into data structures called **factors**, which define distributions over subsets of features. We can then compute any of the probabilities in the joint probability distribution using the product of these factors.

For example, Equation (6.1)[251] listed the joint probability distribution for the four binary features in the meningitis diagnosis dataset in Table 6.1[250]. This distribution contained 16 entries. If, however, it is in fact the case that HEADACHE, FEVER, and VOMITING are conditionally independent of each other given MENINGITIS, then we would need to store only four factors: $P(M)$, $P(H \mid M)$, $P(F \mid M)$, and $P(V \mid M)$. We can recalculate all the elements of the joint probability distribution using the product of these four factors:

$$P(H, F, V, M) = P(M) \times P(H \mid M) \times P(F \mid M) \times P(V \mid M)$$

Because all the features in this example are binary, we need to store only the probabilities for the events where the features are true under the different combinations of values for the conditioning cases, as the probabilities for the complementary events can be computed by subtracting the stored probabilities from 1.0. Consequently, under this factorization, we need to calculate only seven probabilities directly from the data: $P(m)$, $P(h \mid m)$, $P(h \mid \neg m)$, $P(f \mid m)$, $P(f \mid \neg m)$, $P(v \mid m)$, and $P(v \mid \neg m)$. The four factors required to represent the full joint distribution over the features HEADACHE, FEVER, VOMITING, and MENINGITIS (when the first three are assumed to be conditionally independent given MENINGITIS) can be stated as

$$Factor_1 = \langle P(M) \rangle$$
$$Factor_2 = \langle P(h \mid m), P(h \mid \neg m) \rangle$$
$$Factor_3 = \langle P(f \mid m), P(f \mid \neg m) \rangle$$
$$Factor_4 = \langle P(v \mid m), P(v \mid \neg m) \rangle$$

and the product required to calculate the probability of any joint event in the domain using these four factors is

$$P(H, F, V, M) = P(M) \times P(H \mid M) \times P(F \mid M) \times P(V \mid M)$$

So, the assumed conditional independence between the features permits us to factorize the distribution and in doing so reduces the number of probabilities we need to calculate and store from the data. The reduction from 16 to

7 probabilities to represent this domain may not seem to achieve much, but there are two things to bear in mind. First, individually, the 7 probabilities have fewer constraints on them than the 16 in the full joint probability distribution. As a result, it is typically easier to collect the data required to calculate these probabilities. Second, as the number of features in the domain grows, the difference between the number of probabilities required for a factorized representation and the number of probabilities in the full joint probability distribution gets larger. For example, in a domain with one target feature and nine descriptive features, all of which are binary, the full joint probability distribution will contain $2^{10} = 1{,}024$ probabilities. However, if all the descriptive features are conditionally independent given the target feature, we can factorize the joint distribution and represent it using just 19 probabilities (one for the prior of the target and two conditional probabilities for each descriptive feature).

Apart from making a model more compact, conditional independence and factorization also increase the coverage of a probability-based prediction model by allowing the model to calculate reasonable probabilities for queries with combinations of evidence that do not occur in the training dataset. To illustrate this, let's return to the example query instance for the meningitis diagnosis problem, where HEADACHE = *true*, FEVER = *true*, and VOMITING = *false*. When we originally tried to calculate probabilities for this query, a problem arose from the requirement that we have instances in the training dataset where **all** the evidence events hold. If we treat the evidence events as conditionally independent given the target feature, however, then we can factorize the evidence into its component events and calculate probabilities for each of these events separately. By doing this, we relax the requirement that, to avoid probabilities of zero, all the evidence events must hold in at least one instance for each value in the domain of the target. Instead, to avoid zero probabilities, we require only that for each value in the domain of the target feature, there be at least one instance in the dataset where each event in the evidence holds. For example, this allows us to use the probability of a patient having a fever given that the patient has meningitis, rather than the more constrained conditional probability of the patient having a fever given that the patient has meningitis **and** is suffering from a headache.

We reiterate the factors required to represent the full joint distribution for the meningitis diagnosis scenario when we assume that the descriptive features are conditionally independent given the target, this time including the actual probabilities calculated from the dataset:

$$
\begin{aligned}
Factor_1 &= \langle P(m) = 0.3 \rangle \\
Factor_2 &= \langle P(h \mid m) = 0.6666, P(h \mid \neg m) = 0.7413 \rangle \\
Factor_3 &= \langle P(f \mid m) = 0.3333, P(f \mid \neg m) = 0.4286 \rangle \\
Factor_4 &= \langle P(v \mid m) = 0.6666, P(v \mid \neg m) = 0.5714 \rangle
\end{aligned}
\tag{6.15}
$$

Using the factors in Equation (6.15)[266], we calculate the posterior distribution for meningitis given the query instance using Equation (6.14)[263] as

$$
\begin{aligned}
P(m \mid h, f, \neg v) &= \frac{P(h \mid m) \times P(f \mid m) \times P(\neg v \mid m) \times P(m)}{\sum_i P(h \mid M_i) \times P(f \mid M_i) \times P(\neg v \mid M_i) \times P(M_i)} \\[2mm]
&= \frac{0.6666 \times 0.3333 \times 0.3333 \times 0.3}{(0.6666 \times 0.3333 \times 0.3333 \times 0.3) + (0.7143 \times 0.4286 \times 0.4286 \times 0.7)} \\[2mm]
&= 0.1948
\end{aligned}
$$

$$
\begin{aligned}
P(\neg m \mid h, f, \neg v) &= \frac{P(h \mid \neg m) \times P(f \mid \neg m) \times P(\neg v \mid \neg m) \times P(\neg m)}{\sum_i P(h \mid M_i) \times P(f \mid M_i) \times P(\neg v \mid M_i) \times P(M_i)} \\[2mm]
&= \frac{0.7143 \times 0.4286 \times 0.4286 \times 0.7}{(0.6666 \times 0.3333 \times 0.3333 \times 0.3) + (0.7143 \times 0.4286 \times 0.4286 \times 0.7)} \\[2mm]
&= 0.8052
\end{aligned}
$$

As with our previous calculations, the posterior probabilities for meningitis, calculated under the assumption of conditional independence of the evidence, indicates that the patient probably does not have meningitis, and consequently, a MAP Bayesian model would return MENINGITIS = *false* as the prediction for this query instance. However, the posterior probabilities are not as extreme as those calculated when we did not assume conditional independence. What has happened is that asserting conditional independence has allowed the evidence of the individual symptoms to be taken into account, rather than requiring an exact match across all the symptoms taken together. By doing this, the Bayesian prediction model is able to calculate reasonable probabilities for queries with combinations of evidence that do not occur in the dataset. This results in the model having a higher coverage with respect to the possible queries it can handle. Furthermore, the conditional independence assumption enables us to factorize the distribution of the domain, and consequently we need fewer probabilities with fewer constraints to represent the domain. As we will see, a fundamental component of creating probabilistic prediction models is deciding on the conditional independence assumptions we wish to make and the resulting factorization of the domain.

In the next section we introduce the naive Bayes model, a probability-based machine learning algorithm that asserts a global conditional independence between the descriptive features given the target. As a result of this conditional independence assumption, naive Bayes models are very compact and relatively robust to overfitting the data, making them one of the most popular predictive modeling approaches.

6.3   Standard Approach: The Naive Bayes Model

A naive Bayes model returns a **MAP** prediction where the posterior probabilities for the levels of the target feature are computed under the assumption of **conditional independence** between the descriptive features in an instance given a target feature level. More formally, the **naive Bayes model** is defined as

$$\mathbb{M}(\mathbf{q}) = \arg\max_{l \in levels(t)} \left(\left(\prod_{i=1}^{m} P(\mathbf{q}[i] \mid t = l) \right) \times P(t = l) \right) \tag{6.16}$$

where t is a target feature with a set of levels, $levels(t)$, and $\mathbf{q}$ is a query instance with set of descriptive features, $\mathbf{q}[1], \ldots, \mathbf{q}[m]$.

In Section 6.2[249] we described how a full joint probability distribution could be used to compute the probability for any event in a domain. The problem with this, however, is that generating full joint probability distributions suffers from the curse of dimensionality, and as a result, this approach is not tractable for domains involving more than a few features. In Section 6.2.3[262], however, we showed how conditional independence between features allows us to factorize the joint distribution, and this helps with the curse of dimensionality problem by reducing the number of probabilities we are required to calculate from the data as well as the number of conditioning constraints on these probabilities. The naive Bayes model leverages conditional independence to the extreme by assuming conditional independence between the assignment of all the descriptive feature values given the target level. This assumption allows a naive Bayes model to radically reduce the number of probabilities it requires, resulting in a very compact, highly factored representation of a domain.

We say that the naive Bayes model is *naive* because the assumption of conditional independence between the features in the evidence given the target level is a simplifying assumption that is made whether or not it is incorrect.

Despite this simplifying assumption, however, the naive Bayes approach has been found to be surprisingly accurate across a large range of domains. This is partly because errors in the calculation of the posterior probabilities for the different target levels do not necessarily result in prediction errors. As we noted when we dropped the denominator of Bayes' Theorem from the MAP prediction model (Equation (6.11)[260]), for a categorical prediction task, we are primarily interested in the relative size of the posterior probabilities for the different target levels rather than the exact probabilities. Consequently, the relative ranking of the likelihood of the target levels are, to a certain extent, robust to errors in the calculation of the exact probabilities.[13]

The assumption of conditional independence between the features in the evidence given the level of the target feature also makes the naive Bayes model relatively robust to **data fragmentation** and the **curse of dimensionality**. This is particularly important in scenarios with small datasets or with **sparse data**.[14] One application domain where sparse data is the norm rather than the exception is in **text analytics** (for example, **spam filtering**), and naive Bayes models are often successful in this domain.

The naive Bayes model can also be easily adapted to handle missing feature values: we simply drop the conditional probabilities for the evidence events that specify features taking values that are not in the data from the product of the evidence events. Obviously, doing this may have a negative effect on the accuracy of posterior probabilities computed by the model, but again this may not translate directly into prediction errors.

A final advantage of the naive Bayes model is how simple it is to train. For a given prediction task, all that is required to train a naive Bayes model is to calculate the priors for each target level and the conditional probability for each feature given each target level. As a result, a naive Bayes model can be trained relatively quickly compared to many other prediction models. A further advantage that results from this simplicity is the compactness of the naive Bayes model with which a very large dataset can be represented.

13 One consequence of this, however, is that a naive Bayes model is not a good approach for predicting a continuous target, because errors in calculating posterior probabilities do directly affect the accuracy of the model. This is the only modeling approach covered in this book for which we will not present a way to predict both continuous and categorical target features.

14 Recall that **sparse data**, discussed in Section 5.4.5[212], refers to datasets where the majority of descriptive features have a value of zero.

Overall, although naive Bayes models may not be as powerful as some other prediction models, they often provide reasonable accuracy results, for prediction tasks with categorical targets, while being robust to the curse of dimensionality and also being easy to train. As a result, a naive Bayes model is often a good prediction model to use to define a baseline accuracy score or when working with limited data.

6.3.1   A Worked Example

We will use the dataset presented in Table 6.2[270] to illustrate how to create and use a naive Bayes model for a prediction problem. This dataset relates to a **fraud detection** scenario in which we would like to build a model that predicts whether loan applications are fraudulent or genuine. There are three categorical descriptive features in this dataset. CREDIT HISTORY captures the credit history of the applicant, and its levels are *none* (the applicant has no previous loans), *paid* (the applicant had loans previously and has paid them off), *current* (the applicant has existing loans and are current in repayments), and *arrears* (the applicant has existing loans and are in arrears in repayments). The GUARANTOR/COAPPLICANT feature records whether the loan applicant has a guarantor or coapplicant associated with the application. The levels are *none*, *guarantor*, and *coapplicant*. The ACCOMMODATION feature refers to the applicant's current accommodation, and the levels are *own* (the applicant owns their accommodation), *rent* (the applicant rents their accommodation), and *free* (the applicant has free accommodation). The binary target feature, FRAUD, tells us whether the loan application turned out to be fraudulent (*true* or *false*).

To train a naive Bayes model using this data, we need to compute the prior probabilities of the target feature taking each level in its domain, and the conditional probability of each feature taking each level in its domain conditioned for each level that the target can take. There are two levels in the target feature domain, four levels in the CREDIT HISTORY domain, three in the GUARANTOR/COAPPLICANT domain, and three in the ACCOMMODATION domain. This means that we need to calculate $2 + (2 \times 4) + (2 \times 3) + (2 \times 3) = 22$ probabilities. Although this sounds like a lot of probabilities considering the size of the example dataset, it is worth noting that these 22 probabilities would suffice no matter how many new instances are added to the dataset, be it hundreds of thousands, or even millions. This is an example of the compactness of a naive Bayes representation. Be aware, however, that if new

Table 6.2

A dataset from a loan application fraud detection domain.

ID	CREDIT HISTORY	GUARANTOR/ COAPPLICANT	ACCOMMODATION	FRAUD
1	current	none	own	true
2	paid	none	own	false
3	paid	none	own	false
4	paid	guarantor	rent	true
5	arrears	none	own	false
6	arrears	none	own	true
7	current	none	own	false
8	arrears	none	own	false
9	current	none	rent	false
10	none	none	own	true
11	current	coapplicant	own	false
12	current	none	own	true
13	current	none	rent	true
14	paid	none	own	false
15	arrears	none	own	false
16	current	none	own	false
17	arrears	coapplicant	rent	false
18	arrears	none	free	false
19	arrears	none	own	false
20	paid	none	own	false

descriptive features were added to the dataset, then the number of probabilities required would grow by |domain of target| × |domain of new feature|, and, furthermore, if an extra value were added to the domain of the target, then the number of probabilities would grow exponentially. Once the required probabilities are calculated, our naive Bayes model is ready to make predictions for queries. It is that simple! Table 6.3[271] lists the probabilities we need for our naive Bayes fraud detection model.

The following is a query instance for the fraud detection domain:

CREDIT HISTORY = *paid*, GUARANTOR/COAPPLICANT = *none*,
ACCOMMODATION = *rent*

Table 6.4[272] shows the relevant probabilities needed to make a prediction for this query and the calculation of the scores for each possible prediction. Each calculation applies Equation (6.16)[267] and can be understood as a product of the four factors that the naive Bayes model represents: $P(\text{FR})$, $P(\text{CH} \mid \text{FR})$, $P(\text{GC} \mid \text{FR})$, and $P(\text{ACC} \mid \text{FR})$. The scores are 0.0139 for a prediction of *true*

Table 6.3
The probabilities needed by a naive Bayes prediction model, calculated from the data in Table 6.2[270].

$P(fr)$	$=$	0.3		$P(\neg fr)$	$=$	0.7
$P(\text{CH} = none \mid fr)$	$=$	0.1666		$P(\text{CH} = none \mid \neg fr)$	$=$	0
$P(\text{CH} = paid \mid fr)$	$=$	0.1666		$P(\text{CH} = paid \mid \neg fr)$	$=$	0.2857
$P(\text{CH} = current \mid fr)$	$=$	0.5		$P(\text{CH} = current \mid \neg fr)$	$=$	0.2857
$P(\text{CH} = arrears \mid fr)$	$=$	0.1666		$P(\text{CH} = arrears \mid \neg fr)$	$=$	0.4286
$P(\text{GC} = none \mid fr)$	$=$	0.8334		$P(\text{GC} = none \mid \neg fr)$	$=$	0.8571
$P(\text{GC} = guarantor \mid fr)$	$=$	0.1666		$P(\text{GC} = guarantor \mid \neg fr)$	$=$	0
$P(\text{GC} = coapplicant \mid fr)$	$=$	0		$P(\text{GC} = coapplicant \mid \neg fr)$	$=$	0.1429
$P(\text{ACC} = own \mid fr)$	$=$	0.6666		$P(\text{ACC} = own \mid \neg fr)$	$=$	0.7857
$P(\text{ACC} = rent \mid fr)$	$=$	0.3333		$P(\text{ACC} = rent \mid \neg fr)$	$=$	0.1429
$P(\text{ACC} = free \mid fr)$	$=$	0		$P(\text{ACC} = free \mid \neg fr)$	$=$	0.0714

Notation key: FR = FRAUD, CH = CREDIT HISTORY, GC = GUARANTOR/COAPPLICANT, ACC =ACCOMMODATION.

and 0.0245 for a prediction of *false*. It is worth emphasizing that the scores calculated are not the actual posterior probabilities for each target level given the query evidence (to get the actual probabilities we would need to normalize these scores), but they do give us enough information to rank the different target levels based on the relative posterior probabilities. A naive Bayes prediction model returns the MAP prediction, so our naive Bayes model would make a prediction of *false* and so classify this loan application query as not fraudulent.

There is one, non-obvious, aspect of this example that is particularly interesting. If we look for an instance in the dataset in Table 6.2[270] that matches all the descriptive feature values in the query, we won't find one. The fact that despite the lack of any instances that perfectly match the evidence, we were still able to calculate a score for each target level and make a prediction for the query highlights how the conditional independence assumption between the evidence given the target level increases the coverage of the model and allows the model to generalize beyond the data used to induce it.

Table 6.4

The relevant probabilities, from Table 6.3[271], needed by the naive Bayes prediction model to make a prediction for a query with CH = *paid*, GC = *none*, and ACC = *rent*, and the calculation of the scores for each target level.

$P(fr)$	=	0.3	$P(\neg fr)$	=	0.7
$P(\text{CH} = paid \mid fr)$	=	0.1666	$P(\text{CH} = paid \mid \neg fr)$	=	0.2857
$P(\text{GC} = none \mid fr)$	=	0.8334	$P(\text{GC} = none \mid \neg fr)$	=	0.8571
$P(\text{ACC} = rent \mid fr)$	=	0.3333	$P(\text{ACC} = rent \mid \neg fr)$	=	0.1429

$$\left(\prod_{k=1}^{m} P(\mathbf{q}[k] \mid fr) \right) \times P(fr) = 0.0139$$

$$\left(\prod_{k=1}^{m} P(\mathbf{q}[k] \mid \neg fr) \right) \times P(\neg fr) = 0.0245$$

6.4   Extensions and Variations

In this section we discuss extensions and variations of the naive Bayes model that increase its ability to generalize and avoid overfitting (smoothing) and that allow it to handle continuous descriptive features. We also describe Bayesian networks, which are a probability-based modeling approach that allows us to include more subtle assumptions in a model than the global assumption of conditional independence between all descriptive features that the naive Bayes model makes.

6.4.1   Smoothing

Although the assumption of conditional independence extends the coverage of a naive Bayes model and allows it to generalize beyond the contents of the training data, naive Bayes models still do not have complete coverage of the set of all possible queries. We can see the reason for this in in Table 6.3[271], where there are still some probabilities equal to zero, for example, $P(\text{CH} = none \mid \neg fr)$. These arise when there are no instances in the training data that match a specific combination of target feature and descriptive feature levels. Consequently, a model is likely to overfit the data for any query where one or more of the evidence events match the conditioned event of one of these zero probabilities. For example, consider the following query:

Table 6.5

The relevant probabilities, from Table 6.3[271], needed by the naive Bayes prediction model to make a prediction for the query with CH = *paid*, GC = *guarantor*, and ACC = *free*, and the calculation of the scores for each possible target level.

$P(fr)$	$=$	0.3	$P(\neg fr)$	$=$	0.7
$P(\text{CH} = paid \mid fr)$	$=$	0.1666	$P(\text{CH} = paid \mid \neg fr)$	$=$	0.2857
$P(\text{GC} = guarantor \mid fr)$	$=$	0.1666	$P(\text{GC} = guarantor \mid \neg fr)$	$=$	0
$P(\text{ACC} = free \mid fr)$	$=$	0	$P(\text{ACC} = free \mid \neg fr)$	$=$	0.0714

$$\left(\prod_{k=1}^{m} P\left(\mathbf{q}\,[k] \mid fr\right) \right) \times P\left(fr\right) = 0.0$$

$$\left(\prod_{k=1}^{m} P\left(\mathbf{q}\,[k] \mid \neg fr\right) \right) \times P\left(\neg fr\right) = 0.0$$

CREDIT HISTORY = *paid*, GUARANTOR/COAPPLICANT = *guarantor*,
ACCOMMODATION = *free*

Table 6.5[273] lists the relevant probabilities needed to make a prediction for this query, and the calculation of the scores for each of the possible target levels. In this instance, both possible predictions have a score of zero! Both scores are set to zero because one of the conditional probabilities used to calculate them is zero. For *fr* the probability $P(\text{ACC} = free \mid fr)$ causes the problem, and for $\neg fr$ the probability $P(\text{GC} = guarantor \mid \neg fr)$ is the offender. As a result, the model is unable to return a prediction for this query.

The way to solve this problem is by **smoothing** the probabilities used by the model. We know from the definition of probability that the sum of the probabilities of a feature taking each of its possible levels should equal 1.0:

$$\sum_{l \in levels(f)} P(f = l) = 1.0$$

where f is a feature and $levels(f)$ is the set of levels in the domain of the feature. This means that we have a total **probability mass** of 1.0 that is shared out between the different assignments of a level to a feature based on their relative frequency. Smoothing involves taking some of the probability mass from the assignments with probability greater than average and spreading it across the probabilities that are below average, or even equal to zero.

Table 6.6

The posterior probability distribution for the GUARANTOR/COAPPLICANT feature under the condition that FRAUD = *false*.

$P(GC = none \mid \neg fr)$	=	0.8571
$P(GC = guarantor \mid \neg fr)$	=	0
$P(GC = coapplicant \mid \neg fr)$	=	0.1429
$\displaystyle\sum_{l \in levels(GC)} P(GC = l \mid \neg fr)$	=	1.0

For example, if we sum across the posterior probability distribution for the GUARANTOR/COAPPLICANT feature under the condition that FRAUD = *false*, we will get a value of 1.0 (see Table 6.6[274]). Notice that within this set, $P(GC = none \mid \neg fr)$ is quite large, and at the other extreme, $P(GC = guarantor \mid \neg fr) =$ is equal to zero. Smoothing takes some of the probability mass from the events with high probability and shares this with the events with low probabilities. If this is done correctly, then the total probability mass for the set will remain equal to 1.0, but the spread of probabilities across the set will be smoother (hence the name smoothing).

There are several different ways to smooth probabilities. We will use **Laplace smoothing**. Note, that in general, it does not make sense to smooth the unconditional (prior) probabilities for the different target feature levels,[15] so here we will focus on smoothing the conditional probabilities for the features. Laplace smoothing for conditional probabilities is defined as

$$P(f = l \mid t) = \frac{count(f = l \mid t) + k}{count(f \mid t) + (k \times |Domain(f)|)}$$

where $count(f = l \mid t)$ is how often the event $f = l$ occurs in the subset of rows in the dataset where the target level is t, $count(f \mid t)$ is how often the feature, f, took any level in the subset of rows in the dataset where the target level is t, $|Domain(f)|$ is the number of levels in the domain of the feature, and k is a predetermined parameter. Larger values of k mean that more smoothing

---

15 The primary reason that we apply smoothing is to remove zero probabilities from a model's representation of a domain, and in the vast majority of cases, all the unconditional target level probabilities will be non-zero (because there will be at least one instance with each target level in the training data). Even in cases where one of the target levels is very rare, it may not be appropriate to smooth the target level priors. See Bishop (2006, pp. 45) for a discussion on how to train a probability-based prediction model in situations where one of the target levels is rare.

Table 6.7

Smoothing the posterior probabilities for the GUARANTOR/COAPPLICANT feature conditioned on FRAUD = *false*.

Raw	$P(GC = none \mid \neg fr)$	$=$	0.8571
Probabilities	$P(GC = guarantor \mid \neg fr)$	$=$	0
	$P(GC = coapplicant \mid \neg fr)$	$=$	0.1429
Smoothing	k	$=$	3
Parameters	$count(GC \mid \neg fr)$	$=$	14
	$count(GC = none \mid \neg fr)$	$=$	12
	$count(GC = guarantor \mid \neg fr)$	$=$	0
	$count(GC = coapplicant \mid \neg fr)$	$=$	2
	$\lvert Domain(GC) \rvert$	$=$	3
Smoothed	$P(GC = none \mid \neg fr) = \dfrac{12 + 3}{14 + (3 \times 3)}$	$=$	0.6522
Probabilities	$P(GC = guarantor \mid \neg fr) = \dfrac{0 + 3}{14 + (3 \times 3)}$	$=$	0.1304
	$P(GC = coapplicant \mid \neg fr) = \dfrac{2 + 3}{14 + (3 \times 3)}$	$=$	0.2174

occurs—that is more probability mass is taken from the larger probabilities and given to the small probabilities. Typically k takes small values such as 1, 2, or 3.

Table 6.7[275] illustrates the steps in smoothing the posterior probabilities for the GUARANTOR/COAPPLICANT feature when conditioned on FRAUD = *false*. We can see that after smoothing, the probability mass is more evenly distributed across the events in the set. Crucially, the posterior probability for $P(GC = guarantor \mid \neg fr)$ is no longer zero, and as a result, the coverage of the model has been extended to include queries with GUARANTOR/COAPPLI-CANT values of *guarantor*.

Table 6.8[276] lists the prior and smoothed conditional probabilities for the fraud domain that are relevant to a naive Bayes model. Notice that there are no zero probabilities, so the model will be able to return a prediction for any query in this domain. We can illustrate the extended coverage of the model by returning to the query from the beginning of this section:

Table 6.8

The Laplace smoothed (with $k = 3$) probabilities needed by a naive Bayes prediction model, calculated from the dataset in Table 6.2[270].

$P(fr)$	=	0.3	$P(\neg fr)$	=	0.7
$P(\text{CH} = none \mid fr)$	=	0.2222	$P(\text{CH} = none \mid \neg fr)$	=	0.1154
$P(\text{CH} = paid \mid fr)$	=	0.2222	$P(\text{CH} = paid \mid \neg fr)$	=	0.2692
$P(\text{CH} = current \mid fr)$	=	0.3333	$P(\text{CH} = current \mid \neg fr)$	=	0.2692
$P(\text{CH} = arrears \mid fr)$	=	0.2222	$P(\text{CH} = arrears \mid \neg fr)$	=	0.3462
$P(\text{GC} = none \mid fr)$	=	0.5333	$P(\text{GC} = none \mid \neg fr)$	=	0.6522
$P(\text{GC} = guarantor \mid fr)$	=	0.2667	$P(\text{GC} = guarantor \mid \neg fr)$	=	0.1304
$P(\text{GC} = coapplicant \mid fr)$	=	0.2	$P(\text{GC} = coapplicant \mid \neg fr)$	=	0.2174
$P(\text{ACC} = own \mid fr)$	=	0.4667	$P(\text{ACC} = own \mid \neg fr)$	=	0.6087
$P(\text{ACC} = rent \mid fr)$	=	0.3333	$P(\text{ACC} = rent \mid \neg fr)$	=	0.2174
$P(\text{ACC} = free \mid fr)$	=	0.2	$P(\text{ACC} = free \mid \neg fr)$	=	0.1739

Notation key: FR =FRAUD, CH = CREDIT HISTORY, GC = GUARANTOR/COAPPLICANT, ACC =ACCOMMODATION.

CREDIT HISTORY = *paid*, GUARANTOR/COAPPLICANT = *guarantor*, ACCOMMODATION = *free*

Table 6.9[277] illustrates how a naive Bayes model would calculate the scores for each candidate target level for this query using the smoothed probabilities from Table 6.8[276]. Using our smoothed probabilities we are able to calculate a score for both target levels: 0.0036 for *true* and 0.0043 for *false*. The target level *false* has the highest score (if only marginally) and is the MAP prediction for this query. Therefore, our naive Bayes model will predict that this loan application is not fraudulent.

6.4.2   Continuous Features: Probability Density Functions

To calculate the probability of an event, we have simply counted how often the event occurred and divided this number by how often the event could have occurred. A continuous feature can have an infinite number of values in its domain, so any particular value will occur a negligible amount of the time. In

Table 6.9

The relevant smoothed probabilities, from Table 6.8[276], needed by the naive Bayes prediction model to make a prediction for the query with CH = *paid*, GC = *guarantor*, and ACC = *free*, and the calculation of the scores for each target levels.

$P(fr)$	=	0.3	$P(\neg fr)$	=	0.7
$P(\text{CH} = paid \mid fr)$	=	0.2222	$P(\text{CH} = paid \mid \neg fr)$	=	0.2692
$P(\text{GC} = guarantor \mid fr)$	=	0.2667	$P(\text{GC} = guarantor \mid \neg fr)$	=	0.1304
$P(\text{ACC} = free \mid fr)$	=	0.2	$P(\text{ACC} = free \mid \neg fr)$	=	0.1739

$$\left(\prod_{k=1}^{m} P\left(\mathbf{q}\left[m\right] \mid fr\right) \right) \times P(fr) = 0.0036$$

$$\left(\prod_{k=1}^{m} P\left(\mathbf{q}\left[m\right] \mid \neg fr\right) \right) \times P(\neg fr) = 0.0043$$

fact, the relative frequency of any particular value for a continuous feature will be indistinguishable from zero given a large dataset.

The way to solve the problem of zero probabilities is to think in terms of how the probability of a continuous feature taking a value is distributed across the range of values that a continuous feature can take. A **probability density function (PDF)** represents the probability distribution of a continuous feature using a mathematical function, and there are a large number of standard, well-defined probability distributions—such as the **normal distribution**—that we can use to model the probability of a continuous feature taking different values in its range.

Table 6.10[278] shows the definition of some of the standard probability distributions—the **normal**, **exponential**, and **mixture of Gaussians** distributions—that are commonly used in probabilistic prediction models, and Figure 6.3[279] illustrates the shapes of the density curves of these distributions. All standard PDFs have parameters that alter the shape of the density curve defining that distribution. The parameters required for the normal, exponential, and mixture of Gaussians PDFs are shown in Table 6.10[278]. In order to use a PDF to represent the probability of a continuous feature taking different values, we need to choose these parameters to fit the characteristics of the data. We have already described the normal distribution, in some detail, in Section 3.2.1[64], so we won't repeat that introduction here, but we will describe the other distributions in a little detail.

Table 6.10

Definitions of some standard probability distributions.

Normal
$x \in \mathbb{R}$
$\mu \in \mathbb{R}$
$\sigma \in \mathbb{R}_{>0}$

$$N(x, \mu, \sigma) = \frac{1}{\sigma \sqrt{2\pi}} e^{-\frac{(x - \mu)^2}{2\sigma^2}}$$

Student-t
$x \in \mathbb{R}$
$\phi \in \mathbb{R}$
$\rho \in \mathbb{R}_{>0}$
$\kappa \in \mathbb{R}_{>0}$
$z = \frac{x - \phi}{\rho}$

$$\tau(x, \phi, \rho, \kappa) = \frac{\Gamma(\frac{\kappa+1}{2})}{\Gamma(\frac{\kappa}{2}) \times \sqrt{\pi \kappa} \times \rho} \times \left(1 + \left(\frac{1}{\kappa} \times z^2\right)\right)^{-\frac{\kappa+1}{2}}$$

Exponential
$x \in \mathbb{R}$
$\lambda \in \mathbb{R}_{>0}$

$$E(x, \lambda) = \begin{cases} \lambda e^{-\lambda x} & \text{for } x > 0 \\ 0 & \text{otherwise} \end{cases}$$

Mixture of n Gaussians
$x \in \mathbb{R}$
$\{\mu_1, \ldots, \mu_n | \mu_i \in \mathbb{R}\}$
$\{\sigma_1, \ldots, \sigma_n | \sigma_i \in \mathbb{R}_{>0}\}$
$\{\omega_1, \ldots, \omega_n | \omega_i \in \mathbb{R}_{>0}\}$
$\sum_{i=1}^{n} \omega_i = 0$

$$N(x, \mu_1, \sigma_1, \omega_1, \ldots, \mu_n, \sigma_n, \omega_n) = \sum_{i=1}^{n} \frac{\omega_i}{\sigma_i \sqrt{2\pi}} e^{-\frac{(x - \mu_i)^2}{2\sigma_i^2}}$$

The **student-t** distribution is symmetric around a single peak. In fact, it looks very similar to a normal distribution, as shown in Figure 6.3(a)[279]. The definition of the **student-t** probability density function uses the **gamma function**, $\Gamma()$, which is a standard statistical function.[16] The student-t distribution is a member of the **location-scale** family of distributions.[17] These distributions take two parameters: a **location** parameter ϕ, which specifies the position of the peak density of the distribution, and a non-negative **scale** parameter ρ, which specifies how spread out the distribution is; the higher the scale the more spread out the distribution. The normal distribution is a member of this **location-scale** family, with the mean μ specifying the location, and the standard deviation σ

---

16 See Tijms (2012), or any good probability textbook, for an introduction to the gamma function.

17 The student-t distribution can be defined in a number of ways. For example, it can be defined so that it takes only one parameter, degrees of freedom. In this text we use the extended location-scale definition.

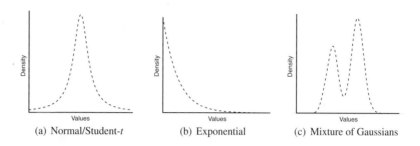

(a) Normal/Student-*t*   (b) Exponential   (c) Mixture of Gaussians

Figure 6.3
Plots of some well-known probability distributions.

acting as the scale parameter. We use different notation for location and scale parameters, ϕ and ρ, than we do for mean and standard deviation parameters of the normal, μ and σ, because the values of these parameters are estimated using different techniques: generally, the location and scale parameters for distributions are fitted to the data using a guided search process.[18] The student-*t* distribution, however, takes an extra parameter κ. This parameter is the **degrees of freedom** of the distribution. In statistics the degrees of freedom of a distribution is the number of variables in the calculation of the statistic that are free to vary. For the student-*t* distribution, the degrees of freedom is always set to the sample size (number of rows in the dataset) minus one.

From a distribution perspective, the main distinction between a normal distribution and a student-*t* is that a normal distribution has **light tails** whereas the student-*t* distribution has **fat tails**. Figure 6.4[280] illustrates the distinction between fat and light tail distributions using histograms of two datasets. The dataset in Figure 6.4(a)[280] follows a light tail distribution—the bars at the extreme left and right of the distribution have zero height. The dataset in Figure 6.4(b)[280] has a fat tail distribution—the bars on the extreme left and right of the distribution are still above zero, if only just. This distinction between fat and light tailed distributions is important because it highlights that when we use a normal distribution, we are implicitly assuming that the likelihood of values that differ from the mean of the distribution drops quite dramatically as

---

18 This guided search process is similar to the **gradient descent** search we use to fit our regression models in Chapter 7[323]. Many data analytics packages and programming APIs provide functions that implement methods to fit a distribution to a dataset.

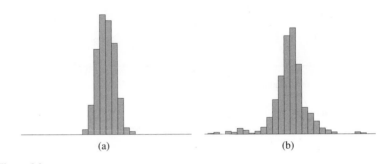

Figure 6.4

Histograms of two unimodal datasets: (a) the distribution has light tails; (b) the distribution has fat tails.

we move away from the mean. A common mistake made by many data analysts is to automatically default to modeling unimodally distributed data with a normal distribution.[19] There are statistical tests (such as the **Kolmogorov-Smirnov test**) that can be use to check whether or not a feature is normally distributed, and in cases where the feature is not normally distributed, another **unimodal** distribution, such as the **student-*t* distribution**, may be a better fit.

Another consequence of the normal distribution having light tails is that it is sensitive to outliers in the data. Figure 6.5[281] illustrates how outliers affect normal and student-*t* distributions. Figure 6.5(a)[281] shows a histogram of a dataset that has been overlaid with the curves of a normal and a student-*t* distribution that have been fitted to the data. The normal and the student-*t* distributions are both very similar, and both do a good job of matching the shape of the density histogram. Figure 6.5(b)[281] shows a histogram of the same dataset after some outliers have been added to the extreme right of the distribution. Again, we have overlaid the histogram with plots of the curves for a normal and a student-*t* distribution that have been fitted to the updated dataset. Comparing Figure 6.5(a)[281] and Figure 6.5(b)[281], we can see clearly that the introduction of outliers has a much larger effect on the normal distribution than it does on

19 Taleb (2008) discusses the problems that arise when analysts use normal distributions to model social and economic features, where the assumptions regarding light tails don't hold.

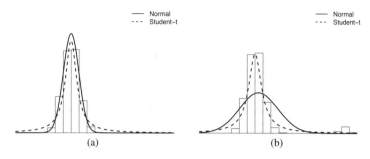

Figure 6.5

Illustration of the robustness of the student-*t* distribution to outliers: (a) a density histogram of a unimodal dataset overlaid with the density curves of a normal and a student-*t* distribution that have been fitted to the data; (b) a density histogram of the same dataset with outliers added, overlaid with the density curves of a normal and a student-*t* distribution that have been fitted to the data. (This figure is inspired by Figure 2.16 in Bishop (2006).)

the student-*t* distribution. The robustness of the student-*t* to outliers is another reason to consider using this distribution, as opposed to a normal distribution, to model unimodal data in situations with relatively small or possibly noisy datasets.

The plot of the density curve for the **exponential distribution** (Figure 6.3(b)[279]) shows that it assigns a high probability to values near the left of the distribution and that the probability of a value occurring drops dramatically as we move to the right. The standard range for the exponential distribution is from zero upward (i.e., the density assigned to values less than zero is zero). However, we can adjust this by offsetting the values input into the distribution. The exponential distribution takes one parameter, λ, known as the **rate**. Varying the value λ changes the rate at which the density drops off. As λ gets larger, the peak of the distribution (on the left) gets larger and the drop-off in density gets steeper. To fit an exponential distribution to a continuous feature, we set λ equal to 1 divided by the mean of the feature. The exponential distribution is often used to model waiting times (for example, how long it will take for a call to be answered at a help desk, how long you will have to wait for a bus, or how long before a piece of hardware fails), where the parameter λ is equal to 1 divided by the average time it takes for the event.

As the name suggests, the **mixture of Gaussians** distribution is the distribution that results when a number of normal (or Gaussian) distributions are merged. Mixture of Gaussians distributions are used to represent data that is composed of multiple subpopulations. Figure 6.6(a)[283] illustrates the profile typical of data with multiple subpopulations. The multiple peaks in the density curve arise from the different subpopulations (a distribution with multiple peaks is called **multimodal**). Using a mixture of Gaussians distribution assumes that all the subpopulations in the data are distributed following a normal distribution, but that each of these subpopulation normal distributions has a different mean and may also have a different standard deviation.

The definition of the mixture of Gaussians distribution in Table 6.10[278] shows how the individual normal distributions in a mixture of Gaussians distribution are combined using a weighted sum. Each normal that is merged is known as a **component** of the mixture. The weight of a component in the sum determines the contribution of the component to the overall density of the resulting mixture. A mixture of Gaussians distribution is defined by three parameters for each component: a mean, μ, a standard deviation, σ, and a weight, ω. The set of weight parameters for the mixture must sum to 1.

There is no closed form solution to calculate the parameters to fit a mixture of Gaussians distribution to a set of feature values, as there is for the exponential and normal distributions. Instead, given the set of values for a continuous feature, we fit a mixture of Gaussians distribution to this data by searching for the number of components and set of parameters for each component that best matches the data. **Guided search** techniques, such as the **gradient descent** algorithm, are used for this task. Analysts will often input a suggested starting point for this search based on their own analysis of the data in order to guide the process.

In Figure 6.6(b)[283] we can see the three normal distributions used to model the multimodal distribution in Figure 6.6(a)[283]. Each normal distribution has a different mean but the same standard deviation. The size of the individual normal density curves is proportional to the weight for that normal used in the mixture. Figure 6.6(c)[283] overlays the multimodal density curve on top of the three weighted normals. It is clear from this figure that the weighted sum of the three normals does an excellent job of modeling the multimodal density distribution.

The fact that we have a range of parameterized distributions to choose from means that in order to define a probability density function (PDF), we must

1. Select which probability distribution we believe will best model the distribution of the values of the feature. The simplest and most direct way to

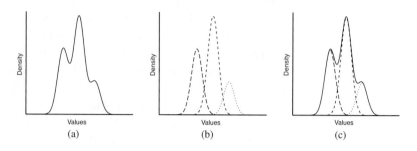

Figure 6.6

Illustration of how a mixture of Gaussians model is composed of a number of normal distributions. The curve plotted using a solid line is the mixture of Gaussians density curve, created using an appropriately weighted summation of the three normal curves, plotted using dashed and dotted lines.

choose a distribution for a feature is to create a density histogram of the feature's values and compare the shape of this histogram to the shapes of the standard distributions. We should choose whichever standard distribution best matches the shape of the histogram to model the feature.

2. Fit the parameters of the selected distribution to the feature values in the dataset. It is relatively straightforward to fit the parameters, μ and σ, of the normal distribution to a dataset by using the sample mean and standard deviation of the feature values in a dataset as estimates of μ and σ respectively. Similar to the normal distribution, the λ parameter for the exponential distribution can be easily calculated by using the value of 1 divided by the mean of the data. However, for many of the other statistical distributions, for example, the mixture of Gaussians distribution, we cannot define an equation over the data that estimates the parameters appropriately. For these distributions, the parameters are set using guided search techniques such as **gradient descent**. Fortunately, most data analytics packages and programming APIs provide functions that implement methods to fit a specified distribution to a given dataset.[20]

---

20 For example, the R language provides the *fitdistr()* method, as part of the *MASS* package, that implements a maximum-likelihood fitting of a number of univariate distributions to a given dataset.

A PDF is an abstraction over a density histogram and, as such, defines a density curve. The shape of the curve is determined by (a) the statistical distribution that is used to define the PDF, and (b) the values of the statistical distribution parameters. To use a PDF to calculate a probability, we need to think in terms of the area under an interval of the PDF curve. Consequently, to calculate a probability using a PDF, we need to first decide on the interval we wish to calculate the probability for, and then calculate the area under the density curve for that interval to give the probability of a value from that interval occurring. There is no hard and fast rule for deciding on **interval size**. Instead, this decision is made on a case by case basis and is dependent on the precision required in answering a question. In some cases, the size of the interval is defined as part of the problem we are trying to solve, or there may be a natural interval to use because of the domain. For example, when we are dealing with a financial feature, we might use intervals that represent cents, while if we were dealing with temperature, we might define the interval to be 1 degree. Once we have selected the interval size, we need to calculate the area under the density curve for that interval.[21]

When we use a PDF to represent the probability distribution of a descriptive feature in a naive Bayes model, however, we don't actually need to calculate exact probabilities. We only need to calculate the relative likelihood of a continuous feature taking a value given different levels of a target feature. The height of the density curve defined by a PDF at a particular feature value gives us this, so we can avoid the effort of calculating the actual probability. We can use a value from a PDF as a relative measure of likelihood because when the interval is very small, the actual area under a PDF curve for that interval can be approximated (with a small error proportional to the width of the interval) by the height of the PDF curve at the center of the interval multiplied by the width of the interval. Figure 6.7[285] illustrates this approximation.

If we were to include the interval width when calculating conditional probabilities for a continuous descriptive feature in a naive Bayes prediction model, using Equation (6.16)[267], we would multiply the value returned by the PDF by the same interval width each time we calculated the likelihood score for a level of the target feature. Consequently, we can drop this multiplication and

---

21 We can do this either by consulting a probability table or by using **integration** to calculate the area under the curve within the bounds of the interval. There are many excellent statistical textbooks that explain how to do both of these, for example, Montgomery and Runger (2010).

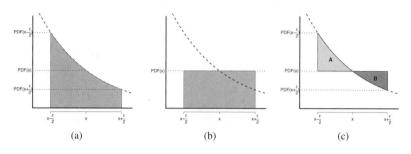

Figure 6.7

(a) The area under a density curve between the limits $x - \frac{\epsilon}{2}$ and $x + \frac{\epsilon}{2}$; (b) the approximation of this area computed by $PDF(x) \times \epsilon$; and (c) the error in the approximation is equal to the difference between area A, the area under the curve omitted from the approximation, and area B, the area above the curve erroneously included in the approximation. Both of these areas will get smaller as the width of the interval gets smaller, resulting in a smaller error in the approximation.

just use the value returned by the PDF as a relative measure of the likelihood that the feature takes a specific value.

To ground our discussion of PDFs, and to illustrate how they can be used in making naive Bayes prediction models, we will extend our loan application fraud detection scenario to have two extra continuous features: ACCOUNT BALANCE, which specifies the amount of money in the account of the loan applicant at the time of the application, and LOAN AMOUNT, which specifies the amount of the loan being applied for. Table 6.11[286] lists this extended dataset. We first use only the extra ACCOUNT BALANCE feature in the dataset (ignoring LOAN AMOUNT, which we return to later in this chapter) to demonstrate how PDFs allow us included continuous features in a naive Bayes model.

To enable the naive Bayes model to handle the ACCOUNT BALANCE feature, we have to extend the set of probabilities used by the model to represent the domain to include the probabilities for this feature. Recall that the naive Bayes domain representation defines a conditional probability for each possible value in the domain of a descriptive feature for each level in the domain of the target. In our example, the target feature, FRAUD, is binary, so we need to define two conditional probabilities for each value in the domain of the new descriptive feature: $P(AB = x \mid fr)$ and $P(AB = x \mid \neg fr)$. Because the descriptive feature ACCOUNT BALANCE is continuous, there is an infinite number of values in the feature's domain. However, we know that using an appropriately defined PDF, we can approximate the probability of

Table 6.11

The dataset from the loan application fraud detection domain (from Table 6.2[270]) with two continuous descriptive features added: ACCOUNT BALANCE and LOAN AMOUNT.

ID	CREDIT HISTORY	GUARANTOR/ COAPPLICANT	ACCOMO- DATION	ACCOUNT BALANCE	LOAN AMOUNT	FRAUD
1	current	none	own	56.75	900	true
2	current	none	own	1,800.11	150,000	false
3	current	none	own	1,341.03	48,000	false
4	paid	guarantor	rent	749.50	10,000	true
5	arrears	none	own	1,150.00	32,000	false
6	arrears	none	own	928.30	250,000	true
7	current	none	own	250.90	25,000	false
8	arrears	none	own	806.15	18,500	false
9	current	none	rent	1,209.02	20,000	false
10	none	none	own	405.72	9,500	true
11	current	coapplicant	own	550.00	16,750	false
12	current	none	free	223.89	9,850	true
13	current	none	rent	103.23	95,500	true
14	paid	none	own	758.22	65,000	false
15	arrears	none	own	430.79	500	false
16	current	none	own	675.11	16,000	false
17	arrears	coapplicant	rent	1,657.20	15,450	false
18	arrears	none	free	1,405.18	50,000	false
19	arrears	none	own	760.51	500	false
20	current	none	own	985.41	35,000	false

the feature taking any value in its domain. As a result, we simply need to define two PDFs for the new feature with each PDF conditioned on a different level of the target feature: $P(\text{AB} = x \,|\, fr) = PDF_1(\text{AB} = x \,|\, fr)$ and $P(\text{AB} = x \,|\, \neg fr) = PDF_2(\text{AB} = x \,|\, \neg fr)$. These two PDFs do not have to be defined using the same distribution. Once we have selected the distributions we wish to use, to define a PDF for a descriptive feature that is conditioned on a particular target, we fit the parameters of the selected distribution to the subset of the data where the target has that value.

The first step in defining the two PDFs is to decide which distribution we will use to define the PDFs for each target feature level. To make this decision, we partition the training data based on the target feature and generate histograms of the values of the descriptive feature for each of the splits. We then select the statistical distribution that is most similar in shape to each of the resulting histograms. Figure 6.8[287] shows the histograms of the values of

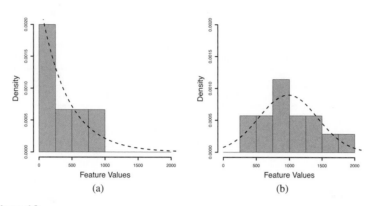

Figure 6.8

Histograms, using a bin size of 250 units, and density curves for the ACCOUNT BALANCE feature:
(a) the fraudulent instances overlaid with a fitted exponential distribution; (b) the non-fraudulent
instances overlaid with a fitted normal distribution.

the ACCOUNT BALANCE feature partitioned on the two levels of the FRAUD
target feature. It is clear from these histograms that the distribution of values
taken by the ACCOUNT BALANCE feature in the set of instances where FRAUD
= *true* follows an exponential distribution; whereas, the distribution of the values taken by the ACCOUNT BALANCE feature in the set of instances where the
FRAUD = *false* is similar to a normal distribution.

Once we have selected the distributions, the next step is to fit the distributions to the data. To fit the exponential distribution we compute the sample
mean of the ACCOUNT BALANCE feature in the set of instances where FRAUD
= *true* and set the λ parameter equal to 1 divided by this value. To fit the normal distribution to the set of instances where FRAUD = *false*, we compute the
sample mean and sample standard deviation for the ACCOUNT BALANCE feature for this set of instances and set the parameters of the normal distribution
to these values. Table 6.12[288] shows how these values are calculated, and the
dashed lines in Figure 6.8[287] plot the density curves that result from this process. Once distributions have been fitted to the data, we can extend the naive
Bayes domain representation to include the PDFs. Table 6.13[289] shows the
extended domain representation.

To use the extended domain representation of the model to make a prediction for a query, we calculate the product of the relevant descriptive feature
probabilities and the priors for the different target levels as before, but using

Table 6.12

Partitioning the dataset based on the value of the target feature and fitting the parameters of a statistical distribution to model the ACCOUNT BALANCE feature in each partition.

(a) Instances where FRAUD = *true* and the fitted parameters for the exponential distribution

(b) Instances where FRAUD = *false* and the fitted parameters for the normal distribution

ID	...	ACCOUNT BALANCE	FRAUD		ID	...	ACCOUNT BALANCE	FRAUD
1		56.75	true		2		1,800.11	false
4		749.50	true		3		1,341.03	false
6		928.30	true		5		1,150.00	false
10	...	405.72	true		7		250.90	false
12		223.89	true		8		806.15	false
13		103.23	true		9		1,209.02	false
$\overline{AB}$		411.22			11	...	550.00	false
$\lambda = {}^{1}/_{\overline{AB}}$		0.0024			14		758.22	false
					15		430.79	false
					16		675.11	false
					17		1,657.20	false
					18		1,405.18	false
					19		760.51	false
					20		985.41	false
					$\overline{AB}$		984.26	
					$sd(AB)$		460.94	

Note: ACCOUNT BALANCE has been shortened to AB in these tables.

PDFs to calculate the probabilities for the continuous feature. Table 6.14[290] shows how a prediction is made for the following query:

CREDIT HISTORY = *paid*, GUARANTOR/COAPPLICANT = *guarantor*, ACCOMMODATION = *free*, ACCOUNT BALANCE = 759.07

The calculations for the probabilities for the ACCOUNT BALANCE feature are made using the equations for the normal and exponential distributions in Table 6.10[278]. The result is that FRAUD = *false* still has the highest score and will be returned as the prediction for this query.

Table 6.13

The Laplace smoothed (with $k = 3$) probabilities needed by a naive Bayes prediction model, calculated from the dataset in Table 6.11[286], extended to include the conditional probabilities for the new ACCOUNT BALANCE feature, which are defined in terms of PDFs.

$P(fr)$	$=$	0.3	$P(\neg fr)$	$=$	0.7
$P(\text{CH} = none \mid fr)$	$=$	0.2222	$P(\text{CH} = none \mid \neg fr)$	$=$	0.1154
$P(\text{CH} = paid \mid fr)$	$=$	0.2222	$P(\text{CH} = paid \mid \neg fr)$	$=$	0.2692
$P(\text{CH} = current \mid fr)$	$=$	0.3333	$P(\text{CH} = current \mid \neg fr)$	$=$	0.2692
$P(\text{CH} = arrears \mid fr)$	$=$	0.2222	$P(\text{CH} = arrears \mid \neg fr)$	$=$	0.3462
$P(\text{GC} = none \mid fr)$	$=$	0.5333	$P(\text{GC} = none \mid \neg fr)$	$=$	0.6522
$P(\text{GC} = guarantor \mid fr)$	$=$	0.2667	$P(\text{GC} = guarantor \mid \neg fr)$	$=$	0.1304
$P(\text{GC} = coapplicant \mid fr)$	$=$	0.2	$P(\text{GC} = coapplicant \mid \neg fr)$	$=$	0.2174
$P(\text{ACC} = own \mid fr)$	$=$	0.4667	$P(\text{ACC} = own \mid \neg fr)$	$=$	0.6087
$P(\text{ACC} = rent \mid fr)$	$=$	0.3333	$P(\text{ACC} = rent \mid \neg fr)$	$=$	0.2174
$P(\text{ACC} = free \mid fr)$	$=$	0.2	$P(\text{ACC} = free \mid \neg fr)$	$=$	0.1739
$P(\text{AB} = x \mid fr)$			$P(\text{AB} = x \mid \neg fr)$		

$$\approx E \begin{pmatrix} x, \\ \lambda = 0.0024 \end{pmatrix} \qquad \approx N \begin{pmatrix} x, \\ \mu = 984.26, \\ \sigma = 460.94 \end{pmatrix}$$

Notation key: FR = FRAUD, CH = CREDIT HISTORY, GC = GUARANTOR/COAPPLICANT, ACC = ACCOMMODATION, AB = ACCOUNT BALANCE.

6.4.3 Continuous Features: Binning

A commonly used alternative to representing a continuous feature using a probability density function is to convert the feature into a categorical feature using **binning**. In Section 3.6.2[94] we explained two of the best known binning techniques, **equal-width binning** and **equal-frequency binning**, and discussed some of the general advantages and disadvantages of each technique. One feature of equal-width binning is that it can result in a very uneven distribution of instances across the bins, with some bins containing a large number of instances and other bins being nearly empty. This uneven distribution of instances across bins can have dramatic and unwanted consequences for probability-based models. Bins that contain only a few instances may have

Table 6.14

The probabilities, from Table 6.13[289], needed by the naive Bayes prediction model to make a prediction for the query with CH = *paid*, GC = *guarantor*, ACC = *free*, and AB=759.07, and the calculation of the scores for each candidate prediction.

$P(fr)$	=	0.3	$P(\neg fr)$	=	0.7
$P(\text{CH} = paid \mid fr)$	=	0.2222	$P(\text{CH} = paid \mid \neg fr)$	=	0.2692
$P(\text{GC} = guarantor \mid fr)$	=	0.2667	$P(\text{GC} = guarantor \mid \neg fr)$	=	0.1304
$P(\text{ACC} = free \mid fr)$	=	0.2	$P(\text{ACC} = free \mid \neg fr)$	=	0.1739
$P(\text{AB} = 759.07 \mid fr)$			$P(\text{AB} = 759.07 \mid \neg fr)$		
$\approx E\left(\begin{array}{c}759.07, \\ \lambda = 0.0024\end{array}\right)$	=	0.00039	$\approx N\left(\begin{array}{c}759.07, \\ \mu = 984.26, \\ \sigma = 460.94\end{array}\right)$	=	0.00077

$$\left(\prod_{k=1}^{m} P\left(\mathbf{q}\,[k] \mid fr\right)\right) \times P\left(fr\right) = 0.0000014$$

$$\left(\prod_{k=1}^{m} P\left(\mathbf{q}\,[k] \mid \neg fr\right)\right) \times P\left(\neg fr\right) = 0.0000033$$

extremely small or extremely large conditional probabilities (depending on how the instances are divided when conditioned on the target feature), and these extreme conditional probabilities may bias a model based on the parameters of the binning technique (for example, the number of bins we choose to have) rather than on real distributions in the data. For this reason, we recommend the use of equal-frequency binning to convert continuous features to categorical ones for probability-based models.

Returning to our loan application fraud detection example, we will show how binning can be used to include the LOAN AMOUNT feature (see Table 6.11[286]) in a naive Bayes prediction model for this scenario. Table 6.15[291] shows the discretization of the LOAN AMOUNT feature into 4 equal-frequency bins. In this table, the instances in the dataset have been reordered in ascending order based on their LOAN AMOUNT values. Even when using equal-frequency binning, there is still chance that the partitioning of the data will give rise to extreme conditional probabilities. For example, all the *bin3* values have a target feature value of *false*. Consequently, the posterior probability of LOAN AMOUNT = *bin3* conditioned on FRAUD = *true* will be 0.0 and LOAN

Table 6.15

The LOAN AMOUNT continuous feature discretized into 4 equal-frequency bins.

ID	LOAN AMOUNT	BINNED LOAN AMOUNT	FRAUD	ID	LOAN AMOUNT	BINNED LOAN AMOUNT	FRAUD
15	500	bin1	false	9	20,000	bin3	false
19	500	bin1	false	7	25,000	bin3	false
1	900	bin1	true	5	32,000	bin3	false
10	9,500	bin1	true	20	35,000	bin3	false
12	9,850	bin1	true	3	48,000	bin3	false
4	10,000	bin2	true	18	50,000	bin4	false
17	15,450	bin2	false	14	65,000	bin4	false
16	16,000	bin2	false	13	95,500	bin4	true
11	16,750	bin2	false	2	150,000	bin4	false
8	18,500	bin2	false	6	250,000	bin4	true

AMOUNT = *bin3* conditioned FRAUD = *false* will be 1.0. **Smoothing** should be used in conjunction with binning to help with these extreme probabilities.

Once we have discretized the data using binning, we need to record the raw continuous feature thresholds between the bins. The reason for this is that we need to be able to bin the features of any query instances appropriately before we make predictions for them. To calculate these thresholds, we take the mid-point in the feature range between the instance with the highest feature value in one bin and the feature with the lowest feature value in the next bin. For example, the instances in Table 6.15[291] are ordered in ascending order based on the magnitude of their original LOAN AMOUNT value. So, the threshold between *bin1* and *bin2* will be the mid-point between the LOAN AMOUNT values for d_{12} (9,850) and d_4 (10,000) which is 9,925. The threshold boundaries for the 4 bins used to discretize the LOAN AMOUNT feature are

$$
\begin{aligned}
&& bin1 &\leqslant 9,925 \\
9,925 <\!\!\!&& bin2 &\leqslant 19,250 \\
19,225 <\!\!\!&& bin3 &\leqslant 49,000 \\
49,000 <\!\!\!&& bin4 &
\end{aligned}
$$

Once we have discretized the continuous features and calculated the thresholds for binning query features, we are ready to create our predictive model. As before, for a naive Bayes model, we calculate the prior probability distribution for the target feature and the posterior distribution for each descriptive feature conditioned on the target feature. Again, we should smooth the resulting probabilities. Table 6.16[293] shows the Laplace smoothed (with $k = 3$) probabilities required by a naive Bayes prediction model calculated from the dataset in Table 6.11[286]. Notice that in this domain representation, we blend different approaches to continuous features: we are retaining the PDFs developed in Section 6.4.2[276] for the ACCOUNT BALANCE feature and extend the representation with the binned version of the LOAN AMOUNT feature, BINNED LOAN AMOUNT.

We are now ready to process a query that has the continuous LOAN AMOUNT feature as part of the evidence:

$$\text{CREDIT HISTORY} = paid, \text{GUARANTOR/COAPPLICANT} = guarantor,$$
$$\text{ACCOMMODATION} = free, \text{ACCOUNT BALANCE} = 759.07,$$
$$\text{LOAN AMOUNT} = 8,000$$

The LOAN AMOUNT value for this query (8,000) is below the threshold for *bin1*. Consequently, the query LOAN AMOUNT feature will be treated as being equal to *bin1* during prediction. Table 6.17[294] lists the calculations of the naive Bayes scores for the candidate predictions for this query: 0.000000462 for *true* and 0.000000633 for *false*. The target level *false* has the highest score and will be the prediction made by the model.

6.4.4   Bayesian Networks

In this chapter we have introduced two ways to represent the probabilities of events in a domain, a **full joint probability distribution** and a **naive Bayes model**. A full joint probability distribution encodes the probabilities for all joint events in the domain. Using a full joint probability distribution, we can do probabilistic inference by summing out the features we are not interested in. Full joint probability distributions, however, grow at an exponential rate as new features or feature levels are added to the domain. This exponential growth rate is partially due to the fact that a full joint probability distribution ignores the structural relationships between features, such as direct influence and conditional independence relationships. As a result, full joint distributions are not tractable for any domain of reasonable complexity. By contrast, a naive Bayes model uses a very compact representation of a domain. The reason for this is that the model assumes that all the descriptive features are **conditionally**

Table 6.16
The Laplace smoothed (with $k = 3$) probabilities needed by a naive Bayes prediction model, calculated from the data in Tables 6.11[286] and 6.15[291].

$P(fr)$	=	0.3	$P(\neg fr)$	=	0.7
$P(CH = none \mid fr)$	=	0.2222	$P(CH = none \mid \neg fr)$	=	0.1154
$P(CH = paid \mid fr)$	=	0.2222	$P(CH = paid \mid \neg fr)$	=	0.2692
$P(CH = current \mid fr)$	=	0.3333	$P(CH = current \mid \neg fr)$	=	0.2692
$P(CH = arrears \mid fr)$	=	0.2222	$P(CH = arrears \mid \neg fr)$	=	0.3462
$P(GC = none \mid fr)$	=	0.5333	$P(GC = none \mid \neg fr)$	=	0.6522
$P(GC = guarantor \mid fr)$	=	0.2667	$P(GC = guarantor \mid \neg fr)$	=	0.1304
$P(GC = coapplicant \mid fr)$	=	0.2	$P(GC = coapplicant \mid \neg fr)$	=	0.2174
$P(ACC = own \mid fr)$	=	0.4667	$P(ACC = own \mid \neg fr)$	=	0.6087
$P(ACC = rent \mid fr)$	=	0.3333	$P(ACC = rent \mid \neg fr)$	=	0.2174
$P(ACC = free \mid fr)$	=	0.2	$P(ACC = free \mid \neg fr)$	=	0.1739
$P(AB = x \mid fr)$			$P(AB = x \mid \neg fr)$		

$$\approx E \begin{pmatrix} x, \\ \lambda = 0.0024 \end{pmatrix} \qquad \approx N \begin{pmatrix} x, \\ \mu = 984.26, \\ \sigma = 460.94 \end{pmatrix}$$

$P(BLA = bin1 \mid fr)$	=	0.3333	$P(BLA = bin1 \mid \neg fr)$	=	0.1923
$P(BLA = bin2 \mid fr)$	=	0.2222	$P(BLA = bin2 \mid \neg fr)$	=	0.2692
$P(BLA = bin3 \mid fr)$	=	0.1667	$P(BLA = bin3 \mid \neg fr)$	=	0.3077
$P(BLA = bin4 \mid fr)$	=	0.2778	$P(BLA = bin4 \mid \neg fr)$	=	0.2308

Notation key: FR =FRAUD, CH = CREDIT HISTORY, GC = GUARANTOR/COAPPLICANT, ACC =ACCOMMODATION, AB =ACCOUNT BALANCE, BLA =BINNED LOAN AMOUNT.

independent of each other given the value of the target feature. The compactness of the representation is at the cost of making a naive assumption that may adversely affect the predictive accuracy of the model.

Bayesian networks use a graph-based representation to encode the structural relationships—such as direct influence and conditional independence—between subsets of features in a domain. Consequently, a Bayesian network representation is generally more compact than a full joint distribution (because

Table 6.17
The relevant smoothed probabilities, from Table 6.16[293], needed by the naive Bayes model to make a prediction for the query with CH = *paid*, GC = *guarantor*, ACC = *free*, AB=759.07, and LA=8,000, and the calculation of the scores for each candidate prediction.

$P(fr)$	=	0.3		$P(\neg fr)$	=	0.7
$P(\text{CH} = paid \mid fr)$	=	0.2222		$P(\text{CH} = paid \mid \neg fr)$	=	0.2692
$P(\text{GC} = guarantor \mid fr)$	=	0.2667		$P(\text{GC} = guarantor \mid \neg fr)$	=	0.1304
$P(\text{ACC} = free \mid fr)$	=	0.2		$P(\text{ACC} = free \mid \neg fr)$	=	0.1739
$P(\text{AB} = 759.07 \mid fr)$				$P(\text{AB} = 759.07 \mid \neg fr)$		
$\approx E\left(\begin{array}{c} 759.07, \\ \lambda = 0.0024 \end{array}\right)$	=	0.00039		$\approx N\left(\begin{array}{c} 759.07, \\ \mu = 984.26, \\ \sigma = 460.94 \end{array}\right)$	=	0.00077
$P(\text{BLA} = bin1 \mid fr)$	=	0.3333		$P(\text{BLA} = bin1 \mid \neg fr)$	=	0.1923

$$\left(\prod_{k=1}^{m} P(\mathbf{q}[k] \mid fr) \right) \times P(fr) = 0.000000462$$

$$\left(\prod_{k=1}^{n} P(\mathbf{q}[k] \mid \neg fr) \right) \times P(\neg fr) = 0.000000633$$

it can encode conditional independence relationships), yet it is not forced to assert a global conditional independence between all descriptive features. As such, Bayesian network models are an intermediary between full joint distributions and naive Bayes models and offer a useful compromise between model compactness and predictive accuracy.

A Bayesian network is a directed acyclical graph (there are no cycles in the graph) that is composed of three basic elements:

- **nodes**: each feature in a domain is represented by a single node in the graph.

- **edges**: nodes are connected by directed links; the connectivity of the links in a graph encodes the influence and conditional independence relationships between nodes.

- **conditional probability tables**: each node has a conditional probability table (**CPT**) associated with it. A CPT lists the probability distribution of the feature represented by the node conditioned on the features represented by the other nodes to which a node is connected by edges.

Figure 6.9(a)[296] illustrates a simple Bayesian network. This network describes a domain consisting of two features A and B. The directed link from A to B indicates that the value of A directly influences the value of B. In probability terms, the directed edge from A to B in Figure 6.9(a)[296] states that

$$P(A,B) = P(B \mid A) \times P(A) \tag{6.17}$$

For example, the probability of the event a and $\neg b$ is

$$P(a, \neg b) = P(\neg b \mid a) \times P(a) = 0.7 \times 0.4 = 0.28$$

where the probabilities used in the calculation are read directly from the CPTs in Figure 6.9(a)[296]. In the terminology of Bayesian networks, node A is a **parent node** of B, and node B is a **child node** of A, because there is a direct edge from A into B. The CPT associated with each node defines the probabilities of each feature taking a value given the value(s) of its parent node(s). Node A has no parents, so the CPT just lists the unconditional probability distribution for A. Notice that each row in the CPT tables sum to 1. Consequently, for a categorical feature with N levels, we need only $N - 1$ probabilities in each row, with the final probability being understood as equal to 1 minus the sum of the other $N - 1$ probabilities. For example, when dealing with binary features, we need simply state the probability of each feature being *true*, and the *false* value is understood as 1 minus this probability. The network in Figure 6.9(a)[296] could be simplified in this way, and we will use this simplification for all networks drawn from now on. The standard approach for handling continuous features in a Bayesian network is to use binning. As a result, the CPT representation is sufficient to handle both categorical and (binned) continuous features.

Equation (6.17)[295] can be generalized to the statement that for any network with N nodes, the probability of an event $x_1, \ldots, x_n$, can be computed using the following formula:

$$P(x_1, \ldots, x_n) = \prod_{i=1}^{n} P(x_i \mid Parents(x_i)) \tag{6.18}$$

where $Parents(x_i)$ describes the set of nodes in the graph that directly link into node x_i. Using this equation, we can compute any joint event in the domain represented by the Bayesian network. For example, using the slightly more complex Bayesian network in Figure 6.9(b)[296], we can calculate the probability

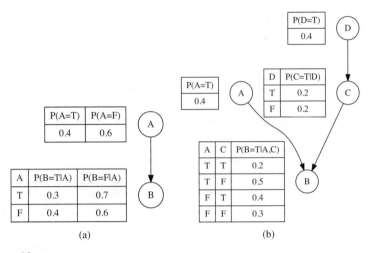

P(A=T)	P(A=F)
0.4	0.6

A

A	P(B=T|A)	P(B=F|A)
T	0.3	0.7
F	0.4	0.6

B

(a)

P(A=T)
0.4

A

P(D=T)
0.4

D

D	P(C=T|D)
T	0.2
F	0.2

C

A	C	P(B=T|A,C)
T	T	0.2
T	F	0.5
F	T	0.4
F	F	0.3

B

(b)

Figure 6.9
(a) A Bayesian network for a domain consisting of two binary features. The structure of the network states that the value of feature A directly influences the value of feature B. (b) A Bayesian network consisting of 4 binary features with a path containing 3 generations of nodes: D, C, and B.

of the joint event $P(a, \neg b, \neg c, d)$ as

$$P(a, \neg b, \neg c, d) = P(\neg b \mid a, \neg c) \times P(\neg c \mid d) \times P(a) \times P(d)$$
$$= 0.5 \times 0.8 \times 0.4 \times 0.4 = 0.064$$

When we are computing a conditional probability, we need to be aware of the state of both the parents of a node and the children of a node and their parents. This is because knowledge of the state of a child node can tell us something about the state of the parent node. For example, returning to our simple Bayesian network in Figure 6.9(a)[296], we can compute $P(a \mid \neg b)$ using

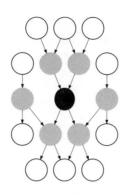

Figure 6.10

A depiction of the Markov blanket of a node. The gray nodes define the Markov blanket of the black node. The black node is conditionally independent of the white nodes given the state of the gray nodes.

Bayes' Theorem as follows:

$$P(a \mid \neg b) = \frac{P(\neg b \mid a) \times P(a)}{P(\neg b)} = \frac{P(\neg b \mid a) \times P(a)}{\sum_i P(\neg b \mid A_i)}$$

$$= \frac{P(\neg b \mid a) \times P(a)}{(P(\neg b \mid a) \times P(a)) + (P(\neg b \mid \neg a) \times P(\neg a))}$$

$$= \frac{0.7 \times 0.4}{(0.7 \times 0.4) + (0.6 \times 0.6)} = 0.4375$$

Essentially, here we are using Bayes' Theorem to invert the dependencies between the nodes. So, for a conditional independence, we need to take into account not only the parents of a node but also the state of its children and their parents. If we have knowledge of these parent and children nodes, however, then the node is **conditionally independent** of the rest of the nodes in the graph. The set of nodes in a graph that make a node independent of the rest of the graph are known as the **Markov blanket** of a node. Figure 6.10[297] illustrates the Markov blanket of a node.

So, the conditional probability of a node x_i in a graph with n nodes can be defined as

$$P(x_i \mid x_1, \ldots, x_{i-1}, x_{i+1}, \ldots, x_n) =$$

$$P(x_i \mid Parents(x_i)) \prod_{j \in Children(x_i)} P(x_j \mid Parents(x_j)) \qquad (6.19)$$

where *Parents*(x_i) describes the set of nodes in the graph that directly link into node x_i, and *Children*(x_i) describes the set of nodes in the graph that x_i directly links into. Applying this definition to the network in Figure 6.9(b)[296], we can calculate the probability of $P(c \mid \neg a, b, d)$ as

$$P(c \mid \neg a, b, d) = P(c \mid d) \times P(b \mid c, \neg a)$$
$$= 0.2 \times 0.4 = 0.08$$

We already used Equation (6.19)[297] when we were making predictions for a naive Bayes classifier. A naive Bayes classifier is a Bayesian network with a specific topological structure. Figure 6.11(a)[299] illustrates the network structure of a naive Bayes classifier and how it encodes the conditional independence between the descriptive features given assumed knowledge of the target. Figure 6.11(b)[299] illustrates the network structure of the naive Bayes model for predicting a fraudulent loan application that was built in Section 6.3.1[269]. We can see in this structure that the target feature, FRAUD, has no parents and is the single parent for all the descriptive feature nodes. This structure directly reflects the assumption, made by naive Bayes models, of the conditional independence between descriptive features given knowledge of the target feature and is why the conditional probabilities of the descriptive features in a naive Bayes model are conditioned only on the target feature.

When we computed a conditional probability for the target feature using a naive Bayes model, we used the following calculation

$$P(t \mid \mathbf{d}[1], \ldots, \mathbf{d}[n]) = P(t) \prod_{j \in Children(t)} P(\mathbf{d}[j] \mid t)$$

This equation is equivalent to Equation (6.19)[297]. The fact that the probability $P(t)$ is an unconditional probability simply reflects that structure of the naive Bayes' network where the target feature has no parent nodes (see Figure 6.11(a)[299]).

Computing a conditional probability for a node becomes more complex if the value of one or more of the parent nodes is unknown. In this situation the node becomes dependent on the ancestors of it unknown parent. This is because if a parent node is unknown, then to compute the distribution for the node, we must sum out this parent. However, to do this summing out, we must know the distribution for the unknown parent, which in turn requires us to sum out the parents of the parent, and so on if necessary. As a result of this recursive summing out, the distribution over a node is dependent on knowledge of the

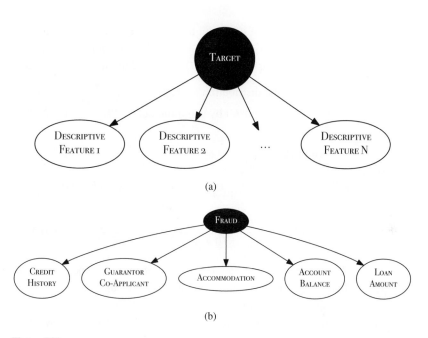

Figure 6.11

(a) A Bayesian network representation of the conditional independence asserted by a naive Bayes model between the descriptive features given knowledge of the target feature; (b) a Bayesian network representation of the conditional independence assumption for the naive Bayes model in the fraud example.

ancestors of any of its parent nodes.[22] For example, in Figure 6.9(b)[296], if the status of node C is not known, then node B becomes dependent on node D. For example, to compute $P(b \mid a, d)$ we would do the following calculations

1. Compute the distribution for C given D: $P(c \mid d) = 0.2$, $P(\neg c \mid d) = 0.8$
2. Compute $P(b \mid a, C)$ by summing out C: $P(b \mid a, C) = \sum_i P(b \mid a, C_i)$

$$
\begin{aligned}
P(b \mid a, C) &= \sum_i P(b \mid a, C_i) = \sum_i \frac{P(b, a, C_i)}{P(a, C_i)} \\
&= \frac{(P(b \mid a, c) \times P(a) \times P(c)) + (P(b \mid a, \neg c) \times P(a) \times P(\neg c))}{(P(a) \times P(c)) + (P(a) \times P(\neg c))} \\
&= \frac{(0.2 \times 0.4 \times 0.2) + (0.5 \times 0.4 \times 0.8)}{(0.4 \times 0.2) + (0.4 \times 0.8)} = 0.44
\end{aligned}
$$

This example illustrates the power of Bayesian networks. When complete knowledge of the state of all the nodes in the network is not available, we clamp the values of nodes that we do have knowledge of and sum out the unknown nodes. Furthermore, during these calculations, we only need to condition a node on its Markov blanket, which dramatically reduces the number of probabilities required by the network.

6.4.4.1   Building Bayesian Networks

Bayesian networks can be constructed by hand or learned from data. Learning both the topology of a Bayesian network and the parameters in the CPTs in the network is a difficult computational task. One of the things that makes learning the structure of a Bayesian network so difficult is that it is possible to define several different Bayesian networks as representations for the same full joint probability distribution. Consider, for example, a probability distribution for three binary features A, B, and C. The probability for a joint event in this domain $P(A, B, C)$ can be decomposed using the **chain rule** in the following way:

$$P(A, B, C) = P(C \mid A, B) \times P(B \mid A) \times P(A) \tag{6.20}$$

---

22 The conditional independence relationship between any two nodes in a Bayesian network can be specified using the framework of **d-separation** (the "d" stands for *directed*) (Pearl, 1988). We don't discuss d-separation in this book as it is not required for our discussion.

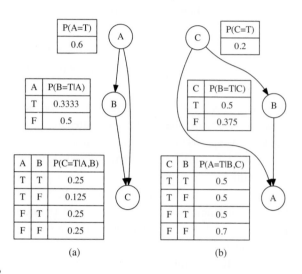

Figure 6.12

Two different Bayesian networks, each defining the same full joint probability distribution.

The chain rule, however, doesn't specify any constraints on which features in the domain we choose to condition on. We could just as easily have decomposed the probability of the joint event as follows:

$$P(A, B, C) = P(A \mid C, B) \times P(B \mid C) \times P(C) \qquad (6.21)$$

Both of these decompositions are valid, and both define different Bayesian networks for the domain. Figure 6.12(a)[301] illustrates the Bayesian network representing the decomposition defined in Equation (6.20)[300], and Figure 6.12(b)[301] illustrates the Bayesian network representing the decompositions defined in Equation (6.21)[301].

We can show that both of the networks in Figure 6.12[301] represent the same joint probability by using each of them to calculate the probability of an arbitrarily chosen joint event from the domain. We should get the same probability for the joint event from both of the networks. For this example, we will calculate the probability of the event $\neg a, b, c$. Using the Bayesian network in Figure 6.12(a)[301], we would carry out the calculation as follows:

$$P(\neg a, b, c) = P(c \mid \neg a, b) \times P(b \mid \neg a) \times P(\neg a)$$
$$= 0.25 \times 0.5 \times 0.4 = 0.05$$

Using the network in Figure 6.12(b)[301], the calculation would be

$$P(\neg a, b, c) = P(\neg a \mid c, b) \times P(b \mid c) \times P(c)$$
$$= 0.5 \times 0.5 \times 0.2 = 0.05$$

Both networks return the same probability for the joint event. In fact, these networks will return identical probabilities for all events in this domain.

The basic approach to learning the structure of a Bayesian network is to use a local search algorithm that moves through the space of possible networks and parameters, and searches for the network topology and CPT parameters, that best fit with the data. To start the search, the algorithm is given a seed network and then iteratively adapts this network by adding, removing, or reversing links (and/or adding and removing hidden nodes), accompanied by iterations of parameter learning after each network structure adaptation. One of the difficulties with learning a network structure is that we can always improve the likelihood of the data given a network by simply adding new links into the network. Each time we add a link to a network we increase the number of CPT entries in the network. The CPT entries are essentially parameters on the network, and the more parameters a network has, the greater its ability to fit (or overfit) the data. So, care must be taken to ensure that the objective function used by the search process avoids overfitting the data by simply creating a very highly connected graph. Consequently, the objective functions used by these algorithms are often based on the **minimum description length principle**, which asserts that the solution with the fewest parameters (shortest description) is the best one. We have already met the minimum description length principle in the more general form of **Occam's razor**. A popular metric used by these algorithms is the **Bayesian information criterion (BIC)**:

$$BIC(\mathcal{G}, D) = log_e \left(P(D \mid \hat{P}, \mathcal{G}) \right) - \left(\frac{d}{2} \times log_e(n) \right) \qquad (6.22)$$

where $\mathcal{G}$ denotes the network graph, D is the training data, $\hat{P}$ is the set of entries in the CPTs of $\mathcal{G}$, d is the number of parameters of $\mathcal{G}$ (i.e., how many entries in the CPTs of $\mathcal{G}$), and n is the number of instances in D. This metric contains a term describing how well the model predicts the data $P(D \mid \hat{P}, \mathcal{G})$ as well as a term that punishes complex models $- \left(\frac{d}{2} \times log_e(n) \right)$. As such, it balances the search goals of model accuracy and simplicity. The term $P(D \mid \hat{P}, \mathcal{G})$ can be computed using metrics such as the **Bayesian score** or the **K2 score**[23]. The search space for these algorithms is exponential in the number of features. Consequently, developing algorithms to learn the structure of Bayesian networks is an ongoing research challenge.[24]

It is much simpler to construct a Bayesian network using a hybrid approach, where the topology of the network is given to the learning algorithm, and the learning task involves inducing the CPT entries from the data. This type of learning illustrates one of the real strengths of the Bayesian network framework, namely, that it provides an approach to learning that naturally accommodates human expert information. In this instance, the human expert specifies that topology of the network, and the learning algorithm induces the CPT entries for nodes in the topology in the same way that we computed the conditional probabilities for the naive Bayes model.[25]

Given that there are multiple Bayesian networks for any domain, an obvious question to ask is what is the best topological structure to give the algorithm as input? Ideally, we would like to use the network whose structure most accurately reflects the causal relationships in the domain. Specifically, if the value of one feature directly influences, or *causes*, the value taken by another feature, then this should be reflected in the structure of the graph by having a link from the cause feature to the effect feature. Bayesian networks whose topological structure correctly reflects the causal relationships between the features in a dataset are called **causal graphs**. There are two advantages to using a causal graph: (1) people find it relatively easy to think in terms of causal relationships, and as a result, networks that encode these relationships are relatively easy to understand; (2) often networks that reflect the causal structure of a domain are more compact in terms of the number of links between nodes and hence are more compact with respect to the number of CPT entries.

We will use an example from **social science** to illustrate how to construct a causal graph using this hybrid approach. In this example, we will build a

---

23 The K2 score is named after the K2 algorithm, one of the earliest and best known algorithms for learning Bayesian networks (Cooper and Herskovits, 1992).

24 See Kollar and Friedman (2009) for a discussion of algorithms that seek to address this research challenge.

25 In some cases we may not have data for all the features, and in these instances, the standard approach to learning the CPT entries is to use a gradient descent approach (similar to the one we introduce in Chapter 7[323]), where the objective function of the local search algorithm is simply how well the product of the induced conditional probabilities match the relative frequency of each joint event in the data. In other words, we choose the set of conditional probabilities that maximize the likelihood of the training data.

Bayesian network that enables us to predict the level of corruption in a country based on a number of macro-economic and social descriptive features. Table 6.18[305] lists some countries described using the following features[26]

- GINI COEF measures the equality in a society, where a larger Gini coefficient indicates a more unequal society.

- LIFE EXP measures life expectancy at birth.

- SCHOOL YEARS refers to the mean number of years spent in school for adult females.

- CPI is the **Corruption Perception Index** (**CPI**), and it is the target feature. The CPI measures the perceived level of corruption in the public sector of a country and ranges from 0 (highly corrupt) to 100 (very clean).

The original feature values shown in Table 6.18[305] are continuous, so we use the standard approach of converting them to categorical features using **equal-frequency binning**, with two bins for each feature: *low* and *high*. The columns labelled binned feature values in Table 6.18[305] show the data after it has been binned.

Once the data has been prepared, there are two stages to building the Bayesian network. First, we define the topology of the network. Second, we create the network CPTs. The topology of the network will be a causal graph that models this domain. In order to build this, we must have a theory of the causal relationships between the features in the domain. A potential causal theory between the features in this dataset is that

the more equal a society, the higher the investment that society will make in health and education, and this in turn results in a lower level of corruption

Figure 6.13[306] illustrates a Bayesian network with a topology that encodes this causal theory. Equality directly affects both health and education, so there are directed arcs from GINI COEF to both LIFE EXP and SCHOOL YEARS. Health and education directly affect corruption, so there is a directed arc from LIFE

---

26 The data listed in this table is real. The Gini coefficient data is for 2013 (or the most recent year prior to 2013 for which the data was available for a country) and was retrieved from the World Bank (data.worldbank.org/indicator/SI.POV.GINI); the life expectancy and mean years in school data was retrieved from Gapminder (www.gapminder.org) and is for 2010/11 (or the most recent year prior to 2010/11 for which the data was available for a country); and the mean years in school were originally sourced from the Institute for Health Metrics and Evaluation (www.healthdata.org). The Corruption Perception Index is for 2011 and was retrieved from Transparency International (www.transparency.org).

Table 6.18
Some socio-economic data for a set of countries, and a version of the data after equal-frequency binning has been applied.

COUNTRY ID	Original Feature Values				Binned Feature Values			
	GINI COEF	SCHOOL YEARS	LIFE EXP	CPI	GINI COEF	SCHOOL YEARS	LIFE EXP	CPI
Afghanistan	27.82	0.40	59.61	1.52	low	low	low	low
Argentina	44.49	10.10	75.77	3.00	high	low	low	low
Australia	35.19	11.50	82.09	8.84	low	high	high	high
Brazil	54.69	7.20	73.12	3.77	high	low	low	low
Canada	32.56	14.20	80.99	8.67	low	high	high	high
China	42.06	6.40	74.87	3.64	high	low	low	low
Egypt	30.77	5.30	70.48	2.86	low	low	low	low
Germany	28.31	12.00	80.24	8.05	low	high	high	high
Haiti	59.21	3.40	45.00	1.80	high	low	low	low
Ireland	34.28	11.50	80.15	7.54	low	high	high	high
Israel	39.2	12.50	81.30	5.81	low	high	high	high
New Zealand	36.17	12.30	80.67	9.46	low	high	high	high
Nigeria	48.83	4.10	51.30	2.45	high	low	low	low
Russia	40.11	12.90	67.62	2.45	high	high	low	low
Singapore	42.48	6.10	81.788	9.17	high	low	high	high
South Africa	63.14	8.50	54.547	4.08	high	low	low	low
Sweden	25.00	12.80	81.43	9.30	low	high	high	high
U.K.	35.97	13.00	80.09	7.78	low	high	high	high
U.S.A	40.81	13.70	78.51	7.14	high	high	high	high
Zimbabwe	50.10	6.7	53.684	2.23	high	low	low	low

EXP and from SCHOOL YEARS to CPI. To complete the network, we need to add the CPTs. To do this, we compute the required conditional probabilities from the binned data in Table 6.18[305]. The CPTs are shown in Figure 6.13[306].

6.4.4.2 Using a Bayesian Network to Make Predictions

Once a network has been created, it is relatively straightforward to use to make a prediction. We simply compute the probability distribution for the target feature conditioned on the state of the descriptive features in the query and return the target feature level with the maximum a posteriori probability:

$$\mathbb{M}(\mathbf{q}) = \arg \max_{l \in levels(t)} BayesianNetwork(t = l, \mathbf{q}) \tag{6.23}$$

where $\mathbb{M}(\mathbf{q})$ is the prediction made by the model for the query $\mathbf{q}$, $levels(t)$ is the set of levels in the domain of the target feature t, and $BayesianNetwork(t =$

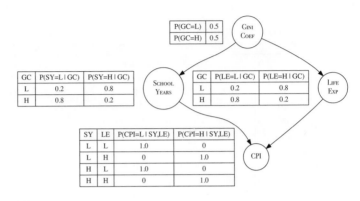

Figure 6.13

A Bayesian network that encodes the causal relationships between the features in the corruption domain. The CPT entries have been calculated using the binned data from Table 6.18[305].

$l, \mathbf{q})$ returns the probability computed by the network for the event $t = l$ given the evidence specified in the query $\mathbf{q}$.

For example, imagine we wanted to use the Bayesian network in Figure 6.13[306] to predict the CPI for a country with the following profile:

GINI COEF = *low*, SCHOOL YEARS = *high*, LIFE EXP = *high*

Because both the parent nodes for CPI are known (SCHOOL YEARS and LIFE EXP), the probability distribution for CPI is independent of the GINI COEF feature. Therefore, we can read the relevant probability distribution for CPI directly from the CPT for the CPI node. From this CPT we can see that when SCHOOL YEARS = *high*, and LIFE EXP = *high*, then the most likely level is CPI = *high*. As a result, CPI = *high* is the MAP CPI value for this query, and this is the prediction the model will return. In other words, countries that are relatively equal and that have good education and high life expectancy are likely to have a low level of corruption.

6.4.4.3   Making Predictions with Missing Descriptive Feature Values

One real advantage of Bayesian networks over the other predictive model types that we discuss in this book is they a provide an elegant solution to making predictions for a target feature when one or more of the descriptive feature values in a query instance are missing.[27] For example, we may wish to predict the CPI for a country with the following profile:

$$\text{GINI COEF} = high, \text{SCHOOL YEARS} = high$$

where the value of the LIFE EXP feature is unknown for the country. This means that in the network, one of the parents of the target feature node, CPI, is unknown. Consequently, we need to sum out this feature for each level of the target. We can calculate the probability for CPI = *high* as follows:[28]

$$
\begin{aligned}
&P(\text{CPI} = high \mid \text{SY} = high, \text{GC} = high) \\[4pt]
&= \frac{P(\text{CPI} = high, \text{SY} = high, \text{GC} = high)}{P(\text{SY} = high, \text{GC} = high)} \\[8pt]
&= \frac{\displaystyle\sum_{i \in \left\{\substack{high,\\ low}\right\}} P(\text{CPI} = high, \text{SY} = high, \text{GC} = high, \text{LE} = i)}{P(\text{SY} = high, \text{GC} = high)}
\end{aligned}
$$

---

27 The most common way to achieve this for the other model types covered in this book is to **impute** the missing values in the query instance using one of the techniques described in Section 3.4.1[73].

28 In the following calculations we have abbreviated feature names as follows: GC = GINI COEF, LE = LIFE EXP, and SY = SCHOOL YEARS.

We calculate the numerator in this term as follows:

$$\sum_{i \in \left\{ {high, \atop low} \right\}} P(\text{CPI} = high, \text{SY} = high, \text{GC} = high, \text{LE} = i)$$

$$= \sum_{i \in \left\{ {high, \atop low} \right\}} \left(\begin{array}{l} P(\text{CPI} = high \mid \text{SY} = high, \text{LE} = i) \\ \times P(\text{SY} = high \mid \text{GC} = high) \\ \times P(\text{LE} = i \mid \text{GC} = high) \\ \times P(\text{GC} = high) \end{array} \right)$$

$$= \Big(P(\text{CPI} = high \mid \text{SY} = high, \text{LE} = high)$$
$$\times P(\text{SY} = high \mid \text{GC} = high)$$
$$\times P(\text{LE} = high \mid \text{GC} = high)$$
$$\times P(\text{GC} = high) \Big)$$

$$+ \Big(P(\text{CPI} = high \mid \text{SY} = high, \text{LE} = low)$$
$$\times P(\text{SY} = high \mid \text{GC} = high)$$
$$\times P(\text{LE} = low \mid \text{GC} = high)$$
$$\times P(\text{GC} = high) \Big)$$

$$= (1.0 \times 0.2 \times 0.2 \times 0.5) + (0 \times 0.2 \times 0.8 \times 0.5) = 0.02$$

and denominator as:

$$P(\text{SY} = high, \text{GC} = high)$$
$$= P(\text{SY} = high \mid \text{GC} = high) \times P(\text{GC} = high)$$
$$= 0.2 \times 0.5 = 0.1$$

We can now calculate the probability for CPI = *high* as

$$P(\text{CPI} = high \mid \text{SY} = high, \text{GC} = high) = \frac{0.02}{0.1} = 0.2$$

We know from this result that the probability for CPI = *low* must be 0.8. So, the network will predict CPI = *low* as the MAP target value for the query. This tells us that an unequal society that has a good education system but for which we have no evidence about the health system is still likely to suffer from corruption.

These calculations make it apparent that even in this small example domain, the calculation of a probability becomes computationally complex very quickly, particularly when we need to sum out one or more features. The complexity of the calculations can be reduced by being careful with the positioning of features with respect to summations and by using dynamic programming techniques to avoid repeated computations. A well-known algorithm that focuses on this approach to reducing the complexity is the **variable elimination** algorithm (Zhang and Poole, 1994). However, even using the variable elimination algorithm, calculating exact probabilities from a Bayesian network when descriptive feature values are missing is prohibitively complex.

Given the complexity of exact probabilistic inference for Bayesian networks, a popular alternative is to approximate the probability distribution required for a prediction using **Monte Carlo methods**.[29] Monte Carlo methods generate a large number of sample events and then use the relative frequency of an event in the set of generated samples as the approximation for the probability of that event in the real distribution. Monte Carlo methods work well in conjunction with Bayesian networks because a Bayesian network models the probability distribution over the features. More specifically, a Bayesian network can be viewed as defining a **Markov chain**. A Markov chain is a system that has a set of finite states and a set of transition probabilities that define the likelihood of the system moving from one state to another. When we view a Bayesian network as a Markov chain, a state is a complete assignment of values to all the nodes in the network (for example, GINI COEF = *high*, SCHOOL YEARS = *low*, LIFE EXP = *high*, *CPI* = *high* would be a state in the Markov chain defined by the network in Figure 6.13[306]), and the CPTs of the network provide a distributed representation of the transition probabilities of the Markov chain. If the distribution used to generate the samples for a Monte Carlo method is a **Markov chain**, then the specific algorithms we use to implement this approach come from a family known as **Markov chain Monte Carlo** (**MCMC**) algorithms. **Gibbs sampling** is one of the best known MCMC algorithms and is particularly suitable when we wish to generate probabilities that are conditioned on some evidence, so this is the algorithm we discuss in this section.

---

29 Monte Carlo methods are named after the Mediterranean principality that is famous for its casino.

The Gibbs sampling algorithm initializes a Bayesian network by clamping the values of the evidence nodes and randomly assigning values to the non-evidence nodes. The algorithm then iteratively generates samples by changing the value of one of the non-evidence nodes. The selection of which non-evidence node to change can be random or follow a predefined list through which the algorithm iterates. The new value for the selected node is drawn from the distribution for the node (the CPT), conditioned on the current state of all the other nodes in the network. Each time a node is updated, a new sample state has been generated. More formally, for a network with three nodes x_1, x_2, x_3, using a predefined node selection order of $x_1, x_2, x_3, x_1, \ldots$ and assuming that at iteration τ each node has the values $x_1^{(\tau)}$, $x_2^{(\tau)}$, $x_3^{(\tau)}$, the next four states generated will be

1. $\left\langle x_1^{(\tau+1)} \leftarrow P\left(x_1 \mid x_2^{(\tau)}, x_3^{(\tau)}\right), x_2^{(\tau)}, x_3^{(\tau)} \right\rangle$

2. $\left\langle x_1^{(\tau+1)}, x_2^{(\tau+2)} \leftarrow P\left(x_2 \mid x_1^{(\tau+1)}, x_3^{(\tau)}\right), x_3^{(\tau)} \right\rangle$

3. $\left\langle x_1^{(\tau+1)}, x_2^{(\tau+2)}, x_3^{(\tau+3)} \leftarrow P\left(x_3 \mid x_1^{(\tau+1)}, x_2^{(\tau+2)}\right) \right\rangle$

4. $\left\langle x_1^{(\tau+4)} \leftarrow P\left(x_1 \mid x_2^{(\tau+2)}, x_3^{(\tau+3)}\right), x_2^{(\tau+2)}, x_3^{(\tau+3)} \right\rangle$

There are three technical requirements that must hold for distribution of states generated from Gibbs sampling to converge with the distribution that we are sampling from—in this case, the distribution defined by the Bayesian network. The first is that the distribution we are sampling from must be a **stationary distribution** (also known as an **invariant distribution**). A stationary distribution is a distribution that doesn't change. The distribution defined by a Bayesian network doesn't change during Gibbs sampling, so this requirement always holds in this context. The second requirement is that the Markov chain used to generate the samples must be **ergodic**. A Markov chain is ergodic if every state is reachable from every other state and there are no cycles in the chain. The Markov chain defined by a Bayesian network is ergodic if there are no zero entries in any of the CPTs.[30] The third requirement is that the generated states should be independent of each other. As each generated state is a modified version of the preceding state, it is clear that successive states will be correlated with each other. So to obtain independent sample states, we often

---

30 If there are one or more zero entries in the CPTs, then the Markov chain may still be ergodic, but it is non-trivial to prove ergodicity in these cases.

subsample from the sequence (subsampling in this way is also known as **thin-ning**). Once these three conditions hold (stationary distribution, ergodicity, and independent states), the samples generated will eventually converge with the distribution, and it is appropriate to use Gibbs sampling.

Because we start sampling from a random state, however, we do not know whether the initial state is an appropriate state from which to start generating samples. It may, for example, be a state that has a very low probability in the distribution. As a result, it is a good idea to run the network for a number of iterations before the generated states are recorded as samples. This **burn-in time** is to allow the Markov chain to settle into a state that is independent of the initial random state and that is a probable state for the distribution we are sampling from. The time it takes for the Markov chain to forget the initial random state is called the **mixing time**. Unfortunately, estimating how long the burn-in should be is difficult. For some Markov chains, mixing may require only a few iterations, but for others, it may require hundreds or thousands of iterations. The topology of the network can provide some insight into this problem. Larger graphs will tend to have longer mixing times. Also, an evenly connected network typically has a relatively short mixing time (for the size of the graph). If, however, a graph is composed of a number of clusters connected via bottleneck nodes, this would typically indicate a longer mixing time. Another approach used to determine the appropriate burn-in time is to start several Markov chains with different initial states and wait until all the chains are generating states with similar distribution characteristics (mean state, mode state, etc.). When this happens, it indicates that all the chains are sampling from the same distribution and, hence, that it is likely that they have all forgotten their starting states. Once this happens, the target probability can be computed by calculating the relative frequency of the event within the selected subset of generated states.

Table 6.19[312] lists a some of the samples generated using Gibbs sampling for the Bayesian network in Figure 6.13[306] for the query

GINI COEF = *high*, SCHOOL YEARS = *high*

A burn-in of 30 iterations was used, and the samples were thinned by subsampling every 7th iteration. When the algorithm was used to generate 500 samples, the relative frequency of CPI = *high* was 0.196. When 2,000 samples were generated, the relative frequency rose to 0.1975. This rise in relative frequency illustrates that, as the number of samples generated increases, the

resulting distribution approaches the actual distribution. Recall that when we
did an exact calculation for this query the probability of CPI = *high* was 0.2.

Table 6.19

Examples of the samples generated using Gibbs sampling.

Sample Number	Gibbs Iteration	Feature Updated	GINI COEF	SCHOOL YEARS	LIFE EXP	CPI
1	37	CPI	high	high	high	low
2	44	LIFE EXP	high	high	high	low
3	51	CPI	high	high	high	low
4	58	LIFE EXP	high	high	low	high
5	65	CPI	high	high	high	low
6	72	LIFE EXP	high	high	high	low
7	79	CPI	high	high	low	high
8	86	LIFE EXP	high	high	low	low
9	93	CPI	high	high	high	low
10	100	LIFE EXP	high	high	high	low
11	107	CPI	high	high	low	high
12	114	LIFE EXP	high	high	high	low
13	121	CPI	high	high	high	low
14	128	LIFE EXP	high	high	high	low
15	135	CPI	high	high	high	low
16	142	LIFE EXP	high	high	low	low

. . .

We can make predictions using Gibbs sampling in the same way that we
made predictions using exact probabilistic inference by predicting the target
level with the maximum a posteriori probability:

$$\mathbb{M}(\mathbf{q}) = \arg\max_{l \in levels(t)} Gibbs\,(t = l, \mathbf{q}) \qquad (6.24)$$

where $\mathbb{M}(\mathbf{q})$ is the prediction made by the model for the query $\mathbf{q}$, $levels(t)$ is
the set of levels in the domain of the target feature t, and $Gibbs(t = l, \mathbf{q})$ returns
the probability for the event $t = l$ given the evidence specified in the query $\mathbf{q}$
using Gibbs sampling.

6.5   Summary

There are two ways to reason with probabilities forward and inverse. Forward probability reasons from causes to effects: if we know that a particular

causal event has happened, then we increase the probability associated with the known effects that it causes. Inverse probability reasons from effects to causes: if we know that a particular event has occurred, then we can increase the probability that one or more of the events that could cause the observed event have also happened. Bayes' Theorem relates these two views of probability by using the notion of a prior probability. Put in subjective terms, Bayes' Theorem tells us that by modifying our initial beliefs about what has happened (our prior beliefs about the world) proportionally with how our observations relate to their potential causes (inverse probability), we can update our beliefs regarding what has happened to cause our observations (forward probability). Put more formally:

$$P(t \mid \mathbf{d}) = \frac{P(\mathbf{d} \mid t) \times P(t)}{P(\mathbf{d})} \qquad (6.25)$$

The use of prior probabilities in Bayes' Theorem is what distinguishes between Bayesian and **maximum likelihood** approaches to probability.

Bayesian prediction is a very intuitive approach to predicting categorical targets. In order to make a prediction, we have to learn two things:

1. the probability of an instance having a particular set of descriptive feature values given that it has a particular target level $P(\mathbf{d} \mid t)$

2. the prior probability of that target level $P(t)$

Given these two pieces of information, we can compute the relative likelihood of a particular instance having a particular target level as

$$P(t \mid \mathbf{d}) = P(\mathbf{d} \mid t) \times P(t) \qquad (6.26)$$

Once the relative likelihoods for each target level have been calculated, we simply return the maximum a posteriori (MAP) prediction.

The biggest challenge in creating a Bayesian prediction model is overcoming the exponential growth in the number of probabilities (model parameters) that are required as the dimensionality of the feature space increases. The standard approach to addressing this problem is to use the **independence** and **conditional independence** relationships between the features in a domain to **factorize** the **full joint distribution** of the domain. Factorizing the domain representation reduces the number of interactions between the features and reduces the number of model parameters.

A naive Bayes model addresses this problem by naively assuming that each of the descriptive features in a domain is conditionally independent of all the other descriptive features, given the state of the target feature. This assumption, although often wrong, enables the naive Bayes model to maximally factorize the representation that it uses of the domain—in other words, to use the smallest possible number of probabilities to represent the domain.

Surprisingly, given the naivety and strength of the assumption it depends upon, naive Bayes models often perform well. This is partly because naive Bayes models are able to make correct predictions even if the probabilities that they calculate are incorrect, so long as the error in the calculated probabilities does not affect the relative rankings of the different target levels. One consequence of this observation is that naive Bayes models are not really suitable for predicting continuous targets. When predicting a continuous target, every error in the calculation of a probability is reflected in reduced model performance.

The conditional independence assumption means that naive Bayes models use very few parameters to represent a domain. One consequence of this is that naive Bayes models can be trained using a relatively small dataset: with so few parameters and so few conditions on each parameter—only the state of the target feature—it is possible to make reasonable estimates for the parameters using a small dataset. Another benefit of the reduced representation of the model is that the behavior of the model is relatively easy to interpret. It is possible to look at the probabilities for each descriptive feature and analyze how that value contributed to the final prediction. This information can be useful in informing the development of more powerful models later in a project. Consequently, a naive Bayes model is often a good model to begin with: it is easy to train and has the potential to provide both a baseline accuracy score and some insight into the problem structure. The major drawback of naive Bayes models is the inability of the model to handle the interactions between features.

Bayesian networks provide a more flexible representation for encoding the conditional independence assumptions between the features in a domain. Ideally, the topology of a network should reflect the causal relationships between the entities in a domain. Properly constructed Bayesian networks are relatively powerful models that can capture the interactions between descriptive features in determining a prediction. Although the task of inducing the optimal network structure from data is strictly intractable, algorithms that encode various assumptions exist that allow good models to be learned. Also, in domains where the causal relationships between features are known, Bayesian networks have the advantage of providing a natural framework for integrating expert human knowledge with data-driven induction. Bayesian networks have been successfully applied across a range of fields, including medical diagnosis, object recognition, and natural language understanding.

Several parallels can be drawn between probability-based learning and the other approaches to machine learning that we present in this book. Intuitively, the prior probability of a **nearest neighbor** model predicting a particular target level is simply the relative frequency of that target level in the dataset. For this reason, in general it is wrong to artificially balance the dataset used by a nearest neighbor model,[31] and doing so biases the target level priors used by the model.

The relationship between probability-based and information-based learning is simply that the amount of information provided by an observation—such as a descriptive feature taking a particular value—is reflected in the difference between the prior and posterior probabilities caused by the observation. If the prior and posterior probabilities are similar, then the information content in the observation was low. If the prior and posterior probabilities are very different, then the information content in the observation was high.

Finally, it can be shown that, under some assumptions, any learning algorithm that minimizes the squared error of the model over the data will output a maximum likelihood prediction.[32] The relevance of this finding is that it provides a probabilistic justification for the approach to learning we present in Chapter 7[323].

6.6 Further Reading

McGrayne (2011) is an accessible book on the development and history of Bayes' Theorem. All data analysts should have at least one good textbook on statistics and probability. We would recommend either Montgomery and Runger (2010) or Tijms (2012) (or both). Jaynes (2003) deals with the use of probability theory in science and is a suitable text for postgraduate students.

Chapter 6 of Mitchell (1997) provides an excellent overview of Bayesian learning. Barber (2012) is a more recent machine learning textbook that adopts a Bayesian approach to learning and inference.

Judea Pearl is recognized as one of the key pioneers in developing the use of Bayesian networks in the field of **artificial intelligence**, and his books (Pearl, 1988, 2000) are accessible and provide good introductions to the theory and methods of Bayesian networks, as well as the more general field of **graphical models**. Neapolitan (2004) is a good textbook on Bayesian networks. Kollar

---

31 See Davies (2005, pp. 693–696).
32 See Mitchell (1997, pp. 164–167).

and Friedman (2009) is a comprehensive text on the theory and methods of graphical models and is a good reference text for postgraduate students who are doing research using graphical models.

6.7 Exercises

1. a. Three people flip a fair coin. What is the probability that exactly two of them will get heads?

   b. Twenty people flip a fair coin. What is the probability that exactly eight of them will get heads?

   c. Twenty people flip a fair coin. What is the probability that at least 4 of them will get heads?

2. The table below gives details of symptoms that patients presented and whether they were suffering from meningitis.

ID	HEADACHE	FEVER	VOMITING	MENINGITIS
1	true	true	false	false
2	false	true	false	false
3	true	false	true	false
4	true	false	true	false
5	false	true	false	true
6	true	false	true	false
7	true	false	true	false
8	true	false	true	true
9	false	true	false	false
10	true	false	true	true

Using this dataset calculate the following probabilities:

   a. $P(\text{VOMITING} = true)$

   b. $P(\text{HEADACHE} = false)$

   c. $P(\text{HEADACHE} = true, \text{VOMITING} = false)$

   d. $P(\text{VOMITING} = false \mid \text{HEADACHE} = true)$

   e. $P(\text{MENINGITIS} \mid \text{FEVER} = true, \text{VOMITING} = false)$

3. Predictive data analytics models are often used as tools for process quality control and fault detection. The task in this question is to create a naive Bayes model to monitor a waste water treatment plant.[33] The table below lists a dataset containing details of activities at a waste water treatment

33 The dataset in this question is inspired by the Waste Water Treatment Dataset that is available from the UCI Machine Learning repository (Bache and Lichman, 2013) at archive.ics.

plant for 14 days. Each day is described in terms of six descriptive features that are generated from different sensors at the plant. SS-IN measures the solids coming into the plant per day; SED-IN measures the sediment coming into the plant per day; COND-IN measures the electrical conductivity of the water coming into the plant.[34] The features SS-OUT, SED-OUT, and COND-OUT are the corresponding measurements for the water flowing out of the plant. The target feature, STATUS, reports the current situation at the plant: *ok*, everything is working correctly; *settler*, there is a problem with the plant settler equipment; or *solids*, there is a problem with the amount of solids going through the plant.

ID	SS -IN	SED -IN	COND -IN	SS -OUT	SED -OUT	COND -OUT	STATUS
1	168	3	1,814	15	0.001	1,879	ok
2	156	3	1,358	14	0.01	1,425	ok
3	176	3.5	2,200	16	0.005	2,140	ok
4	256	3	2,070	27	0.2	2,700	ok
5	230	5	1,410	131	3.5	1,575	settler
6	116	3	1,238	104	0.06	1,221	settler
7	242	7	1,315	104	0.01	1,434	settler
8	242	4.5	1,183	78	0.02	1,374	settler
9	174	2.5	1,110	73	1.5	1,256	settler
10	1,004	35	1,218	81	1,172	33.3	solids
11	1,228	46	1,889	82.4	1,932	43.1	solids
12	964	17	2,120	20	1,030	1,966	solids
13	2,008	32	1,257	13	1,038	1,289	solids

a. Create a naive Bayes model that uses probability density functions to model the descriptive features in this dataset (assume that all the descriptive features are normally distributed).

b. What prediction will the naive Bayes model return for the following query?

$$\text{SS-IN} = 222, \text{SED-IN} = 4.5, \text{COND-IN} = 1{,}518, \text{SS-OUT} = 74$$
$$\text{SED-OUT} = 0.25, \text{COND-OUT} = 1{,}642$$

uci.edu/ml/machine-learning-databases/water-treatment. The creators of this dataset reported their work in Bejar et al. (1991).

34 The conductivity of water is affected by inorganic dissolved solids and organic compounds, such as oil. Consequently, water conductivity is a useful measure of water purity.

4. The following is a description of the causal relationship between storms, the behavior of burglars and cats, and house alarms:

Stormy nights are rare. Burglary is also rare, and if it is a stormy night, burglars are likely to stay at home (burglars don't like going out in storms). Cats don't like storms either, and if there is a storm, they like to go inside. The alarm on your house is designed to be triggered if a burglar breaks into your house, but sometimes it can be set off by your cat coming into the house, and sometimes it might not be triggered even if a burglar breaks in (it could be faulty or the burglar might be very good).

a. Define the topology of a Bayesian network that encodes these causal relationships.

b. The table below lists a set of instances from the house alarm domain. Using the data in this table, create the conditional probability tables (CPTs) for the network you created in part (a) of this question.

ID	STORM	BURGLAR	CAT	ALARM
1	false	false	false	false
2	false	false	false	false
3	false	false	false	false
4	false	false	false	false
5	false	false	false	true
6	false	false	true	false
7	false	true	false	false
8	false	true	false	true
9	false	true	true	true
10	true	false	true	true
11	true	false	true	false
11	true	false	true	false
13	true	true	false	true

c. What value will the Bayesian network predict for ALARM given that there is both a burglar and a cat in the house but there is no storm.

d. What value will the Bayesian network predict for ALARM given that there is a storm but we don't know if a burglar has broken in or where the cat is?

✳ 5. The table below lists a dataset containing details of policy holders at an insurance company. The descriptive features included in the table describe each policy holders' ID, occupation, gender, age, the type of insurance policy they hold, and their preferred contact channel. The preferred contact channel is the target feature in this domain.

ID	OCCUPATION	GENDER	AGE	POLICY TYPE	PREF CHANNEL
1	lab tech	female	43	planC	email
2	farmhand	female	57	planA	phone
3	biophysicist	male	21	planA	email
4	sheriff	female	47	planB	phone
5	painter	male	55	planC	phone
6	manager	male	19	planA	email
7	geologist	male	49	planC	phone
8	messenger	male	51	planB	email
9	nurse	female	18	planC	phone

a. Using **equal-frequency binning** transform the AGE feature into a categorical feature with three levels: *young, middle-aged, mature*.

b. Examine the descriptive features in the dataset and list the features that you would exclude before you would use the dataset to build a predictive model. For each feature you decide to exclude explain why you have made this decision.

c. Calculate the probabilities required by a **naive Bayes model** to represent this domain.

d. What target level will a **naive Bayes model** predict for the following query:

$$\text{GENDER} = female, \text{AGE} = 30, \text{POLICY} = planA$$

* 6. Imagine that you have been given a dataset of 1,000 documents that have been classified as being about *entertainment* or *education*. There are 700 *entertainment* documents in the dataset and 300 *education* documents in the dataset. The tables below give the number of documents from each topic that a selection of words occurred in.

Word-document counts for the *entertainment* dataset

fun	is	machine	christmas	family	learning
415	695	35	0	400	70

Word-document counts for the *education* dataset

fun	is	machine	christmas	family	learning
200	295	120	0	10	105

a. What target level will a **naive Bayes model** predict for the following query document: "*machine learning is fun*"?

b. What target level will a **naive Bayes model** predict for the following query document: "*christmas family fun*"?

c. What target level will a **naive Bayes model** predict for the query document in part (b) of this question, if **Laplace smoothing** with $k = 10$ and a vocabulary size of 6 is used?

7   Error-based Learning

Ever tried. Ever failed. No matter. Try Again. Fail again. Fail better.
—Samuel Beckett

In error-based machine learning, we perform a search for a set of parameters for a parameterized model that minimizes the total error across the predictions made by that model with respect to a set of training instances. The fundamentals section of this chapter introduces the key ideas of a **parameterized model**, measuring **error** and an **error surface**. We then present the standard approach to building error-based predictive models: **multivariable linear regression with gradient descent**. The extensions and variations to this standard approach that we describe are how to handle categorical descriptive features, the use of **logistic regression** to make predictions for categorical target features, fine tuning regression models, techniques for building **non-linear** and **multinomial** models, and **support vector machines**, which take a slightly different approach to using error to build prediction models.

7.1   Big Idea

Anyone who has learned a new sport will have had the, sometimes painful, experience of taking an error-based approach to learning. Take surfing, for example. One of the key skills the novice surfer has to learn is how to successfully *catch a wave*. This involves floating on your surf board until a wave approaches, and then paddling furiously to gain enough momentum for the wave to pick up both you and your board. The position of your body on the board is key to doing this successfully. If you lie too far toward the back of the board, the board will sink and create so much drag that even big waves will pass by, leaving you behind. If you lie too far forward on your board, you will begin to make great progress before the surf board tilts nose down into the water and launches you head over heels into the air. Only when you are positioned at the *sweet spot* in the middle of the board—neither too far forward nor too far back—will you be able to use your paddling efforts to successfully catch a wave.

At their first attempt, new surfers will typically position themselves either too far forward or too far backward on their board when they attempt to catch their first wave, resulting in a bad outcome. The outcome of an attempt to catch a wave is a judgment on how well the surfer is doing, so an attempt constitutes an error function: lying too far back on the board leads to a medium error, lying too far forward on the board leads to a more dramatic error, while successfully catching a wave means really no error at all. Armed with the unsuccessful outcome of their first attempt, surfers usually overcompensate on the second attempt, resulting in the opposite problem. On subsequent attempts, surfers will slowly reduce their error by slightly adjusting their position until they home in on the *sweet spot* at which they can keep their board perfectly balanced to allow a seamless transition to *tickling the face of an awesome toob*!

A family of error-based machine learning algorithms takes the same approach. A parameterized prediction model is initialized with a set of random parameters, and an error function is used to judge how well this initial model performs when making predictions for instances in a training dataset. Based on the value of the error function, the parameters are iteratively adjusted to create a more and more accurate model.

7.2   Fundamentals

In this section we introduce a simple model of linear regression, some metrics for measuring the error of a model, and the concept of an error surface. The discussion in this section, and in the rest of this chapter, assume that you have a basic understanding of differentiation, in particular, what a derivative is, how to calculate a derivative for a continuous function, the chain rule for differentiation, and what a partial derivative is. If you don't understand any of these concepts, see Appendix C[551] for the necessary introduction.

7.2.1   Simple Linear Regression

Table 7.1[325] shows a simple dataset recording the rental price (in Euro per month) of Dublin city-center offices (RENTAL PRICE), along with a number of descriptive features that are likely to be related to rental price: the SIZE of the office (in square feet), the FLOOR in the building in which the office space is located, the BROADBAND rate available at the office (in Mb per second), and the ENERGY RATING of the building in which the office space is located (ratings range from *A* to *C*, where *A* is the most efficient). Over the course of this chapter, we look at the ways in which all these descriptive features can be used to train an error-based model to predict office rental prices. Initially, though, we will focus on a simplified version of this task in which just SIZE is used to predict RENTAL PRICE.

Table 7.1

A dataset that includes office rental prices and a number of descriptive features for 10 Dublin city-center offices.

ID	SIZE	FLOOR	BROADBAND RATE	ENERGY RATING	RENTAL PRICE
1	500	4	8	C	320
2	550	7	50	A	380
3	620	9	7	A	400
4	630	5	24	B	390
5	665	8	100	C	385
6	700	4	8	B	410
7	770	10	7	B	480
8	880	12	50	A	600
9	920	14	8	C	570
10	1,000	9	24	B	620

Figure 7.1(a)[326] shows a scatter plot of the office rentals dataset with RENTAL PRICE on the vertical (or y) axis and SIZE on the horizontal (or x) axis. From this plot, it is clear that there is a strong linear relationship between these two features: as SIZE increases so too does RENTAL PRICES by a similar amount. If we could capture this relationship in a model, we would be able to do two important things. First, we would be able to understand how office size affects office rental price. Second, we would be able to fill in the gaps in the dataset to predict office rental prices for office sizes that we have never actually seen in the historical data—for example, how much would we expect a 730 square foot office to rent for? Both of these things would be of great use to real estate agents trying to make decisions about the rental prices they should set for new rental properties.

There is a simple, well-known mathematical model that can capture the relationship between two continuous features like those in our dataset. Many readers will remember from school geometry that the **equation of a line** can be written as

$$y = mx + b \tag{7.1}$$

where m is the slope of the line, and b is known as the y-intercept of the line (i.e., the position at which the line meets the vertical axis when the value of x is set to zero). The equation of a line predicts a y value for every x value given the slope and the y-intercept, and we can use this simple model to capture the relationship between two features such as SIZE and RENTAL PRICE. Figure

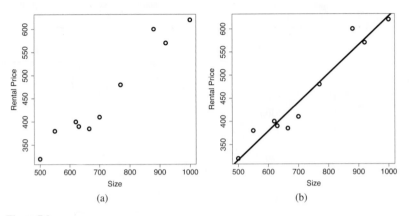

Figure 7.1

(a) A scatter plot of the SIZE and RENTAL PRICE features from the office rentals dataset; (b) the scatter plot from (a) with a linear model relating RENTAL PRICE to SIZE overlaid.

7.1(b)[326] shows the same scatter plot as shown in Figure 7.1(a)[326] with a simple linear model added to capture the relationship between office sizes and office rental prices. This model is

$$\text{RENTAL PRICE} = 6.47 + 0.62 \times \text{SIZE} \tag{7.2}$$

where the slope of the line is 0.62 and the y-intercept is 6.47.

This model tells us that for every increase of a square foot in SIZE, RENTAL PRICE increases by 0.62 Euro. We can also use this model to determine the expected rental price of the 730 square foot office mentioned previously by simply plugging this value for SIZE into the model:

$$\text{RENTAL PRICE} = 6.47 + 0.62 \times 730$$
$$= 459.07$$

So, we can expect our 730 square foot office to rent for about 460 Euro per month. This kind of model is known as a **simple linear regression model**. This approach to modeling the relationships between features is extremely common in both machine learning and statistics.

For consistency with the notation we have used in this book, we can rewrite the simple linear regression model as

$$\mathbb{M}_{\mathbf{w}}(\mathbf{d}) = \mathbf{w}[0] + \mathbf{w}[1] \times \mathbf{d}[1] \tag{7.3}$$

where $\mathbf{w}$ is the vector $\langle \mathbf{w}[0], \mathbf{w}[1] \rangle$, the parameters $\mathbf{w}[0]$ and $\mathbf{w}[1]$ are referred to as weights,[1] $\mathbf{d}$ is an instance defined by a single descriptive feature $\mathbf{d}[1]$, and $\mathbb{M}_{\mathbf{w}}(\mathbf{d})$ is the prediction output by the model for the instance $\mathbf{d}$. The key to using simple linear regression models is determining the optimal values for the weights in the model. The optimal values for the weights are the ones that allow the model to best capture the relationship between the descriptive features and a target feature. A set of weights that capture this relationship well are said to **fit** the training data. In order to find the optimal set of weights, we need some way to measure how well a model defined using a candidate set of weights fits a training dataset. We do this by defining an **error function** to measure the error between the predictions a model makes based on the descriptive features for each instance in the training data and the actual target values for each instance in the training data.

7.2.2   Measuring Error

The model shown in Equation (7.2)[326] is defined by the weights $\mathbf{w}[0] = 6.47$ and $\mathbf{w}[1] = 0.62$. What tells us that these weights suitably capture the relationship within the training dataset? Figure 7.2(a)[328] shows a scatter plot of the SIZE and RENTAL PRICE descriptive features from the office rentals dataset and a number of different simple linear regression models that might be used to capture this relationship. In these models the value for $\mathbf{w}[0]$ is kept constant at 6.47 and the values for $\mathbf{w}[1]$ are set to 0.4, 0.5, 0.62, 0.7, and 0.8 from top to bottom. Out of the candidate models shown, the third model from the top (with $\mathbf{w}[1]$ set to 0.62) passes most closely through the actual dataset and is the one that most accurately fits the relationship between office sizes and office rental prices, but how do we measure this formally?

In order to formally measure the fit of a linear regression model with a set of training data, we require an **error function**. An error function captures the error between the predictions made by a model and the actual values in a training dataset.[2] There are many different kinds of error functions, but for measuring the fit of simple linear regression models, the most commonly used is the **sum of squared errors** error function, or L_2. To calculate L_2 we use our candidate model $\mathbb{M}_{\mathbf{w}}$ to make a prediction for each member of the training dataset,

---

1 Weights are often also known as **model parameters**, so regression models are often known as parameterized models.

2 Error functions are also commonly referred to as **loss functions** because they represent what we *lose* by reducing the training set to a simple model.

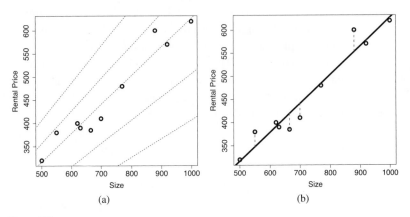

Figure 7.2

(a) A scatter plot of the SIZE and RENTAL PRICE features from the office rentals dataset. A collection of possible simple linear regression models capturing the relationship between these two features are also shown. For all models $\mathbf{w}[0]$ is set to 6.47. From top to bottom, the models use 0.4, 0.5, 0.62, 0.7, and 0.8 respectively for $\mathbf{w}[1]$. (b) A scatter plot of the SIZE and RENTAL PRICE features from the office rentals dataset showing a candidate prediction model (with $\mathbf{w}[0] = 6.47$ and $\mathbf{w}[1] = 0.62$) and the resulting errors.

$\mathcal{D}$, and then calculate the error (or **residual**) between these predictions and the actual target feature values in the training set.

Figure 7.2(b)[328] shows the office rentals dataset and the candidate model with $\mathbf{w}[0] = 6.47$ and $\mathbf{w}[1] = 0.62$ and also includes error bars to highlight the differences between the predictions made by the model and the actual RENTAL PRICE values in the training data. Notice that the model sometimes over estimates the office rental price, and sometimes underestimates the office rental price. This means that some of the errors will be positive and some will be negative. If we were to simply add these together, the positive and negative errors would effectively cancel each other out. This is why, rather than just using the sum of the errors, we use the sum of the *squared* errors because this means all values will be positive.

The sum of squared errors error function, L_2, is formally defined as

$$L_2(\mathbb{M}_\mathbf{w}, \mathcal{D}) = \frac{1}{2} \sum_{i=1}^{n} (t_i - \mathbb{M}_\mathbf{w}(\mathbf{d}_i))^2 \qquad (7.4)$$

where the training set is composed of n training instances, each training instance is composed of descriptive features $\mathbf{d}$ and a target feature t, $\mathbb{M}_\mathbf{w}(\mathbf{d}_i)$

Table 7.2

Calculating the sum of squared errors for the candidate model (with $\mathbf{w}[0] = 6.47$ and $\mathbf{w}[1] = 0.62$) to make predictions for the office rentals dataset.

ID	SIZE	RENTAL PRICE	Model Prediction	Error	Squared Error
1	500	320	316.47	3.53	12.46
2	550	380	347.47	32.53	1,058.20
3	620	400	390.87	9.13	83.36
4	630	390	397.07	-7.07	49.98
5	665	385	418.77	-33.77	1,140.41
6	700	410	440.47	-30.47	928.42
7	770	480	483.87	-3.87	14.98
8	880	600	552.07	47.93	2,297.28
9	920	570	576.87	-6.87	47.20
10	1,000	620	626.47	-6.47	41.86
				Sum	5,674.15
			Sum of squared errors (Sum/2)		2,837.08

is the prediction made by a candidate model $\mathbb{M}_{\mathbf{w}}$ for a training instance with descriptive features $\mathbf{d}_i$, and the candidate model $\mathbb{M}_{\mathbf{w}}$ is defined by the weight vector $\mathbf{w}$. For our simple scenario in which each instance is described with a single descriptive feature, Equation (7.4)[328] expands to

$$L_2(\mathbb{M}_{\mathbf{w}}, \mathcal{D}) = \frac{1}{2} \sum_{i=1}^{n} (t_i - (\mathbf{w}[0] + \mathbf{w}[1] \times \mathbf{d}_i[1]))^2 \qquad (7.5)$$

Table 7.2[329] shows the calculation of the sum of squared errors for the candidate model with $\mathbf{w}[0] = 6.47$ and $\mathbf{w}[1] = 0.62$. In this case, the sum of squared errors is equal to 2,837.08.

If we perform the same calculation for the other candidate models shown in Figure 7.2(a)[328], we find that with $\mathbf{w}[1]$ set to 0.4, 0.5, 0.7, and 0.8, the sums of squared errors are 136,218, 42,712, 20,092, and 90,978 respectively. The fact that the sums of squared errors for these models are larger than for the model with $\mathbf{w}[1]$ set to 0.62 demonstrates that our previous visual intuition that this model most accurately fits the training data was correct.

The sum of squared errors function can be used to measure how well any combination of weights fits the instances in a training dataset. The next section explains how the values of an error function for many different potential models can be combined to form an error surface across which we can search for the optimal weights with the minimum sum of squared errors.[3]

7.2.3   Error Surfaces

For every possible combination of weights, $\mathbf{w}[0]$ and $\mathbf{w}[1]$, there is a corresponding sum of squared errors value. We can think about all these error values joined to make a surface defined by the weight combinations, as shown in Figure 7.3(a)[330]. Here, each pair of weights $\mathbf{w}[0]$ and $\mathbf{w}[1]$ defines a point on the *x-y* plane, and the sum of squared errors for the model using these weights determines the height of the error surface above the *x-y* plane for that pair of weights. The *x-y* plane is known as a **weight space**, and the surface is known as an **error surface**. The model that best fits the training data is the model corresponding to the lowest point on the error surface.

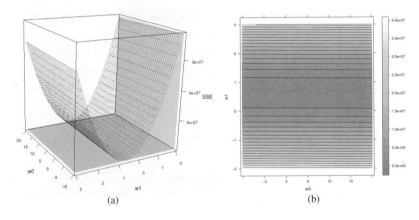

(a)   (b)

Figure 7.3
(a) A 3D surface plot and (b) a bird's-eye view contour plot of the error surface generated by plotting the sum of squared errors for the office rentals training set for each possible combination of values for $\mathbf{w}[0]$ (from the range $[-10, 20]$) and $\mathbf{w}[1]$ (from the range $[-2, 3]$).

---

3 One of the best known and earliest applications of solving a problem by reducing the sum of squared errors occurred in 1801, when **Carl Friedrich Gauss** used it to minimize the measurement error in astronomical data and by doing so was able to extrapolate the position of the dwarf planet Ceres, which had recently been found but then lost behind the glare of the Sun.

Although for some simple problems, like that presented in our office rentals dataset, it is possible to try out every reasonable combination of weights and through this **brute-force search** find the best combination, for most real-world problems this is not feasible—the computation required would take far too long. Instead, we need a more efficient way to find the best combination of weights. Fortunately, for prediction problems like that posed by the office rentals dataset, the associated error surfaces have two properties that help us find the optimal combination of weights: they are **convex**, and they have a **global minimum**. By convex we mean that the error surfaces are shaped like a bowl. Having a global minimum means that on an error surface, there is a unique set of optimal weights with the lowest sum of squared errors. The reason that the error surface always has these properties is that its overall shape is determined by the linearity of the model, rather than the properties of the data. If we can find the global minimum of the error surface, we can find the set of weights defining the model that best fits the training dataset. This approach to finding weights is known as **least squares optimization**.

Because we can expect the error surface to be convex and possess a global minimum, we can find the optimal weights at the point where the **partial derivatives** of the error surface with respect to $\mathbf{w}[0]$ and $\mathbf{w}[1]$ are equal to 0. The partial derivatives of the error surface with respect to $\mathbf{w}[0]$ and $\mathbf{w}[1]$ measure the slope of the error surface at the point $\mathbf{w}[0]$ and $\mathbf{w}[1]$. The point on the error surface at which the partial derivatives with respect to $\mathbf{w}[0]$ and $\mathbf{w}[1]$ are equal to 0 is simply the point at the very bottom of the bowl defined by the error surface—there is no slope at the bottom of the bowl. This point is at the **global minimum** of the error surface and the coordinates of this point define the weights for the prediction model with the lowest sum of squared errors on the dataset. Using Equation (7.5)[329], we can formally define this point on the error surface as the point at which

$$\frac{\partial}{\partial \mathbf{w}[0]} \frac{1}{2} \sum_{i=1}^{n} (t_i - (\mathbf{w}[0] + \mathbf{w}[1] \times \mathbf{d}_i[1]))^2 = 0 \qquad (7.6)$$

and

$$\frac{\partial}{\partial \mathbf{w}[1]} \frac{1}{2} \sum_{i=1}^{n} (t_i - (\mathbf{w}[0] + \mathbf{w}[1] \times \mathbf{d}_i[1]))^2 = 0 \qquad (7.7)$$

There are a number of different ways to find this point. In this chapter we describe a **guided search** approach known as the **gradient descent** algorithm. This is one of the most important algorithms in machine learning and, as we will see in other chapters, can be used for many different purposes. The next section describes how gradient descent can be used to find the optimal weights for linear regression models that handle multiple descriptive features: **multivariable linear regression** models.

7.3   Standard Approach: Multivariable Linear Regression with Gradient Descent

The most common approach to error-based machine learning for predictive analytics is to use **multivariable linear regression** with **gradient descent** to train a best-fit model for a given training dataset. This section explains how this works. First, we describe how we extend the simple linear regression model described in the previous section to handle multiple descriptive features, and then we describe the gradient descent algorithm.

7.3.1   Multivariable Linear Regression

The simple linear regression model we looked at in Section 7.2.1[324] handled only a single descriptive feature. Interesting problems in predictive analytics, however, are multivariable[4] in nature. Fortunately, extending the simple linear regression model to a multivariable linear regression model is straightforward. We can define a multivariable linear regression model as

$$\mathbb{M}_{\mathbf{w}}(\mathbf{d}) = \mathbf{w}[0] + \mathbf{w}[1] \times \mathbf{d}[1] + \cdots + \mathbf{w}[m] \times \mathbf{d}[m]$$

$$= \mathbf{w}[0] + \sum_{j=1}^{m} \mathbf{w}[j] \times \mathbf{d}[j] \tag{7.8}$$

where $\mathbf{d}$ is a vector of m descriptive features, $\mathbf{d}[1] \ldots \mathbf{d}[m]$, and $\mathbf{w}[0] \ldots \mathbf{w}[m]$ are $(m+1)$ weights. We can make Equation (7.8)[332] look a little neater by inventing a dummy descriptive feature, $\mathbf{d}[0]$, that is always equal to 1. This

---

4 The words multivariable and multi-feature are equivalent. The use of multivariable is a sign of the origins of regression in statistics rather than machine learning.

then gives us

$$\mathbb{M}_{\mathbf{w}}(\mathbf{d}) = \mathbf{w}[0] \times \mathbf{d}[0] + \mathbf{w}[1] \times \mathbf{d}[1] + \cdots + \mathbf{w}[m] \times \mathbf{d}[m]$$

$$= \sum_{j=0}^{m} \mathbf{w}[j] \times \mathbf{d}[j]$$

$$= \mathbf{w} \cdot \mathbf{d} \tag{7.9}$$

where $\mathbf{w} \cdot \mathbf{d}$ is the **dot product** of the vectors $\mathbf{w}$ and $\mathbf{d}$. The dot product of two vectors is the sum of the products of their corresponding elements.

The expansion of the sum of squared errors loss function, L_2, that we gave in Equation (7.5)[329] changes slightly to reflect the new regression equation:

$$L_2(\mathbb{M}_{\mathbf{w}}, \mathcal{D}) = \frac{1}{2} \sum_{i=1}^{n} (t_i - \mathbb{M}_{\mathbf{w}}(\mathbf{d}_i))^2$$

$$= \frac{1}{2} \sum_{i=1}^{n} (t_i - (\mathbf{w} \cdot \mathbf{d}_i))^2 \tag{7.10}$$

where the training dataset is composed of n training instances $(\mathbf{d}_i, t_i)$, $\mathbb{M}_{\mathbf{w}}(\mathbf{d}_i)$ is the prediction made by a model $\mathbb{M}_{\mathbf{w}}$ for a training instance with descriptive features $\mathbf{d}_i$, and the model $\mathbb{M}_{\mathbf{w}}$ is defined by the weight vector $\mathbf{w}$.

This multivariable model allows us to include all but one of the descriptive features in Table 7.2[329] in a regression model to predict office rental prices (we will see how to include the categorical ENERGY RATING into the model in Section 7.4.3[351]). The resulting multivariable regression model equation is

$$\text{RENTAL PRICE} = \mathbf{w}[0] + \mathbf{w}[1] \times \text{SIZE} + \mathbf{w}[2] \times \text{FLOOR}$$
$$+ \mathbf{w}[3] \times \text{BROADBAND RATE}$$

We will see in the next section how the best-fit set of weights for this equation are found, but for now we will set $\mathbf{w}[0] = -0.1513$, $\mathbf{w}[1] = 0.6270$, $\mathbf{w}[2] = -0.1781$, and $\mathbf{w}[3] = 0.0714$. This means that the model is rewritten as

$$\text{RENTAL PRICE} = -0.1513 + 0.6270 \times \text{SIZE} - 0.1781 \times \text{FLOOR}$$
$$+ 0.0714 \times \text{BROADBAND RATE}$$

Using this model, we can, for example, predict the expected rental price of a 690 square foot office on the 11th floor of a building with a broadband rate of 50 Mb per second as

$$\text{RENTAL PRICE} = -0.1513 + 0.6270 \times 690 - 0.1781 \times 11 + 0.0714 \times 50$$
$$= 434.0896$$

The next section describes how the weights can be determined using the gradient descent algorithm.

7.3.2   Gradient Descent

In Section 7.2.3[330] we said that the best-fit set of weights for a linear regression model can be found at the global minimum of the error surface defined by the weight space associated with the relevant training dataset. We also mentioned that this global minimum can be found at the point at which the partial derivatives of the error surface, with respect to the weights, are equal to zero. Although it is possible to calculate this point directly for some simpler problems, this approach is not computationally feasible for most interesting predictive analytics problems. The number of instances in the training set and the number of weights for which we need to find values simply make the problem too large. The brute-force search approach that was mentioned in Section 7.2.3[330] is not feasible either—especially as the number of descriptive features, and subsequently the number of weights, increases.

There is, however, a simple approach to learning weights that we can take based on the facts that, even though they are hard to visualize, the error surfaces that correspond to these high-dimensional weight spaces still have the convex shape seen in Figure 7.3[330] (albeit in multiple dimensions), and that a single global minimum exists. This approach uses a guided search from a random starting position and is known as **gradient descent**.

To understand how gradient descent works, imagine a hiker unlucky enough to be stranded on the side of a valley on a foggy day. Because of the dense fog, it is not possible for her to see the way to her destination at the bottom of the valley. Instead, it is only possible to see the ground at her feet to within about a three foot radius. It might, at first, seem like all is lost and that it will be impossible for the hiker to find her way down to the bottom of the valley. There is, however, a reliable approach that the hiker can take that will guide her to the bottom (assuming, somewhat ideally, that the valley is *convex* and has a *global minimum*). If the hiker looks at the slope of the ground at her feet, she will notice that in some directions, the ground slopes up, and in other directions, the ground slopes down. If she takes a small step in the direction in which the ground slopes most steeply downward (the direction of the gradient of the mountain), she will be headed toward the bottom of the mountain. If she repeats this process over and over again, she will make steady progress down the mountain until eventually she arrives at the bottom. Gradient descent works in exactly the same way.

Gradient descent starts by selecting a random point within the weight space (i.e., each weight in the multivariable linear regression equation is assigned a random value within some sensible range) and calculating the sum of squared errors associated with this point based on predictions made for each instance in the training set using the randomly selected weights (as shown in Section 7.2.2[327]). This defines one point on the error surface. Although the error value at this point in the weight space can be calculated, we know very little else about the relative position of this point on the error surface. Just like our imagined mountain climber, the algorithm can use only very localized information. It is possible, however, to determine the slope of the error surface by determining the derivative of the function used to generate it, and then calculating the value of this derivative at the random point selected in the weight space. This means that, again like our mountain climber, the gradient descent algorithm can use the direction of the slope of the error surface at the current location in the weight space. Taking advantage of this information, the randomly selected weights are adjusted slightly in the direction of the error surface gradient to move to a new position on the error surface. Because the adjustments are made in the direction of the error surface gradient, this new point will be closer to the overall global minimum. This adjustment is repeated over and over until the global minimum on the error surface is reached. Figure 7.4[336] shows an error surface (defined over just two weights so that we can visualize the error surface) and some examples of the path down this surface that the gradient descent algorithm would take from different random starting positions.[5]

For the simple version of the office rentals example that uses only the SIZE descriptive feature, described in Section 7.2.1[324], it is easy to visualize how the gradient descent algorithm would move iteratively toward a model that best fits the training data, making small adjustments each time—with each adjustment reducing the error of the model, just as our surfer from Section 7.1[323] did. Figure 7.5[337] shows the journey across the error surface that is taken by the gradient descent algorithm when training this model. Figure 7.6[338] shows a series of snapshots of the candidate models created at steps along this journey toward the best-fit model for this dataset. Notice how the model gets closer and

---

5 In fact, this is the error surface that results from the office rentals dataset when the descriptive features in the dataset are normalized to the range $[-1, 1]$ using range normalization before being used. We discuss normalization later in the chapter.

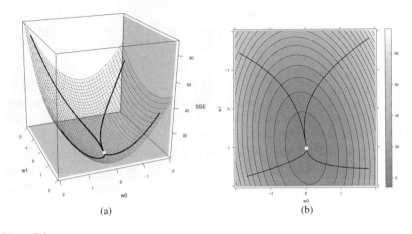

(a)   (b)

Figure 7.4

(a) A 3D plot of an error surface and (b) a bird's-eye view contour plot of the same error surface. The lines indicate the path that the gradient descent algorithm would take across this error surface from 4 different starting positions to the global minimum—marked as the white dot in the center.

closer to a model that accurately captures the relationship between SIZE and RENTAL PRICE. This is also apparent in the final panel in Figure 7.6[338], which shows how the sum of squared errors decreases as the model becomes more accurate.

The gradient descent algorithm for training multivariable regression models is formally presented in Algorithm 7.1[339]. Each weight is iteratively adjusted by a small amount based on the error in the predictions made by the current candidate model so as to generate subsequently more and more accurate candidate models. Eventually, the algorithm will converge to a point on the error surface where any subsequent changes to weights do not lead to a noticeably better model (within some tolerance). At this point we can expect the algorithm to have found the global minimum of the error surface and, as a result, the most accurate predictive model possible.

The most important part to the gradient descent algorithm is the line on which the weights are updated, Line 4[339]. Each weight is considered independently, and for each one a small adjustment is made by adding a small value, called a **delta value**, to the current weight, $\mathbf{w}[j]$. This adjustment should ensure that the change in the weight leads to a move *downward* on the error surface.

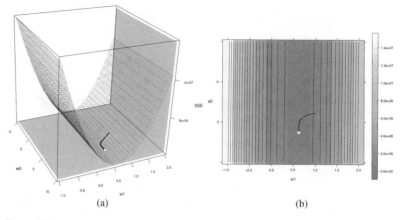

(a)   (b)

Figure 7.5

(a) A 3D surface plot and (b) a bird's-eye view contour plot of the error surface for the office rentals
dataset showing the path that the gradient descent algorithm takes toward the best-fit model.

The learning rate, α, determines the size of the adjustments made to weights at
each iteration of the algorithm and is discussed further in Section 7.3.3[341].

The remainder of this section focuses on the error delta function, which calculates the delta value that determines the direction (either positive or negative)
and the magnitude of the adjustments made to each weight. The direction and
magnitude of the adjustment to be made to a weight is determined by the gradient of the error surface at the current position in the weight space. Recalling
that the error surface is defined by the error function, L_2 (given in Equation
(7.10)[333]), the gradient at any point on this error surface is given by the value
of the partial derivative of the error function with respect to a particular weight
at that point. The error delta function invoked on Line 4[339] of Algorithm 7.1[339]
performs this calculation to determine the delta value by which each weight
should be adjusted.

To understand how to calculate the value of the partial derivative of the error
function with respect to a particular weight, let us imagine for a moment that
our training dataset, $\mathcal{D}$, contains just one training instance: $(\mathbf{d}, t)$, where $\mathbf{d}$ is
a set of descriptive features and t is a target feature. The gradient of the error

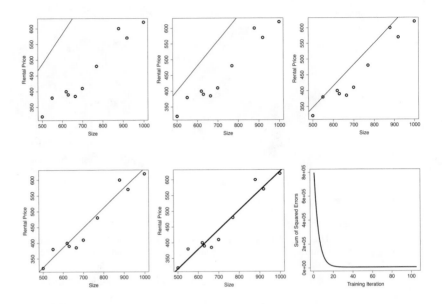

Figure 7.6
A selection of the simple linear regression models developed during the gradient descent process for the office rentals dataset. The bottom-right panel shows the sums of squared errors generated during the gradient descent process.

surface is given as the partial derivative of L_2 with respect to each weight, $\mathbf{w}[j]$:

$$\frac{\partial}{\partial \mathbf{w}[j]} L_2 \left(\mathbb{M}_{\mathbf{w}}, \mathcal{D} \right) = \frac{\partial}{\partial \mathbf{w}[j]} \left(\frac{1}{2} \left(t - \mathbb{M}_{\mathbf{w}}(\mathbf{d}) \right)^2 \right) \tag{7.11}$$

$$= \left(t - \mathbb{M}_{\mathbf{w}}(\mathbf{d}) \right) \times \frac{\partial}{\partial \mathbf{w}[j]} \left(t - \mathbb{M}_{\mathbf{w}}(\mathbf{d}) \right) \tag{7.12}$$

$$= \left(t - \mathbb{M}_{\mathbf{w}}(\mathbf{d}) \right) \times \frac{\partial}{\partial \mathbf{w}[j]} \left(t - (\mathbf{w} \cdot \mathbf{d}) \right) \tag{7.13}$$

$$= \left(t - \mathbb{M}_{\mathbf{w}}(\mathbf{d}) \right) \times -\mathbf{d}[j] \tag{7.14}$$

Equation $(7.12)^{[338]}$ is calculated from Equation $(7.11)^{[338]}$ by applying the differentiation **chain rule**.[6] To understand the move from Equation $(7.13)^{[338]}$ to Equation $(7.14)^{[338]}$ imagine a problem with four descriptive features

6 See Appendix C[551].

Algorithm 7.1 The gradient descent algorithm for training multivariable linear regression models.

Require: set of training instances $\mathcal{D}$
Require: a learning rate α that controls how quickly the algorithm converges
Require: a function, *errorDelta*, that determines the direction in which to adjust a given weight, $\mathbf{w}[j]$, so as to move down the slope of an error surface determined by the dataset, $\mathcal{D}$
Require: a convergence criterion that indicates that the algorithm has completed
 1: $\mathbf{w} \leftarrow$ random starting point in the weight space
 2: **repeat**
 3:    **for** each $\mathbf{w}[j]$ in $\mathbf{w}$ **do**
 4:       $\mathbf{w}[j] \leftarrow \mathbf{w}[j] + \alpha \times errorDelta(\mathcal{D}, \mathbf{w}[j])$
 5: **until** convergence occurs

$\mathbf{d}[1]\dots\mathbf{d}[4]$. Remembering that we always include the dummy feature $\mathbf{d}[0]$ with a value of 1, the dot product $\mathbf{w} \cdot \mathbf{d}$ becomes

$$\mathbf{w} \cdot \mathbf{d} = \mathbf{w}[0] \times \mathbf{d}[0] + \mathbf{w}[1] \times \mathbf{d}[1] + \mathbf{w}[2] \times \mathbf{d}[2]$$
$$+ \mathbf{w}[3] \times \mathbf{d}[3] + \mathbf{w}[4] \times \mathbf{d}[4]$$

If we take the partial derivative of this with respect to $\mathbf{w}[0]$ all the terms that do not contain $\mathbf{w}[0]$ are treated as constants, so

$$\frac{\partial}{\partial \mathbf{w}[0]}\mathbf{w} \cdot \mathbf{d} = \frac{\partial}{\partial \mathbf{w}[0]}(\mathbf{w}[0] \times \mathbf{d}[0] + \mathbf{w}[1] \times \mathbf{d}[1] + \mathbf{w}[2] \times \mathbf{d}[2]$$
$$+ \mathbf{w}[3] \times \mathbf{d}[3] + \mathbf{w}[4] \times \mathbf{d}[4])$$
$$= \mathbf{d}[0] + 0 + 0 + 0 + 0 = \mathbf{d}[0]$$

Similarly, the partial derivative with respect to $\mathbf{w}[4]$ is

$$\frac{\partial}{\partial \mathbf{w}[4]}\mathbf{w} \cdot \mathbf{d} = \frac{\partial}{\partial \mathbf{w}[4]}(\mathbf{w}[0] \times \mathbf{d}[0] + \mathbf{w}[1] \times \mathbf{d}[1] + \mathbf{w}[2] \times \mathbf{d}[2]$$
$$+ \mathbf{w}[3] \times \mathbf{d}[3] + \mathbf{w}[4] \times \mathbf{d}[4])$$
$$= 0 + 0 + 0 + 0 + \mathbf{d}[4] = \mathbf{d}[4]$$

So, in the move between Equations (7.13)[338] and (7.14)[338] $\frac{\partial}{\partial \mathbf{w}[j]}(t - (\mathbf{w} \cdot \mathbf{d}))$ becomes $-\mathbf{d}[j]$ (remember that in this equation, t is a constant and so becomes zero when differentiated).

Equation (7.14)[338] calculates the gradient based only on a single training instance. To take into account multiple training instances, we calculate the sum of the squared errors for each training instance (as we did in all our previous examples). So, Equation (7.14)[338] becomes

$$\frac{\partial}{\partial \mathbf{w}[j]} L_2(\mathbb{M}_\mathbf{w}, \mathcal{D}) = \sum_{i=1}^{n} ((t_i - \mathbb{M}_\mathbf{w}(\mathbf{d}_i)) \times -\mathbf{d}_i[j]) \quad (7.15)$$

where $(\mathbf{d}_1, t_1) \dots (\mathbf{d}_n, t_n)$ are n training instances, and $d_i[j]$ is the jth descriptive feature of training instance $(\mathbf{d}_i, t_i)$. The direction of the gradient calculated using this equation is toward the highest values on the error surface. The error delta function from Line 4[339] of Algorithm 7.1[339] should return a small step toward a lower value on the error surface. Therefore we move in the opposite direction of the calculated gradient, and the error delta function can be written as

$$errorDelta(\mathcal{D}, \mathbf{w}[j]) = -\frac{\partial}{\partial \mathbf{w}[j]} L_2(\mathbb{M}_\mathbf{w}, \mathcal{D})$$

$$= \sum_{i=1}^{n} ((t_i - \mathbb{M}_\mathbf{w}(\mathbf{d}_i)) \times \mathbf{d}_i[j]) \quad (7.16)$$

Line 4[339] of Algorithm 7.1[339] can therefore be rewritten as what is known as the weight update rule for multivariable linear regression with gradient descent:

$$\mathbf{w}[j] \leftarrow \mathbf{w}[j] + \alpha \times \underbrace{\sum_{i=1}^{n} ((t_i - \mathbb{M}_\mathbf{w}(\mathbf{d}_i)) \times \mathbf{d}_i[j])}_{errorDelta(\mathcal{D},\mathbf{w}[j])} \quad (7.17)$$

where $\mathbf{w}[j]$ is any weight, α is a constant learning rate, t_i is the expected target feature value for the ith training instance, $\mathbb{M}_\mathbf{w}(\mathbf{d}_i)$ is the prediction made for this training instance by the current candidate model defined by the weight vector $\mathbf{w}$, and $\mathbf{d}_i[j]$ is the jth descriptive feature of the ith training instance and corresponds with weight $\mathbf{w}[j]$ in the regression model.

To intuitively understand the weight update rule given in Equation (7.17)[340], it helps to think in terms of what the weight update rule does to weights based on the error in the predictions made by the current candidate model:

- If the errors show that, in general, predictions made by the candidate model are too high, then $\mathbf{w}[j]$ should be decreased if $\mathbf{d}_i[j]$ is positive and increased if $\mathbf{d}_i[j]$ is negative.

- If the errors show that, in general, predictions made by the candidate model are too low, then $\mathbf{w}[j]$ should be increased if $\mathbf{d}_i[j]$ is positive and decreased if $\mathbf{d}_i[j]$ is negative.

The approach to training multivariable linear regression models described so far is more specifically known as **batch gradient descent**. The word batch is used because only one adjustment is made to each weight at each iteration of the algorithm based on summing the squared error made by the candidate model for each instance in the training dataset.[7] Batch gradient descent is a straightforward, accurate, and reasonably efficient approach to training multivariable linear regression models and is used widely in practice. The inductive bias encoded in this algorithm includes a preference bias to prefer models that minimize the sum of squared errors function and a restriction bias introduced by the facts that we only consider linear combinations of descriptive features and that we take a single path through the error gradient from a random starting point.

7.3.3   Choosing Learning Rates and Initial Weights

The values chosen for the learning rate and initial weights can have a significant impact on how the gradient descent algorithm proceeds. Unfortunately, there are no theoretical results that help in choosing the optimal values for these parameters. Instead, these algorithm parameters must be chosen using rules of thumb gathered through experience.

The learning rate, α, in the gradient descent algorithm determines the size of the adjustment made to each weight at each step in the process. We can illustrate this using the simplified version of the RENTAL PRICE prediction problem based only on office size (SIZE). A linear regression model for the problem uses only two weights, $\mathbf{w}[0]$ and $\mathbf{w}[1]$. Figure 7.7[342] shows how different learning rates—0.002, 0.08, and 0.18—result in very different journeys across the error surface.[8] The changing sum of squared errors that result from these journeys are also shown.

Figure 7.7(a)[342] shows the impact of a very small learning rate. Although the gradient descent algorithm will converge to the global minimum eventually, it takes a very long time as tiny changes are made to the weights at each iteration

---

7 **Stochastic gradient descent** is a slightly different approach in which an adjustment to each weight is made based on the error in the prediction made by the candidate model for each training instance individually. This means that many more adjustments are made to the weights. We will

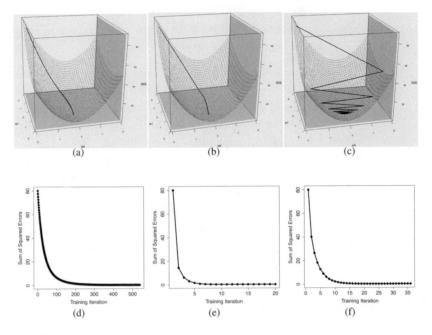

Figure 7.7
Plots of the journeys made across the error surface for the simple office rentals prediction problem
for different learning rates: (a) a very small learning rate (0.002); (b) a medium learning rate (0.08);
and (c) a very large learning rate (0.18). The changing sum of squared errors for these journeys
are also shown.

of the algorithm. Figure 7.7(c)[342] shows the impact of a large learning rate.
The large adjustments made to the weights during gradient descent cause it to
jump completely from one side of the error surface to the other. Although the
algorithm can still converge toward an area of the error surface close to the
global minimum, there is a strong chance that the global minimum itself will
actually be missed, and the algorithm will simply jump back and forth across
it. In fact, if inappropriately large learning rates are used, the jumps from one
side of the error surface to the other can actually cause the sum of squared

---

not discuss stochastic gradient descent in any detail in this book, although the modifications that
need to be made to the gradient descent algorithm for stochastic gradient descent are fairly simple.

8 Note that in this example, we have normalized the RENTAL PRICE and SIZE features to the
range [−1, 1], so the error surfaces shown in this example look slightly different from those shown
in Figure 7.3[330] and Figure 7.5[337].

errors to repeatedly increase rather than decrease, leading to a process that will never converge. Figure 7.7(b)[342] shows that a well-chosen learning rate strikes a good balance, converging quickly but also ensuring that the global minimum is reached. Note that even though the shape of the curve in Figure 7.7(e)[342] is similar to the shape in Figure 7.7(d)[342], it takes far fewer iterations to reach the global minimum.

Unfortunately, choosing learning rates is not a well-defined science. Although there are some algorithmic approaches, most practitioners use rules of thumb and trial and error. A typical range for learning rates is $[0.00001, 10]$, and practitioners will usually try out higher values and observe the resulting learning graph. If the graph looks too much like Figure 7.7(f)[342], a smaller value will be tested until something approaching Figure 7.7(e)[342] is found.

When the gradient descent algorithm is used to find optimal weights for linear regression models, the initial weights are chosen randomly from a predefined range that must be specified as an input to the algorithm. The choice of the range from which these initial weights are selected affects how quickly the gradient descent algorithm will converge to a solution. Unfortunately, as is the case with the learning rate, there are no well-established, proven methods for choosing initial weights. Normalization also has a part to play here. It is much easier to select initial weights for normalized feature values than for raw feature values, as the range in which weights for normalized feature values might reasonably fall (particularly for the intercept weight, $\mathbf{w}[0]$) is much better defined than the corresponding range when raw feature values are used. The best advice we can give is that, based on empirical evidence, choosing random initial weights uniformly from the range $[-0.2, 0.2]$ tends to work well.

7.3.4   A Worked Example

We are now in a position to build a linear regression model that uses all the continuous descriptive features in the office rentals dataset in Table 7.1[325] (i.e., all features except for ENERGY RATING). The general structure of the model is

$$\text{RENTAL PRICE} = \mathbf{w}[0] + \mathbf{w}[1] \times \text{SIZE} + \mathbf{w}[2] \times \text{FLOOR}$$
$$+ \mathbf{w}[3] \times \text{BROADBAND RATE}$$

so there are four weights—$\mathbf{w}[0]$, $\mathbf{w}[1]$, $\mathbf{w}[2]$, and $\mathbf{w}[3]$—for which optimal values must be found. For this example, let's assume that the learning rate, α, is 0.00000002 and the initial weights are chosen from a uniform random distribution in the range $[-0.2, 0.2]$ to be $\mathbf{w}[0] = -0.146$, $\mathbf{w}[1] = 0.185$, $\mathbf{w}[2] = -0.044$, and $\mathbf{w}[3] = 0.119$. Table 7.3[345] details the important values from the first two iterations of the gradient descent algorithm when applied to this data.[9]

Using the initial weights predictions are made for all the instances in the training dataset, as shown in the Predictions column (column 3) of Table 7.3[345]. By comparing these predicted values with the actual RENTAL PRICE (column 2), we can compute an error and a squared error term for each training instance, columns 4 and 5 of the table.

To update the weights, we must first calculate the delta value for each weight. This is calculated by summing over all the instances in the training set the prediction error multiplied by the value of the relevant feature for that instance (see Equation (7.16)[340]). The last four columns on the right of the table list for each instance the product of the prediction error and the feature value. Remember that $\mathbf{d}[0]$ is a dummy descriptive feature, added to match $\mathbf{w}[0]$, with a value of 1 for all training instances. As a result, the values in column 6 are identical to the values in the error column. Focusing on the top cell of column 7, we see the value 113,370.05. This value was calculated by multiplying the prediction error for $\mathbf{d}_1$ (226.74) by the SIZE value for this instance (500). The other cells in these columns are populated with similar calculations. The $errorDelta(\mathcal{D}, \mathbf{w}[j])$ for each weight is then the summation of the relevant column, for example, $errorDelta(\mathcal{D}, \mathbf{w}[0]) = 3,185.61$ and $errorDelta(\mathcal{D}, \mathbf{w}[1]) = 2,412,073.90$

Once the $errorDelta(\mathcal{D}, \mathbf{w}[j])$ for a weight has been calculated, we can then update the weight using Equation (7.17)[340]. This weight update occurs on Line 4[339] of Algorithm 7.1[339]. The update involves multiplying the $errorDelta(\mathcal{D}, \mathbf{w}[j])$ for a given weight by the learning rate and then adding this to the current weight to give a new, updated, weight. The new set of weights is labeled **New Weights (after Iteration 1)** in Table 7.3[345].

---

9 All values in Table 7.3[345], and similar subsequent tables, are reported at a precision of two places of decimal. Because of this, some error values and squared error values may appear inconsistent. This, however, is only due to rounding differences.

Table 7.3

Details of the first two iterations when the gradient descent algorithm is used to train a multivariable linear regression model for the office rentals dataset (using only the continuous descriptive features).

			Initial Weights			
$\mathbf{w}[0]$:	-0.146	$\mathbf{w}[1]$:	0.185	$\mathbf{w}[2]$:	-0.044	$\mathbf{w}[3]$: 0.119

Iteration 1

	RENTAL			Squared	errorDelta($\mathcal{D}, \mathbf{w}[j]$)			
ID	PRICE	Pred.	Error	Error	$\mathbf{w}[0]$	$\mathbf{w}[1]$	$\mathbf{w}[2]$	$\mathbf{w}[3]$
1	320	93.26	226.74	51,411.08	226.74	113,370.05	906.96	1,813.92
2	380	107.41	272.59	74,307.70	272.59	149,926.92	1,908.16	13,629.72
3	400	115.15	284.85	81,138.96	284.85	176,606.39	2,563.64	1,993.94
4	390	119.21	270.79	73,327.67	270.79	170,598.22	1,353.95	6,498.98
5	385	134.64	250.36	62,682.22	250.36	166,492.17	2,002.91	25,036.42
6	410	130.31	279.69	78,226.32	279.69	195,782.78	1,118.76	2,237.52
7	480	142.89	337.11	113,639.88	337.11	259,570.96	3,371.05	2,359.74
8	600	168.32	431.68	186,348.45	431.68	379,879.24	5,180.17	21,584.05
9	570	170.63	399.37	159,499.37	399.37	367,423.83	5,591.23	3,194.99
10	620	187.58	432.42	186,989.95	432.42	432,423.35	3,891.81	10,378.16
			Sum	1,067,571.59	3,185.61	2,412,073.90	27,888.65	88,727.43
		Sum of squared errors (Sum/2)		533,785.80				

			New Weights (after Iteration 1)			
$\mathbf{w}[0]$:	-0.146	$\mathbf{w}[1]$:	0.233	$\mathbf{w}[2]$:	-0.043	$\mathbf{w}[3]$: 0.121

Iteration 2

	RENTAL			Squared	errorDelta($\mathcal{D}, \mathbf{w}[j]$)			
ID	PRICE	Pred.	Error	Error	$\mathbf{w}[0]$	$\mathbf{w}[1]$	$\mathbf{w}[2]$	$\mathbf{w}[3]$
1	320	117.40	202.60	41,047.92	202.60	101,301.44	810.41	1,620.82
2	380	134.03	245.97	60,500.69	245.97	135,282.89	1,721.78	12,298.44
3	400	145.08	254.92	64,985.12	254.92	158,051.51	2,294.30	1,784.45
4	390	149.65	240.35	57,769.68	240.35	151,422.55	1,201.77	5,768.48
5	385	166.90	218.10	47,568.31	218.10	145,037.57	1,744.81	21,810.16
6	410	164.10	245.90	60,468.86	245.90	172,132.91	983.62	1,967.23
7	480	180.06	299.94	89,964.69	299.94	230,954.68	2,999.41	2,099.59
8	600	210.87	389.13	151,424.47	389.13	342,437.01	4,669.60	19,456.65
9	570	215.03	354.97	126,003.34	354.97	326,571.94	4,969.57	2,839.76
10	620	187.58	432.42	186,989.95	432.42	432,423.35	3,891.81	10,378.16
			Sum	886,723.04	2,884.32	2,195,615.84	25,287.08	80,023.74
		Sum of squared errors (Sum/2)		443,361.52				

			New Weights (after Iteration 2)			
$\mathbf{w}[0]$:	-0.145	$\mathbf{w}[1]$:	0.277	$\mathbf{w}[2]$:	-0.043	$\mathbf{w}[3]$: 0.123

We can see from Iteration 2 in the bottom half of Table 7.3[345] that the new set of predictions made using the updated set of weights calculated in iteration 1 result in a lower sum of squared errors, 443,361.52. Based on this error another new set of weights is calculated using the error deltas shown. The algorithm then keeps iteratively applying the weight update rule until it converges on a stable set of weights beyond which little improvement in model accuracy is possible. In our example, convergence occurred after 100 iterations, and the final values for the weights were $\mathbf{w}[0] = -0.1513$, $\mathbf{w}[1] = 0.6270$, $\mathbf{w}[2] = -0.1781$, and $\mathbf{w}[3] = 0.0714$. The sum of squared errors for the final model was 2,913.5.[10]

A last point to make about this example is that careful examination of Table 7.3[345] shows why such a low learning rate is used in this example. The large values of the RENTAL PRICE feature, $[320, 620]$, causes the squared errors and, in turn, the error delta values to become very large. This means that a very low **learning rate** is required in order to ensure that the changes made to the weights at each iteration of the learning process are small enough for the algorithm to work effectively. Using normalization (see Section 3.6.1[92]) on the features can help avoid these large squared errors, and we do this in most examples from now on.

7.4 Extensions and Variations

In this section we discuss common and useful extensions to the basic multi-variable linear regression with gradient descent approach described in Section 7.3[332]. Topics covered include interpreting a linear regression model, using weight decay to set the learning rate, handling categorical descriptive and target features, using feature selection, using multivariable linear regression models to model non-linear relationships, and using support vector machines (SVMs) as an alternative to linear regression models.

---

10 Because this is a higher dimensional problem (three dimensions in the feature space and four dimensions in the weight space), it is not possible to draw the same graphs of the error surfaces that were shown for the previous examples.

Table 7.4
Weights and standard errors for each feature in the office rentals model.

Descriptive Feature	Weight	Standard Error	*t*-statistic	*p*-value
SIZE	0.6270	0.0545	11.504	<0.0001
FLOOR	-0.1781	2.7042	-0.066	0.949
BROADBAND RATE	0.071396	0.2969	0.240	0.816

7.4.1   Interpreting Multivariable Linear Regression Models

A particularly useful feature of linear regression models is that the weights used by the model indicate the effect of each descriptive feature on the predictions returned by the model. First, the signs of the weights indicate whether different descriptive features have a positive or a negative impact on the prediction. Table 7.4[347] repeats the final weights for the office rentals model trained in Section 7.3.4[343]. We can see that increasing office size leads to increasing rental prices; that lower building floors lead to higher rental prices; and that rental prices increase with broadband rates. Second, the magnitudes of the weights show how much the value of the target feature changes for a unit change in the value of a particular descriptive feature. For example, for every increase of a square foot in office size, we can expect the rental price to go up by 0.6270 Euro per month. Similarly, for every floor we go up in an office building, we can expect the rental price to decrease by 0.1781 Euro per month.

It is tempting to infer the relative importance of the different descriptive features in the model from the magnitude of the weights—i.e., the descriptive features associated with higher weights are more predictive than those with lower weights. This is a mistake, however, when the descriptive features themselves have varying scales. For example, in the office rentals dataset, the values of the SIZE feature range from 500 to 1,000 while the values for the FLOOR feature range from only 4 to 14. So, direct comparison of the weights tells us little about their relative importance. A better way to determine the importance of each descriptive feature in the model is to perform a **statistical significance test**.

A statistical significance test works by stating a **null hypothesis** and then determining whether there is enough evidence to accept or reject this hypothesis. This accept/reject decision is carried out in three steps:

1. A **test-statistic** is computed.

2. The probability of a test-statistic value as big as or greater than the one computed being the result of chance is calculated. This probability is called a *p*-value.

3. The *p*-value is compared to a predefined significance threshold, and if the *p*-value is less than or equal to the threshold (i.e., the *p*-value is small), the null hypothesis is rejected. These thresholds are typically the standard statistical thresholds of 5% or 1%.

The statistical significance test we use to analyze the importance of a descriptive feature $\mathbf{d}[j]$ in a linear regression model is the *t*-**test**. The null hypothesis that we adopt for this test is that the feature does not have a significant impact on the model. The test statistic we calculate is called the *t*-statistic. In order to calculate this test statistic, we first have to calculate the **standard error** for the overall model and the standard error for the descriptive feature we are investigating the importance of. The standard error for the overall model is calculated as

$$se = \sqrt{\frac{\sum_{i=1}^{n} (t_i - \mathbb{M}_{\mathbf{w}}(\mathbf{d}_i))^2}{n-2}} \tag{7.18}$$

where n is the number of instances in the training dataset. A standard error calculation is then done for a descriptive feature as follows:

$$se(\mathbf{d}[j]) = \frac{se}{\sqrt{\sum_{i=1}^{n} \left(\mathbf{d}_i[j] - \overline{\mathbf{d}[j]}\right)^2}} \tag{7.19}$$

where $\mathbf{d}[j]$ is some descriptive feature and $\overline{\mathbf{d}[j]}$ is the mean value of that descriptive feature in the training set.

The *t*-statistic for this test is calculated as follows:

$$t = \frac{\mathbf{w}[j]}{se(\mathbf{d}[j])} \tag{7.20}$$

where $\mathbf{w}[j]$ is the weight associated with descriptive feature $\mathbf{d}[j]$. Using a standard *t*-statistic look-up table, we can then determine the *p*-value associated with this test (this is a two tailed *t*-test with degrees of freedom set to the number of instances in the training set minus 2). If the *p*-value is less than the required significance level, typically 0.05, we reject the null hypothesis and say that the descriptive feature has a significant impact on the model; otherwise we say that it does not. We can see from Table 7.4[347] that only the SIZE descriptive feature has a significant impact on the model. If a descriptive feature is found to have a significant impact on the model, this indicates that there is a significant linear relationship between it and the target feature.

7.4.2 Setting the Learning Rate Using Weight Decay

In Section 7.3.3[341] we illustrated the impact of a learning rate parameter on the gradient descent algorithm. In that section we also explained that most practitioners use rules of thumb and trial and error to set the learning rate. A more systematic approach is to use learning rate decay, which allows the learning rate to start at a large value and then decay over time according to a predefined schedule. Although there are different approaches in the literature, a good approach is to use the following decay schedule:

$$\alpha_\tau = \alpha_0 \frac{c}{c + \tau} \tag{7.21}$$

where α_0 is an initial learning rate (this is typically quite large, e.g., 1.0), c is a constant that controls how quickly the learning rate decays (the value of this parameter depends on how quickly the algorithm converges, but it is often set to quite a large value, e.g., 100), and τ is the current iteration of the gradient descent algorithm. Figure 7.8[350] shows the journey across the error surface and related plot of the sums of squared errors for the office rentals problem—using just the SIZE descriptive feature—when error decay is used with $\alpha_0 = 0.18$ and $c = 10$ (this is a pretty simple problem, so smaller values for these parameters are suitable). This example shows that the algorithm converges to the global minimum more quickly than any of the approaches shown in Figure 7.7[342].

The differences between Figures 7.7(f)[342] and 7.8(b)[350] most clearly show the impact of learning rate decay as the initial learning rates are the same in these two instances. When learning rate decay is used, there is much less thrashing back and forth across the error surface than when the large static learning rate is used. Using learning rate decay can even address the problem of inappropriately large error rates causing the sum of squared errors to increase rather than decrease. Figure 7.9[350] shows an example of this in which learning rate decay is used with $\alpha_0 = 0.25$ and $c = 100$. The algorithm starts at the position marked 1 on the error surface, and learning steps actually cause it to move farther and farther up the error surface. This can be seen in the increasing sums of squared errors in Figure 7.9(b)[350]. As the learning rate decays, however, the direction of the journey across the error surface moves back downward, and eventually the global minimum is reached. Although learning rate decay almost always leads to better performance than a fixed learning rate, it still does require that problem-dependent values are chosen for α_0 and c.

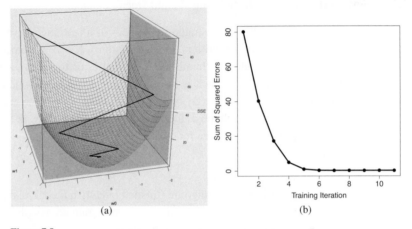

(a) (b)

Figure 7.8

(a) The journey across the error surface for the office rentals prediction problem when learning rate decay is used ($\alpha_0 = 0.18$, $c = 10$); (b) a plot of the changing sum of squared errors during this journey.

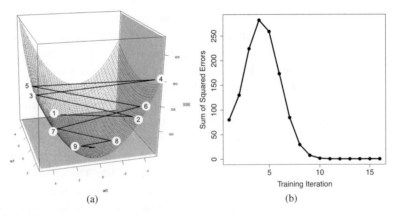

(a) (b)

Figure 7.9

(a) The journey across the error surface for the office rentals prediction problem when learning rate decay is used ($\alpha_0 = 0.25$, $c = 100$); (b) a plot of the changing sum of squared errors during this journey.

7.4.3   Handling Categorical Descriptive Features

The regression equation for a multivariable linear regression model for the full dataset shown in Table 7.1[325] would look like

$$
\begin{aligned}
\textsc{Rental Price} = {}& \mathbf{w}[0] + \mathbf{w}[1] \times \textsc{Size} + \mathbf{w}[2] \times \textsc{Floor} \\
& + \mathbf{w}[3] \times \textsc{Broadband Rate} \\
& + \mathbf{w}[4] \times \textsc{Energy Rating}
\end{aligned}
$$

The multiplication of $\mathbf{w}[4] \times$ Energy Rating causes a problem here. Energy rating is a categorical feature, so multiplying the values of this feature by a numeric weight is simply not sensible. The basic structure of the multivariable linear regression model allows for only continuous descriptive features. Obviously, though, in real-world datasets, we often encounter categorical descriptive features, so for the linear regression approach to be really useful, we need a way to handle these.

The most common approach to handling categorical features in linear regression models is to use a transformation that converts a single categorical descriptive feature into a number of continuous descriptive feature values that can encode the levels of the categorical feature. This is done by creating one new binary descriptive feature for every level of the categorical feature. These new features can then be used to encode a level of the original categorical descriptive feature by setting the value of the new feature corresponding to the level of the categorical feature to 1 and the other new continuous features to 0.

For example, if we were to use the Energy Rating descriptive feature from Table 7.1[325] in a linear regression model, we would convert it into three new continuous descriptive features, as energy rating can have one of three distinct levels: *A, B,* or *C*. Table 7.5[352] shows this transformed dataset in which the energy rating feature has been replaced with Energy Rating A, Energy Rating B and Energy Rating C. For training instances in which the original Energy Rating feature had a value *A*, the new Energy Rating A feature has a value of 1, and the Energy Rating B and Energy Rating C are both set to 0. A similar rule is used for instances with the Energy Rating feature levels of *B* and *C*.

Table 7.5
The office rentals dataset from Table 7.1[325] adjusted to handle the categorical ENERGY RATING descriptive feature in linear regression models.

ID	SIZE	FLOOR	BROADBAND RATE	ENERGY RATING A	ENERGY RATING B	ENERGY RATING C	RENTAL PRICE
1	500	4	8	0	0	1	320
2	550	7	50	1	0	0	380
3	620	9	7	1	0	0	400
4	630	5	24	0	1	0	390
5	665	8	100	0	0	1	385
6	700	4	8	0	1	0	410
7	770	10	7	0	1	0	480
8	880	12	50	1	0	0	600
9	920	14	8	0	0	1	570
10	1,000	9	24	0	1	0	620

Returning to our example, the regression equation for this RENTAL PRICE model would change to

$$
\begin{aligned}
\text{RENTAL PRICE} = \; & \mathbf{w}\,[0] + \mathbf{w}\,[1] \times \text{SIZE} + \mathbf{w}\,[2] \times \text{FLOOR} \\
& + \mathbf{w}\,[3] \times \text{BROADBAND RATE} \\
& + \mathbf{w}\,[4] \times \text{ENERGY RATING A} \\
& + \mathbf{w}\,[5] \times \text{ENERGY RATING B} \\
& + \mathbf{w}\,[6] \times \text{ENERGY RATING C}
\end{aligned}
$$

where the newly added categorical features allow the original ENERGY RATING feature to be included. Everything else about using such a model is exactly the same as before.

The downside to this approach is that it introduces a number of extra weights for which optimal values must be found—in this simple example for only four descriptive features, we need seven weights. This increases the size of the weight space through which we need to search when training the model. One way we can reduce the impact of this is that for each categorical feature we transform, we can reduce the number of newly added features by one by assuming that a zero in all the new features implies that the original feature had the final level. So, for example, for our ENERGY RATING feature, instead of adding three new features (ENERGY RATING A, ENERGY RATING B, and ENERGY RATING C), we could just add ENERGY RATING A and ENERGY

RATING B and assume that whenever they both have a value of 0, ENERGY RATING C is implicitly set.

7.4.4 Handling Categorical Target Features: Logistic Regression

In Section 7.3[332] we described how a multivariable linear regression model trained using gradient descent can be used to make predictions for continuous target features. Although this is useful for a range of real-world predictive analytics problems, we are also interested in prediction problems with categorical target features. This section covers the reasonably simple adjustments that must be made to the multivariable linear regression with gradient descent algorithm to handle categorical target features, in particular, logistic regression.

7.4.4.1 Predicting Categorical Targets Using Linear Regression

Table 7.6[354] shows a sample dataset with a categorical target feature. This dataset contains measurements of the revolutions per minute (RPM) that power station generators are running at, the amount of vibration in the generators (VIBRATION), and an indicator to show whether the generators proved to be working or faulty the day after these measurements were taken. The RPM and VIBRATION measurements come from the day before the generators proved to be operational or faulty. If power station administrators could predict upcoming generator failures before the generators actually fail, they could improve power station safety and save money on maintenance.[11] Using this dataset, we would like to train a model to distinguish between properly operating power station generators and faulty generators using the RPM and VIBRATION measurements.

Figure 7.10(a)[355] shows a scatter plot of this dataset in which we can see that there is a good separation between the two types of generator. In fact, as shown in Figure 7.10(b)[355], we can draw a straight line across the scatter plot that perfectly separates the *good* generators from the *faulty* ones. This line is known as a decision boundary, and because we can draw this line, this dataset is said to be linearly separable in terms of the two descriptive features used. As the decision boundary is a linear separator, it can be defined using the equation

---

11 Gross et al. (2006) describes a real-world example of this kind of application of predictive analytics.

Table 7.6

A dataset listing features for a number of generators.

ID	RPM	VIBRATION	STATUS	ID	RPM	VIBRATION	STATUS
1	568	585	good	29	562	309	faulty
2	586	565	good	30	578	346	faulty
3	609	536	good	31	593	357	faulty
4	616	492	good	32	626	341	faulty
5	632	465	good	33	635	252	faulty
6	652	528	good	34	658	235	faulty
7	655	496	good	35	663	299	faulty
8	660	471	good	36	677	223	faulty
9	688	408	good	37	685	303	faulty
10	696	399	good	38	698	197	faulty
11	708	387	good	39	699	311	faulty
12	701	434	good	40	712	257	faulty
13	715	506	good	41	722	193	faulty
14	732	485	good	42	735	259	faulty
15	731	395	good	43	738	314	faulty
16	749	398	good	44	753	113	faulty
17	759	512	good	45	767	286	faulty
18	773	431	good	46	771	264	faulty
19	782	456	good	47	780	137	faulty
20	797	476	good	48	784	131	faulty
21	794	421	good	49	798	132	faulty
22	824	452	good	50	820	152	faulty
23	835	441	good	51	834	157	faulty
24	862	372	good	52	858	163	faulty
25	879	340	good	53	888	91	faulty
26	892	370	good	54	891	156	faulty
27	913	373	good	55	911	79	faulty
28	933	330	good	56	939	99	faulty

of the line (remember Equation (7.2.1)[325]). In Figure 7.10(b)[355] the decision boundary is defined as

$$\text{VIBRATION} = 830 - 0.667 \times \text{RPM} \tag{7.22}$$

or

$$830 - 0.667 \times \text{RPM} - 1 \times \text{VIBRATION} = 0 \tag{7.23}$$

So, for any instance that is actually on the decision boundary, the RPM and VIBRATION values satisfy the equality in Equation (7.23)[354]. What is more interesting is that instances not actually on the decision boundary behave in

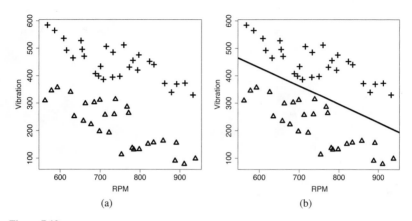

Figure 7.10

(a) A scatter plot of the RPM and VIBRATION descriptive features from the generators dataset shown in Table 7.6[354], where *good* generators are shown as crosses, and *faulty* generators are shown as triangles; (b) as decision boundary separating *good* generators (crosses) from *faulty* generators (triangles).

a very regular way. The descriptive feature values of all instances above the decision boundary will result in a negative value when plugged into the decision boundary equation, while the descriptive features of all instances below the decision boundary will result in a positive value. For example, applying Equation (7.23)[354] to the instance RPM = 810, VIBRATION = 495, which is be above the decision boundary in Figure 7.10(b)[355], gives the following result:

$$830 - 0.667 \times 810 - 495 = -205.27$$

By contrast, if we apply Equation (7.23)[354] to the instance RPM = 650 and VIBRATION = 240, which is be below the decision boundary in Figure 7.10(b)[355], we get

$$830 - 0.667 \times 650 - 240 = 156.45$$

Figure 7.11(a)[356] illustrates the consistent relationship between Equation (7.23)[354] and the decision boundary by plotting the value of Equation (7.23)[354] for all values of RPM and VIBRATION.[12]

---

12 Note that in this figure, both the RPM and VIBRATION features have been normalized to the range $[-1, 1]$ (using **range normalization** as described in Section 3.6.1[92]). It is standard practice

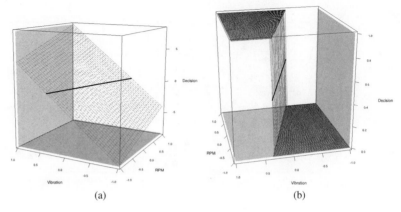

(a)   (b)

Figure 7.11

(a) A surface showing the value of Equation (7.23)[354] for all values of RPM and VIBRATION, with the decision boundary given in Equation (7.23)[354] highlighted; (b) the same surface linearly thresholded at zero to operate as a predictor.

Because the values of this equation are so well behaved, we can use it to predict a categorical target feature. Reverting to our previous notation, we have,

$$\mathbb{M}_{\mathbf{w}}(\mathbf{d}) = \begin{cases} 1 & \text{if } \mathbf{w} \cdot \mathbf{d} \geqslant 0 \\ 0 & \textit{otherwise} \end{cases} \tag{7.24}$$

where $\mathbf{d}$ is a set of descriptive features for an instance, $\mathbf{w}$ is the set of weights in the model, and the *good* and *faulty* generator target feature levels are represented as 0 and 1 respectively. Figure 7.11(b)[356] shows the value of Equation (7.24)[356] for every possible value of RPM and VIBRATION. This surface is known as a **decision surface**.

One problem that we need to solve in order to use the model defined in Equation (7.24)[356] is how to determine the values for the weights, $\mathbf{w}$, that will minimize the error function for our hypothesis $\mathbb{M}_{\mathbf{w}}(\mathbf{d})$. Unfortunately, in this case we cannot just use the gradient descent algorithm. The hard decision boundary given in Equation (7.24)[356] is **discontinuous**, so is not differentiable, which

---

to normalize descriptive features whenever we are using regression models to predict a categorical target feature.

means we cannot calculate the gradient of the error surface using the derivative. Another problem with this model is that the model always makes completely confident predictions of 0 or 1. A model able to distinguish between instances that are very close to the boundary and those that are farther away would be preferable. We can solve both these problems by using a more sophisticated threshold function that is continuous, and therefore differentiable, and that allows for the subtlety desired: the **logistic function**.[13]

The logistic function[14] is given by

$$logistic(x) = \frac{1}{1 + e^{-x}} \qquad (7.25)$$

where x is a numeric value and e is Euler's number and is approximately equal to 2.7183. A plot of the logistic function for values of x in the range $[-10, 10]$ is shown in Figure 7.12(a)[358]. We can see that the logistic function is a threshold function that pushes values above zero to 1 and values below zero to 0. This is very similar to the hard threshold function given in Equation (7.24)[356], except that it has a soft boundary. The next section explains how use of the logistic function allows us to build logistic regression models that predict categorical target features.

7.4.4.2 Logistic Regression

To build a logistic regression model, we threshold the output of the basic linear regression model using the logistic function. So, instead of the regression function simply being the dot product of the weights and the descriptive features (as given in Equation (7.9)[333]), the dot product of weights and descriptive feature values is passed through the logistic function:

$$\mathbb{M}_{\mathbf{w}}(\mathbf{d}) = logistic(\mathbf{w} \cdot \mathbf{d})$$
$$= \frac{1}{1 + e^{-\mathbf{w} \cdot \mathbf{d}}} \qquad (7.26)$$

To see the impact of this, we can build a multivariable logistic regression model for the dataset in Table 7.6[354]. After the training process (which uses

---

13 A hard threshold can be used fairly successfully to train prediction models for categorical targets using the **perceptron learning rule**, although we do not cover that in this book.

14 The logistic function is a real workhorse of mathematical modeling and is used in a huge range of different applications. For example, the logistic function has been used to model how new words enter a language over time, being first used very infrequently before moving through a tipping point to become widespread in a language.

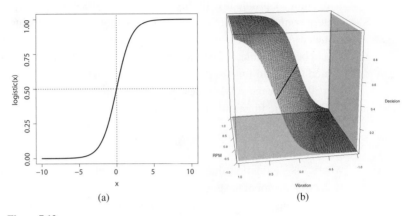

Figure 7.12

(a) A plot of the logistic function (Equation (7.25)[357]) for the range of values $[-10, 10]$; (b) the logistic decision surface that results from training a model to represent the generators dataset given in Table 7.6[354] (note that the data has been normalized to the range $[-1, 1]$).

a slightly modified version of the gradient descent algorithm, which we will explain shortly), the resulting logistic regression model is[15]

$$\mathbb{M}_\mathbf{w}(\langle \text{RPM}, \text{VIBRATION} \rangle) = \frac{1}{1 + e^{-(-0.4077 + 4.1697 \times \text{RPM} + 6.0460 \times \text{VIBRATION})}}$$
(7.27)

The decision surface resulting from Equation (7.27)[358] is shown in Figure 7.12(b)[358]. The important thing to notice about this decision surface, in contrast to the decision surface in Figure 7.11(b)[356], is that there is a gentle transition from predictions of the *faulty* target level to predictions of the *good* generator target level. This is one of the key benefits of using logistic regression. Another benefit of using the logistic function is that logistic regression model outputs can be interpreted as probabilities of the occurrence of a target level. So

$$P(t = faulty|\mathbf{d}) = \mathbb{M}_\mathbf{w}(\mathbf{d})$$

15 Note that in this example, and in the examples that follow, a normalized version of the generators dataset is used (all descriptive features are normalized to the range $[-1, 1]$ using range normalization), so the weights in Equation (7.27)[358] are different from those in Equation (7.23)[354]. If it were not for normalization, these two sets of weights would be the same.

and

$$P(t = good|\mathbf{d}) = 1 - \mathbb{M}_{\mathbf{w}}(\mathbf{d})$$

To find the optimal decision boundary for a logistic regression problem, we use the gradient descent algorithm (Algorithm 7.1[339]) to minimize the sum of squared errors based on the training dataset. Figure 7.13[359] shows a series of the candidate models that were explored on the way to finding this boundary. The final panel in Figure 7.13[359] shows how the sum of squared errors changed during the training process.

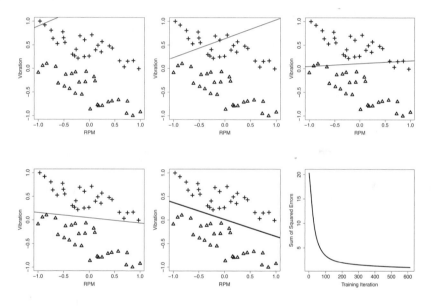

Figure 7.13
A selection of the logistic regression models developed during the gradient descent process for the machinery dataset from Table 7.6[354]. The bottom-right panel shows the sums of squared errors generated during the gradient descent process.

To repurpose the gradient descent algorithm for training logistic regression models, the only change that needs to be made is in the error delta function, which is used in the weight update rule given on Line 4[339] of Algorithm 7.1[339]. To derive this new weight update rule, imagine that there is just a single training instance, $(\mathbf{d}, t)$, in our training dataset. The partial derivative of the error function, L_2, is then

$$\frac{\partial}{\partial \mathbf{w}[j]} L_2(\mathbb{M}_\mathbf{w}, \mathcal{D}) = \frac{\partial}{\partial \mathbf{w}[j]} \frac{1}{2}(t - \mathbb{M}_\mathbf{w}(\mathbf{d}))^2$$

where $\mathbf{w}[j]$ is a single weight from the set of weights $\mathbf{w}$. Applying the chain rule to this, we get

$$\frac{\partial}{\partial \mathbf{w}[j]} L_2(\mathbb{M}_\mathbf{w}, \mathcal{D}) = (t - \mathbb{M}_\mathbf{w}(\mathbf{d})) \times \frac{\partial}{\partial \mathbf{w}[j]}(t - \mathbb{M}_\mathbf{w}(\mathbf{d}))$$

But $\mathbb{M}_\mathbf{w}(d) = logistic(\mathbf{w} \cdot \mathbf{d})$, so

$$\frac{\partial}{\partial \mathbf{w}[j]} L_2(\mathbb{M}_\mathbf{w}, \mathcal{D}) = (t - logistic(\mathbf{w} \cdot \mathbf{d})) \times \frac{\partial}{\partial \mathbf{w}[j]}(t - logistic(\mathbf{w} \cdot \mathbf{d}))$$

Applying the chain rule again to the partial derivative part of this equation, and remembering that $\frac{\partial}{\partial \mathbf{w}[j]} \mathbf{w} \cdot \mathbf{d} = d[j]$, we get

$$\frac{\partial}{\partial \mathbf{w}[j]} L_2(\mathbb{M}_\mathbf{w}, \mathcal{D}) = (t - logistic(\mathbf{w} \cdot \mathbf{d})) \times \frac{\partial}{\partial \mathbf{w}[j]} logistic(\mathbf{w} \cdot \mathbf{d})$$

$$\times \frac{\partial}{\partial \mathbf{w}[j]} \mathbf{w} \cdot \mathbf{d}$$

$$= (t - \mathbb{M}_\mathbf{w}(d)) \times \frac{\partial}{\partial \mathbf{w}[j]} logistic(\mathbf{w} \cdot \mathbf{d}) \times \mathbf{d}[j]$$

Fortunately, the derivative of the logistic function is well known:

$$\frac{d}{dx} logistic(x) = logistic(x)(1 - logistic(x)) \tag{7.28}$$

So

$$\frac{\partial}{\partial \mathbf{w}[j]} L_2(\mathbb{M}_\mathbf{w}, \mathcal{D}) = (t - logistic(\mathbf{w} \cdot \mathbf{d}))$$

$$\times logistic(\mathbf{w} \cdot \mathbf{d})(1 - logistic(\mathbf{w} \cdot \mathbf{d})) \times \mathbf{d}[j] \tag{7.29}$$

Rewriting $logistic(\mathbf{w} \cdot \mathbf{d})$ as $\mathbb{M}_\mathbf{w}(\mathbf{d})$ for readability, we get

$$\frac{\partial}{\partial \mathbf{w}[j]} L_2(\mathbb{M}_\mathbf{w}, \mathcal{D}) = (t - \mathbb{M}_\mathbf{w}(\mathbf{d})) \tag{7.30}$$

$$\times \mathbb{M}_\mathbf{w}(\mathbf{d}) \times (1 - \mathbb{M}_\mathbf{w}(\mathbf{d})) \times \mathbf{d}[j] \tag{7.31}$$

This is the partial derivative of the error surface with respect to a particular weight $\mathbf{w}[j]$ and indicates the gradient of the error surface. Using this formulation for the gradient, we can write the weight update rule for logistic regression as

$$\mathbf{w}[j] \leftarrow \mathbf{w}[j] + \alpha \times (t - \mathbb{M}_{\mathbf{w}}(\mathbf{d})) \times \mathbb{M}_{\mathbf{w}}(\mathbf{d}) \times (1 - \mathbb{M}_{\mathbf{w}}(\mathbf{d})) \times \mathbf{d}[j] \quad (7.32)$$

where $\mathbb{M}_{\mathbf{w}}(\mathbf{d}) = logistic(\mathbf{w} \cdot \mathbf{d}) = \frac{1}{1+e^{-\mathbf{w} \cdot \mathbf{d}}}$.

The rule given in Equation (7.32)[361] assumes that only a single training instance exists. To modify this to take into account a full training dataset, we simply need to a sum across all the training instances as we did before in Equation (7.17)[340]. This gives us the weight update rule for multivariable logistic regression:

$$\mathbf{w}[j] \leftarrow \mathbf{w}[j] + \alpha \times \sum_{i=1}^{n} ((t_i - \mathbb{M}_{\mathbf{w}}(\mathbf{d}_i)) \times \mathbb{M}_{\mathbf{w}}(\mathbf{d}_i) \times (1 - \mathbb{M}_{\mathbf{w}}(\mathbf{d}_i)) \times \mathbf{d}_i[j])$$

$$(7.33)$$

Other than changing the weight update rule, we don't need to make any other changes to the model training process presented for multivariable linear regression models. To further illustrate this process, the next section presents a worked example of training a multivariable logistic regression model for an extended version of the generators dataset.

7.4.4.3   A Worked Example of Multivariable Logistic Regression

One of the advantages of using a logistic regression model is that it works well for datasets in which the instances with target features set to different levels overlap with each other in the feature space. Table 7.7[362] shows an extended version of the generators dataset given in Table 7.6[354], including extra instances that make the separation between *good* generators and *faulty* generators less clear cut. This kind of data is very common in real-world scenarios. A scatter plot of this dataset is shown in Figure 7.14[363],s in which the overlap between the different types of generator in this dataset is clearly visible. Even though the separation between the instances with the different levels of the target feature in this case is not particularly well defined, a logistic regression model can be trained to distinguish between the two types of generator. In the remainder of this section, we examine this in some detail.

There is an on-going argument regarding whether descriptive features should be **normalized** before being used in linear regression models. The main disadvantage of normalization is that the interpretative analysis discussed in Section 7.4.4[353] becomes more difficult as the descriptive feature values used in the model do not relate to the actual feature values in the data. For example,

Table 7.7

An extended version of the generators dataset from Table 7.6[354].

ID	RPM	VIBRATION	STATUS	ID	RPM	VIBRATION	STATUS
1	498	604	faulty	35	501	463	good
2	517	594	faulty	36	526	443	good
3	541	574	faulty	37	536	412	good
4	555	587	faulty	38	564	394	good
5	572	537	faulty	39	584	398	good
6	600	553	faulty	40	602	398	good
7	621	482	faulty	41	610	428	good
8	632	539	faulty	42	638	389	good
9	656	476	faulty	43	652	394	good
10	653	554	faulty	44	659	336	good
11	679	516	faulty	45	662	364	good
12	688	524	faulty	46	672	308	good
13	684	450	faulty	47	691	248	good
14	699	512	faulty	48	694	401	good
15	703	505	faulty	49	718	313	good
16	717	377	faulty	50	720	410	good
17	740	377	faulty	51	723	389	good
18	749	501	faulty	52	744	227	good
19	756	492	faulty	53	741	397	good
20	752	381	faulty	54	770	200	good
21	762	508	faulty	55	764	370	good
22	781	474	faulty	56	790	248	good
23	781	480	faulty	57	786	344	good
24	804	460	faulty	58	792	290	good
25	828	346	faulty	59	818	268	good
26	830	366	faulty	60	845	232	good
27	864	344	faulty	61	867	195	good
28	882	403	faulty	62	878	168	good
29	891	338	faulty	63	895	218	good
30	921	362	faulty	64	916	221	good
31	941	301	faulty	65	950	156	good
32	965	336	faulty	66	956	174	good
33	976	297	faulty	67	973	134	good
34	994	287	faulty	68	1002	121	good

if the age of a customer was used as a descriptive feature in a financial credit scoring model, it is more difficult to talk about changes in normalized age on a scale from 0 to 1 than it is to discuss original age values on their natural scale, about 18 to 80. The main advantages of normalizing descriptive feature values are that all weights become directly comparable with each other (as all descriptive features are on the same scale), and the behavior of the gradient descent algorithm used to train the model becomes much less sensitive to the learning rate and the initial weights. Although it is less important for simple linear regression models, for logistic regression models we recommend that descriptive feature values always be normalized. In this example, before the training process begins, both descriptive features are normalized to the range $[-1,1]$.

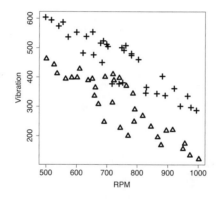

Figure 7.14
A scatter plot of the extended generators dataset given in Table 7.7[362], which results in instances with the different target levels overlapping with each other. Instances representing *good* generators are shown as crosses, and those representing *faulty* generators as triangles.

To begin the gradient descent process, random starting values for the weights within the model, $\mathbf{w}[0], \mathbf{w}[1], \mathbf{w}[2]$, are selected. In this example, random values were selected from the range $[-3,3]$ to give $\mathbf{w}[0] = -2.9465$, $\mathbf{w}[1] = -1.0147$, and $\mathbf{w}[2] = 2.1610$. Using these weights, a prediction is made for every instance in the training dataset, and the resulting sum of squared errors is calculated. The predictions made using these weights and the related error are shown in Table 7.8[364] under **Iteration 1**.

This first candidate model is not particularly accurate with an initial sum of squared errors of 12.2369. In fact, instances 1 and 2 are the only instances at this stage that are given predictions of the *faulty* target level, level 1 (note that their prediction values are the only ones greater than 0.5). This can also

Table 7.8

Details of the first two iterations when the gradient descent algorithm is used to train a logistic regression model for the extended generators dataset given in Table 7.7[362].

Initial Weights

| $\mathbf{w}[0]$: | -2.9465 | $\mathbf{w}[1]$: | -1.0147 | $\mathbf{w}[2]$: | -2.1610 |

Iteration 1

ID	TARGET LEVEL	Pred.	Error	Squared Error	errorDelta($\mathcal{D}$,$\mathbf{w}[j]$) $\mathbf{w}[0]$	$\mathbf{w}[1]$	$\mathbf{w}[2]$
1	1	0.5570	0.4430	0.1963	0.1093	-0.1093	0.1093
2	1	0.5168	0.4832	0.2335	0.1207	-0.1116	0.1159
3	1	0.4469	0.5531	0.3059	0.1367	-0.1134	0.1197
			...				
66	0	0.0042	-0.0042	0.0000	0.0000	0.0000	0.0000
67	0	0.0028	-0.0028	0.0000	0.0000	0.0000	0.0000
68	0	0.0022	-0.0022	0.0000	0.0000	0.0000	0.0000
		Sum		24.4738	2.7031	-0.7015	1.6493
		Sum of squared errors (Sum/2)		12.2369			

New Weights (after Iteration 1)

| $\mathbf{w}[0]$: | -2.8924 | $\mathbf{w}[1]$: | -1.0287 | $\mathbf{w}[2]$: | -2.1940 |

Iteration 2

ID	TARGET LEVEL	Pred.	Error	Squared Error	errorDelta($\mathcal{D}$,$\mathbf{w}[j]$) $\mathbf{w}[0]$	$\mathbf{w}[1]$	$\mathbf{w}[2]$
1	1	0.5817	0.4183	0.1749	0.1018	-0.1018	0.1018
2	1	0.5414	0.4586	0.2103	0.1139	-0.1053	0.1094
3	1	0.4704	0.5296	0.2805	0.1319	-0.1094	0.1155
			...				
66	0	0.0043	-0.0043	0.0000	0.0000	0.0000	0.0000
67	0	0.0028	-0.0028	0.0000	0.0000	0.0000	0.0000
68	0	0.0022	-0.0022	0.0000	0.0000	0.0000	0.0000
		Sum		24.0524	2.7236	-0.6646	1.6484
		Sum of squared errors (Sum/2)		12.0262			

New Weights (after Iteration 2)

| $\mathbf{w}[0]$: | -2.8380 | $\mathbf{w}[1]$: | -1.0416 | $\mathbf{w}[2]$: | -2.2271 |

be seen in the top left hand image of Figure 7.15[366],which shows the candidate model corresponding to this initial set of weights. Based on the errors in these predictions, the delta contributions, labeled as errorDelta($\mathcal{D}$, $\mathbf{w}[0]$), errorDelta($\mathcal{D}$, $\mathbf{w}[1]$) and errorDelta($\mathcal{D}$, $\mathbf{w}[2]$) in Table 7.8[364], from each training instance are calculated according to Equation (7.31)[360]. These individual delta contributions are then summed so that the weight update rule (Equation (7.33)[361]) can be applied, in this example using a learning rate of 0.02. So, for example, the new value of $\mathbf{w}[0]$ is calculated as the old value plus the learning rate times the sum of the *errorDelta*$(\mathcal{D}, \mathbf{w}[0])$ contributions to give $-2.9465 + 0.02 \times 2.7031 = -2.8924$. This gives the new set of weights shown as **New Weights (after Iteration 1)**.

The process then starts again using these new weights as the basis for the predictions and errors marked as **Iteration 2** in Table 7.8[364]. The new weights result in slightly more accurate predictions, evident from the slightly reduced sum of squared errors of 12.0262. Based on the updated errors, a new set of weights is calculated, marked in Table 7.8[364] as **New Weights (after Iteration 2)**. Table 7.8[364] shows just the first two iterations of the gradient descent process for this model. The continuing process that finds the final model is illustrated in Figure 7.15[366], which shows a selection of the candidate models generated on the way to generating the final model, and the bottom-right panel shows how the sum of squared errors changed during the process. The final model trained is

$$\mathbb{M}_{\mathbf{w}}(\langle \text{RPM}, \text{Vibration} \rangle) = \frac{1}{1 + e^{-(-0.4077 + 4.1697 \times \text{RPM} + 6.0460 \times \text{Vibration})}}$$

which has a sum of squared errors of 1.8804. Obviously, because there are instances with different levels for the target feature overlapping in the feature space, it is not possible in this case to build a model that perfectly separates the *good* and *faulty* machines. The model trained, however, strikes a good balance between mistaking *good* machines for *faulty* ones and vice versa.

7.4.5 Modeling Non-linear Relationships

All the simple linear regression and logistic regression models that we have looked at so far model a linear relationship between descriptive features and a target feature. Linear models work very well when the underlying relationships in the data are linear. Sometimes, however, the underlying data will exhibit non-linear relationships that we would like to capture in a model. For example, the dataset in Table 7.9[367] is based on an agricultural scenario and shows rainfall (in mm per day), RAIN, and resulting grass growth (in kilograms per acre per day), GROWTH, measured on a number of Irish farms during July 2012. A scatter plot of these two features is shown in Figure 7.16(a)[368], from which the strong non-linear relationship between rainfall and grass growth is clearly apparent—grass does not grow well when there is very little rain or too

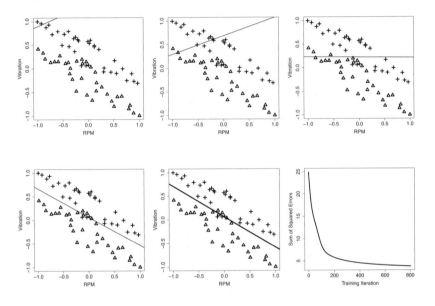

Figure 7.15

A selection of the logistic regression models developed during the gradient descent process for the extended generators dataset in Table 7.7[362]. The bottom-right panel shows the sums of squared errors generated during the gradient descent process.

much rain, but hits a sweet spot at rainfall of about 2.5mm per day. It would be useful for farmers to be able to predict grass growth for different amounts of forecasted rainfall so that they could plan the optimal times to harvest their grass for making hay.

A simple linear regression model cannot handle this non-linear relationship. Figure 7.16(b)[368] shows the best simple linear regression model that can be trained for this prediction problem. This model is

$$\text{GROWTH} = 13.510 + -0.667 \times \text{RAIN}$$

To successfully model the relationship between grass growth and rainfall, we need to introduce non-linear elements. A generalized way in which to do this is to introduce basis functions that transform the raw inputs to the model into non-linear representations but still keep the model itself linear in terms of the weights. The advantage of this is that, except for introducing the mechanism of basis functions, we do not need to make any other changes to the approach

Table 7.9

A dataset describing grass growth on Irish farms during July 2012.

ID	RAIN	GROWTH	ID	RAIN	GROWTH	ID	RAIN	GROWTH
1	2.153	14.016	12	3.754	11.420	23	3.960	10.307
2	3.933	10.834	13	2.809	13.847	24	3.592	12.069
3	1.699	13.026	14	1.809	13.757	25	3.451	12.335
4	1.164	11.019	15	4.114	9.101	26	1.197	10.806
5	4.793	4.162	16	2.834	13.923	27	0.723	7.822
6	2.690	14.167	17	3.872	10.795	28	1.958	14.010
7	3.982	10.190	18	2.174	14.307	29	2.366	14.088
8	3.333	13.525	19	4.353	8.059	30	1.530	12.701
9	1.942	13.899	20	3.684	12.041	31	0.847	9.012
10	2.876	13.949	21	2.140	14.641	32	3.843	10.885
11	4.277	8.643	22	2.783	14.138	33	0.976	9.876

we have presented so far. Furthermore, basis functions work for both simple multivariable linear regression models that predict a continuous target feature and multivariable logistic regression models that predict a categorical target feature.

To use basis functions, we recast the simple linear regression model (see Equation (7.9)[333]) as follows:

$$\mathbb{M}_{\mathbf{w}}(\mathbf{d}) = \sum_{k=0}^{b} \mathbf{w}[k] \times \phi_k(\mathbf{d}) \tag{7.34}$$

where $\mathbf{d}$ is a set of m descriptive features, $\mathbf{w}$ is a set of b weights, and ϕ_0 to ϕ_b are a series of b basis functions that each transform the input vector $\mathbf{d}$ in a different way. It is worth noting that there is no reason that b must equal m, and usually b is quite a bit larger than m—i.e., there are usually more basis functions than there are descriptive features.

One of the most common uses of basis functions in linear regression is to train models to capture **polynomial** relationships. A linear relationship implies that the target is calculated from the descriptive features using only the addition of the descriptive feature values multiplied by weight values. Polynomial relationships allow multiplication of descriptive feature values by each other and raising of descriptive features to exponents. The most common form of polynomial relationship is the **second order polynomial**, also known as the

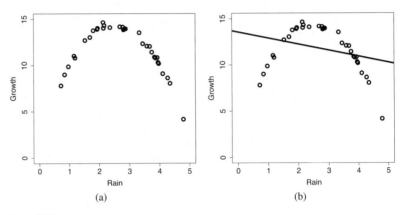

Figure 7.16
(a) A scatter plot of the RAIN and GROWTH feature from the grass growth dataset; (b) the same plot with a simple linear regression model trained to capture the relationship between the grass growth and rainfall.

quadratic function, which takes the general form $a = bx + cx^2$. The relationship between rainfall and grass growth in the grass growth dataset can be accurately represented as a second order polynomial through the following model:

$$\text{GROWTH} = \mathbf{w}[0] \times \phi_0(\text{RAIN}) + \mathbf{w}[1] \times \phi_1(\text{RAIN}) + \mathbf{w}[2] \times \phi_2(\text{RAIN})$$

where

$$\phi_0(\text{RAIN}) = 1$$
$$\phi_1(\text{RAIN}) = \text{RAIN}$$
$$\phi_2(\text{RAIN}) = \text{RAIN}^2$$

What makes this approach really attractive is that, although this new model stated in terms of basis functions captures the non-linear relationship between rainfall and grass growth, the model is still linear in terms of the weights and so can be trained using gradient descent without making any changes to the algorithm. Figure 7.17[369] shows the final non-linear model that results from this training process, along with a number of the interim steps on the way to this model. The final model is

$$\text{GROWTH} = 3.707 \times \phi_0(\text{RAIN}) + 8.475 \times \phi_1(\text{RAIN}) + -1.717 \times \phi_2(\text{RAIN})$$

where ϕ_0, ϕ_1, and ϕ_2 are as described before. This model captures the non-linear relationship in the data very well but was still easy to train using a gradient descent approach. Basis functions can also be used for multivariable simple linear regression models in the same way, the only extra requirement being the definition of more basis functions.

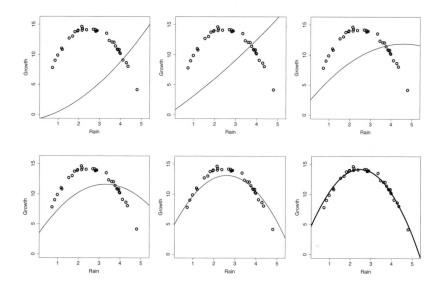

Figure 7.17

A selection of the models developed during the gradient descent process for the grass growth dataset from Table 7.9[367].

Basis functions can also be used to train logistic regression models for categorical prediction problems that involve non-linear relationships. Table 7.10[370] shows a dataset, the EEG dataset, based on a neurological experiment designed to capture how neural responses change when experiment participants view *positive* images (e.g., a picture of a smiling baby) and *negative* images (e.g., a picture of rotting food). In an experiment performed to capture this data, participants were shown a series of different images, and their neural responses were measured using **electroencephalography** (**EEG**). In particular, the values of the commonly used P20 and P45 potentials were measured while a participant viewed each image. These are the descriptive features in this dataset, and the target feature, TYPE, indicates whether the subject was viewing a positive or a negative image. If a model could be trained to classify brain activity as

Table 7.10

A dataset showing participants' responses to viewing *positive* and *negative* images measured on the EEG P20 and P45 potentials.

ID	P20	P45	TYPE	ID	P20	P45	TYPE
1	0.4497	0.4499	negative	26	0.0656	0.2244	positive
2	0.8964	0.9006	negative	27	0.6336	0.2312	positive
3	0.6952	0.3760	negative	28	0.4453	0.4052	positive
4	0.1769	0.7050	negative	29	0.9998	0.8493	positive
5	0.6904	0.4505	negative	30	0.9027	0.6080	positive
6	0.7794	0.9190	negative	31	0.3319	0.1473	positive
⋮				⋮			

being associated with positive images or negative images, doctors could use this model to help in assessing the brain function of people who have suffered severe brain injuries and are non-communicative.[16] Figure 7.18[1370] shows a scatter plot of this dataset, from which it is clear that the decision boundary between the two different types of images is not linear—i.e., the two types of images are not **linearly separable**.

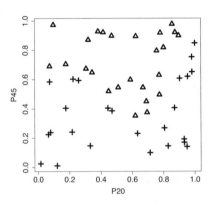

Figure 7.18

A scatter plot of the P20 and P45 features from the EEG dataset. Instances representing *positive* images are shown as crosses, and those representing *negative* images as triangles.

16 This example is very much simplified for illustration purposes, but very interesting work is done on building prediction models from the output of EEG and fMRI scans—for example, Mitchell et al. (2008).

The non-linear decision boundary that is just about perceivable in Figure 7.18[370] can be represented using a third-order polynomial in the two descriptive features, P20 and P45. The simple regression model we trained previously cannot cope with a non-linear decision boundary like the one seen in Figure 7.18[370]. We can, however, rewrite the logistic regression equation from Equation (7.26)[357] to use basis functions as follows:

$$\mathbb{M}_{\mathbf{w}}(\mathbf{d}) = \cfrac{1}{1 + e^{-\left(\sum_{j=0}^{b} \mathbf{w}[j]\,\phi_j(\mathbf{d})\right)}} \qquad (7.35)$$

Using this representation with the following set of basis functions will give the learning process the flexibility to find the non-linear decision boundary required to successfully separate the different types of images in the EEG dataset:[17]

$$\phi_0(\langle P20, P45\rangle) = 1 \qquad \phi_4(\langle P20, P45\rangle) = P45^2$$
$$\phi_1(\langle P20, P45\rangle) = P20 \qquad \phi_5(\langle P20, P45\rangle) = P20^3$$
$$\phi_2(\langle P20, P45\rangle) = P45 \qquad \phi_6(\langle P20, P45\rangle) = P45^3$$
$$\phi_3(\langle P20, P45\rangle) = P20^2 \qquad \phi_7(\langle P20, P45\rangle) = P20 \times P45$$

This model can be trained using gradient descent to find the optimal decision boundary between the two different types of images. Figure 7.19[372] shows a series of the models built during the gradient descent process. The final model can accurately distinguish between the two different types of image based on the measured P20 and P45 activity. Figure 7.19(f)[372] shows a 3D plot of the final decision surface. Note that although this decision surface is more complex than the ones we have seen before (for example, Figure 7.12[358]), the logistic shape is still maintained.

Using basis functions is a simple and effective way in which to capture non-linear relationships within a linear regression model. One way to think about this process is that we change the dataset from two dimensions to a higher dimensional space. There is no limit to the kinds of functions that can be used as basis functions, and as we have seen in the previous example, the basis functions for different descriptive features in a dataset can be quite different. One disadvantage of using basis functions, however, is that the analyst has to

[17] The term arising from ϕ_7 is commonly referred to as an **interaction term** as it allows two descriptive features to *interact* in the model.

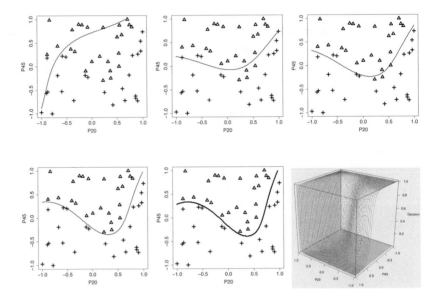

Figure 7.19

A selection of the models developed during the gradient descent process for the EEG dataset from Table 7.10[370]. The final panel shows the decision surface generated.

design the basis function set that will be used. Although there are some well-known sets of functions—for example, different order polynomial functions—this can be a considerable challenge. Second, as the number of basis functions grows beyond the number of descriptive features, the complexity of our models increases, so the gradient descent process must search through a more complex weight space. Using basis functions is an interesting way to change the inductive bias, in particular the restriction bias, encoded in the gradient descent algorithm for learning regression models. By using basis functions such as those given in the examples in this section, we relax the restriction on the algorithm to consider only linear models and instead allow more complex model types such as the higher order polynomial models seen in these examples.

7.4.6   Multinomial Logistic Regression

The **multinomial logistic regression**[18] model is an extension that handles categorical target features with more than two levels. A good way to build multinomial logistic regression models is use a set of **one-versus-all** models.[19] If we have r target levels, we create r **one-versus-all** logistic regression models. A **one-versus-all** model distinguishes between one level of the target feature and all the others. Figure 7.20[373] shows three one-versus-all prediction models for a prediction problem with three target levels (these models are based on the dataset in Table 7.11[374] that is introduced later in this section).

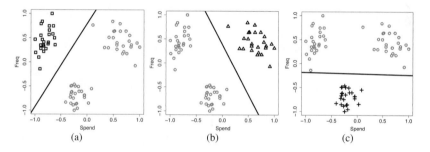

Figure 7.20

An illustration of three different one-versus-all prediction models for the customer type dataset in Table 7.11[374], with three target levels: *single* (squares), *business* (triangles), and *family* (crosses).

For r target feature levels, we build r separate logistic regression models $\mathbb{M}_{\mathbf{w_1}}$ to $\mathbb{M}_{\mathbf{w_r}}$:

$$\mathbb{M}_{\mathbf{w_1}}(\mathbf{d}) = logistic(\mathbf{w_1} \cdot \mathbf{d})$$
$$\mathbb{M}_{\mathbf{w_2}}(\mathbf{d}) = logistic(\mathbf{w_2} \cdot \mathbf{d})$$
$$\vdots \qquad\qquad\qquad\qquad\qquad (7.36)$$
$$\mathbb{M}_{\mathbf{w_r}}(\mathbf{d}) = logistic(\mathbf{w_r} \cdot \mathbf{d})$$

where $\mathbb{M}_{\mathbf{w_1}}$ to $\mathbb{M}_{\mathbf{w_r}}$ are r different one-versus-all logistic regression models, and $\mathbf{w_1}$ to $\mathbf{w_r}$ are r different sets of weights. To combine the outputs of these

---

18 Multinomial logistic regression models are often also known as **maximum entropy**, **conditional maximum entropy**, or **MaxEnt** models.

19 This is an example of an ensemble model like those described in Section 4.4.5[163].

Table 7.11

A dataset of customers of a large national retail chain.

ID	SPEND	FREQ	TYPE	ID	SPEND	FREQ	TYPE
1	21.6	5.4	single	28	122.6	6.0	business
2	25.7	7.1	single	29	107.7	5.7	business
3	18.9	5.6	single			⋮	
4	25.7	6.8	single				
				47	53.2	2.6	family
	⋮			48	52.4	2.0	family
26	107.9	5.8	business	49	46.1	1.4	family
27	92.9	5.5	business	50	65.3	2.2	family
	⋮					⋮	

different models, we normalize their results as follows:

$$\mathbb{M}'_{\mathbf{w_k}}(\mathbf{d}) = \frac{\mathbb{M}_{\mathbf{w_k}}(\mathbf{d})}{\sum\limits_{l \in levels(t)} \mathbb{M}_{\mathbf{w_l}}(\mathbf{d})} \tag{7.37}$$

where $\mathbb{M}'_{\mathbf{w_k}}(\mathbf{d})$ is a revised, normalized prediction for the one-versus-all model for the target level k. The denominator in this equation sums the predictions of each of the one-versus-all models for the r levels of the target feature and acts as a normalization term. This ensures that the output of all models sums to 1. The r one-versus-all logistic regression models used are trained in parallel, and the revised model outputs, $\mathbb{M}'_{\mathbf{w_k}}(\mathbf{d})$, are used when calculating the sum of squared errors for each model during the training process. This means that the sum of squared errors function is changed slightly to

$$L_2(\mathbb{M}_{\mathbf{w_k}}, \mathcal{D}) = \frac{1}{2} \sum_{i=1}^{n} \left(t_i - \mathbb{M}'_{\mathbf{w_k}}(\mathbf{d}_i[1]) \right)^2 \tag{7.38}$$

The revised predictions are also used when making predictions for query instances. The predicted level for a query, $\mathbf{q}$, is the level associated with the one-versus-all model that outputs the highest result after normalization. We can write this as

$$\mathbb{M}(\mathbf{q}) = \arg\max_{l \in levels(t)} \mathbb{M}'_{\mathbf{w_l}}(\mathbf{q}) \tag{7.39}$$

Table 7.11[374] shows a sample from a dataset of mobile customers that includes details of customers' shopping habits with a large national retail chain. Each customer's average weekly spending with the chain, SPEND, and average number of visits per week to the chain, FREQ, are included along with the TYPE of customer: *single*, *business*, or *family*. An extended version of this dataset was used to build a model that can determine the type of a customer based on a few weeks of shopping behavior data. Figure 7.21[375] shows the training sequence for a multinomial logistic regression model trained using this data (after the data had been range normalized to $[-1, 1]$). There are three target levels, so three one-versus-all models are built. The evolution of the decision boundary for each model is shown.

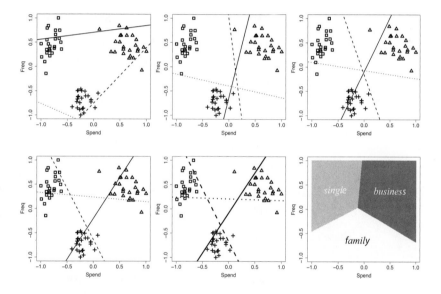

Figure 7.21

A selection of the models developed during the gradient descent process for the customer group dataset from Table 7.11[374]. Squares represent instances with the *single* target level, triangles the *business* level, and crosses the *family* level. The bottom-right panel illustrates the overall decision boundaries between the three target levels.

The final one-versus-all decision boundaries shown in the bottom-middle panel of Figure 7.21[375] do not look like the individual one-versus-all decision boundaries shown in Figure 7.20[373]. The reason for this is that the boundaries shown in Figure 7.20[373] were trained in isolation, whereas the boundaries shown in Figure 7.21[375] were trained in parallel and so are interconnected. While it might look like the decision boundary for the *single* target level shown by the solid line does not discriminate between the instances with the *single* target level and those with the other target levels, when used in conjunction with the other two decision boundaries, it does. We can see this in the **decision boundaries** shown in the bottom-right panel of Figure 7.21[375]. We will use an example to illustrate how a prediction is made using a multinomial regression model.

The parameters of the models learned for the three final decision boundaries in Figure 7.21[375] are

$$\mathbb{M}_{\mathbf{w}_{single}}(\mathbf{q}) = logistic(0.7993 - 15.9030 \times \text{SPEND} + 9.5974 \times \text{FREQ})$$

$$\mathbb{M}_{\mathbf{w}_{family}}(\mathbf{q}) = logistic(3.6526 + -0.5809 \times \text{SPEND} - 17.5886 \times \text{FREQ})$$

$$\mathbb{M}_{\mathbf{w}_{business}}(\mathbf{q}) = logistic(4.6419 + 14.9401 \times \text{SPEND} - 6.9457 \times \text{FREQ})$$

For a query instance with SPEND = 25.67 and FREQ = 6.12, which are normalized to SPEND = −0.7279 and FREQ = 0.4789, the predictions of the individual models would be

$$\mathbb{M}_{\mathbf{w}_{single}}(\mathbf{q}) = logistic(0.7993 - 15.9030 \times (-0.7279) + 9.5974 \times 0.4789)$$
$$= 0.9999$$

$$\mathbb{M}_{\mathbf{w}_{family}}(\mathbf{q}) = logistic(3.6526 + -0.5809 \times (-0.7279) - 17.5886 \times 0.4789)$$
$$= 0.01278$$

$$\mathbb{M}_{\mathbf{w}_{business}}(\mathbf{q}) = logistic(4.6419 + 14.9401 \times (-0.7279) - 6.9457 \times 0.4789)$$
$$= 0.0518$$

These predictions would be normalized as follows:

$$\mathbb{M}'_{\mathbf{w}_{single}}(\mathbf{q}) = \frac{0.9999}{0.9999 + 0.01278 + 0.0518} = 0.9393$$

$$\mathbb{M}'_{\mathbf{w}_{family}}(\mathbf{q}) = \frac{0.01278}{0.9999 + 0.01278 + 0.0518} = 0.0120$$

$$\mathbb{M}'_{\mathbf{w}_{business}}(\mathbf{q}) = \frac{0.0518}{0.9999 + 0.01278 + 0.0518} = 0.0487$$

This means the overall prediction for the query instance is *single*, as this gets the highest normalized score.

7.4.7   Support Vector Machines

Support vector machines (SVM) are another approach to predictive modeling that is based on error-based learning. Figure 7.22(a)[377] shows a scatter plot of a reduced version of the generators dataset (shown in Table 7.6[354]) with a decision boundary drawn across it. The instance nearest the decision boundary, based on perpendicular distance, is highlighted. This distance from the decision boundary to the nearest training instance is known as the **margin**. The dashed lines on either side of the decision boundary show the extent of the margin, and we refer to these as the **margin extents**.

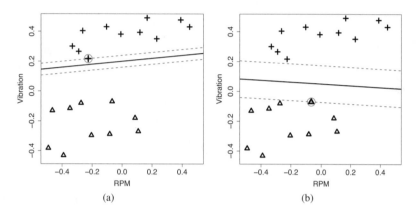

(a)   (b)

Figure 7.22

A small sample of the generators dataset with two features, RPM and VIBRATION, and two target levels, *good* (shown as crosses) and *faulty* (shown as triangles): (a) a decision boundary with a very small margin; (b) a decision boundary with a much larger margin. In both cases, the instances along the margins are highlighted.

Figure 7.22(b)[377] shows a similar diagram but with a different decision boundary, which has a much larger margin. The intuition behind support vector machines is that this second decision boundary should distinguish between the two target levels much more reliably than the first. Training a support vector machine involves searching for the decision boundary, or **separating hyperplane**,[20] that leads to the maximum margin as this will best separate the levels of the target feature. Although the goal of finding the best decision boundary is the same for algorithms that build support vector machines as it is for logistic regression models, the inductive bias encoded in the algorithms to select this boundary is different, which leads to different decision boundaries being found.

---

20 Remember that for problems with more than two descriptive features, the decision boundary is a **hyperplane** rather than a line.

The instances in a training dataset that fall along the margin extents, and so define the margins, are known as the **support vectors**. These are the most important instances in the dataset because they define the decision boundary. There will always be at least one support vector for each level of the target feature, but there is no limit to how many support vectors there can be in total.

We define the separating hyperplane in the same way that we did at the beginning of the discussion of logistic regression:

$$w_0 + \mathbf{w} \cdot \mathbf{d} = 0 \tag{7.40}$$

Note that this time we have separated w_0 from the other weights, $\mathbf{w}$, as this will make later equations simpler.[21] Recall from Section 7.4.4[353] that for instances above a separating hyperplane

$$w_0 + \mathbf{w} \cdot \mathbf{d} > 0$$

and for instances below a separating hyperplane

$$w_0 + \mathbf{w} \cdot \mathbf{d} < 0$$

For support vector machines, we first set the negative target feature level to -1 and the positive target feature level to $+1$. We then build a support vector machine prediction model so that instances with the negative target level result in the model outputting $\leqslant -1$ and instances with the positive target level result in the model outputting $\geqslant +1$. The space between the outputs of -1 and $+1$ allows for the margin.

A support vector machine model is defined as

$$\mathbb{M}_{\boldsymbol{\alpha}, w_0}(\mathbf{q}) = \sum_{i=1}^{s} (t_i \times \boldsymbol{\alpha}[i] \times (\mathbf{d}_i \cdot \mathbf{q}) + w_0) \tag{7.41}$$

where $\mathbf{q}$ is the set of descriptive features for a query instance; $(\mathbf{d}_1, t_1), \ldots, (\mathbf{d}_s, t_s)$ are s support vectors (instances composed of descriptive features and a target feature); w_0 is the first weight of the decision boundary; and $\boldsymbol{\alpha}$ is a set of parameters determined during the training process (there is a parameter for each support vector $\boldsymbol{\alpha}[1], \ldots, \boldsymbol{\alpha}[s]$).[22] When the output of this equation is greater than 1, we predict the positive target level for the query, and

21 This also means that we no longer use the dummy descriptive feature, $\mathbf{d}[0]$, that we previously always set to 1, see Equation (7.9)[333].

22 These parameters are formally known as **Lagrange multipliers**.

when the output is less than -1, we predict the negative target level. An important feature of this equation is that the support vectors are a component of the equation. This reflects the fact that a support vector machine uses the support vectors to define the separating hyperplane and hence to make the actual model predictions.

To train a support vector machine, we need to find values for each of the components in Equation (7.41)[378] (the support vectors, w_0, and the $\boldsymbol{\alpha}$ parameters) that define the optimal decision boundary between the target levels. This is an instance of a **constrained quadratic optimization problem**, and there are well-known approaches to solving this type of problem. In this book we do not describe this step of the process in detail.[23] Instead, we focus on explaining how the process is set up and how the training process reflects the inductive bias of searching for the separating hyperplane with the maximum margin. As the name **constrained quadratic optimization problem** suggests, this type of problem is defined in terms of (1) a set of constraints and (2) an optimization criterion.

When training a support vector machine, we wish to find a hyperplane that distinguishes between the two target levels, -1 and $+1$. So, the required **constraints** required by the training process are

$$w_0 + \mathbf{w} \cdot \mathbf{d} \leqslant -1 \text{ for } t_i = -1 \qquad (7.42)$$

and

$$w_0 + \mathbf{w} \cdot \mathbf{d} \geqslant +1 \text{ for } t_i = +1 \qquad (7.43)$$

Figure 7.23[380] shows two different decision boundaries that satisfy these constraints. Note that the decision boundaries in these examples are equally positioned between positive and negative instances, which is a consequence of the fact that decision boundaries satisfy these constraints. The support vectors are highlighted in Figure 7.23[380] for each of the decision boundaries shown. For simplicity in later calculations, we can combine the two constraints in Equations (7.42)[379] and (7.43)[379] into a single constraint (remember that t_i is always equal to either -1 or $+1$):

$$t_i \times (w_0 + \mathbf{w} \cdot \mathbf{d}) \geqslant 1 \qquad (7.44)$$

---

23 We provide references in Section 7.6[386].

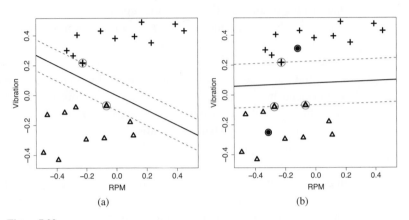

Figure 7.23

Different margins that satisfy the constraint in Equation (7.44)[379], the instances that define the margin are highlighted in each case; (b) shows the maximum margin and also shows two query instances represented as black dots.

The optimization criterion used when training a support vector machine allows us to choose between multiple different decision boundaries that satisfy the constraint given in Equation (7.44)[379], such as those shown in Figure 7.23[380]. The optimization criterion used is defined in terms of the perpendicular distance from any instance to the decision boundary and is given by

$$dist(\mathbf{d}) = \frac{abs(w_0 + \mathbf{w} \cdot \mathbf{d})}{||\mathbf{w}||}$$

where $||\mathbf{w}||$ is known as the **Euclidean norm** of $\mathbf{w}$ and is calculated as

$$||\mathbf{w}|| = \sqrt{\mathbf{w}[1]^2 + \mathbf{w}[2]^2 + \ldots + \mathbf{w}[m]^2}$$

For instances along the margin extents, $abs(w_0 + \mathbf{w} \cdot \mathbf{d}) = 1$ (according to Equation (7.44)[379]). So, the distance from any instance along the margin extents to the decision boundary is $\frac{1}{||\mathbf{w}||}$, and because the margin is symmetrical to either side of the decision boundary, the size of the margin is $\frac{2}{||\mathbf{w}||}$. The goal when training a support vector machine is to maximize $\frac{2}{||\mathbf{w}||}$ subject to the constraint expressed in Equation (7.44)[379].

Once the constraints and optimization criterion have been defined, the solution to the constrained quadratic optimization process will identify and define all the components in Equation $(7.41)^{[378]}$ (the support vectors, w_0, and the $\boldsymbol{\alpha}$ parameters) for the optimal decision boundary.

The optimal decision boundary and associated support vectors for the example we have been following are shown in Figure $7.23(b)^{[380]}$. In this case *good* is the positive level and set to $+1$, and *faulty* is the negative level and set to -1. The descriptive feature values and target feature values for the support vectors in these cases are $(\langle -0.225, 0.217\rangle, +1)$, $(\langle -0.066, -0.069\rangle, -1)$, and $(\langle -0.273, -0.080\rangle, -1)$. The value of w_0 is -0.1838, and the values of the $\boldsymbol{\alpha}$ parameters are $\langle 23.056, 6.998, 16.058\rangle)$. Figure $7.23(b)^{[380]}$ shows the position of two new query instances for this problem. The descriptive feature values for these query instances are $\mathbf{q_1} = \langle -0.314, -0.251\rangle$ and $\mathbf{q_2} = \langle -0.117, 0.31\rangle$. For the first query instance, $\mathbf{q_1}$, the output of the support vector machine model is:

$$\mathbb{M}_{\boldsymbol{\alpha}, w_0}(\mathbf{q_1})$$
$$= (1 \times 23.056 \times ((-0.225 \times -0.314) + (0.217 \times -0.251)) - 0.1838)$$
$$+ (-1 \times 6.998 \times ((-0.066 \times -0.314) + (-0.069 \times -0.251)) - 0.1838)$$
$$+ (-1 \times 16.058 \times ((-0.273 \times -0.314) + (-0.080 \times -0.251)) - 0.1838)$$
$$= -2.145$$

The model output is less than -1, so this query is predicted to be a *faulty* generator. For the second query instance, the model output is calculated similarly and is 1.592. This is greater than $+1$, so this instance is predicted to be a *good* generator.

In the same way we used basis functions with logistic regression models in Section $7.4.5^{[365]}$, basis functions can be used with support vector machines to handle training data that is not linearly separable. In order to use basis functions, we must update Equation $(7.44)^{[379]}$ to

$$t_i \times (w_0 + \mathbf{w} \cdot \boldsymbol{\phi}(\mathbf{d})) \geqslant 1 \text{ for all } i \tag{7.45}$$

where $\boldsymbol{\phi}$ is a set of basis functions applied to the descriptive features $\mathbf{d}$, and $\mathbf{w}$ is a set of weights containing one weight for each member of $\boldsymbol{\phi}$. Typically, the number of basis functions in $\boldsymbol{\phi}$ is larger than the number of descriptive features, so the application of the basis functions moves the data into a higher-dimensional space. The expectation is that a linear separating hyperplane will exist in this higher-dimensional space even though it does not in the original feature space. The prediction model in this case becomes

$$\mathbb{M}_{\boldsymbol{\alpha},\boldsymbol{\phi},w_0}(\mathbf{q}) = \sum_{i=1}^{s} (t_i \times \boldsymbol{\alpha}[i] \times (\boldsymbol{\phi}(\mathbf{d}_i) \cdot \boldsymbol{\phi}(\mathbf{q})) + w_0) \qquad (7.46)$$

Equation $(7.46)^{[382]}$ requires a dot product calculation between the result of applying the basis functions to the query instance and to each of the support vectors. During the training process, this is repeated multiple times. A dot product of two high-dimensional vectors is a computationally expensive operation, but a clever trick—the **kernel trick**—is used to avoid it. The same result obtained by calculating the dot product of the descriptive features of a support vector and a query instance after having applied the basis functions can be obtained by applying a much less costly **kernel function**, *kernel*, to the original descriptive feature values of the support vector and the query.[24] The prediction equation becomes

$$\mathbb{M}_{\boldsymbol{\alpha},kernel,w_0}(\mathbf{q}) = \sum_{i=1}^{s} (t_i \times \boldsymbol{\alpha}[i] \times kernel(\mathbf{d}_i,\mathbf{q}) + w_0) \qquad (7.47)$$

A wide range of standard kernel functions can be used with support vector machines. Some popular options are

Linear kernel $kernel(\mathbf{d},\mathbf{q}) = \mathbf{d} \cdot \mathbf{q} + c$

where c is an optional constant

Polynomial kernel $kernel(\mathbf{d},\mathbf{q}) = (\mathbf{d} \cdot \mathbf{q} + 1)^p$

where p is the degree of a polynomial function

Gaussian radial basis kernel $kernel(\mathbf{d},\mathbf{q}) = \exp(-\gamma \|\mathbf{d} - \mathbf{q}\|^2)$

where γ is a manually chosen tuning parameter

The appropriate kernel function for a particular prediction model should be selected by experimenting with different options. It is best to start with a simple linear or low-degree polynomial kernel function and move to more complex kernel functions only if good performance cannot be achieved with this.

---

24 Question 4, at the end of this chapter, explores the kernel trick in more detail, and worked examples are provided in the solution.

The description of the support vector machine approach given in this section assumes that it is possible to separate the instances with the two different target feature levels with a linear hyperplane. Sometimes this is not possible, even after using a kernel function to move the data to a higher dimensional feature space. In these instances, a margin cannot be defined as we have done in this example. An extension of the standard support vector machine approach that allows a **soft margin**, however, caters for this and allows overlap between instances with target features of the two different levels. Another extension allows support vector machines to handle multinomial target features using a one-versus-all approach similar to that described in Section 7.4.6[373]. There are also extensions to handle categorical descriptive features (similar to the approach described in Section 7.4.3[351]) and continuous target features.

Support vector machines have become a very popular approach to building predictive models in recent times. They can be quickly trained, are not overly susceptible to overfitting, and work well for high-dimensional data. In contrast to logistic regression models, however, they are not very interpretable, and, especially when kernel functions are used, it is very difficult to understand why a particular prediction has been made.

7.5 Summary

The **simple multivariable linear regression** (Section 7.3[332]) model (for convenience, repeated here as Equation (7.48)[383]) makes a prediction for a continuous target feature based on a weighted sum of the values of a set of descriptive features. In an error-based model, learning equates to finding the optimal values for these weights. Each of the infinite number of possible combinations of values for the weights will result in a model that **fits**, to some extent, the relationship present in the training data between the descriptive features and the target feature. The optimal values for the weights are the values that define the model with the minimum prediction error.

$$\mathbb{M}_{\mathbf{w}}(\mathbf{d}) = \mathbf{w} \cdot \mathbf{d}$$
$$= \sum_{j=0}^{m} \mathbf{w}[j] \times \mathbf{d}[j] \tag{7.48}$$

We use an **error function** to measure how well a set of weights fits the relationship in the training data. The most common error function used for error-based models is the **sum of squared errors**. The value of the error function for every possible weight combination defines an error surface, similar to the one shown in Figure 7.24(a)[384]—for each combination of weight values, we get a point on the surface whose coordinates are the weight values, with an elevation defined by the error of the model using the weight values. To find the optimal set of weights, we begin with a set of random weight values that corresponds to some random point on the error surface. We then iteratively make small adjustments to these weights based on the output of the error functio,n which leads to a journey down the error surface that eventually leads to the optimal set of weights. The zig-zagging line in Figure 7.24(a)[384] shows an example journey across an error surface, and Figure 7.24(b)[384] shows the reduction in the sum of squared errors as the search for the optimal weights progresses down the error surface.

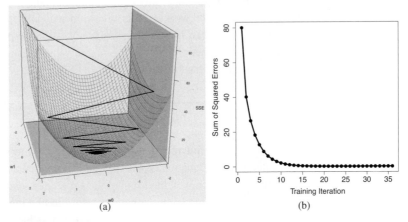

(a)   (b)

Figure 7.24
The journey across an error surface and the changing sums of squared errors during this journey.

To ensure that we arrive at the optimal set of weights at the end of this journey across the error surface, we need to ensure that each step we take moves downward on the error surface. We do this by directing our steps according to the **gradient** of the error surface at each step. This is the **gradient descent algorithm**, which is one of the most important algorithms in all of computer science, let alone machine learning.

The simple multivariable linear regression model that we presented at the beginning of this chapter can be extended in many ways, and we presented some of the most important of these. **Logistic regression** models (Section

$7.4.4^{[353]}$) allow us to predict categorical targets rather than continuous ones by placing a threshold on the output of the simple multivariable linear regression model using the logistic function.

The simple linear regression and logistic regression models that we first looked at were only capable of representing **linear relationships** between descriptive features and a target feature. In many cases, this limits the creation of an accurate prediction model. By applying a set of **basis functions** (Section $7.4.5^{[365]}$) to descriptive features, models that represent **non-linear relationships** can be created. The advantages of using basis functions is that they allow models that represent non-linear relationships to be built even though these models themselves remain a linear combination of inputs (e.g., we still use something very similar to Equation $(7.48)^{[383]}$ to predict continuous targets). Consequently, we can still use the gradient descent process to train them. The main disadvantages of using basis functions are, first, that we must manually decide what set of basis functions to use, and second, that the number of weights in a model using basis functions is usually far greater than the number of descriptive features, so finding the optimal set of weights involves a search across a much larger set of possibilities—i.e., a much larger **weight space**.

It is somewhat surprising how often a linear multivariable regression model can accurately represent the relationship between descriptive features and a target feature without the use of basis functions. We recommend that simple linear models be evaluated first and basis functions introduced only when the performance of the simpler models is deemed unsatisfactory.

The logistic regression approach (and the SVM approach) discussed in this chapter is at a disadvantage to those discussed in the previous chapters in that in its basic form, it can only handle categorical target features with two levels. In order to handle categorical target features with more than two levels, that is **multinomial** prediction problems, we need to use a **one-versus-all** approach in which multiple models are trained. This introduces something of an explosion in the number of weights required for a model, as we have an individual set of weights for every target feature level. This is one reason that other approaches are often favored over logistic regression for predicting categorical targets with many levels.

One of the most attractive features of the regression models discussed in this chapter is that they are based on a large body of research and best-practice in **statistics**, a much older discipline than machine learning. The maturity of regression-based approaches means that they are easily accepted in other disciplines (e.g., biological, physical, and social sciences) and that there is a range

of techniques that allow a degree of analysis of regression models beyond what
is possible for other approaches. We saw some of these techniques in Section
7.4.1[347] when we examined the importance of the different descriptive features in a linear regression model through an analysis of the model weights.
A range of other approaches we do not cover in this book can be used to do
other in-depth analysis of regression models. Section 7.6[386] recommends further reading on this topic.

Near the end of this chapter we covered **support vector machines** (SVM),
a more recent development in error-based learning. SVM models are trained in
a slightly different way than regression models, but the concepts underpinning
both approaches are similar. The main advantages of SVM models are that they
are robust to overfitting and perform well for very high-dimensional problems.
SVM models are just one of a whole range of error-based approaches that are
active areas for machine learning research, and new approaches are constantly
being developed. The next section discusses recommended readings for more
information on the regression approaches discussed in this chapter and on some
of the more recent developments in error-based learning.

7.6   Further Reading

The key component of the gradient descent algorithm presented in this chapter
is the use of **differentiation** to compute the slope of the error surface. Differentiation is a part of calculus, which is a large and very important field of
mathematics. In Appendix C[551] we provide an introduction to differentiation
that covers all the techniques required to understand how the gradient descent
algorithm works. If, however, you wish to get a broader understanding of calculus, we recommend Stewart (2012) as an excellent textbook on all aspects of
calculus.

For a more in-depth treatment of regression models and their underpinnings
in statistics, Chapter 14 of Rice (2006) offers a nice treatment of the topic,
while Kutner et al. (2004) provides massive detail. Ayres (2008) gives a lighter
discussion of the many different ways in which regression models are applied
in practice.

Burges (1998) is still a good, freely available tutorial on support vector machines. For more details, Cristianini and Shawe-Taylor (2000) is a well-respected textbook on the topic and covers the extensions mentioned in Section 7.4.7[376], while Vapnik (2000) gives a good overview of the theoretical underpinnings of support vector machines.

In this chapter we have not covered **artificial neural networks**, another popular error-based approach to learning. One type of artificial neural network can be built by connecting layers of logistic regression models, but there are many other network topologies used in practice. Chapter 5 of Bishop (2006) gives a good introduction to neural networks, and Bishop (1996), by the same author, covers neural networks in great detail.

7.7 Exercises

1. A multivariate linear regression model has been built to predict the **heating load** in a residential building based on a set of descriptive features describing the characteristics of the building. Heating load is the amount of heat energy required to keep a building at a specified temperature, usually 65° Fahrenheit, during the winter regardless of outside temperature. The descriptive features used are the overall surface area of the building, the height of the building, the area of the building's roof, and the percentage of wall area in the building that is glazed. This kind of model would be useful to architects or engineers when designing a new building.[25] The trained model is

$$\text{HEATING LOAD} = -26.030 + 0.0497 \times \text{SURFACE AREA}$$
$$+ 4.942 \times \text{HEIGHT} - 0.090 \times \text{ROOF AREA}$$
$$+ 20.523 \times \text{GLAZING AREA}$$

Use this model to make predictions for each of the query instances shown in the table below.

ID	SURFACE AREA	HEIGHT	ROOF AREA	GLAZING AREA
1	784.0	3.5	220.5	0.25
2	710.5	3.0	210.5	0.10
3	563.5	7.0	122.5	0.40
4	637.0	6.0	147.0	0.60

2. You have been hired by the European Space Agency to build a model that predicts the amount of oxygen that an astronaut consumes when performing five minutes of intense physical work. The descriptive features for the model will be the age of the astronaut and their average heart rate throughout the work. The regression model is

$$\text{OXYCON} = \mathbf{w}[0] + \mathbf{w}[1] \times \text{AGE} + \mathbf{w}[2] \times \text{HEARTRATE}$$

25 This question is inspired by Tsanas and Xifara (2012), and although the data used is artificially generated, it is based on the Energy Efficiency Dataset available from the UCI Machine Learning Repository (Bache and Lichman, 2013) at archive.ics.uci.edu/ml/datasets/ Energy+efficiency/.

The table below shows a historical dataset that has been collected for this task.

ID	OXYCON	AGE	HEART RATE	ID	OXYCON	AGE	HEART RATE
1	37.99	41	138	7	44.72	43	158
2	47.34	42	153	8	36.42	46	143
3	44.38	37	151	9	31.21	37	138
4	28.17	46	133	10	54.85	38	158
5	27.07	48	126	11	39.84	43	143
6	37.85	44	145	12	30.83	43	138

a. Assuming that the current weights in a multivariate linear regression model are $\mathbf{w}[0] = -59.50$, $\mathbf{w}[1] = -0.15$, and $\mathbf{w}[2] = 0.60$, make a prediction for each training instance using this model.

b. Calculate the sum of squared errors for the set of predictions generated in part (a).

c. Assuming a learning rate of 0.000002, calculate the weights at the next iteration of the gradient descent algorithm.

d. Calculate the sum of squared errors for a set of predictions generated using the new set of weights calculated in part (c).

3. A multivariate logistic regression model has been built to predict the propensity of shoppers to perform a repeat purchase of a free gift that they are given. The descriptive features used by the model are the age of the customer, the socio-economic band to which the customer belongs (*a*, *b*, or *c*), the average amount of money the customer spends on each visit to the shop, and the average number of visits the customer makes to the shop per week. This model is being used by the marketing department to determine who should be given the free gift. The weights in the trained model are shown in the table below.

Feature	Weight
Intercept ($\mathbf{w}[0]$)	-3.82398
AGE	-0.02990
SOCIO ECONOMIC BAND B	-0.09089
SOCIO ECONOMIC BAND C	-0.19558
SHOP VALUE	0.02999
SHOP FREQUENCY	0.74572

Use this model to make predictions for each of the following query instances.

ID	AGE	SOCIO ECONOMIC BAND	SHOP FREQUENCY	SHOP VALUE
1	56	b	1.60	109.32
2	21	c	4.92	11.28
3	48	b	1.21	161.19
4	37	c	0.72	170.65
5	32	a	1.08	165.39

4. The use of the **kernel trick** is key in writing efficient implementations of the **support vector machine** approach to predictive modelling. The kernel trick is based on the fact that the result of a **kernel function** applied to a support vector and a query instance is equivalent to the result of calculating the dot product between the support vector and the query instance after a specific set of basis functions have been applied to both—in other words $kernel(\mathbf{d}, \mathbf{q}) = \boldsymbol{\phi}(\mathbf{d}) \cdot \boldsymbol{\phi}(\mathbf{q})$.

   a. Using the support vector $\langle \mathbf{d}[1], \mathbf{d}[2] \rangle$ and the query instance $\langle \mathbf{q}[1], \mathbf{q}[2] \rangle$ as examples, show that applying a polynomial kernel with $p = 2$, $kernel(\mathbf{d}, \mathbf{q}) = (\mathbf{d} \cdot \mathbf{q} + 1)^2$, is equivalent to calculating the dot product of the support vector and query instance after applying the following set of basis functions:

   $$\phi_0(\langle \mathbf{d}[1], \mathbf{d}[2] \rangle) = \mathbf{d}[1]^2 \qquad \phi_1(\langle \mathbf{d}[1], \mathbf{d}[2] \rangle) = \mathbf{d}[2]^2$$
   $$\phi_2(\langle \mathbf{d}[1], \mathbf{d}[2] \rangle) = \sqrt{2} \times \mathbf{d}[1] \times \mathbf{d}[2] \qquad \phi_3(\langle \mathbf{d}[1], \mathbf{d}[2] \rangle) = \sqrt{2} \times \mathbf{d}[1]$$
   $$\phi_4(\langle \mathbf{d}[1], \mathbf{d}[2] \rangle) = \sqrt{2} \times \mathbf{d}[2] \qquad \phi_5(\langle \mathbf{d}[1], \mathbf{d}[2] \rangle) = 1$$

   b. A support vector machine model has been trained to distinguish between dosages of two drugs that cause a dangerous interaction, and those that interact safely. This model uses just two continuous features, DOSE1 and DOSE2, and two target levels, *dangerous* (the positive level, $+1$) and *safe* (the negative level, -1). The support vectors in the trained model are shown in the table below.

DOSE1	DOSE2	CLASS
0.2351	0.4016	+1
-0.1764	-0.1916	+1
0.3057	-0.9394	-1
0.5590	0.6353	-1
-0.6600	-0.1175	-1

In the trained model the value of w_0 is 0.3074, and the values of the α parameters are $\langle 7.1655, 6.9060, 2.0033, 6.1144, 5.9538 \rangle$.

i. Using the version of the support vector machine prediction model that uses basis functions (see Equation 7.46) with the basis functions given in part (a), calculate the output of the model for a query instance with DOSE1 $= 0.90$ and DOSE2 $= -0.90$.

ii. Using the version of the support vector machine prediction model that uses a kernel function (see Equation 7.47) with the polynomial kernel function, calculate the output of the model for a query instance with DOSE1 $= 0.22$ and DOSE2 $= 0.16$.

iii. Verify that the answers calculated in parts (i) and (ii) of this question would have been the same if the alternative approach (basis functions or the polynomial kernel function) had been used in each case.

iv. Compare the amount of computation required to calculate the output of the support vector machine using the polynomial kernel function with the amount required to calculate the output of the support vector machine using the basis functions.

∗ 5. When building multivariate logistic regression models, it is recommended that all continuous descriptive features be normalized to the range $[-1, 1]$. The table below shows a data quality report for the dataset used to train the model described in Question 3.

Feature	Count	% Miss.	Card.	Min.	1st Qrt.	Mean	Median	3rd Qrt.	Max.	Std. Dev.
AGE	5,200	6	40	18	22	32.7	32	32	63	12.2
SHOP FREQUENCY	5,200	0	316	0.2	1.0	2.2	1.3	4.3	5.4	1.6
SHOP VALUE	5,200	0	3,730	5	11.8	101.9	100.14	174.6	230.7	72.1

Feature	Count	% Miss.	Card.	Mode	Mode Count	Mode %	2nd Mode	2nd Mode Count	2nd Mode %
SOCIO ECONOMIC BAND	5,200	8	3	a	2,664	51.2	b	1,315	25.3
REPEAT PURCHASE	5,200	0	2	no	2,791	53.7	yes	2,409	46.3

Based on the information in this report, all continuous features were normalized using **range normalization**, and any missing values were replaced using **mean imputation** for continuous features and **mode imputation** for categorical features. After applying these data preparation operations, a multivariate logistic regression model was trained to give the weights shown in the table below.

Feature	Weight
Intercept ($\mathbf{w}[0]$)	0.6679
AGE	-0.5795
SOCIO ECONOMIC BAND B	-0.1981
SOCIO ECONOMIC BAND C	-0.2318
SHOP VALUE	3.4091
SHOP FREQUENCY	2.0499

Use this model to make predictions for each of the query instances shown in the table below (question marks refer to missing values).

ID	AGE	SOCIO ECONOMIC BAND	SHOP FREQUENCY	SHOP VALUE
1	38	a	1.90	165.39
2	56	b	1.60	109.32
3	18	c	6.00	10.09
4	?	b	1.33	204.62
5	62	?	0.85	110.50

∗ 6. The effects that can occur when different drugs are taken together can be difficult for doctors to predict. Machine learning models can be built to help predict optimal dosages of drugs so as to achieve a medical practitioner's goals.[26] The image below on the left shows a scatter plot of a dataset used

---

26 The data used in this question has been artificially generated for this book. Mac Namee et al. (2002) is, however, a good example of prediction models being used to help doctors select correct drug dosages.

to train a model to distinguish between dosages of two drugs that cause a dangerous interaction and those that cause a safe interaction. There are just two continuous features in this dataset, DOSE1 and DOSE2 (these have both been normalized to the range $(-1, 1)$ using range normalization), and two target levels, *dangerous* and *safe*. In the scatter plot DOSE1 is shown on the horizontal axis, DOSE2 is shown on the vertical axis, and the shapes of the points represent the target level—crosses represent *dangerous* interactions and triangles represent *safe* interactions.

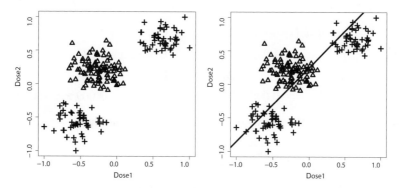

The image above on the right shows a simple linear logistic regression model trained to perform this task. This model is

$$P(\text{TYPE} = dangerous) =$$
$$Logistic(0.6168 + 2.7320 \times \text{DOSE1} - 2.4809 \times \text{DOSE2})$$

Plainly, this model is not performing well.

a. Would the similarity-based, information-based, or probability-based predictive modeling approaches that have already been covered in this book be likely to do a better job of learning this model than the simple linear regression model?

b. A simple approach to adapting a logistic regression model to learn this type of decision boundary is to introduce a set of basis functions that will allow a non-linear decision boundary to be learned. In this case, a set of basis functions that generate a cubic decision boundary will work well. An appropriate set of basis functions is as follows:

$$\phi_0(\langle \text{DOSE1}, \text{DOSE2} \rangle) = 1 \qquad \phi_1(\langle \text{DOSE1}, \text{DOSE2} \rangle) = \text{DOSE1}$$

$$\phi_2(\langle \text{DOSE1}, \text{DOSE2} \rangle) = \text{DOSE2} \qquad \phi_3(\langle \text{DOSE1}, \text{DOSE2} \rangle) = \text{DOSE1}^2$$

$$\phi_4(\langle \text{DOSE1}, \text{DOSE2} \rangle) = \text{DOSE2}^2 \qquad \phi_5(\langle \text{DOSE1}, \text{DOSE2} \rangle) = \text{DOSE1}^3$$

$$\phi_6(\langle \text{DOSE1}, \text{DOSE2} \rangle) = \text{DOSE2}^3 \qquad \phi_7(\langle \text{DOSE1}, \text{DOSE2} \rangle) = \text{DOSE1} \times \text{DOSE2}$$

Training a logistic regression model using this set of basis functions leads to the following model:

$$P(\text{TYPE} = dangerous) =$$
$$Logistic\big(-0.848 \times \phi_0(\langle \text{DOSE1}, \text{DOSE2} \rangle) + 1.545 \times \phi_1(\langle \text{DOSE1}, \text{DOSE2} \rangle)$$
$$- 1.942 \times \phi_2(\langle \text{DOSE1}, \text{DOSE2} \rangle) + 1.973 \times \phi_3(\langle \text{DOSE1}, \text{DOSE2} \rangle)$$
$$+ 2.495 \times \phi_4(\langle \text{DOSE1}, \text{DOSE2} \rangle) + 0.104 \times \phi_5(\langle \text{DOSE1}, \text{DOSE2} \rangle)$$
$$+ 0.095 \times \phi_6(\langle \text{DOSE1}, \text{DOSE2} \rangle) + 3.009 \times \phi_7(\langle \text{DOSE1}, \text{DOSE2} \rangle) \big)$$

Use this model to make predictions for the following query instances:

ID	DOSE1	DOSE2
1	0.50	0.75
2	0.10	0.75
3	-0.47	-0.39
4	-0.47	0.18

* 7. The following **multinomial logistic regression** model predicts the TYPE of a retail customer (*single*, *family*, or *business*) based on the average amount that they spend per visit, SPEND, and the average frequency of their visits, FREQ:

$$\mathbb{M}_{\mathbf{w}_{single}}(\mathbf{q}) = logistic(0.7993 - 15.9030 \times \text{SPEND} + 9.5974 \times \text{FREQ})$$

$$\mathbb{M}_{\mathbf{w}_{family}}(\mathbf{q}) = logistic(3.6526 + -0.5809 \times \text{SPEND} - 17.5886 \times \text{FREQ})$$

$$\mathbb{M}_{\mathbf{w}_{business}}(\mathbf{q}) = logistic(4.6419 + 14.9401 \times \text{SPEND} - 6.9457 \times \text{FREQ})$$

Use this model to make predictions for the following query instances:

ID	SPEND	FREQ
1	-0.62	0.10
2	-0.43	-0.71
3	0.00	0.00

* 8. A support vector machine has been built to predict whether a patient is at
risk of cardiovascular disease. In the dataset used to train the model there
are two target levels—*high risk* (the positive level, $+1$) or *low risk* (the negative level, -1)—and three descriptive features—AGE, BMI, and BLOOD
PRESSURE. The support vectors in trained the model are shown in the table
below (all descriptive feature values have been standardised).

AGE	BMI	BLOOD PRESSURE	RISK
-0.4549	0.0095	0.2203	low risk
-0.2843	-0.5253	0.3668	low risk
0.3729	0.0904	-1.0836	high risk
0.558	0.2217	0.2115	high risk

In the model the value of w_0 is -0.0216, and the values of the α parameters
are $\langle 1.6811, 0.2384, 0.2055, 1.7139 \rangle$. What predictions would this model
make for the following query instances?

ID	AGE	BMI	BLOOD PRESSURE
1	-0.8945	-0.3459	0.552
2	0.4571	0.4932	-0.4768
3	-0.3825	-0.6653	0.2855
4	0.7458	0.1253	-0.7986

8 Evaluation

Essentially, all models are wrong, but some are useful.
—George E. P. Box

In this chapter we describe how to evaluate machine learning models built for predictive data analytics tasks. We start by outlining the fundamental goals of evaluation before describing the standard approach of measuring the **misclassification rate** for a model on a **hold-out test set**. We then present extensions and variations of this approach that describe different performance measures for models predicting categorical, continuous, and multinomial targets; how to design effective evaluation experiments; and how to continually measure the performance of models after deployment.

8.1 Big Idea

The year is 1904, and you are a research assistant working in the lab of physicist Professor René Blondlot, at the University of Nancy, in France. Until recently, spirits have been very high in the lab due to the discovery earlier the previous year of a new form of electromagnetic radiation called **N rays** (Blondlot, 1903). The existence of N rays was first hinted at in an experiment performed at the lab that was designed to answer questions about the exact nature of the recently discovered X ray radiation. This experiment showed behavior uncharacteristic of X rays, which Professor Blondlot interpreted to mean that another, different type of electromagnetic radiation must exist. This new type of radiation was named the N ray (after the University of Nancy), and experiments were designed to demonstrate its existence. These experiments were performed in Nancy and confirmed, to the satisfaction of everyone involved, that N rays did indeed exist. This new discovery caused ripples of great excitement in the international physics community and greatly enhanced the reputations of the lab at Nancy and Professor Blondlot.

Doubt has begun to surround the phenomenon of N rays, however, as a number of international physicists have not been able to reproduce the results of the experiments that demonstrate their existence. You are currently preparing for a visit by the American physicist Professor Robert W. Wood to whom Professor Blondlot has agreed to demonstrate the experiments that show the effects of N rays. In one of these experiments, the brightening of a small spark that occurs when an object that supposedly emits N rays is brought close to it is measured. In a second experiment, the refractive effect of passing N rays through a prism (something that does not happen to X rays) is demonstrated. You carefully prepare the apparatus for these experiments, and on the 21st of September, 1904, you spend three hours assisting Professor Blondlot in demonstrating them to Professor Wood.

Just over a week later, you are very disappointed to read an article published by Wood in the journal *Nature* (Wood, 1904) that completely refutes the existence of N rays. He dismisses the experimental setup for the experiments you demonstrated as entirely inappropriate. Even more dramatically, he reports that he actually interfered with the second experiment by removing the prism from the apparatus during the demonstration (because the experiment was completed in darkness, Wood was able to do this without anybody noticing), which made no difference to the results that you measured and reported, so it completely undermines them. Within a few years of the publication of this article, the consensus within the physics research community is that N rays do not exist.

The story of Professor Blondlot and N rays is true,[1] and it is one of the most famous examples in all of science of how badly designed experiments can lead to completely inappropriate conclusions. There was no fraud involved in the work at the Nancy lab. The experiments designed to show the existence of N rays simply relied too much on subjective measurements (the changes in the brightness of the spark was measured by simple human observation) and did not account for all the reasons other than the presence of N rays that could have created the phenomena observed.

The *big idea* to take from this example to predictive data analytics projects is that when we evaluate predictive models, we must ensure that the evaluation experiments are designed so that they give an accurate estimate of how the models will perform when deployed. The most important part of the design of an evaluation experiment for a predictive model is ensuring that the data used to evaluate the model is not the same as the data used to train the model.

8.2   Fundamentals

Over the last four chapters, we have discussed a range of approaches to building machine learning models that make various kinds of predictions. The question that we must answer in the **Evaluation** phase of the **CRISP-DM** process

---

1 Detailed descriptions of the story of Professor Blondlot and N rays are available in Klotz (1980) and Ashmore (1993).

(recall Section 1.5[12]) is can the model generated do the job that it has been built for? The purpose of evaluation is threefold:

- to determine which of the models that we have built for a particular task is most suited to that task
- to estimate how the model will perform when deployed
- to convince the business for whom a model is being developed that the model will meet their needs

The first two items in this list focus on measuring and comparing the performance of a group of models to determine which model *best* performs the prediction task that the models have been built to address. The definition of *best* is important here. No model will ever be perfect, so some fraction of the predictions made by every model will be incorrect. There are, though, a range of ways in which models can be incorrect, and different analytics projects will emphasize some over others. For example, in a medical diagnosis scenario, we would require that a prediction model be very accurate in its diagnoses and, in particular, never incorrectly predict that a sick patient is healthy, as that patient will then leave the health-care system and could subsequently develop serious complications. On the other hand, a model built to predict which customers would be most likely to respond to an online ad only needs to do a slightly better than random job of selecting those customers that will actually respond in order to make a profit for the company. To address these different project requirements, there is a spectrum of different approaches to measuring the performance of a model, and it is important to align the correct approach with a given modeling task. The bulk of this chapter discusses these different approaches and the kinds of modeling tasks that they best suit.

As indicated by the third item in the list above, there is more to evaluation than measuring model performance. For a model to be successfully deployed, we must consider issues like how quickly the model makes predictions, how easy it easy for human analysts to understand the predictions made by a model, and how easy it is to retrain a model should it go stale over time. We return to these issues in the final section of this chapter.

8.3   Standard Approach: Misclassification Rate on a Hold-out Test Set

The basic process for evaluating the effectiveness of predictive models is simple. We take a dataset for which we know the predictions that we expect the model to make, referred to as a **test set**, present the instances in this dataset to a trained model, and record the predictions that the model makes. These predictions can then be compared to the predictions we expected the model to make. Based on this comparison, a **performance measure** can be used to capture, numerically, how well the predictions made by the model match those that were expected.

There are different ways in which a test set can be constructed from a dataset, but the simplest is to use what is referred to as a **hold-out test set**. A hold-out test set is created by randomly sampling a portion of the data in the ABT we created in the **Data Preparation** phase. This random sample *is never used in the training process* but reserved until after the model has been trained, when we would like to evaluate its performance. Figure 8.1[400] illustrates this process.

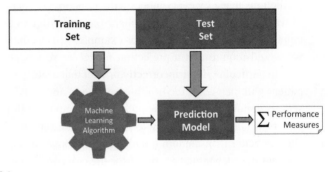

Figure 8.1
The process of building and evaluating a model using a hold-out test set.

Using a hold-out test set avoids the issue of **peeking**, which arises when the performance of a model is evaluated on the same data used to train it; because the data was used in the training process, the model has already *seen* this data, so it is probable that it will perform very well when evaluated on this data. An extreme case of this problem happens when k nearest neighbor models are used. If the model is asked to make a prediction about an instance that was used to train it, the model will find as the nearest neighbor, for this instance, the instance itself. Therefore, if the entire training set is presented to this model, its performance will appear to be perfect. Using a hold-out test set avoids this problem, because none of the instances in the test set will have been used in the training process. Consequently, the performance of the model on the test set is a better measure of how the model is likely to perform when actually deployed and shows how well the model can **generalize** beyond the instances

Table 8.1

A sample test set with model predictions.

ID	Target	Pred.	Outcome	ID	Target	Pred.	Outcome
1	spam	ham	FN	11	ham	ham	TN
2	spam	ham	FN	12	spam	ham	FN
3	ham	ham	TN	13	ham	ham	TN
4	spam	spam	TP	14	ham	ham	TN
5	ham	ham	TN	15	ham	ham	TN
6	spam	spam	TP	16	ham	ham	TN
7	ham	ham	TN	17	ham	spam	FP
8	spam	spam	TP	18	spam	spam	TP
9	spam	spam	TP	19	ham	ham	TN
10	spam	spam	TP	20	ham	spam	FP

used to train it. The most important rule in evaluating models is not to use the same data sample both to evaluate the performance of a predictive model and to train it.

For a first example of how to evaluate the performance of a predictive model, let us assume that we are dealing with an email classification problem with a binary categorical target feature distinguishing between *spam* and *ham* emails. When making predictions about categorical targets, we need performance measures that capture how often the model makes correct predictions and the severity of the mistakes that the model makes when it is incorrect. Table 8.1[401] shows the expected targets for a small sample test set and a set of predictions made by a model trained for this prediction problem (the FP and FN comments in the Outcome column will be explained shortly).

The simplest performance measure we can use to asses how well this model has performed for this problem is the **misclassification rate**. The misclassification rate is the number of incorrect predictions made by the model divided by the total number of predictions made:

$$\textit{misclassification rate} = \frac{\textit{number incorrect predictions}}{\textit{total predictions}} \tag{8.1}$$

In the example in Table 8.1[401], 20 predictions are made in total, and out of these, 5 are incorrect (instances $\mathbf{d}_1$, $\mathbf{d}_2$, $\mathbf{d}_{12}$, $\mathbf{d}_{17}$, and $\mathbf{d}_{20}$). Therefore, the misclassification rate is calculated as $\frac{5}{20} = 0.25$, which is usually expressed as a percentage: 25%. This tells us that the model is incorrect about a quarter of the time. Misclassification rate can assume values in the range $[0, 1]$, and lower values indicate better performance.

The **confusion matrix** is a very useful analysis tool to capture what has happened in an evaluation test in a little more detail and is the basis for calculating many other performance measures. The confusion matrix calculates the frequencies of each possible outcome of the predictions made by a model for a test dataset in order to show, in detail, how the model is performing. For a prediction problem with a binary target feature (where, by convention, we refer to the two levels as **positive** and **negative**), there are just four outcomes when the model makes a prediction:

- **True Positive (TP):** an instance in the test set that had a positive target feature value and that was predicted to have a positive target feature value

- **True Negative (TN):** an instance in the test set that had a negative target feature value and that was predicted to have a negative target feature value

- **False Positive (FP):** an instance in the test set that had a negative target feature value but that was predicted to have a positive target feature value

- **False Negative (FN):** an instance in the test set that had a positive target feature value but that was predicted to have a negative target feature value

The Outcome column of Table 8.1[401] shows the category to which each prediction made by the model belongs. One thing worth keeping in mind is that there are two ways in which the prediction made by a model can be correct—true positive or true negative—and two ways in which the prediction made by a model can be incorrect—false positive or false negative.[2] The confusion matrix allows us to capture these different types of correct and incorrect predictions made by the model.

Each cell in a confusion matrix represents one of these outcomes (TP, TN, FP, FN) and counts the number of times this outcome occurred when the test dataset was presented to the model. The structure of a confusion matrix for a simple prediction task with two target levels is shown in Table 8.2[403]. The columns in the table are labeled *Prediction-positive* and *Prediction-negative* and represent the predictions generated by a model, that is either positive or negative. The rows in the table are labeled *Target-positive* and *Target-negative* and represent the target feature values that were expected. The top left cell in the confusion matrix, labeled TP, shows the number of instances in a test set that have a positive target feature value that were also predicted by the

_____

2 Statisticians will often refer to false positives as **type I errors** and false negatives as **type II errors**. Similarly, false positives are often also referred to as **false alarms**, true positives as **hits**, and false negatives as **misses**.

Table 8.2

The structure of a confusion matrix.

		Prediction	
		positive	negative
Target	positive	TP	FN
	negative	FP	TN

Table 8.3

A confusion matrix for the set of predictions shown in Table 8.1[401].

		Prediction	
		spam	ham
Target	spam	6	3
	ham	2	9

model to have a positive target feature value. Similarly, the bottom left cell in the matrix, labeled FP, shows the number of instances in a test set that have a negative target feature value that were in fact predicted by the model to have a positive target feature value. TN and FN are defined similarly.

At a glance, the confusion matrix can show us that a model is performing well if the numbers on its diagonal, representing the true positives and true negatives, are high. Looking at the other cells within the confusion matrix can show us what kind of mistakes the model is making. Table 8.3[403] shows the confusion matrix for the set of predictions shown in Table 8.1[401] (in this case, we refer to the *spam* target level as the positive level and *ham* as the negative level).[3]

It is clear from the values along the diagonal, the true positives and true negatives, that the model is doing a reasonably good job of making accurate predictions. We can actually calculate the **misclassification rate** directly from the confusion matrix as follows:

$$misclassification\ rate = \frac{(FP + FN)}{(TP + TN + FP + FN)} \qquad (8.2)$$

---

3 Typically, the level that is of most interest is referred to as the positive level. In email classification, identifying spam emails is the most important issue, so the *spam* level is referred to as the positive level. Similarly, in fraud detection, the fraud events would most likely be the positive level; in credit scoring, the default events would most likely be the positive level; and in disease diagnosis, a confirmation that a patient has the disease would most likely be the positive level. The choice, however, is arbitrary.

In the email classification example we have been following, the misclassification rate would be

$$misclassification\ rate = \frac{(2+3)}{(6+9+2+3)} = 0.25$$

For completeness, it is worth noting that **classification accuracy** is the opposite of misclassification rate. Again, using the confusion matrix, classification accuracy is defined as

$$classification\ accuracy = \frac{(TP + TN)}{(TP + TN + FP + FN)} \qquad (8.3)$$

Classification accuracy can assume values in the range $[0, 1]$, and higher values indicate better performance. For the email classification task, classification accuracy would be

$$classification\ accuracy = \frac{(6+9)}{(6+9+2+3)} = 0.75$$

We can also use the confusion matrix to begin to investigate the kinds of mistakes that the prediction model is making. For example, the model makes a prediction of *ham* incorrectly 3 times out of the 9 times that the correct prediction should be *spam* (33.333% of the time), while it makes a prediction of *spam* incorrectly just 2 times out the 11 times that the correct prediction should be *ham* (18.182% of the time). This suggests that when the model makes mistakes, it more commonly incorrectly predicts the *spam* level than the *ham* level. This kind of insight that we can get from the confusion matrix can help in trying to improve a model as it can suggest to us where we should focus our work.

This section has presented a basic approach to evaluating prediction models. The most important things to take away from this example are

1. It is crucial to use data to evaluate a model that has not been used to train the model.
2. The overall performance of a model can be captured in a single performance measure, for example, misclassification rate.
3. To fully understand how a model is performing, it can often be useful to look beyond a single performance measure.

There are, however, a range of variations to this standard approach to evaluating prediction model performance, and the remainder of this chapter covers the most important of these.

8.4   Extensions and Variations

When evaluating the performance of prediction models, there is always a tension between the need to fully understand the performance of the model and the need to reduce model performance to a single measure that can be used to rank models by performance. For example, a set of confusion matrices gives a detailed description of how a set of models trained on a categorical prediction problem performed and can be used for a detailed comparison of performances. Confusion matrices, however, cannot be ordered and so cannot be used to rank the performance of the set of models. To perform this ranking, we need to reduce the information contained in the confusion matrix to a single measure, for example, misclassification rate. Any information reduction process will result in some information loss, and a single measure of model performance will be designed to emphasize some aspects of model performance and de-emphasize, or lose, others. For this reason, there are a variety of different performance measures and no single approach that is appropriate for all scenarios.

This section covers a selection of the most important performance measures. We also describe different experimental designs for evaluating prediction models and ways to monitor model performance after a model has been deployed.

8.4.1   Designing Evaluation Experiments

As well as being required to select appropriate performance measures to use when evaluating trained models, we also need to ensure that we are using the appropriate evaluation experiment design. The goal here is to ensure that we calculate the best estimate of how a prediction model will perform when actually deployed *in the wild*. In this section we will describe the most important evaluation experiment designs and indicate when each is most appropriate.

8.4.1.1   Hold-out Sampling

In Section 8.3[399] we used a **hold-out test set** to evaluate the performance of a model. The important characteristic of this test set was that it was not used in the process of training the model. Therefore, the performance measured on this test set should be a good indicator of how well the model will perform on future unseen data for which it will be used to make predictions after deployment. This is an example of using a **sampling method** to evaluate the performance of a model, as we take distinct, random, non-overlapping **samples** from a larger dataset and use these for training and testing a prediction model. When we use a hold-out test set, we take one sample from the overall dataset to use to train a model and another separate sample to test the model.

Hold-out sampling is probably the simplest form of sampling that we can use and is most appropriate when we have very large datasets from which we can take samples. This ensures that the training set and test set are sufficiently large to train an accurate model and fully evaluate the performance of that model. Hold-out sampling is sometimes extended to include a third sample, the **validation set**. The validation set is used when data outside the training set is required in order to tune particular aspects of a model. For example, when **wrapper-based feature selection** techniques are used, a validation set is required in order to evaluate the performance of the different feature subsets on data not used in training. It is important that after the feature selection process is complete, a separate test set still exists that can be used to evaluate the expected performance of the model on future unseen data after deployment. Figure 8.2[406] illustrates how a large ABT can be divided into a **training set**, a **validation set**, and a **test set**. There are no fixed recommendations for how large the different datasets should be when hold-out sampling is used, although training:validation:test splits of 50:20:30 or 40:20:40 are common.

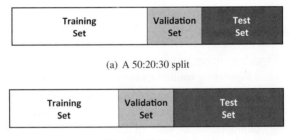

(a) A 50:20:30 split

(b) A 40:20:40 split

Figure 8.2
Hold-out sampling can divide the full data into training, validation, and test sets.

One of the most common uses of a validation set is to avoid **overfitting** when using machine learning algorithms that iteratively build more and more complex models. The **ID3** algorithm for building **decision trees** and the **gradient descent** algorithm for building regression models are two examples of this type of approach. As the algorithm proceeds, the model that it is building will become more and more fitted to the nuances of the training data. We can see this in the solid line in Figure 8.3[407]. This shows how the misclassification rate made by a model on a set of training instances changes as the training process continues. This will continue almost indefinitely as the model becomes more and more tuned to the instances in the training set. At some point in this process, however, overfitting will begin to occur, and the ability of the model to generalize well to new query instances will diminish.

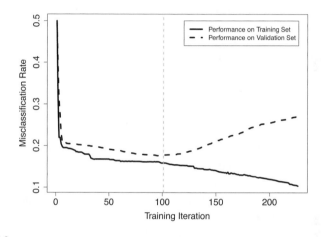

Figure 8.3

Using a validation set to avoid overfitting in iterative machine learning algorithms.

We can find the point at which overfitting begins to happen by comparing the performance of a model at making predictions for instances in the training dataset used to build it versus its ability to make predictions for instances in a validation dataset as the training process continues. The dashed line in Figure 8.3[407] shows the performance of the model being trained on a validation dataset. We can see that, initially, the performance of the model on the validation set falls almost in line with the performance of the model on the training dataset (we usually expect the model to perform slightly better on the training set). About halfway through the training process, however, the performance of the model on the validation set begins to disimprove. This is the point at which we say overfitting has begun to occur (this is shown by the vertical dashed line, at Training Iteration = 100, in Figure 8.3[407]). To combat overfitting, we allow algorithms to train models beyond this point but save the model generated at each iteration. After the training process has completed, we find the point at which performance on the validation set began to disimprove and revert back to the model trained at that point. This process is essentially the same as the decision tree post-pruning process described in Section 4.4.4[158].

Two issues arise when using hold-out sampling. First, using hold-out sampling requires that we have enough data available to make suitably large training, test, and if required, validation sets. This is not always the case, and making any of these partitions too small can result in a poor evaluation. Second, performance measured using hold-out sampling can be misleading if we happen to make a **lucky split** of the data that places the *difficult* instances into the training set and the *easy* ones into the test set. This will make the model appear much more accurate than it will actually be when deployed. An example of a commonly used sampling method that attempts to address these two issues is **k-fold cross validation**.

8.4.1.2   *k*-Fold Cross Validation

When **k-fold cross validation** is used, the available data is divided into k equal-sized **folds** (or partitions), and k separate evaluation experiments are performed. In the first evaluation experiment, the data in the 1st fold is used as the test set, and the data in the remaining $k - 1$ folds is used as the training set. A model is trained using the training set, and the relevant performance measures on the test set are recorded. A second evaluation experiment is then performed using the data in the 2nd fold as the test set and the data in the remaining $k - 1$ folds as the training set. Again the relevant performance measures are calculated on the test set and recorded. This process continues until k evaluation experiments have been conducted and k sets of performance measures have been recorded. Finally, the k sets of performance measures are aggregated to give one overall set of performance measures. Although k can be set to any value, 10-fold cross validation is probably the most common variant used in practice. Figure 8.4[410] illustrates how the available data is split during the k-fold cross validation process. Each row represents a fold in the process, in which the black rectangles indicate the data used for testing while the white spaces indicate the data used for training.

Let's consider an example. As part of a medical decision making system, a prediction system that can automatically determine the orientation of chest x-rays (the orientations can be *lateral* or *frontal*) is built.[4] Based on a full

---

4 Lehmann et al. (2003) discusses building prediction models to perform this task.

Table 8.4

The performance measures from the five individual evaluation experiments and an overall aggregate from the 5-fold cross validation performed on the chest X ray classification dataset.

Fold	Confusion Matrix				Classification Accuracy
1			Prediction		81%
			lateral	*frontal*	
	Target	*lateral*	43	9	
		frontal	10	38	
2			Prediction		88%
			lateral	*frontal*	
	Target	*lateral*	46	9	
		frontal	3	42	
3			Prediction		82%
			lateral	*frontal*	
	Target	*lateral*	51	10	
		frontal	8	31	
4			Prediction		85%
			lateral	*frontal*	
	Target	*lateral*	51	8	
		frontal	7	34	
5			Prediction		84%
			lateral	*frontal*	
	Target	*lateral*	46	9	
		frontal	7	38	
Overall			Prediction		84%
			lateral	*frontal*	
	Target	*lateral*	237	45	
		frontal	35	183	

dataset of 1,000 instances we decide to evaluate the performance of this system with classification accuracy using 5-fold cross validation. So, the full dataset is

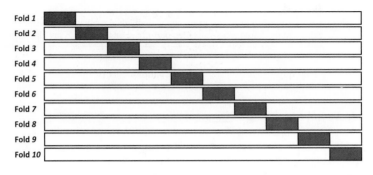

Figure 8.4

The division of data during the *k*-fold cross validation process. Black rectangles indicate test data, and white spaces indicate training data.

divided into 5 folds (each containing 200 instances) and five evaluation experiments are performed using 1 fold as the test set and the remaining folds as the training set. The confusion matrices and class accuracy measures arising from each fold are shown in Table 8.4[409].

The performance measures for each fold (in this case, a confusion matrix and a class accuracy measure) can be aggregated into summary performance measures that capture the overall performance across the 5 folds. The aggregate confusion matrix, generated by summing together the corresponding cells in the individual confusion matrices for each fold, is shown at the bottom of Table 8.4[409]. The aggregate class accuracy measure can then be calculated from this combined confusion matrix and, in this case, turns out to be 84%. When different performance measures are used, the aggregates can be calculated in the same way.

There is a slight shift in emphasis here from evaluating the performance of one model, to evaluating the performance of a set of *k* models. Our goal, however, is still to estimate the performance of a model after deployment. When we have a small dataset (introducing the possibility of a lucky split) measuring aggregate performance using a set of models gives a better estimate of post-deployment performance than measuring performance using a single model. After estimating the performance of a deployed model using *k*-fold cross validation, we typically train the model that will be deployed using all of the available data. This contrasts with the hold-out sampling design, in which we simply deploy the model that has been evaluated.

8.4.1.3 Leave-one-out Cross Validation

Leave-one-out cross validation, also known as **jackknifing**, is an extreme form of k-fold cross validation in which the number of folds is the same as the number of training instances. This means that each fold of the test set contains only one instance, and the training set contains the remainder of the data. Leave-one-out cross validation is useful when the amount of data available is too small to allow big enough training sets in a k-fold cross validation. Figure 8.5[411] illustrates how the available data is split during the leave-one-out cross validation process. Each row represents a fold in the process, in which the black rectangles indicate the instance that is used for testing while the white spaces indicate the data used for training.

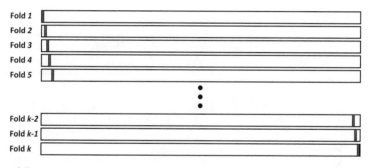

Figure 8.5

The division of data during the leave-one-out cross validation process. Black rectangles indicate instances in the test set, and white spaces indicate training data.

At the conclusion of the leave-one-out cross validation process, a performance measure will have been calculated for every instance in the dataset. In the same way as we saw in Table 8.4[409] for k-fold cross validation, these performance measures are aggregated across all the folds to arrive at an overall measure of model performance.

8.4.1.4 Bootstrapping

The next sampling method we will look at is **bootstrapping**, and in particular the $\epsilon 0$ **bootstrap**. Bootstrapping approaches are preferred over cross validation approaches in contexts with very small datasets (approximately fewer than 300 instances). Similar to k-fold cross validation, the $\epsilon 0$ bootstrap iteratively performs multiple evaluation experiments using sightly different training and test sets each time to evaluate the expected performance of a model. To generate these partitions for an iteration of the $\epsilon 0$ bootstrap, a random selection of m instances is taken from the full dataset to generate a test set, and the remaining instances are used as the training set. Using the training set to train a model and the test set to evaluate it, a performance measure (or measures) is calculated for this iteration. This process is repeated for k iterations, and the average of the individual performance measures, the titular $\epsilon 0$, gives the overall performance of the model. Typically, in the $\epsilon 0$ bootstrap, k is set to values greater than or equal to 200, much larger values than when k-fold cross validation is used. Figure 8.6[412] illustrates how the data is divided during the $\epsilon 0$ bootstrap process. Each row represents an iteration of the process, in which the black rectangles indicate the data used for testing while the white spaces indicate the data used for training.

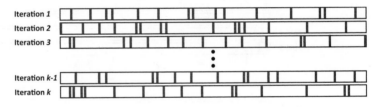

Figure 8.6
The division of data during the $\epsilon 0$ bootstrap process. Black rectangles indicate test data, and white spaces indicate training data.

8.4.1.5   Out-of-time Sampling

The sampling methods discussed in the previous section all rely on random sampling from a large dataset in order to create test sets. In some applications there is a natural structure in the data that we can take advantage of to form test sets. In scenarios that include a time dimension, this can be particularly effective and is often referred to as **out-of-time sampling**, because we use data from one period to build a training set and data out of another period to build a test set. For example, in a customer churn scenario, we might use details of customer behavior from one year to build a training set and details of customer behavior from a subsequent year to build a test set. Figure 8.7[413] illustrates the process of out-of-time sampling.

Out-of-time sampling is essentially a form of hold-out sampling in which the sampling is done in a targeted rather than a random fashion. When using

Figure 8.7
The out-of-time sampling process.

out-of-time sampling, we should be careful to ensure that the times from which
the training and test sets are taken do not introduce a bias into the evaluation
process, because the two different time samples are not really representative.
For example, imagine we wished to evaluate the performance of a prediction
model built to estimate the daily energy demand in a residential building based
on features describing the family that live in the house, the weather on a given
day, and the time of the year. If the training sample covered a period in the
summer and the testing sample covered a period in the winter, the results of any
evaluation would not provide a reliable measure of how likely the model might
actually perform when deployed. It is important when choosing the periods for
out-of-time sampling that the time spans are large enough to take into account
any cyclical behavioral patterns or that other approaches are used to account
for these.

8.4.2   Performance Measures: Categorical Targets

This section describes the most important performance measures for evaluating
the performance of models with categorical target features.

8.4.2.1   Confusion Matrix-based Performance Measures

Confusion matrices are a convenient way to fully describe the performance of a
predictive model when applied to a test set. They are also the basis for a whole
range of different performance measures that can highlight different aspects
of the performance of a predictive model. The most basic of these measures
are **true positive rate (TPR)**, **true negative rate (TNR)**, **false negative rate
(FNR)**, and **false positive rate (FPR)**, which convert the raw numbers from

the confusion matrix into percentages.[5] These measures are defined as follows:

$$TPR = \frac{TP}{(TP + FN)} \tag{8.4}$$

$$TNR = \frac{TN}{(TN + FP)} \tag{8.5}$$

$$FPR = \frac{FP}{(TN + FP)} \tag{8.6}$$

$$FNR = \frac{FN}{(TP + FN)} \tag{8.7}$$

There are strong relationships between these measures, for example: $FNR = 1 - TPR$, and $FPR = 1 - TNR$.

All these measures can have values in the range $[0, 1]$. Higher values of TPR and TNR indicate better model performance, while the opposite is the case for FNR and FPR. Confusion matrices are often presented containing these measures rather than the raw counts, although we recommend using raw counts so that the number of instances with each of the different levels of the target feature remains apparent.

For the email classification data given in Table 8.1[401], the confusion matrix-based values can be calculated as follows:

$$TPR = \frac{6}{(6+3)} = 0.667$$

$$TNR = \frac{9}{(9+2)} = 0.818$$

$$FPR = \frac{2}{(9+2)} = 0.182$$

$$FNR = \frac{3}{(6+3)} = 0.333$$

These values immediately suggest that the model is better at predicting the *ham* level (TNR) than it is at predicting the *spam* level (TPR).

8.4.2.2   Precision, Recall and F_1 Measure

Precision, recall, and the **F_1 measure** are another frequently used set of performance measures that can be calculated directly from the confusion matrix.

---

5 The terms **sensitivity** and **specificity** are often used for true positive rate and true negative rate.

Precision and **recall** are defined as follows:

$$precision = \frac{TP}{(TP + FP)} \qquad (8.8)$$

$$recall = \frac{TP}{(TP + FN)} \qquad (8.9)$$

Recall is equivalent to true positive rate (TPR) (compare Equations (8.4)[414] and (8.9)[415]). Recall tells us how confident we can be that all the instances with the positive target level have been found by the model. Precision captures how often, when a model makes a positive prediction, this prediction turns out to be correct. Precision tells us how confident we can be that an instance predicted to have the positive target level actually has the positive target level. Both precision and recall can assume values in the range $[0, 1]$, and higher values in both cases indicate better model performance.

Returning to the email classification example, and assuming again that *spam* emails are the positive level, precision measures how often the emails marked as spam actually are spam, whereas recall measures how often the spam messages in the test set were actually marked as *spam*. The precision and recall measures for the email classification data shown in Table 8.1[401] are

$$precision = \frac{6}{(6 + 2)} = 0.750$$

$$recall = \frac{6}{(6 + 3)} = 0.667$$

Email classification is a good application scenario in which the different information provided by precision and recall is useful. The precision value tells us how likely it is that a genuine *ham* email could be marked as *spam* and, presumably, deleted: 25% $(1 - precision)$. Recall, on the other hand, tells us how likely it is that a spam email will be missed by the system and end up in our inbox: 33.333% $(1 - recall)$. Having both of these numbers is useful as it allows us to think about tuning the model toward one kind of error or the other. Is it better for a genuine email to be marked as *spam* and deleted, or for a spam email to end up in our inbox? The performance recorded in Table 8.1[401] shows that this system is slightly more likely to make the second kind of mistake than the first.

Precision and recall can be collapsed to a single performance measure known as the **F_1 measure**,[6] which offers a useful alternative to the simpler misclassification rate. The F_1 measure is the **harmonic mean** of precision and recall and is defined as

$$F_1 \; measure = 2 \times \frac{(precision \times recall)}{(precision + recall)} \tag{8.10}$$

In Section A.1[525] we talk about how measures of **central tendency** attempt to capture the average value of a list of numbers. Although the **arithmetic mean** and **median** are two of the most commonly known such measures, there are more, including the **harmonic mean**. The harmonic mean tends toward the smaller values in a list of numbers and so can be less sensitive to large outliers than the arithmetic mean, which tends toward higher values. This characteristic is useful in the generation of performance measures like the F_1 measure, as we typically prefer measures to highlight shortcomings in our models rather than hide them. The F_1 measure can assume values in the range $(0, 1]$, and higher values indicate better performance.

For the email classification dataset shown in Table 8.1[401], the F_1 measure (again assuming that the *spam* level is the positive level) is calculated as

$$F_1 \; measure = 2 \times \frac{\left(\frac{6}{(6+2)} \times \frac{6}{(6+3)} \right)}{\left(\frac{6}{(6+2)} + \frac{6}{(6+3)} \right)}$$
$$= 0.706$$

Precision, recall, and the F_1 measure work best in prediction problems with binary target features and place an emphasis on capturing the performance of a prediction model on the positive, or most important, level. These measures place less emphasis on the performance of the model on the negative target level. This is appropriate in many applications. For example, in medical applications, a prediction that a patient has a disease is much more important than a prediction that a patient does not. In many cases, however, it does not make sense to consider one target level as being more important. The **average class accuracy** performance measure can be effective in these cases.

---

6 The F_1 measure is often also referred to as the **F measure**, **F score**, or **F_1 score**.

Table 8.5

A confusion matrix for a *k*-NN model trained on a churn prediction problem.

		Prediction	
		non-churn	*churn*
Target	*non-churn*	90	0
	churn	9	1

Table 8.6

A confusion matrix for a naive Bayes model trained on a churn prediction problem.

		Prediction	
		non-churn	*churn*
Target	*non-churn*	70	20
	churn	2	8

8.4.2.3   Average Class Accuracy

Classification accuracy can mask poor performance. For example, the confusion matrices shown in Tables 8.5[417] and 8.6[417] show the performance of two different models on a test dataset that relates to a prediction problem in which we would like to predict whether a customer will churn or not. The accuracy for the model associated with the confusion matrix shown in Table 8.5[417] is 91%, while for the model associated with the confusion matrix shown in Table 8.6[417], the accuracy is just 78%. In this example the test dataset is quite **imbalanced**, containing 90 instances with the *non-churn* level and just 10 instances with the *churn* level. This means that the performance of the model on the *non-churn* level overwhelms the performance on the *churn* level in the accuracy calculation and illustrates how classification accuracy can be a misleading measure of model performance.

To address this issue, we can use **average class accuracy**[7] instead of classification accuracy.[8] The average class accuracy is calculated as

$$average\ class\ accuracy = \frac{1}{|levels(t)|} \sum_{l \in levels(t)} recall_l \qquad (8.11)$$

where $levels(t)$ is the set of levels that the target feature, t, can assume; $|levels(t)|$ is the size of this set; and $recall_l$ refers to the recall achieved by

---

7 Sometimes target levels in categorical prediction problems are referred to as classes, which is where this name comes from.

8 Target level imbalance affects misclassification rate in the same way, and average misclassification rate can also be calculated to combat this problem.

a model for level $l.^9$ The average class accuracies for the model performances shown in Tables 8.5[417] and 8.6[417] are $\frac{1}{2}(1+0.1) = 55\%$ and $\frac{1}{2}(0.778+0.8) = 78.889\%$ respectively, which would indicate that the second model is actually a better performer than the first. This result is contrary to the conclusion drawn from classification accuracy but is more appropriate in this case due to the target level imbalance present in the data.

The average class accuracy measure shown in Equation (8.11)[417] uses an **arithmetic mean** and so can be more fully labeled *averageclassaccuracy$_{AM}$*. While this is an improvement over raw classification accuracy, many people prefer to use a **harmonic mean**[10] instead of an arithmetic mean when calculating average class accuracy. Arithmetic means are susceptible to influence of large outliers, which can inflate the apparent performance of a model. The **harmonic mean**, on the other hand, emphasizes the importance of smaller values and so can give a slightly more realistic measure of how well a model is performing. The harmonic mean is defined as follows:

$$average\ class\ accuracy_{HM} = \frac{1}{\frac{1}{|levels(t)|} \sum\limits_{l \in levels(t)} \frac{1}{recall_l}} \tag{8.12}$$

where the notation meanings are the same as for Equation (8.11)[417]. The *average class accuracy$_{HM}$* for the model performances shown in Tables 8.5[417] and 8.6[417] are

$$\frac{1}{\frac{1}{2}\left(\frac{1}{1.0} + \frac{1}{0.1}\right)} = \frac{1}{5.5} = 18.2\%$$

and

$$\frac{1}{\frac{1}{2}\left(\frac{1}{0.778} + \frac{1}{0.800}\right)} = \frac{1}{1.268} = 78.873\%$$

The harmonic mean results in a more pessimistic view of model performance than an arithmetic mean. To further illustrate the difference between arithmetic mean and harmonic mean, Figure 8.8[419] shows the arithmetic mean and the harmonic mean of all combinations of two features A and B that range from

9 Whereas before we referred to recall as something calculated only for the positive level, we can calculate recall for any level as the accuracy of the predictions made for that level.

10 Remember that a harmonic mean is used in the F_1 measure given in Equation (8.10)[416].

0 to 100. The curved shape of the harmonic mean surface shows that the harmonic mean emphasizes the contribution of smaller values more than the arithmetic mean—note how the sides of the surface are pulled down to the base of the graph by the harmonic mean. We recommend that, in general, when calculating average class accuracy, the harmonic mean should be used rather than the arithmetic mean.

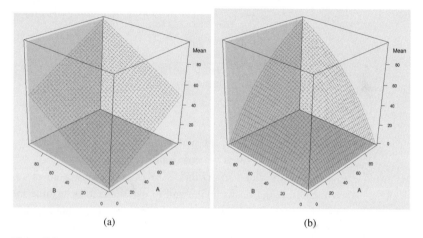

(a)   (b)

Figure 8.8
Surfaces generated by calculating (a) the arithmetic mean and (b) the harmonic mean of all combinations of features A and B that range from 0 to 100.

8.4.2.4 Measuring Profit and Loss

One of the problems faced by all the performance measures discussed so far is that they place the same value on all the cells within a confusion matrix. For example, in the churn prediction example, correctly classifying a customer as likely to churn is *worth* the same as correctly classifying a customer as not likely to churn. It is not always correct to treat all outcomes equally. For example, if a customer who really was not a churn risk is classified as likely to churn, the cost incurred by the company because of this mistake is the cost of a small bonus offer that would be given to the customer to entice the customer to stay with the company. On the other hand, misclassifying a customer who really was a churn risk probably has a much larger cost associated with it because that customer will be lost when a small bonus may have enticed the customer

Table 8.7

The structure of a profit matrix.

		Prediction	
		positive	negative
Target	positive	TP_{Profit}	FN_{Profit}
	negative	FP_{Profit}	TN_{Profit}

Table 8.8

The profit matrix for the pay-day loan credit scoring problem.

		Prediction	
		good	bad
Target	good	140	−140
	bad	−700	0

to stay. When evaluating the performance of models, it would be useful to be able to take into account the costs of different outcomes.

One way in which to do this is to calculate the profit or loss that arises from each prediction we make and to use these to determine the overall performance of a model. To do this we first need to create a **profit matrix** that records these. Table 8.7[420] shows the structure of a profit matrix, which is the same as the structure of a confusion matrix. TP_{Profit} represents the profit arising from a correct positive prediction, FN_{Profit} is the profit arising from an incorrect negative prediction, and so on (note that profit can refer to a positive or a negative value). The actual values in a profit matrix are determined through domain expertise.

To see the use of a profit matrix in action, consider a prediction problem in which a pay-day loan company has built a credit scoring model to predict the likelihood that a borrower will default on a loan. Based on a set of descriptive features extracted from the loan application (e.g., AGE, OCCUPATION, and ASSETS), the model will classify potential borrowers as belonging to one of two groups: *good* borrowers, who will repay their loans in full, and *bad* borrowers, who will default on some portion of their loans. The company can run this model whenever a new loan application is made and only extend credit to those borrowers predicted to belong to the *good* target level. Table 8.8[420] shows the profit matrix for this problem.

The values in this matrix are based on historical data that the company has on loans given out in the past. The typical value of a loan is $1,000, and the interest rate charged is 14%. So, when a loan is repaid in full, the profit made by

Table 8.9

(a) The confusion matrix for a k-NN model trained on the pay-day loan credit scoring problem (*average class accuracy$_{HM}$* = 83.824%); (b) the confusion matrix for a decision tree model trained on the pay-day loan credit scoring problem (*average class accuracy$_{HM}$* = 80.761%).

		(a) k-NN model					(b) decision tree		
		Prediction					Prediction		
		good	bad				good	bad	
Target	good	57	3		Target	good	43	17	
	bad	10	30			bad	3	37	

the company is usually $140. Therefore, the profit arising from correctly predicting the *good* level for a potential borrower is $140. Incorrectly predicting the *bad* level for a potential borrower who would have repaid the loan in full will result in a negative profit (or loss) of −$140, as the company has forgone potential interest payments. Correctly predicting the *bad* level for a potential borrower results in no profit as no money is loaned.[11] Incorrectly predicting the *good* level for a potential borrower who goes on to default on the loan, however, results in a loan not being repaid. Based on historical examples, the expected loss in this case, referred to as the **loss given default**, is $700 (most borrowers will repay some of their loan before defaulting). The values in Table 8.8[420] are based on these figures. It is clear that the different outcomes have different profit and loss associated with them. In particular, extending a loan to a borrower who turns out to be *bad* is a very costly mistake.

Tables 8.9(a)[421] and 8.9(b)[421] show confusion matrices for two different prediction models, a k-NN model and a decision tree model, trained for the pay-day loans credit scoring problem. The average class accuracy (using a harmonic mean) for the k-NN model is 83.824% and for the decision tree model is 80.761%, which suggests that the k-NN model is quite a bit better than the decision tree.

We can, however, use the values in the profit matrix to calculate the overall profit associated with the predictions made by these two models. This is achieved by multiplying the values in the confusion matrix by the corresponding values in the profit matrix and summing the results. Tables 8.10(a)[422] and 8.10(b)[422] show this calculation for the k-NN and the decision tree models. The overall profit for the k-NN model is $560, while it is $1,540 for the decision

---

11 This is always an interesting category to determine a value for. Some people might argue that some profit arises as no loss was made.

Table 8.10
(a) Overall profit for the *k*-NN model using the profit matrix in Table 8.8[420] and the confusion matrix in Table 8.9(a)[421]; (b) overall profit for the decision tree model using the profit matrix in Table 8.8[420] and the confusion matrix in Table 8.9(b)[421].

(a) *k*-NN model		Prediction			(b) decision tree		Prediction	
		good	bad				good	bad
Target	good	7,980	−420		Target	good	6,020	−2,380
	bad	−7,000	0			bad	−2,100	0
	Profit		560			Profit		1,540

tree model. As well as showing that it is hard to make money in the pay-day loans business, this reverses the ordering implied using the average class accuracy. The predictions made by the decision tree model result in a higher profit than those made by the *k*-NN model. This is because the *k*-NN makes the mistake of misclassifying a *bad* borrower as *good* more often than the decision tree model, and this is the more costly mistake. Ranking the models by profit, we are able to take this into account, which is impossible using classification accuracy or average class accuracy.

It is worth mentioning that to use profit as a performance measure, we don't need to quantify the profit associated with each outcome as completely as we have done in this example. The minimal amount of information we need is the relative profit associated with each of the different outcomes (TP, TN, FP, or FN) that can arise when a model makes a prediction. For example, in the spam filtering problem described previously, all we need to use are the relative profits of classifying a *ham* email as *spam*, classifying a *spam* email as *ham*, and so on.

While using profit might appear to be the ideal way to evaluate model performance for categorical targets, unfortunately, this is not the case. It is only in very rare scenarios that we can accurately fill in a profit matrix for a prediction problem. In many cases, although it may be possible to say that some outcomes are more desirable than others, it is simply not possible to quantify this. For example, in a medical diagnosis problem, we might confidently say that a false negative (telling a sick patient that they do not have a disease) is worse than a false positive (telling a healthy patient that they do have a disease), but it is unlikely that we will be able to quantify this as twice as bad, or four times as bad, or 10.75 times as bad. When a profit matrix is available, however, profit is a very effective performance measure to use.

8.4.3   Performance Measures: Prediction Scores

Careful examination of the workings of the different classification models that we have discussed in Chapters 4[117] to 7[323] shows that none of them simply produces a target feature level as its output. In all cases, a **prediction score** (or scores) is produced, and a threshold process is used to convert this score into one of the levels of the target feature. For example, the naive Bayes model produces probabilities that are converted into categorical predictions using the maximum a posteriori probability approach, and logistic regression models produce a probability for the positive target level that is converted into a categorical prediction using a threshold. Even in decision trees, the prediction is based on the majority target level at a leaf node, and the proportion of this level gives us a prediction score. In a typical scenario with two target levels, a prediction score in the range $[0, 1]$ is generated by a model, and a threshold of 0.5 is used to convert this score into a categorical prediction as follows:

$$threshold(score, 0.5) = \begin{cases} positive & \text{if } score \geqslant 0.5 \\ negative & otherwise \end{cases} \qquad (8.13)$$

To illustrate this, Table 8.11[424] shows the underlying scores that the predictions shown in Table 8.1[401] were based on, assuming a threshold of 0.5—that is, instances with a prediction score greater than or equal to 0.5 were given predictions of the *spam* (positive) level, and those with prediction scores less than 0.5 were given predictions of the *ham* (negative) level. The instances in this table have been sorted by these scores in ascending order; as a result, the thresholding on the scores to generate predictions is very much apparent. An indication of the performance of the model is also evident from this ordering— the Target column shows that the instances that actually should get predictions of the *ham* level generally have lower scores, and those that should get predictions of the *spam* level generally have higher scores.

A range of performance measures use this ability of a model, to rank instances that should get predictions of one target level higher than the other, to better assess how well a prediction model is performing. The basis of most of these approaches is measuring how well the distributions of scores produced by the model for different target levels are separated. Figure 8.9[424] illustrates this: assuming that prediction scores are normally distributed, the distributions of the scores for the two target levels are shown for two different classification models. The prediction score distributions shown in Figure 8.9(a)[424] are much better separated than those in Figure 8.9(b)[424]. We can use the separation of

Table 8.11
A sample test set with model predictions and scores.

ID	Target	Prediction	Score	Outcome	ID	Target	Prediction	Score	Outcome
7	ham	ham	0.001	TN	5	ham	ham	0.302	TN
11	ham	ham	0.003	TN	14	ham	ham	0.348	TN
15	ham	ham	0.059	TN	17	ham	spam	0.657	FP
13	ham	ham	0.064	TN	8	spam	spam	0.676	TP
19	ham	ham	0.094	TN	6	spam	spam	0.719	TP
12	spam	ham	0.160	FN	10	spam	spam	0.781	TP
2	spam	ham	0.184	FN	18	spam	spam	0.833	TP
3	ham	ham	0.226	TN	20	ham	spam	0.877	FP
16	ham	ham	0.246	TN	9	spam	spam	0.960	TP
1	spam	ham	0.293	FN	4	spam	spam	0.963	TP

the prediction score distributions to construct performance measures for categorical prediction models.

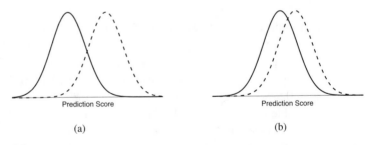

(a)   (b)

Figure 8.9
Prediction score distributions for two different prediction models. The distributions in (a) are much better separated than those in (b).

If the distributions of prediction scores from predictive models perfectly followed a normal distribution, similar to those in Figure 8.9[424], calculating the degree of separation between distributions would be very simple and only involve a simple comparison of means and standard deviations. Unfortunately, this is not the case, as the distribution of prediction scores for a model can follow any distribution. For example, the density histograms in Figure 8.10[425] show the distributions of prediction scores for the *spam* and *ham* target levels based on the data in Table 8.11[424]. There are a number of performance measures based on the idea of comparing prediction score distributions that attempt to cater for the peculiarities of real data. This section describes some of the most important of these measures.

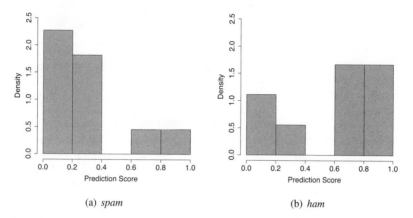

(a) *spam*   (b) *ham*

Figure 8.10
Prediction score distributions for the (a) *spam* and (b) *ham* target levels based on the data in Table 8.11[424].

8.4.3.1   Receiver Operating Characteristic Curves

The **receiver operating characteristic index** (**ROC index**), which is based on the **receiver operating characteristic curve** (**ROC curve**),[12] is a widely used performance measure that is calculated using prediction scores. We saw in Section 8.4.2[413] how the true positive rate (TPR) and true negative rate (TNR) can be calculated from a confusion matrix. These measures, however, are intrinsically tied to the threshold used to convert prediction scores into target levels. The predictions shown in Table 8.11[424] and in the confusion matrix in Table 8.3[403], are based on a prediction score threshold of 0.5. This threshold can be changed, however, which leads to different predictions and a different confusion matrix. For example, if we changed the threshold used to generate the predictions shown in Table 8.11[424] from 0.5 to 0.75, the predictions for instances d_{17}, d_8, and d_6 would change from *spam* to *ham*, resulting in their outcomes changing to TN, FN, and FN respectively. This would mean that the confusion

---

12 The slightly strange name *receiver operating characteristic* comes from the fact that this approach was first used for tuning radar signals in World War II.

Table 8.12

Confusion matrices for the set of predictions shown in Table 8.11[424] using (a) a prediction score threshold of 0.75 and (b) a prediction score threshold of 0.25.

<table>
<tr><td colspan="4">(a) Threshold: 0.75</td><td colspan="4">(b) Threshold: 0.25</td></tr>
<tr><td></td><td></td><td colspan="2">Prediction</td><td></td><td></td><td colspan="2">Prediction</td></tr>
<tr><td></td><td></td><td>spam</td><td>ham</td><td></td><td></td><td>spam</td><td>ham</td></tr>
<tr><td rowspan="2">Target</td><td>spam</td><td>4</td><td>4</td><td rowspan="2">Target</td><td>spam</td><td>7</td><td>2</td></tr>
<tr><td>ham</td><td>2</td><td>10</td><td>ham</td><td>4</td><td>7</td></tr>
</table>

matrix would change to that shown in Table 8.12(a)[426] and, in turn, that the TPR and TNR measures would change to 0.5 and 0.833 respectively.

Similarly, if we changed the threshold from 0.5 to 0.25, the predictions for instances d_{14}, d_5, and d_1 would change from *ham* to *spam*, resulting in their outcomes changing to FP, FP, and TP respectively. This would mean that the confusion matrix would change to that shown in Table 8.12(b)[426] and, in turn, that the TPR and TNR measures would change to 0.777 and 0.636 respectively.

For every possible value of the threshold, in the range $[0, 1]$, there are corresponding TPR and TNR values. The pattern that is evident in the two examples presented above continues as the threshold value is modified: as the threshold increases, TPR decreases and TNR increases, and as the threshold decreases, the opposite occurs. Table 8.13[427] shows how the predictions made for test instances change as the threshold changes. Also shown are the resulting TPR, TNR, FPR, and FNR values, as well as the misclassification rate for each threshold. We can see that the misclassification rate doesn't change that much as the threshold changes. This is due to the trade-offs between false positives and false negatives.

Figure 8.11(a)[428] shows the changing values for TPR and TNR for the prediction scores shown in Table 8.13[427] as the threshold is varied from 0 to 1.[13] This graph shows that changing the value of the threshold results in a trade-off between accuracy for predictions of positive target levels and accuracy for predictions of negative target levels. Capturing this trade-off is the basis of the ROC curve.

To plot an ROC curve, we create a chart with true positive rate on the vertical access and false positive rate (or $1 -$ true negative rate) on the horizontal

13 The staircase nature of this graph arises from the fact that there are ranges for the threshold in which no instances occur (for example, from 0.348 to 0.657), during which the TPR and TNR values do not change. Larger test sets cause these curves to smoothen significantly.

Table 8.13

A sample test set with prediction scores and resulting predictions based on different threshold values.

ID	Target	Score	Pred. (0.10)	Pred. (0.25)	Pred. (0.50)	Pred. (0.75)	Pred. (0.90)
7	ham	0.001	ham	ham	ham	ham	ham
11	ham	0.003	ham	ham	ham	ham	ham
15	ham	0.059	ham	ham	ham	ham	ham
13	ham	0.064	ham	ham	ham	ham	ham
19	ham	0.094	ham	ham	ham	ham	ham
12	spam	0.160	spam	ham	ham	ham	ham
2	spam	0.184	spam	ham	ham	ham	ham
3	ham	0.226	spam	ham	ham	ham	ham
16	ham	0.246	spam	ham	ham	ham	ham
1	spam	0.293	spam	spam	ham	ham	ham
5	ham	0.302	spam	spam	ham	ham	ham
14	ham	0.348	spam	spam	ham	ham	ham
17	ham	0.657	spam	spam	spam	ham	ham
8	spam	0.676	spam	spam	spam	ham	ham
6	spam	0.719	spam	spam	spam	ham	ham
10	spam	0.781	spam	spam	spam	spam	ham
18	spam	0.833	spam	spam	spam	spam	ham
20	ham	0.877	spam	spam	spam	spam	ham
9	spam	0.960	spam	spam	spam	spam	spam
4	spam	0.963	spam	spam	spam	spam	spam
		Misclassification Rate	0.300	0.300	0.250	0.300	0.350
		True Positive Rate (TPR)	1.000	0.778	0.667	0.444	0.222
		True Negative rate (TNR)	0.455	0.636	0.818	0.909	1.000
		False Positive Rate (FPR)	0.545	0.364	0.182	0.091	0.000
		False Negative Rate (FNR)	0.000	0.222	0.333	0.556	0.778

axis.[14] The values for these measures, when any threshold value is used on a collection of score predictions, gives a point on this plot, or a point in **receiver operating characteristic space** (**ROC space**). Figure 8.11(b)[428] shows three such points in ROC space and associated confusion matrices for the email classification dataset for thresholds of 0.25, 0.5, and 0.75.

---

14 ROC curves are often plotted with sensitivity on the vertical axis and 1 − specificity on the horizontal axis. Recall that sensitivity is equal to TPR, and specificity is equal to TNR, so these are equivalent.

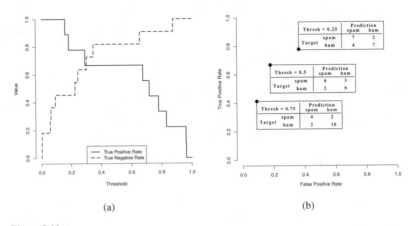

Figure 8.11

(a) The changing values of TPR and TNR for the test data shown in Table 8.13[427] as the threshold is altered; (b) points in ROC space for thresholds of 0.25, 0.5, and 0.75.

The ROC curve is drawn by plotting a point for every feasible threshold value and joining them. Figure 8.12(a)[429] shows a complete ROC curve for the email predictions in Table 8.13[427]. A line along the diagonal of ROC space from $(0,0)$ to $(1,0)$, shown as a dotted line in Figure 8.12(a)[429], is a reference line representing the expected performance of a model that makes random predictions. We always expect the ROC curve for a trained model to be above this random reference line.[15] In fact as the strength of a predictive model increases, the ROC curve moves farther away from the random line toward the top left hand corner of ROC space—toward a TPR of 1.0 and an FPR of 0.0. So, the ROC curve gives us an immediate visual indication of the strength of a model—the closer the curve is to the top left, the more predictive the model.

Often the ROC curves for multiple predictive models will be plotted on a single ROC plot, allowing easy comparison of their performance. Figure 8.12(b)[429] shows ROC curves for four models tested on a version of the email classification test set in Table 8.13[427], containing many more instances than the one we have been discussing so far, which is why the curves are so much

---

15 If an ROC curve appears below the diagonal random reference line, this means that the model is consistently making predictions of the positive level for instances that should receive predictions of the negative level and vice versa, and that it could actually be quite a powerful model. This usually arises when a transcription error of some kind has been made and should be investigated.

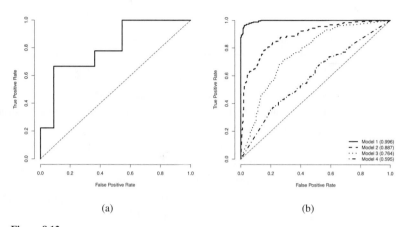

Figure 8.12

(a) A complete ROC curve for the email classification example; (b) a selection of ROC curves for different models trained on the same prediction task.

smoother than the curve shown in Figure 8.12(a)[429]. These smoother curves are more representative of the kind of ROC curves we typically encounter in practice. In this example, Model 1 approaches perfect performance, Model 4 is barely better than random guessing, and Models 2 and 3 sit somewhere in between these two extremes.

Although it is useful to visually compare the performance of different models using an ROC curve, it is often preferable to have a single numeric performance measure with which models can be assessed. Fortunately, there is an easy calculation that can be made from the ROC curve that achieves this. The **ROC index** or **area under the curve** (**AUC**) measures the area underneath an ROC curve. Remembering that the perfect model will appear in the very top left hand corner of ROC space, it is fairly intuitive that curves with higher areas will be closer to this maximum possible value. The area under an ROC curve is calculated as the integral of the curve. Because ROC curves are discrete and stepped in nature, finding their integrals is actually very easily done using the

trapezoidal method. The ROC index can be calculated as

$$ROC\ index =$$

$$\sum_{i=2}^{|\mathbf{T}|} \frac{(FPR(\mathbf{T}[i]) - FPR(\mathbf{T}[i-1])) \times (TPR(\mathbf{T}[i]) + TPR(\mathbf{T}[i-1]))}{2} \quad (8.14)$$

where $\mathbf{T}$ is a set of thresholds, $|\mathbf{T}|$ is the number of thresholds tested, and $TPR(\mathbf{T}[i])$ and $FPR(\mathbf{T}[i])$ are the true positive and false positive rates at threshold i respectively.

The ROC index can take values in the range $[0, 1]$ (although values less than 0.5 are unlikely and indicative of a target labeling error), and larger values indicate better model performance. So, for example, the ROC index for the ROC curve shown in Figure 8.12(a)[429] is 0.798, and the ROC indices for Models 1 to 4 in Figure 8.12(b)[429] are 0.996, 0.887, 0.764, and 0.595 (as shown in the legend). While there are no hard and fast rules about what constitutes an acceptable value for the ROC index, and this is really an application-specific decision, a good rule of thumb is that a value above 0.7 indicates a *strong* model, while a value below 0.6 indicates a *weak* model. The ROC index is quite robust in the presence of imbalanced data, which makes it a common choice for practitioners, especially when multiple modeling techniques are being compared to one another.

The ROC index can be interpreted probabilistically as the probability that a model will assign a higher rank to a randomly selected positive instance than to a randomly selected negative instance.[16] The **Gini coefficient**[17] is another commonly used performance measure that is just a linear rescaling of the ROC index:

$$Gini\ coefficient = (2 \times ROC\ index) - 1 \quad (8.15)$$

The Gini coefficient can take values in the range $[0, 1]$, and higher values indicate better model performance. The Gini coefficient for the model shown in Figure 8.12(a)[429] is 0.596, and the Gini coefficients for the four models shown in Figure 8.12(a)[429] are 0.992, 0.774, 0.527, and 0.190. The Gini coefficient is very commonly used in financial modeling scenarios such as credit scoring.

---

16 The ROC index is in fact equivalent to the **Wilcoxon-Mann-Whitney statistic** used in significance testing.

17 The Gini coefficient should not be confused with the **Gini index** described in Section 4.4.1[144]. Their only connection is that they are both named after the Italian statistician Corrado Gini.

8.4.3.2 Kolmogorov-Smirnov Statistic

The **Kolmogorov-Smirnov statistic** (**K-S statistic**) is another performance measure that captures the separation between the distribution of prediction scores for the different target levels in a classification problem. To calculate the K-S statistic, we first determine the cumulative probability distributions of the prediction scores for the positive and negative target levels. This is done as follows:

$$CP(positive, ps) = \frac{\text{num positive test instances with score} \leqslant ps}{\text{num positive test instances}} \quad (8.16)$$

$$CP(negative, ps) = \frac{\text{num negative test instances with score} \leqslant ps}{\text{num negative test instances}} \quad (8.17)$$

where ps is a prediction score value, $CP(positive, ps)$ is the cumulative probability distribution of positive value scores, and $CP(negative, ps)$ is the cumulative probability distribution of negative value scores. These cumulative probability distributions can be plotted on a **Kolmogorov-Smirnov chart** (**K-S chart**). Figure 8.13[431] shows the K-S chart for the test set predictions shown in Table 8.11[424]. We can see how the cumulative likelihood of finding a *ham* (or negative) instance increases much more quickly than that of finding a *spam* (or positive) instance. This makes sense because if a model is performing accurately, we would expect negative instances to have low scores (close to 0.0) and positive instances to have high scores (close to 1.0).

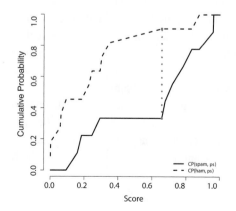

Figure 8.13

The K-S chart for the email classification predictions shown in Table 8.11[424].

The K-S statistic is calculated by determining the maximum difference between the cumulative probability distributions for the positive and negative target levels. This can be given formally as

$$K\text{-}S = \max_{ps}\left(CP(positive, ps) - CP(negative, ps)\right) \qquad (8.18)$$

where $CP(positive, ps)$ and $CP(negative, ps)$ are as described above. This distance is indicated by the vertical dotted line in Figure 8.13[431], from which it is clear that the K-S statistic is the largest distance between the positive and negative cumulative distributions. The K-S statistic ranges from 0 to 1, and higher values indicate better model performance, reflecting the fact that there is a clear distinction between the distributions of the scores predicted by the model for the negative and the positive instances.

In practice, the simplest way to calculate a K-S statistic for the predictions made by a model for a test dataset is to first tabulate the positive and negative cumulative probabilities for the scores predicted for each instance in the test dataset, in ascending order by prediction score. For the score predicted by the model for each instance in the test set, the distance between the positive and negative cumulative probabilities at that score can then be calculated. The K-S statistic is the maximum of these distances. Table 8.14[433] shows an example for the email classification problem predictions given in Table 8.11[424]. We have highlighted in bold and marked with a * the instance that results in the maximum distance between $CP(spam, ps)$ and $CP(ham, ps)$. This distance is 0.576, which is the K-S statistic for this example.

To illustrate how a K-S statistic and K-S chart can give insight into model performance, Figure 8.14[434] shows a series of charts for the four different prediction models trained on the email classification task and evaluated on a large test set. The charts are a histogram of the *spam* scores predicted by the model, a histogram of the *ham* scores predicted by the model, and the resulting K-S chart with the K-S statistic highlighted.

The resulting K-S statistics are 0.940, 0.631, 0.432, and 0.164. These results show that Model 1 is doing a much better job of separating the two target levels than the other models. We can see this in the score histograms and the K-S charts, but it is also nicely captured in the K-S statistics.

8.4.3.3   Measuring Gain and Lift

In scenarios in which we have a positive target level that we are especially interested in (for example, spam emails, fraudulent transactions, or customers

Table 8.14

Tabulating the workings required to generate a K-S statistic.

ID	Prediction Score	Positive (spam) Cumulative Count	Negative (ham) Cumulative Count	Positive (spam) Cumulative Probability	Negative (ham) Cumulative Probability	Distance
7	0.001	0	1	0.000	0.091	0.091
11	0.003	0	2	0.000	0.182	0.182
15	0.059	0	3	0.000	0.273	0.273
13	0.064	0	4	0.000	0.364	0.364
19	0.094	0	5	0.000	0.455	0.455
12	0.160	1	5	0.111	0.455	0.343
2	0.184	2	5	0.222	0.455	0.232
3	0.226	2	6	0.222	0.545	0.323
16	0.246	2	7	0.222	0.636	0.414
1	0.293	3	7	0.333	0.636	0.303
5	0.302	3	8	0.333	0.727	0.394
14	0.348	3	9	0.333	0.818	0.485
17	**0.657**	**3**	**10**	**0.333**	**0.909**	**0.576***
8	0.676	4	10	0.444	0.909	0.465
6	0.719	5	10	0.556	0.909	0.354
10	0.781	6	10	0.667	0.909	0.242
18	0.833	7	10	0.778	0.909	0.131
20	0.877	7	11	0.778	1.000	0.222
9	0.960	8	11	0.889	1.000	0.111
4	0.963	9	11	1.000	1.000	0.000

* marks the maximum distance, which is the K-S statistic.

that will respond to an offer), it can often be useful to focus in on how well a model is making predictions for just those instances, rather than how well the model is distinguishing between two target levels. This is a subtle difference but can lead to a change in the ordering of models compared to other performance measures. Two useful performance measures in this regard are **gain** and **lift** (we will see that the related performance measures of **cumulative gain** and **cumulative lift** are also useful).

The basic assumption behind both gain and lift is that if we were to rank the instances in a test set in descending order of the prediction scores assigned to them by a well-performing model, we would expect the majority of the positive instances to be toward the top of this ranking. The gain and lift measures attempt to measure to what extent a set of predictions made by a model meet this assumption.

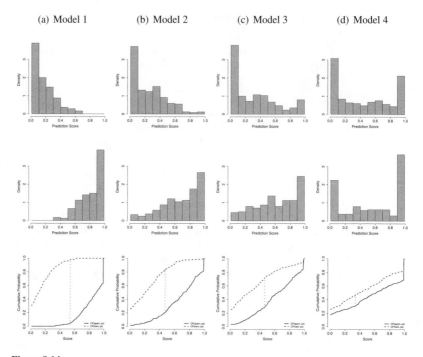

Figure 8.14

A series of charts for different model performance on the same large email classification test set used to generate the ROC curves in Figure 8.12(b)[429]. Each column from top to bottom: a histogram of the *ham* scores predicted by the model, a histogram of the *spam* scores predicted by the model, and the K-S chart.

To calculate gain and lift, we first rank the predictions made for a test set in descending order by prediction score and then divide them into **deciles**.[18] A decile is a group containing 10% of a dataset. Table 8.15[435] shows the data from Table 8.11[424] divided into deciles. There are 20 instances, so each decile contains just 2 instances. The first decile contains instances 9 and 4, the second decile contains instances 18 and 20, and so on.

Gain is a measure of how many of the positive instances in the overall test set are found in a particular decile. To find this, we count the number of positive instances (based on the known target values) found in each decile and divide

---

18 Any **percentiles** (see Section A.1[525]) can be used, but deciles are particularly common.

Table 8.15
The test set with model predictions and scores from Table 8.11[424] extended to include deciles.

Decile	ID	Target	Prediction	Score	Outcome
1st	9	spam	spam	0.960	TP
	4	spam	spam	0.963	TP
2nd	18	spam	spam	0.833	TP
	20	ham	spam	0.877	FP
3rd	6	spam	spam	0.719	TP
	10	spam	spam	0.781	TP
4th	17	ham	spam	0.657	FP
	8	spam	spam	0.676	TP
5th	5	ham	ham	0.302	TN
	14	ham	ham	0.348	TN
6th	16	ham	ham	0.246	TN
	1	spam	ham	0.293	FN
7th	2	spam	ham	0.184	FN
	3	ham	ham	0.226	TN
8th	19	ham	ham	0.094	TN
	12	spam	ham	0.160	FN
9th	15	ham	ham	0.059	TN
	13	ham	ham	0.064	TN
10th	7	ham	ham	0.001	TN
	11	ham	ham	0.003	TN

these by the total number of positive instances in the test set. So, the gain in a given decile is calculated as

$$gain(dec) = \frac{\text{num positive test instances in decile } dec}{\text{num positive test instances}} \quad (8.19)$$

where *dec* refers to a particular decile. Table 8.16[436] shows how gain is calculated for each decile in the email classification test set. The number of positive and negative instances in each decile is shown. Based on these numbers, the gain for each decile is calculated using Equation (8.19)[435] (the calculation of some other measures are also included in this table, and these will be explained shortly).

Figure 8.15(a)[437] graphs the gain for each decile to produce a **gain chart**. We can see from this chart that the gain is higher for the lower deciles, which contain the instances with the highest scores. This is indicative of the fact that the model is performing reasonably well. **Cumulative gain** is calculated as the fraction of the total number of positive instances in a test set identified up to a

Table 8.16

Tabulating the workings required to calculate gain, cumulative gain, lift, and cumulative lift for the data given in Table 8.11[424].

Decile	Positive (*spam*) Count	Negative (*ham*) Count	Gain	Cum. Gain	Lift	Cum. Lift
1st	2	0	0.222	0.222	2.222	2.222
2nd	1	1	0.111	0.333	1.111	1.667
3rd	2	0	0.222	0.556	2.222	1.852
4th	1	1	0.111	0.667	1.111	1.667
5th	0	2	0.000	0.667	0.000	1.333
6th	1	1	0.111	0.778	1.111	1.296
7th	1	1	0.111	0.889	1.111	1.270
8th	1	1	0.111	1.000	1.111	1.250
9th	0	2	0.000	1.000	0.000	1.111
10th	0	2	0.000	1.000	0.000	1.000

particular decile (i.e., in that decile and all deciles below it):

$$cumulative\ gain(dec) = \frac{\text{num positive test instances in all deciles up to } dec}{\text{num positive test instances}}$$

(8.20)

The cumulative gain for each decile of the email classification dataset is shown in Table 8.16[436]. Figure 8.15(b)[437] shows a **cumulative gain chart** of this data. That cumulative gain chart allows us to understand how many of the positive instances in a complete test set we can expect to have identified at each decile of the dataset. So, for example, Figure 8.15(b)[437] shows that by the 4th decile (40% of the test data), 66.667% of the spam emails in the entire test set will have been identified. This is evidence of just how well the model is performing. The dotted diagonal line on the cumulative gain chart shows the performance we would expect from random guessing, and the closer the cumulative gain line is to the top left hand corner of the chart, the better the model is performing.

The **gain** in a particular decile can be interpreted as a measure of how much better than random guessing the predictions made by a model are. **Lift** captures this more formally. If a model were performing no better than random guessing, we would expect that within each decile, the percentage of positive instances should be the same as the percentage of positive instances overall in the complete dataset. Lift tells us how much higher the actual percentage of positive instances in a decile *dec* is than the rate expected. So, the lift at decile

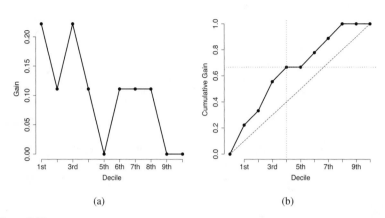

Figure 8.15
The (a) gain and (b) cumulative gain at each decile for the email predictions given in Table 8.11[424].

dec is the ratio between the percentage of positive instances in that decile and the percentage of positive instances overall in the population:

$$lift(dec) = \frac{\% \text{ of positive test instances in decile } dec}{\% \text{ of positive test instances}} \tag{8.21}$$

In the email classification example, the percentage of positive (*spam*) instances in the full test dataset is $\frac{9}{20} = 0.45$. Therefore, the lift at each decile *dec* is the percentage of *spam* instances in that decile divided by 0.45. Table 8.16[436] shows the lift for each decile for the predictions shown in Table 8.11[424] for the email classification problem. If we compare the visualization of lift for these predictions shown in Figure 8.16(a)[438] to the gain chart for the same set of predictions in Figure 8.15(a)[437], we can see that the shapes are the same. For a well-performing model, the lift curve should start well above 1.0 and cross 1.0 at one of the lower deciles. Lift can take values in the range $[0, \infty]$, and higher values indicate that a model is performing well at a particular decile.

In the same way we calculated cumulative gain, we can calculate lift cumulatively. The **cumulative lift** at decile *dec* is defined as

$$cumulative\ lift(dec) = \frac{\% \text{ of positive instances in all deciles up to } dec}{\% \text{ of positive test instances}}$$

$$\tag{8.22}$$

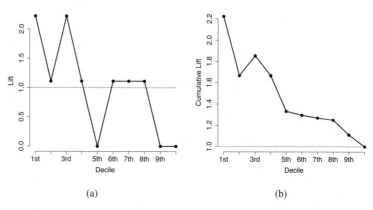

(a)   (b)

Figure 8.16

The (a) lift and (b) cumulative lift at each decile for the email predictions given in Table 8.11[424].

Table 8.16[436] shows the cumulative lift for each decile for the predictions shown in Table 8.11[424] for the email classification problem, and these values are plotted in a **cumulative lift curve** in Figure 8.16(b)[438].

Figure 8.17[439] shows cumulative gain, lift, and cumulative lift charts (the gain chart is not shown as it is essentially the same as the lift chart) for four different sets of model predictions for the larger version of the email classification test set (these are the same predictions for which ROC charts and K-S charts were plotted in Figures 8.12(b)[429] and 8.14[434]). Focusing on the cumulative gain charts, we can see that for Model 1, 80% of the spam messages are identified in the top 40% of the model predictions. For Model 2, we need to look almost as far as the top 50% of predictions to find the same percentage of spam messages. For Models 3 and 4, we need to go as far as 60% and 75% respectively. This indicates that Model 1 distinguishes between the target levels most effectively.

Cumulative gain is especially useful in **customer relationship management (CRM)** applications such as **cross-sell** and **upsell** models. The cumulative gain tells us how many customers we need to contact in order to reach a particular percentage of those who are likely to respond to an offer, which is an incredibly useful piece of information to know when planning customer contact budgets.

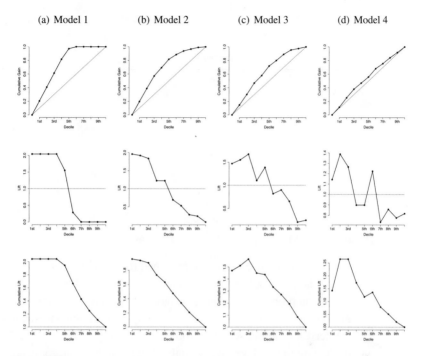

Figure 8.17

Cumulative gain, lift, and cumulative lift charts for four different models for the extended email classification test set.

Table 8.17

The structure of a confusion matrix for a multinomial prediction problem with *l* target levels.

		Prediction					Recall
		level 1	*level 2*	*level 3*	⋯	*level l*	
	level 1	-	-	-		-	-
	level 2	-	-	-		-	-
Target	*level 3*	-	-	-		-	-
	⋮				⋱		⋮
	level l	-	-	-		-	-
	Precision	-	-	-	⋯	-	

8.4.4   Performance Measures: Multinomial Targets

All the performance measures described in the previous section assumed that the prediction problem being evaluated had only two target levels. Many of the prediction problems for which we build models are **multinomial**, that is, there are multiple target levels. When we deal with multinomial prediction problems, we need a different set of performance measures. This section describes the most common of these. We begin by discussing how the confusion matrix can be extended to handle multiple target levels.

If we have multiple target levels, the structure of the confusion matrix shown in Figure 8.2[403] no longer fits the data. Similarly, the notion of thinking about a positive level and a negative level doesn't apply any more. The confusion matrix can, however, be easily extended to handle multiple target levels by including a row and column for each one. Table 8.17[440] shows the structure of a confusion matrix for a multinomial prediction problem in which the target feature has *l* levels.

In Table 8.17[440] we have included precision and recall measures for each target level. Precision and recall are calculated in almost exactly the same way for multinomial problems as for binary problems. Abandoning the notion of positive and negative target levels, we get

$$precision(l) = \frac{TP(l)}{TP(l) + FP(l)} \tag{8.23}$$

$$recall(l) = \frac{TP(l)}{TP(l) + FN(l)} \tag{8.24}$$

Table 8.18

A sample test set with model predictions for a bacterial species identification problem.

ID	Target	Prediction	ID	Target	Prediction
1	durionis	fructosus	16	ficulneus	ficulneus
2	ficulneus	fructosus	17	ficulneus	ficulneus
3	fructosus	fructosus	18	fructosus	fructosus
4	ficulneus	ficulneus	19	durionis	durionis
5	durionis	durionis	20	fructosus	fructosus
6	pseudo.	pseudo.	21	fructosus	fructosus
7	durionis	fructosus	22	durionis	durionis
8	ficulneus	ficulneus	23	fructosus	fructosus
9	pseudo.	pseudo.	24	pseudo.	fructosus
10	pseudo.	fructosus	25	durionis	durionis
11	fructosus	fructosus	26	pseudo.	pseudo.
12	ficulneus	ficulneus	27	fructosus	fructosus
13	durionis	durionis	28	ficulneus	ficulneus
14	fructosus	fructosus	29	fructosus	fructosus
15	fructosus	ficulneus	30	fructosus	fructosus

where $TP(l)$ refers to the number of instances correctly given a prediction of the target level l, $FP(l)$ refers to the number of instances that are incorrectly given a prediction of target level l, and $FN(l)$ refers to the number of instances that should have been given a prediction of target level l but were given some other prediction.

Table 8.18[441] shows the expected targets and a set of model predictions for a multinomial prediction problem in which the species of a bacteria present in a sample is determined using the results of spectrography performed on the sample.[19] In this example, we are trying to distinguish between four species of the bacterial genus *Fructobacillus*, namely, *durionis*, *ficulneus*, *fructosus*, and *pseudoficulneus* (abbreviated as *pseudo.* in all tables). Table 8.19[442] shows the associated confusion matrix for these predictions, including measures of precision and recall.

While the overall classification accuracy for this set of predictions is 80%,[20] the individual recall scores for each target level show that the performance of the model is not the same for all four levels: the accuracy on the *ficulneus*

19 See De Bruyne et al. (2011) for an example of machine learning models being used for this task.

20 It is important to remember that for a prediction problem with four target levels, uniform random guessing will give an accuracy of just 25%.

Table 8.19

A confusion matrix for a model trained on the bacterial species identification problem.

		Prediction				Recall
		durionis	*ficulneus*	*fructosus*	*pseudo.*	
	durionis	5	0	2	0	0.714
Target	*ficulneus*	0	6	1	0	0.857
	fructosus	0	1	10	0	0.909
	pseudo.	0	0	2	3	0.600
	Precision	1.000	0.857	0.667	1.000	

and *fructosus* levels is quite high (85.714% and 90.909% respectively), while for the *durionis* and *pseudoficulneus* levels, the accuracy is considerably lower (71.429% and 60.000%). The *averageclassaccuracy$_{HM}$* performance measure can be applied to multinomial prediction problems and is an effective option for measuring performance. Using Equation (8.12)[418], we can calculate the average class accuracy for this problem:

$$\frac{1}{\frac{1}{4}\left(\frac{1}{0.714}+\frac{1}{0.857}+\frac{1}{0.909}+\frac{1}{0.600}\right)} = \frac{1}{1.333} = 75.000\%$$

It is not easy to apply the measures based on prediction scores to multinomial problems. Although there are some examples of doing it, there is no broad consensus in the community on how it should best be done in all cases, so we do not discuss it further in this book.

8.4.5 Performance Measures: Continuous Targets

All the performance measures that we have discussed so far focus on prediction problems with categorical targets. When evaluating the performance of prediction models built for continuous targets, there are fewer options to choose from. In this section we describe the most popular performance measures used for continuous targets. The basic process is the same as for categorical targets. We have a test set containing instances for which we know the correct target values, and we have a set of predictions made by a model. We would like to measure how accurately the predicted values match the correct target values.

8.4.5.1 Basic Measures of Error

In Section 7.2.2[327], when covering error-based learning, we discussed the basis of the most common performance measure for continuous targets: **sum of squared errors**. The sum of squared errors function, L_2, for a set of predictions made by a model, $\mathbb{M}$, is defined as

$$sum\ of\ squared\ errors = \frac{1}{2}\sum_{i=1}^{n}(t_i - \mathbb{M}(\mathbf{d}_i))^2 \qquad (8.25)$$

where $t_1 \ldots t_n$ is a set of n expected target values, and $\mathbb{M}(d_1) \ldots \mathbb{M}(d_n)$ is a set of n predictions for a set of test instances, $d_1 \ldots d_n$. We modify this very slightly to give us the **mean squared error** performance measure, which captures the average difference between the expected target values in the test set and the values predicted by the model. The **mean squared error** (**MSE**) performance measure is defined as

$$mean\ squared\ error = \frac{\sum_{i=1}^{n}(t_i - \mathbb{M}(\mathbf{d}_i))^2}{n} \qquad (8.26)$$

The mean squared error allows us to rank the performance of multiple models on a prediction problem with a continuous target. Mean squared error values fall in the range $[0, \infty]$, and smaller values indicate better model performance.

Table 8.20[445] shows the expected target values for a test set, the predictions made by two different models (a multivariable linear regression model and a k-NN model), and the resulting errors based on these predictions (the additional error measures will be explained shortly). The prediction problem in this case is to determine the dosage of a blood thinning drug (in milligrams) that should be given to a patient in order to achieve a particular level of blood thinning. The descriptive features in this case would be the level of blood thinning desired, demographic details for the patient, and the results of various medical tests performed on the patient. Doctors could use the outputs of such a system to help them make better dosing decisions.[21] The mean squared error for the multivariable linear regression model is 1.905 and for the k-NN model is 4.394. This indicates that the regression model is more accurately predicting the correct drug dosages than the nearest neighbor model.

21 A nice example of building machine learning models for drug dosage prediction can be found in Mac Namee et al. (2002).

One complaint that is often leveled against mean squared error is that, although it can be used to effectively rank models, the actual mean squared error values themselves are not especially meaningful in relation to the scenario that a model is being used for. For example, in the drug dosage prediction problem, we cannot say by how many milligrams we expect the model to be incorrect based on the mean squared error values. This is due to the use of the squared term in the mean squared error calculation but can easily be addressed by using **root mean squared error** instead. The **root mean squared error** (**RMSE**) for a set of predictions made by a model on a test set is calculated as

$$root\ mean\ squared\ error = \sqrt{\frac{\sum_{i=1}^{n}(t_i - \mathbb{M}(\mathbf{d}_i))^2}{n}} \tag{8.27}$$

where the terms have the same meaning as before. Root mean squared error values are in the same units as the target value and so allow us to say something more meaningful about what the error for predictions made by the model will be. For example, for the drug dosage prediction problem, the root mean squared error value is 1.380 for the regression model and 2.096 for the nearest neighbor model. This means that we can expect the predictions made by the regression model to be 1.38mg out on average, whereas those made by the nearest neighbor model will be, on average, 2.096mg out.

Due to the inclusion of the squared term, the root mean squared error tends to overestimate error slightly as it overemphasizes individual large errors. An alternative measure that addresses this problem is the **mean absolute error** (**MAE**), which does not include a squared term.[22] Mean absolute error is calculated as

$$mean\ absolute\ error = \frac{\sum_{i=1}^{n} abs(t_i - \mathbb{M}(\mathbf{d}_i))}{n} \tag{8.28}$$

where the terms in the equation have the same meaning as before, and *abs* refers to the absolute value. Mean absolute error values fall in the range $[0, \infty]$, and smaller values indicate better model performance.

For the drug dosage predictions given in Table 8.20[445], the mean absolute error is 0.975 for the regression model and 1.750 for the nearest neighbor

22 This is very similar to the difference between **Euclidean distance** and **Manhattan distance** discussed in Section 5.2.2[183].

Table 8.20

The expected target values for a test set, the predictions made by a model, and the resulting errors based on these predictions for a blood thinning drug dosage prediction problem.

ID	Target	Linear Regression		k-NN	
		Prediction	Error	Prediction	Error
1	10.502	10.730	0.228	12.240	1.738
2	18.990	17.578	-1.412	21.000	2.010
3	20.000	21.760	1.760	16.973	-3.027
4	6.883	7.001	0.118	7.543	0.660
5	5.351	5.244	-0.107	8.383	3.032
6	11.120	10.842	-0.278	10.228	-0.892
7	11.420	10.913	-0.507	12.921	1.500
8	4.836	7.401	2.565	7.588	2.752
9	8.177	8.227	0.050	9.277	1.100
10	19.009	16.667	-2.341	21.000	1.991
11	13.282	14.424	1.142	15.496	2.214
12	8.689	9.874	1.185	5.724	-2.965
13	18.050	19.503	1.453	16.449	-1.601
14	5.388	7.020	1.632	6.640	1.252
15	10.646	10.358	-0.288	5.840	-4.805
16	19.612	16.219	-3.393	18.965	-0.646
17	10.576	10.680	0.104	8.941	-1.634
18	12.934	14.337	1.403	12.484	-0.451
19	10.492	10.366	-0.126	13.021	2.529
20	13.439	14.035	0.596	10.920	-2.519
21	9.849	9.821	-0.029	9.920	0.071
22	18.045	16.639	-1.406	18.526	0.482
23	6.413	7.225	0.813	7.719	1.307
24	9.522	9.565	0.043	8.934	-0.588
25	12.083	13.048	0.965	11.241	-0.842
26	10.104	10.085	-0.020	10.010	-0.095
27	8.924	9.048	0.124	8.157	-0.767
28	10.636	10.876	0.239	13.409	2.773
29	5.457	4.080	-1.376	9.684	4.228
30	3.538	7.090	3.551	5.553	2.014
	MSE		1.905		4.394
	RMSE		1.380		2.096
	MAE		0.975		1.750
	R^2		0.889		0.776

model. Mean absolute errors are in the same units as the predictions themselves, so we can say that, based on mean absolute error, we can expect the

regression model to make errors of approximately 0.9575mg in each of its predictions and the nearest neighbor model to be out by approximately 4.020mg.
These are not massively different from the values calculated using root mean
squared error. As we recommended the use of harmonic mean over arithmetic
mean when calculating average class accuracy, we recommend the use of root
mean squared error over mean absolute error because it is better to be pessimistic when estimating the performance of models.

8.4.5.2   Domain Independent Measures of Error

The fact that root mean squared error and mean absolute error are in the same
units as the target feature itself can be attractive as it gives a very intuitive
measure of how well a model is performing—for example, a model is typically 1.38mg out in its dosage predictions. The disadvantage of this, however,
is that these types of measure by themselves are not sufficient to judge whether
a model is making accurate predictions without deep knowledge of a domain.
For example, how can we judge whether a drug dosage prediction model that
has a root mean squared error of 1.38mg is actually making accurate predictions without also understanding the domain of drug dosage prediction. To
make these judgements it is necessary to have a normalised, domain independent measure of model performance.

The R^2 coefficient is a domain independent measure of model performance
that is frequently used for prediction problems with a continuous target. The
R^2 coefficient compares the performance of a model on a test set with the
performance of an imaginary model that always predicts the average values
from the test set. The R^2 coefficient is calculated as

$$R^2 = 1 - \frac{sum\ of\ squared\ errors}{total\ sum\ of\ squares} \tag{8.29}$$

where the **sum of squared errors** is computed using Equation (8.25)[443], and
the **total sum of squares** is given by

$$total\ sum\ of\ squares = \frac{1}{2} \sum_{i=1}^{n} (t_i - \bar{t})^2 \tag{8.30}$$

R^2 coefficient values fall in the range $[0, 1)$ and larger values indicate better model performance. A useful interpretation of the R^2 coefficient is as the
amount of variation in the target feature that is explained by the descriptive
features in the model.

The average target value for the drug dosage prediction test set given in Table 8.20[445] is 11.132. Using this, the R^2 coefficient for the regression model can be calculated as 0.889 and for the nearest neighbor model as 0.776. This leads to the same conclusion with regard to model ranking as the root mean squared error measures: namely, that the regression model has better performance on this task than the nearest neighbor model. The R^2 coefficient has the advantage in general, however, that it allows assessment of model performance in a domain independent way.

8.4.6   Evaluating Models after Deployment

Predictive models are based on the assumption that the patterns learned in the training data will be relevant to unseen instances that are presented to the model in the future. Data, however, like everything else in the world, is not constant. People grow older, inflation drives up salaries, the content of the spam emails changes, and the way people use technologies changes. This phenomenon is often referred to as **concept drift**. Concept drift means that almost all the predictive models that we build will at some point go **stale**, and the relationships that they have learned between descriptive features and target features will no longer apply. It is important that once a model is deployed, we put in place an **on-going model validation** scheme to monitor the model to catch the point at which it begins to go stale. If we can catch this point, we can take appropriate action.

To monitor the on-going performance of a model, we need a signal that indicates that something has changed. There are three sources from which we can extract such a signal:

- The performance of the model measured using appropriate performance measures
- The distributions of the outputs of a model
- The distributions of the descriptive features in query instances presented to the model

Once a signal has identified that concept drift has occurred and that a model has indeed gone stale, corrective action is required. The nature of this corrective action depends on the application and the type of model being used. In most cases, however, corrective action involves gathering a new labeled dataset and restarting the model building process using this new dataset.

8.4.6.1   Monitoring Changes in Performance Measures

The simplest way to get a signal that concept drift has occurred is to repeatedly evaluate models with the same performance measures used to evaluate them before deployment. We can calculate performance measures for a deployed model and compare these to the performance achieved in evaluations before the model was deployed. If the performance changes significantly, this is a strong indication that concept drift has occurred and that the model has gone stale. For example, if we had used root mean squared error on a hold-out test set to evaluate the performance of a model before deployment, we could collect all the query instances presented to the model for a period after deployment and, once their true target feature values became available, calculate the root mean squared error on this new set of query instances. A *large* change in the root mean squared error value would flag that the model had gone stale. One of the drawbacks of using this method to detect that a model has gone stale is that estimating how *large* this change needs to be in order to signal that the model has gone stale is entirely domain dependent.[23]

Although monitoring changes in the performance of a model is the easiest way to tell whether it has gone stale, this method makes the rather large assumption that the correct target feature value for a query instance will be made available shortly after the query has been presented to a deployed model. There are many scenarios in which this is the case. For example, for churn models, customers will either churn or not churn; for credit scoring models, customers will either repay their loans or not; and for models predicting athlete performance, athletes will either match expectations or not. There are many more scenarios, however, in which the correct target feature values either never become available or do not become available early enough to be useful for on-going model validation. In these scenarios, this approach to on-going model validation simply doesn't work.

8.4.6.2   Monitoring Model Output Distribution Changes

An alternative to using changing model performance is to use changes in the distribution of model outputs as a signal for concept drift. If the distribution of model outputs changes dramatically, for example, if a model that previously

---

23 Systems like the **Western Electric rules** (Montgomery, 2004), used widely in process engineering to detect *out-of-control* processes, can be useful in this regard.

made positive predictions 80% of the time is suddenly making positive predictions only 20% of the time, then we can assume that there is a strong possibility that concept drift has occurred and that the model has gone stale. In order to compare distributions, we measure the distribution of model outputs on the test set that was used to originally evaluate a model and then repeat this measurement on new sets of query instances collected during periods after the model has been deployed. We then use an appropriate measure to calculate the difference between the distributions collected after deployment and the original distribution. One of the most commonly used measures for this is the **stability index**. The stability index is calculated as

$$stability\ index = \sum_{l \in levels(t)} \left(\left(\frac{|\mathcal{A}_{t=l}|}{|\mathcal{A}|} - \frac{|\mathcal{B}_{t=l}|}{|\mathcal{B}|} \right) \times log_e \left(\frac{|\mathcal{A}_{t=l}|}{|\mathcal{A}|} \middle/ \frac{|\mathcal{B}_{t=l}|}{|\mathcal{B}|} \right) \right)$$

(8.31)

where $|\mathcal{A}|$ refers to the size of the test set on which performance measures were originally calculated, $|\mathcal{A}_{t=l}|$ refers to the number of instances in the original test set for which the model made a prediction of level l for target t, $|\mathcal{B}|$ and $|\mathcal{B}_{t=l}|$ refer to the same measurements on the newly collected dataset, and log_e is the **natural logarithm**.[24] In general,

- If the value of the stability index is less than 0.1, then the distribution of the newly collected test set is broadly similar to the distribution in the original test set.

- If the value of the stability index is between 0.1 and 0.25, then some change has occurred and further investigation may be useful.

- A stability index value greater than 0.25 suggests that a significant change has occurred and corrective action is required.

Table 8.21[450] shows an example of how the stability index could be calculated for two different sets of query instances collected at two different times after model deployment based on the bacterial species identification problem given in Table 8.18[441]. For the original test set and the two new test sets, referred to as New Sample 1 and New Sample 2, the count and percentage for each target value is given (note that the tests sets do not have to be the same size because relative distributions are used). The original baseline target

---

24 The natural logarithm of a value a, $log_e(a)$, is the logarithm of a to the base e, where e is **Euler's number**, equal to approximately 2.718.

Table 8.21

Calculating the stability index for the bacterial species identification problem given new test data for two periods after model deployment.

| | Original | | New Sample 1 | | | New Sample 2 | | |
Target	Count	%	Count	%	SI_t	Count	%	SI_t
durionis	7	0.233	12	0.267	0.004	12	0.200	0.005
ficulneus	7	0.233	8	0.178	0.015	9	0.150	0.037
fructosus	11	0.367	16	0.356	0.000	14	0.233	0.060
pseudo.	5	0.167	9	0.200	0.006	25	0.417	0.229
Sum	30		45		0.026	60		0.331

The frequency and percentage of each target level are shown for the original test set and for two samples collected after deployment. The column marked SI_t shows the different parts of the stability index sum based on Equation (8.31)[449].

frequencies are based on the predictions in Table 8.18[441] and are visualized in Figure 8.18(a)[451].

Figures 8.18(b)[451] and 8.18(c)[451] show the target distributions for the two points in time after deployment for which the stability index is to be calculated. These bar plots show that the distribution of target levels for New Sample 1 is similar to the original test set, but that the distribution of target levels for New Sample 2 is quite different. This is reflected in the stability index calculations in Table 8.21[450], which are determined using Equation (8.31)[449]. For example, for New Sample 1, the stability index is

$$
\begin{aligned}
stability\ index = &\left(\frac{7}{30} - \frac{12}{45}\right) \times log_e\left(\frac{7}{30} / \frac{12}{45}\right) \\
+ &\left(\frac{7}{30} - \frac{8}{45}\right) \times log_e\left(\frac{7}{30} / \frac{8}{45}\right) \\
+ &\left(\frac{11}{30} - \frac{16}{45}\right) \times log_e\left(\frac{11}{30} / \frac{16}{45}\right) \\
+ &\left(\frac{5}{30} - \frac{9}{45}\right) \times log_e\left(\frac{5}{30} / \frac{9}{45}\right) \\
= &\ 0.026
\end{aligned}
$$

where the counts come from Table 8.21[450]. The stability index for New Sample 2, calculated in the same way, is 0.331. This suggests that at the point in time at which New Sample 1 was collected, the outputs produced by the model followed much the same distribution as when the model was originally evaluated, but that when New Sample 2 was collected, the distribution of the outputs produced by the model had changed significantly.

To monitor models for the occurrence of concept drift, it is important that the stability index be continuously tracked over time. Figure 8.18(d)[451] shows how the stability index could be tracked for the bacterial species identification problem every month for a period of twelve months after model deployment. The dotted line indicates a stability index value of 0.1, above which a model should be closely monitored, and the dashed line indicates a stability index of 0.25, above which corrective action is recommended.

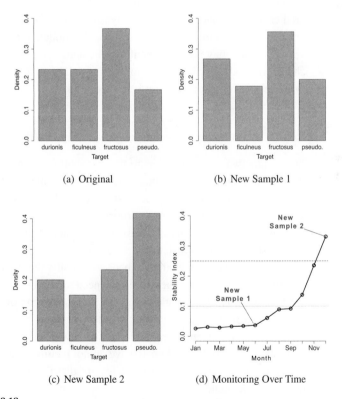

(a) Original

(b) New Sample 1

(c) New Sample 2

(d) Monitoring Over Time

Figure 8.18

The distributions of predictions made by a model trained for the bacterial species identification problem for (a) the original evaluation test set and for (b) and (c) two periods of time after model deployment; (d) shows how the stability index should be tracked over time to monitor for concept drift.

The stability index can be used for both categorical and continuous targets. When a model predicts a continuous target, the target range is divided into bins, and the distribution of values into these bins is used in the calculation. It is particularly common to use deciles for this task. The same can actually be done for models that predict binary categorical targets by dividing the prediction scores into deciles. The stability index is just one measure of the difference between two different distributions, and there are many other options that can be used. For example, for categorical targets, the χ^2 statistic is often used, and for continuous targets, the **K-S statistic** can also be used.

The advantage of using evaluation approaches based on comparing the distribution of a model's output, such as the stability index, is that they do not require that the true targets for query instances become available shortly after predictions have been made. The downside, however, is that such measures do not directly measure the performance of the model, and consequently, a high stability index may reflect a change in the underlying population rather than a change in model performance. So, relying solely on a stability index can lead to models being rebuilt when it is not required.

8.4.6.3   Monitoring Descriptive Feature Distribution Changes

In the same way we can compare the distributions of model outputs between the time that the model was built and after deployment, we can also make the same type of comparison for the distributions of the descriptive features used by the model. We can use any appropriate measure that captures the difference between two different distributions for this, including the stability index, the χ^2 statistic, and the K-S statistic.

There is, however, a challenge here, as usually, there are a large number of descriptive features for which measures need to be calculated and tracked. Furthermore, it is unlikely that a change in the distribution of just one descriptive feature in a multi-feature model will have a large impact on model performance. For this reason, unless a model uses a very small number of descriptive features (generally fewer than 10), we do not recommend this approach. Measuring the difference in descriptive feature distributions can be useful, however, in understanding what has changed to make a model go stale. So, we recommend that if a model has been flagged as having gone stale using either performance measure monitoring or output distribution monitoring, then the distributions of the descriptive features at the time that the model was built and the distributions of the features at the time that the model went stale should be compared in an effort to understand what has changed. This information should help if the model is to be rebuilt to address the fact that it has gone stale.

8.4.6.4 Comparative Experiments Using a Control Group

At the beginning of this chapter, we emphasized that it is important that the evaluation of prediction models not just focus on predictive power but also take into account the suitability of the model for the task to which it will be deployed. As part of this type of broader evaluation, the use of **comparative experiments** that include a **control group** can be quite effective. The idea of a control group might be familiar to readers from reading about medical trials. To test a new medicine, doctors typically assemble a group of patients who suffer from the problem that the medicine is designed to address. During a trial period, half of the patients, the **treatment group**, are given the new drug, and the other half, the control group, are given a **placebo** (essentially a fake drug that has no actual medical effect). Patients are not aware which group they have been assigned to during the trial (hence the need for the placebo). As long as both the treatment group and the control group are representative of the overall population, at the end of the trial period, the doctors running the trial can be confident that any improvement they see in the patients in the treatment group that they do not see in the control group is due to the new medicine.

We can use exactly the same idea to evaluate the impact of predictive models. It is important to note here that we use control groups not to evaluate the predictive power of the models themselves, but rather to evaluate how good they are at helping with the business problem when they are deployed. If we have developed a predictive model that is used in a particular business process, we can run that business process in parallel both with the predictive model, the treatment group, and without the predictive model, the control group, in order to evaluate how much the use of the predictive model has improved the business process.

For example, consider a mobile phone network operator that has built a churn prediction model to help address a problem with customers leaving to join other networks. The company would like to evaluate how well the model is helping to address the churn problem. Before the churn model was put in place, every week the company would randomly select 1,000 customers from their customer base and have their customer contact center call these customers to discuss how satisfied they were with the network's performance and offer

Table 8.22

The number of customers who left the mobile phone network operator each week during the comparative experiment from both the control group (random selection) and the treatment group (model selection).

Week	Control Group (Random Selection)	Treatment Group (Model Selection)
1	21	23
2	18	15
3	28	18
4	19	20
5	18	15
6	17	17
7	23	18
8	24	20
9	19	18
10	20	19
11	18	13
12	21	16
Mean	20.500	17.667
Std. Dev.	3.177	2.708

assistance with any issues. This was based on the assumption that such a call made to customers considering switching to a different network would encourage them to stay with their current network. The churn model replaced the random selection of customers by assigning every customer in the company's customer base a churn risk score and selecting the 1,000 customers with the highest churn risk scores to receive a call from the customer contact center. Everything else about the process was the same as before.

In order to evaluate the effect this model was having on the company's churn problem, they performed a comparative experiment. The company's entire customer base was divided randomly into two groups, the treatment group and the control group—each group contained approximately 400,000 customers. For the customers in the treatment group, the company applied the process using the predictive model to determine which customers to contact regarding customer satisfaction. For the customers in the control group, the random selection process was used. These two approaches ran in parallel for twelve weeks, and at the end of this period, the company measured the number of customers within each group who had left the company to join another network. Table 8.22[454] shows the number of customers who churned from each of these two groups during the twelve weeks of the trial, and the associated means and standard deviations. These figures show that, on average, fewer customers churn when the churn prediction model is used to select which customers to call. This tells us not only something about how accurate the churn prediction model is but, more importantly, that using the model actually made a difference in the business problem that the company were trying to address.[25]

In order to use control groups in evaluation, we need to be able to divide a population into two groups, run two versions of a business process in parallel, and accurately measure the performance of the business process. Therefore, using control groups is not suitable in all scenarios, but when it is applicable, it adds an extra dimension to our evaluations that takes into account not just how well a model can make predictions, but also how much the predictive model helps to address the original business problem.

8.5 Summary

This chapter covers a range of approaches for evaluating the performance of prediction models. The choice of the correct performance measure for a particular problem depends on a combination of the nature of the prediction problem (e.g., continuous versus categorical), the characteristics of the dataset (e.g., balanced versus imbalanced), and the needs of the application (e.g., medical diagnosis versus marketing response prediction). This last issue is interesting because sometimes particular performance measures become especially popular in certain industries, and in many cases, this dictates the choice of performance measure. For example, in financial credit scoring, the **Gini coefficient** is almost always used to evaluate model performance.

For those struggling to choose an appropriate performance measure, in the absence of other information, we recommend:

- For categorical prediction problems use **average class accuracy** based on a **harmonic mean**.
- For continuous prediction problems use the R^2 coefficient.

There are also a number of different ways in which evaluation experiments can be performed, as described in Section 8.4.1[405]. The choice of which one to use mostly depends on how much data is available. The following rules

---

25 A formal test for **statistical significance** could easily be used to reinforce this conclusion.

of thumb may be useful (although the usual caveats that all scenarios are slightly different apply). In cases with very small datasets (approximately fewer than 300 instances), bootstrapping approaches are preferred over cross validation approaches. Cross validation approaches are generally preferred unless datasets are very large, in which case the likelihood of the **lucky split** becomes very low, and hold-out approaches can be used. As with everything else, there is an application-specific component to the selection of an experimental design—for example, **out-of-time sampling** is a good choice in scenarios where a time dimension is important.

8.6   Further Reading

The evaluation of machine learning models is a live research issue, and a large body of material addresses all the questions that have been discussed in this chapter. For a detailed discussion of the issues associated with evaluating models for categorical prediction problems (and model evaluation in general) Japkowicz and Shah (2011) is excellent. David Hand has also written extensively on the appropriateness of different evaluation measures and is always worth reading. For example, Hand and Anagnostopoulos (2013) discusses issues with the use of the ROC index.

Japkowicz and Shah (2011) also discusses the issue of performing statistical significance tests to compare the performance of multiple models. Demsar (2006) gives another excellent overview of comparing multiple modeling types and has been the basis for much discussion in the machine learning community. This is slightly more of a concern to machine learning researchers who are interested in comparing the overall power of different machine learning algorithms. By contrast, in most predictive analytics projects, our focus is on determining the best model for a specific problem.

The design of model evaluation experiments is an example of the application of techniques from the larger discipline of experimental design, which is used extensively in the manufacturing industry amongst others. Montgomery (2012) is an excellent reference for this topic and well worth reading.

Finally, for those interested in experimenting with different evaluation measures, the ROCR package (Sing et al., 2005) for the R programming language includes a wide range of measures.

8.7   Exercises

1. The table below shows the predictions made for a categorical target feature by a model for a test dataset. Based on this test set, calculate the evaluation measures listed below.

ID	Target	Prediction	ID	Target	Prediction	ID	Target	Prediction
1	false	false	8	true	true	15	false	false
2	false	false	9	false	false	16	false	false
3	false	false	10	false	false	17	true	false
4	false	false	11	false	false	18	true	true
5	true	true	12	true	true	19	true	true
6	false	false	13	false	false	20	true	true
7	true	true	14	true	true			

a. A confusion matrix and the misclassification rate

b. The average class accuracy (harmonic mean)

c. The precision, recall, and F_1 measure

2. The table below shows the predictions made for a continuous target feature by two different prediction models for a test dataset.

ID	Target	Model 1 Prediction	Model 2 Prediction	ID	Target	Model 1 Prediction	Model 2 Prediction
1	2,623	2,664	2,691	16	2,570	2,577	2,612
2	2,423	2,436	2,367	17	2,528	2,510	2,557
3	2,423	2,399	2,412	18	2,342	2,381	2,421
4	2,448	2,447	2,440	19	2,456	2,452	2,393
5	2,762	2,847	2,693	20	2,451	2,437	2,479
6	2,435	2,411	2,493	21	2,296	2,307	2,290
7	2,519	2,516	2,598	22	2,405	2,355	2,490
8	2,772	2,870	2,814	23	2,389	2,418	2,346
9	2,601	2,586	2,583	24	2,629	2,582	2,647
10	2,422	2,414	2,485	25	2,584	2,564	2,546
11	2,349	2,407	2,472	26	2,658	2,662	2,759
12	2,515	2,505	2,584	27	2,482	2,492	2,463
13	2,548	2,581	2,604	28	2,471	2,478	2,403
14	2,281	2,277	2,309	29	2,605	2,620	2,645
15	2,295	2,280	2,296	30	2,442	2,445	2,478

    a. Based on these predictions, calculate the evaluation measures listed below for each model.

       i. The sum of squared errors

      ii. The R^2 measure

    b. Based on the evaluation measures calculated, which model do you think is performing better for this dataset?

3. A credit card issuer has built two different credit scoring models that predict the propensity of customers to default on their loans. The outputs of the first model for a test dataset are shown in the table below.

ID	Target	Score	Prediction	ID	Target	Score	Prediction
1	bad	0.634	bad	16	good	0.072	good
2	bad	0.782	bad	17	bad	0.567	bad
3	good	0.464	good	18	bad	0.738	bad
4	bad	0.593	bad	19	bad	0.325	good
5	bad	0.827	bad	20	bad	0.863	bad
6	bad	0.815	bad	21	bad	0.625	bad
7	bad	0.855	bad	22	good	0.119	good
8	good	0.500	good	23	bad	0.995	bad
9	bad	0.600	bad	24	bad	0.958	bad
10	bad	0.803	bad	25	bad	0.726	bad
11	bad	0.976	bad	26	good	0.117	good
12	good	0.504	bad	27	good	0.295	good
13	good	0.303	good	28	good	0.064	good
14	good	0.391	good	29	good	0.141	good
15	good	0.238	good	30	good	0.670	bad

The outputs of the second model for the same test dataset are shown in the table below.

ID	Target	Score	Prediction	ID	Target	Score	Prediction
1	bad	0.230	bad	16	good	0.421	bad
2	bad	0.859	good	17	bad	0.842	good
3	good	0.154	bad	18	bad	0.891	good
4	bad	0.325	bad	19	bad	0.480	bad
5	bad	0.952	good	20	bad	0.340	bad
6	bad	0.900	good	21	bad	0.962	good
7	bad	0.501	good	22	good	0.238	bad
8	good	0.650	good	23	bad	0.362	bad
9	bad	0.940	good	24	bad	0.848	good
10	bad	0.806	good	25	bad	0.915	good
11	bad	0.507	good	26	good	0.096	bad
12	good	0.251	bad	27	good	0.319	bad
13	good	0.597	good	28	good	0.740	good
14	good	0.376	bad	29	good	0.211	bad
15	good	0.285	bad	30	good	0.152	bad

Based on the predictions of these models, perform the following tasks to compare their performance.

a. The image below shows an **ROC curve** for each model. Each curve has a point missing.

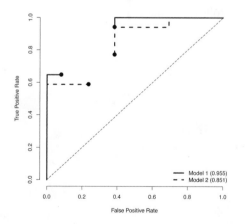

Calculate the missing point in the ROC curves for Model 1 and Model 2. To generate the point for Model 1, use a threshold value of 0.51. To generate the point for Model 2, use a threshold value of 0.43.

b. The **area under the ROC curve** (AUC) for Model 1 is 0.955 and for Model 2 is 0.851. Which model is performing best?

c. Based on the AUC values for Model 1 and Model 2, calculate the **Gini coefficient** for each model.

4. A retail supermarket chain has built a prediction model that recognizes the household that a customer comes from as being one of *single*, *business*, or *family*. After deployment, the analytics team at the supermarket chain uses the **stability index** to monitor the performance of this model. The table below shows the frequencies of predictions of the three different levels made by the model for the original validation dataset at the time the model was built, for the month after deployment, and for a month-long period six months after deployment.

Target	Original Sample	1st New Sample	2nd New Sample
single	123	252	561
business	157	324	221
family	163	372	827

Bar plots of these three sets of prediction frequencies are shown in the following images.

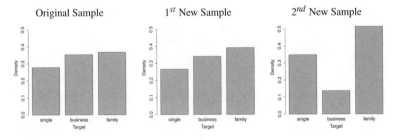

Calculate the **stability index** for the two new periods and determine whether the model should be retrained at either of these points.

* 5. Explain the problem associated with measuring the performance of a predictive model using a single accuracy figure.

* 6. A marketing company working for a charity has developed two different models that predict the likelihood that donors will respond to a mail-shot asking them to make a special extra donation. The prediction scores generated for a test set for these two models are shown in the table below.

ID	Target	Model 1 Score	Model 2 Score	ID	Target	Model 1 Score	Model 2 Score
1	false	0.1026	0.2089	16	true	0.7165	0.4569
2	false	0.2937	0.0080	17	true	0.7677	0.8086
3	true	0.5120	0.8378	18	false	0.4468	0.1458
4	true	0.8645	0.7160	19	false	0.2176	0.5809
5	false	0.1987	0.1891	20	false	0.9800	0.5783
6	true	0.7600	0.9398	21	true	0.6562	0.7843
7	true	0.7519	0.9800	22	true	0.9693	0.9521
8	true	0.2994	0.8578	23	false	0.0275	0.0377
9	false	0.0552	0.1560	24	true	0.7047	0.4708
10	false	0.9231	0.5600	25	false	0.3711	0.2846
11	true	0.7563	0.9062	26	false	0.4440	0.1100
12	true	0.5664	0.7301	27	true	0.5440	0.3562
13	true	0.2872	0.8764	28	true	0.5713	0.9200
14	true	0.9326	0.9274	29	false	0.3757	0.0895
15	false	0.0651	0.2992	30	true	0.8224	0.8614

a. Using a classification threshold of 0.5, and assuming that *true* is the positive target level, construct a **confusion matrix** for each of the models.

b. Calculate the simple accuracy and **average class accuracy** (using an **arithmetic mean**) for each model.

c. Based on the average class accuracy measures, which model appears to perform best at this task?

d. Generate a **cumulative gain chart** for each model.

e. The charity for which the model is being built typically has only enough money to send a mailshot to the top 20% of its contact list. Based on the cumulative gain chart generated in the previous part, would you recommend that Model 1 or Model 2 would perform best for the charity?

* 7. A prediction model is going to be built for in-line quality assurance in a factory that manufactures electronic components for the automotive industry. The system will be integrated into the factory's production line and determine whether components are of an acceptable quality standard based on a set of test results. The prediction subject is a component, and the descriptive features are a set of characteristics of the component that can be gathered on the production line. The target feature is binary and labels components as *good* or *bad*.

     It is extremely important that the system not in any way slow the production line and that the possibility of defective components being passed by the system be minimized as much as possible. Furthermore, when the system makes a mistake, it is desirable that the system can be retrained immediately using the instance that generated the mistake. When mistakes are made, it would be useful for the production line operators to be able to query the model to understand why it made the prediction that led to a mistake. A large set of historical labeled data is available for training the system.

     a. Discuss the different issues that should be taken into account when evaluating the suitability of different machine learning approaches for use in this system.

     b. For this task, discuss the suitability of the decision tree, k nearest neighbor, naive Bayes, and logistic regression models. Which one do you think would be most appropriate?

9   Case Study: Customer Churn

There is only one boss. The customer. And he can fire everybody in the company from the chairman on down, simply by spending his money somewhere else.
—Sam Walton

Acme Telephonica (AT) is a mobile phone operator that has customers across every state of the U.S.A. Like every telecommunications company, AT struggles with customer **churn**—customers leaving AT for other mobile phone operators. AT is always looking for new ways to address the churn issue and in 2008 founded a **customer retention** team. The customer retention team monitors the number of calls made to the AT customer support center by each customer and identifies the customers who make a large number of customer support calls as churn risks. The customer retention team contacts these customers with special offers designed to entice them to stay with AT. This approach, however, has not proved particularly successful, and churn has been steadily increasing over the last five years.

In 2010 AT hired Ross, a predictive data analytics specialist, to take a new approach to reducing customer churn. This case study describes the work carried out by Ross when he took AT through the CRISP-DM process[1] in order to develop a predictive data analytics solution to this business problem. The remainder of this chapter will discuss how each phase of the CRISP-DM process was addressed in this project.

9.1   Business Understanding

As is the case in most predictive data analytics projects, AT did not approach Ross with a well-specified predictive analytics solution. Instead, the company approached him with a business problem—reducing customer churn. Therefore, Ross's first goal was to convert this business problem into a concrete analytics solution. Before attempting this conversion, Ross had to fully understand the business objectives of AT. This was reasonably straightforward as AT management had stated that their goal was to reduce their customer churn rates. The only factor left unspecified was what the magnitude of that reduction was expected to be. Based on previous projects he had worked on, the current approach to customer retention that AT was taking, and AT's historical data, Ross agreed with AT management that a target reduction from the current

---

1 See Section 1.5[12].

high of approximately 10% to approximately 7.5% was realistic and probably achievable. Ross did stress to AT management that until he actually examined the data, he could not know how useful a model he would be able to build.

Ross's next task was to fully assess the current situation within AT. In particular, Ross needed to understand the current analytics capability of the company and its readiness to take action in response to the insights that an analytics solution would provide. AT already had a customer retention team proactively making interventions in an effort to reduce customer churn. Furthermore, this team was already using data from within the organization to choose which customers to target for intervention, which suggested that the team members were in a position to use predictive data analytics models.

Ross spent a significant amount of time meeting with Kate, the leader of the customer retention team, in order to understand how they worked. Kate explained that at the end of every month, a call list was generated, capturing the customers who had made more than three calls to the AT customer support service in the previous two months. These customers were deemed to be at risk of churning in the coming month, so the customer retention team set about contacting them with a special offer. Typically, the offer was a reduced call rate for the next three months, although retention team members had the freedom to make other offers.

Ross also spoke to the chief technology officer (CTO) at AT, Grace, in order to understand the available data resources. Ross learned that AT had reasonably sophisticated transactional systems for recording recent call activity and billing information. Historic call and bill records as well as customer demographic information were stored in a data warehouse. Grace had played a significant role in developing the process that had made information about customer support contacts available to the customer retention team. Ross hoped that this would make his task a little easier because Grace was the main gate-keeper to all the data resources at AT, and having her support for the project would be important. Other parts of the business that Ross spent significant time interviewing included the billing department, the sales and marketing team, and the network management.

Throughout the early stages of the project, Ross had been consciously working on developing his **situational fluency**. Through his discussions with the AT management team, Kate, and Grace, he had learned a lot about the mobile phone industry. The basic structure of the AT business was that customers had a contract for call services that AT provided. These contracts did not have a fixed time and were essentially renewed every month when a customer paid a fixed **recurring charge** for that month. Paying the recurring charge entitled a customer to a **bundle** of minutes of call time that were offered at a reduction to the standard call rate. For different recurring fees, customers received different sized bundles of call time. When a customer used up all the call time in his or her bundle, subsequent call time was referred to as **over bundle minutes**. These tended to be more expensive than the minutes included as part of a customer's bundle. At AT, all calls were classified as either **peak time calls** or **off-peak time calls**. Peak time was 08:00 to 18:00 from Monday to Friday, and calls made during peak time were more expensive than calls made during off-peak times.

Based on his assessment of the current situation within AT, Ross developed a list of ways that predictive analytics could help address the customer churn problem at AT. These included finding answers to the following questions:

- **What is the overall lifetime value of a customer?** A model could be built to predict the overall value that AT was likely to receive from a particular customer over the person's entire customer lifecycle. This could be used to identify customers that currently did not look valuable but that were likely to be valuable customers later in their customer lifecycles (college students often fall into this category). By offering these customers incentives now to prevent them from churning, AT would ensure that it received the full value from these customers in the future.

- **Which customers were most likely to churn in the near future?** A prediction model could be trained to identify the customers from the AT customer base that were most likely to churn in the near future. The retention team could focus their retention efforts on these customers. The process that the AT retention team had in place at the beginning of the project to identify customers likely to churn took a single feature approach to this identification—they looked only at how many calls a customer had made to the AT customer support service. It was likely that a machine learning model that looked at multiple features would do a better job of identifying customers likely to churn.

- **What retention offer would a particular customer best respond to?** A system could be built to predict which offer, from a set of possible retention offers, a particular customer would be most likely respond to when contacted by the AT retention team. This could help the retention team convince more customers to stay with AT.

- **Which pieces of the network infrastructure were likely to fail in the near future?** Using information about network loads, network usage, and equipment diagnostics, a predictive model could be built to flag upcoming equipment failures so that pre-emptive action could be taken. Network outages are a driver of customer dissatisfaction and ultimately customer churn, so reducing these could have a positive impact on churn rates.

After discussion with the AT executive team, it was decided that the analytics solution most appropriate to focus on was predicting *which customers are most likely to churn in the near future.* There were a number of reasons this project was selected:

- Ross's previous discussions with Grace, the AT CTO, had established that the data required to build a churn prediction model were likely to be available and reasonably easily accessible.

- The prediction model could be easily integrated with AT's current business processes. AT already had a retention team in place that was making proactive interventions to help prevent churn, albeit using a very simple system to identify which customers to contact. By creating a more sophisticated model to identify those customers, this existing process would be improved.

- Building a churn prediction model was also attractive to the AT executive team, as they hoped that as well as being useful in reducing churn rates, it would help to explain the main drivers behind customer churn. Better understanding of the main drivers of customer churn would be useful to many other parts of the AT business.

By contrast, the other analytics solutions developed suffered from a lack of available data (e.g., AT had no data available on the success or otherwise of various retention offers made); from being too significant a change in the business processes used by AT to be considered achievable at the time (e.g., generating a prediction of the overall lifetime value of a customer); or from not being based on sufficiently well-grounded assumptions (e.g., the fact that customer churn is heavily influenced by network failures).

Once the analytics solution had been defined, the next step was to agree on the expected performance of the new analytics model. Based on a recent evaluation of historical performance, AT management believed at the time of this project that their current system for identifying likely churners had an accuracy of approximately 60%, so any newly developed system would have to perform considerably better than this to be deemed worthwhile. In consultation with the members of the AT executive team and the retention team, Ross agreed that his goal would be to create a churn prediction system that would achieve a prediction accuracy in excess of 75%.

9.2   Data Understanding

During the process of determining which analytics solution was most suitable for the current situation at AT, Ross had already begun to understand the data resources available. His next task was to add much more depth to this understanding, following the process described in Section 2.3[27]. This involved working very closely with Grace to understand what data was available, the formats that the data was kept in, and where the data resided. This understanding would form the basis of Ross's work on designing the **domain concepts** and **descriptive features** that would make up the **analytics base table** (**ABT**), which would drive the creation of the predictive model. This was an iterative process in which Ross moved back and forth between Kate at the AT retention team, Grace, the CTO, and other parts of the business identified as having insight into the data associated with customer churn. It quickly became apparent that the key data resources within AT that would be important for this project were

- The customer demographic records from the AT data warehouse
- The customer billing records stored in the AT billing database, records stretch back over a time horizon of 5 years
- The transactional record of calls made by individuals, stretching back over a time horizon of 18 months
- The sales team's transactional database, containing details of phone handsets issued to customers
- The retention team's simple transactional database, containing all the contacts they had made with customers, and the outcomes of these contacts, stretching back to a time horizon of 12 months

Before going any further, Ross had to define the **prediction subject** for the ABT and the target feature. The goal was to develop a model that would predict whether a customer would churn in the coming months. This meant that the prediction subject in this case was a customer, so the ABT would need to be built to contain one row per customer.

Predicting churn is a form of **propensity modeling**,[2] where the event of interest in this case is a customer making the decision to churn. Consequently, Ross needed to agree with the business (in particular the customer retention team) on a definition of churn. The definition would be used to identify churn events in AT's historical data and, consequently, was fundamental to building the ABT for the project. The business agreed that a customer who had been inactive for 1 month (i.e., had not made any calls or paid a bill) or who had explicitly canceled or not renewed a contract would be considered to have churned. Ross also needed to define the lengths of the **observation period** and the **outcome period** for the model. He decided that the **observation period**, during which he would collect data on customer behavior, would stretch back for 12 months. This was a decision made based on the data available and Ross's expectation that anything further back than this was likely to have little impact on predicting churn. With regard to defining the **outcome period**, the company agreed that it would be most useful to make a prediction that a customer was likely to churn three months before the churn event took place, as this gave them time to take retention actions. Consequently, the outcome period was defined as three months.[3]

With the target feature suitably defined, Ross's next task was to determine the domain concepts that would underpin the design of the ABT. The domain concepts are those areas that the business believes have an impact on a customer's decision to churn. The domain concepts were developed through a series of workshops with representatives of various parts of the AT business—in particular the retention team, but also sales and marketing and billing. AT believed that the main concepts that affected churn were underlying customer demographics (e.g., perhaps younger customers were more likely to churn); customer billing information, and in particular changes in billing patterns (e.g., perhaps customers whose bill suddenly increased were more likely to churn); the details of a customer's handset (e.g., perhaps customers who have had a handset for a long time are more likely to churn); the interactions a customer has had with AT customer care (e.g., perhaps customers who are making a large number of calls to customer care are having difficulties with the AT network and so are likely to churn); and the actual calls the customer is making,

---

2 See Section 2.4.3[37].

3 Obviously, churn events will happen on different dates for different customers; therefore to build the ABT, the observation and outcome periods for different customers would have to be aligned. This situation is an example of the propensity model scenario illustrated in Figure 2.6[39] in Section 2.4.3[37].

in particular, changing call patterns (e.g., perhaps customers who have started making calls to new groups of people are more likely to churn). This set of domain concepts was felt to be extensive enough to cover all the characteristics that were likely to contribute toward a customer's likelihood to churn and is shown in Figure 9.1[469].

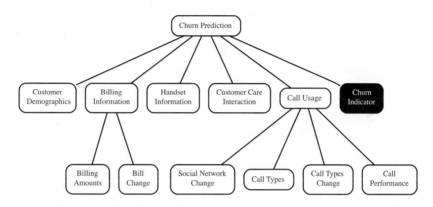

Figure 9.1

The set of domain concepts for the Acme Telephonica customer churn prediction problem.

From these domain concepts, Ross worked on deriving a set of descriptive features. Some of the descriptive features were simply copies of available raw data. For example, the AGE, GENDER, CREDITRATING, and OCCUPATION columns from the customer demographics data warehouse could be directly included as descriptive features in the ABT to capture the CUSTOMER DEMOGRAPHICS domain concept. The more interesting descriptive features were ones that had to be derived from the raw data sources. For example, Ross learned that the retention team believed that one of the main reasons customers churned was the availability of new, high-end handsets at other networks. To try to capture the HANDSET INFORMATION domain concept Ross, designed three descriptive features:

- SMARTPHONE: This feature indicated whether the customer's current handset was a smart phone, this was derived from the customer's most recent handset entry.

- NUMHANDSETS: This was a count of how many different handsets the customer had had in the past three years. This was derived from a count of all the handset entries for a particular customer.

- HANDSETAGE: Based on a customer's latest handset entry, this feature captured the number of days that the customer had had his or her current handset.

In churn analysis, and in any sort of propensity modeling, change is usually a key driver of customer behavior. For this reason, and based on discussions with the AT team, Ross included the BILL CHANGE and SOCIAL NETWORK CHANGE domain concepts. It was understood by the AT retention team that customers often made a decision to churn if their bill increased significantly due to changing call patterns, or when they began to make large numbers of calls to new friends or colleagues on other networks. For these reasons, Ross designed the following descriptive features:

- CALLMINUTESCHANGEPCT: Derived from the raw call data, this feature captured the amount by which the number of minutes a customer used had changed that month compared to the previous month.

- BILLAMOUNTCHANGEPCT: Derived from the raw call data, this feature captured the amount by which a customer's bill had changed that month compared to previous month.

- NEWFREQUENTNUMBERS: Derived from analysis of the actual numbers dialed in the raw call data, this feature attempted to capture how many new numbers a customer has begun calling frequently that month. A frequent number was defined as a number that constituted more than 15% of a customer's total calls.

Often descriptive features that are likely to be very useful cannot be implemented due to the unavailability of data. For example, the AT team felt that a customer beginning to frequently call other networks would be a good indicator of churn, but a suitable data feature could not be extracted to capture this. In its call records, AT did not include information about which network calls are made to, and with the free movement of numbers among operators, numbers themselves were no longer a reliable indicator of network.

The full set of descriptive features Ross developed, along with a short description of each, is shown in Table 9.1[471].

Table 9.1

The descriptive features in the ABT developed for the Acme Telephonica churn prediction task.

Feature	Description
BILLAMOUNTCHANGEPCT	The percentage by which the customer's bill has changed from last month to this month
CALLMINUTESCHANGEPCT	The percentage by which the call minutes used by the customer has changed from last month to this month
AVGBILL	The average monthly bill amount
AVGRECURRINGCHARGE	The average monthly recurring charge paid by the customer
AVGDROPPEDCALLS	The average number of customer calls dropped each month
PEAKRATIOCHANGEPCT	The percentage by which the customer's peak calls to off-peak calls ratio has changed from last month to this month
AVGRECEIVEDMINS	The average number of calls received each month by the customer
AVGMINS	The average number of call minutes used by the customer each month
AVGOVERBUNDLEMINS	The average number of out-of-bundle minutes used by the customer each month
AVGROAMCALLS	The average number of roaming calls made by the customer each month
PEAKOFFPEAKRATIO	The ratio between peak and off-peak calls made by the customer this month
NEWFREQUENTNUMBERS	How many new numbers the customer is frequently calling this month
CUSTOMERCARECALLS	The number of customer care calls made by the customer last month
NUMRETENTIONCALLS	The number of times the customer has been called by the retention team
NUMRETENTIONOFFERS	The number of retention offers the customer has accepted
AGE	The customer's age
CREDITRATING	The customer's credit rating
INCOME	The customer's income level
LIFETIME	The number of months the customer has been with AT
OCCUPATION	The customer's occupation
REGIONTYPE	The type of region the customer lives in
HANDSETPRICE	The price of the customer's current handset
HANDSETAGE	The age of the customer's current handset
NUMHANDSETS	The number of handsets the customer has had in the past 3 years
SMARTPHONE	Whether the customer's current handset is a smart phone
CHURN	The target feature

9.3 Data Preparation

With help from Grace to implement the actual data manipulation and data integration scripts using the tools available at AT, Ross populated an ABT containing all the features listed in Table 9.1[471]. Ross sampled data from the period 2008 to 2013. Using the definition of churn as a customer who had not made any calls or paid a bill for 1 month, Ross was able to identify churn events throughout this time period. To collect instances of customers who had not

churned, Ross randomly sampled customers who did not match the churn definition but who also could be deemed active customers. Working with Kate,
Ross defined an active customer as current customer who made at least 5 calls
per week and who had been a customer for at least 6 months.[4] This definition ensured that the non-churn instances in the dataset would include only
customers with a relatively normal behavior profile and for which there was a
long enough data history that realistic descriptive features could be calculated
for them.

The final ABT contained 10,000 instances equally split between customers
who churned and customers who did not churn. In the raw data, customers who
did not churn outnumber those that churned at a ratio of over 10 to 1. This is an
example of an **imbalanced dataset**, in which the different levels of the target
feature—in this case, churners and non-churners—are not equally represented
in the data. Some of the machine learning approaches we have discussed in
the preceding chapters perform better when a **balanced sample** is used to train
them, and this is why Ross created an ABT with equal numbers of instances
with each target level.[5]

Ross then developed a full data quality report for the ABT including a
range of data visualizations. The data quality report tables are shown in Table
9.2[476]. Ross first assessed the level of **missing values** within the data. Within
the continuous features, only AGE stood out with 11.47% of values missing.
This could be handled reasonably easily using an imputation approach,[6] but
Ross held off on performing this at this stage. The REGIONTYPE and OCCU-
PATION categorical features both suffered from a significant number of missing values—74% and 47.8% respectively. Ross strongly considered removing
these features entirely.

When he considered **cardinality**, Ross noticed that a number of the
continuous features had very low cardinality—for example, INCOME, AGE,
NUMHANDSETS, HANDSETPRICE, and NUMRETENTIONCALLS. In most
cases, Ross confirmed with Kate and Grace that these were valid because the

---

4 The fact that active customers were defined as *current customers* means that they were all active
on the same date—namely, whatever day the ABT was generated. This could be problematic: a
model trained on this data might ignore seasonal effects such as Christmas. The alternative is
to define active customers as any customer in the AT data that was active at some point. Such
a definition, however, has the complication that the same customer could appear in the ABT as
both an active and a churn customer, although admittedly the descriptive features for these two
instances would be calculated over different periods of dates.

5 We return to this discussion in Section 9.5[479] and Section 10.4.1[500].

6 See Section 3.4[73].

range of values that the features could take was naturally low. For example, HANDSETPRICE can take only a small number of values—e.g., 59.99, 129.99, 499.99, and so on. The INCOME feature stood out as unusual with only 10 distinct values (the histogram for this feature confirmed this; see Figure 9.2(a)[474]). Grace explained to Ross that incomes were actually recorded in bands rather than as exact values, so this was really a categorical feature. The cardinality of the CREDITCARD and REGIONTYPE categorical features were higher than expected (the histograms for these features are shown in Figures 9.2(b)[474] and 9.2(c)[474]). The issue was that some levels had multiple representations—for example, for the REGIONTYPE feature, towns were represented as *town* and as *t*. Ross easily corrected this issue by mapping the levels of the feature to one consistent labeling scheme.

Four continuous features stood out as possibly suffering from the presence of **outliers**: HANDSETPRICE, with a minimum value of 0, which seemed unusual; AVGMINS, with a maximum of 6,336.25, which was very different from the mean and the 3rd quartile values for that feature; AVGRECEIVEDMINS, with a maximum of 2,006.29, which was also very different from the mean and the 3rd quartile values for that feature; and AVGOVERBUNDLEMINS, with minimum, 1st quartile, and median values of 0 compared to a mean of 40. Figure 9.2[474] presents the histograms for these features. Ross confirmed with Grace and Kate that these were valid outliers—for example, some handsets are given away for free, and some customers just make a lot of calls. They did spend some time, however, discussing the AVGOVERBUNDLEMINS. The histogram for this feature has an unusual shape that results in the unusual minimum, 1st quartile, and median values (see Figure 9.2(g)[474]). By examining the data for this feature more closely, they eventually explained this shape by the fact that most customers did not go over the number of minutes in their bundle, which accounts for the large bar for 0 in this histogram. The values above zero seem to follow something close to a wide normal distribution, and the large number of, albeit valid, zero values account for the unusual minimum, 1st quartile, and median values. At this point Ross just made note of these outliers as something he might have to deal with during the modeling phase.

Ross then turned his attention to examining the data visualizations of the relationship between each descriptive feature and the target feature. No individual feature stood out as having a very strong relationship, but the evidence of connections between the descriptive features and the target feature could be

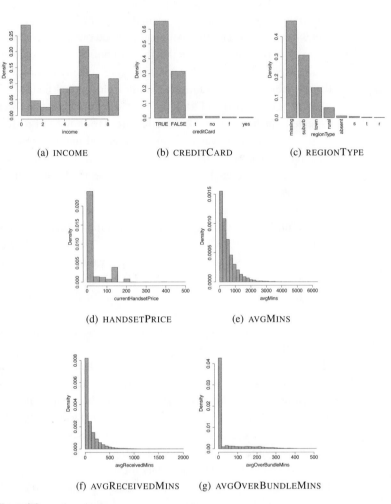

Figure 9.2

(a)–(c) Histograms for the features from the AT ABT with irregular cardinality; (d)–(g) histograms for the features from the AT ABT that are potentially suffering from outliers.

seen. For example, Figure 9.3(a)[475] shows a slightly higher propensity of people in rural areas to churn. Similarly, Figure 9.3(b)[475] shows that customers who churned tended to make more calls outside their *bundle* than those who did not.

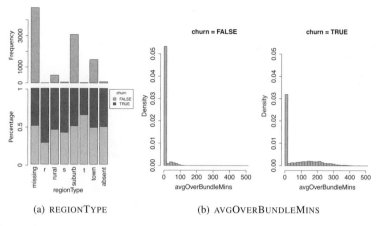

(a) REGIONTYPE   (b) AVGOVERBUNDLEMINS

Figure 9.3

(a) A stacked bar plot for the REGIONTYPE feature; (b) histograms for the AVGOVER-BUNDLEMINS feature by target feature value.

Once Ross had reviewed the full data quality report in detail, he made the following decisions regarding the problematic features he had identified. First, he decided to delete the AGE and OCCUPATION features because of the level of missing values in each of these features. He decided to keep the REGION-TYPE feature, however, because it appeared to have some relationship with the target. He also applied the planned mapping of the REGIONTYPE values to a consistent labeling scheme: $\{s|suburb\} \rightarrow suburb$; $\{t|town\} \rightarrow town$; $\{missing|absent\} \rightarrow missing$.

Ross further divided this dataset into three randomly sampled partitions—a training partition (50%), a validation partition (20%) and a test partition (30%). The training partition was used as the core training data for the prediction models built. The validation partition was used for tuning tasks, and the test partition was used for nothing other than a final test of the model to evaluate its performance.

Table 9.2

A data quality report for the Acme Telephonic ABT.

(a) Data quality report for continuous features

Feature	Count	% Miss.	Card.	Min.	1st Qrt.	Mean	Median	3rd Qrt.	Max.	Std. Dev.
AGE	10,000	11.47	40	0.00	0.00	30.32	34.00	48.00	98.00	22.16
INCOME	10,000	0.00	10	0.00	0.00	4.30	5.00	7.00	9.00	3.14
NUMHANDSETS	10,000	0.00	19	1.00	1.00	1.81	1.00	2.00	21.00	1.35
HANDSETAGE	10,000	0.00	1,923	52.00	590.00	905.52	887.50	1,198.00	2,679.00	453.75
HANDSETPRICE	10,000	0.00	16	0.00	0.00	35.73	0.00	59.99	499.99	57.07
AVGBILL	10,000	0.00	5,588	0.00	33.33	58.93	49.21	71.76	584.23	43.89
AVGMINS	10,000	0.00	4,461	0.00	150.63	521.17	359.63	709.19	6,336.25	540.44
AVGRECURRINGCHARGE	10,000	0.00	1,380	0.00	30.00	46.24	44.99	59.99	337.98	23.97
AVGOVERBUNDLEMINS	10,000	0.00	2,808	0.00	0.00	40.65	0.00	37.73	513.84	81.12
AVGROAMCALLS	10,000	0.00	850	0.00	0.00	1.19	0.00	0.26	177.99	6.05
CALLMINUTESCHANGEPCT	10,000	0.00	10,000	-16.422	-1.49	0.76	0.50	2.74	19.28	3.86
BILLAMOUNTCHANGEPCT	10,000	0.00	10,000	-31.67	-2.63	2.96	1.96	7.56	42.89	8.51
AVGRECEIVEDMINS	10,000	0.00	7,103	0.00	7.69	115.27	52.54	154.38	2,006.29	169.98
AVGOUTCALLS	10,000	0.00	524	0.00	3.00	25.29	13.33	33.33	610.33	35.66
AVGINCALLS	10,000	0.00	310	0.00	0.00	8.37	2.00	9.00	304.00	17.68
PEAKOFFPEAKRATIO	10,000	0.00	8,307	0.00	0.78	2.22	1.40	2.50	160.00	3.88
PEAKRATIOCHANGEPCT	10,000	0.00	10,000	-41.32	-6.79	-0.05	0.01	6.50	37.78	9.97
AVGDROPPEDCALLS	10,000	0.00	1,479	0.00	0.00	0.50	0.00	0.00	9.89	1.41
LIFETIME	10,000	0.00	56	6.00	11.00	18.84	17.00	24.00	61.00	9.61
CUSTOMERCARECALLS	10,000	0.00	109	0.00	0.00	1.74	0.00	1.33	365.67	5.76
NUMRETENTIONCALLS	10,000	0.00	5	0.00	0.00	0.05	0.00	0.00	4.00	0.23
NUMRETENTIONOFFERS	10,000	0.00	5	0.00	0.00	0.02	0.00	0.00	4.00	0.155
NEWFREQUENTNUMBERS	10,000	0.00	4	0.00	0.00	0.20	0.00	0.00	3.00	0.64

(b) Data quality report for categorical features

Feature	Count	% Miss.	Card.	Mode	Mode Freq.	Mode %	2nd Mode	2nd Mode Freq.	2nd Mode %
OCCUPATION	10,000	74.00	8	professional	1,705	65.58	crafts	274	10.54
REGIONTYPE	10,000	47.80	8	suburb	3,085	59.05	town	1,483	28.39
MARRIAGESTATUS	10,000	0.00	3	unknown	3,920	39.20	yes	3,594	35.94
CHILDREN	10,000	0.00	2	false	7,559	75.59	true	2,441	24.41
SMARTPHONE	10,000	0.00	2	true	9,015	90.15	false	985	9.85
CREDITRATING	10,000	0.00	7	b	3,785	37.85	c	1,713	17.13
HOMEOWNER	10,000	0.00	2	false	6,577	65.77	true	3,423	34.23
CREDITCARD	10,000	0.00	6	true	6,537	65.37	false	3,146	31.46
CHURN	10,000	0.00	2	false	5,000	50.00	true	5,000	50.00

9.4   Modeling

The requirements for this model were that it be accurate, that it be capable of being integrated into the wider AT processes, and, possibly, that it act as a source of insight into the reasons people might churn. In selecting the appropriate model type to use, all these aspects, along with the structure of the data, should be taken into account. In this case, the ABT was composed of a mixture of continuous and categorical descriptive features and had a categorical target feature. The categorical target feature, in particular, makes decision trees a suitable choice for this modeling task. Furthermore, decision tree algorithms are capable of handling both categorical and continuous descriptive features as well as handling missing values and outliers without any need to transform the data. Finally, decision trees are relatively easy to interpret, which means that the structure of the model can give some insight into customer behavior. All these factors taken together indicated that decision trees were an appropriate modeling choice for this problem.

Ross used the ABT to train, tune, and test a series of decision trees to predict churn given the set of descriptive features. The first tree that Ross built used an entropy-based information gain as the splitting criterion, limited continuous splits to binary choices, and no pruning. Ross had decided, again in consultation with the business, that a simple classification accuracy rate was the most appropriate evaluation measure for this task. The first tree constructed achieved an **average class accuracy**[7] of 74.873% on the hold-out test set, which was reasonably encouraging.

Figure 9.4

An unpruned decision tree built for the AT churn prediction problem (shown only to indicate its size and complexity). The excessive complexity and depth of the tree are evidence that overfitting has probably occurred.

---

7 All average class accuracies used in this section use a **harmonic mean**.

This tree is shown in Figure 9.4[477] and the lack of pruning is obvious in its complexity. This complexity and the excessive depth of the tree suggest over-fitting. In the second tree that he built, Ross employed **post-pruning** using **reduced error pruning**,[8] which used the validation partition that was created from the initial dataset. The reasonably large dataset that Ross had to begin with, which in turn led to a reasonably large validation partition, meant that reduced error pruning was appropriate in this case.[9] Figure 9.5[478] shows the tree resulting from this training iteration. It should be clear that this is a much simpler tree than the previous one. The features used at the top levels of both trees, and deemed most informative by the algorithm, were the same: AVGOVERBUNDLEMINS, BILLAMOUNTCHANGEPCT, and HANDSETAGE.

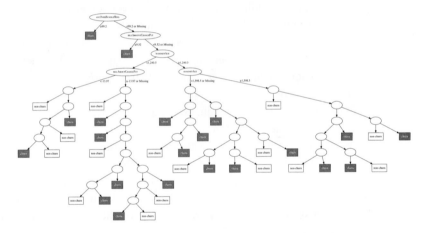

Figure 9.5

A pruned decision tree built for the AT churn prediction problem. Gray leaf nodes indicate a churn prediction, while clear leaf nodes indicate a non-churn prediction. For space reasons, we show only the features tested at the top level nodes.

Using pruning, Ross was able to increase the average class accuracy on the hold-out test set to 79.03%, a significant improvement over the previous model. Table 9.3[479] shows the confusion matrix from this test. The confusion matrix shows that this model was slightly more accurate when classifying instances with the *non-churn* target level than with the *churn* target level. Based on these,

---

8 See Section 4.4.4[158].

9 If data had been more scarce, pruning using a statistical test, such as χ^2, would have been a more sensible route to take.

Table 9.3

The confusion matrix from the test of the AT churn prediction stratified hold-out test set using the pruned decision tree in Figure 9.5[478].

| | | \multicolumn{2}{c}{Prediction} | |
		churn	non-churn	Recall
Target	churn	1,058	442	70.53
	non-churn	152	1,348	89.86

Table 9.4

The confusion matrix from the test of the AT churn prediction non-stratified hold-out test set.

| | | \multicolumn{2}{c}{Prediction} | |
		churn	non-churn	Recall
Target	churn	1,115	458	70.88
	non-churn	1,439	12,878	89.95

results Ross was confident that this tree was a good solution for the AT churn prediction problem.

9.5 Evaluation

The model evaluations based on misclassification rate described in the previous section are the first step in evaluating the performance of the prediction model created. The classification accuracy of 79.03% is well above the target agreed on with the business. This is misleading, however. This performance is based on a stratified hold-out test set, which contains the same number of churners and non-churners. The underlying distribution of churners and non-churners within the larger AT customer base, however, is much different. Rather than a 50:50 split of churners to non-churners, the actual underlying ratio is, in fact, closer to 10:90. For this reason, it is very important to perform a second evaluation in which the test data reflect the actual distribution of target feature values in the business scenario.

Ross had AT generate a second data sample (which did not overlap with the sample taken previously) that was not stratified according to the target feature values. The confusion matrix illustrating the performance of the prediction model on this test set is shown in Table 9.4[479].

The average class accuracy on the non-stratified hold-out test set was 79.284%. Ross also generated **cumulative gain**, **lift**, and **cumulative lift** charts for the dataset.[10] These are shown in Figure 9.6[480]. The cumulative gain chart in particular shows that if AT were to call just 40% of their customer base, they would identify approximately 80% of the customers who are likely to churn, which is strong evidence that the model is doing a good job of distinguishing between different customer types.

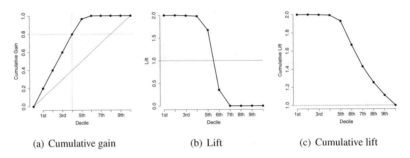

(a) Cumulative gain   (b) Lift   (c) Cumulative lift

Figure 9.6
(a) Cumulative gain, (b) lift, and (c) cumulative lift charts for the predictions made on the large test data sample.

Given these good results Ross decided that it was appropriate to present the model to other parts of the business. This was an important step in gaining credibility for the model. The tree shown in Figure 9.5[478] is reasonably straight forward to interpret, but when taken out to other parts of the business, it may be hard for people to deal with this much information, so Ross decided to create a purposefully stunted version of the decision tree, with only a small number of levels shown for the presentation of the model to the business (although he intended to use the larger pruned tree for actual deployment). The idea behind this was that stunting the tree made it more interpretable. The fact that the most informative features occupy berths toward the top of a tree means that stunted trees usually capture the most important information. Many machine learning tools will allow the maximum depth of a tree to be specified as a parameter, which allows for the creation of such **stunted trees**.

Figure 9.7[481] shows the stunted tree Ross generated for the churn problem, where the depth of the tree is limited to 5 generations. This tree results in a slightly lower classification accuracy on the test partition, 78.5%, but

10 **Cumulative gain**, **lift**, and **cumulative lift** are introduced in Section 8.4.3.3[432].

is very easy to interpret—the key features in determining churn are clearly AVGOVERBUNDLEMINS, BILLAMOUNTCHANGEPCT, and HANDSETAGE. It seems, from this data, that customers are most likely to churn when their bill changes dramatically, when they begin to exceed the bundled minutes in their call package, or when they have had a handset for a long time and are considering changing to something newer. This is useful information that the business can use to attempt to devise other churn handling strategies in parallel to using this model to create call lists for the retention team. The business was interested in the features that were selected as important to the tree, and there was a good deal of discussion on the omission of the features describing customers' interactions with AT customer care (these had been the basis of the organization's previous model).

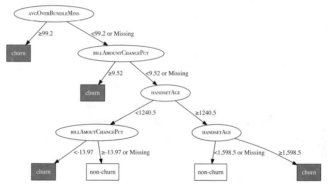

Figure 9.7
A pruned and stunted decision tree built for the Acme Telephonica churn prediction problem.

To further support his model, Ross organized a control group test (see Section 8.4.6[447]) in which for two months, the AT customer base was randomly divided into two groups, and call lists for the retention team were selected from the first group using the old approach based on calls to customer care, and for the second group using the new decision tree model. It was shown after two months that the churn rate within the sample for which the retention team used the new model to build their call list was approximately 7.4%, while for the group using the old model, it was over 10%. This experiment showed the AT executive team that the new decision tree model could significantly reduce churn rates within the AT customer base.

9.6 Deployment

Because AT was already using a process in which its retention team generated call lists based on collected data, deployment of the new decision tree model was reasonably straightforward. The main challenge was a return to the Data Preparation phase to make the routines used to extract the data for the ABT robust and reliable enough to be used to generate new query instances every month. This involved working with the AT IT department to develop deployment-ready **extract-transform-load** (ETL) routines. Code was then written to replace the previous simple rule about customer care contacts with the decision tree when retention call lists were generated.

The last step in deployment was to put in place an **on-going model validation** plan to raise an alarm if evidence arose indicating that the deployed model had gone **stale**. In this scenario, feedback on the performance of the model implicitly arises within a reasonably short amount of time after predictions are made—churn predictions can be easily compared to actual customer behavior (taking into account interventions made by the business). The monitoring system that Ross put in place generated a report at the end of every quarter that evaluated the performance of the model in the previous quarter by comparing how many of the people not contacted by the retention team actually churned. If this number changed significantly from what was seen in the data used to build the model, the model would be deemed stale, and retraining would be required.

10 Case Study: Galaxy Classification

The history of astronomy is a history of receding horizons.
—Edwin Powell Hubble

Astronomy has gone through a revolution in recent years as the reducing costs of digital imaging has made it possible to collect orders of magnitude more data than ever before. Large-scale sky scanning projects are being used to map the whole of the night sky in intricate detail. This offers huge potential for new science based on this massive data collection effort. This progress comes at a cost, however, as all this data must be labeled, tagged, and cataloged. The old approach of doing all this manually has become obsolete because the volume of data involved is just too large.

The **Sloan Digital Sky Survey** (**SDSS**) is a landmark project that is cataloging the night sky in intricate detail and is facing exactly the problem described above.[1] The SDSS telescopes collect over 175GB of data every night, and for the data collected to be fully exploited for science, each night sky object captured must be identified and cataloged within this data in almost real time. Although the SDSS has been able to put in place algorithmic solutions to identifying certain objects within the images collected, there have been a number of difficulties. In particular, it has not been possible for the SDSS to develop a solution to automatically categorize galaxies into the different **morphological** groups—for example, spiral galaxies or elliptical galaxies.

This case study[2] describes the work undertaken when, in 2011, the SDSS hired Jocelyn, an analytics professional, to build a galaxy morphology classification model to include in their data processing pipeline. The remainder of this chapter describes the work undertaken by Jocelyn on this project within each phase of the CRISP-DM process.

10.1 Business Understanding

When Jocelyn first arrived at SDSS, she was pleased to find that the business problem she was being asked to help with was already pretty well defined in predictive analytics terms. The SDSS pipeline takes the data captured by the

---

1 Full details of the SDSS project, which is fascinating, are available at `www.sdss.org`.

2 Although this case study is based on real data downloaded from the SDSS, the case study itself is entirely fictitious and developed only for the purposes of this book. Very similar work to that described in this section has, however, actually been undertaken, and details of representative examples are given in Section 10.6[509].

SDSS instruments and processes it, before storing the results of this processing in a centrally accessible database. At the time Jocelyn arrived, the SDSS pipeline included rule-based systems that could classify night sky objects into broad categories—for example, stars and galaxies. SDSS scientists, however, were struggling to build rule-based systems that could accurately perform more fine-grained classifications. In particular, the SDSS scientists wanted a system that could reliably classify galaxies into the important morphological (i.e., shape) types: **elliptical galaxies** and **spiral galaxies**. Classifying galaxies according to **galaxy morphology** is standard practice in astronomy,[3] and morphological categories have been shown to be strongly correlated with other important galaxy features. So, grouping galaxies by morphological type is a fundamentally important step in analyzing the characteristics of galaxies.

This was the challenge that the SDSS had hired Jocelyn to address. The scientists at SDSS wanted Jocelyn to build a machine learning model that could examine sky objects that their current rule-based system had flagged as being galaxies and categorize them as belonging to the appropriate morphological group. Although there remained some details left to agree on, the fact that the SDSS had defined their problem in terms of analytics meant that Jocelyn very easily completed the important step of converting a business problem into an analytics solution. Edwin was assigned to Jocelyn as her key scientific contact from SDSS and was eager to answer any questions Jocelyn had as he saw real value in the model she was developing.

The first detail that Jocelyn needed to agree on with Edwin was the set of categories into which sky objects should be categorized. The scientists at SDSS listed two key galaxy morphologies of interest: *elliptical* and *spiral*. The spiral category further divided into *clockwise spiral* and *anti-clockwise spiral* subcategories. Figure 10.1[485] shows illustrations of these different galaxy types. Jocelyn suggested that she would first work on the coarse classification of galaxies into elliptical and spiral categories, and then, depending on how this model performed, look at classifying spirals into the more fine-grained categories. Jocelyn also suggested that a third *other* category be included to take into account the fact that all the sky objects labeled as galaxies in the previous step in the SDSS may not actually be galaxies. Edwin agreed with both of these suggestions.

The second detail that Jocelyn needed to agree on with Edwin was the target accuracy that would be required by the system she would build in order

---

3 This practice was first systematically applied by Edwin Hubble in 1936 (Hubble, 1936).

(a) Elliptical   (b) Clockwise spiral   (c) Anti-clockwise spiral

Figure 10.1
Examples of the different galaxy morphology categories into which SDSS scientists categorize galaxy objects. Credits for these images belong to the Sloan Digital Sky Survey, `www.sdss3.org`.

for it to be of use to scientists at SDSS. It is extremely important that analytics professionals manage the expectations of their clients during the business understanding process, and agreeing on expected levels of model performance is one of the easiest ways in which to do this. This avoids disappointment and difficulties at later stages in a project. After lengthy discussion, both Jocelyn and Edwin agreed that in order for the system to be useful, a classification accuracy of approximately 80% would be required. Jocelyn stressed that until she had looked at the data and performed experiments, she could not make any predictions as to what classification accuracy would be possible. She did, however, explain to Edwin that because the categorization of galaxy morphologies is a somewhat subjective task (even human experts don't always fully agree on the category that a night sky object should belong to), it was unlikely that classification accuracies beyond 90% would be achievable.

Finally, Edwin and Jocelyn discussed how fast the model built would need to be to allow its inclusion in the existing SDSS pipeline. Fully processed data from the SDSS pipeline is available to scientists approximately one week after images of night sky objects are captured by the SDSS telescopes.[4] The system that Jocelyn built would be added to the end of this pipeline because it would require outputs from existing data processing steps. It was important that the

---

4 In an interesting example of the persistence of good solutions using older technology, the data captured by the telescopes at the SDSS site in New Mexico is recorded onto magnetic tapes that are then couriered to the Feynman Computing Center at Fermilab in Illinois, over 1,000 miles away. This is the most effective way to transport the massive volumes of data involved!

model Jocelyn deployed not add a large delay to data becoming available to scientists. Based on the expected volumes of images that would be produced by the SDSS pipeline, Jocelyn and Edwin agreed that the model developed should be capable of performing approximately 1,000 classifications per second on a dedicated server of modest specification.

10.1.1   Situational Fluency

The notion of **situational fluency**[5] is especially important when dealing with scientific scenarios. It is important that analytics professionals have a basic grasp of the work their scientific partners are undertaking so that they can converse fluently with them. The real skill in developing situational fluency is determining how much knowledge about the application domain the analytics professional requires in order to complete the project successfully. It was not reasonable, nor necessary, to expect that Jocelyn would become fully familiar with the intricacies of the SDSS and the astronomy that it performs. Instead, she needed enough information to understand the key pieces of equipment involved, the important aspects of the night sky objects that she would be classifying, and the key terminology involved.

While complex scientific scenarios can make this process more difficult than is the case for more typical business applications, there is also the advantage that scientific projects typically produce publications clearly explaining their work. These kinds of publications are an invaluable resource for an analytics professional trying to come to grips with a new topic. Jocelyn read a number of publications by the SDSS team[6] before spending several sessions with Edwin discussing the work that he and his colleagues did. The following short summary of the important things she learned illustrates the level of situational fluency required for this kind of scenario.

The SDSS project captures two distinct kinds of data—images of night-sky objects and **spectrographs** of night sky objects—using two distinct types of instrument, an imaging camera and a spectrograph.

---

5 See Chapter 2[21].

6 Stoughton et al. (2002) provides an in-depth discussion of the data collected by the SDSS. A shorter overview is provided at `skyserver.sdss3.org/dr9/en/sdss/data/data.asp`.

The SSDS imaging camera captures images in *five* distinct **photometric bands**:[7] ultra-violet (*u*), green (*g*), red (*r*), far-red (*i*), and near infra-red (*z*). The raw imaging data captured from the SDSS telescopes is passed through a processing pipeline that identifies individual night sky objects and extracts a number of properties for each object. For galaxy classification, the most important properties extracted from the images are brightness, color, and shape. The measure of brightness used in the SDSS pipeline is referred to as **magnitude**. **Flux** is another measure that attempts to standardize measures of brightness, taking into account how far away different objects are from the telescope. Measures of flux and magnitude are made in each of the five photometric bands used by the SDSS imaging system. To measure the **color** of night sky objects, the flux measured in different photometric bands is compared. The image-based measures of overall galaxy shape are extracted from the images using **morphological** and **moment** image processing operations. These measures capture how well objects match template shapes—although none is accurate enough to actually perform the galaxy morphology prediction itself.

A **spectrograph** is a device that disperses the light emitted by an object into different wavelengths and measures the intensity of the emission of each wavelength—this set of measures is referred to as a **spectrogram**. The SDSS spectrographs perform this task for manually identified night sky objects and produce spectrograms across wavelengths from visible blue light to near-infrared light. Spectrography data may be useful in galaxy classification because different galaxy types are likely to emit different amounts of different light wavelengths, so spectrograms might be a good indicator for galaxy type. Spectrography also allows measurement of **redshift**, which is used to determine the distance of night sky objects from the viewer.

Once Jocelyn felt that she was suitably fluent with the SDSS situation, she proceeded to the Data Understanding phase of the CRISP-DM process so as to better understand the data available.

---

7 Most consumer digital cameras capture full color images by capturing separate images on red, green, and blue imaging sensors and combining these. The colors red, green, and blue are known as **photometric bands**. The photometric bands captured by the SDSS imaging camera are the same as these bands; they are just defined on different parts of the spectrum.

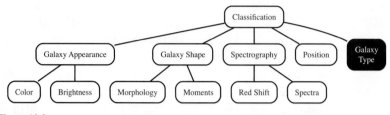

Figure 10.2
The first draft of the domain concepts diagram developed by Jocelyn for the galaxy classification task.

10.2   Data Understanding

Jocelyn's first step in fully understanding the data available to her was to define the **prediction subject**. In this case the task was to categorize galaxies according to morphology, and therefore galaxy made sense as the prediction subject. The structure of the dataset required for this task would contain one row per galaxy, and each row would include a set of descriptive features describing the characteristics of that galaxy object and a target feature indicating the morphological category of the galaxy object.

Based on her understanding of the SDSS process , Jocelyn sketched out the first draft of the domain concepts diagram for the galaxy classification problem shown in Figure 10.2[488]. Jocelyn felt that the important **domain concepts** were likely to be the target (galaxy type), galaxy appearance measures (e.g., color), spectrography information (e.g., red shift), and position information (the position of each object in the night sky was also available from the SDSS pipeline). Data with which to implement features based on these domain concepts would likely come from the raw camera imaging and spectrograph images themselves, or from the results of the SDSS processing pipeline.

Jocelyn took this first domain concept draft along to a meeting with Ted, the SDSS chief data architect, to discuss the data resources that would be available for model building. Ted quickly made two observations. First, the spectrograph data collected by the SDSS telescopes was not nearly as extensive as the camera imaging data collected—while there was imaging data for millions of galaxies, there were spectrograms for only hundreds of thousands. Collecting spectrographic information involves a much more complicated process than capturing imaging data, so it is done for a much smaller portion of the sky. This was likely to continue to be the case, so any solution that relied on spectrographic data as well as imaging data to classify galaxy types would work for only a fraction of the observations made by the SDSS telescopes.

Ted's second observation was that, although there was a huge amount of data available on past observations of night sky objects, only a tiny fraction of these contained manual labels indicating the morphological category to which they belonged. This meant that the data available at the SDSS did not contain a suitable target feature that Jocelyn could use to train prediction models. This is a very common scenario and a real thorn in the side of the predictive model builder—although there is often an almost endless amount of data available for training, little or none of it is labeled with the relevant target feature, making it effectively useless.

Jocelyn's options at this stage were (1) to embark on a large-scale manual data labeling project for which she would hire experts to manually label a suitably large set of historical night sky object observations, or (2) to find some other data source that she could add to the SDSS data to use as a target feature. While the first option is often used, Jocelyn was lucky that another data source became available. Through conversations with Edwin, Jocelyn became aware of a parallel project to the SDSS that offered an intriguing solution to her problem. **Galaxy Zoo**[8] is a **crowdsourced**, **citizen science** effort in which people can log onto a website and categorize images of galaxies—taken from the SDSS—into different groups. The Galaxy Zoo project started in 2007 and since then has collected millions of classifications of hundreds of thousands of galaxies.

The galaxy types that Galaxy Zoo citizen scientists could choose from were *elliptical, clockwise spiral, anti-clockwise spiral, edge-on disk, merger,* and *don't know*. The first three types are self-explanatory and match directly with the categories of interest to the SDSS project. An *edge-on disk* is a spiral galaxy viewed from the edge, which makes the direction of the spiral arms unclear. A *merger* is a sky object in which multiple galaxies appear grouped together. Examples were labeled as *don't know* when a Galaxy Zoo participant could not place the object in question into one of the other categories.

---

8 Full details of the Galaxy Zoo project and the data released by it are described in Lintott et al. (2011, 2008). The Galaxy Zoo (www.galaxyzoo.org) project referred to in this example is Galaxy Zoo I.

Table 10.1

The structure of the SDSS and Galaxy Zoo combined dataset.

Name	Type	Description
OBJID	Continuous	Unique SDSS object identifier
P_EL	Continuous	Fraction of votes for elliptical galaxy category
P_CW	Continuous	Fraction of votes for clockwise spiral galaxy category
P_ACW	Continuous	Fraction of votes for anti-clockwise spiral galaxy category
P_EDGE	Continuous	Fraction of votes for edge-on disk galaxy category
P_MG	Continuous	Fraction of votes for merger category
P_DK	Continuous	Fraction of votes for don't know category

The data from the Galaxy Zoo project was publicly available and therefore easily accessible to Jocelyn. Galaxy Zoo labels were available for approximately 600,000 SDSS galaxies, which Jocelyn felt would be more than enough to use to train and test a galaxy morphology classification model. Conveniently, this also determined the subset of the SDSS dataset (those galaxies used in the Galaxy Zoo project) that Jocelyn would use for this project. With the knowledge that the Galaxy Zoo labels would provide her with a target feature, Jocelyn returned to speak with Ted again about getting access to the SDSS data.

Accessing the results of the SDSS processing pipeline turned out to be reasonably straightforward as it was already collected into a single large table in the SDSS data repository. Ted organized a full download of the SDSS photo imaging data repository for all the objects for which Galaxy Zoo labels existed. This dataset contained 600,000 rows and 547 columns,[9] with one row for each galaxy observation, containing identifiers, position information, and measures describing the characteristics of the galaxy.

Jocelyn decided to begin her data exploration work by focusing on the target feature. The structure of the data available from the Galaxy Zoo project is shown in Table 10.1[490]. The category of each galaxy is voted on by multiple Galaxy Zoo participants, and the data includes the fraction of these votes for each of the categories.

9 The fact that the SDSS and Galaxy Zoo make all their data available for free online is a massive contribution to global science. The data used in this case study can be accessed by performing a simple SQL query at `skyserver.sdss3.org/dr9/en/tools/search/sql.asp`. The query to select all the camera imaging data from the SDSS data release for each of the objects covered by the Galaxy Zoo project along with the Galaxy Zoo classifications is `SELECT * FROM PhotoObj AS p JOIN ZooSpec AS zs ON zs.objid = p.objid ORDER BY p.objid`. Full details of all the data tables available from the SDSS are available at `skyserver.sdss3.org/dr9/en/help/docs/tabledesc.asp`.

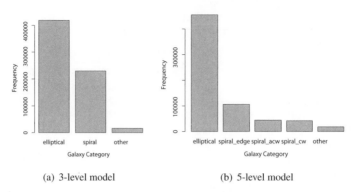

(a) 3-level model   (b) 5-level model

Figure 10.3
Bar plots of the different galaxy types present in the full SDSS dataset for the 3-level and 5-level target features.

The raw data did not contain a single column that could be used as a target feature, so Jocelyn had to design one from the data sources that were present. She generated two possible target features from the data provided. In both cases, the target feature level was set to the galaxy category that received the majority of the votes. In the first target feature, just three levels were used: *elliptical* (P_EL majority), *spiral* (P_CW, P_ACW, or P_EDGE majority), and *other* (P_MG or P_DK majority). The second target feature allowed three levels for spiral galaxies: *spiral_cw* (P_CW majority), *spiral_acw* (P_ACW majority), and *spiral_edge* (P_EDGE majority). Figure 10.3[491] shows bar plots of the frequencies of the 3-level and the 5-level target features. The main observation that Jocelyn made from these is that galaxies in the dataset were not evenly distributed across the different morphology types. Instead, the *elliptical* level was much more heavily represented than the others in both cases. Using the 3-level target feature as her initial focus, Jocelyn began to look at the different descriptive features in the data downloaded from the SDSS repository that might be useful in building a model to predict galaxy morphology.

The SDSS download that Jocelyn had access to was a big dataset—over 600,000 rows. Although modern predictive analytics and machine learning tools can handle data of this size, a large dataset can be cumbersome when performing data exploration operations—calculating summary statistics, generating visualizations, and performing correlation tests can just take too long.

Table 10.2

Analysis of a subset of the features in the SDSS dataset.

Feature	Count	% Miss.	Card.	Min.	1st Qrt.	Mean	Median	3rd Qrt.	Max.	Std. Dev.
RUN	10,000	0.00	380	109.00	2,821.00	3,703.45	3,841.00	4,646.00	8,095.00	1,378.82
RA.1	10,000	0.00	9,964	0.03	151.38	185.26	185.02	220.56	359.99	59.12
DEC.1	10,000	0.00	9,928	-11.23	9.71	24.87	23.41	39.11	69.83	18.92
ROWC_U	10,000	0.00	1	0.00	0.00	0.00	0.00	0.00	0.00	0.00
ROWC_G	10,000	0.00	1	0.00	0.00	0.00	0.00	0.00	0.00	0.00
ROWC_R	10,000	0.00	1	0.00	0.00	0.00	0.00	0.00	0.00	0.00
ROWC_I	10,000	0.00	1	0.00	0.00	0.00	0.00	0.00	0.00	0.00
ROWC_Z	10,000	0.00	1	0.00	0.00	0.00	0.00	0.00	0.00	0.00
SKYIVAR_U	10,000	0.00	9,986	-9,999.00	459.81	78.89	798.27	1,083.65	2,197.09	450.26
SKYIVAR_G	10,000	0.00	9,989	-9,999.00	439.55	965.88	2,957.92	6,005.71	9,913.59	2,766.70
SKYIVAR_R	10,000	0.00	9,988	-9,999.00	123.31	201.91	1,091.78	3,347.77	4,623.07	1,514.50
SKYIVAR_I	10,000	0.00	9,986	-9,999.00	46.02	174.79	434.48	1,825.93	2,527.57	851.42
SKYIVAR_Z	10,000	0.00	9,986	-9,999.00	13.60	-234.23	49.57	75.39	205.07	44.51
PSFMAG_U	10,000	0.00	9,768	7.47	20.60	21.08	21.13	21.598	26.19	0.85
PSFMAG_G	10,000	0.00	9,743	8.30	19.06	19.48	19.54	19.967	26.17	0.78
PSFMAG_R	10,000	0.00	9,744	7.45	18.23	18.65	18.68	19.113	26.49	0.76
PSFMAG_I	10,000	0.00	9,744	7.33	17.83	18.27	18.26	18.722	25.46	0.80
PSFMAG_Z	10,000	0.00	9,747	7.40	17.47	17.93	17.90	18.381	23.92	0.82
DEVFLUX_U	10,000	0.00	9,990	-3.68	11.64	43.05	23.07	44.31	28,616.04	194.73
DEVFLUX_G	10,000	0.00	9,987	-1,278.28	48.79	143.71	77.06	133.46	614,662.80	2,401.59
DEVFLUX_R	10,000	0.00	9,983	-4.37	111.04	267.74	152.75	250.65	137,413.00	993.65
DEVFLUX_I	10,000	0.00	9,980	-4.06	160.42	390.98	216.57	351.21	608,862.80	3,041.20
DEVFLUX_Z	10,000	0.00	9,983	-14.72	204.72	528.69	276.99	447.45	2,264,700.00	9,073.95

For this reason, Jocelyn extracted a small sample of 10,000 rows from the full dataset for exploratory analysis using **stratified sampling**.

Given that (1) the SDSS data that Jocelyn downloaded was already in a single table; (2) the data was already at the right prediction subject level (one row per galaxy); and (3) many of the columns in this dataset would most likely be used directly as features in the ABT that she was building, Jocelyn decided to produce a **data quality report** on this dataset. Table 10.2[492] shows an extract from this data quality report. At this point Jocelyn was primarily interested in understanding the amount of data available, any issues that might arise from missing values, and the types of each column in the dataset.

Jocelyn was surprised that none of the columns had any missing values. Although this is not unheard of (particularly in cases like the SDSS project

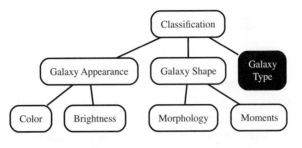

Figure 10.4

The revised domain concepts diagram for the galaxy classification task.

in which data is generated in a fully automated process) it is very unusual. The minimum values of −9,999 for the SKYIVAR_U/G/R/I/Z columns (and some others not shown in Table 10.2[492]), which were so different from the means for those columns, suggested that maybe there were missing values after all.[10] There were also a number of columns, such as ROWC_U/G/R/I/Z, that had cardinality of 1 (and standard deviations of zero) indicating that every row had the same. These features contained no actual information, so should be removed from the dataset.

Having performed this initial analysis, Jocelyn met again with Edwin and Ted to discuss the data quality issues and, more generally, to review the domain concepts outlined in Figure 10.2[488] so as to begin designing the actual descriptive features that would populate the ABT. Edwin was broadly in agreement with the set of domain concepts that Jocelyn had developed and was very positive about the use of Galaxy Zoo classifications as a source for generating the target feature. He did explain, however, that Jocelyn's suggestion of using position information was very unlikely to be useful, so that was removed from the set of domain concepts. Edwin also agreed that Ted was correct about the unavailability of spectrograph data for most objects, so this was also removed. The final domain concept diagram is shown in Figure 10.4[493]. Edwin helped Jocelyn align the columns in the raw SDSS dataset with the different domain concepts, which generated a good set of descriptive features within each domain concept.

Both Edwin and Ted were surprised to see missing values in the data as it was produced through a fully automated process. Simply through eye-balling

10 Many systems use values like −9,999 to indicate that values are actually missing.

the data, Jocelyn uncovered the fact that, in almost all cases, when one suspect −9,999 value was present in a row in the dataset, that row contained a number of suspect −9,999 values (this was the case for 2% of the rows in the dataset). Although neither Edwin nor Ted could understand exactly how this had happened, they agreed that something had obviously gone wrong in the processing pipeline in those cases and that the −9,999 values must refer to missing values.[11] **Complete case analysis** was used to entirely remove any rows containing two or more −9,999, or missing, values. Before performing this operation, however, Jocelyn first checked that the percentage of missing values was approximately 2% in each of the 3 levels (and in each of the levels in the 5-level model) to ensure that there was no relationship between missing values and galaxy type. There was no obvious relationship, so Jocelyn was confident that removing rows containing missing values would not affect one target level more than the others.

One of the advantages of working in scientific scenarios is that there is a body of literature that discusses how other scientists have addressed similar problems. Working with Edwin, Jocelyn reviewed the relevant literature and discovered a number of very informative articles discussing descriptive features that were likely to be useful in classifying galaxy morphologies.[12] In particular, a number of interesting features that could be derived from the flux and magnitude measurements already in the SDSS dataset were described in the literature. Jocelyn implemented these derived features for inclusion in the final ABT.

In many instances the SDSS dataset contained the same measurement for a night sky object measured separately for each of the five photometric bands covered by the SDSS telescope. Because of this, Jocelyn suspected that there would be a large amount of redundancy in the data as the measurements in the different bands were likely to be highly correlated. To investigate this idea, she generated SPLOM charts for different photometric band versions of a selection of columns from the dataset (see Figure 10.5[495]), and these showed significant relationships, which confirmed her suspicion. Jocelyn showed these charts to

---

11 The co-occurrence of multiple missing values in a row is something that it is hard to find through summary analysis of the data and one of the reasons analytics practitioners should always eye-ball extracts from a dataset during the data exploration process.

12 Interested readers might find Tempel et al. (2011), Ball et al. (2004) and Banerji et al. (2010) good references on this topic.

Edwin. Edwin agreed that it was likely that correlations existed between measurements in the different photometric bands but stressed, however, that differences across these bands would exist and might be quite important in predicting galaxy morphology. The existence of a high level of correlation between
measurements indicated to Jocelyn that feature selection would be important
later during the modeling phase as it had the potential to massively reduce the
dimensionality of the dataset.

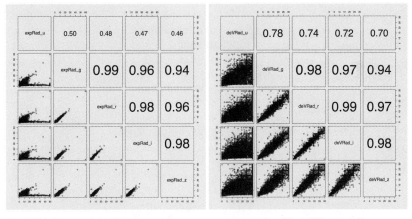

(a) EXPRAD   (b) DEVRAD

Figure 10.5
SPLOM diagrams of (a) the EXPRAD and (b) DEVRAD measurements from the raw SDSS dataset.
Each SPLOM shows the measure across the five different photometric bands captured by the SDSS
telescope (u, g, r, i, and z).

At this point the design of the ABT had fallen into place. For the most part,
Jocelyn would use descriptive features directly from the raw SDSS data. These
would be augmented with a small number of derived features that the literature review undertaken with Edwin had identified. Jocelyn was now ready to
move into the **Data Preparation** phase, during which she would populate the
ABT, analyze its contents in detail, and perform any transformations that were
required to handle data quality issues.

10.3   Data Preparation

After removing a large number of the columns from the raw SDSS dataset,
introducing a number of derived features, and generating two target features,

Table 10.3

Features from the ABT for the SDSS galaxy classification problem.

Feature	Feature	Feature
SKYIVAR_U/G/R/I/Z	UERR_U/G/R/I/Z	EXPFLUX_U/G/R/I/Z
PSFMAG_U/G/R/I/Z	ME1_U/G/R/I/Z	EXPFLUXIVAR_U/G/R/I/Z
PSFMAGERR_U/G/R/I/Z	ME2_U/G/R/I/Z	MODELFLUXIVAR_U/G/R/I/Z
FIBERMAG_U/G/R/I/Z	ME1E1ERR_U/G/R/I/Z	CMODELFLUX_U/G/R/I/Z
FIBERMAGERR_U/G/R/I/Z	ME1E2ERR_U/G/R/I/Z	CMODELFLUXIVAR_U/G/R/I/Z
FIBER2MAG_U/G/R/I/Z	ME2E2ERR_U/G/R/I/Z	APERFLUX7_U/G/R/I/Z
FIBER2MAGERR_U/G/R/I/Z	MRRCC_U/G/R/I/Z	APERFLUX7IVAR_U/G/R/I/Z
PETROMAG_U/G/R/I/Z	MRRCCERR_U/G/R/I/Z	LNLSTAR_U/G/R/I/Z
PETROMAGERR_U/G/R/I/Z	MCR4_U/G/R/I/Z	LNLEXP_U/G/R/I/Z
PSFFLUX_U/G/R/I/Z	DEVRAD_U/G/R/I/Z	LNLDEV_U/G/R/I/Z
PSFFLUXIVAR_U/G/R/I/Z	DEVRADERR_U/G/R/I/Z	FRACDEV_U/G/R/I/Z
FIBERFLUX_U/G/R/I/Z	DEVAB_U/G/R/I/Z	DERED_U/G/R/I/Z
FIBERFLUXIVAR_U/G/R/I/Z	DEVABERR_U/G/R/I/Z	DEREDDIFF_U_G
FIBER2FLUX_U/G/R/I/Z	DEVMAG_U/G/R/I/Z	DEREDDIFF_G_R
FIBER2FLUXIVAR_U/G/R/I/Z	DEVMAGERR_U/G/R/I/Z	DEREDDIFF_R_I
PETROFLUX_U/G/R/I/Z	DEVFLUX_U/G/R/I/Z	DEREDDIFF_I_Z
PETROFLUXIVAR_U/G/R/I/Z	DEVFLUXIVAR_U/G/R/I/Z	PETRORATIO_I
PETRORAD_U/G/R/I/Z	EXPRAD_U/G/R/I/Z	PETRORATIO_R
PETRORADERR_U/G/R/I/Z	EXPRADERR_U/G/R/I/Z	AE_I
PETROR50_U/G/R/I/Z	EXPAB_U/G/R/I/Z	PETROMAGDIFF_U_G
PETROR50ERR_U/G/R/I/Z	EXPABERR_U/G/R/I/Z	PETROMAGDIFF_G_R
PETROR90_U/G/R/I/Z	EXPMAG_U/G/R/I/Z	PETROMAGDIFF_R_I
PETROR90ERR_U/G/R/I/Z	EXPMAGERR_U/G/R/I/Z	PETROMAGDIFF_I_Z
Q_U/G/R/I/Z	CMODELMAG_U/G/R/I/Z	GALAXY_CLASS_3
QERR_U/G/R/I/Z	CMODELMAGERR_U/G/R/I/Z	GALAXY_CLASS_5
U_U/G/R/I/Z		

Jocelyn generated an ABT containing 327 descriptive features and two target features. Table 10.3[496] lists these features (features that occur over all five photometric bands are listed as NAME_U/G/R/I/Z to save space).[13]

Once Jocelyn had populated the ABT, she generated a data quality report (the initial data quality report covered the data in the raw SDSS dataset only, so a second one was required that covered the actual ABT) and performed an in-depth analysis of the characteristics of each descriptive feature. An extract from this data quality report is shown in Table 10.4[498].

---

13 We direct the interested reader to http://skyserver.sdss3.org/dr9/en/sdss/data/data.asp for a overview of what these features represent.

The magnitude of the maximum values for the FIBER2FLUXIVAR_U feature in comparison to the median and 3rd quartile value was unusual and suggested the presence of outliers. The difference between the mean and median values for the SKYIVAR_R feature also suggested the presence of outliers. Similarly, the difference between the mean and median values for the LNLSTAR_R feature suggested that the distribution of this feature was heavily skewed and also suggested the presence of outliers. Figure 10.6[497] shows histograms for these features. The problems of outliers and skewed distributions is clearly visible in these distributions. A number of other features exhibited a similar pattern.

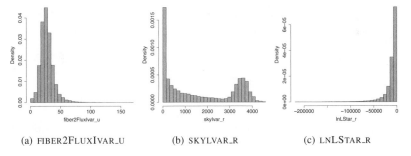

(a) FIBER2FLUXIVAR_U   (b) SKYLVAR_R   (c) LNLSTAR_R

Figure 10.6

Histograms of a selection of features from the SDSS dataset.

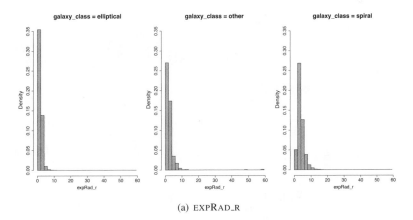

(a) EXPRAD_R

Figure 10.7

Histograms of the EXPRAD_R feature by target feature level.

Table 10.4

A data quality report for a subset of the features in the SDSS ABT.

Feature	Count	% Miss.	Card.	Min.	1st Qrt.	Mean	Median	3rd Qrt.	Max.	Std. Dev.
SkyIvar_U	640,432	0.00	639,983	0.00	465.53	784.78	793.20	1,079.53	2,190.05	447.36
SkyIvar_G	640,432	0.00	640,081	0.00	442.55	3,318.72	2,949.62	6,008.31	9,898.47	2,769.84
SkyIvar_R	640,432	0.00	640,178	0.00	127.18	1,629.86	1,094.93	3,342.65	4,596.46	1,513.38
SkyIvar_I	640,432	0.00	640,042	0.00	48.28	842.18	436.13	1,825.88	2,515.35	852.73
SkyIvar_Z	640,432	0.00	640,042	0.00	13.90	52.19	49.76	75.10	205.69	44.19
ME2_G	640,432	0.00	629,246	-0.96	-0.13	0.01	0.01	0.15	0.97	0.28
Fiber2FluxIvar_U	640,432	0.00	639,827	0.00	20.31	27.24	25.96	32.40	170.70	11.02
PsfMag_U	640,432	0.00	632,604	13.76	20.59	21.05	21.12	21.58	25.56	0.81
PetroFluxIvar_U	640,432	0.00	627,391	0.00	0.16	0.40	0.31	0.53	6.29	0.36
LnL_Star_R	640,432	0.00	639,690	-218,875.30	-12,623.05	-12,009.95	-6,771.37	-4,308.99	0.00	16,193.73
PetroMag_R	640,432	0.00	628,562	11.72	16.76	17.08	17.29	17.61	22.72	0.75
ExpAB_I	640,432	0.00	623,467	0.05	0.49	0.65	0.67	0.81	1.00	0.20
DeredDiff_U_G	640,432	0.00	630,319	-2.47	1.29	1.61	1.67	1.89	6.67	0.40
DeredDiff_G_R	640,432	0.00	631,627	-1.06	0.64	0.82	0.84	0.99	4.70	0.27
DeredDiff_R_I	640,432	0.00	611,597	-4.46	0.36	0.39	0.40	0.44	2.22	0.10
DeredDiff_I_Z	640,432	0.00	615,131	-2.29	0.23	0.28	0.30	0.34	5.33	0.11
PetroRatio_I	640,432	0.00	640,432	1.12	2.33	2.67	2.68	3.01	25.52	0.46
PetroRatio_R	640,432	0.00	640,432	1.18	2.29	2.63	2.64	2.96	10.05	0.42
AE_I	640,432	0.00	640,432	0.00	0.13	0.27	0.23	0.38	0.90	0.18
ModelMagDiff_U_G	640,432	0.00	630,476	-2.45	1.33	1.65	1.71	1.94	6.83	0.40
ModelMagDiff_G_R	640,432	0.00	630,437	-1.05	0.68	0.85	0.87	1.03	4.75	0.27
ModelMagDiff_R_I	640,432	0.00	613,667	-4.46	0.38	0.41	0.42	0.47	2.25	0.10
ModelMagDiff_I_Z	640,432	0.00	615,346	-2.27	0.25	0.29	0.32	0.35	5.34	0.11
PetroMagDiff_G_R	640,432	0.00	631,901	-1.99	0.64	0.83	0.84	1.00	5.13	0.28
PetroMagDiff_R_I	640,432	0.00	612,827	-3.32	0.35	0.39	0.41	0.45	2.83	0.11
PetroMagDiff_I_Z	640,432	0.00	620,422	-4.43	0.19	0.24	0.27	0.33	3.69	0.15

With Edwin's help, Jocelyn investigated the actual data in the ABT to determine whether the extreme values in the features displaying significant skew or
the presence of outliers were due to **valid outliers** or **invalid outliers**. In all
cases the extreme values were determined to be valid outliers. Jocelyn decided
to use the **clamp transformation** to change the values of these outliers to
something closer to the central tendency of the features. Any values beyond the
1st quartile value plus 2.5 times the inter-quartile range were reduced to this
value. The standard value of 1.5 times the inter-quartile range was changed to
2.5 to slightly reduce the impact of this operation.

Jocelyn also made the decision to normalize all the descriptive features
into **standard scores**.The differences in the ranges of values of the set of
descriptive features in the ABT was huge. For example, DEVAB_R had a
range as small as $[0.05, 1.00]$ while APERFLUX7IVAR_U had a range as large
as $[-265,862, 15,274]$. Standardizing the descriptive feature in this way was
likely to improve the accuracy of the final predictive models. The only drawback to standardization is that the models become less interpretable. Interpretability, however, was not particularly important for the SDSS scenario (the
model built would be added to the existing SDSS pipeline and process thousands of galaxy objects per day), so standardization was appropriate.

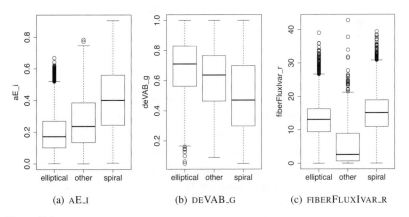

(a) AE_I   (b) DEVAB_G   (c) FIBERFLUXIVAR_R

Figure 10.8
Small multiple box plots (split by the target feature) of some of the features from the SDSS ABT.

Jocelyn also performed a simple first-pass feature selection using the 3-level
model to see which features might stand out as predictive of galaxy morphology. Jocelyn used the **information gain** measure to rank the predictiveness
of the different features in the dataset (for this analysis, missing values were

simply omitted). The columns identified as being most predictive of galaxy morphology were expRad_g (0.3908), expRad_r (0.3649), deVRad_g (0.3607), expRad_i (0.3509), deVRad_r (0.3467), expRad_z (0.3457), and mRrCc_g (0.3365). Jocelyn generated histograms for all these features compared to the target feature—for example, Figure 10.7[497] shows the histograms for the EXPRAD_R feature. It was encouraging that in many cases distinct distributions for each galaxy type were apparent in the histograms. Figure 10.8[499] shows small multiple box plots divided by galaxy type for a selection of features from the ABT. The differences between the three box plots in each plot gives an indication of the likely predictiveness of each feature. The presence of large numbers of outliers can also be seen.

10.4   Modeling

The descriptive features in the SDSS dataset are primarily continuous. For this reason, Jocelyn considered trying a similarity-based model, the **k nearest neighbor**, and two error-based models, the **logistic regression** model and the **support vector machine**. Jocelyn began by constructing a simple baseline model using the 3-level target feature.

10.4.1   Baseline Models

Because of the size of the ABT, Jocelyn decided to split the dataset into a **training set** and a large **hold-out test set**. Subsets of the training set would be also used for **validation** during the model building process. The training set consisted of 30% of the data in the ABT (approximately 200,000 instances), and the test set consisted of the remaining 70% (approximately 450,000 instances).[14] Using the training set, Jocelyn performed a 10-fold cross validation experiment on models trained to use the full set of descriptive features to predict the 3-level target. These would act as baseline performance scores that she would try to improve upon. The classification accuracies achieved during the cross validation experiment were 82.912%, 86.041%, and 85.942% by the k nearest neighbor, logistic regression, and support vector

---

14 It is more common to split an ABT in the opposite proportions (70% for the training set and 30% for the test set). In this case, however, because the ABT was so large it was more useful to have a very large test sample as 200,000 instances should be more than enough for the training set.

Table 10.5

The confusion matrices for the baseline models.

(a) *k* nearest neighbor model (classification accuracy: 82.912%, average class accuracy: 54.663%)

		Prediction			Recall
		elliptical	*spiral*	*other*	
	elliptical	115,438	10,238	54	91.814%
Target	*spiral*	19,831	50,368	18	71.731%
	other	2,905	1,130	18	0.442%

(b) logistic regression model (classification accuracy: 86.041%, average class accuracy: 62.137%)

		Prediction			Recall
		elliptical	*spiral*	*other*	
	elliptical	115,169	10,310	251	91.600%
Target	*spiral*	13,645	56,321	251	80.209%
	other	2,098	1,363	592	14.602%

(c) support vector machine model (classification accuracy: 85.942%, average class accuracy: 58.107%)

		Prediction			Recall
		elliptical	*spiral*	*other*	
	elliptical	114,721	10,992	18	91.244%
Target	*spiral*	13,089	57,092	36	81.307%
	other	2,654	1,327	72	1.770%

machine models respectively. The confusion matrices from the evaluation of these models are shown in Table 10.5[501].

These initial baseline results were promising; however, one key issue did emerge. It was clear that the performance of the models trained using the SDSS data was severely affected by the **target level imbalance** in the data—there were many more examples of the *elliptical* target level than either the *spiral* or, especially, the *other* target level. Having a dominant target level, like the *elliptical* target level in this example, means that models trained on this data can over-compensate for the majority target level and ignore the minority ones. For example, based on the confusion matrix in Table 10.5(c)[501], the misclassification rate for the *elliptical* target level is only 8.756%, while for the *spiral* target level, it is higher, at 18.693%, and for the *other* target level, it is a fairly dire 98.230%. The single classification accuracy performance measure hides this poor performance on the minority target levels. An average class accuracy performance measure, however, brings this issue to the fore. The average class accuracy scores achieved by the models were 54.663%, 62.137%, and 58.107% by the k nearest neighbor, logistic regression, and support vector machine models respectively. Jocelyn decided to build a second set of models in which she would address the target level imbalance issue.

The target level imbalance in the SDSS dataset arises through **relative rarity**.[15] In the large SDSS dataset, there are plenty of galaxies in the *other* and *spiral* categories; there are just many more in the *elliptical* category. In this case, Jocelyn addressed the target level imbalance problem by using **under-sampling** to generate a new training dataset in which all three target levels had an equal distribution. This was referred to as the **under-sampled training set**. Jocelyn performed the same baseline test on the three model types using this new dataset. The resulting confusion matrices are shown in Table 10.6[503].

The resulting classification accuracies (average class accuracies and classification accuracies are the same in this case because the dataset is balanced) from the 10-fold cross validation experiment were 73.965%, 78.805%, and 78.226% for the k nearest neighbor, logistic regression, and support vector machine models respectively. The overall performance on this balanced dataset was not as good as the performance on the original dataset; however, balancing the training set did result in the performance on each target level being more equal. Predictions for the *other* target level are actually being performed this time, whereas in the previous example, this target level was essentially being ignored. Choosing between models in this sort of scenario is difficult as it really comes down to balancing the needs of the application—when the system makes errors (as it inevitably will from time to time), what error is least bad? In this example, is it better to classify a galaxy that should be *other* as an *elliptical* galaxy or vice versa? Jocelyn discussed this issue and the results of these two baseline experiments with Edwin, and both decided that it would be best to pursue the optimal performance measured by overall classification accuracy because, in practice, the important thing for the SDSS system was to classify *elliptical* and *spiral* galaxies as accurately as possible.

---

15 Target level imbalance typically arises through either **absolute rarity** or **relative rarity** of the minority target levels. Absolute rarity refers to scenarios in which there simply do not exist many examples of the minority target levels—for example, in automated inspection tasks on production lines, it is often the case that there are simply very few examples of defective products that can be used for training. Relative rarity, on the other hand, refers to scenarios in which the proportion of examples of the majority target levels in a dataset is much higher than the proportion of examples of the minority target level, but there is actually no shortage of examples of the minority target level.

Table 10.6

The confusion matrices showing the performance of models on the under-sampled training set.

(a) *k* nearest neighbor model (classification accuracy: 73.965%)

		Prediction			Recall
		elliptical	*spiral*	*other*	
	elliptical	23,598	4,629	5,253	70.483%
Target	*spiral*	4,955	24,734	3,422	74.700%
	other	3,209	4,572	25,628	76.711%

(b) logistic regression model (classification accuracy: 78.805%)

		Prediction			Recall
		elliptical	*spiral*	*other*	
	elliptical	25,571	4,203	3,706	76.378%
Target	*spiral*	3,677	26,267	3,166	79.331%
	other	2,684	3,763	26,963	80.705%

(c) support vector machine model (classification accuracy: 78.226%)

		Prediction			Recall
		elliptical	*spiral*	*other*	
	elliptical	24,634	4,756	4,089	73.579%
Target	*spiral*	3,763	26,310	3,038	79.460%
	other	2,584	3,550	27,275	81.640%

With these baseline performance measures established, Jocelyn turned her attention to feature selection in an effort to improve on these performance scores.

10.4.2 Feature Selection

In the SDSS dataset, many of the features are represented multiple times for each of the five different photometric bands, and this made Jocelyn suspect that many of these features might be redundant and so ripe for removal from the dataset. **Feature selection** approaches that search through subsets of features (known as **wrapper** approaches) are better at removing redundant features than rank and prune approaches because they consider groups of features together. For this reason, Jocelyn chose to use a **step-wise sequential search** for feature selection for each of the three model types. In all cases overall classification accuracy was used as the fitness function that drove the search. After feature selection, the classification accuracy of the models on the test

Table 10.7

The confusion matrices for the models after feature selection.

(a) k nearest neighbor model (classification accuracy: 85.557%, average class accuracy: 57.617%)

		Prediction			Recall
		elliptical	*spiral*	*other*	
	elliptical	116,640	9,037	54	92.770%
Target	*spiral*	15,833	54,366	18	77.426%
	other	2,815	1,130	108	2.655%

(b) logistic regression model (classification accuracy: 88.829%, average class accuracy: 67.665%)

		Prediction			Recall
		elliptical	*spiral*	*other*	
	elliptical	117,339	8,302	90	93.326%
Target	*spiral*	10,812	59,297	108	84.448%
	other	1,757	1,273	1,022	25.221%

(c) support vector machine model (classification accuracy: 87.188%, average class accuracy: 60.868%)

		Prediction			Recall
		elliptical	*spiral*	*other*	
	elliptical	115,152	10,561	18	91.586%
Target	*spiral*	11,243	58,938	36	83.938%
	other	2,528	1,237	287	7.080%

set were 85.557%, 88.829%, and 87.188% for the k nearest neighbor, logistic regression, and support vector machine models respectively. The resulting confusion matrices are shown in Table 10.7[504]. In all cases performance of the models improved with feature selection. The best performing model is the logistic regression model. For this model, just 31 out of the total 327 features were selected.[16] This was not surprising given the large amount of redundancy within the feature set.

16 The features selected were AE_I, APERFLUX7IVAR_G, APERFLUX7IVAR_I, APERFLUX7_U, DERED_U, DEVAB_R, DEVRADERR_Z, DEVRAD_U, DEREDDIFF_G_R, EXPRAD_G, EXPRAD_R, FIBER2FLUXIVAR_Z, FIBER2MAGERR_G, FIBERFLUXIVAR_R, FRACDEV_Z, LNLDEV_G, LNLDEV_R, LNLDEV_U, LNLDEV_Z, MCR4_Z, PETROFLUXIVAR_G, PETROFLUXIVAR_I, PETROR50ERR_R, PETROR50_G, PETROR90_G, PETRORATIO_R, PSFFLUXIVAR_I, PSF-MAGERR_R, PSFMAG_R, SKYIVAR_U, and SKYIVAR_Z.

Based on these results, Jocelyn determined that the logistic regression model trained using the reduced set of features was the best model to use for galaxy classification. This model gave the best prediction accuracy and offered the potential for very fast classification times, which was attractive for integration into the SDSS pipeline. Logistic regression models also produce confidences along with the predictions, which was attractive to Edwin as it meant that he could build tests into the pipeline that would redirect galaxies with low confidence classifications for manual confirmation of the predictions made by the automated system.

10.4.3   The 5-level Model

To address the finer grained 5-level (*elliptical*, *spiral_cw*, *spiral_acw*, *spiral_eo*, and *other*) classification task, Jocelyn attempted two approaches. First, she used a 5-target-level model to make predictions. Second, she used a **two-stage model**. In this case the logistic regression model used for the 3-level target feature would first be used, and then a model trained to distinguish only between different spiral galaxy types (*clockwise*, *anti-clockwise*, and *edge-on*) would be used to further classify those galaxy objects classified as *spiral* by the first stage.

Based on the performance of the logistic regression model on the 3-level classification problem, Jocelyn trained a logistic regression classifier on the 5-level dataset and evaluated it using a 10-fold cross validation. Following the same approach as in earlier models, Jocelyn performed feature selection using a **step-wise sequential search** to find the best subset of features for this model. Just 11 features from the full set were selected.[17] The resulting classification accuracy on the best performing model that Jocelyn could build was 77.528% (with an average class accuracy of 43.018%). The confusion matrix from this test is shown in Table 10.8[506]. The overall accuracy of this model is somewhat comparable with the overall accuracy of the 3-level model. The classifier accurately predicts the type of galaxies with the *elliptical* target level and, to a lesser extent, with the *spiral_eo* target level. The ability of the model to distinguish between clockwise (*spiral_cw*) and anti-clockwise (*spiral_acw*) spiral galaxies, however, is extremely poor.

---

17 The features selected were SKYIVAR_U, PETROFLUXIVAR_I, PETROR50ERR_G, DEVRAD_G, DEVRADERR_R, DEVRADERR_I, DEVAB_G, EXPFLUX_Z, APERFLUX7_Z, APERFLUX7IVAR_R, and MODELMAGDIFF_I_Z.

Table 10.8

The confusion matrix for the 5-level logistic regression model (classification accuracy: 77.528%, average class accuracy: 43.018%).

		Prediction					Recall
		elliptical	*spiral_cw*	*spiral_acw*	*spiral_eo*	*other*	Recall
	elliptical	120,625	46	1,515	3,450	95	95.939%
	spiral_cw	7,986	373	4,715	2,176	30	2.443%
Target	*spiral_acw*	8,395	435	4,928	2,272	35	30.673%
	spiral_eo	8,719	75	1,018	28,981	78	74.556%
	other	3,038	30	218	619	148	3.660%

Table 10.9

The confusion matrix for the logistic regression model that distinguished between only the spiral galaxy types (classification accuracy: 68.225%, average class accuracy: 56.621%).

		Prediction			Recall
		spiral_cw	*spiral_acw*	*spiral_eo*	Recall
	spiral_cw	5,753	6,214	3,319	37.636%
Target	*spiral_acw*	6,011	6,509	3,540	40.528%
	spiral_eo	1,143	2,084	35,643	91.698%

To test the two-stage classifier, Jocelyn extracted a small ABT containing only spiral galaxies from the original ABT. Using this new ABT, Jocelyn trained a logistic regression model to distinguish between the three spiral galaxy types (*spiral_cw*, *spiral_acw*, and *spiral_eo*). She used step-wise sequential feature selection again, and this time 32 features were chosen.[18] This model was able to achieve a classification accuracy of 68.225% (with an average class accuracy of 56.621%). The resulting confusion matrix is shown in Table 10.9[506]. Although it is evident from the confusion matrix that the model could distinguish between the edge-on spiral galaxies and the other two types, it could not accurately distinguish between the clockwise and anti-clockwise spiral galaxies.

---

18 The features selected were AE_I, APERFLUX7IVAR_R, CMODELFLUXIVAR_U, DEV-ABERR_G, DEVABERR_Z, DEVAB_G, DEVAB_I, DEVFLUXIVAR_U, DEVMAGERR_U, DEVRAD_G, DEVRAD_U, DEREDDIFF_U_G, EXPABERR_U, EXPAB_G, EXPMAG_Z, EXPRADERR_U, FIBER2FLUXIVAR_R, FIBER2MAG_I, FIBERFLUXIVAR_G, FIBERFLUX_G, FIBERFLUX_R, FIBERFLUX_Z, LNLDEV_R, MCR4_Z, ME1E1ERR_Z, ME1_U, MODEL-MAGDIFF_R_I, PETROMAGDIFF_R_I, PETROR90_R, PSFMAG_U, SKYIVAR_U, and U_R.

Table 10.10

The confusion matrix for the 5-level two-stage model (classification accuracy: 79.410%, average class accuracy: 53.118%).

		Prediction					Recall
		elliptical	*spiral_cw*	*spiral_acw*	*spiral_eo*	*other*	
	elliptical	117,339	76	2,510	5,716	90	93.326%
	spiral_cw	2,354	4,859	5,242	2,802	23	31.799%
Target	*spiral_acw*	2,473	5,079	5,499	2,990	25	34.229%
	spiral_eo	5,985	965	1,760	30,102	60	77.439%
	other	1,757	98	341	834	1,022	25.222%

In spite of the model's difficulty distinguishing between the clockwise and anti-clockwise spiral galaxies, Jocelyn did perform an evaluation of the **two-stage model**. This model first used a 3-level logistic regression model to distinguish between the *elliptical*, *spiral*, and *other* target levels. Any objects classified as belonging to the *spiral* target level were then presented to a model trained to distinguish between the three different spiral types. The two-stage model achieved a classification accuracy of 79.410%. The resulting confusion matrix is shown in Table 10.10[507].

Although the performance of the two-stage model was better than the performance of the simpler 5-level model, it still did a very poor job of distinguishing between the different spiral galaxy types. Jocelyn discussed this model with Edwin, and they both agreed that the performance was not at the level required by the SDSS scientists for inclusion in the SDSS processing pipeline. It would most likely be possible to create a model that could distinguish between the clockwise and anti-clockwise spiral galaxies, but this would probably require the calculation of new features based on the application of image processing techniques to the raw galaxy images. Based on the time available to the project, Jocelyn did not pursue this avenue and, in consultation with Edwin, decided to continue with just the 3-level model. The best performing model was the 3-level logistic regression model after feature selection (the performance of this model is shown in Table 10.7(b)[504]). With this model selected as the best performing approach, Jocelyn was ready to perform the final evaluation experiment.

Table 10.11
The confusion matrix for the final logistic regression model on the large hold-out test set (classification accuracy: 87.979%, average class accuracy: 67.305%).

		Prediction			Recall
		elliptical	spiral	other	
	elliptical	251,845	19,159	213	92.857%
Target	spiral	25,748	128,621	262	83.179%
	other	4,286	2,648	2,421	25.879%

10.5   Evaluation

The final evaluation that Jocelyn performed was in two parts. In the first part, she performed a performance test of the final model selected—the 3-level logistic regression model using the selected feature subset—on the large test dataset mentioned at the beginning of Section 10.4[500]. This dataset had not been used in the training process, so the performance of the model on this dataset should give a fair indication of how well the model would perform when deployed on real, unseen data. The confusion matrix resulting from this test is shown in Table 10.11[508]. The classification accuracy was 87.979% (with an average class accuracy of 67.305%), which was similar to performance on the training data and well above the target that Jocelyn and Edwin had agreed on at the beginning of the project.

The purpose of the second part of the evaluation was to encourage confidence in the models that Jocelyn had built amongst the SDSS scientists. In this evaluation, Edwin and four of his colleagues independently examined 200 galaxy images randomly selected from the final test set and classified them as belonging to one of the three galaxy types. A single majority classification was calculated from the five manual classifications for each galaxy. Jocelyn extracted two key measurements by comparing these manual classifications to the classifications made by the model she had built. First, Jocelyn calculated an average class accuracy by comparing the predictions made by her model for the same 200 galaxies with the manual classifications made by the SDSS scientists. The average class accuracy was 78.278%, which was similar to the accuracies measured on the overall test set.

Second, Jocelyn calculated an **inter-annotator agreement** statistic for the manual classifications given by the five SDSS scientists. Using the **Cohen's**

kappa[19] measure of **inter-annotator agreement** to measure how closely the manual classifications matched each other, Jocelyn calculated a measure of 0.6. Jocelyn showed that even the SDSS scientists themselves disagreed on the types of certain galaxies. This is not uncommon in this kind of scenario, in which the classifications have a certain amount of fuzziness around their boundaries—e.g., the exact line between an *elliptical* and a *spiral* galaxy can be hard to define—and led to very interesting discussions for the scientists!

Together the strong performance by the model on the large test dataset and the confidence built through the manual annotation exercise meant that Edwin and his colleagues were happy to integrate the 3-level model into the SDSS processing pipeline.

10.6   Deployment

Once Edwin had approved the models that Jocelyn had built, Jocelyn met again with Ted to begin the process of integrating the models into the SDSS processing pipeline. This was a reasonably straightforward process with just a few issues that needed discussion. First, Jocelyn had put the SDSS data through a preprocessing step, standardizing all descriptive features. The standardization parameters (the mean and standard deviation of each feature) needed to be included in the pipeline so that the same preprocessing step could be applied to newly arriving instances before presenting them to the models.

Second, a process was put in place that allowed manual review by SDSS experts to be included in the galaxy classification process. One of the advantages of using a logistic regression model is that along with classifications, it also produces probabilities. Given that there are three target levels, a prediction probability of approximately 0.333 indicates that the prediction made by the model is really quite unsure. A system was put in place in the SDSS processing pipeline to flag for manual review any galaxies given low probability predictions.

Last, a strategy needed to be put in place to monitor the performance of the models over time so that any **concept drift** that might take place could be flagged. Jocelyn agreed with Ted to put in place an alert system using the

---

19 The Cohen's kappa statistic was first described in Cohen (1960). Using the Cohen's kappa statistic, a value of 1.0 indicates total agreement, while a value of 0.0 indicates agreement no better than chance. Values around 0.6 are typically understood to indicate an *acceptable* level of agreement, although the exact nature of what is and is not acceptable is very task dependent.

stability index. This would raise an alert whenever the stability index went above 0.25 so that someone could consider retraining the model.

11   The Art of Machine Learning for Predictive Data Analytics

It is a capital mistake to theorize before one has data. Insensibly one begins to twist facts to suit theories, instead of theories to suit facts.
—Sherlock Holmes

Predictive data analytics projects use machine learning to build models that capture the relationships in large datasets between descriptive features and a target feature. A specific type of learning, called inductive learning, is used, where learning entails inducing a general rule from a set of specific instances. This observation is important because it highlights that machine learning has the same properties as inductive learning. One of these properties is that a model learned by induction is not guaranteed to be correct. In other words, the general rule that is induced from a sample may not be true for all instances in a population.

Another important property of inductive learning is that learning cannot occur unless the learning process is biased in some way. This means that we need to tell the learning process what types of patterns to look for in the data. This bias is referred to as inductive bias. The inductive bias of a learning algorithm comprises the set of assumptions that define the search space the algorithm explores and the search process it uses.

On top of the inductive bias encoded in a machine learning algorithm, we also bias the outcome of a predictive data analytics project in lots of other ways. Consider the following questions:

What is the predictive analytics target? What descriptive features will we include/exclude? How will we handle missing values? How will we normalize our features? How will we represent continuous features? What types of models will we create? How will we set the parameters of the learning algorithms? What evaluation process will we follow? What performance measures will we use?

These questions are relevant when building any prediction model, and the answer to each one introduces a specific bias. Often we are forced to answer these questions, and others like them, based on intuition, experience, and experimentation. This is what makes machine learning something of an art, rather than strictly a science. But it is also what makes machine learning such a fascinating and rewarding area to work in.

En masse all the questions that must be answered to successfully complete a predictive data analytics project can seem overwhelming. This is why we recommend using the **CRISP-DM** process to manage a project through its

Table 11.1

The alignment between the phases of CRISP-DM, key questions for analytics projects, and the chapters and sections of this book.

CRISP-DM	Open Questions	Chapter
Business Understanding	*What is the organizational problem being addressed? In what ways could a prediction model address the organizational problem? Do we have situational fluency? What is the capacity of the organization to utilize the output of a prediction model? What data is available?*	Chapter 2[21]
Data Understanding	*What is the prediction subject? What are the domain concepts? What is the target feature? What descriptive features will be used?*	Chapter 2[21]
Data Preparation	*Are there data quality issues? How will we handle missing values? How will we normalize our features? What features will we include?*	Chapter 3[55]
Modeling	*What types of models will we use? How will we set the parameters of the machine learning algorithms? Have underfitting or overfitting occurred?*	Chapters 4[117], 5[179], 6[247] and 7[323]
Evaluation	*What evaluation process will we follow? What performance measures will we use? Is the model fit for purpose?*	Chapter 8[397]
Deployment	*How will we continue to evaluate the model after deployment? How will the model be integrated into the organization?*	8.4.6[447] and Chapters 9[463] and 10[483]

lifecycle. Table 11.1[512] shows the alignment between the phases of CRISP-DM, some of the key questions that must be answered during a predictive data analytics project, and the chapters in this book dealing with these questions.

Remember, an analytics project is often iterative, with different stages of the project feeding back into later cycles. It is also important to remember that the purpose of an analytics project is to solve a real-world problem and to keep focus on this rather than being distracted by the, admittedly sometimes fascinating, technical challenges of model building. We strongly believe that the best way to keep an analytics project focused, and to improve the likelihood of a successful conclusion, is to adopt a structured project lifecycle, such as CRISP-DM, and we recommend its use.

11.1   Different Perspectives on Prediction Models

A key step in any predictive analytics project is deciding which type of predictive analytics model to use. In this book we have presented some of the most commonly used prediction models and the machine learning algorithms used to build them. We have structured this presentation around four approaches to learning: information-based, similarity-based, probability-based, and error-based. The mathematical foundation of these approaches can be described using four simple (but important) equations: Claude Shannon's model of **entropy** (Equation (11.1)[513]), **Euclidean distance** (Equation (11.2)[513]), **Bayes' Theorem** (Equation (11.3)[513]), and the **sum of squared errors** (Equation (11.4)[513]).

$$H(t, \mathcal{D}) = - \sum_{l \in levels(t)} (P(t = l) \times log_2(P(t = l))) \qquad (11.1)$$

$$dist(\mathbf{q}, \mathbf{d}) = \sqrt{\sum_{i=1}^{m}(\mathbf{q}\,[i] - \mathbf{d}\,[i])^2} \qquad (11.2)$$

$$P(t = l | \mathbf{q}) = \frac{P(\mathbf{q} | t = l)P(t = l)}{P(\mathbf{q})} \qquad (11.3)$$

$$L_2(\mathbb{M}_{\mathbf{w}}, \mathcal{D}) = \frac{1}{2} \sum_{i=1}^{n}(t_i - \mathbb{M}_{\mathbf{w}}(\mathbf{d}_i))^2 \qquad (11.4)$$

An understanding of these four equations is a strong basis for understanding the mathematical fundamentals of many areas of scientific modeling. Adding an understanding of how these four equations are used in the machine learning algorithms we have described (ID3, k nearest neighbor, multivariable linear regression with gradient descent, and naive Bayes) is a strong foundation on which to build a career in predictive data analytics.

The taxonomy we have used to distinguish between different machine learning algorithms is based on human approaches to learning that the algorithms can be said to emulate. This is not the only set of distinctions that can be made between the algorithms and the resulting models. It is useful to understand some of the other commonly used distinctions, because this understanding can provide insight into which learning algorithm and related model is most appropriate for a given scenario.

The first distinction between models that we will discuss is the distinction between **parametric** and **non-parametric** models. This distinction is not absolute, but it generally describes whether the size of the **domain representation** used to define a model is solely determined by the number of features in the domain or is affected by the number of instances in the dataset. In a parametric model the size of the domain representation (i.e., the number of parameters) is independent of the number of instances in the dataset. Examples of parametric models include the naive Bayes and Bayesian network models in Chapter 6[247] and the simple linear and logistic regression models in Chapter 7[323]. For example, the number of factors required by a naive Bayes model is only dependent on the number of features in the domain and is independent of the number of instances. Likewise, the number of weights used in a linear regression model is defined by the number of descriptive features and is independent of the number of instances in the training data.

In a non-parametric model the number of parameters used by the model increases as the number of instances increases. Nearest neighbor models are an obvious example of a non-parametric model. As new instances are added to the feature space, the size of the model's representation of the domain increases. Decision trees are also considered non-parametric models. The reason for this is that when we train a decision tree from data, we do not assume a fixed set of parameters prior to training that define the tree. Instead, the tree branching and the depth of the tree are related to the complexity of the dataset it is trained on. If new instances were added to the dataset and we rebuilt the tree, it is likely that we would end up with a (potentially very) different tree. Support vector machines are also non-parametric models. They retain some instances from the dataset—potentially all of them, although in practice, relatively few—as part of the domain representation. Hence, the size of the domain representation used by a support vector machine may change as instances are added to the dataset.

In general, parametric models make stronger assumptions about the underlying distributions of the data in a domain. A linear regression model, for example, assumes that the relationship between the descriptive features and the target is linear (this is a strong assumption about the distribution in the domain). Non-parametric models are more flexible but can struggle with large datasets. For example, a 1-NN model has the flexibility to model a discontinuous decision surface; however, it runs into time and space complexity issues as the number of instances grows.

When datasets are small, a parametric model may perform well because the strong assumptions made by the model—if correct—can help the model to avoid overfitting. However, as the size of the dataset grows, particularly if the decision boundary between the classes is very complex, it may make more sense to allow the data to inform the predictions more directly. Obviously the computational costs associated with non-parametric models and large datasets cannot be ignored. However, support vector machines are an example of a non-parametric model that, to a large extent, avoids this problem. As such, support vector machines are often a good choice in complex domains with lots of data.

The other important distinction that is often made between classification models is whether they are **generative** or **discriminative**. A model is generative if it can be used to generate data that will have the same characteristics as the dataset from which the model was produced. In order to do this, a generative model must learn, or encode, the distribution of the data belonging to each class. The Bayesian network models described in Chapter 6[247] are examples of generative models.[1] Indeed, Markov chain Monte Carlo methods for estimating probabilities are based on the fact that we can run these models to generate data that approximate the distributions of the dataset from which the model was induced. Because they explicitly model the distribution of the data for each class k nearest neighbor models are also generative models.

In contrast, discriminative models learn the boundary between classes rather than the characteristics of the distributions of the different classes. Support vector machines and the other classification models described in Chapter 7[323] are examples of discriminative prediction models. In some cases they learn a hard boundary between the classes; in other cases—such as logistic regression—they learn a soft boundary, which takes into account the distance from the boundary. However, all these models learn a boundary. Decision trees are also discriminative models. Decision trees are induced by recursively partitioning the feature space into regions belonging to the different classes, and consequently they define a decision boundary by aggregating the neighboring regions belonging to the same class. Decision tree **model ensembles** based on **bagging** and **boosting** are also discriminative models.

This generative versus discriminative distinction is more than just a labeling exercise. Generative and discriminative models learn different concepts. In

1 In this discussion, when we categorize models as being generative or discriminative, we are speaking in the general case. In fact, all models can be trained in either a generative or a discriminative manner. However, some models lend themselves to generative training and others to discriminative training, and it is this perspective that we use in this discussion.

probabilistic terms, using $\mathbf{d}$ to represent the vector of descriptive feature values and t_l to represent a target level, a generative model works by

1. learning the class conditional densities (i.e., the distribution of the data for each target level) $P(\mathbf{d}|t_l)$ and the class priors $P(t_l)$;

2. then using Bayes' Theorem to compute the class posterior probabilities $P(t_l|\mathbf{d})$;[2]

3. and then applying a decision rule over the class posteriors to return a target level.

By contrast, a discriminative model works by

1. learning the class posterior probability $P(t_l|\mathbf{d})$ directly from the data,

2. and then applying a decision rule over the class posteriors to return a target level.

This distinction between what generative and discriminative models try to learn is important because the class conditional densities, $P(\mathbf{d}|t_l)$, can be very complex compared to the class posteriors, $P(t_l|\mathbf{d})$ (see Figure 11.1[517]). Consequently, generative models try to learn more complex solutions to the prediction problem than discriminative models.

The potential difficulty in learning the class conditional densities, relative to the posterior class probabilities, is exacerbated in situations where we have a lot of descriptive features because, as the dimensionality of $\mathbf{d}$ increases, we will need more and more data to create good estimates for $P(t_l|\mathbf{d})$. So, in complex domains, discriminative models are likely to be more accurate. However, as is so often the case in machine learning, this is not the end of the generative versus discriminative debate. Generative models tend to have a higher bias—they make more assumptions about the form of the distribution they are learning. For example, as we discussed in Chapter 6[247] on probability, generative models encode independence assumptions about the descriptive features in $\mathbf{d}$. This may sound like another problem for generative models. However, in domains where we have good prior knowledge of the independence relationships between features, we can encode this prior structural information into a generative model. This structural information can bias the model in such as way as to help it avoid overfitting the data. As a result, a generative model

---

2 We could also formulate the generative model as learning the joint distribution $P(\mathbf{d}, t_l)$ directly and then computing the required posteriors from this distribution.

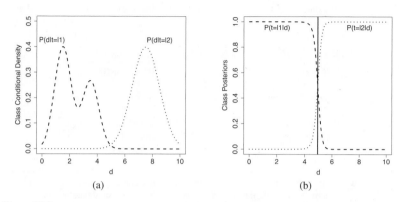

Figure 11.1

(a) The class conditional densities for two classes (*l1,l2*) with a single descriptive feature **d**. The height of each curve reflects the density of the instances from that class for that value of **d**. (b) The class posterior probabilities plotted for each class for different values of **d**. Notice that the class posterior probability $P(t = l1|\mathbf{d})$ is not affected by the multimodal structure of the corresponding class conditional density $P(\mathbf{d}|t = l1)$. This illustrates how the class posterior probabilities can be simpler than the class conditional densities. The solid vertical line in (b) plots the decision boundary for **d** that gives the minimum misclassification rate assuming uniform prior for the two target levels (i.e., $P(t = l1) = P(t = l2)$). This figure is based on Figure 1.27 from Bishop (2006).

may outperform a discriminative model when trained on a small dataset with good prior knowledge. Conversely, however, as the amount of training data increases. the bias imposed on a generative model can become larger than the error of the trained model. Once this tipping point in dataset size has been surpassed, a discriminative model will out perform a generative model.

The debate regarding the advantages and disadvantages of generative and discriminative models can be extended beyond model accuracy to include their ability to handle missing data, unlabeled data, and feature preprocessing, among other topics. We will not discuss these topics here. Instead we will simply note that the appropriate choice of generative versus discriminative model is context-dependent, and evaluating a range of different types of models is the safest option. Table 11.2[518] summarizes the different perspectives on the model types that we have presented in this book.

Table 11.2
A taxonomy of models based on the parametric versus non-parametric and generative versus discriminative distinctions.

Model	Parametric/ Non-Parametric	Generative/ Discriminative
k Nearest Neighbor	Non-Parametric	Generative
Decision Trees	Non-Parametric	Discriminative
Bagging/Boosting	Parametric*	Discriminative
Naive Bayes	Parametric	Generative
Bayesian Network	Parametric	Generative
Linear Regression	Parametric	Discriminative
Logistic Regression	Parametric	Discriminative
SVM	Non-Parametric	Discriminative

*Although the individual models in an ensemble could be non-parametric (for example, when decision trees are used), the ensemble model itself is considered parametric.

11.2   Choosing a Machine Learning Approach

Each of the approaches to machine learning that we have presented in this book induces distinct types of prediction models with different strengths and weaknesses. This raises the question of when to use which machine learning approach. The first thing to understand is that there is not one best approach that always outperforms the others. This is known as the **No Free Lunch Theorem** (Wolpert, 1996). Intuitively, this theorem makes sense because each algorithm encodes a distinct set of assumptions (i.e., the **inductive bias** of the learning algorithm), and a set of assumptions that are appropriate in one domain may not be appropriate in another domain.

We can see the assumptions encoded in each algorithm reflected in the distinctive characteristics of the **decision boundaries** that they learn for categorical prediction tasks. To illustrate these characteristics, we have created three artificial datasets and trained four different models on each of these datasets. The top row of images in Figure 11.2[520] illustrates how the three artificial datasets were created. Each of the images in the top row shows a feature space defined by two continuous descriptive features, F1 and F2, partitioned into *good* and *bad* regions by three different, artificially created decision boundaries.[3] In the subsequent images, we show the decision boundaries that

---

3 This example is partly inspired by the "machine learning classifier gallery" by Tom Fawcett at home.comcast.net/~tom.fawcett/public_html/ML-gallery/pages/

are learned by four different machine learning algorithms based on training datasets generated according to the decision boundaries shown in the top row. In order from top to bottom, we show decision trees (without pruning), nearest neighbor models (with $k = 3$ and using majority voting), naive Bayes models (using normal distributions to represent the two continuous feature values), and logistic regression models (using a simple linear model). In these images the training data instances are shown as symbols on the feature space (triangles for *good* and crosses for *bad*), the decision boundaries learned by each algorithm are represented by thick black lines, and the underlying *actual* decision boundaries are shown by the background shading.

These examples show two things. First, the decision boundaries learned by each algorithm are characteristic of that algorithm. For example, the decision boundaries associated with decision trees have a characteristic stepped appearance because of the way feature values are split in a decision tree, while the decision boundaries associated with k-NN models are noticeably jagged because of their local focus. The characteristic appearance of the decision boundaries is related to the representations used within the models and the inductive biases that the algorithms used to build them encode. The second thing that is apparent from the images in Figure 11.2[520] is that some of the models do a better job of representing the underlying decision boundaries than others. The decision boundary learned by the logistic regression model best matches the underlying decision boundary for the dataset in the first column, the decision tree model seems most appropriate for the dataset in the second column, and the k-NN model appears best for the dataset in the third column.

Real predictive data analytics projects use datasets that are much more complex than those shown in Figure 11.2[520]. For this reason selecting which type of model to use should be informed by the specific priorities of a project and the types of the descriptive and target features in the data. Also, in general, it is not a good idea to select just one machine learning approach at the beginning of a project and to exclusively use that. Instead, it is better to choose a number of different approaches and to run experiments to evaluate which is best for the particular project. However, this still requires the selection of a set of initial approaches. There are two questions to consider:

1. Does a machine learning approach match the requirements of the project?

2. Is the approach suitable for the type of prediction we want to make and the types of descriptive features we are using?

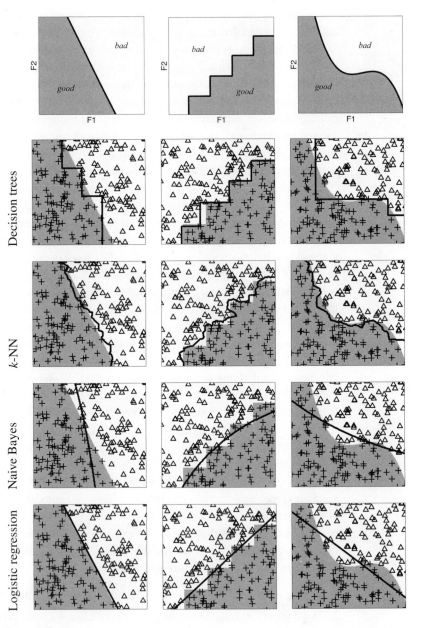

Figure 11.2

An illustration of the decision boundaries learned by different machine learning algorithms for three artificial datasets.

11.2.1   Matching Machine Learning Approaches to Projects

In many cases the primary requirement of a project is to create an accurate prediction model. Accuracy can often be related to the power of a machine learning algorithm to capture the interaction between descriptive features and the target feature. Caruana and Niculescu-Mizil (2006) and Caruana et al. (2008) report empirical evaluations of the accuracy of a range of model types across a range of domains. They found that on average, ensemble models and support vector machines were among the most accurate models. A consistent finding in both of these experiments, however, was the fact that for some domains, these more powerful models performed quite poorly, and other models, that in other domains were quite weak, achieved the best results. The main conclusions from this, and other similar studies, is that no machine learning approach is universally best, and experimentation with different approaches is the best way to ensure that an accurate model is built.

When evaluating models against a particular deployment scenario, model accuracy is not the only issue we need to consider. In order to successfully address a business problem, a model must be accurate, but it must also meet the other requirements of the business scenario. Three issues are important to consider:

- **Prediction speed:** How quickly can a model make predictions? Logistic regression models, for example, are very fast at making predictions as all that is involved is calculating the regression equation and performing a thresholding operation. On the other hand, k nearest neighbor models are very slow to make predictions as they must perform a comparison of a query instance to every instance in a, typically large, training set. The time differences arising from these different computational loads can have an influence on model selection. For example, in a real-time credit card fraud prediction system, it may be required that a model perform thousands of predictions per second. Even if significant computational resources were to be deployed for such a problem, it may not be possible for a k nearest neighbor model to perform fast enough to meet this requirement.

- **Capacity for retraining:** In Section 8.4.6[447] we discussed approaches that can be used to monitor the performance of a model so as to flag the occurrence of concept drift and indicate if a model has gone stale. When this occurs, the model needs to be changed in some way to adapt to the new scenario. For some modeling approaches this is quite easy, while for others it is almost impossible to adapt a model, and the only option is to discard the current model and train a new one using an updated dataset. Naive Bayes and *k* nearest neighbor models are good examples of the former type, while decision trees and regression models are good examples of the latter.

- **Interpretability:** In many instances a business will not be happy to simply accept the predictions made by a model and incorporate these into their decision making. Rather, they will require the predictions made by a model to be explained and justified. Different models offer different levels of explanation capacity and therefore different levels of interpretability. For example, decision trees and linear regression models are very easily interpreted, while support vector machines and ensembles are almost entirely uninterpretable (because of this, they are often referred to as a **black box**).

In summary, ensembles, support vector machines, and Bayesian networks are, in general, more powerful machine learning approaches than the others we have presented. However, these approaches are more complex, take a longer time to train, leverage more inductive bias, and are harder to interpret than the simpler approaches that we have presented. Furthermore, the selection of a machine learning approach also depends on the aspects of an application scenario described above (speed, capacity for retraining, interpretability), and often, these factors are a bigger driver for the selection of a machine learning approach than prediction accuracy.

11.2.2   Matching Machine Learning Approaches to Data

When matching machine learning approaches to the characteristics of a dataset, it is important to remember that almost every approach can be made to work for both continuous and categorical descriptive and target features. Certain approaches, however, are a more natural fit for some kinds of data than others, so we can make some recommendations. The first thing to consider in regard to data is whether the target feature is continuous or categorical. Models trained by reducing the sum of squared errors, for example, linear regression, are the most natural fit for making predictions for continuous target features. Out of the different approaches we have considered, the information-based and probability-based approaches are least well suited in this case. If, on the other hand, the target feature is categorical, then information-based and probability-based approaches are likely to work very well. Models trained using error-based approaches can become overly complicated when the number of levels of the target feature goes above two.

If all the descriptive features in a dataset are continuous, then a similarity-based approach is a natural fit, especially when there is also a categorical target feature. Error-based models would be preferred if the target feature is also continuous. When there are many continuous features, probability-based and information-based models can become complicated, but if all the features in a dataset are categorical, then information-based and probability-based models are appropriate. Error-based models are less suitable in this case as they require categorical features to be converted into sets of binary features, which causes an increase in dimensionality. In many cases datasets will contain both categorical and continuous descriptive features. The most naturally suited learning approaches in these scenarios are probably those that are best suited for the majority feature type.

The last issue to consider in relation to data when selecting machine learning approaches is the **curse of dimensionality**. If there are a large number of descriptive features, then we will need a large training dataset. **Feature selection** is an important process in any machine learning project and should generally be applied no matter what type of models are being developed. That said, some models are more susceptible to the curse of dimensionality than others. Similarity-based approaches are particularly sensitive to the curse of dimensionality and can struggle to perform well for a dataset with large numbers of descriptive features. Decision tree models have a feature selection mechanism built into their induction algorithm and so are more robust to this issue.

11.3   Your Next Steps

In many ways, the easy part of a predictive data analytics project is building the models. The machine learning algorithms tell us how to do this. What makes predictive data analytics difficult, but also fascinating, is figuring out how to answer all the questions that surround the modeling phase of a project. Throughout the course of a predictive data analytics project, we are forced to use our intuition and experience, and experimentation, to steer the project toward the best solution. To ensure a successful project outcome, we should inform the decisions that we make by

- becoming situationally fluent so that we can converse with experts in the application domain;
- exploring the data to understand it correctly;

- spending time cleaning the data;
- thinking hard about the best ways to represent features;
- and spending time designing the evaluation process correctly.

A distinctive aspect of this book is that we have chosen to present machine learning in context. In order to do this, we have included topics that are not covered in many machine learning books, including discussions on business understanding, data exploration and preparation, and case studies. We have also provided an in-depth introduction to some of the most popular machine learning approaches with examples that illustrate how these algorithms work. We believe that this book will provide you with an understanding of the broader context and core techniques of machine learning that will enable you to have a successful career in predictive data analytics.

Machine learning is a huge topic, however, and one book can only be so long. As a result, we have had to sacrifice coverage of some aspects of machine learning in order to include other topics and worked examples. We believe that this book will give you the knowledge and skills that you will need to explore these topics yourself. To help with this, we would recommend Hastie et al. (2001), Bishop (2006), and Murphy (2012) for broad coverage of machine learning algorithms, including unsupervised and reinforcement learning approaches not covered in this book. These books are suitable as reference texts for experienced practitioners and postgraduate researchers in machine learning. Some of the other machine learning topics that you might like to explore include **deep learning** (Bengio, 2009; Hinton and Salakhutdinov, 2006), **multi-label classification** (Tsoumakas et al., 2012), and **graphical models** (Kollar and Friedman, 2009). Finally, we hope that you find machine learning as fascinating and rewarding a topic as we do, and we wish you the best in your future learning.

A Descriptive Statistics and Data Visualization for Machine Learning

In this appendix we introduce the fundamental statistical measures of **central tendency** and **variation**. We also introduce three of the most important and useful data visualization techniques that can be used to visualize a single feature: the **bar plot**, the **histogram**, and the **box plot**.

A.1 Descriptive Statistics for Continuous Features

To understand the characteristics of a continuous feature, there are two things that are important to measure: the **central tendency** of the feature and the **variation** within the feature. These are the basic building blocks of everything else that will follow, so it is important to fully understand them.

A.1.1 Central Tendency

The central tendency of a sample refers to the value that is *typical* of the sample and therefore can be used to summarize it. Measures of central tendency are an approximation of this notional value. The **arithmetic mean** (or **sample mean** or just **mean**) is the best known measure of central tendency. The arithmetic mean of a set of n values for a feature a is denoted by the symbol $\bar{a}$ and is calculated as

$$\bar{a} = \frac{1}{n} \sum_{i=1}^{n} a_i \tag{1}$$

Figure A.1[526] shows a group of players on a school basketball team and their heights. Using Equation (1)[525] we can calculate the arithmetic mean of these players' heights as

$$\overline{\text{HEIGHT}} = \frac{1}{8} \times (150 + 163 + 145 + 140 + 157 + 151 + 140 + 149)$$

$$= 149.375$$

This mean height is shown by the dashed gray line in Figure A.1[526]. The arithmetic mean is one measure of the central tendency of a **sample** (for our purposes, a sample is just a set of values for a feature in an ABT). Because it is easy to calculate and easy to interpret, the mean is commonly used as part of the data exploration process as a good estimate of the central tendencies of features in an ABT.

150 163 145 140 157 151 140 149

Figure A.1

The members of a school basketball team. The height of each player is listed below the player. The dashed gray line shows the arithmetic mean of the players' heights.

Any measure of central tendency is, however, just an approximation, so we must be aware of the limitations of any measure that we use. The arithmetic mean, for example, is very sensitive to very large or very small values in a sample. For example, suppose our basketball team manage to sign a *ringer* measuring in at 229cm, as shown in Figure A.2(a)[526]. The arithmetic mean for the full group is now 158.222cm and, as shown by the dashed gray line in Figure A.2(a)[526], no longer really represents the central tendency of the group. An unusually large or small value like this is referred to as an **outlier**, and the arithmetic mean is very sensitive to the presence of outliers.

150 163 145 140 157 151 140 149 229   140 140 145 149 **150** 151 157 163 229

(a) Mean   (b) Median

Figure A.2

The members of the school basketball team from Figure A.1[526] with one very tall *ringer* added: (a) the dashed gray line shows the mean of the players' heights; (b) the dashed gray line shows the median of the players' heights, with the players ordered by height.

There are other statistics that we can use to measure central tendency that are not as sensitive to outliers. The **median** is another very useful measure of the central tendency of a sample. The median of a set of values can be calculated by ordering the values from lowest to highest and selecting the middle value. If there is an even number of values in the sample, then the median is obtained by calculating the arithmetic mean of the middle two values. The median is not as sensitive to outliers as the arithmetic mean and therefore can be a more accurate estimate of the central tendency of a set of values if outliers exist.

In fact, a large difference between the mean and median of a feature is an indication that there may be outliers among the feature values.

Figure A.2(b)[526] shows the extended basketball team ordered from smallest to tallest, with the height of the each player listed below the player. The median value of this set is 150 and is shown as the dashed gray line in Figure A.2(b)[526]. In this case the median better captures the central tendency of the set of values.

Another commonly used measure of central tendency is the **mode**. The mode is simply the most commonly occurring value in a sample (determined by counting the frequency with which each value occurs in the sample). If all values in a sample occur with equal frequency, then there is no mode. For the heights of the players in the extended basketball team in Figure A.2[526], the mode is 140 as it is the only value that appears twice. The mode is not particularly effective in this case at measuring the central tendency of the values. Mode is more frequently useful for categorical features than for continuous ones, but it can be useful for continuous features when the sample is large enough.

A.1.2 Variation

Having used the measures of central tendency to describe where our data is centered, we will now turn our attention to the **variation** in our data. Figure A.3[527] shows a rival school basketball team to that shown in Figure A.1[526]. The height of each player is listed below the player, and the dashed gray line shows the arithmetic mean of the players' heights, which is 149.375, the same as for the original team. The heights of the players in this second team vary much more than those of the first team (see Figures A.1[526] and A.3[527]). Descriptive statistics provides us with a range of tools that we can use to formally measure variation and so distinguish between the sets of heights in the two basketball teams. In essence, most of statistics, and in turn analytics, is about describing and understanding variation.

192 102 145 165 126 154 123 188

Figure A.3
The members of a rival school basketball team. Player heights are listed below each player. The dashed gray line shows the arithmetic mean of the players' heights.

The most easily calculated measure of variation is **range**. The range of a sample of n values for a feature a is calculated as

$$range = max(a) - min(a) \qquad (2)$$

The range of the basketball player heights in Figure A.1[526] is $163 - 140 = 23$ and for those in Figure A.3[527] is $192 - 102 = 90$. These measures match what we intuitively see in these figures—the heights of the second team vary much more than those of the first team. The main advantage of using the range is the ease with which it is calculated. The major disadvantage of the range, however, is that it is highly sensitive to outliers.

The **variance** of a sample is a more useful measure of variation. Variance measures the average difference between each value in a sample and the mean of that sample. The variance of the n values of a feature a is denoted $var(a)$ and is calculated as

$$var(a) = \frac{\sum_{i=1}^{n} (a_i - \bar{a})^2}{n-1} \qquad (3)$$

In order to allow for the fact that some of the differences between values and the mean will be positive and some will be negative, we square each difference.[1]

For the players' heights given in Figure A.1[526], the mean is 149.375, so the variance can be calculated as

$$var(\text{HEIGHT}) = \frac{(150 - 149.375)^2 + (163 - 149.375)^2 + \ldots + (149 - 149.375)^2}{8 - 1}$$

$$= 63.125$$

For the players' heights given in Figure A.3[527], the mean is also 149.375, so the variance can be calculated as

$$var(\text{HEIGHT}) = \frac{(192 - 149.375)^2 + (102 - 149.375)^2 + \ldots + (188 - 149.375)^2}{8 - 1}$$

$$= 1{,}011.411$$

This example illustrates that the variance also captures the intuition that the heights of the players in the second team vary much more than those in the

---

1 We divide by $n - 1$ (as opposed to n) because we are calculating the variance using only a sample, and on average, dividing by $n - 1$ gives a better estimate of the population variance than using n.

first team. It also, however, illustrates an issue with using variance. Due to the fact that the differences are squared, variances are not in the same units as the original values, so they are not especially informative—telling someone that the variance of the heights on one team is 63.125 and on another is 1,011.411 doesn't give them any particularly useful information other than the fact that the variance of one team is bigger than that of the other.

The **standard deviation**, *sd*, of a sample is calculated by taking the square root of the variance of the sample:

$$sd(a) = \sqrt{var(a)}$$

$$= \sqrt{\frac{\sum_{i=1}^{n} (a_i - \overline{a})^2}{n - 1}} \qquad (4)$$

This means that the standard deviation is measured in the original units of the sample, which makes it much more interpretable than the variance. It is very common to see the mean and standard deviation provided as a full description of a sample.

The standard deviation of the heights of the players on the first basketball team is 7.945 and for the second team is 31.803. As these measures are in the same units as the heights, they afford us a more intuitive understanding of the data and make comparison easier. We can say that, on average, players on the first team vary by almost 8cm from the average of 149.375cm, while on the second team, they vary by approximately 32cm.

Percentiles are another useful measure of the variation of the values for a feature. A proportion of $\frac{i}{100}$ of the values in a sample take values equal to or lower than the ith percentile of that sample. Conversely, a proportion of $(100 - i)/100$ values in a sample take values larger than the ith percentile. To calculate the ith percentile of the n values of a feature a, we first order the values in ascending order and then multiply n by $\frac{i}{100}$ to determine the *index*. If the *index* is a whole number, we take the value at that position in the ordered list of values as the ith percentile. If *index* is not a whole number, then we interpolate the value for the ith percentile as

$$i^{th}\ percentile = (1 - index\_f) \times a_{index\_w} + index\_f \times a_{index\_w+1} \qquad (5)$$

where *index_w* is the whole part of *index*, *index_f* is the fractional part of *index*, and a_{index_w} is the value in the ordered list at position *index_w*.

102 123 126 145 154 165 188 192

Figure A.4
The members of the rival school basketball team from Figure A.3[527] ordered by height.

For example, Figure A.4[530] shows the basketball team from Figure A.3[527] ordered by height. To calculate the 25th percentile, we first calculate *index* as $\frac{25}{100} \times 8 = 2$. So, the 25th percentile is the second value in the ordered list, which is 123. To calculate the 80th percentile, we first calculate *index* as $\frac{80}{100} \times 8 = 6.4$. Because *index* is not a whole number, we set *index_w* to the whole part of *index*, 6, and *index_f* to the fractional part, 0.4. Then we can calculate the 80th percentile as

$$(1 - 0.4) \times 165 + 0.4 \times 188 = 174.2$$

using the 6th and 7th values in the list, 165 and 188. We have actually already come across a percentile in the measures of central tendency. The median is the 50th percentile.

We can use percentiles to describe another measure of variation known as the **inter-quartile range** (**IQR**). The inter-quartile range is calculated as the difference between the 25th percentile and the 75th percentile. These percentiles are also known as the **lower quartile** (or 1st quartile) and the **upper quartile** (or 3rd quartile), hence the name inter-quartile range. For the heights of the first basketball team, the inter-quartile range is $151 - 140 = 11$, while for the second team, it is $165 - 123 = 42$.

A.2   Descriptive Statistics for Categorical Features

The statistics outlined in the previous section work well to describe continuous features, but they do not work for categorical features. For categorical features we are interested primarily in **frequency counts** and **proportions**. The frequency count of each level[2] of a categorical feature is calculated by

---

2 Remember, we refer to each value that a particular categorical feature can take as the levels of the categorical feature.

Table A.1

A dataset showing the positions and monthly training expenses of a school basketball team.

ID	POSITION	TRAINING EXPENSES	ID	POSITION	TRAINING EXPENSES
1	center	56.75	11	center	550.00
2	guard	1,800.11	12	center	223.89
3	guard	1,341.03	13	center	103.23
4	forward	749.50	14	forward	758.22
5	guard	1,150.00	15	forward	430.79
6	forward	928.30	16	forward	675.11
7	center	250.90	17	guard	1,657.20
8	guard	806.15	18	guard	1,405.18
9	guard	1,209.02	19	guard	760.51
10	forward	405.72	20	forward	985.41

Table A.2

A frequency table for the POSITION feature from the school basketball team dataset in Table A.1[531].

Level	Count	Proportion
guard	8	40%
forward	7	35%
center	5	25%

counting the number of times that level appears in the sample. The proportion for each level is calculated by dividing the frequency count for that level by the total sample size. Frequencies and proportions are typically presented in a **frequency table**, which shows the frequency and proportion of each level for a particular feature—usually sorted by descending frequency.

For example, Table A.1[531] lists the position that each player on a school basketball team plays at, and the average training expenses accrued each month by each player on the team. Table A.2[531] shows the frequencies and proportions of the positions that players in the team play at, based on counts of the occurrences of the different levels of the POSITION feature in Table A.1[531]. We can see from this example that the *guard* level is the most frequent, followed by *forward* and *center*.

Based on these frequency counts and proportions, the **mode** of a categorical feature can be calculated. The mode is a measure of the central tendency of a categorical feature and is simply the most frequent level. Based on the counts in Table A.2[531], the mode of the POSITION feature is *guard*. We often also calculate a **second mode**, which is just the second most common level of a feature. In this example, the second mode is *forward*.

A.3   Populations and Samples

Throughout the discussion in the previous sections about central tendency and variation, we consistently used the word **sample** to refer to the set of values in an ABT for a particular feature. In statistics it is very important to understand the difference between a **population** and a sample. The term population is used in statistics to represent all possible measurements or outcomes that are of interest to us in a particular study or piece of analysis. The term sample refers to the subset of the population that is selected for analysis.

For example, consider Table A.3[533], which shows a set of results for polls run shortly before the 2012 United States presidential election, in which Mitt Romney and Barack Obama were the front runners.[3] In the first poll in the table, from Pew Research, we can see that a sample of just 2,709 likely voters[4] was used. This poll put Obama ahead of Romney in the race to the White House. In this example the actual population of interest was the voting population of the United States, which was approximately 240,926,957 people. It would be almost impossible to ask the full voting population their voting intentions before an actual election—after all, that is what the actual election is for—so polling companies take a sample.

While the sample of 2,709 voters out of a population of 240,926,957 might appear quite small, we can also see from the table that the **margin of error** for the poll is given as $\pm 2.2\%$. The margin of error takes into account the fact that this is just a sample from a much larger population.[5] All the other polls in the table were conducted with similar sized samples. You should notice, however, that, in general, the larger the sample, the smaller the margin of error. This reflects the fact that if we use a bigger sample, we can be more confident in our approximations of the characteristics of the full population.

3 This data is taken from the collection at Real Clear Politics: `www.realclearpolitics.com/epolls/2012/president/us/general_election_romney_vs_obama-1171.html`.

4 Likely voters are the subset of registered voters who have been identified as most likely to actually vote in an election.

5 This size of margin of error is common for these types of election polls.

Table A.3
A number of poll results from the run-up to the 2012 US presidential election.

Poll	Obama	Romney	Other	Date	Margin of Error	Sample Size
Pew Research	50	47	3	04-Nov	±2.2	2,709
ABC News/Wash Post	50	47	3	04-Nov	±2.5	2,345
CNN/Opinion Research	49	49	2	04-Nov	±3.5	963
Pew Research	50	47	3	03-Nov	±2.2	2,709
ABC News/Wash Post	49	48	3	03-Nov	±2.5	2,069
ABC News/Wash Post	49	49	2	30-Oct	±3.0	1,288

In choosing a sample, it is important that it be representative of the population. In this example the sample should represent the voting population—for example, there should be a representative proportion of males compared to females and of different age categories within the sample. If a sample is not representative, we say that the sample is **biased**. Using a **simple random sample** is the most straightforward way of avoiding biased samples. In a simple random sample, each item in the population is equally likely to make it into the sample. Other, more sophisticated sampling methods can be used to ensure that a sample maintains relationships that exist in a population. We discuss sampling methods in more detail in Section 3.6.3[98].

In the context of a predictive analytics scenario, the sample is the set of values that occur in an ABT. The population is the set of all the values that could possibly occur. For example, in an ABT for a motor insurance claims fraud prediction problem, we may include details of 500 claims that have happened in the past. This would be our sample. The population would be all the claims that have ever happened.

Up to this point we have outlined descriptive statistics that we can use to describe the values in a sample. How do we relate these values to the actual underlying population? Statistics that describe the population are referred to as **population parameters**. In general we use the sample statistics, which we have already calculated, as estimates for the population parameters. The population mean of a feature is usually denoted by μ, and in general, given a sufficiently large sample, we use the sample mean $\bar{a}$ as a point estimate of μ. The population variance of a feature is usually denoted by σ^2. In general, given a sufficiently large sample, we use the sample variance, $var(a)$, as a point estimate of σ^2. This process is known as statistical inference.

Careful readers will have noticed that in the equation for variance given in Equation (3)[528], we divided the sum of the differences between the values of the feature a and $\bar{a}$ not by n, the number of values for a in the ABT, but by $n-1$. We divide by $n-1$ so that the sample variance is an unbiased estimate of the population variance. We say that the estimate is unbiased if its variance, on average, equals that of the population variance. If we divided by n, we would have a biased estimator that on average underestimates the variance. It is in small differences like this that we see the impact of working on samples rather than populations.

A.4   Data Visualization

When performing data exploration, **data visualization** can help enormously. In this section we describe three important data visualization techniques that can be used to visualize the values in a single feature: the **bar plot**, the **histogram**, and the **box plot**. For the examples throughout this section, we will use the dataset in Table A.1[531], which lists the position that each player on a school basketball team plays at and the average training expenses they accrue each month.

A.4.1   Bar Plots

The simplest form of data visualization we can use for data exploration is the bar plot. A bar plot includes a vertical bar for each level of a categorical feature. The height of each bar indicates the frequency of the associated level (readers will most likely already be familiar with the bar plot). In a slight variation of the bar plot, we can show **densities** rather than frequencies by dividing each frequency by the total number of values in the dataset. This makes bar plots comparable across datasets or samples of different sizes and is referred to as a **probability distribution**, because the densities actually tell us the probability that we would pick each level if we were to select one instance at random from the dataset.

Another simple variant of the basic bar plot orders the bars in descending order.[6] Typically we use bar plots to discover the most frequent levels for a feature, and this ordering makes this more apparent. Figure A.5[535] shows example

---

6 These charts are often referred to as **Pareto charts**, especially when they also include a line indicating the cumulative total frequency or density.

bar plots of all three types for the POSITION feature from the dataset in Table A.1[531]. We can see that *guard* is the most frequent level.

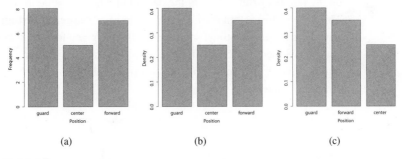

(a)   (b)   (c)

Figure A.5
Example bar plots for the POSITION feature in Table A.1[531]: (a) frequency bar plot, (b) density bar plot, and (c) order density bar plot.

A.4.2 Histograms

Figure A.6[535] is a bar plot of the TRAINING EXPENSES feature from Table A.1[531]. The figure illustrates why a bar plot is not an appropriate graphic to use to visualize a continuous feature: as is generally the case with a continuous feature, there are as many distinct values as there are instances in the dataset, and therefore there are as many bars in the histogram as there are instances, each bar having a height of 1.0.

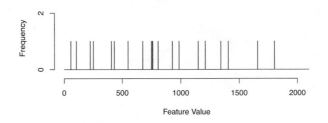

Figure A.6
Bar plot of the continuous TRAINING EXPENSES feature from Table A.1[531].

The way to solve this problem is to visualize intervals rather than specific values, and this is what a **histogram** does. Figure A.7(a)[536] shows the frequency histogram for the TRAINING EXPENSES feature when we define ten

200-unit intervals spanning the range that this feature can take (the frequencies come from Table A.4(a)[537]). In this histogram the width of each bar indicates the extent of the interval the bar represents, and the height of each bar is based on the number of instances in the dataset that have a value inside the interval. This type of histogram is often referred to as a **frequency histogram**. Generally, there is not an optimal set of intervals for a given feature. For example, we could have used four 500-unit intervals to generate the histogram instead—see Figure A.7(b)[536], based on frequencies from Table A.4(b)[537]—or, indeed, any other set of intervals.

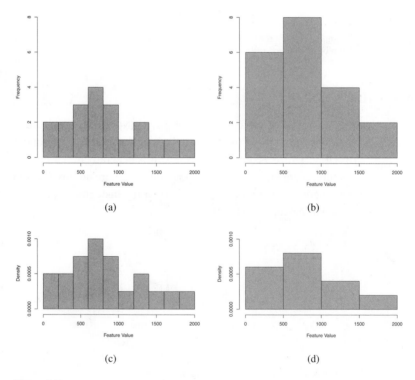

Figure A.7

(a) and (b) frequency histograms and (c) and (d) density histograms for the continuous TRAINING EXPENSES feature from Table A.1[531], illustrating how using intervals overcomes the problem seen in Figure A.6[535] and the effect of varying interval sizes.

Table A.4

The density calculation for the TRAINING EXPENSES feature from Table A.1[531] using (a) ten 200-unit intervals and (b) four 500-unit intervals.

(a) 200-unit intervals

Interval	Count	Density	Prob
$[0, 200)$	2	0.00050	0.1
$[200, 400)$	2	0.00050	0.1
$[400, 600)$	3	0.00075	0.15
$[600, 800)$	4	0.00100	0.2
$[800, 1000)$	3	0.00075	0.15
$[1000, 1200)$	1	0.00025	0.05
$[1200, 1400)$	2	0.00050	0.1
$[1400, 1600)$	1	0.00025	0.05
$[1600, 1800)$	1	0.00025	0.05
$[1800, 2000)$	1	0.00025	0.02

(b) 500-unit intervals

Interval	Count	Density	Prob
$[0, 500)$	6	0.0006	0.3
$[500, 1000)$	8	0.0008	0.4
$[1000, 1500)$	4	0.0004	0.2
$[1500, 2000)$	2	0.0002	0.1

We can convert a histogram to a probability distribution by dividing the count for each interval by the total number of observations in the dataset multiplied by the width of the interval. As a result, the area of each bar (the bar height times the bar width) gives the probability for the feature taking a value in the interval represented by that bar. The resulting histogram is called a **density histogram** because the height of each bar represents how densely the instances in the dataset that fall within the interval are packed into the area of the bar.

Figure A.7(c)[536] illustrates the density histogram of the TRAINING EXPENSES feature using ten 200-unit intervals, and Figure A.7(d)[536] illustrates the density histogram using four 500-unit intervals. Notice that the vertical axes in these histograms are labeled **density**, rather than frequency. Table A.4(a)[537] shows the density and probability calculations for the TRAINING EXPENSES feature when we use ten 200-unit intervals, and Table A.4(b)[537] shows the same calculations when we use four 500-unit intervals.[7] Recall that we compute the density for each interval by dividing the number of observations in the interval by the width of the interval multiplied by the total number of observations. Notice that the sum of the probabilities (the bar areas in the histograms) in both of these tables is 1.0, which is what we would expect with a probability distribution—all probability distributions sum to 1.0.

---

7 When defining intervals, a square bracket, [or], indicates that the boundary value is included in the interval, and a curved bracket, (or), indicates that it is excluded from the interval.

A.4.3   Box Plots

The last data visualization technique we will discuss for visualizing the values of a single feature is the **box plot**.[8] A box plot is a visual representation of the five key descriptive statistics for a continuous feature: minimum, 1st quartile, median, 3rd quartile, and maximum. Figure A.8(a)[538] shows the structure of a box plot. In a box plot the vertical axis shows the range of values that a feature can take. The extent of the rectangular box in the middle of the plot is determined by the 3rd quartile at the top and the 1st quartile at the bottom. The height of this rectangle, then, also shows the inter-quartile range. The strong black line across the middle of the rectangle shows the median.

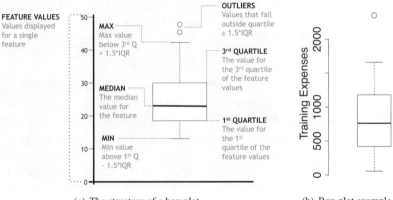

(a) The structure of a box plot   (b) Box plot example

Figure A.8

(a) The structure of a box plot; (b) a box plot for the TRAINING EXPENSES feature from the basketball team dataset in Table A.1[531].

The whiskers that emerge from the top and bottom of the main rectangle in a box plot are designed to show the range of the data. The top whisker extends to whichever is lower of the maximum value of the feature or the upper quartile plus 1.5 times the IQR. Similarly, the bottom whisker extends to whichever is higher of the minimum value of the feature or the lower quartile minus 1.5 times the IQR. Values that fall outside the whiskers are referred to as outliers and are shown as small circles.

---

8 Box plots are one of the collection of visual data exploration techniques first presented in Tukey's influential 1977 book *Exploratory Data Analysis* (Tukey, 1977).

Figure A.8(b)[538] shows a box plot for the TRAINING EXPENSES feature from the dataset in Table A.1[531]. From this plot we can get a concise, but detailed, description of the feature and notice the inclusion of an outlier value. In comparison with a box plot, an individual histogram provides more information; for example, histograms show the distribution of the values of a feature. Box plots, however, can be placed side by side, and in Section 3.5.1.2[80] we see that the ability to place multiple box plots side by side is the main advantage box plots have over histograms.

B Introduction to Probability for Machine Learning

In this appendix we introduce the fundamental concepts of **probability theory** that are used in probability-based machine learning algorithms. Specifically, we present the basics of calculating probabilities based on **relative frequencies**, calculating **conditional probabilities**, the probability **product rule**, the probability **chain rule**, and the **Theorem of Total Probability**.

B.1 Probability Basics

Probability is the branch of mathematics that deals with measuring the likelihood (or uncertainty) around events. The roots of probability are in gambling, where, understandably, gamblers wanted to be able to predict future events based on their likelihood. There are two ways of computing the likelihood of a future event: (1) use the **relative frequency** of the event in the past, or (2) use a **subjective estimate** (ideally from an expert!). In the predictive analytics context, the standard approach is to use relative frequency, and we focus on this approach in this chapter.

Probability has a longer history, and broader applicability, than predictive analytics. Consequently, the standard language of probability has developed some esoteric terminology, including terms such as **sample space**, **experiment**, **outcome**, **event**, and **random variable**. So we will begin by first explaining this terminology and aligning it with the more familiar terminology of predictive analytics.

In probability a **domain** of interest is represented by a set of **random variables**. For example, if we want to model the behavior of a die using probability, we would begin by creating a random variable, let us call it X, that has a domain equal to the set of possible outcomes when we roll the die, namely the set $\{ \boxdot, \boxdot, \boxdot, \boxdot, \boxdot, \boxdot \}$. Extending this example, if we wanted to study the behavior of two dice, we would create two random variables, we might call them $Dice_1$ and $Dice_2$, each having the domain $\{ \boxdot, \boxdot, \boxdot, \boxdot, \boxdot, \boxdot \}$. In this extended context, an **experiment** involves rolling the two dice, and the **sample space** defines the set of all possible outcomes for this experiment (see Figure B.1[542]). An **event** is then an experiment whose **outcome** fixes the values of the random variables. For example, an **event** in this domain would be represented as $Dice_1 = \boxdot, Dice_2 = \boxdot$.

Table B.1[542] lists a small dataset of instances from the sample space shown in Figure B.1[542]. We will use this example dataset to illustrate how to map the terminology of probability into the language of predictive analytics:

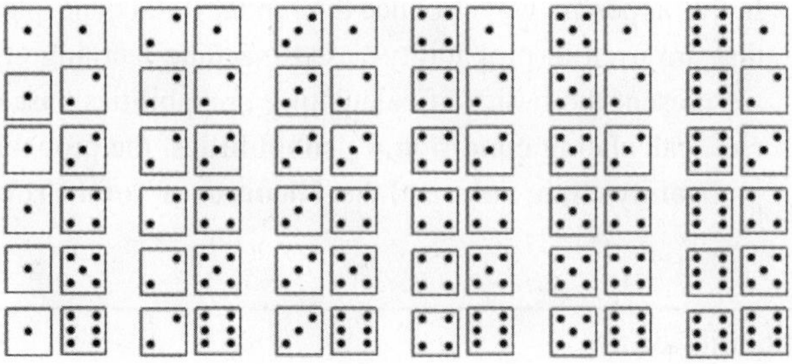

Figure B.1

The **sample space** for the domain of two dice.

Table B.1

A dataset of instances from the sample space in Figure B.1[542].

ID	DICE1	DICE2
1	⚂	⚃
2	⚀	⚅
3	⚅	⚄
4	⚂	⚂
5	⚀	⚀

- The set of **random variables** in a domain maps to the set of features in a dataset (both descriptive and target). DICE1 and DICE2 are the equivalent of random variables.

- The **sample space** for a domain is the set of all possible combinations of assignments of values to features.

- An **experiment** whose outcome has been already been recorded is a row in the dataset. Each row in Table B.1[542] records the outcome of a previous experiment.

- An **experiment** whose outcome we do not yet know but would like to predict is the prediction task for which we are building a model.

- An **event** is any subset of an experiment. An event may describe an assignment of values to all the features in the domain (e.g., a full row in the dataset) or an assignment to one or more features in the domain. DICE1 = ⚂ is an example of an event. DICE1 = ⚀, DICE2 = ⚄ is also an event.

So that we are consistent with the terminology throughout this book, in the rest of this chapter, we use the predictive analytics terms (feature, dataset, prediction, and event) rather than the traditional terms from probability.

A feature can take one or more values from a domain, and we can find out the likelihood of a feature taking any particular value using a **probability function**, $P()$. A probability function is a function that takes an event (an assignment of values to features) as a parameter and returns the likelihood of that event. For example, $P(\textsc{Dice}1 = \square)$ will return the likelihood of the event $\textsc{Dice}1 = \square$, and $P(\textsc{Dice}1 = \square, \textsc{Dice}2 = \square)$ will return the likelihood of the event where $\textsc{Dice}1 = \square$ and $\textsc{Dice}2 = \square$. If we are defining the probability function for a categorical feature, then the function is known as a **probability mass function** because it can be understood as returning a discrete **probability mass** for each level in the domain of the feature. The probability mass is simply the probability of an event. Conversely, if the feature we are dealing with is a continuous feature, the probability function is known as a **probability density function**. For this introduction, we focus on categorical features and probability mass functions.

Probability mass functions have two properties: (1) they always return a value between 0.0 and 1.0; and (2) the sum of the probabilities over the set of events covering all the possible assignments of values to features must equal 1.0. Formally these properties are defined as follows:

$$0 \leqslant P(f = level) \leqslant 1$$

$$\sum_{l \in levels(f)} P(f = l) = 1.0$$

where $levels(f)$ returns the set of levels in the domain of the feature f.

Probability functions are the basic building blocks of probability theory, and they are very easy to create from a dataset. The value returned by a probability function for an event is simply the **relative frequency** of that event in the dataset. The relative frequency of an event is calculated as how often the event happened divided by how often could it have happened. For example, the relative frequency of the event $\textsc{Dice}1 = \square$ is simply the count of all the rows in the dataset where $\textsc{Dice}1$ has a value of $\square$ divided by the number of rows in the dataset. Based on Table B.1[542], the probability of the event $\textsc{Dice}1 = \square$ is[1]

$$P(\textsc{Dice}1 = \square) = \frac{|\{\mathbf{d}_1, \mathbf{d}_4\}|}{|\{\mathbf{d}_1, \mathbf{d}_2, \mathbf{d}_3, \mathbf{d}_4, \mathbf{d}_5\}|} = \frac{2}{5} = 0.4$$

---

1 In the notation used in this book, $\mathbf{d}_1$ refers to the instance in a dataset with an ID of 1 and so on.

So far we have focused on calculating the probability of an individual event. In a predictive analytics task, we will often be interested in calculating the probability of more than one event. For example, we might want to know the probability of the target feature taking a particular value and one of the descriptive features taking a particular value at the same time. Technically, if an event involves more than one feature, it can be considered to be composed of several *simple* events. In these cases the probability calculated is known as a **joint probability**. The probability of a joint event is simply the relative frequency of the joint event within the dataset. In terms of rows in a dataset, this computation is simply the number of rows where the set of assignments listed in the joint event holds divided by the total number of rows in the dataset. For example, the probability of the joint event[2] $\text{DICE}1 = \boxdot, \text{DICE}2 = \boxdot$ would be calculated as

$$ P(\text{DICE}1 = \boxdot, \text{DICE}2 = \boxdot) = \frac{|\{\mathbf{d}_3\}|}{|\{\mathbf{d}_1, \mathbf{d}_2, \mathbf{d}_3, \mathbf{d}_4, \mathbf{d}_5\}|} = \frac{1}{5} = 0.2 $$

The type of probabilities we have calculated so far are known as **prior probabilities** or **unconditional probabilities**. Often, however, we want to know the probability of an event in the context where one or more other events are known to have happened. This type of probability, where we take one or more events to already hold, is known as a **posterior probability**, because it is calculated *after* other events have happened. It is also commonly known as a **conditional probability**, because the probability calculated is valid conditional on the given events (or evidence). When we want to express this type of probability, formally we use a vertical bar, |, to separate the events we want the probability for (listed on the left hand side of the bar) from the events that we know have already happened. The vertical bar symbol can be read as *given that*. So the probability of $\text{DICE}1 = \boxdot$ *given that* $\text{DICE}2 = \boxdot$ would be written as

$$ P(\text{DICE}1 = \boxdot \mid \text{DICE}2 = \boxdot) $$

The **conditional probability** for an event given that we know another event is true is calculated by dividing the number of rows in the dataset where both events are true by the number of rows in the dataset where just the given event is true. For example, the conditional probability for the event $\text{DICE}1 = \boxdot$ *given*

---

2 When listing a joint event, we use a comma , to denote logical *and*.

Table B.2

A simple dataset for MENINGITIS with three common symptoms of the disease listed as descriptive features: HEADACHE, FEVER, and VOMITING.

ID	HEADACHE	FEVER	VOMITING	MENINGITIS
11	true	true	false	false
37	false	true	false	false
42	true	false	true	false
49	true	false	true	false
54	false	true	false	true
57	true	false	true	false
73	true	false	true	false
75	true	false	true	true
89	false	true	false	false
92	true	false	true	true

that DICE2 = ⊡ would be calculated as

$$P(\text{DICE1} = \boxplus \mid \text{DICE2} = \boxdot) = \frac{|\{\mathbf{d}_3\}|}{|\{\mathbf{d}_2, \mathbf{d}_3\}|} = \frac{1}{2} = 0.5$$

We now understand the theory of how to calculate a simple unconditional probability, a joint probability, and a conditional probability using a dataset. Now is a good point to ground this knowledge in a more interesting example focused on predictive data analytics. We will use the dataset in Table B.2[545] for this.[3] The target being predicted in this dataset is whether or not a patient is suffering from meningitis, and the descriptive features are common symptoms associated with meningitis.

A quick comment on our notation. Throughout this chapter, named features will be denoted by the uppercase initial letters of their names—for example, a feature named MENINGITIS will be denoted by M. Also, where a named feature is binary, we will use the lowercase initial letter of the feature name to denote the event where the feature is true and the lowercase initial letter preceded by the $\neg$ symbol to denote the event where it is false. So, m will denote the event MENINGITIS = *true* and $\neg m$ will denote MENINGITIS = *false*. Given the dataset in Table B.2[545], the probability of a patient having a headache is

$$P(h) = \frac{|\{\mathbf{d}_{11}, \mathbf{d}_{42}, \mathbf{d}_{49}, \mathbf{d}_{57}, \mathbf{d}_{73}, \mathbf{d}_{75}, \mathbf{d}_{92}\}|}{|\{\mathbf{d}_{11}, \mathbf{d}_{37}, \mathbf{d}_{42}, \mathbf{d}_{49}, \mathbf{d}_{54}, \mathbf{d}_{57}, \mathbf{d}_{73}, \mathbf{d}_{75}, \mathbf{d}_{89}, \mathbf{d}_{92}\}|} = \frac{7}{10} = 0.7 \quad (1)$$

---

3 This data has been artificially generated for this example.

the probability of a patient having a headache and meningitis is

$$P(m,h) = \frac{|\{\mathbf{d}_{75}, \mathbf{d}_{92}\}|}{|\{\mathbf{d}_{11}, \mathbf{d}_{37}, \mathbf{d}_{42}, \mathbf{d}_{49}, \mathbf{d}_{54}, \mathbf{d}_{57}, \mathbf{d}_{73}, \mathbf{d}_{75}, \mathbf{d}_{89}, \mathbf{d}_{92}\}|} = \frac{2}{10} = 0.2 \quad (2)$$

and the probability of a patient having meningitis given that we know that the patient has a headache is

$$P(m \mid h) = \frac{|\{\mathbf{d}_{75}, \mathbf{d}_{92}\}|}{|\{\mathbf{d}_{11}, \mathbf{d}_{42}, \mathbf{d}_{49}, \mathbf{d}_{57}, \mathbf{d}_{73}, \mathbf{d}_{75}, \mathbf{d}_{92}\}|} = \frac{2}{7} = 0.2857 \quad (3)$$

B.2   Probability Distributions and Summing Out

Sometimes it is useful to talk about the probabilities for all the possible assignments to a feature. To do this we use the concept of a **probability distribution**. A probability distribution is a data structure that describes the probability of a feature taking a value for all the possible values the feature can take. The probability distribution for a categorical feature is a vector that lists the probabilities associated with each of the values in the domain of the feature. A vector is an ordered list, so the mechanism for matching a probability in the vector with a particular value in the domain is just to look up the position of the probability within the vector. We use bold notation $\mathbf{P}()$ to distinguish between a probability distribution and a probability function $P()$. For example, the probability distribution for the binary feature MENINGITIS from Table B.2[545], with a probability of 0.3 of being *true* and using the convention of the first element in the vector being the probability for a *true* value, would be written as $\mathbf{P}(M) = \langle 0.3, 0.7 \rangle$.

The concept of a probability distribution also applies to joint probabilities, which gives us the concept of a **joint probability distribution**. A joint probability distribution is a multi-dimensional matrix where each cell in the matrix lists the probability for one of the events in the sample space defined by the combination of feature values. The dimensions of the matrix are dependent on the number of features and the number of values in the domains of the features. The joint probability distribution for the four binary features from Table B.2[545]

(HEADACHE, FEVER, VOMITING, and MENINGITIS) would be written as

$$\mathbf{P}(H,F,V,M) = \begin{bmatrix} P(h,f,v,m), & P(\neg h,f,v,m) \\ P(h,f,v,\neg m), & P(\neg h,f,v,\neg m) \\ P(h,f,\neg v,m), & P(\neg h,f,\neg v,m) \\ P(h,f,\neg v,\neg m), & P(\neg h,f,\neg v,\neg m) \\ P(h,\neg f,v,m), & P(\neg h,\neg f,v,m) \\ P(h,\neg f,v,\neg m), & P(\neg h,\neg f,v,\neg m) \\ P(h,\neg f,\neg v,m), & P(\neg h,\neg f,\neg v,m) \\ P(h,\neg f,\neg v,\neg m), & P(\neg h,\neg f,\neg v,\neg m) \end{bmatrix}$$

Remember that the sum of all the elements in a probability distribution must be 1.0. Consequently, the sum of all the cells in a joint probability distribution must be 1.0. A **full joint probability distribution** is simply a joint probability distribution over all the features in a domain. Given a full joint probability distribution we can compute the probability of any event in a domain by summing over the cells in the distribution where that event is true. For example, imagine we want to compute the probability of $P(h)$ in the domain specified by the joint probability distribution $\mathbf{P}(H,F,V,M)$. To do this we simply sum the values in the cells containing h, in other words, the cells in the first column of the distribution. Calculating probabilities in this way is known as **summing out** or **marginalization**.[4]

We can also use summing out to compute conditional probabilities from a joint probability distribution. For example, imagine we wish to calculate the probability of h given f when we don't care what values V or M take. In this context, V and M are examples of **hidden features**. A hidden feature is a feature whose value is not specified as part of the evidence. We can calculate $P(h, V = ?, M = ? \,|\, f)$ from $\mathbf{P}(H,F,V,M)$ by summing the values in all the cells where h and f are the case (the top four cells in the first column).

The process of **summing out** is a key concept in probability-based prediction. In order to make a prediction, a model must compute the probability for a target event in the context where some other events are known (the evidence) and where there are potentially one or more hidden features. As we have seen, using a joint probability distribution, a model can carry out this calculation by simply conditioning on the evidence features and summing out the hidden

---

4 Summing out is sometimes referred to as marginalization because statisticians used to carry out these calculations in the margins of the probability tables they were working with!

features. Unfortunately, the size of a joint probability distribution grows exponentially as the number of features and the number of values in the domains
of the features grow. Consequently, they are difficult to generate because of
the curse of dimensionality: computing the probability for each cell in a joint
probability table requires a set of instances and, because the number of cells
grows exponentially as features and feature values are added, so does the size
of the dataset required to generate the joint probability distribution. As a result,
for any domain of reasonable complexity, it is not tractable to define the full
joint probability distribution, and therefore probability-based prediction models build more compact representations of full joint probability distributions
instead.

B.3   Some Useful Probability Rules

Several important rules in probability theory allow us to compute new probabilities in terms of previously computed probabilities. Note that throughout
the rest of the chapter, we use uppercase letters to denote generic events where
an unspecified feature (or set of features) is assigned a value (or set of values).
Typically we will use letters from the end of the alphabet (e.g., X, Y, Z) for
this purpose. Also, we will use subscripts on uppercase letters to iterate over
events. So, $\sum_i P(X_i)$ should be interpreted as summing over all the possible
combinations of value assignments to the features in X.

The first rule we will introduce defines **conditional probability** in terms of
joint probability:

$$P(X \mid Y) = \frac{P(X,Y)}{P(Y)} \qquad (4)$$

We have already calculated the conditional probability of the event m given h
directly from the dataset in Table B.2[545] as $P(m \mid h) = 0.2857$ (see Equation
(3)[546]). We will now recalculate this probability using our rule-based definition
of conditional probability. From our previous calculations, we already know
that $P(h) = 0.7$ (see Equation (1)[545]) and $P(m,h) = 0.2$ (see Equation (2)[546]).
So our calculation for $P(m \mid h)$ is

$$P(m \mid h) = \frac{P(m,h)}{P(h)} = \frac{0.2}{0.7} = 0.2857$$

Using Equation (4)[548], we can provide a second definition for the probability of a joint event, which is known as the **product rule**:

$$P(X, Y) = P(X \mid Y) \times P(Y) \tag{5}$$

We can demonstrate the product rule by recalculating the probability $P(m, h)$ using previously computed probabilities:

$$P(m, h) = P(m \mid h) \times P(h) = 0.2857 \times 0.7 = 0.2$$

Again, the result of the calculation matches the probability computed directly from the dataset (see Equation (2)[546]).

There are a few points worth noting about the product rule. First, it defines the probability of a joint event $P(X, Y)$ in terms of a conditional (or posterior) probability $P(X \mid Y)$ multiplied by an unconditional (or prior) probability $P(Y)$. Second, the order of the events in the product rule is not important, and we can condition the calculation on any of the events listed in the *and* (in logic, the *and* operation is symmetric):

$$P(X, Y) = P(X \mid Y)P(Y) = P(Y \mid X)P(X)$$

We can also extend the product rule to define the joint probability of more than two events. When we generalize the rule in this way, it is known as the probability **chain rule**:

$$P(A, B, C, \dots, Z) = P(Z) \times P(Y \mid Z) \times P(X \mid Y, Z) \times \cdots \times P(A \mid B, \dots, X, Y, Z) \tag{6}$$

As with the simple two event version, the order of events in the chain rule is not important.

Finally, the **Theorem of Total Probability** defines the unconditional probability for any event X as

$$P(X) = \sum_i P(X \mid Y_i)P(Y_i) \tag{7}$$

where each Y_i is one of a set of events Y_1 to Y_k that cover all the possible outcomes in a domain and have no overlap between them. Because an event defines a partition of a dataset (the rows from the dataset that match the event), then each Y_i defines a set of rows from a dataset, and the set of data partitions defined by Y_1 to Y_k must cover the full dataset and not overlap with each other. The Theorem of Total Probability is a formal specification of the **summing out** process we introduced earlier in Section B.2[546].

To illustrate how the Theorem of Total Probability can be used to calculate probabilities, we will compute $P(h)$ by summing out M (note: earlier, in Equation (1)[545], we computed $P(h) = 0.7$):

$$P(h) = (P(h \mid m) \times P(m)) + (P(h \mid \neg m) \times P(\neg m))$$
$$= (0.6666 \times 0.3) + (0.7143 \times 0.7) = 0.7$$

We can, if we wish, sum out more than one feature. For example, we could compute $P(h)$ by summing out all the other features in the dataset:

$$P(h) = \sum_{i \in level(M)} \sum_{j \in level(F)} \sum_{k \in level(V)} P(h \mid M_i, F_j, V_k) \times P(M_i, F_j, V_k)$$

We will, however, leave this calculation to the interested reader (the result should still be 0.7).

B.4   Summary

Probability theory underpins a great deal of machine learning. This section has provided an overview of the aspects of probability that readers need to understand in order to follow the other sections in this book. One thing to note is that many of the rules and techniques we presented were different ways of achieving the same thing—for example, we can calculate $P(h)$ by simple counting, by summing out from a full joint probability distribution, or by using the Theorem of Total Probability. This is an aspect of probability theory with which beginners sometimes struggle. The important thing to remember, though, is that the different approaches exist because in different scenarios it will be often be easier to apply one approach over the others. Just like the proverbial cat, there is more than one way to skin a probability problem!

C Differentiation Techniques for Machine Learning

In this appendix we present the basic differentiation techniques that are required to understand how linear regression can be used to build predictive analytics models. In particular we explain what a derivative is, how to calculate derivatives for continuous functions, the chain rule for differentiation, and what a partial derivative is.

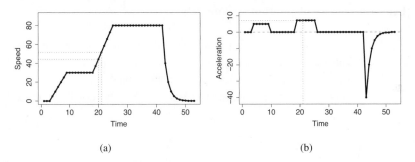

(a)   (b)

Figure C.1

(a) The speed of a car during a journey along a minor road before joining a highway and finally coming to a sudden halt; (b) the acceleration, the derivative of speed with respect to time, for this journey.

To begin, imagine a car journey where we start out driving on a minor road at about 30mph and then move onto a highway, where we drive at about 80mph before noticing an accident and braking suddenly. Figure C.1(a)[551] shows a profile of the *speed* during this journey measured at different points in time. Figure C.1(b)[551] shows a profile of the *acceleration* during this journey. We can see that when the car is driving at a constant speed, on the minor road or the highway, acceleration is zero as the speed is not changing. In contrast, acceleration has modest positive values when we are taking off initially and slightly larger positive values when we increase speed on reaching the highway. The sudden braking at the end of the journey results in large negative values that slowly taper off to match the speed profile in Figure C.1(a)[551].

Acceleration is a measure of the rate of change of speed over time. We can say more formally that acceleration is, in fact, the **derivative** of speed *with respect to* time. **Differentiation** is the set of techniques from **calculus** (the branch of mathematics that deals with how things change) that allows us to calculate **derivatives**. In an example like the car journey just described, where we have a set of discrete measurements, calculating the derivative is simply a matter of determining the difference between subsequent pairs of measure-ments. For example, the derivative of speed with respect to time at time index 21 is the speed at time index 21 minus the speed at time index 20, which is $44.28 - 51.42 = 7.14$. These values are marked in Figure C.1[551]. All the values of acceleration have been calculated in this way.

C.1   Derivatives of Continuous Functions

While it is interesting to see how derivatives can be calculated for discrete examples, it is much more common that we need to calculate the derivative of a continuous function. A continuous function, $f(x)$, generates an output for every value of a variable x based on some expression involving x. For example:

$$f(x) = 2x + 3$$
$$f(x) = x^2$$
$$f(x) = 3x^3 + 2x^2 - x - 2$$

are continuous functions with a single variable x. Graphs of these functions are shown in Figure C.2[553]. Each graph also shows the derivative of the function. We will return to these shortly.

The function $f(x) = 2x + 3$ is known as a **linear function** because the output is a combination of only additions and multiplications[1] involving x. The other two functions are known as **polynomial functions** as they include addition, multiplication, and raising to exponents. Of those, $f(x) = x^2$ is an example of a **second order polynomial function**, also known as a **quadratic function**, as its highest exponent is 2, and $f(x) = 3x^3 + 2x^2 - x - 2$ is a **third order polynomial function**, also known as a **cubic function**, as its highest exponent is 3.

Looking first at Figure C.2(a)[553], the function here is very simple, $f(x) = 2x + 3$, which results in a straight diagonal line. A straight diagonal line gives us a constant rate of change (in this case an increase of 2 in the value of the function for every change of 1 in x), so the derivative of this function with respect to x is just a constant. This is represented by the horizontal dashed line.

We can intuitively see from Figure C.2(b)[553] for $f(x) = x^2$ that the rate of change of the value of this function is likely to be high at the steep edges of the

---

1 Note that subtraction is viewed as addition of negative numbers, and division is seen as multiplication by reciprocals, so both are also allowed.

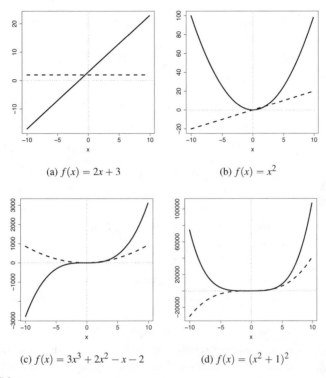

(a) $f(x) = 2x + 3$

(b) $f(x) = x^2$

(c) $f(x) = 3x^3 + 2x^2 - x - 2$

(d) $f(x) = (x^2 + 1)^2$

Figure C.2
Examples of continuous functions (shown as solid lines) and their derivatives (shown as dashed lines).

curve and low at the bottom (imagine a ball rolling around inside this shape!). This intuition is mirrored in the derivative of the function with respect to x. We can see that at the left hand side of the graph (for large negative values of x), the rate of change has a high negative value, while at the right hand side of the graph (for large positive values of x), the rate of change has a large positive value. In the middle of the graph, at the bottom of the curve, the rate of change is zero. It should be no surprise to learn that the derivative of the function with respect to x also gives us the slope of the function at that value of x. The shape of the derivative in Figure C.2(c)[553] can be understood similarly.

To actually calculate the derivative, referred to as $\frac{d}{dx}f(x)$, of a simple continuous function, $f(x)$, we use a small number of differentiation rules:

1. $\dfrac{d}{dx}\alpha$ $\quad=\quad$ 0 $\qquad$ (where α is any constant)

2. $\dfrac{d}{dx}\alpha x^n$ $\quad=\quad$ $\alpha \times n \times x^{n-1}$

3. $\dfrac{d}{dx}a+b$ $\quad=\quad$ $\dfrac{d}{dx}a + \dfrac{d}{dx}b$ $\qquad$ (where a and b are expressions that may or may not contain x)

4. $\dfrac{d}{dx}a \times c$ $\quad=\quad$ $a \times \dfrac{d}{dx}c$ $\qquad$ (where α is any constant and c is an expression containing x)

Applying these rules to the first of our previous examples, $f(x) = 2x + 3$ (Figure C.2(a)[553]), we first apply Rule 3 to split this function into two parts, $2x$ and 3, and then apply differentiation rules to each. By Rule 2 we can differentiate $2x$ to 2 (remember that x is really x^1). The 3 is a constant, so by Rule 1 differentiates to zero. The derivative of the function, then, is $\frac{d}{dx}f(x) = 2$.

For the last function, $f(x) = 3x^3 + 2x^2 - x - 2$ (Figure C.2(c)[553]), we first apply Rule 3 to divide this into four parts: $3x^3$, $2x^2$, x, and 2. Applying Rule 2 to each of the first three parts gives $9x^2$, $4x$, and -1. The final part, 2, is a constant and so differentiates to zero. The derivative of this function then is $\frac{d}{dx}f(x) = 9x^2 + 4x - 1$.

We can see from these examples that calculating derivatives of simple functions is a matter of, fairly mechanically, applying these four simple rules. Calculating the derivatives of the other two functions are left as exercises for the reader. Some of the functions that we will encounter later on in this chapter will be a little more complex, and we need two more differentiation rules to handle these.

C.2   The Chain Rule

The function $f(x) = (x^2 + 1)^2$ (shown in Figure C.2(d)[553]) cannot be differentiated using the rules just described because it is a **composite function**— it is a *function of a function*. We can rewrite $f(x)$ as $f(x) = (g(x))^2$ where $g(x) = x^2 + 1$. The differentiation **chain rule** allows us to differentiate functions of this kind.[2] The chain rule is

$$\frac{d}{dx}f(g(x)) = \frac{d}{d\,g(x)}f(g(x)) \times \frac{d}{dx}g(x) \qquad (1)$$

2 This is not to be confused with the probability **chain rule** discussed in Section B.3[548]. These are two completely different operations.

The differentiation is performed in two steps. First, treating $g(x)$ as a unit, we differentiate $f(g(x))$ with respect to $g(x)$, and then we differentiate $g(x)$ with respect to x, in both cases using the differentiation rules from the previous section. The derivative of $f(g(x))$ with respect to x is the product of these two pieces.

Applying this to the example $f(x) = (x^2 + 1)^2$ we get

$$\frac{d}{dx}(x^2 + 1)^2 = \frac{d}{d\,(x^2 + 1)}(x^2 + 1)^2 \times \frac{d}{dx}(x^2 + 1)$$

$$= \left(2 \times (x^2 + 1)\right) \times (2x)$$

$$= 4x^3 + 4x$$

Figure C.2(d)[553] shows this example function and its derivative calculated using the chain rule.

C.3 Partial Derivatives

Some functions are not defined in terms of just one variable. For example, $f(x,y) = x^2 - y^2 + 2x + 4y - xy + 2$ is a function defined in terms of two variables, x and y. Rather than defining a curve (as was the case for all the previous examples), this function defines a surface, as shown in Figure C.3(a)[556]. Using **partial derivatives** offers us an easy way to calculate the derivative of a function like this. A partial derivative (denoted by the symbol ∂) of a function of more than one variable is its derivative with respect to one of those variables with the other variables held constant.

For the example function $f(x,y) = x^2 - y^2 + 2x + 4y - xy + 2$, we get two partial derivatives:

$$\frac{\partial}{\partial x}(x^2 - y^2 + 2x + 4y - xy + 2) = 2x + 2 - y$$

where the terms y^2 and $4y$ are treated as constants as they do not include x, and

$$\frac{\partial}{\partial y}(x^2 - y^2 + 2x + 4y - xy + 2) = -2y + 4 - x$$

where the terms x^2 and $2x$ are treated as constants as they do not include y. Figures C.3(b)[556] and C.3(c)[556] show these partial derivatives.

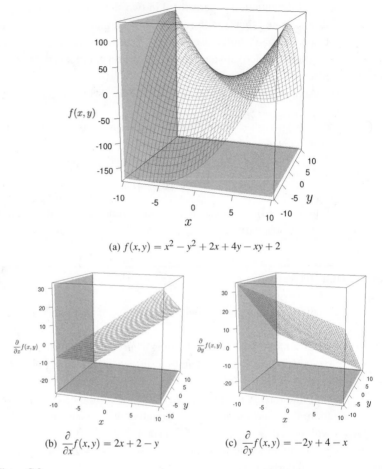

(a) $f(x,y) = x^2 - y^2 + 2x + 4y - xy + 2$

(b) $\dfrac{\partial}{\partial x}f(x,y) = 2x + 2 - y$

(c) $\dfrac{\partial}{\partial y}f(x,y) = -2y + 4 - x$

Figure C.3

(a) A continuous function in two variables, x and y; (b) the partial derivative of this function with respect to x; and (c) the partial derivative of this function with respect to y.

Bibliography

Andoni, A. and P. Indyk (2006). Near-optimal hashing algorithms for approximate nearest neighbor in high dimensions. In *Foundations of Computer Science, 2006. FOCS'06. 47th Annual IEEE Symposium on*, pp. 459–468. IEEE.

Anscombe, F. J. (1973). Graphs in statistical analysis. *American Statistician 27*(1), 17–21.

Anton, H. and C. Rorres (2010). *Elementary Linear Algebra: Applications Version*. John Wiley & Sons.

Ashenfelter, O. (2008). Predicting the quality and prices of bordeaux wine*. *The Economic Journal 118*(529), F174–F184.

Ashmore, M. (1993). The theatre of the blind: Starring a promethean prankster, a phoney phenomenon, a prism, a pocket, and a piece of wood. *Social Studies of Science 23*(1), 67–106.

Ayres, I. (2008). *Super Crunchers: Why Thinking-By-Numbers is the New Way To Be Smart*. Bantam.

Bache, K. and M. Lichman (2013). UCI machine learning repository.

Ball, N. M., J. Loveday, M. Fukugita, O. Nakamura, S. Okamura, J. Brinkmann, and R. J. Brunner (2004). Galaxy types in the sloan digital sky survey using supervised artificial neural networks. *Monthly Notices of the Royal Astronomical Society 348*(3), 1038–1046.

Banerji, M., O. Lahav, C. J. Lintott, F. B. Abdalla, K. Schawinski, S. P. Bamford, D. Andreescu, P. Murray, M. J. Raddick, A. Slosar, A. Szalay, D. Thomas, and J. Vandenberg (2010). Galaxy zoo: Reproducing galaxy morphologies via machine learning. *Monthly Notices of the Royal Astronomical Society 406*(1), 342–353.

Barber, D. (2012). *Bayesian reasoning and machine learning*. Cambridge University Press.

Batista, G. E. A. P. A. and M. C. Monard (2003). An analysis of four missing data treatment methods for supervised learning. *Applied Artificial Intelligence 17*(5-6), 519–533.

Bayes, T. and R. Price (1763). An essay towards solving a problem in the doctrine of chances. by the late rev. mr. bayes, frs communicated by mr. price, in a letter to john canton, amfrs. *Philosophical Transactions (1683-1775)*, 370 – 418.

Bejar, J., U. Cortés, and M. Poch (1991). Linneo+: A classification methodology for ill-structured domains. Research report RT-93-10-R, Dept. Llenguatges i Sistemes Informatics. Barcelona.

Bengio, Y. (2009). Learning deep architectures for ai. *Foundations and trends in Machine Learning 2*(1), 1–127.

Bentley, J. L. (1975). Multidimensional binary search trees used for associative searching. *Commun. ACM 18*(9), 509–517.

Berk, R. A. and J. Bleich (2013). Statistical procedures for forecasting criminal behavior. *Criminology & Public Policy 12*(3), 513–544.

Bertin, J. (2010). *Semiology of Graphics: Diagrams, Networks, Maps*. ESRI Press.

Bishop, C. (2006). *Pattern recognition and machine learning*. Springer.

Bishop, C. M. (1996). *Neural Networks for Pattern Recognition*. Oxford University Press.

Blondot, R. (1903). Sur une nouvelle action produite par les rayons n et sur plusieurs fait relatifs à ces radiations. *Comptes Rendus de l'Académie des Sciences de Paris 137*, 166–169.

Breiman, L. (1993). *Classification and regression trees*. CRC press.

Breiman, L. (1996). Bagging predictors. *Machine learning 24*(2), 123–140.

Breiman, L. (2001). Random forests. *Machine learning 45*(1), 5–32.

Burges, C. J. C. (1998). A tutorial on support vector machines for pattern recognition. *Data Min. Knowl. Discov. 2*(2), 121–167.

Caruana, R., N. Karampatziakis, and A. Yessenalina (2008). An empirical evaluation of supervised learning in high dimensions. In *Proceedings of the 25th international conference on Machine learning*, pp. 96–103. ACM.

Caruana, R. and A. Niculescu-Mizil (2006). An empirical comparison of supervised learning algorithms. In *Proceedings of the 23rd international conference on Machine learning*, pp. 161–168. ACM.

Casscells, W., A. Schoenberger, and T. B. Graboys (1978). Interpretation by physicians of clinical laboratory results. *The New England Journal of Medicine 299*(18), 999–1001.

Chang, W. (2012). *R Graphics Cookbook: Practical Recipes for Visualizing Data*. O'Reilly Media.

Chapman, P., J. Clinton, R. Kerber, T. Khabaza, T. Reinartz, C. Shearer, and R. Wirth (2000, August). CRISP-DM 1.0 Step-by-step data mining guide. Technical report, The CRISP-DM consortium.

Cleary, D. and R. I. Tax (2011). Predictive analytics in the public sector: Using data mining to assist better target selection for audit. In *The Proceedings of the 11th European Conference on EGovernment: Faculty of Administration, University of Ljubljana, Ljubljana, Slovenia, 16-17 June 2011*, pp. 168. Academic Conferences Limited.

Cohen, J. (1960). A coefficient of agreement for nominal scales. *Educational and Psychological Measurement 20*(1), 34–46.

Cooper, G. F. and E. Herskovits (1992). A bayesian method for the induction of probabilistic networks from data. *Machine learning 9*(4), 309–347.

Cover, T. and J. Thomas (1991). *Elements of information theory*. Wiley New York.

Cristianini, N. and J. Shawe-Taylor (2000). *An Introduction to Support Vector Machines and Other Kernel-based Learning Methods*. Cambridge University Press.

Cunningham, P. (2009). A taxonomy of similarity mechanisms for case-based reasoning. *IEEE Transactions on Knowledge and Data Engineering 21*(11), 1532–1543.

Daelemans, W. and A. van den Bosch (2005). *Memory-based language processing*. Studies in natural language processing. Cambridge University Press.

Dalgaard, P. (2008). *Introductory Statistics with R*. Springer.

Davenport, T. H. (2006, January). Competing on Analytics. *Harvard Business Review 84*(1), 98–107.

Davenport, T. H. and J. Kim (2013). *Keeping Up with the Quants: Your Guide to Understanding and Using Analytics*. Harvard Business Press Books.

Davies, E. (2005). *Machine vision: theory, algorithms, practicalities* (3rd Edition ed.). Elsevier.

De Bruyne, K., B. Slabbinck, W. Waegeman, P. Vauterin, B. De Baets, and P. Vandamme (2011). Bacterial species identification from maldi-tof mass spectra through data analysis and machine learning. *Systematic and applied microbiology 34*(1), 20–29.

Demsar, J. (2006). Statistical comparisons of classifiers over multiple data sets. *Journal of Machine Learning Research 7*, 1–30.

Doctorow, C. (2010). *Little Brother*. Macmillan.

Eco, U. (1999). *Kant and the platypus*. Vintage U.K. Random House.

Esposito, F., D. Malerba, and G. Semeraro (1997). A comparative analysis of methods for pruning decision trees. *Pattern Analysis and Machine Intelligence, IEEE Transactions on 19*(5), 476–491.

Fanaee-T, H. and G. Gama (2014, June). Event labeling combining ensemble detectors and background knowledge. *Progress in Artifical Intelligence 2*(2-3), 113–127.

Frank, E. (2000). *Pruning decision trees and lists*. Ph. D. thesis, Department of Computer Science, The University of Waikato.

Franklin, J. (2009). *Mapping Species Distributions: Spatial Inference and Prediction (Ecology, Biodiversity and Conservation)*. Cambridge Univ Press.

Franklin, J., P. McCullough, and C. Gray (2000). Terrain variables used for predictive mapping of vegetation communities in southern california. In J. C. G. John P. Wilson (Ed.), *Terrain analysis: principles and applications*. Wiley.

Freund, Y. and R. E. Schapire (1995). A desicion-theoretic generalization of on-line learning and an application to boosting. In *Computational learning theory*, pp. 23–37. Springer.

Friedman, J., J. Bently, and R. Finkel (1977). An algorithm for finding the best matches in logarithmic expected time. *ACM Transactions on Mathematical Software 3*(3), 209–226.

Friedman, J., T. Hastie, and R. Tibshirani (2000). Additive logistic regression: a statistical view of boosting. *The Annals of Statistics 28*(2), 337–407.

Fry, B. (2007). *Visualizing Data: Exploring and Explaining Data with the Processing Environment*. O'Reilly Media.

Gädenfors, P. (2004). *Conceptual Spaces: The geometry of throught*. MIT Press.

Gleick, J. (2011). *The information: A history, a theory, a flood*. HarperCollins UK.

Gross, P., A. Boulanger, M. Arias, D. L. Waltz, P. M. Long, C. Lawson, R. Anderson, M. Koenig, M. Mastrocinque, W. Fairechio, J. A. Johnson, S. Lee, F. Doherty, and A. Kressner (2006). Predicting electricity distribution feeder failures using machine learning susceptibility analysis. In *AAAI*, pp. 1705–1711. AAAI Press.

Guisan, A. and N. E. Zimmermann (2000). Predictive habitat distribution models in ecology. *Ecological modelling 135*(2), 147–186.

Gwiazda, J., E. Ong, R. Held, and F. Thorn (2000, 03). Vision: Myopia and ambient night-time lighting. *Nature 404*(6774), 144–144.

Hand, D. J. and C. Anagnostopoulos (2013). When is the area under the receiver operating characteristic curve an appropriate measure of classifier performance? *Pattern Recognition Letters 34*(5), 492–495.

Hart, P. (1968). The condensed nearest neighbor rule. *Information Theory, IEEE Transactions on 14*(3), 515 – 516.

Hastie, T., R. Tibshirani, and J. Friedman (2009). *The Elements of Statistical Learning*. Springer, New York.

Hastie, T., R. Tibshirani, and J. J. H. Friedman (2001). *The elements of statistical learning*. Springer.

Hinton, G. E. and R. R. Salakhutdinov (2006). Reducing the dimensionality of data with neural networks. *Science 313*(5786), 504–507.

Hirschowitz, A. (2001). Closing the crm loop: The 21st century marketer's challenge: Transforming customer insight into customer value. *Journal of Targeting, Measurement and Analysis for Marketing 10*(2), 168–178.

Hubble, E. (1936). *The Realm of the Nebulæ*. Yale University Press.

Japkowicz, N. and M. Shah (2011). *Evaluating Learning Algorithms: A Classification Perspective*. Cambridge University Press.

Jaynes, E. T. (2003). *Probability theory: the logic of science*. Cambridge University Press.

Jurafsky, D. and J. H. Martin (2008). *Speech and language processing: an introduction to natural language processing, computational linguistics, and speech recognition (Second Edition)*. Prentice Hall.

Keri, J. (2007). *Baseball Between the Numbers: Why Everything You Know About the Game is Wrong.* Basic Books.

Klotz, I. M. (1980). The n-ray affair. *Scientific American 242*(5), 122–131.

Kohavi, R. (1996). Scaling up the accuracy of naive-bayes classifiers: A decision-tree hybrid. In *KDD*, pp. 202–207.

Kollar, D. and N. Friedman (2009). *Probabilistic graphical models: principles and techniques.* The MIT Press.

Kuncheva, L. I. (2004). *Combining Pattern Classifiers: Methods and Algorithms.* Wiley.

Kutner, M., C. Nachtsheim, J. Neter, and W. Li (2004). *Applied Linear Statistical Models.* McGraw-Hill.

Lehmann, T. M., M. O. Güld, D. Keysers, H. Schubert, M. Kohnen, and B. B. Wein (2003). Determining the view of chest radiographs. *J. Digital Imaging 16*(3), 280–291.

Levitt, Steven, D. and J. Dubner, Stephen (2005). *Freakonomics: A Rogue Economist Explores the Hidden Side of Everything.* Penguin.

Lewis, M. (2004). *Moneyball: The Art of Winning an Unfair Game.* W.W. Norton and Company.

Lintott, C., K. Schawinski, S. Bamford, A. Slosar, K. Land, D. Thomas, E. Edmondson, K. Masters, R. C. Nichol, M. J. Raddick, A. Szalay, D. Andreescu, P. Murray, and J. Vandenberg (2011, January). Galaxy Zoo 1: data release of morphological classifications for nearly 900 000 galaxies. *Monthly Notices of the Royal Astronomical Society 410*, 166–178.

Lintott, C. J., K. Schawinski, A. Slosar, K. Land, S. Bamford, D. Thomas, M. J. Raddick, R. C. Nichol, A. Szalay, D. Andreescu, P. Murray, and J. Vandenberg (2008, September). Galaxy Zoo: morphologies derived from visual inspection of galaxies from the Sloan Digital Sky Survey. *Monthly Notices of the Royal Astronomical Society 389*, 1179–1189.

Loh, W.-Y. (2011). Classification and regression trees. *Wiley Interdisciplinary Reviews: Data Mining and Knowledge Discovery 1*(1), 14–23.

Mac Namee, B., P. Cunningham, S. Byrne, and O. I. Corrigan (2002). The problem of bias in training data in regression problems in medical decision support. *Artificial Intelligence in Medicine 24*(1), 51–70.

MacKay, D. J. (2003). *Information theory, inference and learning algorithms.* Cambridge university press.

McGrayne, S. B. (2011). *The Theory that Would Not Die: How Bayes' Rule Cracked the Enigma Code, Hunted Down Russian Submarines, and Emerged Triumphant from Two Centuries of Controversy.* Yale University Press.

Mingers, J. (1987). Expert systems - rule induction with statistical data. *Journal of the Operational Research Society 38*, 39–47.

Mingers, J. (1989). An empirical comparison of selection measures for decision-tree induction. *Machine learning 3*(4), 319–342.

Mitchell, T. (1997). *Machine Learning.* McGraw Hill.

Mitchell, T. M., S. V. Shinkareva, A. Carlson, K.-M. Chang, V. L. Malave, R. A. Mason, and M. A. Just (2008, May). Predicting Human Brain Activity Associated with the Meanings of Nouns. *Science 320*(5880), 1191–1195.

Montgomery, D. (2004). *Introduction to Statistical Quality Control.* Wiley.

Montgomery, D. C. (2012). *Design and Analysis of Experiments.* Wiley.

Montgomery, D. C. and G. C. Runger (2010). *Applied statistics and probability for engineers.* Wiley. com.

Murphy, K. P. (2012). *Machine learning: a probabilistic perspective.* The MIT Press.

Neapolitan, R. E. (2004). *Learning bayesian networks*. Pearson Prentice Hall Upper Saddle River.

OECD (2013). *The OECD Privacy Framework*. Organisation for Economic Co-operation and Development.

Osowski, S., L. T. Hoai, and T. Markiewicz (2004, April). Support vector machine-based expert system for reliable heartbeat recognition. *Biomedical Engineering, IEEE Transactions on 51*(4), 582–589.

Palaniappan, S. and R. Awang (2008). Intelligent heart disease prediction system using data mining techniques. *International Journal of Computer Science and Network Security 8*(8), 343–350.

Pearl, J. (1988). *Probabilistic reasoning in intelligent systems: networks of plausible inference*. Morgan Kaufmann.

Pearl, J. (2000). *Causality: models, reasoning and inference*, Volume 29. Cambridge Univ Press.

Quinlan, J. R. (1986). Induction of decision trees. *Machine learning 1*(1), 81–106.

Quinlan, J. R. (1987). Simplifying decision trees. *International Journal of Man-Machine Studies 27*(3), 221–234.

Quinlan, J. R. (1993). *C4. 5: programs for machine learning*. Morgan Kaufmann.

Quinn, G. E., C. H. Shin, M. G. Maguire, and R. A. Stone (1999, 05). Myopia and ambient lighting at night. *Nature 399*(6732), 113–114.

Rice, J. A. (2006). *Mathematical Statistics and Data Analysis*. Cengage Learning.

Richter, M. M. and R. O. Weber (2013). *Case-Based Reasoning: A Textbook*. Springer Berlin Heidelberg.

Samet, H. (1990). *The design and analysis of spatial data structures*, Volume 199. Addison-Wesley Reading, MA.

Schapire, R. E. (1990). The strength of weak learnability. *Machine learning 5*(2), 197–227.

Schapire, R. E. (1999). A brief introduction to boosting. In *Ijcai*, Volume 99, pp. 1401–1406.

Schwartz, P. M. (2010). Data protection law and the ethical use of analytics. Technical report, The Centre for Information Policy Leadership (at Hunton & Williams LLP).

Segata, N., E. Blanzieri, S. J. Delany, and P. Cunningham (2009). Noise reduction for instance-based learning with a local maximal margin approach. *Journal of Intelligent Information Systems 35*, 301–331.

Shannon, C. E. and W. Weaver (1949). *The mathematical theory of communication*. Urbana: University of Illinois Press.

Siddiqi, N. (2005). *Credit Risk Scorecards: Developing and Implementing Intelligent Credit Scoring*. Wiley.

Siegel, E. (2013). *Predictive Analytics: The Power to Predict Who Will Click, Buy, Lie, or Die* (1st ed.). Wiley Publishing.

Silver, N. (2012). *The Signal and the Noise: Why So Many Predictions Fail — but Some Don't*. The Penguin Press.

Sing, T., O. Sander, N. Beerenwinkel, and T. Lengauer (2005). Rocr: visualizing classifier performance in r. *Bioinformatics 21*(20), 3940–3941.

Smyth, B. and M. Keane (1995). Remembering to forget: A competence preserving case deletion policy for cbr systems. In C. Mellish (Ed.), *The Fourteenth International Joint Conference on Artificial Intelligence*, pp. 337–382.

Stewart, J. (2012). *Calculus* (7e ed.). Cengage Learning.

Stoughton, C., R. H. Lupton, M. Bernardi, M. R. Blanton, S. Burles, F. J. Castander, A. J. Con-
nolly, D. J. Eisenstein, J. A. Frieman, G. S. Hennessy, R. B. Hindsley, Ž. Ivezić, S. Kent, P. Z.
Kunszt, B. C. Lee, A. Meiksin, J. A. Munn, H. J. Newberg, R. C. Nichol, T. Nicinski, J. R.
Pier, G. T. Richards, M. W. Richmond, D. J. Schlegel, J. A. Smith, M. A. Strauss, M. Sub-
baRao, A. S. Szalay, A. R. Thakar, D. L. Tucker, D. E. V. Berk, B. Yanny, J. K. Adelman,
J. John E. Anderson, S. F. Anderson, J. Annis, N. A. Bahcall, J. A. Bakken, M. Bartelmann,
S. Bastian, A. Bauer, E. Berman, H. Böhringer, W. N. Boroski, S. Bracker, C. Briegel, J. W.
Briggs, J. Brinkmann, R. Brunner, L. Carey, M. A. Carr, B. Chen, D. Christian, P. L. Cole-
stock, J. H. Crocker, I. Csabai, P. C. Czarapata, J. Dalcanton, A. F. Davidsen, J. E. Davis,
W. Dehnen, S. Dodelson, M. Doi, T. Dombeck, M. Donahue, N. Ellman, B. R. Elms, M. L.
Evans, L. Eyer, X. Fan, G. R. Federwitz, S. Friedman, M. Fukugita, R. Gal, B. Gillespie,
K. Glazebrook, J. Gray, E. K. Grebel, B. Greenawalt, G. Greene, J. E. Gunn, E. de Haas,
Z. Haiman, M. Haldeman, P. B. Hall, M. Hamabe, B. Hansen, F. H. Harris, H. Harris, M. Har-
vanek, S. L. Hawley, J. J. E. Hayes, T. M. Heckman, A. Helmi, A. Henden, C. J. Hogan, D. W.
Hogg, D. J. Holmgren, J. Holtzman, C.-H. Huang, C. Hull, S.-I. Ichikawa, T. Ichikawa, D. E.
Johnston, G. Kauffmann, R. S. J. Kim, T. Kimball, E. Kinney, M. Klaene, S. J. Kleinman,
A. Klypin, G. R. Knapp, J. Korienek, J. Krolik, R. G. Kron, J. Krzesiński, D. Q. Lamb, R. F.
Leger, S. Limmongkol, C. Lindenmeyer, D. C. Long, C. Loomis, J. Loveday, B. MacKinnon,
E. J. Mannery, P. M. Mantsch, B. Margon, P. McGehee, T. A. McKay, B. McLean, K. Menou,
A. Merelli, H. J. Mo, D. G. Monet, O. Nakamura, V. K. Narayanan, T. Nash, J. Eric H. Neilsen,
P. R. Newman, A. Nitta, M. Odenkirchen, N. Okada, S. Okamura, J. P. Ostriker, R. Owen, A. G.
Pauls, J. Peoples, R. S. Peterson, D. Petravick, A. Pope, R. Pordes, M. Postman, A. Prosapio,
T. R. Quinn, R. Rechenmacher, C. H. Rivetta, H.-W. Rix, C. M. Rockosi, R. Rosner, K. Ruth-
mansdorfer, D. Sandford, D. P. Schneider, R. Scranton, M. Sekiguchi, G. Sergey, R. Sheth,
K. Shimasaku, S. Smee, S. A. Snedden, A. Stebbins, C. Stubbs, I. Szapudi, P. Szkody, G. P.
Szokoly, S. Tabachnik, Z. Tsvetanov, A. Uomoto, M. S. Vogeley, W. Voges, P. Waddell, R. Wal-
terbos, S. i Wang, M. Watanabe, D. H. Weinberg, R. L. White, S. D. M. White, B. Wilhite,
D. Wolfe, N. Yasuda, D. G. York, I. Zehavi, and W. Zheng (2002). Sloan digital sky survey:
Early data release. *The Astronomical Journal 123*(1), 485.

Svolba, G. (2007). *Data Preparation for Analytics Using SAS*. SAS Institute.

Svolba, G. (2012). *Data Quality for Analytics Using SAS*. SAS Institute.

Taleb, N. N. (2008). *The Black Swan: The Impact of the Highly Improbable*. Penguin.

Tempel, E., E. Saar, L. J. Liivamägi, A. Tamm, J. Einasto, M. Einasto, and V. Müller (2011).
Galaxy morphology, luminosity, and environment in the sdss dr7. *A&A 529*, A53.

Tene, O. and J. Polonetsky (2013). Big data for all: Privacy and user control in the age of
analytics. *Northwestern Journal of Technology and Intellectual Property 11*(5), 239–247.

Tijms, H. (2012). *Understanding probability*. Cambridge University Press.

Tsanas, A. and A. Xifara (2012). Accurate quantitative estimation of energy performance of
residential buildings using statistical machine learning tools. *Energy and Buildings 49*, 560–
567.

Tsoumakas, G., M.-L. Zhang, and Z.-H. Zhou (2012). Introduction to the special issue on
learning from multi-label data. *Machine Learning 88*(1-2), 1–4.

Tufte, E. R. (2001). *The Visual Display of Quantitative Information*. Graphics Press.

Tukey, J. W. (1977). *Exploratory Data Analysis*. Addison-Wesley.

Vapnik, V. (2000). *The Nature of Statistical Learning Theory*. Springer.

Widdows, D. (2004). *Geometry and Meaning*. Stanford, CA: Center for the Study of Language
and Information.

Wirth, R. and J. Hipp (2000). Crisp-dm: Towards a standard process model for data mining. In
*Proceedings of the 4th International Conference on the Practical Applications of Knowledge
Discovery and Data Mining*, pp. 29–39. Citeseer.

Wolpert, David, H. (1996). The lack of a priori distinctions between learning algorithms. *Neural Computation 8*(7), 1341–1390.

Wood, R. W. (1904). The n-rays. *Nature 70*, 530–531.

Woolery, L., J. Grzymala-Busse, S. Summers, and A. Budihardjo (1991). The use of machine learning program lers lb 2.5 in knowledge actuitiion for expert system development in nursing. *Computers in Nursing 9*, 227–234.

Zadnik, K., L. A. Jones, B. C. Irvin, R. N. Kleinstein, R. E. Manny, J. A. Shin, and D. O. Mutti (2000, 03). Vision: Myopia and ambient night-time lighting. *Nature 404*(6774), 143–144.

Zhang, N. L. and D. Poole (1994). A simple approach to bayesian network computations. In *Proceedings of the Tenth Biennial Canadian Artificial Intelligence Conference*, pp. 171–178.

Zhou, Z.-H. (2012). *Ensemble methods: foundations and algorithms*. CRC Press.

List of Figures

List of Tables

Index